Microsoft® Office 365®

ALL-IN-ONE

2nd Edition

by Peter Weverka with Matt Wade

A Wiley Brand

Microsoft® Office 365® All-in-One For Dummies®, 2nd Edition

Published by: **John Wiley & Sons, Inc.**, 111 River Street, Hoboken, NJ 07030-5774, www.wiley.com

For general information on our other products and services, please contact our Customer Care Department within the U.S. at 877-762-2974, outside the U.S. at 317-572-3993, or fax 317-572-4002. For technical support, please visit https://hub.wiley.com/community/support/dummies.

Wiley publishes in a variety of print and electronic formats and by print-on-demand. Some material included with standard print versions of this book may not be included in e-books or in print-on-demand. If this book refers to media such as a CD or DVD that is not included in the version you purchased, you may download this material at http://booksupport.wiley.com. For more information about Wiley products, visit www.wiley.com.

Library of Congress Control Number: 2021950056

ISBN: 978-1-119-83070-2

ISBN 978-1-119-83071-9 (ebk); ISBN ePDF 978-1-119-83073-3 (ebk)

SKY10029804_111821

Contents at a Glance

Table of Contents

Introduction

This book is for users of Microsoft Office 365 who want to get to the heart of Office without wasting time. Don't look in this book to find out how the different Office 365 applications work. Look in this book to find out how *you* can get *your* work done better and faster with these applications.

We show you everything you need to make the most of each of the Office applications. On the way, you have a laugh or two. No matter how much or how little skill you bring to the table, this book will make you a better, more proficient, more confident user of the Office 365 applications.

Comprising 11 minibooks, this book is your guide to making the most of the Office applications. It's jam-packed with how-to's, advice, shortcuts, and tips.

Book 1, "Common Office Tasks," looks into the many commands and features that are common to all or several of the Office programs. Book 1 explains handling text, the proofing tools, and speed techniques that can make you more productive in most of the Office applications.

Book 2, "Word 365," explains the numerous features in Office's word processor, including how to create documents from letters to reports. Use the techniques described here to construct tables, manage styles, turn Word into a desktop-publishing program, and quickly dispatch office tasks such as mass mailings. You also discover how to get Word's help in writing indexes, bibliographies, and other items of interest to scholars and report writers.

Book 3, "Excel 365," shows the many different ways to crunch the numbers with the bean counter in the Office suite. You find out how to design worksheets that are easy to read and understand, use data-validation rules to cut down on entry mistakes, write meaningful formulas, and analyze your data with PivotTables and the goal-analysis tools. You also find out just how useful Excel can be for financial analyses, data tracking, and forecasting.

Book 4, "PowerPoint 365," demonstrates how to construct a meaningful presentation that makes the audience say "Wow!" See how to make a presentation livelier and more original, both when you create your presentation and when you deliver it.

Book 5, "Outlook 365," shows you how to send and receive email messages and files, as well as track tasks, maintain an address book, and keep a calendar with Outlook. You will also be delighted to discover all the ways to track and manage email — and junk email — in Outlook.

Book 6, "Access 365," describes how to create a relational database for storing information, as well as query the database for information and gather the data into meaningful reports. Don't be frightened by the word *database*. You will be surprised to discover how useful Access can be in your work.

Book 7, "Publisher 365," shows you how to create brochures, pamphlets, news-letters, and other publications with the "print shop in a can."

Book 8, "Working with Charts and Graphics," explains how to present informa-tion in charts and diagrams, and how to use photos and graphics in your Word documents, PowerPoint presentations, and Excel spreadsheets. You also discover how to create lines, shapes, and text boxes to illustrate your ideas.

Book 9, "Office 365: One Step Beyond," delves into customizing the Office 365 applications and distributing your work.

Book 10, "Microsoft Teams," shows how to use Microsoft Teams to hold meetings online, chat, create channels, and otherwise organize coworkers into Teams.

Book 11, "File Sharing and Collaborating," explores how coworkers can join forces to store and share files and work together through OneDrive and SharePoint.

What Makes This Book Different

You are holding in your hands a computer book designed to make learning the Office 365 applications as easy and comfortable as possible. Besides the fact that this book is easy to read, it's different from other books about Office:

>> **Easy-to-look-up information:** This book is a reference, which means that readers have to be able to find instructions quickly. To that end, I have taken great pains to make sure that the material in this book is well organized and easy to find. The descriptive headings help you find information quickly. The bulleted and numbered lists make following instructions simpler. The tables make options easier to understand and compare. I want you to be able to look down the page and see a heading or list with the name of the topic that concerns you. I want you to be able to find instructions quickly. Compare the table of contents in this book to the book next to it on the bookstore shelf. The table of contents in this book is put together better and presents topics so that you can find them in a hurry.

>> **A task-oriented approach:** Most computer books describe what the software is, but this book explains how to complete tasks with the software. I assume that you came to this book because you want to know how to *do* something — print form letters, create a worksheet, or query a database. You came to the right place. This book describes how to get tasks done.

>> **Meaningful screen shots:** The screen shots in this book show only the part of the screen that illustrates what is being explained in the text. When instructions refer to one part of the screen, only that part of the screen is shown. I took great care to make sure that the screen shots in this book serve to help you understand the Office 365 applications and how they work. Compare this book to the one next to it on the bookstore shelf. Do you see how clean the screenshots in this book are?

Foolish Assumptions

Please forgive me, but I made one or two foolish assumptions about you, the reader of this book. I assumed that:

>> You own a copy of Office 365, the latest edition of Office, and you have installed it on your computer.

>> You use the Windows 10 or 11 operating system. Office 365 works on machines that run Windows 10 or higher, not machines that run Windows 8.1, Windows 8, or Windows 7.

>> You are kind to foreign tourists and furry creatures.

Conventions Used in This Book

I want you to understand all the instructions in this book, and in that spirit, I've adopted a few conventions.

Where you see boldface letters or numbers in this book, it means to type the letters or numbers. For example, "Enter **25** in the Percentage text box" means to do exactly that: Enter the number 25.

To give most commands, you can press combinations of keys. For example, pressing Ctrl+S saves the file you're working on. In other words, you can hold down the Ctrl key and press the S key to save a file. Where you see Ctrl+, Alt+, or Shift+ and a key name or key names, press the keys simultaneously.

On a computer with a touchscreen, you can click a mouse button or tap your finger on the screen to do tasks. In this book, the word *click* does double duty. *Click* means to click a mouse button or tap your finger. Either action will suffice. To keep from littering the pages of the book with instructions to "click or tap," I just use the word *click.*

Icons Used in This Book

To help you get the most out of this book, I've placed icons here and there. Here's what the icons mean:

TIP

Next to the Tip icon, you can find shortcuts and tricks of the trade to make your visit to Officeland more enjoyable.

WARNING

Where you see the Warning icon, tread softly and carefully. It means that you are about to do something that you may regret later.

REMEMBER

When I explain a juicy little fact that bears remembering, I mark it with a Remember icon. When you see this icon, prick up your ears. You will discover something that you need to remember throughout your adventures with Word, Excel, Power-Point, or the other Office application I am demystifying.

TECHNICAL STUFF

When I am forced to describe high-tech stuff, a Technical Stuff icon appears in the margin. You don't have to read what's beside the Technical Stuff icons if you don't want to, although these technical descriptions often help you understand how a software feature works.

Beyond the Book

In addition to the information you find in the book, this book includes these online bonuses:

>> **Cheat Sheet:** Go to www.dummies.com and search *Office 365 All-in-One For Dummies* to find the Cheat Sheet for this book. Here you'll find some extra goodies to make your time with Office 365 a little more productive.

>> **Updates:** Occasionally, there are updates to technology books. If this book does have technical updates, they will be posted at www.dummies.com (search this book's title to get to the right page).

1

Common Office Tasks

Contents at a Glance

Chapter **1**

Office Nuts and Bolts

C hapter 1 is where you get your feet wet with Office 365. Walk right to the shore and sink your toes in the water. Don't worry; I won't push you from behind.

In this chapter, you meet the Office applications and discover speed techniques for opening files. I show you around the Ribbon, Quick Access toolbar, and other Office landmarks. I also show you how to open files, save files, and clamp a password on a file.

Introducing Office 365

Office 365 is a subscription service from Microsoft. Subscribers can install and run Office applications on their computers; they can also take advantage of the Office cloud-based services. In computer jargon, *the cloud* is the name for servers on the Internet where individuals can store files and run online software. Microsoft offers many different versions of Office 365, some aimed at home users and some at business users. Visit this web page to compare and contrast the different versions of Office:

```
https://products.office.com
```

Office 365 applications

Table 1-1 describes the Office 365 applications. Not all versions of Office 365 include Outlook, Access, and Publisher.

TABLE 1-1

Office 365 Applications

Application	Description
Word	A word processor for writing letters, reports, and so on. A Word file is called a *document* (see Book 2).
Excel	A number cruncher for performing numerical analyses. An Excel file is called a *workbook* (see Book 3).
PowerPoint	A means of creating slide presentations to give in front of audiences. A PowerPoint file is called a *presentation*, or sometimes a *slide show* (see Book 4).
Outlook	A personal information manager, scheduler, and emailer (see Book 5).
Access	A database management application (see Book 6).
Publisher	A means of creating desktop-publishing files — pamphlets, notices, newsletters, and the like (see Book 7).

WARNING

Windows 10 must be installed on your computer to run Office 365 applications. The applications don't run on computers running earlier versions of the Windows operating system.

REMEMBER

If you're new to Office, don't be daunted by the prospect of having to study so many different applications. The applications have much in common, with the same commands showing up throughout. For example, the method of choosing fonts is the same in Word, Outlook, PowerPoint, Excel, Access, and Publisher. Master one Office program and you're well on your way to mastering the next.

Office 365 cloud services

Besides the applications described in Table 1-1, an Office 365 subscription entitles you to these goodies from the cloud:

» The opportunity to install Word, Excel, and PowerPoint on iPads and Windows tablets.

» Automatic updates to the Office software on your computer. As long as your subscription is paid up, Microsoft updates the Office software automatically.

>> Storing and sharing files with OneDrive, Microsoft's cloud service. As well as keep files on your computer, you can keep them on the Internet so that you can open them wherever your travels take you. At minimum, subscribers to Office 365 get 5 gigabytes of free storage space for their files on OneDrive (some plans offer more free storage than others). You can invite others to work on files you store on OneDrive. (Book 11 explains how to store and share files with OneDrive.)

>> The opportunity to use the web (online) versions of Word, Excel, and PowerPoint. To use a Web application, you open it in a browser and give commands through the browser window.

>> Microsoft Teams for sharing files, chatting, and participating in voice and video calls with coworkers. (Book 10 and Book 11 explain Microsoft Teams, a service available only to Office 365 Business subscribers.)

Finding out what software and Office version you have

Follow these steps to find out which version of Office 365 you have and which Office applications are installed on your computer:

1. **Open any Office 365 application.**

2. **Click the File tab.**

This tab is located in the upper-left corner of the screen. The Backstage window opens after you click the File tab.

TIP

Here's a fast way to open the Backstage window: Click your name in the upper-right corner of any Office application window and choose the Office User Info link on the drop-down menu.

3. **Select the Account category.**

As shown in Figure 1-1, the Account window opens. Under "This Product Contains" is an icon for each Office application that is installed on your computer.

4. **Click the Manage Account button.**

Your web browser opens to a Microsoft web page that tells you, among other things, what type of Office 365 account you have and how much free OneDrive storage space you are entitled to use. (If you aren't signed in to your Microsoft account, sign in to view the web page.)

5. **Return to the Office 365 application and click the Back button in the Account window.**

The Back button, a left-pointing arrow, is located in the upper-left corner of the Account window.

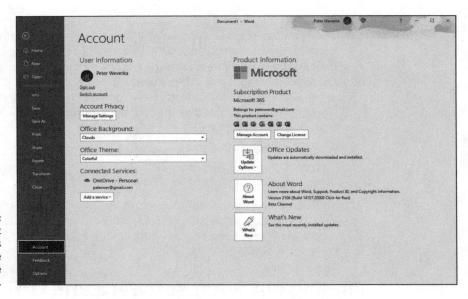

UPDATING OFFICE 365

From time to time, Microsoft updates Office 365 software. The updates are performed automatically. Follow these steps to find out when your version of Office 365 was last updated and update your software, if necessary:

1. **In any Office application, click the File tab.**

2. **In the Backstage window, click Account to open the Account window (refer to Figure 1-1).**

3. **Click the Update Options button and choose an option on the drop-down menu.**

   The options are the following:

   • **Update Now:** Checks whether an update is needed and updates the software, if need be.

   • **View Updates:** Opens a web page where you see when the software was last updated.

Managing your Microsoft account

All subscribers to Office 365 must have a Microsoft account. To find out whether your account is paid up, change the password to your account, pay your subscription fee, and do all else pertaining to your account, follow these steps:

1. **Open any Office 365 application.**

2. **In the upper-right corner of the screen, click your name.**

A drop-down menu appears.

If you don't see your name in the upper-right corner of the screen, you aren't signed in to your Microsoft account. Click the Sign In button and enter your sign-in credentials.

3. **Select the My Microsoft Account link on the drop-down menu.**

Your web browser opens to a page at Microsoft.com where you can investigate everything you need to know about your account.

Beside your name in the upper-right corner of the screen is a diamond-shaped button called Your Subscription Benefits Center. You may click this button to open a screen that tells you how wonderful it is to have a subscription to Office 365. Most people click the button only once.

Finding Your Way Around the Office Interface

Interface, also called the *user interface*, is a computer term that describes how a software program presents itself to the people who use it (and you probably thought *interface* meant two people kissing). Figure 1-2 shows the Word interface. You will be glad to know that the interface of all the Office programs is pretty much the same.

These pages give you a quick tour of the Office interface and explain what the various parts of the interface are. Click along with me as I describe the interface and you'll know what's what by the time you finish reading these pages.

File tab

Quick Access toolbar

Ribbon

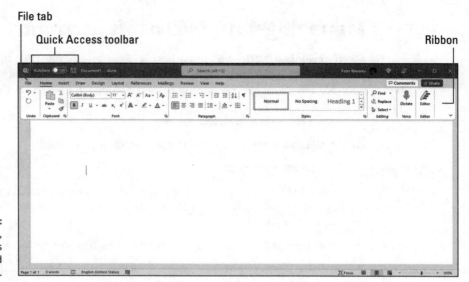

FIGURE 1-2:
The File tab,
Quick Access
toolbar, and
Ribbon.

The File tab and Backstage

In the upper-left corner of the window is the *File tab* (see Figure 1-2). Clicking the File tab opens the Backstage (Microsoft's word, not mine). As shown in Figure 1-3, the *Backstage* offers commands for creating, saving, printing, and sharing files, as well as performing other file-management tasks. Notice the Options command on the Backstage. You can choose Options to open the Options dialog box and tell the application you are working in how you want it to work.

REMEMBER

To leave the Backstage and return to the application window, click the Back button. This button, an arrow, is located in the upper-left corner of the Backstage.

The Quick Access toolbar

No matter where you travel in an Office program, you see the *Quick Access toolbar* in the upper-left corner of the screen (refer to Figure 1-2). This toolbar offers the AutoSave button and the all-important Save button. You can place more buttons on the Quick Access toolbar as well as move the toolbar lower in the window. I explain how to customize the Quick Access toolbar in Book 9, Chapter 1.

FIGURE 1-3:
Go to the Backstage to manage, print, and export files.

The Ribbon and its tabs

Across the top of the screen is the *Ribbon,* an assortment of different *tabs* (see Figure 1-2); click a tab to view a different set of commands and undertake a task. For example, click the Home tab to format text; click the Insert tab to insert a table or chart. Each tab offers a different set of buttons, menus, and galleries.

Context-sensitive tabs

To keep the Ribbon from getting too crowded with tabs, Microsoft has arranged for some tabs to appear only in context — that is, they appear on the Ribbon after you insert or click something. These tabs are called *context-sensitive* tabs.

In Figure 1-4, for example, I inserted a table, and two additional tabs — the Table Design and the Layout tab — appear on the Ribbon. These context-sensitive tabs offer commands for designing and laying out tables. The idea behind context-sensitive tabs is to direct you to the commands you need and exclude all other commands.

COLLAPSING AND SHOWING THE RIBBON

To get more room to view items onscreen, consider collapsing the Ribbon. When the Ribbon is collapsed, only tab names on the Ribbon appear; the buttons and galleries are hidden from view.

Use these techniques to collapse the Ribbon:

- Click the Collapse the Ribbon button (the little upward-pointing arrow located to the right of the Ribbon).
- Press Ctrl+F1.
- Right-click a tab on the Ribbon and select Collapse the Ribbon on the shortcut menu.
- Click the Ribbon Display options button and choose Show Tabs.

Use these techniques to show the Ribbon when it is collapsed:

- Click a tab to display the Ribbon and then click the Pin the Ribbon button.
- Press Ctrl+F1.
- Right-click a tab and deselect Collapse the Ribbon.
- Click the Ribbon Display options button and choose Show Tabs and Commands.

Office provides the Ribbon Display Options button so that you can hide the Ribbon altogether. This button is located in the upper-right corner of the screen. Click it and choose Auto-Hide Ribbon on the drop-down list to hide the ribbon. To see the Ribbon again, click the top of the application. When you want to unhide the Ribbon, click the Ribbon Display Options button and choose Show Tabs and Commands.

Select or insert an item...   and you get context-sensitive tabs

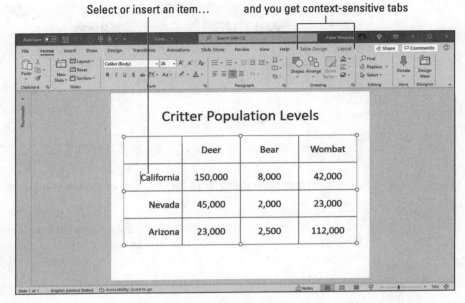

Critter Population Levels

	Deer	Bear	Wombat
California	150,000	8,000	42,000
Nevada	45,000	2,000	23,000
Arizona	23,000	2,500	112,000

FIGURE 1-4:
After you insert
or select an item,
context-sensitive
tabs appear on
the Ribbon.

REMEMBER

If you can't find a tab on the Ribbon, the tab is probably context sensitive. You have to insert or select an item to make some tabs appear on the Ribbon. Context-sensitive tabs always appear on the right side of the Ribbon after the names of other tabs.

The anatomy of a tab

All tabs are different in terms of the commands they offer, but all are the same insofar as how they present commands. On every tab, commands are organized in groups. On every tab, you find group buttons, buttons, and galleries. Group buttons, buttons, galleries — what's up with that?

Groups and group buttons

Commands on each tab are organized into *groups*. The names of these groups appear below the buttons and galleries on tabs. For example, the Home tab in Excel is organized into several groups, including the Clipboard, Font, Alignment, and Number group, as shown in Figure 1-5.

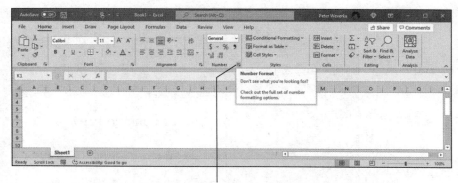

FIGURE 1-5:
Each tab is organized into groups; some groups offer group buttons.

Move the pointer over a group button to see what clicking the button does

Groups tell you what the buttons and galleries above their names are used for. On the Home tab in Excel, for example, the buttons in the Font group are for formatting text. Read group names to help find the command you need.

REMEMBER

Many groups have a *group button* that you can click to open a dialog box or task pane. (Officially, Microsoft calls these little buttons *dialog box launchers,* but let's act like grownups, shall we?) Group buttons are found to the right of group names. Move the pointer over a group button to open a pop-up help box with a description of the dialog box or task pane that appears when the button is clicked (refer to Figure 1-5).

Buttons and galleries

Go to any tab and you find buttons of all shapes and sizes. What matters isn't a button's shape or size but whether a down-pointing arrow appears on its face. Click a button *with* an arrow and you get a drop-down list with options you can choose.

TIP

You can find out what clicking a button does by moving the pointer over it, which makes a pop-up description of the button appear.

Built in to some tabs are galleries. A *gallery* presents you with visual options for changing an item. When you move the pointer over a gallery choice, the item on your page or slide — the table, chart, or diagram, for example — changes appearance. In galleries, you can preview different choices before you click to select the choice you want.

Mini-toolbars and shortcut menus

A *mini-toolbar* is a toolbar that appears onscreen to help you do a task, as shown in Figure 1-6. You can select an option from a drop-down list or click a button on the mini-toolbar to complete a task. Mini-toolbars are very convenient. They save you the trouble of going to a different tab to complete a task.

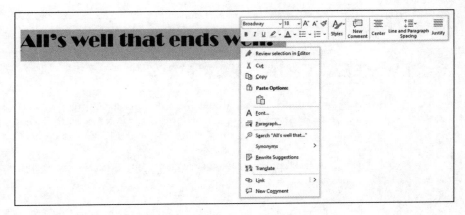

FIGURE 1-6:
A mini-toolbar (top) and shortcut menu (bottom).

Similar to mini-toolbars are the shortcut menus you get when you right-click, as shown in Figure 1-6. *Right-click* means to click the right, not the left, mouse button. Right-click just about anywhere and you get a shortcut menu of some kind.

In Word, Excel, and PowerPoint, you see a mini-toolbar *and* a shortcut menu when you right-click text.

Office 365 for keyboard lovers

People who like to give commands by pressing keyboard shortcuts will be glad to know that Office offers Alt+key shortcuts. Press the Alt key, and letters — they're called *KeyTips* — appear on tab names. After you press the Alt key, follow these instructions to make use of KeyTips:

>> **Go to a tab:** Press a KeyTip on a tab to visit a tab.

>> **Make KeyTips appear on menu items:** Press a KeyTip on a button or gallery to make KeyTips appear on menu items, as shown in Figure 1-7. After the KeyTips appear, press a letter or letter combination to give a command.

SEARCHING FOR HELP

In all Office applications, the Search box (look for the image of a magnifying glass) appears at the top of the screen on the title bar. The Search box is meant to help you complete tasks when you can't locate a command you're looking for.

Follow these steps the next time you can't seem to locate a command in an Office application:

1. Click the magnifying glass or the word *Search* (or press Alt+Q). Your Office application presents a list of tasks in a drop-down menu. On the list, tasks you attempted recently appear under the heading "Recently Used"; tasks Office thinks you'd like to try appear under the heading "Suggested."

2. If the task you want to complete is on the list, select it. Otherwise, enter a word or two to describe the task that needs completing. A new task list appears.

3. Select your task on the list, enter a different term to describe the task, or choose a Help topic on the list. If you select a task on the list, you see a dialog box to help you complete the task.

Saving Your Files

Soon after you create a new file, be sure to save it. And save your file from time to time while you work on it as well. Until you save your work, it resides in the computer's electronic memory (RAM), a precarious location. If a power outage occurs or your computer stalls, you lose all the work you did since the last time you saved your file. Make it a habit to save files every ten minutes or so, or when you complete an important task.

These pages explain how to save a file, declare where you want to save files by default, and handle how files are saved automatically in the background.

Saving a file

To save a file:

>> Click the Save button (you'll find it on the Quick Access toolbar).

>> Press Ctrl+S.

>> Go to the File tab and choose Save.

Saving a file for the first time

The first time you save a file, the Save As window opens. It invites you to give the file a name and choose a folder in which to store it. Enter a descriptive name in the File Name text box. To locate a folder for storing your presentation, see "Navigating the Save As and Open Windows," later in this chapter.

Saving AutoRecovery information

To ensure against data loss owing to computer and power failures, Office saves files on its own every ten minutes. These files are saved in an AutoRecovery file. After your computer fails, you can try to recover some of the work you lost by getting it from the AutoRecovery file.

Office saves AutoRecovery files every ten minutes, but if you want the program to save the files more or less frequently, you can change the AutoRecovery setting. Auto-recovering taxes a computer's memory. If your computer is sluggish, consider making AutoRecovery files at intervals longer than ten minutes; if your computer fails often and you're worried about losing data, make AutoRecovery files more frequently.

Follow these steps to tell Office how often to save data in an AutoRecovery file:

1. **On the File tab, choose Options.**

   The Options dialog box appears.

2. **Select the Save category.**

3. **Enter a Minutes setting in the Save AutoRecover Information Every box.**

4. **Click OK.**

Navigating the Save As and Open Windows

The Open window and Save As window offer a bunch of different ways to locate a file you want to open or the folder where you want to save a file. Figure 1–8 shows the Open and Save As windows. To open these windows, click the File tab and choose Open or Save As.

Follow these steps to open a file or save a file for the first time (or save a file under a different name or in a different location):

1. **Click the File tab.**

2. **Choose Open or Save As.**

   The Open or Save As window opens (refer to Figure 1-8).

REMEMBER

   On the Recent list, the Open window lists files you recently opened. You can open a file on this list by clicking its name. To list files you open frequently at the top of the Recent list, click the Pin This Item button (it looks like a pushpin). You see this button when you move the pointer over a filename on the list.

3. **Select the location where you expect to find or want to save the file (select This PC, most likely).**

   Select This PC to rummage in folders on your computer. You can also list network and OneDrive locations in the Open and Save As windows. (See Book 11, Chapter 2 to learn more about OneDrive.)

4. **Select the folder where you expect to find or want to save the file.**

   The window provides a couple of shortcuts for finding that folder:

   - **Recent Folders:** Click the name of a folder you opened recently.

   - **Browse button:** Click the Browse button, and in the Open or Save As dialog box (refer to Figure 1-8), locate and select a folder.

   The Open or Save As dialog box appears.

5. Open or save the file.

At last, the moment of truth:

- **Open the file:** Select the filename and click the Open button (or double-click the filename).

- **Save the file:** Enter a descriptive name for the file and click the Save button.

Select a location   Select a folder (or click Browse)

FIGURE 1-8:
The Open window
(top) and Save As
window (bottom)
work much the
same way.

Opening and Closing Files

To get to work on a file, you have to open it first. And, of course, you close a file when you're finished working on it and want to stop and smell the roses.

Opening a file

Follow these steps to open a file:

1. **On the File tab, choose Open (or press Ctrl+O).**

You see the Open window (refer to Figure 1-8). It lists files you recently opened (and files you pinned to the Recent list).

2. **If the name of the file you want to open is on the Recent list, click the name to open the file.**

If the name isn't on the list, go to Step 3.

3. **Click the location — This PC, OneDrive, a network folder — where the file is located.**

Click This PC if the file is located on your computer.

4. **Select the folder where the file you want to open is stored; if the folder isn't listed in the Open window, click the Browse button and select the folder in the Open dialog box.**

The Open dialog box appears.

5. **Select the file.**

6. **Click the Open button.**

Your file opens. You can also double-click a filename in the Open dialog box to open a file.

TIP

The fastest way to open a file is to locate it in File Explorer, the Windows file-management application, and double-click its name.

Closing a file

Closing a file is certainly easier than opening one. To close a file, save your file and use one of these techniques:

>> On the File tab, choose Close. The program remains open although the file is closed.

>> Click the Close button — the *X* in the upper-right corner of the window.

>> Press Alt+F4.

Reading and Recording File Properties

Properties are a means of describing a file. If you manage two dozen or more files, you owe it to yourself to record properties. You can use them later to identify files.

To read property descriptions, go to the File tab, choose Info, and examine the Info window. Property descriptions are found on the right side of the window, as shown in Figure 1-9.

FIGURE 1-9:
View and enter properties in the Info window.

To record even more descriptions, click the Properties button (located at the top of the file descriptions) and choose Advanced Properties on the drop-down menu. The Properties dialog box appears. Enter information about your file on the Summary and Custom tabs.

TIP

You can read a file's properties without opening a file. In File Explorer or the Open dialog box, right-click a file's name and choose Properties. You see the Properties dialog box. Go to the Details tab to see descriptions you entered.

Locking a File with a Password

Perhaps you want to submit your file to others for critical review but don't want just any Tom, Dick, or Harriet to look at your file. In that case, lock your file with a password and give out the password only to people whose opinions you trust. These pages explain how to password-protect a file, open a file that is locked with a password, and remove the password from a file.

Password-protecting a file

Follow these steps to clamp a password on a file, such that others need a password to open and perhaps also edit it:

1. Go to the File tab and choose Info.

2. In the Info window, click the Protect Document (or Workbook or Presentation) button, and choose Encrypt with Password on the drop-down list.

The Encrypt dialog box appears, as shown in Figure 1-10.

3. Enter a password in the Password text box and click OK.

Others will need the password you enter to open the file. No ifs, ands, or buts. They have to enter the password.

WARNING

Passwords are case-sensitive. In other words, you have to enter the correct combination of upper- and lowercase letters to successfully enter the password. If the password is *Valparaiso* (with an uppercase *V*), entering **valparaiso** (with a lowercase v) is deemed the wrong password and doesn't open the file.

4. In the Confirm Password dialog box, enter the password again.

Refer to Figure 1-10 for the Confirm Password dialog box.

5. Click OK.

The Info window informs you that a password is required to open the file.

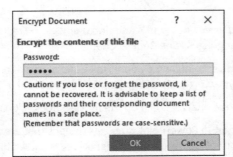

FIGURE 1-10:
Enter passwords
for the file in this
dialog box.

Removing a password from a file

Follow these steps to remove a password from a file:

1. **Open the file that needs its password removed.**

2. **Go to the File tab and choose Info to open the Info window.**

3. **Click the Protect Document (or Workbook or Presentation) button, and choose Encrypt with Password.**

The Encrypt dialog box appears (refer to Figure 1-10).

4. **Delete the password and click OK.**

Trusting (or not Trusting) Microsoft with Your "Content"

In the interest of serving you better, Microsoft wants to see your content. Content (Microsoft's word, not mine) refers to the words, numbers, and other data in Office files. If Microsoft's artificial intelligence (AI) software can read your content, the thinking goes, Microsoft can improve your Office experience. Microsoft can deduce from your history with Office what you like and want to do next.

Some very useful Office features run only if you trust Microsoft with your content. These include:

» **Editor:** In Word, identifies words and phrases that might be misunderstood and presents alternative words and phrases. (See Book 2, Chapter 5.)

» **Research**: In Word, enables you to conduct research in the Researcher task pane. (See Book 2, Chapter 5.)

- » **Translator:** In Word, translates words and documents into English and from English into other languages. (See Book 2, Chapter 5)

- » **Dictate:** In Word, PowerPoint, and Outlook, takes dictation so that you can speak rather than type words. (See Chapter 2 of this minibook.)

- » **Analyze Data:** In Excel, analyzes data on the fly. (See Book 3, Chapter 5.)

- » **PowerPoint Designer:** In PowerPoint, suggests designs that are appropriate for you based on your history with slide designs. (See Book 4, Chapter 2.)

- » **Presenter Coach:** In PowerPoint, critiques your presentation. (See Book 4, Chapter 5.)

Microsoft calls these features "experiences that analyze your content" or "connected experiences." If you don't trust Microsoft to analyze these "connected experiences" and you try to use one, you see the dialog box shown in Figure 1-11. In this dialog box, you can click the File ➪ Account ➪ Account Privacy link to open the Privacy Settings dialog box, where you can — to use Microsoft's words — enable an experience. (I explain the privacy settings and how to find them on your own very, very shortly.)

FIGURE 1-11:
Sorry, this experience is disabled.

What if you don't trust Microsoft? Some people get squeamish when an artificial-intelligence robot peers over their shoulder. Some people get the willies knowing that their private data is available to a faceless corporate behemoth.

Follow these steps to trust or not trust Microsoft with your content:

1. **On the File tab in any Office application, choose Options.**

   The Options dialog box opens.

2. **Select Trust Center on the left side of the dialog box.**

3. **Click the Trust Center Settings button.**

4. **Select Privacy Options on the left side of the dialog box.**

5. **Click the Privacy Settings button.**

   The Privacy Settings dialog box opens, as shown in Figure 1-12. Now you're getting somewhere. Throughout this dialog box are Learn More links that you can click to visit a Microsoft web page that describes privacy settings.

6. **Scroll to "All Connected Experiences" at the bottom of the dialog box and use the Turn On All Connected Experiences check box to tell Microsoft how you want to guard your privacy.**

   Select the check box if you trust Microsoft to examine your use of the Office applications; deselect the check box to prevent Microsoft from analyzing the data and content in your Office files.

   If you deselect the check box, skip to Step 8.

7. **Scroll to "Connected Experiences" in the middle of the dialog box and tell Microsoft which experiences you do or don't want.**

   Your choices under "Connected Experiences" are

   - **Experiences that analyze your content:** Select the Turn On check box if you want the "connected experiences" I described earlier — Editor, Research, Translator, and so on.

   - **Experiences that download online content:** Select the Turn On check box to permit Microsoft to present online content based on its analysis of your Office files. In Word, for example, you can download templates from Office.com. By selecting the Turn On check box, you allow Microsoft to examine your Word files so that it can present you with templates it thinks you will like.

8. **Click OK to close the Privacy Settings dialog box.**

   If you changed your privacy settings, you have to close and restart Office before the settings take effect. The Restart Required dialog box appears if you changed settings. Click OK in this dialog box.

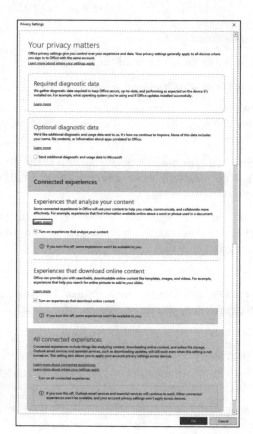

FIGURE 1-12:
To trust or not to
trust Microsoft,
that is the
question.

Chapter **2**

Wrestling with the Text

To enter text, you wiggle your fingers over the keyboard. Everybody knows that. Did you know you can also dictate words to PowerPoint, Word, and Outlook? This chapter explains how to enter words as well as change the look and size of text in an Office 365 file. It explains how to move, copy, and delete text. You find out how to quickly change a letter's case and enter a symbol or foreign character. Finally, I show you how to link your files to the Internet by fashioning a hyperlink.

Manipulating the Text

This short but important part of Chapter 2 describes the many techniques for selecting, deleting, copying, and moving text. You find an inordinate number of tips on these pages because so many shortcuts for manipulating text are available. Master the many shortcuts and you cut down considerably on the time you spend editing text.

Selecting text

Before you can do anything to text — move it, boldface it, delete it, translate it — you have to select it. Here are speed techniques for selecting text:

To Select	Do This
A word	Double-click the word.
A few words	Drag over the words.
A paragraph	Triple-click inside the paragraph (in Word, PowerPoint, and Outlook messages).
A block of text	Click the start of the text, hold down the Shift key, and click the end of the text. In Word you can also click the start of the text, press F8, and click at the end of the text.
All text	Press Ctrl+A.

TIP

Word offers a special command for selecting text with similar formats throughout a document. You can use this command to make wholesale changes to text. Select an example of the text that needs changing, and on the Home tab, click the Select button and choose Select All Text with Similar Formatting (you may have to click the Editing button first). Then choose formatting commands to change all instances of the text that you selected.

Moving and copying text

Office offers a number of different ways to move and copy text from place to place. Drum roll, please . . . . Select the text you want to move or copy and then use one of these techniques to move or copy it:

» **Dragging and dropping:** Move the mouse over the text and then click and drag the text to a new location. *Drag* means to hold down the mouse button while you move the pointer onscreen. If you want to copy rather than move the text, hold down the Ctrl key while you drag.

» **Using the Clipboard:** Move or copy the text to the Clipboard by clicking the Cut or Copy button, pressing Ctrl+X or Ctrl+C, or right-clicking and choosing Cut or Copy on the shortcut menu. The text is moved or copied to an electronic holding tank called the *Clipboard.* Paste the text by clicking the Paste button, pressing Ctrl+V, or right-clicking and choosing Paste. You can find the Paste, Cut, and Copy buttons on the Home tab.

A LOOK AT THE PASTE OPTIONS

Text adopts the formatting of neighboring text when you move or copy it to a new location. Using the Paste options, however, you can decide for yourself what happens to text formatting when you move or copy text from one place to another. To avail yourself of the Paste options:

- On the Home tab, open the drop-down list on the Paste button to see the Paste Options submenu.

- Right-click to see the Paste options on the shortcut menu.

- Click the Paste Options button to open the Paste Options submenu. This button appears after you paste text by clicking the Paste button or pressing Ctrl+V.

Choose a Paste option to determine what happens to text formatting when you move or copy text to a new location:

- **Keep Source Formatting:** The text keeps its original formatting. Choose this option to move or copy text formatting along with text to a different location.

- **Merge Formatting (Word only):** The text adopts the formatting of the text where it is moved or copied.

- **Keep Text Only:** The text is stripped of all formatting.

In Word, you can decide for yourself what the default activity is when you paste within a document, between documents, and between programs. Go to the File tab and choose Options. In the Options dialog box, go to the Advanced category, and under Cut, Copy, and Paste, choose default options.

Taking advantage of the Clipboard task pane

The Windows Clipboard is a piece of work. After you copy or cut text with the Cut or Copy command, the text is placed on the Clipboard. The Clipboard holds the last 24 items that you cut or copied. You can open the Clipboard task pane and view the last 24 items you cut or copied to the Clipboard and cut or copy them anew, as shown in Figure 2-1.

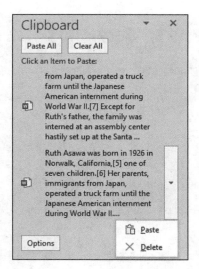

FIGURE 2-1:
The Clipboard
task pane in
action.

To open the Clipboard task pane, go to the Home tab and click the Clipboard group button (it's to the right of the word *Clipboard* in the upper-left corner of the screen). Icons next to the items tell you where they came from. To copy an item, click it or open its drop-down list and choose Paste. The Clipboard, which is available to all Office applications, is especially useful for copying text and graphics from one Office application to another.

Deleting text

To delete text, select it and press the Delete key. By the way, you can kill two birds with one stone by selecting text and then starting to type. The letters you type immediately take the place of and delete the text you selected.

REMEMBER

You can always click the Undo button (or press Ctrl+Z) if you regret deleting text. The Undo button is located on the Home tab.

Speaking, not Typing, the Words

Where Word, PowerPoint, and Outlook are concerned, you can be a dictator. You can dictate words rather than type them. As long as you speak slowly, and as long as the microphone on your computer works, Office can understand the words (most of them, anyway) and enter them for you.

Start by making sure that Office knows which language you want to speak. On the Home tab, click the down arrow on the Dictate button and select a language or regional language from the drop-down list.

Place the cursor where you want the words to appear and follow these steps to dictate to Word, PowerPoint, or Outlook:

1. **On the Home tab (or the Message tab in Outlook), click the Dictate button.**

A dialog box for recording your voice appears at the bottom of the screen, as shown in Figure 2-2.

2. **Click the Microphone button.**

3. **Start talking slowly and clearly.**

To enter a punctuation mark, say its name. For example, to enter a period, say "period."

To start a new paragraph, say "new paragraph."

REMEMBER

Don't use your keyboard while dictating. Using your keyboard tells Office that you want to type the words, not speak them.

4. **Click the Microphone button again to stop dictating.**

Dictation is one of Office's "connected experiences." In theory, dictation works better the more you use it as Office learns to recognize your speech inflections. For dictation to work, you have to trust Microsoft with your private data. Chapter 1 of this minibook explains how to trust (or not trust) Microsoft.

FIGURE 2-2:
Dictating to
Microsoft Word.

Changing the Look of Text

What text looks like is determined by its font, the size of the letters, the color of the letters, and whether text effects or font styles such as italic or boldface are in the text. What text looks like really matters in Word and PowerPoint because files you create in those applications are meant to be read by all and sundry. Even in Excel, Access, and Outlook messages, however, font choices matter because the choices you make determine whether your work is easy to read and understand.

A *font* is a collection of letters, numbers, and symbols in a particular typeface, including all italic and boldface variations of the letters, numbers, and symbols. Fonts have beautiful names, and some of them are many centuries old. Most computers come with these fonts: Arial, Calibri, Tahoma, Times New Roman, and Verdana.

THE FORMAT PAINTER: A FAST WAY TO CHANGE THE LOOK OF TEXT

When you're in a hurry to change the look of text and reformat paragraphs, consider using the Format Painter. This nifty tool works something like a paintbrush. You drag it over text to copy formats from place to place. Follow these instructions to use the Format Painter:

1. **Click a place with text and paragraph formats that you want to copy elsewhere (or select the text).**

2. **On the Home tab (or the Format Text tab in an Outlook message), click or double-click the Format Painter button (or press Ctrl+Shift+C).**

   You can find the Format Painter button in the Clipboard group. Click the button to copy formats once; double-click to copy formats to more than one location. The pointer changes into a paintbrush.

3. **Drag the pointer across text to which you want to copy the formats.**

   You can go from place to place with the Format Painter.

4. **Click the Format Painter button a second time or press Esc when you finish using the Format Painter.**

   Press Esc or click the Format Painter button again to cease using the Format Painter if you used it to copy formats to more than one location.

At the opposite end of the spectrum from the Format Painter button is the Clear All Formatting button on the Home tab (look for it in the Font group). You can select text and click this button to strip text of all its formats, whatever they may be.

Font styles include boldface, italic, and underline. By convention, headings are boldface. Italic is used for emphasis and to mark foreign words in text. Office provides a number of text effects. *Text effects*, also known as *text attributes*, include strikethrough and superscript. Use text effects sparingly.

The following pages look at the different ways to change the font, font size, and color of text, as well as how to assign font styles and text effects to text.

Choosing fonts for text

If you aren't happy with the fonts you choose, select the text that needs a font change and change fonts with one of these techniques:

» **Mini-toolbar:** Move the pointer over the selected text. You see the mini-toolbar. Move the pointer over this toolbar and choose a font in the Font drop-down list, as shown in Figure 2-3.

» **Shortcut menu:** Right-click the selected text, choose Font to open the Font dialog box, and choose a font.

» **Font drop-down list:** On the Home tab, open the Font drop-down list and choose a font.

» **Font dialog box:** On the Home tab, click the Font group button (or press Ctrl+D). You see the Font dialog box. Choose a font and click OK.

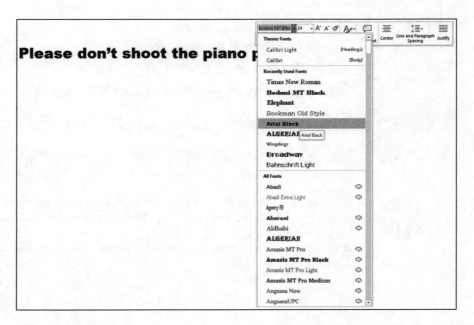

FIGURE 2-3:
Changing fonts by way of the mini-toolbar.

INSTALLING AND REMOVING FONTS ON YOUR COMPUTER

If Windows is installed on your computer, so are many different fonts. The names of these fonts appear on the Font drop-down list, in the Font dialog box, and on the mini-toolbar. Do you have enough fonts on your computer? Do you want to remove fonts to keep the Font drop-down list from being overcrowded?

Font files are kept in the `C:\Windows\Fonts` folder on your computer. Here are instructions for handling fonts:

- **Installing new fonts:** Place the font file in the `C:\Windows\Fonts` folder.

- **Removing a font:** Move the font file out of the `C:\Windows\Fonts` folder. Store font files that you don't want in another folder where you can resuscitate them if need be.

- **Examining fonts:** Double-click a font file in the `C:\Windows\Fonts` folder to examine a font more closely. A window opens, and you see precisely what the font looks like. Do you know why "The quick brown fox jumps over the lazy dog" appears in this window? Because that sentence includes every letter in the alphabet.

TIP

Avoid using too many different fonts because a file with too many fonts looks like alphabet soup. The object is to choose a font that helps set the tone. An aggressive sales pitch calls for a strong, bold font; a technical presentation calls for a font that is clean and unobtrusive. Make sure that the fonts you select help communicate your message.

Changing the font size of text

Font size is measured in *points*; a point is $\frac{1}{72}$ of an inch. The golden rule of font sizes goes something like this: the larger the font size, the more important the text. This is why headings are larger than footnotes. Select your text and use one of these techniques to change the font size of the letters:

>> **Mini-toolbar:** Move the pointer over the text, and when you see the mini-toolbar, move the pointer over the toolbar and choose a font size on the Font Size drop-down list (refer to Figure 2-3).

>> **Font Size drop-down list:** On the Home tab, open the Font Size drop-down list and choose a font size. You can live-preview font sizes this way.

>> **Font dialog box:** On the Home tab, click the Font group button (or press Ctrl+D), and in the Font dialog box, choose a font size and click OK.

>> **Increase Font Size and Decrease Font Size buttons:** Click these buttons (or press Ctrl+] or Ctrl+[) to increase or decrease the point size by the next interval on the Font Size drop-down list. You can find the Increase Font Size and Decrease Font Size buttons on the Home tab and the mini-toolbar. Watch the Font Size list or your text and note how the text changes size. This is an excellent technique when you want to "eyeball it" and you don't care to fool with the Font Size drop-down list or Font dialog box.

TIP

Click the Increase Font Size and Decrease Font Size buttons when you're dealing with fonts of different sizes and you want to proportionally change the size of all the letters. Drag the pointer over the text to select it before clicking one of the buttons.

TIP

If the font size you want isn't on the Font Size drop-down list, enter the size. For example, to change the font size to 13.5 points, type **13.5** in the Font Size box and press Enter.

Applying font styles to text

There are four — count 'em, four — font styles: regular, bold, italic, and underline:

>> **Regular:** This style is just Office's way of denoting an absence of any font style.

>> **Italic:** Italic is used for emphasis, when introducing a new term, and to mark foreign words such as *violà, gung hay fat choy,* and *Qué magnifico!* You can also italicize titles to make them a little more elegant.

- » **Bold:** Bold text, like the word at the start of this bullet, calls attention to itself.

- » **Underline:** Underlined text also calls attention to itself, but use underlining sparingly. Later in this chapter, "Underlining text" looks at all the ways to underline text.

Select text and use one of these techniques to apply a font style to it:

- » **Home tab:** Click the Bold, Italic, or Underline button.

- » **Keyboard:** Press Ctrl+B to boldface text, Ctrl+I to italicize it, or Ctrl+U to underline it.

- » **Mini-toolbar:** The mini-toolbar offers the Bold, Italic, and Underline buttons.

- » **Font dialog box:** Select a Font Style option in the Font dialog box. To open this dialog box, visit the Home tab and click the Font group button (or press Ctrl+D).

To remove a font style, click the Bold, Italic, or Underline button a second time. You can also select text and then click the Clear Formatting button on the Home tab (in Word, PowerPoint, and Publisher).

Applying text effects to text

Text effects have various uses, some utilitarian and some strictly for yucks. Be careful with text effects. Use them sparingly and to good purpose. To apply a text effect, start on the Home tab (or the Format Text tab in Outlook messages) and do one of the following:

- » Click a text effect button on the Home tab.

- » Click the Font group button (or press Ctrl+D) and choose a text effect in the bottom half of the Font dialog box, as shown in Figure 2-4.

Here's a rundown of the different text effects (not all these effects are available in PowerPoint, Excel, Publisher, and Outlook):

- » **Strikethrough and double strikethrough:** By convention, *strikethrough* is used to show where passages are struck from a contract or other important document. Double strikethrough, for all I know, is used to show where passages are struck out forcefully. Use these text effects to demonstrate ideas that you reject.

FIGURE 2-4:
Text effects in the
Font dialog box
(Word).

>> **Subscript:** A *subscripted* letter is lowered in the text. In the following chemical formula, the 2 is lowered to show that two atoms of hydrogen are needed along with one atom of oxygen to form a molecule of water: H_2O. (Press Ctrl+=.)

>> **Superscript:** A *superscripted* letter or number is one that is raised in the text. Superscript is used in mathematical and scientific formulas, in ordinal numbers (1st, 2nd, 3rd), and to mark footnotes. In the theory of relativity equation, the 2 is superscripted: $E = mc^2$. (Press Ctrl+Shift+plus sign.)

>> **Small Caps:** A *small cap* is a small capital letter. You can find many creative uses for small caps. An all-small-cap title looks elegant. Be sure to type lowercase letters in order to create small caps. Type an uppercase letter, and Office refuses to turn it into a small cap. Not all fonts can produce small capital letters.

>> **All Caps:** The All Caps text effect merely capitalizes all letters. Use it in styles to make sure that you enter text in all capital letters.

>> **Equalize Character Height (PowerPoint only):** This effect makes all characters the same height and stretches the characters in text. You can use it to produce interesting effects in text box announcements.

Underlining text

You can choose among 17 ways to underline text, with styles ranging from Words Only to Wavy Line, and you can select a color for the underline in Word,

PowerPoint, and Outlook. If you decide to underline titles, do it consistently. To underline text, select the text that you want to underline, go to the Home tab, and pick your poison:

» On the Home tab, click the Underline button. A single line runs under all the words you selected. In Word, you can open the drop-down list on the Underline button and choose from several ways to underline text.

» Click the Font group button (or press Ctrl+D) to open the Font dialog box (refer to Figure 2-4) and then choose an underline style from the drop-down list. You can also choose an underline color from the Underline Color drop-down list (in Word, PowerPoint, and Outlook). The color you select applies to the underline, not to the words being underlined.

REMEMBER

To remove an underline from text, select the text and then click the Underline button on the Home tab.

Changing the color of text

Before you change the color of text, peer at your computer screen and examine the background theme or color you chose. Unless the color of the text is different from the theme or color, you can't read the text. Besides choosing a color that contributes to the overall tone, choose a color that is easy to read.

Select the text that needs touching up and then use one of these techniques to change its color:

» Right-click to see the mini-toolbar, open the drop-down list on the Font Color button, and choose a color, as shown in Figure 2-5.

» On the Home tab, open the drop-down list on the Font Color button and choose a color.

» On the Home tab, click the Font group button (or press Ctrl+D) to open the Font dialog box, open the Font Color drop-down list, and choose a color.

TIP

The Font Color drop-down list offers theme colors and standard colors. You are well advised to choose a theme color. These colors are deemed *theme colors* because they jibe with the theme you chose for your file.

FIGURE 2-5:
Choosing a font
color on the
mini-toolbar.

Quick Ways to Handle Case, or Capitalization

Case refers to how letters are capitalized in words and sentences. Table 2-1 explains the different cases, and Figure 2-6 demonstrates why paying attention to case matters. In the figure, the PowerPoint slide titles are presented using different cases, and the titles are inconsistent with one another. In one slide, only the first letter in the title is capitalized (sentence case); in another slide, the first letter in each word is capitalized (capitalize each word); in another, none of the letters is capitalized (lowercase); and in another, all the letters are capitalized (uppercase). In your titles and headings, decide on a capitalization scheme and stick with it for consistency's sake.

TABLE 2-1   **Cases for Headings and TITLES**

Case	Description	Example
Sentence case	The first letter in the first word is capitalized; all other words are lowercase unless they are proper names.	Man bites dog in January
Lowercase	All letters are lowercase unless they are proper names.	man bites dog in January
Uppercase	All letters are uppercase no matter what.	MAN BITES DOG IN JANUARY
Capitalize each word	The first letter in each word is capitalized.	Man Bites Dog In January

Looking to gain ground

Our Plan For Tomorrow

FIGURE 2-6:
Capitalization
schemes
(clockwise from
upper-left):
sentence case;
capitalize each
word; uppercase;
lowercase.

by hook or by crook

RAISING THE BAR

To change case in Word and PowerPoint, all you have to do is select the text, go to the Home tab, click the Change Case button, and choose an option on the drop-down list:

>> **Sentence case:** Renders the letters in sentence case.

>> **lowercase:** Makes all the letters lowercase.

>> **UPPERCASE**: Renders all the letters as capital letters.

>> **Capitalize Each Word:** Capitalizes the first letter in each word. If you choose this option for a title or heading, go into the title and lowercase the first letter of articles *(the, a, an)*, coordinate conjunctions *(and, or, for, nor)*, and preposi-tions unless they're the first or last word in the title.

>> **tOGGLE cASE:** Choose this option if you accidentally enter letters with the Caps Lock key pressed.

TIP

You can also change case by pressing Shift+F3. Pressing this key combination in Word and PowerPoint changes characters to uppercase, lowercase, each word cap-italized, and back to uppercase again.

Entering Symbols and Foreign Characters

Don't panic if you need to enter an umlaut, grave accent, or cedilla because you can do it by way of the Symbol dialog box, shown in Figure 2-7. You can enter just about any symbol and foreign character by way of this dialog box. Click where you want to enter a symbol or foreign character and follow these steps to enter it:

1. **On the Insert tab, click the Symbol button.**

    In Word, Outlook, and Publisher, click More Symbols after you click the Symbol button if no symbol on the drop-down list does the job for you. You see the Symbol dialog box (refer to Figure 2-7).

2. **If you're looking to insert a symbol, not a foreign character, choose Webdings or Wingdings 1, 2, or 3 in the Font drop-down list.**

    Webdings and the Wingdings fonts offer all kinds of weird and wacky symbols.

3. **Select a symbol or foreign character.**

    You may have to scroll to find the one you want.

4. **Click the Insert button to enter the symbol and then click Close to close the dialog box.**

    TIP

    The Symbol dialog box lists the last several symbols or foreign characters you entered under Recently Used Symbols. See whether the symbol you need is listed there. It spares you the trouble of rummaging in the Symbol dialog box. In Word, Outlook, and Publisher, you see the last several symbols or foreign characters you entered on a drop-down list after you click the Symbol button.

FIGURE 2-7:
To enter a symbol or foreign character, select it and click the Insert button.

Creating Hyperlinks

A *hyperlink* is an electronic shortcut from one place to another. If you've spent any time on the Internet, you know what a hyperlink is. Clicking hyperlinks on the Internet takes you to different web pages or different places on the same web page. In the Office applications, you can use hyperlinks to connect readers to your favorite web pages or to a different page, slide, or file. You can fashion a link out of a word or phrase as well as any object — a graphic image, text box, shape, or picture.

These pages explain how to insert a hyperlink to another place in your file as well as create links to web pages. You also discover how to enter an email hyperlink that makes it easy for others to email you. By the way, the Office applications create a hyperlink for you automatically when you type a word that begins with *www.* and ends with *.com* or *.net.* The programs create an automatic email hyperlink when you enter letters that include the at symbol (@) and end in *.com* or *.net.*

Linking a hyperlink to a web page

It could well be that a web page on the Internet has all the information your readers need. In that case, you can link to the web page so that viewers can visit it in the course of viewing your file. When a viewer clicks the link, a web browser opens and the web page appears.

Follow these steps to hyperlink your file to a web page on the Internet:

1. **Select the text or object that will form the hyperlink.**

    For example, select a line of text or phrase if you want viewers to be able to click it to go to a web page.

2. **On the Insert tab, click the Link button (or press Ctrl+K).**

    You see the Insert Hyperlink dialog box, as shown in Figure 2-8. (Depending on the size of your screen, you may have to click the Links button before you can get to the Hyperlink button.) You can also open the dialog box by right-clicking an object or text and choosing Link on the shortcut menu.

3. **Under Link To, select Existing File or Web Page.**

4. **In the Address text box, enter the address of the web page to which you want to link, as shown in Figure 2-8.**

    From easiest to hardest, here are techniques for entering web page addresses:

    - **Click the Browse the Web button:** Your web browser opens after you click this button. Go to the web page you want to link to, copy the page's address in your web browser, and paste the address in the Address text box.

- **Click Browsed Pages:** The dialog box lists web pages you recently visited after you click this button. Choose a web page.

- **Type (or copy) a web page address into the Address text box:** Enter the address of the web page. You can right-click the text box and choose Paste to copy a web page address into the text box.

5. **Click the ScreenTip button, enter a ScreenTip in the Set Hyperlink ScreenTip dialog box, and click OK.**

Viewers can read the ScreenTip you enter when they move their pointers over the hyperlink.

6. **Click OK in the Insert Hyperlink dialog box.**

I would test the hyperlink if I were you to make sure that it takes viewers to the right web page. To test a hyperlink, Ctrl+click it or right-click it and choose Open Hyperlink on the shortcut menu.

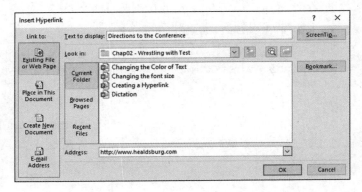

FIGURE 2-8:
Enter the web page target in the Address text box to create a hyperlink to a web page.

Creating a hyperlink to another place in your file

Follow these steps to create a hyperlink to another place in your file:

1. **Select the text or object that will form the hyperlink.**

2. **On the Insert tab, click the Link button (or press Ctrl+K).**

You see the Insert Hyperlink dialog box. Another way to open this dialog box is to right-click and choose Link in the shortcut menu.

3. **Under Link To, select Place in This Document.**

   What you see in the dialog box depends on which program you're working in:

   - **Word:** You see bookmarks and headings to which you've assigned a heading style.

   - **PowerPoint:** You see a list of slides in your presentation, as well as links to the first, last, next, and previous slide, as shown in Figure 2-9.

   - **Excel:** You see boxes for entering cell references and defined cell names.

4. **Select the target of the hyperlink.**

5. **Click the ScreenTip button.**

   You see the Set Hyperlink ScreenTip dialog box, as shown in Figure 2-9.

6. **Enter a ScreenTip and click OK.**

   When viewers move their pointers over the link, they see the words you enter. Enter a description of where the hyperlink takes you.

7. **Click OK in the Insert Hyperlink dialog box.**

   To test your hyperlink, move the pointer over it. You should see the ScreenTip description you wrote. Ctrl+click the link to see whether it takes you to the right place.

FIGURE 2-9:
You can also create a hyperlink to a different place in a file.

Creating an email hyperlink

An *email hyperlink* is one that opens an email program. These links are sometimes found on web pages so that anyone visiting a web page can conveniently send an email message to the person who manages the web page. When you click an email hyperlink, your default email program opens. And if the person who set up the link was thorough about it, the email message is already addressed and given a subject line.

TIP

Include an email hyperlink in a file if you're distributing the file to others and would like them to be able to comment on your work and send the comments to you.

Follow these steps to put an email hyperlink in a file:

1. **Select the words or object that will constitute the link.**

2. **On the Insert tab, click the Link button (or press Ctrl+K).**

The Insert Hyperlink dialog box appears.

3. **Under Link To, click E-Mail Address.**

Text boxes appear for entering an email address and a subject message.

4. **Enter your email address and a subject for the messages that others will send you.**

Office inserts the word *mailto:* before your email address as you enter it.

5. **Click OK.**

Test the link by Ctrl+clicking it. Your default email program opens. The email message is already addressed and given a subject.

Repairing and removing hyperlinks

From time to time, check the hyperlinks in your file to make sure that they still work. Clicking a hyperlink and having nothing happen is disappointing. Hyperlinks get broken when web pages and parts of files are deleted.

To repair or remove a hyperlink, right-click the link and choose Edit Link on the shortcut menu (or click in the link and then click the Link button on the Insert tab). You see the Edit Hyperlink dialog box. This dialog box looks and works just like the Insert Hyperlink dialog box. Sometimes you can repair a link simply by editing it in this dialog box.

>> **Repairing a link:** Select a target in your file or a web page and click OK.

>> **Removing a link:** Click the Remove Link button. You can also remove a hyperlink by right-clicking the link and choosing Remove Link on the shortcut menu.

Chapter **3**

Speed Techniques Worth Knowing About

This brief chapter takes you on a whirlwind tour of shortcut commands that can save you time and effort no matter which Office application you're working in. This chapter is devoted to people who want to get a task done quickly and get away from their computers. It explains the Undo and Repeat commands, zooming in and out, and opening more than one window on the same file. You also discover how to display windows in different ways, correct your typos automatically, and enter hard-to-type terminology with a simple flick of the wrist.

Undoing and Repeating Commands

If I were to choose two commands for the Hall of Fame, they would be the Undo command and the Repeat command. One allows you to reverse actions you regret doing, and the other repeats a previous action without your having to choose the same commands all over again. Undo and Repeat are explained forthwith.

Undoing a mistake

Fortunately for you, all is not lost if you make a big blunder because Office has a marvelous little tool called the Undo command. This command "remembers" your previous editorial and formatting changes. As long as you catch your error in time, you can undo your mistake.

Click the Undo button on the Home tab (or press Ctrl+Z) to undo your most recent change. If you made your error and went on to do something else before you caught it, open the drop-down list on the Undo button. It lists your previous actions, as shown in Figure 3-1. Click the action you want to undo, or if it isn't on the list, scroll until you find the error and then click it.

REMEMBER

Remember, however, that choosing an action far down the Undo list also reverses the actions before it on the list. For example, if you undo the 19th action on the list, you also undo the 18 more recent actions above it.

Repeating an action — and quicker this time

The Home tab offers a button called Repeat that you can click to repeat your last action. This button can be a mighty, mighty timesaver. For example, if you just changed fonts in one heading and you want to change another heading in the same way, select the heading and click the Repeat button (or press F4 or Ctrl+Y). Move the pointer over the Repeat button to see, in a pop-up box, what clicking it does.

After you click the Undo button, the Repeat button changes names and becomes the Redo button. Click the Redo button to "redo" the command you "undid." In other words, if you regret clicking the Undo button, you can turn back the clock by clicking Redo.

Zooming In, Zooming Out

Eyes weren't meant to stare at the computer screen all day, which makes the Zoom controls all the more valuable. You can find these controls on the View tab and in the lower-right corner of the window, as shown in Figure 3-2. Use them freely and often to enlarge or shrink what is on the screen and preserve your eyes for important things, such as gazing at the sunset.

Meet the Zoom controls:

>> **Zoom dialog box:** Click the Zoom button on the View tab or the Zoom box (the % listing) to display the Zoom dialog box, as shown in Figure 3-2. From there, you can select an option button or enter a Percent measurement.

>> **Zoom buttons:** Click the Zoom In or Zoom Out button on the Zoom slider to zoom in or out in 10-percent increments.

>> **Zoom slider:** Drag the *Zoom slider* left to shrink or right to enlarge what is on your screen.

>> **Mouse wheel:** If your mouse has a wheel, you can hold down the Ctrl key and spin the wheel to quickly zoom in or out.

TIP

Each Office program offers its own special Zoom commands in the Zoom group on the View tab. In Word, for example, you can display one page or two pages; in Excel, you can click the Zoom to Selection button to enlarge a handful of cells. Make friends with the Zoom commands. They never let you down.

FIGURE 3-2:
The Zoom controls.

Viewing a File Through More Than One Window

By way of the commands in the Window group in the View tab, you can be two places simultaneously, at least where Office is concerned. You can work on two files at one time. You can place files side by side on the screen and do a number of other things to make your work a little easier.

On the View tab, Word, Excel, and PowerPoint offer these buttons in the Window group:

>> **New Window:** Opens another window on your file so that you can be two places simultaneously in the same file. To go back and forth between windows, click a taskbar button or click the Switch Windows button and choose a window name on the drop-down list. Click a window's Close button when you finish looking at it.

>> **Arrange All:** Arranges open windows onscreen so that all are visible. Similar to Arrange All, the Cascade command in PowerPoint displays open windows so that they overlap.

>> **Switch Windows:** Opens a drop-down list with open windows so that you can travel between windows.

You can also take advantage of these Window buttons in Word and Excel to compare files:

>> **View Side by Side:** Displays files side by side so that you can compare and contrast them.

>> **Synchronous Scrolling:** Permits you to scroll two files at the same rate so that you can proofread one against the other. To use this command, start by clicking the View Side by Side button. After you click the Synchronous Scrolling button, click the Reset Window Position button so that both files are displayed at the same size onscreen.

>> **Reset Window Position:** Makes files being shown side by side the same size onscreen to make them easier to compare.

Correcting Typos on the Fly

The unseen hand of Office 365 corrects some typos and misspellings automatically. For example, try typing **accomodate** with one *m* — Office corrects the misspelling and inserts the second *m* for you. Try typing **perminent** with an *i* instead of an *a* — the invisible hand of Office corrects the misspelling, and you get *permanent.* While you're at it, type a colon and a close parenthesis :) — you get a smiley face.

As good as the AutoCorrect feature is, you can make it even better. You can also add the typos and misspellings you often make to the list of words that are corrected automatically.

Office corrects common spelling errors and turns punctuation mark combinations into symbols as part of its AutoCorrect feature. To see which typos are corrected and which punctuation marks are turned into symbols, open the AutoCorrect dialog box by following these steps:

1. **On the File tab, choose Options.**

You see the Options dialog box.

2. Go to the Proofing category.

3. Click the AutoCorrect Options button.

The AutoCorrect dialog box opens.

4. Go to the AutoCorrect tab.

As shown in Figure 3-3, the AutoCorrect tab lists words that are corrected automatically. Scroll down the Replace list and have a look around. Go ahead. Make yourself at home.

Enter a typo and its replacement

FIGURE 3-3:
As you type, words in the Replace column are replaced automatically with words in the With column.

No doubt, you make the same typing errors and spelling errors time and time again. To keep from making these errors, you can tell Office to correct them for you automatically. You do that by entering the misspelling and its corrected spelling in the AutoCorrect dialog box (see Figure 3-3).

TIP

You can also remove misspellings and typos from the list of words that are corrected automatically. To remove a word from the list of corrected words, select it in the AutoCorrect dialog box and click the Delete button.

Entering Text Quickly with the AutoCorrect Command

TIP

The preceding part of this chapter explains how you can use the AutoCorrect command to help correct typing errors, but with a little cunning, you can also use it to quickly enter hard-to-type jargon, scientific names, and the like. To open the AutoCorrect dialog box, click the File tab, choose Options, go to the Proofing category in the Options dialog box, and then click the AutoCorrect Options button. Select the AutoCorrect tab in the AutoCorrect dialog box, as shown in Figure 3-4.

Enter text to trigger AutoCorrect

What's entered when you type the text

AutoCorrect: English (United States)	?	×

AutoFormat		Actions
AutoCorrect	Math AutoCorrect	AutoFormat As You Type

☑ Show AutoCorrect Options buttons

☑ Correct TWo INitial CApitals   Exceptions...
☑ Capitalize first letter of sentences
☑ Capitalize first letter of table cells
☑ Capitalize names of days
☑ Correct accidental usage of cAPS LOCK key

☑ Replace text as you type
Replace: With: ● Plain text ○ Formatted text
/cs	cordyceps sinensis

(c)	©
(e)	€
(r)	®
(tm)	™
...	…
:(	☹

Add   Delete

☑ Automatically use suggestions from the spelling checker

OK   Cancel

FIGURE 3-4:
With a little
cunning, you can
use AutoCorrect
to enter hard-
to-type text.

In the Replace column in the AutoCorrect tab are hundreds of common typing errors and codes that Office corrects automatically. The program corrects the errors by entering text in the With column whenever you mistakenly type the letters in the Replace column. However, you can also use this dialog box for the secondary purpose of quickly entering text.

To make AutoCorrect work as a means of entering text, you tell Office to enter the text whenever you type three or four specific characters. In Figure 3-4, for example, Office is instructed to insert the words *cordyceps sinensis* (a mushroom genus) whenever I enter the characters **/cs** (and press the spacebar). Follow these steps to use AutoCorrect to enter text:

1. **Open the AutoCorrect tab of the AutoCorrect dialog box (see Figure 3-4).**

2. **In the Replace text box, enter the three or four characters that will trigger the AutoCorrect mechanism and make it enter your text.**

WARNING

Don't enter a word, or a sequence of characters that you might really type someday, in the Replace box. If you do, the AutoCorrect mechanism might kick in when you least expect it. Enter three or four characters that never appear together. Also, start all AutoCorrect entries with a slash (/). You might forget which characters trigger the AutoText entry or decide to delete your AutoCorrect entry someday. By starting it with a slash, you can find it easily in the AutoCorrect dialog box at the top of the Replace list.

3. **In the With text box, enter the hard-to-type name or word(s) that will appear when you enter the Replace text.**

4. **Click the Add button.**

5. **Click OK.**

Test your AutoCorrect entry by typing the Replace text you entered in Step 2 (which, of course, includes the slash I recommended) and pressing the spacebar. (AutoCorrect doesn't do its work until you press the spacebar.)

To delete an AutoCorrect entry, open the AutoCorrect dialog box, select the entry, and click the Delete button.

2

Word 365

Contents at a Glance

Chapter **1**

Speed Techniques for Using Word

This chapter explains shortcuts and commands that can help you become a speedy user of Word 365. Everything in this chapter was put here so that you can get off work earlier and take the slow, scenic route home. Starting here, you discover how to create and change your view of documents. You find out how to select text, get from place to place, and mark your place in long documents. You also explore how to insert one document into another, have Word read aloud to you, and create data-entry forms to make entering information a little easier.

Book 1, Chapter 2 explains the basics of entering and formatting text in Word 365 and the other Office 365 applications.

Introducing the Word Screen

Seeing the Word screen for the first time is like trying to find your way through Tokyo's busy Ikebukuro subway station. It's intimidating. But when you start using Word, you quickly learn what everything is. To help you get going, Figure 1-1 shows you the different parts of the screen. Here are shorthand descriptions of these screen parts:

>> **Quick Access toolbar:** This toolbar offers the AutoSave and Save buttons. (Book 1, Chapter 1 explains the toolbar in detail; Book 9, Chapter 1 explains how to customize and move the Quick Access toolbar.)

>> **Minimize, Restore, Close buttons:** These three magic buttons make it very easy to shrink, enlarge, and close the window you are working in.

>> **The Ribbon:** Select a tab on the Ribbon to undertake a new task. Tab names — File, Home, Insert, and so on — are located along the top of the Ribbon. (Book 1, Chapter 1 explains the Ribbon in detail, and Book 9, Chapter 1 explains how to customize the Ribbon.)

>> **Status bar:** The status bar gives you basic information about where you are and what you're doing in a document. It tells you what page and what section you're in, and the total number of pages and words in your document. Book 9, Chapter 1 explains how to customize the status bar.

Quick Access toolbar

The Ribbon

Minimize, Maximize, and Close buttons

Status bar

View buttons

Zoom controls

FIGURE 1-1:
The Word screen.

>> **View buttons:** Click one of these buttons — Focus Mode, Read Mode, Print Layout, or Web Layout — to change your view of a document. (Later in this chapter, "Getting a Better Look at Your Documents" describes the different ways to view a document.)

>> **Zoom controls:** Use these controls to zoom in and out on your work.

Creating a New Document

Document is just a fancy word for a letter, report, announcement, or proclamation that you create with Word. All documents are created using a special kind of file called a *template.* The template provides the formats — the fonts, styles, margin specifications, layouts and other stuff — that give a document its appearance.

When you create a document, you are asked to choose a template to establish what your document will look like. If your aim is to create an academic report, flyer, newsletter, calendar, résumé, or other sophisticated document, see whether you can spare yourself the formatting work by choosing the appropriate template when you create your document. (Chapter 3 of this minibook explains templates in detail and how to create your own templates.)

Follow these basic steps to create a document:

1. **On the File tab, choose New.**

   The New window, shown in Figure 1-2, appears.

2. **Click to select a template.**

   A preview window appears with a description of the template you chose, as shown in Figure 1-2.

3. **Click the Create button in the preview window.**

   Your new Word document opens.

Use these techniques in the New window to choose a template and create a document:

>> **Choose the Blank Document template:** Choose Blank Document to create a bare-bones document with few styles. Blank Document is the default template for creating documents. (By pressing Ctrl+N, you can create a new document without opening the New window.)

Speed Techniques for Using Word

Search for a template   A preview window

FIGURE 1-2:
To create a
document,
choose a
template in the
New window.

>> **Search online for a template:** Enter a search term in the Search box and
click the Start Searching button (or click a suggested search term). Templates
appear in the New window. You can click a template to examine it closely in a
preview window (refer to Figure 1-2). Click the Create button to create a
document from the template.

>> **Choose a template:** Select a template to examine it in a preview window
(refer to Figure 1-2). Click the Create button in the preview window to create a
document from the template.

>> **Choose a personal template:** On the Personal tab, click to select a template
and create a document. A personal template is one that you created or copied
to your computer or network. Chapter 3 of this minibook explains how to
create templates. The Personal tab appears in the New window only if you've
created templates or copied them to your computer.

WELCOME BACK!

To help you pick up where you left off, the Welcome back! notice appears when you reopen a Word document. It tells you which page you read most recently, the heading on that page, and when you last viewed the page.

Click the Welcome back! notice (or the Welcome back! icon) to go to directly to the page you last read.

> **Welcome back!**
> Pick up where you left off:
>
> Chapter 7: TV Guidance
> 9 minutes ago

If your search for the perfect template takes you too far afield, you can click the Home button to return to the New window.

To find out which template was used to create a document, go to the File tab, choose Info, and in the Info window, click the Show All Properties link (it's located in the lower-right corner of the window). The Properties list appears. Among other things, it tells you the template with which the document was created.

Book 1, Chapter 1 explains how to save documents after you create them, as well as how to open a document you want to work on.

Getting a Better Look at Your Documents

A computer screen can be kind of confining. There you are, staring at the darn thing for hours at a stretch. Do you wish the view were better? The Word screen can't be made to look like the Riviera, but you can examine documents in different ways and work in two places at one time in the same document. Better read on.

Viewing documents in different ways

In word processing, you want to focus sometimes on the writing, sometimes on the layout, and sometimes on the organization of your work. To help you stay in focus, Word offers different ways of viewing a document. Figure 1-3 shows these views. These pages explain how to change views, the six different views, and why to select one view over another. (Be sure to visit Book 1, Chapter 3 as well; it describes how to view a document through more than one window and how to open a second window in a document.)

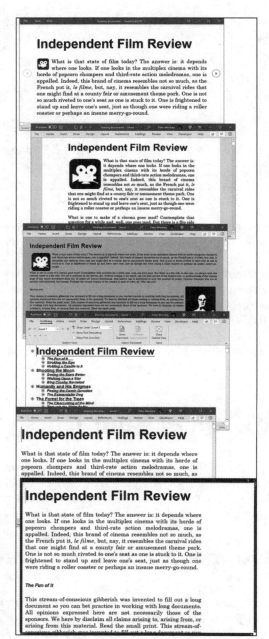

FIGURE 1-3:
The different document views (top to bottom): Read Mode, Print Layout, Web Layout, Outline, Draft, and Focus Mode.

64   BOOK 2 **Word 365**

Changing views

Use these techniques to change views:

>> Click one of the four View buttons on the right side of the status bar.

>> On the View tab, click one of the five buttons in the Views group or the Focus button in the Immersive group.

Read mode

Switch to Read mode to focus on the text itself and proofread your documents. You can't enter or edit text in Read mode. Everything is stripped away — the Ribbon, scroll bars, status bar, and all. All you see are the text and artwork in your documents. Read mode is designed for reading documents on tablet computers. (To leave Read mode, select View on the menu bar and the top of the screen and choose Edit Document on the drop-down list.)

Print Layout view

Switch to Print Layout view to see the big picture. In this view, you can see what your document will look like when you print it. You can see graphics, headers, footers, and even page borders in Print Layout view. You can also see clearly where page breaks occur (where one page ends and the next begins). In Print Layout view, you can click the One Page, Multiple Pages, or Page Width button on the View tab to display more or fewer pages on your screen.

Web Layout view

Switch to Web Layout view to see what your document would look like as a web page. Background colors appear (if you chose a theme or background color for your document). Text is wrapped to the window rather than around the artwork in the document. Book 9, Chapter 2 explains how to save an Office file, including a Word document, as a web page.

Outline view

Switch to Outline view to see how your work is organized. In this view, you can see only the headings in a document. You can get a sense of how your document unfolds and easily move sections of text backward and forward in a document. In other words, you can reorganize a document in Outline view. Chapter 8 of this minibook explains outlines in torturous detail.

READ MODE ZOOMING

While you're in Read mode, you can double-click a table, image, or chart to enlarge it onscreen and get a better look at it. Moreover, after the item gets enlarged, you can click the Zoom button (the magnifying glass) to enlarge it several times more.

To shrink an item back to size, press Esc or click onscreen (don't click the item itself).

Draft view

Switch to Draft view when you're writing a document and you want to focus on the words. Pictures, shapes, and other distractions don't appear in this view, nor do page breaks (although you can clearly see section breaks). Draft view is best for writing first drafts.

Focus Mode view

Switch to Focus Mode view to make reading a document easier. This view is designed to prevent eyestrain. You can enter text in Focus Mode view, but that's about it. All editing commands text are stripped from the screen. Press the Esc key to leave Focus Mode view.

TIP

Word provides a special screen called the Immersive Reader for people who have poor eyesight and need help reading. The screen offers tools for focusing on lines of text, breaking words into syllables, changing the background color of the page, and hearing the words read aloud. Go to the View tab and click the Immersive Reader button to open the Immersive Reader screen. (Later in this chapter, "Getting Word to Read It" explains how to make Word read aloud starting on the Review tab.)

Splitting the screen

Besides opening a second window on a document (a subject of Book 1, Chapter 3), you can be two places at one time in a Word document by splitting the screen. One reason you might do this: You're writing a long report and want the introduction to support the conclusion, plus you want the conclusion to fulfill all promises made by the introduction. Achieving both goals can be difficult to do sometimes, but you can make it easier by splitting the screen so that you can be two places at one time as you write your introduction and conclusion.

Splitting a window means to divide it into north and south halves, as shown in Figure 1-4. In a split screen, two sets of scroll bars appear so that you can travel in one half of the screen without disturbing the other half. Follow these steps to split the screen:

1. **On the View tab, click the Split button.**

A gray line appears onscreen.

2. **Drag the gray line until the gray line is where you want the split to be.**

You get two screens split down the middle. You can also split the screen by pressing Ctrl+Alt+S.

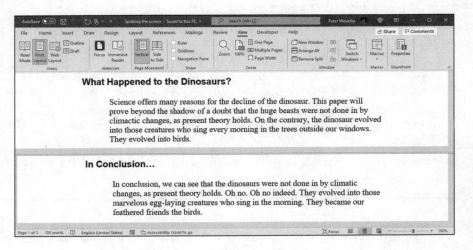

FIGURE 1-4:
A split screen.

When you tire of this split-screen arrangement, click the Remove Split button on the View tab, drag the line to the top or bottom of the screen, or press Ctrl+Alt+S again. You can also double-click the line that splits the screen in two.

TIP

In a split screen, you can choose a different view for the different halves. For example, click in the top half of the screen and choose Outline view to see your document in outline form, and click in the bottom half and choose Draft view to see the other half in Draft view. This way, for example, you can see the headings in a document while you write the introduction.

Selecting Text in Speedy Ways

Book 1, Chapter 2 explains how to enter text and change its appearance and size. After you enter text, you inevitably have to copy, move, or delete it, but you can't do those tasks until you select it first. Table 1-1 describes shortcuts for selecting text.

TABLE 1-1   **Shortcuts for Selecting Text**

To Select This	Do This
A word	Double-click the word.
A line	Click in the left margin next to the line.
Some lines	Drag the mouse pointer over the lines or drag it down the left margin.
A sentence	Ctrl+click the sentence.
A paragraph	Double-click in the left margin next to the paragraph.
A mess of text	Click at the start of the text, hold down the Shift key, and click at the end of the text.
A gob of text	Put the cursor where you want to start selecting, press F8, and press an arrow key, drag the mouse, or click at the end of the selection.
Text with the same formats	On the Home tab, click the Select button and choose Select Text with Similar Formatting (you may have to click the Editing button first).
A document	Hold down the Ctrl key and click in the left margin; triple-click in the left margin; press Ctrl+A; or go to the Home tab, click the Select button, and choose Select All (you may have to click the Editing button first).

REMEMBER

If a bunch of highlighted text is onscreen and you want it to go away but it won't (because you pressed F8), press the Esc key.

TIP

After you press F8, all the keyboard shortcuts for moving the cursor also work for selecting text. For example, press F8 and then press Ctrl+Home to select everything from the cursor to the top of the document. Later in this chapter, "Keys for getting around quickly" describes keyboard shortcuts for getting from place to place.

VIEWING THE HIDDEN FORMAT SYMBOLS

Sometimes it pays to see the hidden format symbols when you're editing and laying out a document. The symbols show line breaks, tab spaces, paragraph breaks, and the space or spaces between words. To see the hidden format symbols, go to the Home tab and click the Show/Hide ¶ button (or press Ctrl+Shift+8). Click the button again to hide the symbols.

Here's what the hidden symbols look like onscreen.

Symbol	How to Enter
Line break (↵)	Press Shift+Enter
Optional hyphen -(-)	Press Ctrl+hyphen
Paragraph (¶)	Press Enter
Space (·)	Press the spacebar
Tab (→)	Press Tab

Moving Around Quickly in Documents

Besides sliding the scroll bar, Word offers a handful of very speedy techniques for jumping around in documents: pressing shortcut keys, using the Go To command, and navigating with the Navigation pane. Read on to discover how to get there faster, faster, faster.

Keys for getting around quickly

One of the fastest ways to go from place to place is to press the keys and key combinations listed in Table 1-2.

TIP

Here's a useful keystroke for getting from place to place: Shift+F5. Press it once to go to the location of your most recent edit. Press it two or three times to go back one or two edits before that. Pressing Shift+F5 is useful when you want to return to the place where you made an edit but can't quite remember where that place is.

TABLE 1-2   ## Keys for Moving Around Documents

Key to Press	Where It Takes You
PgUp	Up the length of one screen
PgDn	Down the length of one screen
Home	To the start of the line
End	To the end of the line
Ctrl+PgUp	To the previous page in the document
Ctrl+PgDn	To the next page in the document
Ctrl+Home	To the top of the document
Ctrl+End	To the bottom of the document

Navigating from page to page or heading to heading

In lengthy documents such as the one in Figure 1-5, the best way to get from place to place is to make use of the Navigation pane. Click a heading or a page in the Navigation pane, and Word takes you there in the twinkling of an eye.

To display the Navigation pane, go to the View tab and click the Navigation Pane check box (you may have to click the Show button first). Then select a tab in the Navigation pane and go to it:

>> **Going from heading to heading:** Select the Headings tab. Headings in your document appear (provided you assigned heading styles to headings, a subject of Book 2, Chapter 3). You can use the Navigation pane like a table of contents and click headings to get from place to place. Right-click a heading and choose a Show Heading Levels option on the shortcut menu to tell Word which headings to display. You can also right-click a heading and choose Expand All or Collapse All to see or hide lower-level headings.

>> **Going from page to page:** Select the Pages tab. A thumbnail image of each page in the document appears. To quickly move from page to page, use the scroll bar in the Navigation pane or click a page thumbnail. Each thumbnail is numbered so that you always know which page you're viewing.

Click a page thumbnail

Click a heading

Click Navigation Pane

FIGURE 1-5:
In the Navigation pane, click a heading or page thumbnail to go from place to place.

Going there fast with the Go To command

Another fast way to go from place to place in a document is to use the Go To command. On the Home tab, open the drop-down list on the Find button and choose Go To (you may have to click the Editing button first). You see the Go To tab of the Find and Replace dialog box, shown in Figure 1-6. You can also open this dialog box by pressing Ctrl+G or F5.

FIGURE 1-6:
Using the Go To
command.

The Go to What menu in this dialog box lists everything that can conceivably be numbered in a Word document, and other things, too. Click a menu item, enter a number, choose an item from the drop-down list, or click the Previous, Next, or Go To buttons to go elsewhere.

Bookmarks for hopping around

Rather than press PgUp or PgDn or click the scroll bar to thrash around in a long document, you can use *bookmarks.* All you do is put a bookmark in an important spot in your document that you'll return to many times. To return to that spot, open the Bookmark dialog box and select a bookmark name, as shown in Figure 1-7. True to the craft, the mystery writer whose bookmarks are shown in Figure 1-7 wrote the end of the story first and used bookmarks to jump back and forth between the beginning and end to make all the clues fit together.

Follow these instructions to handle bookmarks:

>> **Inserting a bookmark:** Click where you want the bookmark to go, visit the Insert tab, and click the Bookmark button (you may have to click the Links button first, depending on the size of your screen). Then, in the Bookmark dialog box, type a descriptive name in the Bookmark Name box, and click the Add button. Bookmarks can't start with numbers or include blank spaces. You can also open the Bookmark dialog box by pressing Ctrl+Shift+F5.

>> **Going to a bookmark:** On the Insert tab, click the Bookmark button (you may have to click the Links button first), double-click the bookmark in the Bookmark dialog box, and click the Close button.

>> **Deleting a bookmark:** Select the bookmark in the Bookmark dialog box and click the Delete button.

TECHNICAL
STUFF

Word uses bookmarks for many purposes. For example, bookmarks indicate where cross-references are located in a document.

FIGURE 1-7:
The Bookmark
dialog box.

Inserting a Whole File into a Document

One of the beautiful things about word processing is being able to recycle documents. Say that you wrote an essay on the Scissor-Tailed Flycatcher that would fit very nicely in a broader report on North American birds. You can insert the Scissor-Tailed Flycatcher document into your report document:

1. **Place the cursor where you want to insert the document.**

2. **On the Insert tab, open the drop-down list on the Object button and choose Text from File.**

You see the Insert File dialog box. (The Object button is located in the Text group on the right side of the Ribbon.)

3. **Find and select the file you want to insert.**

4. **Click the Insert button.**

TIP

You can insert more than one file with the Text from File command. Select more than one file in the Insert File dialog box and click the Insert button. Files land in the document in the order in which they appear in the Insert File dialog box.

Getting Word to Read It

Rather than read it yourself, you can get Word to read it aloud. Word can read you a bedtime story if you open it onscreen first. Follow these steps to hear Word read all or part of a document:

1. **Open the document that needs to be read.**

2. **Switch to Print Layout view or Web Layout view, if necessary.**

   Earlier in this chapter, "Getting a Better Look at Your Documents" explains views.

3. **On the Review tab, click the Read Aloud button.**

   A toolbar appears with buttons you can click to make Word pause or stop reading. Click the Settings button on the toolbar to change reading speeds or choose a different reading voice.

   To start reading in the middle of a document, click where you want the reading to start before you click the Read Aloud button. To read a passage, select it before clicking the Read Aloud button.

4. **Click the Stop button on the toolbar or the Read Aloud button a second time to tell Word to stop reading.**

Entering Information Quickly in a Computerized Form

A *form* is a means of soliciting and recording information. You can use forms like the one shown in Figure 1-8 to enter data faster and to reduce data-entry errors. Instead of entering all the information manually, which takes time, you or a data-entry clerk can choose entries from combo boxes, drop-down lists, and date pickers. Information you enter manually is more likely to be accurate because you choose it from prescribed lists instead of entering it yourself.

To create a form like the one shown in Figure 1-8, start by creating a template for your form and putting *data-entry controls* — the combo boxes, drop-down lists, and date pickers — in the form. To fill out a form, you create a document from the form template and go to it. These pages explain how to create a form and use forms to record information.

FIGURE 1-8:
A data-entry
form.

Creating a computerized form

The first step in creating a data-entry form is to create a template for holding the form. After that, you design the form itself by labeling the data fields and creating the data-entry controls. Better keep reading.

Creating a template to hold the form

Follow these steps to create a new template:

1. **Press Ctrl+N to create a new document.**

2. **On the File tab, choose Save As.**

   You see the Save As window.

3. **Click the Browse button.**

   The Save As dialog box opens.

4. **Open the Save As Type menu and choose Word Template.**

5. **Enter a descriptive name for your template and click the Save button.**

   Word stores your template in the Default Personal Templates Location folder. Chapter 3 of this minibook explains templates in detail, as well as where this folder is located.

Creating the form and data-entry controls

Your next task is to create the form and data-entry controls for your template. Enter labels on the form where you will enter information. The form in Figure 1-8, for example, has five labels: Name, Phone, Fee Paid?, Association, and Date. After you enter the labels, follow these steps to create the data-entry controls:

1. Display the Developer tab, if necessary.

If this tab isn't showing, go to the File tab, choose Options, and on the Customize Ribbon category of the Word Options dialog box, look for the Developer check box on the right side of the screen, select this check box, and click OK. (Book 9, Chapter 1 explains in detail how to customize the Ribbon.)

2. Click where you want to place a control, and then create the control by clicking a Controls button followed by the Properties button on the Developer tab.

Here are instructions for creating three types of controls:

- **Drop-down list:** A *drop-down list* is a menu that "drops" when you open it to reveal different option choices (refer to Figure 1-8). Click the Drop-Down List Content Control button and then the Properties button. You see the Content Control Properties dialog box, as shown in Figure 1-9. For each option you want to place on the drop-down list, click the Add button, and in the Add Choice dialog box, enter the option's name in the Display Name text box and click OK, as shown in Figure 1-9.

- **Combo box:** As with a drop-down list, a *combo box* "drops" to reveal choices. However, as well as choose an option on the drop-down list, data-entry clerks can enter information in the box (refer to Figure 1-8). Click the Combo Box Content Control button and then the Properties button. In the Content Control Properties dialog box, enter option names the same way you enter them in a drop-down list, as shown in Figure 1-9.

- **Date picker:** A *date picker* is a mini-calendar from which data-entry clerks can enter a date (refer to Figure 1-8). Click the Date Picker Content Control button and then the Properties button. In the Content Control Properties dialog box, choose a display format for dates and click OK.

3. Click the Save button to save your template.

Now you're ready to use your newly made form to enter data.

FIGURE 1-9:
Click the Add button to create options for a drop-down list or combo box.

Entering data in the form

Now that you have the template, you or someone else can enter data cleanly in easy-to-read forms by following these steps:

1. On the File tab, choose New.

You see the New window.

2. Click the Personal tab.

This tab lists templates stored on your computer.

3. Double-click the name of the template you created for entering data in your form.

The form appears.

4. Enter information in the input fields.

Press the up or down arrow, or press Tab and Shift+Tab to move from field to field. You can also click an input field to move the cursor there.

5. When you're done, print the document or save it.

Chapter **2**

Laying Out Text and Pages

This chapter explains how to format text and pages. A well-laid-out document says a lot about how much time and thought was put into it. This chapter presents tips, tricks, and techniques for making pages look just right.

In this chapter, you learn what section breaks are and why they are so important to formatting. You discover how to establish the size of margins, indent text, number pages, construct headers and footers, determine how much space appears between lines of text, handle lists, and hyphenate text.

Paragraphs and Formatting

Back in English class, your teacher taught you that a paragraph is a part of a longer composition that presents one idea or, in the case of dialogue, presents the words of one speaker. Your teacher was right, too, but for word-processing purposes, a paragraph is a lot less than that. In word processing, a paragraph is simply what you put onscreen before you press the Enter key.

For instance, a heading is a paragraph. If you press Enter on a blank line to go to the next line, the blank line is considered a paragraph. If you type **Dear John** at the top of a letter and press Enter, "Dear John" is a paragraph.

REMEMBER

Knowing what Word considers to be a paragraph is important because paragraphs have a lot to do with formatting. If you click the Paragraph group button on the Home tab and monkey around with the paragraph formatting in the Paragraph dialog box, your changes affect everything in the paragraph where the cursor is located. To make format changes to a whole paragraph, all you have to do is place the cursor there. You don't have to select the paragraph. And if you want to make format changes to several paragraphs, simply select those paragraphs first.

Inserting a Section Break for Formatting Purposes

When you want to change page-numbering schemes, headers and footers, margin sizes, and page orientations in a document, you have to create a *section break* to start a new section. Word creates a new section for you when you create newspaper-style columns or change the size of margins.

Follow these steps to create a new section:

1. **Click where you want to insert a section break.**

2. **On the Layout tab, click the Breaks button.**

   You open a drop-down list.

3. **Under Section Breaks on the drop-down list, select a section break.**

Figure 2-1 shows what the different section breaks look like in Draft view. All four section break options create a new section, but they do so in different ways:

>> **Next Page:** Inserts a page break as well as a section break so that the new section can start at the top of a new page (the next one). Select this option to start a new chapter, for example.

>> **Continuous:** Inserts a section break in the middle of a page. Select this option if, for example, you want to introduce newspaper-style columns in the middle of a page.

>> **Even Page:** Starts the new section on the next even page. This option is good for two-sided documents in which the headers on the left- and right-side pages are different.

>> **Odd Page:** Starts the new section on the next odd page. You might choose this option if you have a book in which chapters start on odd pages. (By convention, that's where they start.)

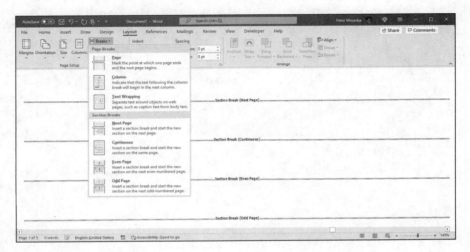

FIGURE 2-1: Section breaks in Draft view.

REMEMBER

To delete a section break, make sure that you are in Draft view so that you can see section breaks, click the dotted line, and press the Delete key.

WARNING

In the same way that paragraph marks store formats for a paragraph, section breaks store formats for an entire section. When you delete a section break, you apply new formats, because the section is folded into the section that formerly followed it and the section you deleted adopts that next section's formats. Because it's easy to accidentally delete a section break and create havoc, I recommend working in Draft view when your document has many section breaks. In Draft view, you can tell where a section ends because Section Break and a double dotted line appear onscreen. The only way to tell where a section ends in Print Layout view is to click the Show/Hide¶ button on the Home tab. (You can make section information appear on the status bar. Right-click the status bar and choose Section on the pop-up menu.)

SEEING WHAT THE FORMATS ARE

Sometimes seeing how text was formatted merely by looking is difficult. However, by pressing Shift+F1, you can see precisely how text and paragraphs were formatted in the Reveal Formatting task pane. It describes how the text, paragraph, and section where the cursor is located are formatted.

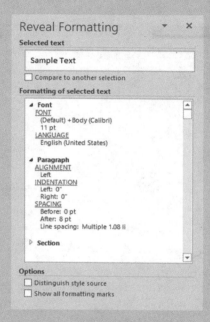

While the Reveal Formatting task pane is open, you can take advantage of these amenities:

- **Compare one part of a document to another:** Click the Compare to Another Section check box and then click another part of your document. The Reveal Formatting task pane describes how the two parts differ. Knowing how parts of a document differ can be invaluable when you're creating and modifying styles.

- **Find out which style was assigned:** Click the Distinguish Style Source check box. The task pane lists the style you assigned to the part of your document where the cursor is located.

- **See the formatting marks:** Click the Show All Formatting Marks check box. You can see where paragraphs end, where line breaks are, and where tab spaces were entered. Clicking this check box is the equivalent to clicking the Show/Hide¶ button on the Home tab.

Breaking a Line

To break a line of text before it reaches the right margin without starting a new paragraph, press Shift+Enter. Figure 2-2 shows how you can press Shift+Enter to make lines break better. The paragraphs are identical, but I broke lines in the right-side paragraph to make the text easier to read. Line breaks are marked with the ↵ symbol. To erase line breaks, click the Show/Hide¶ button to see these symbols and then backspace over them.

FIGURE 2-2:
Break lines to make reading easier.

| "A computer in every home and a chicken in every pot is our goal!" stated Rupert T. Verguenza, president and CEO of the New Technics Corporation International at the annual shareholder meeting yesterday. | "A computer in every home and a chicken in every pot is our goal!" stated Rupert T. Verguenza, president and CEO of the New Technics Corporation International at the annual shareholder meeting yesterday. |

Starting a New Page

Word gives you another page so that you can keep going when you fill up one page. But what if you're impatient and want to start a new page right away? Whatever you do, *don't* press Enter again and again until you fill up the page. Instead, create a *hard page break* by doing one the following on the Insert tab:

» Click the Page Break button (or press Ctrl+Enter). Word starts a new page at the cursor position. (You can also go to the Layout tab, click the Breaks button, and choose Page on the drop-down list.)

» Click the Blank Page button. Word enters two hard page breaks to create an empty, blank page at the cursor position.

REMEMBER

Figure 2-3 shows, in Draft view, the difference between a soft page break and a hard page break. Word inserts a *soft page break* when the page is full and another page is needed; only you can create a hard page break. In Draft view, soft page breaks are marked with a dotted line; hard page breaks are marked with the words Page Break and a dotted line. You can tell where hard page breaks are in Print Layout and Draft view by clicking the Show/Hide¶ button on the Home tab.

To delete a hard page break, switch to Draft view (or click the Show/Hide¶ button), double-click the words Page Break, and press the Delete key.

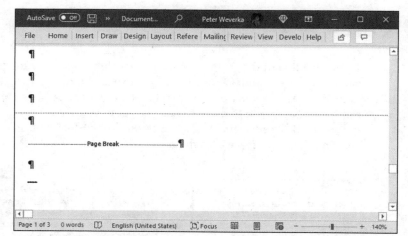

FIGURE 2-3:
In Draft view, a soft page break (top) and hard page break (bottom).

Setting Up and Changing the Margins

Margins are the empty spaces along the left, right, top, and bottom of a page, as shown in Figure 2-4. Headers and footers fall, respectively, in the top and bottom margins. And you can put graphics, text boxes, and page numbers in the margins as well. Margins serve to frame the text and make it easier to read.

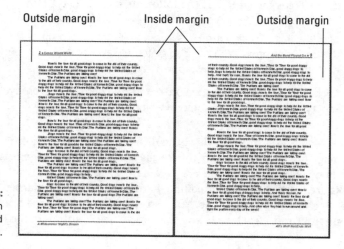

Outside margin   Inside margin   Outside margin

FIGURE 2-4:
Margins in a two-sided document.

REMEMBER

When you start a new document, give a moment's thought to the margins. Changing the size of margins after you have entered the text, graphics, and whatnot can be disastrous. Text is indented from the left and right margins. Pages break on the bottom margin. If you change margin settings, indents and page breaks change for good or ill throughout your document. By setting the margins carefully from the beginning, you can rest assured that text will land on the page where you want it to land.

WARNING

Don't confuse margins with indents. Text is indented from the margin, not from the edge of the page. If you want to change how far text falls from the page edge, indent it. To change margin settings in the middle of a document, you have to create a new section.

To set up or change the margins, go to the Layout tab and click the Margins button. You see a drop-down list with margin settings. Either choose a setting on the drop-down list or select Custom Margins to open the Margins tab of the Page Setup dialog box and choose among these commands for handling margins:

>> **Changing the size of the margins:** Enter measurements in the Top, Bottom, Left, and Right boxes to tell Word how much blank space to put along the sides of the page.

>> **Making room for the gutter:** The *gutter* is the part of the paper that the binding eats into when you bind a document. Enter a measurement in the Gutter box to increase the left or inside margin and make room for the binding. Notice on the pages of this book, for example, that the margin closest to the binding is wider than the outside margin. Choose Top on the Gutter Position menu if you intend to bind your document from the top, not the left, or inside, of the page. Some legal documents are bound this way.

>> **Using mirror margins (inside and outside margins) in two-sided documents:** In a bound document in which text is printed on both sides of the pages, the terms *left margin* and *right margin* are meaningless. What matters instead is in the *inside margin,* which is the margin in the middle of the page spread next to the bindings, and the *outside margin,* which is the margin on the outside of the page spread that isn't affected by the bindings (refer to Figure 2-4). Choose Mirror Margins on the Multiple Pages drop-down list and adjust the margins accordingly if you intend to print on both sides of the paper.

>> **Applying margin changes:** On the Apply To drop-down list, choose Whole Document to apply your margin settings to the entire document; choose This Section to apply them to a section; or choose This Point Forward to change margins in the rest of a document. When you choose This Point Forward, Word creates a new section.

If you're in a hurry to change margins, you can change them on the ruler. Display the ruler (select the Ruler check box on the View tab) and drag the Left Margin, Right Margin, or Top Margin marker. You can find these markers by moving the pointer onto a ruler and looking for the two-headed arrow near a margin boundary. It appears, along with a pop-up label, when the pointer is over a margin marker.

TIP

To get a good look at where margins are, go to the File tab and choose Options. In the Word Options dialog box, select the Advanced category and click the Show Text Boundaries check box (you find it under "Show Document Content").

Indenting Paragraphs and First Lines

An *indent* is the distance between a margin and the text, not the edge of the page and the text. Word offers a handful of ways to change the indentation of paragraphs. You can change the indentation of first lines as well as entire paragraphs. To start, select all or part of the paragraphs you want to re-indent (just click in a paragraph if you want to re-indent only one paragraph). Then click an Indent button, fiddle with the indentation marks on the ruler, or go to the Paragraph dialog box. All three techniques are described here.

Clicking an Indent button (for left-indents)

On the Home tab, click the Increase Indent or Decrease Indent button (or press Ctrl+M or Ctrl+Shift+M) to move a paragraph a half-inch farther away from or closer to the left margin. If you created tab stops, text is indented to the next or previous tab stop as well as to the next or previous half-inch. This is the fastest way to indent text, although you can't indent first lines or indent from the right margin this way.

"Eyeballing" it with the ruler

You can also change indentations by using the ruler to "eyeball" it. This technique requires some dexterity with the mouse or your finger, but it allows you to see precisely where paragraphs and the first lines of paragraphs are indented. If necessary, display the ruler by going to the View tab and clicking the Ruler check box. Then click in or select the paragraph or paragraphs that need indenting and use these techniques to re-indent them:

>> **Indenting an entire paragraph from the left margin:** Drag the *left-indent marker* on the ruler to the right. Figure 2-5 shows where this marker is located. Dragging the left-indent marker moves the first-line indent marker as well.

>> **Indenting the first line of a paragraph:** Drag the *first-line indent marker* to the right (refer to Figure 2-5). This marker determines how far the first line of the paragraph is indented.

>> **Making a hanging indent:** Drag the *hanging indent marker* to the right of the first-line indent marker (refer to Figure 2-5). A *hanging indent* is one in which the first line of a paragraph appears to "hang" into the left margin because the second and subsequent lines are indented to the right of the start of the first line. Bulleted and numbered lists employ hanging indents.

>> **Indenting an entire paragraph from the right margin:** Drag the *right-indent marker* to the left (refer to Figure 2-5).

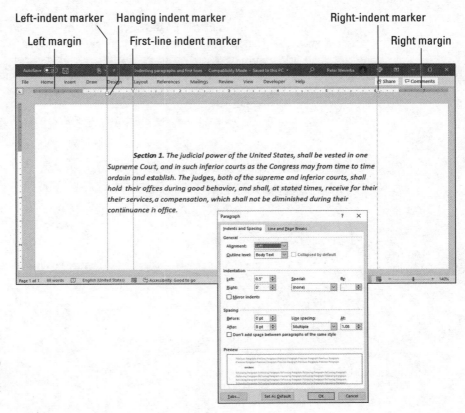

FIGURE 2-5: Indenting with the ruler (top) and Paragraph dialog box (bottom).

Notice the shaded areas on the left and right side of the ruler. These areas represent the page margins.

Indenting in the Paragraph dialog box

Yet another way to indent a paragraph or first line is to visit the Paragraph dialog box, as shown in Figure 2-5. Click in or select the paragraph or paragraphs in question, go to the Home or Layout tab, and click the Paragraph group button (the small button to the right of the word "Paragraph" in the Paragraph group). You see the Indents and Spacing tab of the Paragraph dialog box. Change the indentation settings. If you want to indent the first line or create a hanging indent, choose First Line or Hanging on the Special drop-down list and enter a measurement in the By box.

Numbering the Pages

How do you want to number the pages in your document? You can number them in sequence starting with the number 1, start numbering pages with a number other than 1, use Roman numerals or other number formats, and include chapter numbers in page numbers. What's more, you can number the pages differently in each section of your document as long as you divided your document into sections.

When it comes to numbering pages, you can proceed in two ways, as shown in Figure 2-6:

>> Put a page number by itself on the pages of your document.

>> Include the page number in the header or footer.

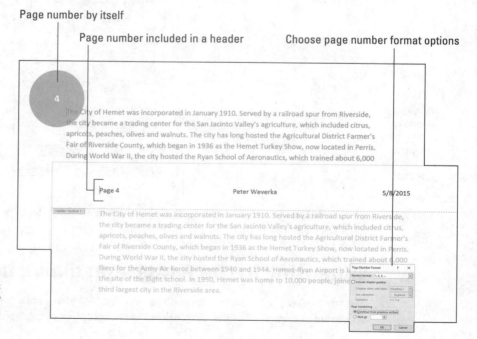

FIGURE 2-6: Ways to display page numbers on document pages.

After you enter a page number, you can format it in different ways in the Page Number Format dialog box (refer to Figure 2-6) and (Header & Footer Tools) Design tab.

REMEMBER

To handle page numbers (as well as headers and footers), you must be in Print Layout view. Click the Print Layout view button on the status bar or go to the View tab and click the Print Layout button.

Numbering with page numbers only

Follow these steps to insert a page number by itself in the header, footer, or margin of the pages:

1. On the Insert tab, click the Page Number button (it's in the Header & Footer group).

2. On the drop-down list, choose where on the page you want to put the page number (Top of Page, Bottom of Page, Page Margins, or Current Position).

3. On the submenu that appears, choose a page number option.

The farther you scroll on the submenu, the fancier the page number formats are.

REMEMBER

If you change your mind about the page number format you choose, switch to Print Layout view and double-click in the header or footer where the page number is displayed. The Header & Footer tab opens. Click the Page Number button and make a different choice, or choose Remove Page Numbers.

Including a page number in a header or footer

To put the page number part in a header or footer, double-click in the header or footer where you want the page number to appear (later in this chapter, "Putting Headers and Footers on Pages" explains headers and footers). Then follow these steps to insert the page number:

1. On the Header & Footer tab, click the Page Number button.

2. Choose Current Position.

You see a submenu with page number choices.

3. Scroll through the submenu and choose a page number format.

The "Page X of Y" option is for listing the total number of pages in a document as well as the page number. For example, page 2 of a ten-page document is numbered "Page 2 of 10."

Changing page number formats

Change page number formats in the Page Number Format dialog box (refer to Figure 2-6). To display this dialog box, make sure you're in Print Layout view and double-click your header or footer. Then use one of the following methods to change page number formats:

>> On the Insert tab, click the Page Number button and choose Format Page Numbers.

>> On the Header & Footer tab, click the Page Number button and choose Format Page Numbers.

In the Page Number Format dialog box, make your page numbers just so:

>> **Choosing a different number format:** Open the Number Format drop-down list and choose a page-numbering format. You can use numbers, letters, or roman numerals.

>> **Including chapter numbers in page numbers:** If your document generates chapter numbers automatically from headings assigned the same style (a subject not covered in this book), you can include the chapter number in the page number. Click the Include Chapter Number check box, choose a style, and choose a separator to go between the chapter number and page number.

>> **Numbering each section separately:** Click the Start At option button (not the Continue from Previous Section button) to begin counting pages anew at each section in your document. Earlier in this chapter, "Inserting a Section Break for Formatting Purposes" explains sections.

>> **Start numbering pages at a number other than 1:** Click the Start At option button and enter a number other than 1.

TIP

To keep some pages in a document from being numbered, create a section for those pages, and then remove page numbers from the section. To paginate your document, Word skips the section you created and resumes numbering pages in the following section.

EDITING PDF FILES

PDF stands for *portable document format*. PDFs are designed to be read with the Adobe Reader application and most web browsers. Almost anywhere you go on the Internet, you stumble upon PDFs. The PDF format is a popular means of sharing and distributing files.

You can edit a PDF file in Word. Open the PDF as you would any text file and start editing. In my experiments, most of the PDF formats carry over to Word. I had some trouble with tables and images, but I didn't have any serious trouble.

Book 9, Chapter 2 explains how to save a Word file as a PDF file.

Putting Headers and Footers on Pages

A *header* is a little description that appears along the top of a page so that the reader knows what's what. Usually, headers include the page number and a title, and often the author's name appears in the header as well. A *footer* is the same thing as a header except that it appears along the bottom of the page, as befits its name.

These pages explain everything a mere mortal needs to know about headers and footers. Meanwhile, here are the ground rules for managing them:

>> **Switching to Print Layout view:** To enter, read, edit or delete headers and footers, you must be in Print Layout view. You can't see headers and footers in the other views.

>> **Displaying the Header & Footer tab:** As shown in Figure 2-7, you manage headers and footers by way of buttons on the Header & Footer tab. To display this tab after you create a header or footer, switch to Print Layout view and double-click a header or footer.

>> **Closing the Header & Footer tab:** Click the Close Header and Footer button or double-click outside the header or footer.

>> **Placing different headers and footers in the same document:** To change headers or footers in the middle of a document, you have to create a new section. See "Inserting a Section Break for Formatting Purposes," earlier in this chapter.

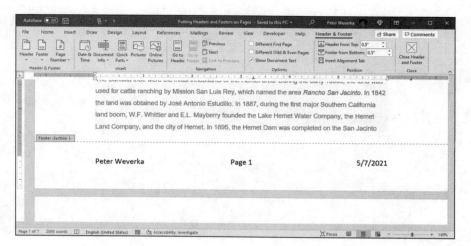

FIGURE 2-7:
Manage headers
and footers on
the Header &
Footer tab.

Creating, editing, and removing headers and footers

Follow these instructions to create, edit, and delete headers and footers:

» **Creating a header or footer:** On the Insert tab, click the Header or the Footer button, and choose a header or footer on the gallery. The gallery presents headers or footers with preformatted page numbers, dates, and places to enter a document title and author's name. Click More Headers (or Footers) from Office.com to download headers or footers from Microsoft. (Later in this chapter, "Fine-tuning a header or footer" explains how to insert the date and time and change headers and footers from section to section.)

» **Choosing a different header or footer:** Don't like the header or footer you chose? If necessary, double-click your header or footer to display it. Then click the Header or Footer button and choose a new header or footer from the gallery.

» **Editing a header or footer:** Double-click the header or footer. The cursor moves into the header or footer so that you can enter or format text. You can also click the Header or the Footer button and choose Edit Header or Edit Footer on the drop-down list.

» **Changing the appearance of a header or footer:** Click a shape or text box in a header or footer and visit a Format tab to change the shape or text box's color, background, or size. (Book 8, Chapter 4 describes the Office 365 drawing tools.)

» **Removing a header or footer:** On the Header & Footer tab, click the Header or Footer button and choose Remove Header or Remove Footer on the drop-down list.

CREATING YOUR OWN HEADER OR FOOTER FOR THE GALLERY

When you click the Header or the Footer button on the Insert tab, a gallery appears with headers or footers. You can create your own header or footer and place it on this gallery. For example, create a header or footer with your company logo. After you design and create your header or footer, follow these instructions to wrangle with it:

- **Placing a header or footer in the gallery:** Select your header or footer by dragging over it or by clicking in the margin to its left. On the Header & Footer tab, click the Quick Parts button and choose Save Selection to Quick Part Gallery. You see the Create New Building Block dialog box. Enter a descriptive name for the header or footer, choose Footers or Headers on the Gallery drop-down list, and click OK.

- **Inserting a header or footer you created:** On the Insert tab, click the Header or Footer button and choose your header or footer in the gallery. It is located in the Built-In or General category, depending on where you chose to put it.

- **Removing and editing headers or footers:** On the Insert tab, click the Quick Parts button and choose Building Blocks Organizer. The Building Blocks Organizer dialog box appears. Select your header or footer and click the Delete button to remove it from the gallery or the Edit Properties button to change its name, gallery assignment, or category assignment.

To switch back and forth between the header and footer, click the Go to Header or Go to Footer button on the Header & Footer tab.

TIP

As you work away on your header and footer, you can call on most of the text-formatting commands on the Home tab. You can change the text's font and font size, click an alignment button, and paste text from the Clipboard. Tabs are set up in most headers and footers to enable you to center, left-align, and right-align text. You can click the Insert Alignment Tab button on the Header & Footer tab to insert a new tab.

Fine-tuning a header or footer

Here is advice for making a perfect header on the Header & Footer tab:

>> **Inserting a page number:** See "Including a page number in a header or footer" and "Changing page number formats," earlier in this chapter.

>> **Inserting the date and time:** Click the Date & Time button, choose a date format in the Date and Time dialog box, and click OK. Click the Update Automatically check box if you want the date to record when you print the document, not when you created your header or footer.

>> **Changing headers and footers from section to section:** Use the Link to Previous button to determine whether headers and footers are different from section to section (you must divide a document into sections to have different headers and footers). Deselecting this button tells Word that you want your header or footer to be different from the header or footer in the previous section of the document; selecting this button (clicking it so that it looks selected) tells Word that you want your header or footer to be the same as the header or footer in the previous section of your document. To make a different header or footer, deselect the Link to Previous button and enter a different header or footer.

REMEMBER

When the header or footer is the same as that of the previous section, the Header or Footer box reads Same as Previous; when the header or footer is different from that of the previous section, the words Same as Previous don't appear. You can click the Previous or Next button to examine the header or footer in the previous or next section.

>> **Different headers and footers for odd and even pages:** Click the Different Odd & Even Pages check box to create different headers and footers for odd and even pages. As "Setting Up and Changing the Margins" explains, earlier in this chapter, documents in which text is printed on both sides of the page can have different headers and footers for the left and right side of the page spread. The Header or Footer box reads Odd or Even to tell you which side of the page spread you're dealing with as you enter your header or footer.

>> **Removing headers and footers from the first page:** Click the Different First Page check box to remove a header or footer from the first page of a document or section. Typically, the first page of letters and reports is not numbered.

Adjusting the Space Between Lines

To change the spacing between lines, select the lines whose spacing you want to change, or simply put the cursor in a paragraph if you're changing the line spacing throughout a paragraph. (If you're just starting a document, you're ready to go.) Then, on the Home tab, click the Line and Paragraph Spacing button and choose an option on the drop-down list.

To take advantage of more line-spacing options, open the Paragraph dialog box, as shown in Figure 2-8. Use either of these techniques to open the Paragraph dialog box:

>> Go to the Home tab or Layout tab and click the Paragraph group button.

>> On the Home tab, click the Line and Paragraph Spacing button and choose Line Spacing Options on the drop-down list.

FIGURE 2-8:
In the Paragraph dialog box, choose Spacing options to decide the amount of space between paragraphs and lines.

Besides single-, 1.5-, and double-spacing, the Paragraph dialog box offers these Line Spacing options:

>> **At Least:** Choose this one if you want Word to adjust for tall symbols or other unusual text. Word adjusts the lines but makes sure there is, at minimum, the number of points you enter in the At box between each line.

>> **Exactly:** Choose this one and enter a number in the At box if you want a specific amount of space between lines.

>> **Multiple:** Choose this one and put a number in the At box to get triple-spaced, quadruple-, quintuple-, or any other number of spaced lines.

TIP

To quickly single-space text, click the text or select it if you want to change more than one paragraph, and press Ctrl+1. To quickly double-space text, select the text and press Ctrl+2. Press Ctrl+5 to put one and a half lines between lines of text.

The Design tab offers a command called Paragraph Spacing for changing the over-all look of paragraphs. Click the Paragraph Spacing button and choose an option on the drop-down list to make paragraphs and lines of text more compact, tight, open, or relaxed.

Adjusting the Space Between Paragraphs

Rather than press Enter to put a blank line between paragraphs, you can open the Paragraph dialog box and enter a point-size measurement in the Before or After text box (see Figure 2-8). The Before and After measurements place a specific amount of space before and after paragraphs.

WARNING

Truth be told, the Before and After options are for use with styles (a subject of the next chapter). When you create a style, you can tell Word to always follow a paragraph in a certain style with a paragraph in another style. For example, a paragraph in the Chapter Title style might always be followed by a paragraph in the Chapter Intro style. In cases like these, when you know that paragraphs assigned to one type of style will always follow paragraphs assigned to another style, you can confidently put space before and after paragraphs. But if you use the Before and After styles indiscriminately, you can end up with large blank spaces between paragraphs.

Go to the Home tab and use one of these techniques to adjust the amount of space between paragraphs:

>> Click the Line and Paragraph Spacing button and choose Add Space Before Paragraph or Add Space after Paragraph on the drop-down list. These commands place 10 points of blank space before or after the paragraph that the cursor is in.

>> Click the Paragraph group button to open the Paragraph dialog box (see Figure 2-8), and enter point-size measurements in the Before and After boxes (or choose Auto in these boxes to enter one blank line between paragraphs in whatever your line-spacing choice is). The Don't Add Space between Paragraphs of the Same Style check box tells Word to ignore Before and After measurements if the previous or next paragraph is assigned the same style as the paragraph that the cursor is in.

Creating Numbered and Bulleted Lists

What is a document without a list or two? It's like an emperor with no clothes. Numbered lists are invaluable in manuals and books like this one that present a lot of step-by-step procedures. Use bulleted lists when you want to present alternatives to the reader. A *bullet* is a black, filled-in circle or other character. These pages explain numbered lists, bulleted lists, and multilevel lists.

Simple numbered and bulleted lists

The fastest, cleanest, and most honest way to create a numbered or bulleted list is to enter the text without any concern for numbers or bullets. Just press Enter at the end of each step or bulleted entry. When you're done, select the list, go to the Home tab, and click the Numbering or Bullets button. You can also click the Numbering or Bullets button and start typing the list. Each time you press Enter, Word enters the next number or another bullet.

Meanwhile, here are some tricks for handling lists:

>> **Ending a list:** Press the Enter key twice after typing the last entry in the list.

>> **Removing the numbers or bullets:** Select the list and click the Numbering or Bullets button.

>> **Adjusting how far a list is indented:** Right-click anywhere in the list, choose Adjust List Indents, and enter a new measurement in the Text Indent box.

AUTOMATIC LISTS AND WHAT TO DO ABOUT THEM

Word creates automatic lists for you whether you like it or not. To see what I mean, type the number 1, type a period, and press the spacebar. Word immediately creates a numbered list. In the same manner, Word creates a bulleted list when you type an asterisk (*) and press the spacebar.

Some people find this kind of behind-the-scenes skullduggery annoying. If you are one such person, do one of the following to keep Word from making lists automatically:

- Click the AutoCorrect Options button — it appears automatically — and choose Stop Automatically Creating Lists.

- On the File tab, choose Options, select the Proofing category in the Word Options dialog box, and click the AutoCorrect Options button. On the AutoFormat As You Type tab in the AutoCorrect dialog box, deselect the Automatic Numbered Lists and Automatic Bulleted Lists check boxes.

>> **Resuming a numbered list:** Suppose that you want a numbered list to resume where a list you entered earlier ended. In other words, suppose that you left off writing a four-step list, put in a graphic or some paragraphs, and now you want to resume the list at Step 5. Click the Numbering button to start numbering again. The AutoCorrect Options button appears. Click it and choose Continue Numbering, or right-click and choose Continue Numbering on the shortcut menu.

>> **Starting a new list:** Suppose that you want to start a brand-new list right away. Right-click the number Word entered and choose Restart at 1 on the shortcut menu.

Constructing lists of your own

If you're an individualist and you want numbered and bulleted lists to work your way, follow these instructions for choosing unusual bullet characters and number formats:

>> **Choosing a different numbering scheme:** On the Home tab, open the drop-down list on the Numbering button and choose a numbering scheme. You can also choose Define New Number Format. As shown in Figure 2-9, you see the Define New Number Format dialog box, where you can choose a number format, choose a font for numbers, and toy with number alignments.

>> **Choosing a different bullet character:** On the Home tab, open the drop-down list on the Bullets button and choose a different bullet character on the drop-down list. You can also choose Define New Bullet to open the Define New Bullet dialog box, shown in Figure 2-9, and click the Symbol button to choose a bullet character in the Symbol dialog box (Book 1, Chapter 2 describes symbols). The dialog box also offers opportunities for indenting bullets and the text that follows them in unusual ways.

FIGURE 2-9: Customizing a numbered or bulleted list.

Managing a multilevel list

A *multilevel list*, also called a *nested list*, is a list with subordinate entries, as shown in Figure 2-10. To create a multilevel list, you declare what kind of list you want, and then, as you enter items for the list, you indent the items that you want to be subordinate. Follow these steps to create a multilevel list:

1. **On the Home tab, click the Multilevel List button and choose what kind of list you want.**

   If none of the lists suit you, you can choose Define New Multilevel List and create a new kind of list in the Define New Multilevel List dialog box.

2. **Enter the items for the list, pressing Enter as you complete each one.**

3. **Select a list item (or items) and click the Increase Indent button (or press Ctrl+M) to make the items subordinate in the list; click the Decrease Indent button (or press Ctrl+Shift+M) to raise their rank in the list.**

   Repeat Step 3 until the list is just so.

❖ *Radiata*
   ➤ Ctenophora
   ➤ Cnidaria
❖ *Bilateria*
   ➤ Acoelomorpha
   ➤ Myxozoa
   ➤ **Superphylum Deuterostomia**
      • Chordata
      • Hemichordata
      • Echinodermata
      • Chaetognatha
   ➤ **Superphylum Ecdysozoa**
      • Kinorhyncha
      • Loricifera
      • Priapulida

1) *Radiata*
   a) Ctenophora
   b) Cnidaria
2) *Bilateria*
   a) Acoelomorpha
   b) Myxozoa
   c) **Superphylum Deuterostomia**
      i) Chordata
      ii) Hemichordata
      iii) Echinodermata
      iv) Chaetognatha
   d) **Superphylum Ecdysozoa**
      i) Kinorhyncha
      ii) Loricifera
      iii) Priapulida

1. *Radiata*
   1.1. Ctenophora
   1.2. Cnidaria
2. *Bilateria*
   2.1. Acoelomorpha
   2.2. Myxozoa
   2.3. **Superphylum Deuterostomia**
      2.3.1. Chordata
      2.3.2. Hemichordata
      2.3.3. Echinodermata
      2.3.4. Chaetognatha
   2.4. **Superphylum Ecdysozoa**
      2.4.1. Kinorhyncha
      2.4.2. Loricifera
      2.4.3. Priapulida

FIGURE 2-10: Examples of multilevel lists.

Working with Tabs

Tabs are a throwback to the days of the typewriter, when it was necessary to make tab stops in order to align text. Except for making leaders and aligning text in headers and footers, everything you can do with tabs can also be done by creating a table — and it can be done far faster. All you have to do is align the text inside the table and then remove the table borders. (Chapter 4 of this minibook explains tables.)

A *tab stop* is a point around which or against which text is formatted. As shown in Figure 2-11, Word offers five tab types for aligning text: Left, Center, Right, Decimal, and Bar (a bar tab stop merely draws a vertical line on the page). When you press the Tab key, you advance the text cursor by one tab stop. Tab stops are shown on the ruler; symbols on the ruler tell you what type of tab you're dealing with.

By default, tabs are left-aligned and are set at half-inch intervals. Display the ruler (click the Ruler check box on the View tab) and follow these steps to change tabs or change where tabs appear on the ruler:

FIGURE 2-11: Different kinds of tab stops.

1. **Select the paragraphs that need different tab settings.**

2. **Click the Tab box on the left side of the ruler as many times as necessary to choose the kind of tab you want.**

   Symbols on the tab box indicate which type of tab you're choosing.

3. **Click the ruler where you want the tab to go.**

   You can click as many times as you want and enter more than one kind of tab.

ALL ABOUT TAB LEADERS

In my opinion, the only reason to fool with tabs and tab stops is to create tab leaders like the ones shown here. A *leader* is a series of punctuation marks — periods in the illustration — that connect text across a page. Leaders are very elegant. For the figure, I used left-aligned tab stops for the characters' names and right-aligned tab stops for the players' names. I included leaders so that you can tell precisely who played whom.

THE PLAYERS

Romeo	McGeorge Wright
Juliet	Gabriela Hernandez
Mercutio	Chris Suzuki
Lady Capulet	Mimi Hornstein

Follow these steps to create tab leaders:

1. **Enter the text and, in each line, enter a tab space between the text on the left side and the text on the right side.**

2. **Select the text you entered.**

3. **On the Home tab, click the Paragraph group button, and in the Paragraph dialog box, click the Tabs button.**

   You see the Tabs dialog box.

4. **Enter a position for the first new tab in the Tab Stop Position box (for example, enter .5).**

5. **Under Leader in the dialog box, select the punctuation symbol that you want for the leader.**

6. **Click OK, display the ruler, and drag tab markers to adjust the space between the text on the left and right.**

To move a tab stop, drag it to a new location on the ruler. Text that is aligned with the tab stop moves as well. To remove a tab stop, drag it off the ruler. When you remove a tab stop, text to which it was aligned is aligned to the next remaining tab stop on the ruler, or to the next default tab stop if you didn't create any tab stops of your own.

Sometimes it's hard to tell where tabs were put in the text. To find out, click the Show/Hide¶ button on the Home tab to see the formatting characters, including the arrows that show where the Tab key was pressed.

Hyphenating Text

The first thing you should know about hyphenating words is that you may not need to do it. Text that hasn't been hyphenated is much easier to read, which is why the majority of text in this book, for example, isn't hyphenated. It has a *ragged right margin*, to borrow typesetter lingo. Hyphenate only when text is trapped in columns or in other narrow places, or when you want a very formal-looking document.

WARNING

Do not insert a hyphen simply by pressing the hyphen key, because the hyphen will stay there even if the word moves to the middle of a line and doesn't need to be broken in half. Instead, when a big gap appears in the right margin and a word is crying out to be hyphenated, put the cursor where the hyphen needs to go and press Ctrl+hyphen. This way, you enter what is called a *discretionary hyphen* or *optional hyphen*, and the hyphen appears only if the word breaks at the end of a line. (To remove a discretionary hyphen, press the Show/Hide¶ button so that you can see it, and then backspace over it.)

Automatically and manually hyphenating a document

Select text if you want to hyphenate part of a document, not all of it, and use one of these techniques to hyphenate words that break on the end of a line of text:

>> **Automatic hyphenation:** On the Layout tab, click the Hyphenation button and choose Automatic on the drop-down list. Word hyphenates your document (or a portion of your document, if you selected it first).

You can tell Word how to hyphenate automatically by clicking the Hyphenation button and choosing Hyphenation Options. You see the Hyphenation dialog box, shown in Figure 2-12. Deselect the Hyphenate Words in CAPS check box if you don't care to hyphenate words in uppercase. Words that fall in the hyphenation zone are hyphenated, so enlarging the hyphenation zone means a less ragged right margin but more ugly hyphens, and a small zone means fewer ugly hyphens but a more ragged right margin. You can limit how many hyphens appear consecutively by entering a number in the Limit Consecutive Hyphens To box.

>> **Manual hyphenation:** On the Layout tab, click the Hyphenation button and choose Manual on the drop-down list. Word displays a box with some hyphenation choices in it, as shown in Figure 2-12. The cursor blinks on the spot where Word suggests putting a hyphen. Click Yes or No to accept or reject Word's suggestion. Keep accepting or rejecting Word's suggestions until the text is hyphenated.

FIGURE 2-12:
Telling Word how to hyphenate (left) and deciding where a hyphen goes (right).

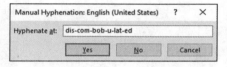

Unhyphenating and other hyphenation tasks

More hyphenation esoterica:

>> **Unhyphenating:** To "unhyphenate" a document or text you hyphenated automatically, go to the Layout tab, click the Hyphenation button, and choose None on the drop-down list.

>> **Preventing text from being hyphenated:** Select the text and, on the Home tab, click the Paragraph group button. In the Paragraph dialog box, select the Line and Page Breaks tab, and select the Don't Hyphenate check box. (If you can't hyphenate a paragraph, it's probably because this box was selected unintentionally.)

EM AND EN DASHES

Here is something about hyphens that editors and typesetters know, but the general public does not know: There is a difference between hyphens and dashes. Most people insert a hyphen where they ought to use an em dash or an en dash:

- An *em dash* looks like a hyphen but is wider — it's as wide as the letter *m*. It's used as a way to separate parts of a sentence. The first sentence in this paragraph has an em dash in it. Did you notice?

- An *en dash* is the width of the letter *n*. Use en dashes to show inclusive numbers or time periods, like so: pp. 45–50; Aug.–Sept. 1998; Exodus 16:11–16:18. An en dash is a little bit longer than a hyphen.

To place an em or en dash in a document and impress your local typesetter or editor, not to mention your readers, use these techniques:

- **Em dash:** Press Ctrl+Alt+ – (the minus sign key on the Numeric keypad).
- **En dash:** Press Ctrl+ – (on the numeric keypad).

You can also enter an em or en dash by following these steps:

1. **Go to the Insert tab.**
2. **Click the Symbol button and choose More Symbols on the drop-down list.**

   The Symbol dialog box opens.
3. **Go to the Special Characters tab.**
4. **Choose Em Dash or En Dash and click the Insert button.**

Chapter **3**

Word Styles

W elcome to what may be the most important chapter of this book — or the most important in Book 2, anyway. Styles can save a ridiculous amount of time that you would otherwise spend formatting and wrestling with text. And many Word features rely on styles. You can't create a table of contents or use the Navigation pane unless each heading in your document has been assigned a heading style. Nor can you take advantage of Outline view and the commands for moving text around in that view. You can't cross-reference headings or number the headings in a document.

If you want to be stylish, at least where Word is concerned, you have to know about styles.

All About Styles

A *style* is a collection of formatting commands assembled under one name. When you apply a style, you give many formatting commands simultaneously, and you spare yourself the trouble of visiting numerous tabs and dialog boxes to format text. Styles save time and make documents look more professional. Headings assigned the same style — Heading1, for example — all look the same. When readers see that headings and paragraphs are consistent with one another across all the pages of a document, they get a warm, fuzzy feeling. They think the person who created the document really knew what he or she was doing.

Styles and templates

REMEMBER

Every document comes with built-in styles that it inherits from the template with which it was created. You can create your own styles to supplement styles from the template. For that matter, you can create a template, populate it with styles you design, and use your new template to create distinctive letters or reports for your company.

A simple document created with the Blank Document template — a document that you create by pressing Ctrl+N — has only a few styles, but a document that was created with a sophisticated template comes with many styles. The Oriel Report template, for example, comes with styles for formatting titles, subtitles, headings, and quotations. Figure 3-1 illustrates how choosing styles from a template changes text formatting. Notice how choosing style options in the Styles pane reformats the text.

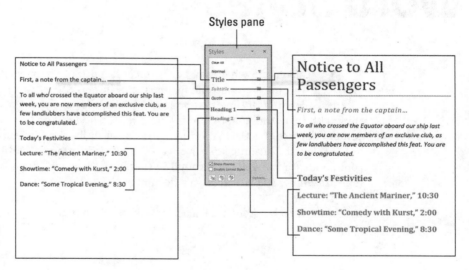

FIGURE 3-1: Apply styles to reformat text.

Types of styles

In the Styles pane (refer to Figure 3-1), the symbol next to each style name tells you what type of style you're dealing with (click the Styles group button on the Home tab to open the Styles pane). Word offers three style types:

>> **Paragraph styles:** Determine the formatting of entire paragraphs. A paragraph style can include these settings: font, paragraph, tab, border, language, bullets, numbering, and text effects. Paragraph styles are marked with the paragraph symbol (¶).

>> **Character styles:** Apply to text, not to paragraphs. You select text before you apply a character style. Create a character style for text that is hard to lay out and for foreign language text. A character style can include these settings: font, border, language, and text effects. When you apply a character style to text, the character-style settings override the paragraph-style settings. For example, if the paragraph style calls for 14-point Arial font but the character style calls for 12-point Times Roman font, the character style wins. Character styles are marked with the letter *a*.

>> **Linked (paragraph and character):** Apply paragraph formats as well as text formats throughout a paragraph. These styles are marked with the paragraph symbol (¶) as well as the letter *a*.

Applying Styles to Text and Paragraphs

Word offers several ways to apply a style, and you are invited to choose the one that works best for you. These pages explain how to apply a style and tell Word how to present style names in the various places where style names are presented for your enjoyment and pleasure.

Applying a style

REMEMBER

The first step in applying a style is to select the part of your document that needs a style change:

>> **A paragraph or paragraphs:** Because paragraph styles apply to all the text in a paragraph, you need only click in a paragraph before applying a style to make a style apply throughout the paragraph. To apply a style to several paragraphs, select all or part of them (Chapter 1 of this minibook explains how to select text).

>> **Text:** To apply a character style, select the letters whose formatting you want to change.

Next, apply the style with one of these techniques:

>> **Styles gallery:** On the Home tab, choose a style in the Styles gallery. (Depending on the size of your screen, you may have to click the Styles button first.) Figure 3-2 shows where the Styles gallery is located. The formatted letters above each style name in the gallery show you what your style choice will do to paragraphs or text. You can "live-preview" styles on the Styles gallery by moving the pointer over style names.

>> **Styles pane:** On the Home tab, click the Styles group button to open the Styles pane, and select a style, as shown in Figure 3-2. Click the Show Preview check box at the bottom of the Styles pane to see formatted style names in the pane and get an idea of what the different styles are. You can drag the Styles pane to different locations on your screen. It remains onscreen after you leave the Home tab.

>> **Apply Styles task pane:** Choose a style on the Apply Styles task pane, as shown in Figure 3-2. To display this task pane, go to the Home tab, open the Styles gallery, and choose Apply Styles (look for this option at the bottom of the gallery). You can drag the Apply Styles task pane to a corner of the screen. As does the Styles pane, the Apply Styles task pane remains onscreen after you leave the Home tab.

REMEMBER

To strip a paragraph or text of its style and give it the generic Normal style, select it and choose Clear Formatting in the Styles gallery or Clear All at the top of the Styles pane.

FIGURE 3-2:
The three ways to apply a style.

Experimenting with style sets

A *style set* is a slight variation on the styles in the template that you chose when you created your document. Figure 3-3 shows examples of style sets. Style sets include Classic, Elegant, Fancy, and Modern. Choosing a style set imposes a slightly different look on your document — you can make it classier, more elegant, fancier, or more modern. All templates, even those you create yourself, offer style sets. Style sets are a convenient way to experiment with the overall look of a document.

To experiment with style sets, go to the Design tab and choose an option in the Style Set gallery.

To return to the original styles in a template, open the Style Set gallery and choose Reset to the Default Style Set.

Choosing which style names appear on the Style menus

One of the challenges of applying styles is finding the right style to apply in the Styles gallery, Styles pane, or Apply Styles task pane (refer to Figure 3-2). All three can become crowded with style names. To make finding and choosing styles names easier, you can decide for yourself which names appear on the three style menus.

Word Styles

FIGURE 3-3:
Examples of
style sets.

Styles gallery

In the Styles gallery, remove a style name by right-clicking it and choosing Remove from Style gallery.

Styles pane and Apply Styles task pane

To decide for yourself which style names appear in the Styles pane and Apply Styles task pane, click the Styles group button on the Home tab, and in the Styles pane, click the Options button (found near the bottom of the pane). You see the Style Pane Options dialog box, shown in Figure 3-4. Choose options to tell Word which style names appear in the Styles pane and Apply Styles task pane:

» **Select Styles to Show:** Choose All Styles to show all style names. The other options place a subset of names in the window and task pane. Recommended style names are those that Microsoft thinks you need most often.

» **Select How List Is Sorted:** Choose an option to describe how to list styles. Except for Based On, these options are, I think, self-explanatory. The Based On option lists styles in alphabetical order according to which style each style is based on (later in this chapter, "Creating a style from the ground up" explains how the Based On setting is used in constructing styles).

» **Select Formatting to Show As Styles:** Choose options to declare which styles to list — those that pertain to paragraph level formatting, fonts, and bulleted and numbered lists.

» **Select How Built-In Style Names Are Shown:** Choose options to tell how to handle built-in styles, the obscure styles that Word applies on its own when you create tables of contents and other self-generating lists.

» **Apply to this document or to the template as well:** Click the Only in This Document option button to apply your choices only to the document you're working on; click the New Documents Based on This Template option button to apply your choices to your document and to all future documents that you create with the template you're using.

FIGURE 3-4:
Deciding which
names to put in
the Styles pane
and Apply Styles
task pane.

DETERMINING WHICH STYLE IS IN USE

How can you tell which style has been applied to a paragraph or text? Sometimes you need to know which style is in play before you decide whether applying a different style is necessary.

Click the paragraph or text and use these techniques to find out which style was applied to it:

- **Glance at the Styles gallery and Styles pane to see which style is selected.** The selected style is the one that was applied to your paragraph or text.

- **Click the Style Inspector button (located at the bottom of the Style pane).** The Style Inspector pane opens and lists the current style.

- **Press Shift+F1.** The Reveal Formatting task pane opens. It lists the style that was applied to the paragraph or text.

If you're especially keen to know about styles in your document, you can make style names appear to the left of the text in Outline and Draft view. On the File tab, choose Options. In the Word Options dialog box, go to the Advanced tab and enter .5 or another measurement in the Style Area Pane Width in Draft and Outline Views box (look for this box under "Display"). You can drag the border of the Style Area pane to enlarge or shrink it.

Creating a New Style

You can create a new style by creating it from a paragraph or building it from the ground up. To do a thorough job, build it from the ground up because styles you create this way can be made part of the template you are currently working in and can be copied to other templates. (Later in this chapter, "Creating and Managing Templates" explains templates.)

Creating a style from a paragraph

Follow these steps to create a new style from a paragraph:

1. **Click in a paragraph whose formatting you want to turn into a style.**

2. **On the Home tab, open the Styles gallery and choose Create a Style.**

You see the Create New Style from Formatting dialog box.

3. **Enter a name for your new style.**

4. **Click OK.**

A style you create this way becomes a part of the document you're working on; it isn't made part of the template from which you created your document.

REMEMBER

Creating a style from the ground up

To make a style available in documents you will create in the future, make it part of a template and build it from the ground up. In the Styles pane, click the New Style button (you can find it at the bottom of the pane). You see the Create New Style from Formatting dialog box, shown in Figure 3-5. Fill in the dialog box and click OK.

FIGURE 3-5: Creating a brand-spanking-new style.

Here's a rundown of the options in the Create New Style from Formatting dialog box:

>> **Name:** Enter a descriptive name for the style.

>> **Style Type:** On the drop-down list, choose a style type ("Types of styles," earlier in this chapter, describes the style types).

WARNING

>> **Style Based On:** If your new style is similar to a style that is already part of the template with which you created your document, choose the style to get a head start on creating the new one. Be warned, however, that if you or someone else changes the Based On style, your new style will inherit those changes and be altered as well.

>> **Style for Following Paragraph:** Choose a style from the drop-down list if the style you're creating is always followed by an existing style. For example, a new style called Chapter Title might always be followed by a style called Chapter Intro Paragraph. For convenience, someone who applies the style you're creating and presses Enter automatically applies the style you choose here on the next line of the document. Applying a style automatically to the following paragraph saves you the trouble of having to apply the style yourself.

>> **Formatting:** Choose options from the menus or click buttons to fashion or refine your style. (You can also click the Format button to do this.)

>> **Add to Styles Gallery:** Select this check box to make the style's name appear in the Styles gallery, Styles pane, and Apply Styles task pane.

>> **Automatically Update:** Normally, when you make a formatting change to a paragraph, the style assigned to the paragraph does not change at all, but the style does change if you select this box. Selecting this box tells Word to alter the style itself each time you alter a paragraph to which you've assigned the style. With this box selected, all paragraphs in the document that were assigned the style are altered each time you change a single paragraph that was assigned the style.

>> **Only in This Document/New Documents Based on This Template:** To make your style a part of the template from which you created your document as well as the document itself, click the New Documents Based on This Template option button. This way, new documents you create that are based on the template you are using can also make use of the new style.

>> **Format:** This is the important one. Click the button and make a formatting choice. Word takes you to dialog boxes so that you can create or refine the style.

Modifying a Style

What if you decide at the end of an 80-page document that all 35 introductory paragraphs to which you assigned the Intro Para style look funny? If you clicked the Automatically Update check box in the Create New Style from Formatting dialog box when you created the style, all you have to do is alter a paragraph to which you assigned the Intro Para style to alter all 35 introductory paragraphs. However, if you decided against updating styles automatically, you can still change the introductory paragraphs throughout your document.

Follow these steps to modify a style that isn't updated automatically:

1. **Click in any paragraph, table, or list to which you've assigned the style; if you want to modify a character style, select the characters to which you've assigned the style.**

2. **In the Styles pane or Apply Styles task pane, make sure that the name of the style that you want to modify is selected.**

   If the right name isn't selected, select it now in the Styles pane or Apply Styles task pane.

3. **In the Styles pane, open the style's drop-down list and choose Modify, as shown in Figure 3-6; in the Apply Styles task pane, click the Modify button.**

   You see the Modify Style dialog box. Does the dialog box look familiar? It is identical to the Create New Style from Formatting dialog box that you used to create the style in the first place (refer to Figure 3-5).

4. **Change the settings in the Modify Styles dialog box and click OK.**

   The previous section in this chapter explains the settings.

After you modify a style, all paragraphs or text to which the style was assigned are instantly changed. You don't have to go back and reformat text and paragraphs throughout your document.

FIGURE 3-6:
Choosing to
modify a style.

Creating and Managing Templates

As I explain at the start of this chapter, every document you create is fashioned from a *template.* The purpose of a template is to store styles for documents. In the act of creating a document, you choose a template, and the styles on the template become available to you when you work on your document (Chapter 1 of this minibook explains how to choose a template when you create a new document).

For example, when you select Blank Template in the New window or press Ctrl+N, you create a document with the Normal template, a relatively simple template with few styles. When you create a document with a template from Office.com or a template from the New window, more styles are available to you because these templates are more sophisticated.

To save time formatting your documents, you are invited to create templates with styles that you know and love. You can create a new template on your own or create a template by assembling styles from other templates and documents. Styles in templates can, like styles in documents, be modified, deleted, and renamed.

REMEMBER

To create a document from a template you created yourself, open the New window (on the File tab, choose New), click the Personal tab, and select your template (see Chapter 1 of this minibook for details).

TIP

To find out which template was used to create a document, go to the File tab and choose Info. Then click the Show All Properties link in the Info window. You see a list of document properties, including the name of the template used to create the document.

Creating a new template

How do you want to create a new template? You can do it on your own or assemble styles from other templates. Read on.

Creating a template on your own

One way to create a template is to start by opening a document with many or all the styles you know and love. When you save this document as a template, you pass along the styles in the document to the template, and you save yourself the trouble of creating styles for the template after you create it.

Follow these steps to create a template on your own:

1. **Create a new document or open a document with styles that you can recycle.**

2. **On the File tab, choose Save As.**

The Save As window opens.

3. **Click This PC.**

4. **Click the Browse button.**

The Save As dialog box appears.

5. **Open the Save As Type menu and choose Word Template.**

The Save As dialog box opens to the folder where templates are stored on your computer.

6. **Enter a name for your template.**

7. **Click the Save button.**

Create, modify, and delete styles as necessary (see "Creating a New Style" and "Modifying a Style," earlier in this chapter).

TELLING WORD WHERE TEMPLATES ARE STORED

The first time you create a template, Word stores it in this folder:

- `C:\Users\`*Username*`\Documents\Custom Office Templates`

However, in previous versions of Word, templates were stored in one of these folders:

- `C:\Users\`*Owner*`\Documents\Custom Office Templates`
- `C:\Users\`*Username*`\AppData\Roaming\Microsoft\Templates`

To keep all your templates in one place, either move them to the `C:\Users\`*Username*`\Documents\Custom Office Templates` folder or tell Word where you prefer to store templates.

Follow these steps to tell Word where you keep templates on your computer:

1. **On the File tab, choose Options.**

   The Word Options dialog box opens.

2. **Go to the Save category.**

3. **In the Default Personal Templates Location text box, enter the path to the folder where you prefer to store templates.**

4. **Click OK.**

Assembling styles from different documents and templates

Suppose that you like a style in one document and you want to copy it to another so that you can use it there. Or you want to copy it to a template to make it available to documents created with the template. Read on to find out how to copy styles between documents and between templates.

COPYING A STYLE FROM ONE DOCUMENT TO ANOTHER

Copy a style from one document to another when you need the style on a one-time basis. Follow these steps:

1. **Select a paragraph that was assigned the style you want to copy.**

   Be sure to select the entire paragraph. If you want to copy a character style, select text to which you have assigned the character style.

2. **Press Ctrl+C or right-click and choose Copy to copy the paragraph to the Clipboard.**

3. **Switch to the document you want to copy the style to and press Ctrl+V or click the Paste button on the Home tab.**

4. **Delete the text you just copied to your document.**

   The style remains in the Styles pane and Styles gallery even though the text is deleted. You can call upon the style whenever you need it.

COPYING STYLES TO A TEMPLATE

Use the Organizer to copy styles from a document to a template or from one template to another. After making a style a part of a template, you can call upon the style in other documents. You can call upon it in each document you create or created with the template. Follow these steps to copy a style into a template:

1. **Open the document or template with the styles you want to copy.**

   Later in this chapter, "Opening a template so that you can modify it" explains how to open a template.

2. **In the Styles pane, click the Manage Styles button.**

   This button is located at the bottom of the window. The Manage Styles dialog box appears.

3. **Click the Import/Export button.**

   You see the Organizer dialog box, shown in Figure 3-7. Styles in the document or template that you opened in Step 1 appear in the In list box on the left side.

4. **Click the Close File button on the right side of the dialog box.**

   The button changes names and becomes the Open File button.

5. **Click the Open File button and, in the Open dialog box, find and select the template to which you want to copy styles; then, click the Open button.**

   See the sidebar "Telling Word where templates are stored," earlier in this chapter, if you have trouble finding the Templates folder.

   The names of styles in the template you chose appear on the right side of the Organizer dialog box.

Select the styles you want to copy

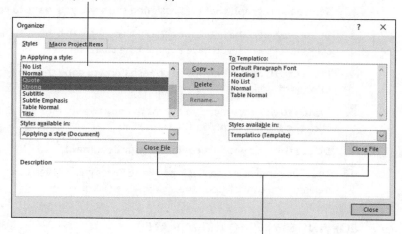

FIGURE 3-7:
Copying styles to a template.

Click to close one template and open another

6. **In the Organizer dialog box, Ctrl+click to select the names of styles on the left side of the dialog box that you want to copy to the template listed on the right side of the dialog box.**

As you click the names, they become highlighted.

7. **Click the Copy button.**

The names of styles that you copied appear on the right side of the Organizer dialog box.

8. **Click the Close button and click Save when Word asks whether you want to save the new styles in the template.**

Opening a template so that you can modify it

Follow these steps to open a template in Word and be able to modify it:

1. **On the File tab, choose Open.**

You see the Open window.

2. **Click This PC.**

3. **Click the Browse button.**

ATTACHING A DIFFERENT TEMPLATE TO A DOCUMENT

It happens in the best of families. You create or are given a document, only to discover that the wrong template is attached to it. For times like those, Word gives you the opportunity to switch templates. Follow these steps:

1. **On the Developer tab, click the Document Template button.**

   You see the Templates and Add-Ins dialog box. If the Developer tab isn't displayed on your screen, go to the File tab, choose Options, visit the Customize Ribbon category in the Word Options dialog box, select the Developer check box, and click OK.

2. **Click the Attach button to open the Attach Template dialog box.**

3. **Find and select the template you want and click the Open button.**

   You return to the Templates and Add-ins dialog box, where the name of the template you chose appears in the Document Template box.

4. **Click the Automatically Update Document Styles check box.**

   Doing so tells Word to apply the styles from the new template to your document.

5. **Click OK.**

4. **In the Open dialog box, go to the Templates folder where you store templates.**

   See the sidebar "Telling Word where templates are stored," earlier in this chapter, if you have trouble finding the Templates folder.

5. **Select the template.**

6. **Click the Open button.**

The template opens in the Word window. Style modifications that you make in the template become available to all documents that were fashioned from the template.

Modifying, deleting, and renaming styles in templates

Modify, delete, and rename styles in a template the same way you do those tasks to styles in a document (see "Modifying a Style," earlier in this chapter). However, in the Modify Style dialog box, select the New Documents Based on This Template option button before clicking OK.

Your style modifications will apply to all documents you create in the future with your template. For the style modifications to take effect in documents you already created with your template, tell Word to automatically update document styles in those documents. Follow these steps:

1. **Save and close your template if it is still open.**

   If any documents you fashioned from the template are open, close them as well.

2. **Open a document that you want to update with the style modifications you made to the template.**

3. **Go to the Developer tab.**

   To display this tab if necessary, open the File tab, choose Options, go to the Customize Ribbon category in the Word Options dialog box, select the Developer check box, and click OK.

4. **Click the Document Template button.**

   The Templates and Add-ins dialog box opens. It should list the path to the Templates folder and the template you modified. If the wrong template is listed, click the Attach button and select the correct template in the Attach Template dialog box.

5. **Select the Automatically Update Document Styles check box.**

6. **Click OK.**

Chapter **4**

Constructing the Perfect Table

The best way to present a bunch of data at one time in Word is to do it in a table. Viewers can compare and contrast the data. They can compare Elvis sightings in different cities or income from different businesses. They can contrast the number of socks lost in different washing machine brands. A table is a great way to plead your case or defend your position. Readers can see right away whether the numbers back you up. They can refer to your table to get the information they need.

As everyone who has worked on tables knows, however, tables are a chore. Getting all the columns to fit, making columns and rows the right width and height, and editing the text in a table isn't easy. This chapter explains how to create tables, enter text in tables, change the number and size of columns and rows, lay out tables, format tables, and do the math in tables. You'll also discover a few tricks — including using a picture for the background — that only magicians know. And to start you on the right foot, I begin by explaining table jargon.

Talking Table Jargon

As with much else in Computerland, tables have their own jargon. Figure 4-1 describes this jargon. Sorry, but you need to catch up on these terms to construct the perfect table:

>> **Cell:** The box that is formed where a row and column intersect. Each cell holds one data item.

>> **Header row:** The name of the labels along the top row that explain what is in the columns below.

>> **Row labels:** The labels in the first column that describe what is in each row.

>> **Borders:** The lines in the table that define where the rows and columns are.

>> **Gridlines:** The gray lines that show where the columns and rows are. Unless you've drawn borders around all the cells in a table, you can't tell where rows and columns begin and end without gridlines. To display or hide the gridlines, go to the (Table) Layout tab and click the View Gridlines button.

Row labels   Header row

	Qtr 1	Qtr 2	Qtr 3	Qtr 4
East	4	8	5	6
West	3	4	4	9
North	3	8	9	6
South	8	7	7	6

Borders   Gridlines   Cells

FIGURE 4-1:
The parts of a table.

Creating a Table

Starting on the Insert tab, Word offers several ways to create a table:

>> **Drag on the Table menu.** On the Insert tab, click the Table button, point in the drop-down list to the number of columns and rows you want, click, and let go of the mouse button, as shown in Figure 4-2.

>> **Use the Insert Table dialog box.** On the Insert tab, click the Table button and choose Insert Table on the drop-down list. The Insert Table dialog box appears (see Figure 4-2). Enter the number of columns and rows you want and click OK.

>> **Draw a table.** On the Insert tab, click the Table button and then choose Draw Table on the drop-down list. The pointer changes into a pencil. Use the pencil to draw table borders, rows, and columns. If you make a mistake, click the Eraser button on the (Table) Layout tab and drag it over the parts of the table you regret drawing. (You may have to click the Draw Borders button first.) When you finish drawing the table, press Esc.

>> **Create a quick table.** On the Insert tab, click the Table button and choose Quick Tables on the drop-down list. Then select a ready-made table on the submenu. You have to replace the sample data in the quick table with your own data.

>> **Construct a table from an Excel worksheet.** On the Insert tab, click the Table button, and choose Excel Spreadsheet. An Excel worksheet appears and — *gadzooks!* — you see Excel tabs and commands where Word tabs and commands used to be. The worksheet you just created is embedded in your file. Whenever you click the worksheet, Excel menus and commands instead of Word menus and commands appear onscreen. Click outside the worksheet to return to Word.

FIGURE 4-2:
Some techniques for creating a table.

TURNING A LIST INTO A TABLE

To turn a list into a table, you need to have all components of the list — each name, address, city name, state, and ZIP code listing, for example — separated from the next component by a tab space or a comma. Word looks for tab spaces or commas when it turns a list into a table, and the program separates data into columns according to where the tab spaces or commas are located. You have to prepare your list carefully by entering tab spaces or commas in all the right places before you can turn a list into a table.

Follow these steps to turn a list into a table after you've done all the preliminary work:

1. **Select the list.**

2. **On the Insert tab, click the Table button and choose Convert Text To Table on the drop-down list.**

   You see the Convert Text to Table dialog box.

   Note the number in the Number of Columns box. It should list the number of components into which you separated your list. If the number doesn't match the number of components, you misplaced a tab entry or comma in your list. Click Cancel, return to your list, and examine it to make sure that each line has been divided into the same number of components.

3. **Under Separate Text At, choose the Tabs or Commas option, depending on which you used to separate the components on the list.**

4. **Click OK.**

You can turn a table into a list by clicking the Convert to Text button on the (Table) Layout tab. (You may have to click the Data button first, depending on the size of your screen.)

REMEMBER

After you create a table, you get two new tabs on the Ribbon. The Table Design tab offers commands for changing the look of the table; the (Table) Layout tab — not to be confused with the other Layout tab on the left side of the Ribbon — is for changing around the rows and columns.

To delete a table, go to the (Table) Layout tab, click the Delete button, and choose Delete Table on the drop-down list.

Entering the Text and Numbers

After you've created the table, you can start entering text and numbers. All you have to do is click in a cell and start typing. Select your table and take advantage of these techniques to make the onerous task of entering table data a little easier:

TIP

» **Quickly changing a table's size:** Drag the bottom or side of a table to change its overall size. To make the table stretch from page margin to page margin, go to the (Table) Layout tab, click the AutoFit button, and choose AutoFit Window.

» **Moving a table:** Switch to Print Layout view and drag the table selector (the square in the upper-left corner of the table).

» **Choosing your preferred font and font size:** Entering table data is easier when you're working in a font and font size you like. Select the table, visit the Home tab, and choose a font and font size there. To select a table, go to the (Table Tools) Layout tab, click the Select button, and choose Select Table on the drop-down list.

» **Quickly inserting a new row:** Click in the last column of the last row in your table and press the Tab key to quickly insert a new row at the bottom of the table.

Here are some shortcuts for moving the cursor in a table:

Press	Moves the Cursor to
Tab	Next column in row
Shift+Tab	Previous column in row
↓	Row below
↑	Row above
Alt+Home	Start of row
Alt+End	End of row
Alt+Page Up	Top of column
Alt+Page Down	Bottom of column

Selecting Different Parts of a Table

It almost goes without saying, but before you can reformat, alter, or diddle with table cells, rows, or columns, you have to select them:

>> **Selecting cells:** To select a cell, click in it. You can select several adjacent cells by dragging the pointer over them.

>> **Selecting rows:** Move the pointer to the left of the row and click when you see the right-pointing arrow; click and drag to select several rows. You can also go to the (Table) Layout tab, click inside the row you want to select, click the Select button, and choose Select Row on the drop-down list. To select more than one row at a time, select cells in the rows before choosing the Select Row command.

>> **Selecting columns:** Move the pointer above the column and click when you see the down-pointing arrow; click and drag to select several columns. You can also start from the (Table) Layout tab, click in the column you want to select, click the Select button, and choose Select Column in the drop-down list. To select several columns, select cells in the columns before choosing the Select Column command.

>> **Selecting a table:** On the (Table) Layout tab, click the Select button, and choose Select Table on the drop-down list (or press Alt+5 on the numeric keypad).

Laying Out Your Table

Very likely, you created too many or too few columns or rows for your table. Some columns are probably too wide and others too narrow. If that's the case, you have to change the table layout by deleting, inserting, and changing the size of columns and rows, not to mention changing the size of the table itself. In other words, you have to modify the table layout. (Later in this chapter, "Decorating your table with borders and colors" shows how to put borders around tables and embellish them in other ways.)

Changing the size of a table, columns, and rows

The fastest way to adjust the width of columns, the height of rows, and the size of a table itself is to "eyeball" it and drag the mouse:

>> **Column or row:** Move the pointer onto a gridline or border, and when the pointer changes into a double-headed arrow, start dragging. Tug and pull, tug and pull until the column or row is the right size.

You can also go to the (Table) Layout tab and enter measurements in the Height and Width text boxes to change the width of a column or the height of a row. The measurements affect entire columns or rows, not individual cells.

>> **A table:** Select your table and use one of these techniques to change its size:

- **Dragging:** Drag the top, bottom, or side of the table. You can also drag the lower-right corner to change the size vertically and horizontally.

- **Height and Width text boxes:** On the (Table) Layout tab, enter measurements in the Height and Width text boxes.

- **Table Properties dialog box:** On the (Table) Layout tab, click the Cell Size group button, and on the Table tab of the Table Properties dialog box, enter a measurement in the Preferred Width text box.

Adjusting column and row size

Resizing columns and rows can be problematic in Word. For that reason, Word offers special commands on the (Table) Layout tab for adjusting the width and height of rows and columns:

>> **Making all columns the same width:** Click the Distribute Columns button to make all columns the same width. Select columns before giving this command to make only the columns you select the same width.

>> **Making all rows the same height:** Click the Distribute Rows button to make all rows in the table the same height. Select rows before clicking the button to make only the rows you select the same height.

You can also click the AutoFit button on the (Table) Layout tab, and take advantage of these commands on the drop-down list for handling columns and rows:

>> **AutoFit Contents:** Make each column wide enough to accommodate its widest entry.

>> **AutoFit Window:** Stretch the table so that it fits across the page between the left and right margin.

>> **Fixed Column Width:** Fix the column widths at their current settings.

Inserting columns and rows

REMEMBER

The trick to inserting (and deleting) columns and rows is to correctly select part of the table first. You can insert more than one column or row at a time by selecting more than one column or row before giving the Insert command. To insert two columns, for example, select two columns and choose an Insert command; to insert three rows, select three rows and choose an Insert command. Earlier in this chapter, "Selecting Different Parts of a Table" explains how to make table selections.

Word offers many, many ways to insert columns and rows. Too many ways, if you ask me.

On the (Table) Layout tab

Go to the (Table) Layout tab and follow these instructions to insert and delete columns and rows:

>> **Inserting columns:** Select a column or columns and click the Insert Left or Insert Right button.

>> **Inserting rows:** Select a row or rows and click the Insert Above or Insert Below button.

TIP

To insert a row at the end of a table, move the pointer into the last cell in the last row and press the Tab key.

Right-clicking

Follow these steps to insert columns or rows by right-clicking:

1. Select column or rows.

2. Right-click to display the mini-toolbar.

Figure 4-3 shows the mini-toolbar you see when you right-click a table.

3. Click Insert on the mini-toolbar.

4. Choose an Insert command (Left, Right, Above, or Below).

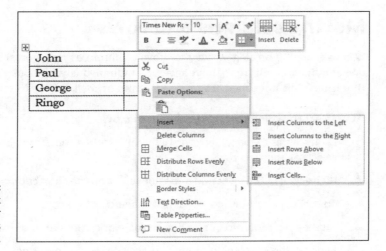

FIGURE 4-3:
The right-click technique for inserting columns and rows.

One-Click Row and One-Click Column buttons

To insert one row or one column, click a One–Click button. The One–Click Column button appears when you move the pointer between columns at the top of a table; the One–Click Row button appears when you move the pointer between rows on the left side of a table. Click a One–Click button to insert one column or one row.

Deleting columns and rows

Go to the (Table) Layout tab and use these techniques to delete columns and rows:

» **Deleting columns:** Click in the column you want to delete, click the Delete button, and choose Delete Columns on the drop-down list. Select more than one column to delete more than one. (You can also right-click and choose Delete Columns.)

» **Deleting rows:** Click in the row you want to delete, click the Delete button, and choose Delete Rows. Select more than one row to delete more than one. (You can also right-click and choose Delete Rows.)

REMEMBER

Pressing the Delete key after you select a column or row deletes the data in the column or row, not the column or row itself.

Constructing the
Perfect Table

Moving columns and rows

Because there is no elegant way to move a column or row, you should move only one at a time. If you try to move several simultaneously, you open a can of worms that is best left unopened. To move a column or row:

1. **Select the column or row you want to move.**

    Earlier in this chapter, "Selecting Different Parts of a Table" explains how to select columns and rows.

2. **Right-click in the selection and choose Cut on the shortcut menu.**

    The column or row is moved to the Clipboard.

3. **Insert a new column or row where you want the column or row to be.**

    Earlier in this chapter, "Inserting columns and rows" explains how.

4. **Move the column or row:**

    - **Column:** Click in the topmost cell in your new column and then click the Paste button (on the Home tab) or press Ctrl+V.
    - **Row:** Click in the first column of the row you inserted and then click the Paste button (on the Home tab) or press Ctrl+V.

SORTING, OR REORDERING A TABLE

On the subject of moving columns and rows, the fastest way to rearrange the rows in a table is to sort the table. *Sorting* means to rearrange all the rows in a table on the basis of data in one or more columns. For example, a table that shows candidates and the number of votes they received could be sorted in alphabetical order by the candidates' names or in numerical order by the number of votes each candidate received. Both tables present the same information, but the information is sorted in different ways.

The difference between ascending and descending sorts is as follows:

- Ascending arranges text from A to Z, numbers from smallest to largest, and dates from earliest to latest.

- Descending arranges text from Z to A, numbers from largest to smallest, and dates from latest to earliest.

When you rearrange a table by sorting it, Word rearranges the formatting as well as the data. Do your sorting before you format the table.

Follow these steps to sort a table:

1. **On the (Table) Layout tab, click the Sort button.**

   You see the Sort dialog box. Depending on the size of your screen, you may have to click the Data button before you see the Sort button.

2. **In the first Sort By drop-down list, choose the column you want to sort with.**

3. **If necessary, open the first Type drop-down list and choose Text, Number, or Date to describe what kind of data you're dealing with.**

4. **Select the Ascending or Descending option button to declare whether you want an ascending or descending sort.**

5. **If necessary, on the first Then By drop-down list, choose the tiebreaker column.**

   If two items in the Sort By columns are alike, Word looks to your Then By column choice to break the tie and place one row before another in the table.

6. **Click OK.**

When you sort a table, Word ignores the *header row* — the first row in the table — and doesn't move it. However, if you want to include the header row in the sort, click the No Header Row option button in the Sort dialog box.

Aligning Text in Columns and Rows

Aligning text in columns and rows is a matter of choosing how you want the text to line up vertically and how you want it to line up horizontally. Follow these steps to align text in a table:

1. **Select the cells, columns, or rows, with text that you want to align (or select your entire table).**

2. **Go to the (Table) Layout tab.**

3. **Click an Align button. (You may have to click the Alignment button first, depending on the size of your screen.)**

Figure 4-4 shows where the Align buttons are on the (Table) Layout tab and how these options align text in a table.

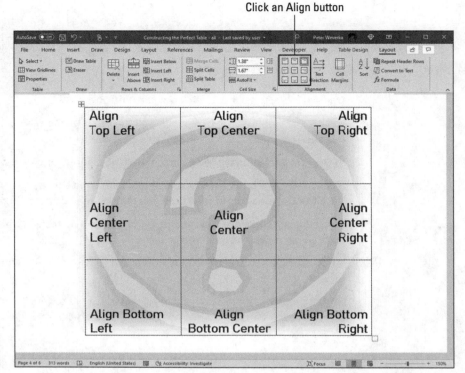

FIGURE 4-4:
Word offers nine
ways to align text.

Merging and Splitting Cells

Merge and split cells to make your tables a little more elegant than run-of-the-mill tables. *Merge* cells to break down the barriers between cells and join them into one cell; *split* cells to divide a single cell into several cells (or several cells into several more cells). In the table shown in Figure 4-5, cells in rows and columns have been split or merged to create a curious-looking little table.

Select the cells you want to merge or split, go to the (Table) Layout tab, and follow these instructions to merge or split cells:

>> **Merging cells:** Click the Merge Cells button. (You can also right-click and choose Merge Cells.)

>> **Splitting cells:** Click the Split Cells button. (You can also right-click and choose Split Cells.) In the Split Cells dialog box, declare how many columns and rows you want to split the cell into and then click OK.

Merge and split table cells

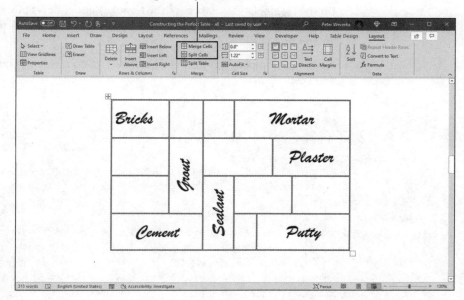

FIGURE 4-5:
Merge and split cells to create unusual tables.

Another way to merge and split cells is to click the Draw Table or Eraser button on the (Table) Layout tab. Click the Draw Table button and then draw lines through cells to split them. Click the Eraser button and drag over or click the boundary between cells to merge cells. Press Esc when you finish drawing or erasing table cell boundaries.

Need to split a table? Place the cursor in what you want to be the first row of the new table, go to the (Table) Layout tab, and click the Split Table button.

Repeating Header Rows on Subsequent Pages

TIP

Making sure that the *header row*, sometimes called the *heading row*, appears on a new page if the table breaks across pages is essential. The header row is the first row in the table, the one that usually describes what is in the columns below. Without a header row, readers can't tell what the information in a table means. Follow these steps to make the header row (or rows) repeat on the top of each new page that a table appears on:

1. **Place the cursor in the header row or select the header rows if your table includes more than one header row.**

Constructing the Perfect Table

2. **On the (Table) Layout tab, click the Repeat Header Rows button. (Depending on the size of your screen, you may have to click the Data button first.)**

Header rows appear only in Print Layout view, so don't worry if you can't see them in Draft view.

FITTING A TABLE ON THE PAGE

Ideally, a table should fit on a single page, because studying table data that is spread across two or more pages can be difficult. Here are some suggestions for fitting a table on a single page:

- **Present the table in landscape mode:** In Landscape mode, a page is turned on its ear so that it is wider than it is tall and you have room for more table columns. To print in Landscape mode, however, you must create a new section for the pages in question. To change the page orientation, go to the Layout tab, click the Orientation button, and choose Landscape.

- **Shrink the font size:** Sometimes shrinking the font size throughout a table shrinks the table just enough to fit it on a page. To shrink fonts throughout a table, go to the Home tab and click the Decrease Font Size button (or press Ctrl+[). Keep decreasing the font size until the table fits on one page.

- **Shrink the columns:** On the (Table) Layout tab, click the AutoFit button, and choose AutoFit Contents on the drop-down list to make each column only wide enough to accommodate its widest entry.

- **Change the orientation of header row text:** In a top-heavy table in which the header row cells contain text and the cells below contain numbers, you can make the entire table narrower by changing the orientation of the text in the header row. To turn text on its ear, select the cells whose text needs a turn, go to the (Table) Layout tab, and click the Text Direction button. Keep clicking until the text turns the direction you want.

Chances are, if your table can't fit on one page, presenting the information in a table isn't the best option. Try presenting it in bulleted or numbered lists. Or present the information in short paragraphs under small fourth- or fifth-level headings.

Formatting Your Table

After you enter text in the table, lay out the columns and rows, and make them the right size, the fun begins. Now you can dress up your table and make it look snazzy. You can choose colors for columns and rows. You can play with the borders that divide the columns and rows and shade columns, rows, and cells by filling them with gray shades or a black background. Read on to find out how to do these tricks.

Designing a table with a table style

TIP

The fastest way to get a good-looking table is to select a table style in the Table Styles gallery, as shown in Figure 4-6. A *table style* is a ready-made assortment of colors and border choices. You can save yourself a lot of formatting trouble by selecting a table style. After you select a table style, you can modify it by selecting or deselecting check boxes in the Table Style Options group on the Table Design tab.

FIGURE 4-6: You have many opportunities for designing tables.

Click anywhere in your table and follow these steps to choose a table style:

1. **Go to the Table Design tab.**

2. **Open the Table Styles gallery and move the pointer over table style choices to live-preview the table.**

3. **Select a table style.**

   To remove a table style, open the Table Styles gallery and choose Clear.

For consistency's sake, choose a similar table style — or better yet, the same table style — for all the tables in your document. This way, your work doesn't become a showcase for table styles.

Calling attention to different rows and columns

On the Table Design tab, Word offers Table Style Options check boxes for calling attention to different rows or columns (refer to Figure 4-6). For example, you can make the first row in the table, called the header row, stand out by selecting the Header Row check box. If your table presents numerical data with total figures in the last row, you can call attention to the last row by selecting the Total Row check box. Select or deselect these check boxes on the Table Design tab to make your table easier to read and understand:

» **Header Row and Total Row:** These check boxes make the first row and last row in a table stand out. Typically, the header row is a different color or contains boldface text because it is the row that identifies the data in the table. Click the Header Row check box to make the first row stand out; if you also want the last row to stand out, click the Total Row check box.

» **Banded Columns and Banded Rows:** *Banded* means "striped" in Office lingo. For striped columns or striped rows — columns or rows that alternate in color — select the Banded Columns or Banded Rows check box.

» **First Column and Last Column:** Often the first column stands out in a table because it identifies what type of data is in each row. Select the First Column check box to make it a different color or boldface its text. Check the Last Column check box if you want the rightmost column to stand out.

Decorating your table with borders and colors

Besides relying on a table style, you can play interior decorator on your own. You can slap color on the columns and rows of your table, draw borders around columns and rows, and choose a look for borders. The Table Design tab offers many commands that pertain to table decoration. Use these commands to shade table columns and rows and draw table borders.

Designing borders for your table

Follow these steps to fashion a border for your table or a part of your table:

1. **Go to the Table Design tab.**

2. **Select the part of your table that needs a new border.**

To select the entire table, go to the (Table) Layout tab, click the Select button, and choose Select Table.

3. **Create a look for the table borders you will apply or draw.**

Use all or some of these techniques to devise a border:

- **Border style:** Open the drop-down list on the Border Styles button and choose the border style that most resembles the one you want.

- **Line style:** Open the Line Style drop-down list and choose a style.

- **Line weight:** Open the Line Weight drop-down list and choose a line thickness.

TIP

If a table on the page you're looking at already has the border you like, you can "sample" the border. Open the drop-down list on the Border Styles button and choose Border Sampler. The pointer changes to an eyedropper. Click the border you want to select its style, weight, and color settings.

4. **Open the drop-down list on the Borders button and choose where to place borders on the part of the table you selected in Step 2.**

You can also change borders by clicking the Borders group button and making selections in the Borders and Shading dialog box, as shown in Figure 4-7.

FIGURE 4-7:
You can draw
borders with
the Borders
and Shading
dialog box.

Selecting colors for columns, rows, or your table

Follow these steps to paint columns, rows, or your table a new color:

1. **Select the part of the table that needs a paint job.**

2. **In the Table Design tab, open the drop-down list on the Shading button and choose a color.**

Later in this chapter, "Using a picture as the table background" explains how to use a picture as the background in a table.

Using Math Formulas in Tables

No, you don't have to add the figures in columns and rows yourself; Word gladly does that for you. Word can perform other mathematical calculations as well. Follow these steps to perform mathematical calculations and tell Word how to format sums and products:

1. **Put the cursor in the cell that will hold the sum or product of the cells above, below, to the right, or to the left.**

2. **On the (Table) Layout tab, click the Formula button.**

    Depending on the size of your screen, you may have to click the Data button first. The Formula dialog box appears, as shown in Figure 4-8. In its wisdom, Word makes an educated guess about what you want the formula to do and places a formula in the Formula box.

3. **If this isn't the formula you want, delete everything except the equals sign in the Formula box, open the Paste Function drop-down list, and choose another function for the formula.**

   For example, choose PRODUCT to multiply figures. You may have to type **left**, **right**, **above**, or **below** in the parentheses to tell Word where to find the figures you want to compute.

4. **In the Number Format drop-down list, choose a format for your number.**

5. **Click OK.**

Units Sold	Price Unit ($)	Total Sale
13	178.12	$2,315.56
15	179.33	$2,689.95
93	178.00	$16,554.00
31	671.13	
24	411.12	
9	69.13	
11	79.40	
196	$1,766.23	

Formula   ?   ×

Formula:
=SUM(LEFT)

Number format:
#,##0

Paste function: Paste bookmark:

ABS
AND
AVERAGE
COUNT
DEFINED
FALSE
IF
INT

OK   Cancel

FIGURE 4-8:
A math formula
in a table.

TIP

Word doesn't calculate blank cells in formulas. Enter 0 in blank cells if you want them to be included in calculations. You can copy functions from one cell to another to save yourself the trouble of opening the Formula dialog box.

Neat Table Tricks

The rest of this chapter details a handful of neat table tricks to make your tables stand out in a crowd. Why should all tables look alike? Read on to discover how to make text in the header row stand on its ear, wrap text around a table, put a picture behind a table, draw diagonal border lines, draw on top of a table, and wrap text around a table.

Changing the direction of header row text

In a top-heavy table in which the cells in the first row contain text and the cells below contain numbers, consider changing the direction of the text in the first row to make the table easier to read. Changing text direction in the first row is also a good way to squeeze more columns into a table. Consider how wide the table shown in Figure 4-9 would be if the words in the first row were displayed horizontally.

FIGURE 4-9:
Change the direction of text to squeeze more columns on a table.

	Yes	No	Maybe	Often	Never
Prof. Plum in the Library	✓				
Miss Scarlet in the Drawing Room				✓	
Col. Mustard in the Dining Room		✓			

Follow these steps to change the direction of text on a table.

1. **Select the row that needs a change of text direction.**

   Usually, that's the first row in a table.

2. **Go to the (Table) Layout tab.**

3. **Keep clicking the Text Direction button until text lands where you want it to land.**

   You may have to click the Alignment button before you can see the Text Direction button.

4. **Change the height of the row to make the vertical text fit.**

   As "Changing the size of a table, columns, and rows" explains, earlier in this chapter, you can change the height of a row by going to the (Table) Layout tab and entering a measurement in the Height box.

Wrapping text around a table

Nothing is sadder than a forlorn little table all alone on a page. To keep tables from being lonely, you can wrap text around them, as shown in Figure 4-10.

FIGURE 4-10:
Wrap text to keep
tables from being
lonely.

Fujita Scale

Scale	Wind Speed (mph)
F0	40–72
F1	73–112
F2	113–157
F3	158–206
F4	207–260
F5	261–318

The Fujita scale measures tornado intensity primarily on the damage a tornado does to buildings and vegetation. Meteorologists determine official Fujita scale measurements by surveying damage on the ground and by air. They take into account eyewitness testimony, media reports, ground-swirl patterns, radar tracking imagery, and, if video is available, videogrammetry.

To wrap text around a table, drag it into the text (drag the selection handle in the upper-left corner of the table). Nine times out of ten, that's all there is to it, but if the text doesn't wrap correctly, follow these steps to wrap your table:

1. **On the (Table) Layout tab, click the Cell Size group button.**

   The Table Properties dialog box opens.

2. **On the Table tab, under Text Wrapping, select the Around option.**

3. **Click the Positioning button.**

   The Table Positioning dialog box appears.

4. **Select the Move with Text check box and click OK.**

   By selecting Move with Text, you make sure that the table stays with the surrounding text when you insert or delete text.

5. **Click OK in the Table Properties dialog box.**

Using a picture as the table background

As Figure 4-11 demonstrates, a picture used as the background in a table looks mighty nice. To make it work, however, you need a graphic that serves well as the background. For Figure 4-11, I got around this problem by recoloring my graphic. (Book 8, Chapter 3 explains how to recolor a graphic.) You also need to think about font colors. Readers must be able to read the table text, and that usually means choosing a white or light font color for text so that the text can be read over the graphic. For Figure 4-11, I selected a white font color.

Placing a graphic behind a table requires a fair bit of work, but the results are well worth the effort. First you insert the graphic and perhaps recolor it. Then you create the table. Lastly, you make the table fit squarely on top of the graphic and perhaps group the objects together.

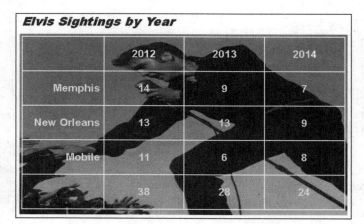

Elvis Sightings by Year

	2012	2013	2014
Memphis	14	9	7
New Orleans	13	13	9
Mobile	11	6	8
	38	28	24

FIGURE 4-11:
A well-chosen graphic in a table background helps indicate what the table is all about.

Follow these steps to place a graphic behind a table:

1. **Insert the graphic, resize it, and format the graphic.**

   Book 8, Chapter 3 explains how to insert and resize graphics. To insert a graphic, go to the Insert tab, click the Pictures button, and choose an option on the drop-down list. To resize your picture, drag a selection handle; make the graphic as big as you want your table to be. To recolor a graphic similar to the job done to the graphic in Figure 4-12, select the Picture Format tab, click the Color button, and choose an option.

2. **Click the Layout Options button (located to the right of the picture) and choose Behind Text on the drop-down list.**

   Choosing Behind Text tells Word to put the graphic behind the text. You can also go to the Picture Format tab, click the Wrap Text button, and choose Behind Text.

3. **Insert the table and make it roughly the same size as the graphic.**

   These tasks are explained earlier in this chapter. To change the size of a table, drag a selection handle on its corner or side. Place the table nearby the graphic, but not right on top of it.

4. **On the Table Design tab, open the Table Styles gallery and choose Clear.**

   With the table styles out of the way, you can see the graphic clearly through your table.

5. **Enter the data in the table, select a font and font color, select a border and border color, and align the text.**

   These tasks (except for selecting fonts) are described throughout this chapter. The easiest way to choose a font and font color for a table is to select the table, go to the Home tab, and select a font and font size.

6. **Move the table squarely on top of the graphic and then make the table and graphic roughly the same size.**

Here are a few tricks that are worth knowing when you're handling a graphic and table:

» If the graphic is in front of the table, select the graphic, go to the Picture Format tab, open the drop-down list on the Send Backward button, and choose Send Behind Text.

» To make the text in the table legible, use a light-colored font. As well, use white or light-colored table borders so that the borders can be clearly seen.

Drawing diagonal lines on tables

Draw diagonal lines across table cells to cancel out those cells or otherwise make cells look different. In Figure 4-12, diagonal lines are drawn on cells to show that information that would otherwise be in the cells is either not available or not relevant.

FIGURE 4-12: Diagonal lines mark off cells as different.

	Mon.	Tues.	Wed.	Thurs.	Fri.	Sat.	Sun.
McKeef	8:00			3:00		8:00	2:15
Arnez	9:00	6:00	2:30	12:00	8:15		4:00
Danes	9:30		2:00	7:30		3:30	7:30
Minor		12:00	4:15	5:15	2:00		
Krupf	3:30	6:00		12:00	2:30	9:00	9:00
Gough	3:00			7:00	3:30	4:530	3:30
Gonzalez	12:00	7:15	8:30				10:15

To draw diagonal lines across cells, select the cells that need diagonal lines, and on the Table Design tab, open the drop-down list on the Borders button and choose Diagonal Down Border or Diagonal Up Border.

To remove diagonal lines, open the drop-down list on the Borders button and choose Diagonal Down Border or Diagonal Up Border again.

Drawing on a table

When you want to call attention to data in one part of a table, draw a circle around the data. By "draw," I mean make an Oval shape and place it over the data you want to highlight, as shown in Figure 4-13. Book 8, Chapter 4 explains the drawing tools in detail. To spare you the trouble of turning to that chapter, here are shorthand instructions for drawing on a table:

1. On the Insert tab, click the Shapes button and select the Oval shape on the drop-down list.

2. On a corner of your page, away from the table, drag to draw the oval.

3. On the Shape Format tab, open the drop-down list on the Shape Fill button and choose No Fill.

4. Open the drop-down list on the Shape Outline button and choose a very dark color.

5. Open the drop-down list on the Shape Outline button, choose Weight, and choose a thick line.

6. Drag the oval over the data on your table that you want to highlight.

   If the oval is obscured by the table, go to the Shape Format tab and click the Bring Forward button. (Click the Arrange button, if necessary, to see this button.) While you're at it, consider rotating the oval a little way to make it appear as though it were drawn manually on the table.

	Qtr 1	Qtr 2	Qtr 3	Qtr 4
East	4	8	5	6
West	3	4	4	9
North	3	8	9	6
South	8	7	7	6

FIGURE 4-13: You can circle data to highlight it.

Chapter **5**

Taking Advantage of the Proofing Tools

I was going to call this chapter "Foolproofing Your Work," but that seemed kind of presumptuous because keeping every error from slipping into your work is well-nigh impossible. Still, you can do a good job of proofing your work and eliminating errors by using the tools that Word provides for that purpose. This chapter describes how to proof your work for misspellings, grammatical errors, and awkward writing. It shows how to find text, and if you're so inclined, find and replace text. You also discover how to translate text and proof foreign language text. The proofing tools are not foolproof, but they're close to it.

REMEMBER

The F7 key is the key to the kingdom when it comes to proofing Word documents. Here is the magic of pressing F7 and various key combinations:

>> **F7:** Open the Editor to search misspellings and grammatical errors

>> **Alt+F7:** Scroll to the next misspelling

>> **Shift+F7:** Open the Thesaurus

Correcting Your Spelling Errors

Word keeps a dictionary in its hip pocket, which is a good thing for you. Who wants to be embarrassed by a spelling error? Word consults its dictionary when you enter text in a document. To correct misspellings, you can either address them one at a time or start the spell checker and proof many pages simultaneously.

WARNING

Don't trust the smell checker to be accurate all the time. It doesn't really locate misspelled words — it locates words that aren't in its dictionary. For example, if you write "Nero diddled while Rome burned," the spell checker doesn't catch the error. Nero *fiddled* while Rome burned, but because *diddle* is a legitimate word in the spelling dictionary, the spell checker overlooks the error. The moral: Proof-read your documents carefully and don't rely on the spell checker to catch all your smelling errors.

Correcting misspellings one at a time

One way to handle misspelled words is to use the one-at-a-time method of spell checking. As shown in Figure 5-1, you can click (or right-click) each word that is underlined in red and choose a correct spelling from the Spelling shortcut menu. After you choose a word from the shortcut menu, it replaces the misspelling that you clicked.

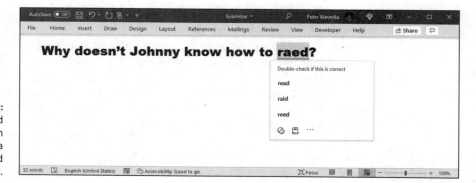

FIGURE 5-1:
Click a word underlined in red to correct a typo or repeated word.

You can also click Ignore All on the Spelling shortcut menu to tell Word when a word is correctly spelled and shouldn't be flagged, or click Add to Dictionary, which adds the word to the Office spelling dictionary and declares it a correctly spelled word.

GETTING RID OF THE SQUIGGLY RED LINES

More than a few people think that the squiggly red lines that appear under misspelled words are annoying. To keep those lines from appearing, go to the File tab, choose Options, and go to the Proofing category in the Options dialog box. Then deselect the Check Spelling As You Type check box.

Even with the red lines gone, you can do a quick one-at-a time spell check. Press Alt+F7 to scroll to the next misspelling and display a shortcut menu for fixing it.

Words entered twice are also flagged in red, in which case the Spelling short-cut menu offers the Delete Repeated Word option so that you can delete the second word.

Running a spell check

Instead of correcting misspellings one at a time, you can run a spell check on your work. Start your spell check with one of these methods:

>> Press F7.

>> Go to the Review tab and click the Editor button.

>> On the status bar, click the Proofing Errors button. (Move the pointer over this button to see a pop-up message that tells you whether Word has found proofing errors in your document.)

You see the Editor task pane. Under Corrections, it declares how many spelling errors are in your document. Select Spelling in the task pane to see suggestions for correcting a misspelling, as shown in Figure 5-2.

Here are options for correcting known misspellings in the Editor task pane:

>> Select the correct spelling.

>> Click in the page you're working on and correct the misspelling there; then click the Resume button in the Editor task plane.

Taking Advantage of the Proofing Tools

Misspelled word   Choose the correct spelling

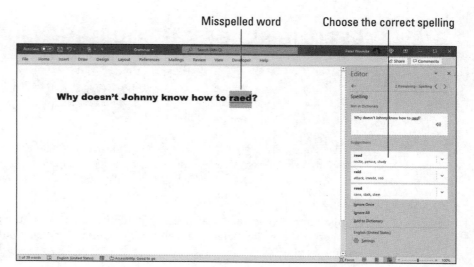

FIGURE 5-2:
Correcting a
misspelling in the
Editor task pane.

If the word in question isn't a misspelling, tell Word how to handle the word by choosing one of these options:

>> **Ignore Once:** Ignores this instance of the misspelling but stops on it again if the same misspelling appears later.

>> **Ignore All:** Ignores the misspelling throughout the document you're working on and in all other open documents as well.

>> **Delete Repeated Word:** Deletes the second word in a pair of repeating words.

>> **Add to Dictionary:** Adds the misspelling to the Office spelling dictionary. By choosing this option, you tell Word that the misspelling is a legitimate word or name.

TIP

Word offers the Change All option to correct a misspelling that occurs throughout a document. In the Editor task pane, open the drop-down menu on a spelling suggestion and choose Change All on the shortcut menu to correct all instances of a misspelling.

REMEMBER

Office programs share the same spelling dictionary. For example, words you add to the spelling dictionary in Word are deemed correct spellings in PowerPoint presentations, Excel spreadsheets, Publisher publications, Access databases, and Outlook emails.

Preventing text from being spell checked

Spell checking address lists, lines of computer code, and foreign languages such as Spanglish for which Microsoft doesn't offer foreign language dictionaries is a thorough waste of time. Follow these steps to tell the spell checker to ignore text:

1. Select the text.

2. In the Review tab, click the Language button and choose Set Proofing Language on the drop-down list.

You see the Language dialog box.

3. Select the Do Not Check Spelling or Grammar check box.

4. Click OK.

Correcting Grammatical Errors

Much of what constitutes good grammar is, like beauty, in the eye of the beholder. Still, you can do your best to repair grammatical errors in Word documents by getting the assistance of the Editor. The Editor identifies grammatical errors, explains what the errors are, and gives you the opportunity to correct the errors.

Word identifies grammatical errors by double-underlining them in blue. Here are ways to correct grammatical errors:

>> **Correct errors one at a time:** Click (or right-click) and choose an option on the Grammar menu, as shown in Figure 5-3.

>> **Correct errors throughout a document:** Press F7 or click the Editor button on the Home tab. The Editor task pane opens, as shown in Figure 5-3. Under Corrections, it reports how many grammatical errors are in your document. Select Grammar in the task pane to visit a grammatical error in your document and, if you want to, repair it by selecting an option under Suggestions.

If you want to fine-tune how Word runs its grammar checker, go to the File tab and choose Options, and in the Word Options dialog box, go to the Proofing category. Under When Correcting Spelling and Grammar in Word, choose whether to mark grammatical errors with blue lines, and in the Writing Style drop-down list, how stringent you want the rules of grammar to be.

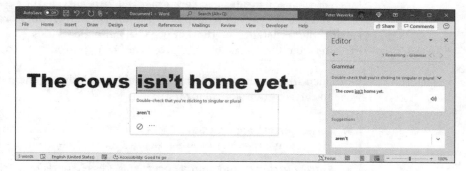

FIGURE 5-3: Fixing grammatical errors.

Refining Your Work with the Editor

If you read the start of this chapter, you know that the Editor can alert you to misspellings and grammatical errors. It can also suggest ways to improve your writing.

When the Editor sees what it thinks is a suspect word or phrase, it marks the word or phrase with a dotted blue line. Click this line to see a pop-up box that explains why the word or phrase was flagged. In some cases, the pop-up box also offers a suggestion for changing the words around. You can click the suggestion to enter it in your document.

Besides addressing errant words and phrases one at a time, you can address them *en masse* in the Editor task pane. Follow these steps:

1. **On the Home tab, click the Editor button (or press F7).**

The Editor task pane opens, as shown in Figure 5-4. Errors in your document that have to do with Clarity, Conciseness, Formality, and similar criteria are tabulated in the task pane under the heading "Refinements."

2. **Select a Refinement category to investigate errors of a certain type.**

For example, to see where your writing could be clearer, select the Clarity category. Word scrolls in your document to an error. Meanwhile, the Editor task pane says why the error was flagged, displays the sentence with the error in a text box, and in some cases offers a suggestion for correcting the error.

3. **Correct the error or let it stand.**

The Editor, as editors sometimes are, can be awfully finicky. The error might not need correcting. Correct it or let it stand as you see fit:

- **Correct the error:** Either correct it in the text box or choose a suggestion.

- **Let the error stand:** Click the Next arrow to scroll to and examine the next error. This arrow is located in the upper-right corner of the Edit task pane.

4. **Repeat Step 3 as many times as necessary to examine errors in the category you chose.**

I hope the Editor helps improve your writing.

To return to the Refinements list in the Editor task pane (see Figure 5-4) and examine errors in a different category, click the Back arrow. You can find this arrow in the upper-left corner of the Editor task pane.

TIP

If you think the dotted blue lines made by the Editor are a distraction, you can remove them. Go to the File tab, choose Options, and visit the Proofing category in the Options dialog box. Then deselect the Mark Grammar Errors As You Type check box. Whether or not the dotted blue lines appear, you can always run an edit check by pressing F7.

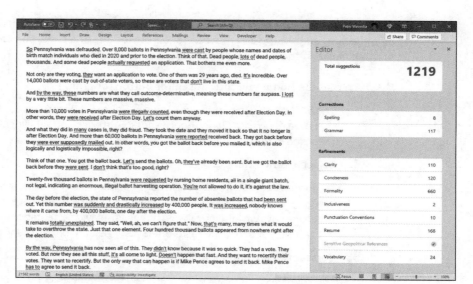

So Pennsylvania was defrauded. Over 8,000 ballots in Pennsylvania were cast by people whose names and dates of birth match individuals who died in 2020 and prior to the election. Think of that. Dead people, lots of dead people, thousands. And some dead people actually requested an application. That bothers me even more.

Not only are they voting, they want an application to vote. One of them was 29 years ago, died. It's incredible. Over 14,000 ballots were cast by out-of-state voters, so these are voters that don't live in this state.

And by the way, these numbers are what they call outcome-determinative, meaning these numbers far surpass. I lost by a very little bit. These numbers are massive, massive.

More than 10,000 votes in Pennsylvania were illegally counted, even though they were received after Election Day. In other words, they were received after Election Day. Let's count them anyway.

And what they did in many cases is, they did fraud. They took the date and they moved it back so that it no longer is after Election Day. And more than 60,000 ballots in Pennsylvania were reported received back. They got back before they were ever supposedly mailed out. In other words, you got the ballot back before you mailed it, which is also logically and logistically impossible, right?

Think of that one. You got the ballot back. Let's send the ballots. Oh, they've already been sent. But we got the ballot back before they were sent. I don't think that's too good, right?

Twenty-five thousand ballots in Pennsylvania were requested by nursing home residents, all in a single giant batch, not legal, indicating an enormous, illegal ballot harvesting operation. You're not allowed to do it, it's against the law.

The day before the election, the state of Pennsylvania reported the number of absentee ballots that had been sent out. Yet this number was suddenly and drastically increased by 400,000 people. It was increased, nobody knows where it came from, by 400,000 ballots, one day after the election.

It remains totally unexplained. They said, "Well, ah, we can't figure that." Now, that's many, many times what it would take to overthrow the state. Just that one element. Four hundred thousand ballots appeared from nowhere right after the election.

By the way, Pennsylvania has now seen all of this. They didn't know because it was so quick. They had a vote. They voted. But now they see all this stuff, it's all come to light. Doesn't happen that fast. And they want to recertify their votes. They want to recertify. But the only way that can happen is if Mike Pence agrees to send it back. Mike Pence has to agree to send it back.

FIGURE 5-4:
You can use the Editor to improve your writing.

Finding and Replacing Text

Use the Find command to locate a name or text passage. Use its twin, the powerful Replace command, to find and replace a name or text passage throughout a document. For an idea of how useful the Replace command is, imagine that the company you work for just changed its name and the old company name is in many different places. By using the Replace command, you can replace the old company name with the new name throughout a long document in a matter of seconds.

The basics: Finding stray words and phrases

To locate stray words, names, text passages, and formats, follow these basic steps:

1. **Press Ctrl+F or go to the Home tab and click the Find button.**

You may have to click the Editing button before you can see the Find button. The Navigation pane appears so that you can enter search criteria in the Results tab, as shown in Figure 5-5.

2. **Enter the word or phrase in the search text box.**

After you enter the word or phrase, the Navigation pane lists each instance of the term you're looking for and the term is highlighted in your document wherever it is found.

Enter a word or phrase   Click Find

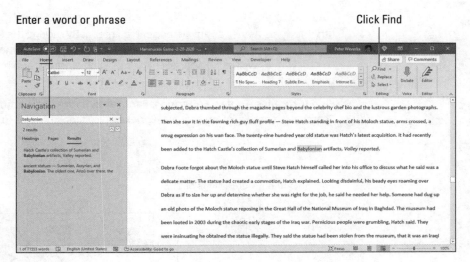

FIGURE 5-5:
Conducting a
Find operation in
Word.

3. **If you want to conduct a narrow search, click the Search for More Things button — located to the right of the Search text box in the Navigation pane — and make a choice on the drop-down list.**

In the next section, "Narrowing your search" explains how to make searches more efficient by choosing options on this drop-down list.

4. **Click an instance of the search term in the Navigation pane to scroll to a location in your document where the search term is located.**

To go from search term to search term, you can also scroll in the Navigation pane, click the Previous button or Next button (located below the Search text box), or press Ctrl+Page Up or Ctrl+Page Down.

Narrowing your search

To narrow your search, click the Search for More Things button in the Navigation pane, as shown in Figure 5-6. Then choose an option on the drop-down list:

» **Options:** Opens the Find Options dialog box so that you can select options to narrow your search (see Figure 5-6). Table 5-1 explains these options.

» **Advanced Find:** Opens the Find tab of the Find and Replace dialog box so that you can select options to narrow the search (see Figure 5-6). Table 5-1 explains these options. (You can also open this dialog box on the Home tab by opening the drop-down menu on the Find button and choosing Advanced Find.) Choose Advanced Find if you want to search using font, paragraph, and other formats as well as advanced search criteria. By clicking the Format button and Special button, you can search for text that was formatted a certain way, as well as for special characters such as paragraph marks and page breaks.

» **Find (Graphics, Tables, Equations, Footnotes/Endnotes, Comments):** Search for a particular object type. For example, choose Tables to search for tables.

Search for More Things button

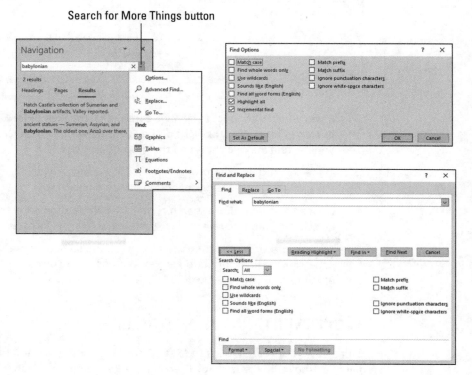

FIGURE 5-6:
Conducting a narrow search.

REMEMBER

Click the More button in the Find and Replace dialog box to see all the search options.

WARNING

After you finish conducting a search for formatted text, don't forget to click the No Formatting button in the Find and Replace dialog box. (You can't conduct a normal search again unless you turn format searching off.)

TABLE 5-1   ## Search Options in the Find Options and Find and Replace Dialog Box

Option	Description
Match Case	Searches for words with upper- and lowercase letters that exactly match those in the search text box. When the Match Case option is selected, a search for *bow* finds *bow*, but not *Bow* or *BOW*.
Find Whole Words Only	Normally, a search for *bow* yields *elbow, bowler, bow-wow,* and all other words with the letters *b-o-w* (in that order). Choose this option and you get only *bow*.
Use Wildcards	Choose this option to use wildcards in searches. (See "Using wildcard operators to refine searches," later in this chapter.)
Sounds Like	Search for words that sound like the one in the Search text box. A search for *bow* with this option selected finds *beau,* for example. However, it doesn't find *bough.* This command isn't very reliable.
Find All Word Forms	Takes into account verb conjugations and plurals in searches. With this option, you get *bows, bowing,* and *bowed* as well as *bow*.
Highlight All[1]	Highlights search results on the page. (Click the Reading Highlight button in the Find and Replace dialog box.)
Incremental Find[1]	Searches for and highlights text as you type it in the Search text box.
Match Prefix	A *prefix* is a syllable appearing before the root or stem of a word to alter its meaning. For example, *co, mid, non,* and *un* are prefixes in the words *coauthor, midtown, nonviolent,* and *unselfish.* Choose this option and enter a prefix in the Find What text box to locate words that begin with the prefix you enter.
Match Suffix	A *suffix* is a syllable or two appearing at the end of a word that alters its meaning. For example, *age, ish,* and *ness* are suffixes in the words *spillage, smallish,* and *darkness.* Choose this option and enter a suffix in the Find What text box to find words that end with the same suffix.
Ignore Punctuation Characters	Search in text for word phrases without regard for commas, periods, and other punctuation marks. For example, a search for *Yuma Arizona* finds *Yuma, Arizona* (with a comma) in the text.
Ignore White Space Characters	Search in text for word phrases without regard for white space caused by multiple blank spaces or tab entries.
Format (button)[2]	Search for text formatted a certain way. For example, search for boldface text. After you click the Format button in the Find and Replace dialog box, you can choose a format type on the drop-down list — Font, Paragraph, Tabs, Language, Frame, Style, or Highlight. A Find dialog box opens so that you can describe the format you're looking for. Select options in the dialog box to describe the format and click OK.
Special (button)[2]	Search for special characters such as paragraph marks and em dashes. (See "Searching for special characters," later in this chapter.)

[1] *Find Options dialog box only*

[2] *Find and Replace dialog box only*

Taking Advantage of
the Proofing Tools

Using wildcard operators to refine searches

Word permits you to use wildcard operators in searches. A *wildcard operator* is a character that represents characters in a search expression. Wildcards aren't for everybody. Using them requires a certain amount of expertise, but after you know how to use them, wildcards can be invaluable in searches and macros. Table 5-2 explains the wildcard operators that you can use in searches. Click the Use Wildcards check box if you want to search using wildcards.

TABLE 5-2 ## Wildcards for Searches

Operator	What It Finds	Example
?	Any single character	**b?t** finds *bat, bet, bit,* and *but.*
*	Zero or more characters	**t*o** finds *to, two,* and *tattoo.*
[xyz]	A specific character, *x, y,* or *z*	**t[aeiou]pper** finds *tapper, tipper,* and *topper.*
[x-z]	A range of characters, *x* through *z*	**[1-4]000** finds *1000, 2000, 3000,* and *4000,* but not *5000.*
[!xy]	Not the specific character or characters, *xy*	**p[!io]t** finds *pat* and *pet,* but not *pit* or *pot.*
<	Characters at the beginning of words	**<info** finds *information, infomaniac,* and *infomercial.*
>	Characters at the end of words	**ese>** finds *these, journalese,* and *legalese.*
@	One or more instances of the previous character	**sho@t** finds *shot* and *shoot.*
{n}	Exactly *n* instances of the previous character	**sho{2}t** finds *shoot* but not *shot.*
{n,}	At least *n* instances of the previous character	**^p{3,}** finds three or more paragraph breaks in a row, but not a single paragraph break or two paragraph breaks in a row.
{n,m}	From *n* to *m* instances of the previous character	**10{2,4}** finds *100, 1000,* and *10000,* but not *10* or *100000.*

WARNING

You can't conduct a whole-word-only search with a wildcard. For example, a search for **f*s** not only finds *fads* and *fits* but also all text strings that begin with *f* and end with *s*, such as *for the birds.* Wildcard searches can yield many, many results and are sometimes useless.

TIP

To search for an asterisk (*), question mark (?), or other character that serves as a wildcard search operator, place a backslash (\) before it in the text box.

Searching for special characters

Table 5-3 describes the *special characters* you can look for in Word documents. To look for the special characters listed in the table, enter the character directly in the text box or click the Special button in the Find and Replace dialog box, and then choose a special character from the pop-up list. Be sure to enter lowercase letters. For example, you must enter **^n**, not **^N**, to look for a column break. *Note:* A caret (^) precedes special characters.

TABLE 5-3

Special Characters for Searches

To Find/Replace	Enter
Manual Formats That Users Insert	
Column break	^n
Field[1]	^d
Manual line break (↵)	^l
Manual page break	^m
No-width non break	^z
No-width optional break	^x
Paragraph break (¶)	^p
Section break[1]	^b
Section character	^%
Tab space (→)	^t
Punctuation Marks	
1/4 em space	^q
Caret (^)	^^
Ellipsis	^i
Em dash (—)	^+
En dash (–)	^=
Full-width ellipses	^j
Nonbreaking hyphen	^~
Optional hyphen	^_
White space (one or more blank spaces)[1]	^w

(continued)

TABLE 5-3 *(continued)*

To Find/Replace	Enter
Characters and Symbols	
Foreign character	You can type foreign characters in the Find What and Replace With text boxes
ANSI and ASCII characters and symbols	^*nnnn,* where *nnnn* is the four-digit code
Any character[1]	^?
Any digit[1]	^#
Any letter[1]	^$
Clipboard contents[2]	^c
Contents of the Find What box[2]	^&
Elements of Reports and Scholarly Papers	
Endnote mark[1]	^e
Footnote mark[1]	^f
Graphic[1]	^g

[1] *For use in Find operations only*

[2] *For use in Replace operations only*

TIP

Before searching for special characters, go to the Home tab and click the Show/Hide¶ button. That way, you see special characters — also known as *hidden format symbols* — onscreen when Word finds them.

TIP

Creative people find many uses for special characters in searches. The easiest way to find section breaks, column breaks, and manual line breaks in a document is to enter **^b**, **^n**, or **^l**, respectively, and start searching. By combining special characters with text, you can make find-and-replace operations more productive. For example, to replace all double hyphens (--) in a document with em dashes (—), enter -- in the Find What text box and **^m** in the Replace With text box. This kind of find-and-replace operation is especially useful for cleaning documents that were created in another application and then imported into Word.

Conducting a find-and-replace operation

Conducting a find-and-replace operation is the spitting image of conducting a Find operation. Figure 5-7 shows the Replace dialog box, the place where you declare what you want to find and what to replace it with. Do the options and buttons in the dialog box look familiar? They do if you read the previous handful of pages about searching because the Replace options are the same as the Find options.

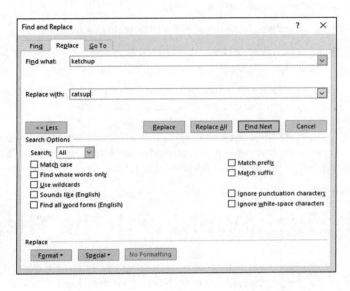

FIGURE 5-7:
Using the powerful Replace command.

TIP

The key to a successful find-and-replace operation is making sure you *find* exactly what you want to find and replace. One way to make sure that you find the right text is to start by running a Find operation. If the program finds precisely the text you want, you're in business. Click the Replace tab in the Find and Replace dialog box and then enter the replacement text.

To locate and replace words, names, or text passages with the Find command, follow these steps:

1. **Press Ctrl+H or go to the Home tab and click the Replace button.**

You may have to click the Editing button before you can see the Replace button. The Find and Replace dialog box appears (see Figure 5-7).

2. **Describe the text that needs replacing.**

Earlier in this chapter, "The basics: Finding stray words and phrases" explains how to construct a search. Try to narrow your search so you find only the text you're looking for.

3. **Click the Find Next button.**

Did your program find what you're looking for? If it didn't, describe the search again.

4. Enter the replacement text in the Replace With text box.

You can select replacement text from the drop-down list.

5. Either replace everything simultaneously or do it one at a time.

Click one of these buttons:

- Click Replace All to make all replacements in an instant.

- Click Find Next and then either click Replace to make the replacement or Find Next to bypass it.

Click the Replace All button only if you are very, very confident that the thing your program found is the thing you want to replace.

WARNING

Be sure to examine your document after you conduct a find-and-replace operation. You never know what the powerful Replace command will do. If the command makes a hash of your document, click the Undo button.

Finding the Right Word with the Thesaurus

If you can't find the right word or if the word is on the tip of your tongue but you can't quite remember it, you can always give the Thesaurus a shot. To find synonyms for a word, start by right-clicking the word and choosing Synonyms on the shortcut menu, as shown in Figure 5-8. With luck, the synonym you're looking for appears on the submenu, and all you have to do is click to enter the synonym. Usually, however, finding a good synonym is a journey, not a Sunday stroll.

To search for a good synonym, click the word in question and open the Thesaurus task pane with one of these techniques:

» Press Shift+F7.

» Right-click the word and choose Synonyms ➪ Thesaurus.

» Go to the Review tab and click the Thesaurus button.

The Thesaurus task pane opens, as shown in Figure 5-9. It offers a list of synonyms and sometimes includes an antonym or two at the bottom. Now you're getting somewhere:

» **Choosing a synonym:** Move the pointer over the synonym you want, open its drop-down list, and choose Insert.

>> **Finding a synonym for a synonym:** If a synonym intrigues you, click it. The task pane displays a new list of synonyms.

>> **Searching for antonyms:** If you can't think of the right word, type its antonym in the text box and then look for an "antonym of an antonym" in the task pane.

FIGURE 5-8:
Searching for a synonym by right-clicking.

FIGURE 5-9:
Searching for a synonym in the Thesaurus task pane.

Taking Advantage of
the Proofing Tools

Proofing Text Written in a Foreign Language

In the interest of cosmopolitanism, Word gives you the opportunity to make foreign languages a part of documents. To enter and edit text in a foreign language, start by installing proofing tools for the language. With the tools installed, you tell Word where in your document a foreign language is used. After that, you can spell check text written in the language.

To spell check text written in Uzbek, Estonian, Afrikaans, and other languages apart from English, French, and Spanish, you have to obtain additional proofing tools from Microsoft. These can be obtained at the Microsoft Download Center at www.microsoft.com/en-us/download (enter **proofing tools** in the Search box). Proofing tools include a spell checker, grammar checker, thesaurus, hyphenator, AutoCorrect list, and translation dictionary, but not all these tools are available for every language.

Telling Office which languages you will use

Follow these steps to inform Word that you will use a language or languages besides English in your documents:

1. **On the Review tab, click the Language button and choose Language Preferences.**

The Word Options dialog box opens to the Language category.

2. **Click the Add a Language button.**

The Add an Authoring Language dialog box appears.

3. **Select a language and click the Add button.**

The name of the language you selected appears in the Word Options dialog box. If proofing tools are available for this language, the Proofing Available link appears next to the name of the language you selected.

4. **Click the Proofing Available link.**

Your browser opens to a web page at Microsoft.com so that you can download the proofing tools.

5. **Click the Download button and follow the instructions for downloading the language's proofing tools to your computer.**

Marking text as foreign language text

The next step is to tell Office where in your document you're using a foreign language. After you mark the text as foreign language text, Office can spell check it with the proper dictionaries. Follow these steps to mark text so that Office knows in which language it was written:

1. Select the text that you wrote in a foreign language.

2. Go to the Review tab.

3. Click the Language button and choose Set Proofing Language on the drop-down list.

You see the Language dialog box, as shown in Figure 5-10.

4. Select a language and click OK.

REMEMBER

The status bar along the bottom of the screen tells you which language was assigned to text in a document. Click a word and glance at the status bar if you aren't sure which language was assigned to text.

FIGURE 5-10: Identifying foreign language words for spell checking.

Translating Foreign Language Text

Office offers a gizmo for translating words and phrases from one language to another. The translation gizmo gives you the opportunity to translate single words and phrases as well as entire documents, although, in my experience, it is good only for translating words and phrases. To translate an entire document, you have to seek the help of a real, native speaker.

Follow these steps to translate foreign language text:

1. **Select the word or phrase that needs translating.**

2. **On the Review tab, click the Translate button and choose a Translate option on the drop-down list.**

   Office offers these ways to translate words:

   - **Translate Selection:** The Translator task pane opens, as shown in Figure 5-11. Click the Insert button to replace the original text with the translated text. If Word failed to detect the language that needs translating, open the From drop-down menu and choose a different language.

   - **Translate Document:** The Translator task pane opens, and if Word is able, the translation is made and entered into a new document. If Word can't detect the language that needs translating, open the From drop-down menu, choose a language, and click the Translate button.

FIGURE 5-11:
Use the Translator task pane to translate a word or phrase.

Chapter **6**

Desktop Publishing with Word

Once upon a time, word processors were nothing more than glorified type-writers. They were good for typing and basic formatting, and not much else. But over the years, Microsoft Word has become a desktop-publishing program in its own right. This chapter explains a few desktop-publishing features that can make your documents stand out in the crowd — themes, columns, text boxes, page borders, watermarks, video, and drop caps, to name a few. (Book 7 describes Publisher 365, another desktop-publishing application.)

Experimenting with Themes

A *theme* is a colorful, ready-made design for headings and text. Each theme imposes a slightly different look on a document. If you want to experiment with themes, theme style sets, theme colors, and theme fonts, more power to you, but be prepared to click the Undo button and backtrack as you rummage around for the right look for your document. Figure 6-1 shows some theme experiments.

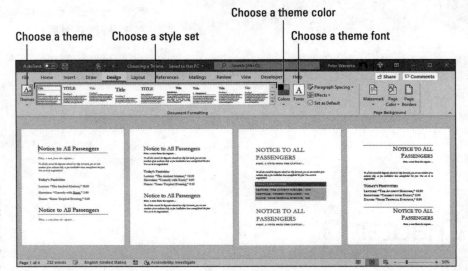

Choose a theme color

Choose a theme   Choose a style set   Choose a theme font

FIGURE 6-1:
On the Design tab, experiment with themes, style sets, theme colors, and theme fonts.

Starting on the Design tab, follow these instructions to experiment with themes:

>> **Choosing a new theme:** Click the Themes button and choose a theme on the drop-down list.

>> **Choosing a new style set:** On the Theme Styles gallery, choose a style set.

>> **Choosing a new set of colors for your theme:** Click the Theme Colors button, slide the pointer over the different color sets on the drop-down list, and see what effect they have on your document.

>> **Changing the fonts:** Click the Theme Fonts button and choose a combination of fonts on the drop-down list for the headings and text in your document.

Sprucing Up Your Pages

You can play interior decorator with the pages of a document by putting a border around pages, splashing color on pages, and taking advantage of the predesigned cover pages that Word provides for you. Keep reading if making the pages of your document a little prettier interests you.

Decorating a page with a border

Word offers a means of decorating title pages, certificates, menus, and similar documents with a page border. Besides lines, you can decorate the sides of a page with stars, pieces of cake, and other artwork. If you want to place a border around a page in the middle of a document, you must create a section break where the page is.

Before you create your border, place the cursor on the page where the border is to appear. Place the cursor on the first page of a document if you want to put a border around only the first page. If your document is divided into sections and you want to put borders around certain pages in a section, place the cursor in the section — either in the first page if you want the borders to go around it, or in a subsequent page.

With the cursor in the right place, follow these steps to decorate your page or pages with a border:

1. **Go to the Design tab and click the Page Borders button.**

    You see the Borders and Shading dialog box, as shown in Figure 6-2.

2. **Under Setting, choose which kind of border you want.**

    Use the None setting to remove borders.

3. **On the Apply To drop-down menu, tell Word which page or pages in the document get borders.**

4. **Select options to construct the border you want and then click OK.**

FIGURE 6-2:
Putting borders
on pages.

The Page Border tab offers a bunch of tools for fashioning a border:

>> **Line for borders:** Under Style, scroll down the list and choose a line for the borders. You will find interesting choices at the bottom of the menu. Be sure to look in the Preview window to see what your choices in this dialog box add up to.

>> **Color for borders:** Open the Color drop-down list and choose a color for the border lines if you want a color border.

>> **Width of borders:** Use the Width drop-down list to tell Word how wide the lines or artwork should be.

>> **Artwork for borders:** Open the Art drop-down list and choose a symbol, illustration, star, or other artwork, if that is what you want for the borders. You will find some ornate choices at the bottom of the long list.

>> **Borders on different sides of the page:** Use the four buttons in the Preview window to tell Word on which sides of the page to draw borders. Click these buttons to remove or add borders, as you wish.

>> **Distance from edge of page:** Click the Options button and fill in the Border and Shading Options dialog box if you want to get specific about how close the borders can come to the edge of the page or pages.

Putting a background color on pages

Especially if you intend to save your Word document as a web page, you will be glad to know that putting a background color on pages is easy. You can't, however, pick and choose which pages get a background color. Putting background colors on the pages of a document is an all-or-nothing proposition.

To grace a page with a background color or gradient color mixture, go to the Design tab, click the Page Color button, and choose a color on the drop-down list. Choose Fill Effects to open the Fill Effects dialog box and apply gradient color mixtures or patterns to the pages.

Getting Word's help with cover letters

Writing and designing a cover page for a letter, resume, or report is a chore. Word can't dictate a cover page for you, but it can provide a handsome preformatted cover page that looks nice at the front of a report or article. Figure 6-3 shows examples of cover pages.

FIGURE 6-3:
Examples of
ready-made
cover pages.

To place a cover page at the start of a document, go to the Insert tab, click the Cover Page button, and choose a cover page on the gallery.

Making Use of Charts, Diagrams, Shapes, and Photos

Figure 6-4 shows a newsletter that includes a chart, diagram, shape, and photo. You are invited to include these items in your Word documents, and you'll be glad to know that including them isn't very much trouble.

>> **Charts:** A chart is an excellent way to present data for comparison purposes. The pie slices, bars, columns, or lines tell readers right away which business is more productive, for example, or who received the most votes. Book 8, Chapter 1 explains how to create charts.

>> **Diagrams:** A diagram allows readers to quickly grasp an idea, relationship, or concept. Instead of explaining an abstract idea, you can portray it in a diagram. Book 8, Chapter 2 explains diagrams.

>> **Shapes and lines:** Shapes and lines can also illustrate ideas and concepts. You can also use them for decorative purposes in Word documents. Book 8, Chapter 4 explains how to draw lines, arrows, and shapes.

>> **Photos:** Photos make a document livelier. They add a little color to documents. Book 8, Chapter 3 explains how to place photos in documents.

FIGURE 6-4:
This newsletter includes a photo, chart, diagram, shape, and image.

Working with the Drawing Canvas

As Book 8, Chapter 4 explains, shapes and lines are a great way to illustrate ideas. You can in effect doodle on the page and give readers another insight into what you want to explain. In Word, however, drawing lines and shapes is problematic unless you draw them on the drawing canvas.

The *drawing canvas* works like a corral to hold lines and shapes. After you create a drawing canvas, you can draw inside it as though you were drawing on a little page, as shown in Figure 6-5. You can treat the drawing canvas as an object in its own right. You can move it, along with the things inside it, to new locations. You can also, by way of the Shape Format tab, give the drawing canvas an outline shape and fill color. The drawing canvas makes working with objects on a page, especially lines and shapes, that much easier.

Follow these steps to create a drawing canvas for holding lines and shapes:

1. Place the cursor roughly where you want the drawing canvas to be.

2. Go to the Insert tab or the Draw tab.

3. Create the drawing canvas.

How you create the drawing canvas depends on where you are:

- **Insert tab:** Click the Shapes button and choose New Drawing Canvas (the bottommost option on the drop-down menu).

- **Draw tab:** Click the Drawing Canvas button.

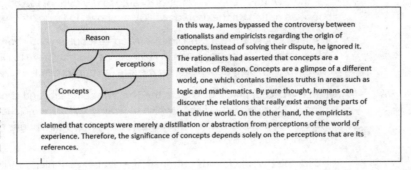

In this way, James bypassed the controversy between rationalists and empiricists regarding the origin of concepts. Instead of solving their dispute, he ignored it. The rationalists had asserted that concepts are a revelation of Reason. Concepts are a glimpse of a different world, one which contains timeless truths in areas such as logic and mathematics. By pure thought, humans can discover the relations that really exist among the parts of that divine world. On the other hand, the empiricists claimed that concepts were merely a distillation or abstraction from perceptions of the world of experience. Therefore, the significance of concepts depends solely on the perceptions that are its references.

FIGURE 6-5: The drawing canvas — a corral for shapes and lines.

REMEMBER

The drawing canvas is an object in its own right. You can wrap text around it, give it an outline, and give it a color fill. You can drag it to a new location. To change its size, drag a handle on the side or corner.

Positioning and Wrapping Objects Relative to the Page and Text

"Object" is just Office's generic term for a shape, line, text box, image, photo, diagram, WordArt image, or chart that you insert in a document. Book 8, Chapter 4 explains how to manipulate an object — how to change its size, shape, and other qualities. When you place an object in a Word document, you have to consider more than its size and shape. You also have to consider where to position it on the page and how to wrap text around it. In Word lingo, *wrap* refers to what text does when it butts heads with a shape, text box, photo, diagram, or other object. You must be in Print Layout view to wrap and position objects on a page.

WARNING

When you insert an object, it lands *inline with text.* That means it lands against the left margin and text doesn't wrap around its side. Before you can change the position of an object, you must select it and choose a text–wrapping option apart from Inline with Text.

Wrapping text around an object

Figure 6-6 illustrates the 15 different ways you can wrap text around an object. Select the object you want to wrap text around and use one of these techniques to wrap text around the object:

>> Click the Layout Options button (it's located to the right of the object) and choose an option on the drop-down list, as shown in Figure 6-7.

>> On the Layout or Format tab, click the Wrap Text button and choose an option on the drop-down list, as shown in Figure 6-7. (You may have to click the Arrange button first, depending on the size of your screen.)

>> Open the Layout dialog box, go to the Text Wrapping tab, and choose a wrapping style and side around which to wrap text. Figure 6-6 shows what the different combinations of Wrapping Style and Wrap Text options do. To open the Layout dialog box:

- Click the Layout Options button (to the right of the object) and click the See More link on the drop-down list.

- Click the Wrap Text button and choose More Layout Options on the drop-down list.

TIP

Wrapped text looks best when it is justified and hyphenated. That way, text can get closer to the object that is being wrapped.

FIGURE 6-6:
All the ways to wrap text in a Word document.

Choose a text wrap option

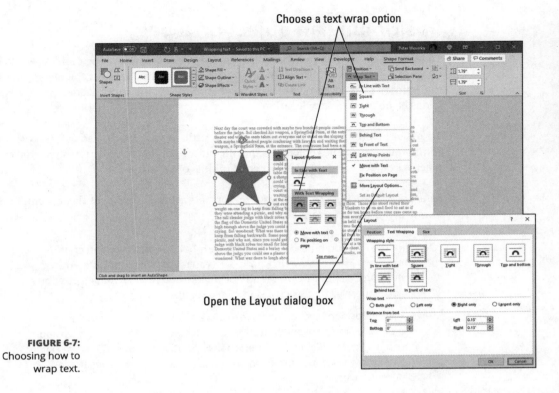

Open the Layout dialog box

FIGURE 6-7:
Choosing how to
wrap text.

WRAPPING TEXT WITH PRECISION

You can decide for yourself how close or far text is from an object when you wrap text. Select the object, and on the Format tab, click the Wrap Text button and choose Edit Wrap Points on the drop-down list. Small black squares called *wrap points* appear around the object, as shown in this illustration. Click and drag the wrap points to push text away from or bring text closer to the object in question.

Positioning an object on a page

To position an object in a Word page, you can drag it to a new location. As Book 8, Chapter 4 explains in torturous detail, dragging means to select the object, move the pointer over its perimeter, click when you see the four-headed arrow, and slide the object to a new location.

To make positioning objects on a page a little easier, Word also offers Position commands for moving objects to specific places on the page. For example, you can place an object squarely in a corner or middle of the page.

Select your object, go to the Layout or Format tab, and use one of these techniques to move your object precisely into place:

>> Click the Position button and select a With Text Wrapping option on the drop-down list, as shown in Figure 6-8. (You may have to click the Arrange button first, depending on the size of your screen.) These options position an object squarely in a corner, a side, or the middle of the page.

>> Click the Position button and choose More Layout Options on the drop-down list, or click the Size group button on the Format tab and select the Position tab in the Layout dialog box. Then choose position options. Go to the Layout dialog box when you want to place objects in the very same position on different pages.

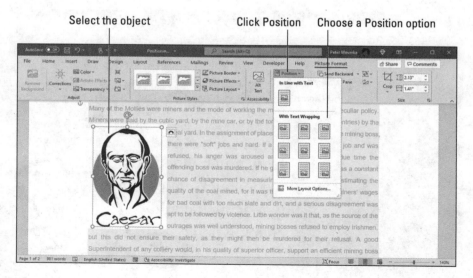

FIGURE 6-8:
The Position options place an object on one part of the page.

REMEMBER

When you insert an object, Word attaches it to the paragraph where the cursor is located when you make the insertion. For that reason, if you move that paragraph to another page or the paragraph gets moved as you edit text, the object moves right along with the paragraph. You can locate the paragraph to which an object is connected by clicking the object. The anchor symbol appears beside the paragraph to which the object is connected.

Working with Text Boxes

Put text in a text box when you want a notice or announcement to stand out on the page. Like other objects, text boxes can be shaded, filled with color, and given borders, as the examples in Figure 6-9 demonstrate. You can also lay them over graphics to make for interesting effects. I removed the borders and the fill color from the text box on the right side of Figure 6-9, but rest assured, the text in this figure lies squarely in a text box. (Book 8, Chapter 4 explains how to give borders, shading, and color to objects such as text boxes.)

FIGURE 6-9:
Examples of text boxes.

You can move a text box around at will on the page until it lands in the right place. You can even use text boxes as columns and make text jump from one text box to the next in a document — a nice feature, for example, when you want a news-letter article on page 1 to be continued on page 2. Instead of cutting and pasting text from page 1 to page 2, Word moves the text for you as the column on page 1 fills up.

Inserting a text box

To create a text box, go to the Insert tab, click the Text Box button, and use one of these techniques:

>> **Choose a ready-made text box:** Scroll in the drop-down list and choose a preformatted text box.

>> **Draw a conventional text box:** Choose Draw Text Box on the drop-down list, and then click and drag to draw the text box. Lines show you how big it will be when you release the mouse button.

After you insert the text box, you can type text in it and call on all the formatting commands on the (Drawing) Format tab. These commands are explained in Book 8, Chapter 4. It also describes how to turn a shape such as a circle or triangle into a text box (create the shape, right-click it and choose Add Text, and start typing).

TIP

Here's a neat trick: You can turn the text in a text box on its side so that it reads from top to bottom or bottom to top, not from left to right. Create a text box, enter the text, go to the Shape Format tab, click the Text Direction button, and choose a Rotate option on the drop-down list.

Making text flow from text box to text box

As I mention earlier, you can link text boxes so that the text in the first box is pushed into the next one when it fills up. To link text boxes, start by creating all the text boxes that you need. You can't link one text box to another if the second text box already has text in it. Starting on the Shape Format tab, follow these directions to link text boxes:

>> **Creating a forward link:** Click a text box and then click the Create Link button to create a forward link. The pointer changes into a very odd-looking pointer that is supposed to look like a pitcher. Move the odd-looking pointer to the next text box in the chain and click there to create a link.

>> **Breaking a link:** To break a link, click the text box that is to be the last in the chain, and then click the Break Link button.

Dropping In a Drop Cap

A *drop cap* is a large capital letter that "drops" into the text, as shown in Figure 6-10. Drop caps appear at the start of chapters in many books, this book included, and you can find other uses for them, too. In Figure 6-10, one drop cap marks the A side of a list of songs on a homemade music CD.

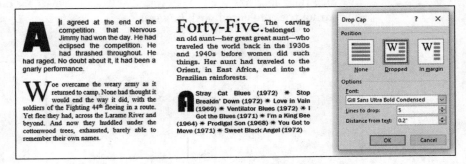

FIGURE 6-10: Creating a drop cap.

To create a drop cap, start by clicking anywhere in the paragraph whose first letter you want to "drop." If you want to "drop" more than one character at the start of the paragraph, select the characters. Then go to the Insert tab, click the Drop Cap button, and choose Dropped or Drop Cap Options. Choosing Drop Cap Options opens the Drop Cap dialog box shown in Figure 6-10, where you can experiment with these options:

- » **Position:** Choose which kind of drop cap you want. In Margin places the drop cap to the left of the paragraph, in the margin, not in the paragraph itself.

- » **Font:** Choose a font from the Font drop-down list. Choose a different font from the text in the paragraph.

- » **Lines to Drop:** Enter the number of text lines to drop the letter.

- » **Distance from Text:** Keep the 0 setting unless you're dropping an *l, 1,* or other skinny letter or number.

Click the Drop Cap button and choose None to remove a drop cap.

Watermarking for the Elegant Effect

A *watermark* is a pale image or set of words that appears behind text on each page in a document. True watermarks are made in the paper mold and can be seen only when the sheet of paper is held up to a light. You can't make true watermarks with Word, but you can make the closest thing to them that can be attained in the debased digital world in which we live. Figure 6-11 shows two pages of a letter in which the paper has been "watermarked." Watermarks are one of the easiest formatting tricks to accomplish in Word.

FIGURE 6-11: Watermarks showing faintly on the page.

To create a watermark for every page of a document, go to the Design tab and click the Watermark button. From the drop-down list, create your watermark:

>> **Prefabricated text watermark:** Scroll down the list and choose an option. You will find "Confidential," "Urgent," and other text watermarks.

>> **Picture watermark:** Choose Custom Watermark, and in the Printed Watermark dialog box, click the Picture Watermark option button. Then click the Select Picture button. In the Insert Pictures dialog box, select a graphics file to use for the watermark and click the Insert button. Back in the Printed Watermark dialog box, choose or enter a size for the graphic on the Scale drop-down menu. I don't recommend deselecting the Washout check box — do so and your image may be so dark it obscures the text.

>> **Text watermark:** Choose Custom Watermark and, in the Printed Watermark dialog box, click the Text Watermark option button. Type a word or two in the Text box (or choose an entry from the drop-down menu). Choose a font, size, color, and layout for the words. If you deselect the Semitransparent check box, you do so at your peril because the watermark words may be too dark on the page.

To tinker with a watermark, reopen the Printed Watermark dialog box. To remove a watermark, click the Watermark button and choose Remove Watermark on the drop-down list.

Putting Newspaper-Style Columns in a Document

Columns look great in newsletters and similar documents. And you can pack a lot of words in columns. I should warn you, however, that the Columns command is good only for creating columns that appear on the same page. Running text to the next page with the Columns command can be problematic. If you're serious about running text in columns, I suggest either constructing the columns from text boxes or using Publisher, another Office program. Book 7 explains Publisher.

TIP

Sometimes it is easier to create columns by creating a table or by using text boxes, especially when the columns refer to one another. In a two-column résumé, for example, the left-hand column often lists job titles ("Facsimile Engineer") whose descriptions are found directly across the page in the right-hand column ("I Xeroxed stuff all day long"). Creating a two-column résumé with Word's Columns command would be futile because making the columns line up is nearly impossible. Each time you add something to the left-hand column, everything *snakes* — it gets bumped down in the left-hand column and the right-hand column as well.

Doing the preliminary work

TIP

Before you put text in newspaper-style columns, write it. Take care of the spelling, grammar, and everything else first because making text changes to words after they've been arranged in columns is difficult. Columns appear only in Print Layout view.

Running text into columns

To "columunize" text, select it, go to the Layout tab, and click the Columns button. Then either choose how many columns you want on the drop-down list or choose More Columns to create columns of different widths.

You see the Columns dialog box shown in Figure 6-12 if you choose More Columns. Here are the options in the Columns dialog box:

» **Preset columns:** Select a Presets box to choose a preset number of columns. Notice that, in some of the boxes, the columns aren't of equal width.

» **Number of columns:** If a preset column doesn't do the trick, enter the number of columns you want in the Number of Columns box.

» **Line between columns:** A line between columns is mighty elegant and is difficult to draw on your own. Choose the Line Between check box to run lines between columns.

» **Columns width:** If you deselect the Equal Column Width check box, you can make columns of unequal width. Change the width of each column by using the Width boxes.

» **Space between columns:** Enter a measurement in the Spacing boxes to determine how much space appears between columns.

» **Start New Column:** Select this check box to put empty space in a column, perhaps to insert a text box or picture. Place the cursor where you want the empty space to begin, choose This Point Forward on the Apply To drop-down list, and click the Start New Column check box.

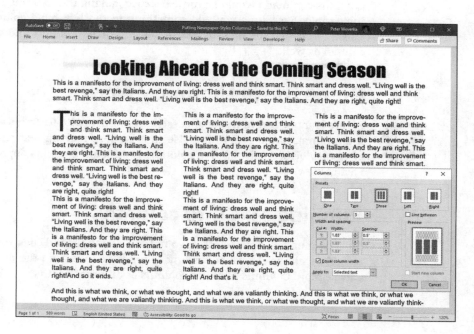

FIGURE 6-12:
Running text in columns.

Word creates a new section if you selected text before you columnized it, and you see your columns in Print Layout view. Chapter 2 of this minibook explains sections.

TIP

To "break" a column in the middle and move text to the next column, click where you want the column to break and press Ctrl+Shift+Enter or go to the Layout tab, click the Breaks button, and choose Column on the drop-down list.

Landscape Documents

A *landscape* document is one in which the page is wider than it is long, like a painting of a landscape, as shown on the right side of Figure 6-13. Most documents, like the pages of this book, are printed in *portrait* style, with the short sides of the page on the top and bottom. However, creating a landscape document is sometimes a good idea because a landscape document stands out from the usual crowd of portrait documents and sometimes printing in landscape mode is necessary to fit text, tables, and graphics on a single page.

FIGURE 6-13:
A portrait document (left) and landscape document (right).

You're ready to go if you want to turn all the pages in your document into landscape pages. To turn some of the pages into landscape pages, create a section for the pages that need to appear in Landscape mode and click in the section (Chapter 2 of this minibook explains sections). Starting on the Layout tab, use these techniques to change the page orientation:

>> **Landscape pages:** Click the Orientation button and choose Landscape on the drop-down list.

>> **Portrait pages:** Click the Orientation button and choose Portrait on the drop-down list.

Printing on Different Size Paper

You don't have to print exclusively on standard 8.5 x 11 paper; you can print on legal–size paper, A4 paper, and other sizes of paper as well. A newsletter with an unusual shape really stands out in a crowd and gets people's attention. Go to the Layout tab and use one of these techniques to change the size of the paper on which you intend to print a document:

>> Click the Size button and choose an option on the drop-down list.

>> Click the Size button and choose More Paper Sizes. You see the Paper tab in the Page Setup dialog box. Choose a setting on the Paper Size drop-down list. If none of the settings suits you, enter your own settings in the Width and Height text boxes.

Showing Online Video in a Document

When words and pictures don't do the job, consider making video a part of your document with the Online Video command. This command establishes a link between your document and a video on the Internet. After you establish the link, the first frame of the video appears in the Word document.

Before you insert a video, go online to the video you want to insert and copy its URL (its address) to the Clipboard. Then follow these steps to insert the video in your document:

1. **On the Insert tab, click the Online Video button.**

   The Insert a Video dialog box appears.

2. **Paste the URL you copied into the textbox.**

   The easiest way to do that is to click in the textbox and press Ctrl+V.

3. **Click the Insert button.**

   The video lands in your Word document.

Click the Play button to open a video viewer and play the video. Press Esc to return to your document and cease watching the video.

Chapter **7**

Getting Word's Help with Office Chores

This chapter is dedicated to the proposition that everyone should get their work done sooner. It explains how Word can be a help in the office, especially when it comes to working on team projects. This chapter explains comments, using revision marks to record edits, and mail merging, Microsoft's term for generating form letters, labels, and envelopes for mass mailings.

Highlighting Parts of a Document

In my work, I often use the Highlight command to mark paragraphs and text that need reviewing later. And on rainy days, I use it to splash color on my documents and keep myself amused. Whatever your reasons for highlighting text in a document, go to the Home tab and use one of these techniques to do it:

>> **Select text and then choose a highlighter:** Select the text you want to highlight. Then, on the Home tab or pop-up menu, click the Text Highlight Color button (if it's displaying your color choice) or open the drop-down list on the button and choose a color.

>> **Choose a highlighter and then select text:** Either click the Text Highlight Color button (if it's already displaying your color choice) or open the drop-down list on the button and choose a color. The pointer changes into a crayon. Drag across the text you want to highlight. When you finish highlighting, click the Text Highlight Color button again or press Esc.

To remove highlights, select the highlighted text, open the drop-down list on the Text Highlight Color button, and choose No Color. Select the entire document (press Ctrl+A) and choose No Color to remove all highlights from a document.

TIP

Highlight marks are printed along with the text. To keep highlights from being printed, go to the File tab, choose Options, visit the Display category in the Word Options dialog box, and deselect the Show Highlighter Marks check box.

Commenting on a Document

People collaborating on a document can write comments and in so doing prove that two heads are better than one. Comments give you the opportunity to suggest improvements, plead with your collaborators, debate your editor, and praise others, all in the interest of turning out a better document.

To enter and read comments, go to the Review tab, as shown in Figure 7-1. These pages explain how to enter comments, examine comments, hide and display comments, and do all else that pertains to commenting on a document.

REMEMBER

Comments appear in the Comments pane on the right side of the screen and in balloons as well, if you so choose (refer to Figure 7-1). To choose where comments appear, click the Show Markup button on the Review tab, choose Balloons, and choose an option on the submenu. See "Viewing and displaying comments," later in this chapter, for details.

Entering comments

In my experience, Print Layout view is the best view for entering and reading comments. Comments are marked with the writer's name, the writer's initials, and the date on which the comment was made. Follow these steps to write comments in Print Layout view:

1. Select the word or sentence that you want to comment on.

2. **Choose a Comment command.**

   Word offers two ways to do it:

   - Click the Comments button in the upper-right corner of the screen to display the Comments task pane; then click the New button.

   - On the Review tab, click the New Comment button.

   Either the Comments pane appears on the right side of the screen, or a balloon for entering a comment appears on the right side. See "Viewing and displaying comments," later in this chapter, for details.

3. **Enter your comment.**

4. **Click the Post Comment button (or press Ctrl+Enter).**

Write, delete, and show comments   Comments

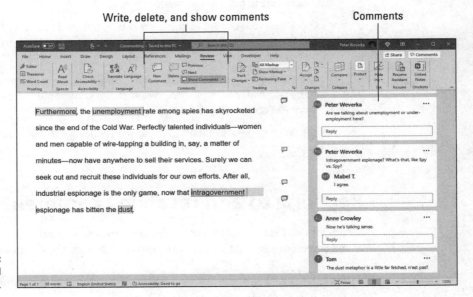

FIGURE 7-1:
Comments in All
Markup view.

TIP

Each comment lists the name of the person who wrote it. If a comment you wrote doesn't list your name, go to the File tab, click Options, and enter your username in the General tab of the Word Options dialog box. Select the Always Use These Values Regardless of Sign In to Office check box if you are enrolled in Office 365 and you sign in to Office.com under a different name than the one you entered.

Viewing and displaying comments

The makers of Word want you to be able to view comments when necessary but shunt them aside when comments get in the way. To tell Word how to display comments, go to the Review tab and choose an option on the Display for Review drop-down list:

- >> **Simple Markup:** Choose Simple Markup to keep comments from crowding the screen. Then click the Show Comments button if necessary:
  - **Show Comments button clicked.** Comments appear in balloons on the right side of the screen or in the Comments task pane. Move the pointer over a comment to see what it refers to on the page.
  - **Show Comments button not clicked.** Comments are marked by icons on the right side of the page. Click an icon to read a comment in a balloon.
- >> **All Markup:** Choose All Markup to see where all the comments are (refer to Figure 7-1). Then click the Show Markup button and choose an option on the drop-down list to display comments:
  - Choose Balloons ⇨ Show Revisions in Balloons (or Show Only Comments and Formatting in Balloons) to show comments in balloons on the right side of the screen.
  - Choose Balloons ⇨ Show All Revisions Inline to show commenters' initials in the text. You can move the pointer over a commenter's initials to read his or her comment in a pop-up box.
- >> **No Markup:** Choose No Markup to cease displaying comment icons or comments.

Replying to and resolving comments

To reply to and resolve comments, display comments in balloons on the right side of the screen or click the Comments button to display the Comments task pane.

- >> **Replying to a comment:** Enter your comment in the Reply text box and click the Post Reply button (or press Ctrl+Enter).
- >> **Resolving a comment:** Click the More Thread Actions button (the three dots) and choose Resolve Thread on the drop-down menu.

Caring for and feeding comments

Starting on the Review tab, here is a handful of tasks that deserve comment (if you'll pardon my little pun):

- » **Editing a comment:** Display the comment, click the More Thread Actions button, and choose Edit comment. Then edit the text.

- » **Going from comment to comment:** Click the Previous or Next button on the Revision tab. You can also scroll to see comments.

- » **Displaying comments by a specific reviewer:** Click the Show Markup button, choose Specific People, and deselect All Reviewers on the submenu. Then click the button again, choose Specific People, and choose the name of a reviewer. To see all comments again, click the Show Markup button and choose Specific People ⇨ All Reviewers.

- » **Deleting comments:** Delete one, all, or some comments:

  - **Deleting a comment:** Select a comment and click the Delete button. You can also click the More Thread Actions button and choose Delete Comment.

  - **Deleting all the comments in the document:** Open the drop-down list on the Delete button and choose Delete All Comments in Document. You can also choose Delete All Resolved Comments to remove comments that were marked "resolved."

  - **Deleting comments made by one or two people:** First, isolate comments made by people whose comments you want to delete (see "Displaying comments by a specific reviewer," earlier in this list). Then open the drop-down list on the Delete button and choose Delete All Comments Shown.

Tracking Changes to Documents

When many hands go into revising a document, figuring out who made changes to what is impossible. What's more, it's impossible to tell what the first draft looked like. Sometimes it's hard to tell whether the changes were for good or ill. To help you keep track of changes to documents, Word offers the Track Changes command. When this command is in effect:

- » Changes to a document are recorded in a different color, with one color for each reviewer.

- » New text is underlined; deleted text is crossed out. (If deleted text isn't crossed out in your documents, go to the Review tab, click the Show Markup button, choose Balloons on the drop-down menu, and choose Show All Revisions Inline on the submenu.)

By moving the pointer over a change, you can read the name of the person who made it as well as the words that were inserted or deleted. You can see changes as well in the Reviewing pane. As you review changes, you can accept or reject each change. You can also see the original document, a copy with revisions, or the final copy simply by making a choice from the Display for Review drop-down list on the Review tab.

To give you an idea of what tracking marks look like, Figure 7-2 shows the first two sentences of Vladimir Nabokov's autobiography *Speak, Memory* with marks showing where the author made additions and deletions to the original draft.

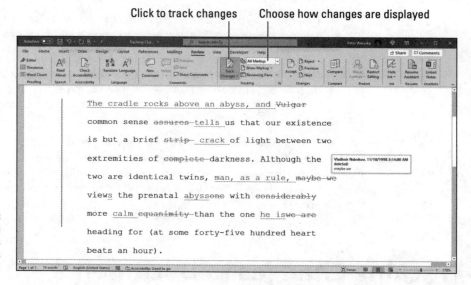

FIGURE 7-2: A document with revision marks and changes showing.

Telling Word to start marking changes

To start tracking where editorial changes are made to a document, turn Track Changes on. You can do that with one of these techniques:

>> On the Review tab, click the Track Changes button (or open its drop-down list and choose Track Changes).

>> Press Ctrl+Shift+E.

>> On the status bar, click the words *Track Changes* so that the status bar reads "Track Changes: On." If you don't see the words *Track Changes* on the status bar and you want to see them there, right-click the status bar and select Track Changes on the pop-up menu.

To stop tracking changes to a document, click the Track Changes button again, press Ctrl+Shift+E again, or click the words *Track Changes* on the status bar so that the words read "Track Changes: Off."

Reading and reviewing a document with revision marks

Reading and reviewing a document with revision marks isn't easy. The marks can get in the way. Fortunately, Word offers the Display for Review menu on the Review tab for dealing with documents that have been scarred by revision marks. Choose options on the Display for Review drop-down list to get a better idea of how your changes are taking shape:

>> **Get an idea where changes were made:** Choose Simple Markup. A vertical line appears on the left side of the page to show where changes were made. (This line doesn't appear in Draft and Outline view.)

>> **See where additions and deletions were made:** Choose All Markup (refer to Figure 7-2). Additions are underlined and deleted text is crossed through.

>> **See what the document would look like if you accepted all changes:** Choose No Markup. All revision marks are stripped away and you see what your document would look like if you accepted all changes made to it.

>> **See what the document would look like if you rejected all changes:** Choose Original. You get the original, pristine document back.

Marking changes when you forgot to turn on revision marks

Suppose that you write the first draft of a document and someone revises it, but that someone doesn't track changes. How can you tell where changes were made? For that matter, suppose that you get hold of a document, you change it around without tracking changes, and now you want to see what your editorial changes did to the original copy. I have good news: You can compare documents to see the editorial changes that were made to them. Word offers a command for comparing the original document to a revised edition and another for comparing two different revised editions of the same document.

After you make the comparison, Word creates a third document similar to the one shown in Figure 7-3. In the Source Document pane on the right side of the window, you can see the documents you're comparing. The Compared Document pane, meanwhile, shows who made changes and what those changes are.

REQUIRING YOUR COLLABORATORS TO TRACK CHANGES

As well as insist that your collaborators track the changes they make to a document, you can compel them to do so. You can lock your document so that all editorial changes made to it are tracked with revision marks.

To lock a document against anyone's making changes without the changes being tracked, go to the Review tab, open the drop-down list on the Track Changes button, and choose Lock Tracking. Then enter and reenter a password in the Lock Tracking dialog box.

All changes are tracked automatically in a document that has been locked against anyone's turning off the track changes mechanism.

To unlock a document so that you and your collaborators can once again turn the track changes feature on or off, open the drop-down list on the Track Changes button and deselect Lock Tracking. Then enter the password in the Unlock Tracking dialog box.

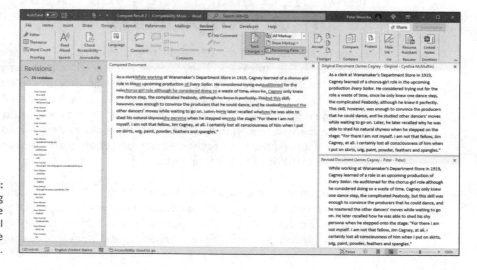

FIGURE 7-3:
Comparing documents to see where editorial changes were made.

Follow these steps to compare an original document to its revised copy or two revised copies:

1. **On the Review tab, click the Compare button.**

   You see a drop-down list (depending on the size of your screen, you may have to choose Compare more than once to get to the drop-down list).

2. **On the drop-down list, choose Compare to compare the original document to its revised edition; choose Combine to compare two editions of the same document that were revised separately.**

   You see the Compare Documents dialog box or the Combine Documents dialog box, as shown in Figure 7-4. These dialog boxes work the same way.

3. **On the Original Document drop-down list, choose the original or a revised edition of the document; if its name isn't there, click the Browse button and select it in the Open dialog box.**

4. **On the Revised Document drop-down list, choose a revised copy, or else click the Browse button and select it in the Open dialog box.**

5. **Click the More button.**

   You see more options for comparing or combining documents.

6. **If you so desire, deselect Comparison Settings check boxes to tell Word what you want to compare.**

7. **Click OK.**

   Word creates a new document that shows where changes were made to the original copy, or where the revised copies differ (refer to Figure 7-3). You can save this document if you want to.

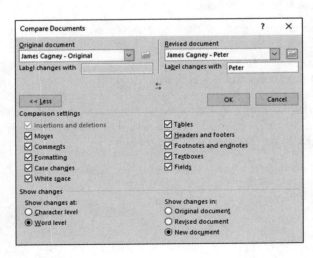

FIGURE 7-4: Choosing which documents to compare.

TIP

To help with document comparisons, you can tell Word what to display in the Source Documents pane on the right side of the screen. On the Review tab, click the Compare button, choose Show Source Documents, and choose an option on the submenu. You can hide the source documents, show the original document, show the revised edition, or show both editions.

Accepting and rejecting changes to a document

TIP

Word gives you the chance to accept or reject changes one at a time, but in my considerable experience with changes (I am a sometime editor), I find that the best way to handle changes is to go through the document, reject the changes you don't care for, and when you have finished reviewing, accept all the remaining changes. That way, reviewing changes is only half as tedious.

Whatever your preference for accepting or rejecting changes, start by selecting a change. To do so, either click it or click the Previous or Next button on the Review tab to locate it in your document. With the change selected, do one of the following:

>> **Accept a change:** Click the Accept button or open the drop-down list on the Accept button and choose Accept This Change or Accept and Move to Next. You can also right-click and choose Accept.

>> **Reject a change:** Click the Reject button or open the drop-down list on the Reject button and choose Reject Change or Reject and Move to Next. You can also right-click and choose Reject.

>> **Accept all changes:** Open the drop-down list on the Accept button and choose Accept All Changes.

>> **Reject all changes:** Open the drop-down list on the Reject button and choose Reject All Changes.

TIP

By way of the Accept and Reject buttons, you can also accept or reject all changes made by a single reviewer. First, isolate the reviewer's changes by clicking the Show Markup button, choosing Specific People, and selecting a reviewer's name. Then open the drop-down list on the Accept or Reject button, and choose Accept All Changes Shown or Reject All Changes Shown.

Printing an Address on an Envelope

Printing addresses gives correspondence a formal, official look. It makes you look like a big shot. (Later in this chapter, "Churning Out Letters, Envelopes, and Labels for Mass Mailings" explains how to print more than one envelope at a time). Here's how to print an address and a return address on an envelope:

1. **To save a bit of time, open the document that holds the letter you want to send; then select the name and address of the person you want to send the letter to.**

By doing so, you save yourself from having to type the address. However, you don't have to open a document to start with.

2. **On the Mailings tab, click the Envelopes button (you may have to click the Create button first, depending on the size of your screen).**

The Envelopes tab of the Envelopes and Labels dialog box appears, as shown in Figure 7-5.

3. **Enter a name and address in the Delivery Address box (the address is already there if you selected it in Step 1).**

4. **Enter your return address in the Return Address box, if you want.**

5. **Click the Omit check box if you don't want your return address to appear on the envelope.**

6. **Click the Options button, and in the Envelope Options dialog box, tell Word what size your envelopes are and how your printer handles envelopes.**

Tell Word about your envelopes on the Envelope Options and Printing Options tabs, and click OK:

- **Envelope Options tab:** Choose an envelope size, a font for printing the delivery and return address, and a position for the addresses. The sample envelope in the Preview shows you what your position settings do when the envelope is printed.

- **Printing Options tab:** Choose a technique for feeding envelopes to your printer. Consult the manual that came with your printer, select one of the Feed Method boxes, click the Face Up or Face Down option button, and open the Feed From drop-down list to tell Word which printer tray the envelope is in or how you intend to stick the envelope in your printer.

7. **Click the Print button.**

All that trouble just to print an address on an envelope!

FIGURE 7-5:
Printing on an envelope.

Printing a Single Address Label (Or a Page of the Same Label)

If you need to print a single label or a sheet of labels that are all the same, you can do it. Before you start printing, however, take note of the label's brand name and product number. You are asked about brand names and product numbers when you print labels. (Later in this chapter, "Churning Out Letters, Envelopes, and Labels for Mass Mailings" explains how to print multiple labels as part of a mass mailing.)

Follow these steps to print a single label or a sheet full of identical labels:

1. On the Mailings tab, click the Labels button (you may have to click the Create button first, depending on the size of your screen).

You see the Labels tab of the Envelopes and Labels dialog box, as shown in Figure 7-6.

2. Enter the label — the name and address — in the Address box.

3. Either click the Options button or click the label icon in the Label box to open the Label Options dialog box.

4. In the Printer Information area, select either Continuous-Feed Printers or Page Printers to declare which kind of printer you have; on the Tray drop-down list, choose the option that describes how you will feed labels to your printer.

5. **Open the Label Vendors drop-down list and choose the brand or type of labels that you have.**

   If your brand is not on the list, click the Details button, and describe your labels in the extremely confusing Information dialog box. A better way, however, is to measure your labels and see whether you can find a label of the same size by experimenting with Product Number and Label Information combinations.

6. **In the Product Number menu, select the product number listed on the box that your labels came in.**

   Look in the Label Information box on the right to make sure that the Height, Width, and Page Size measurements match those of the labels you have.

7. **Click OK to return to the Envelopes and Labels dialog box.**

8. **Choose a Print option.**

   Tell Word to print a single label or a sheet full of labels:

   - **Full Page of the Same Label:** Select this option button if you want to print a pageful of the same label. Likely, you'd choose this option to print a pageful of your own return addresses. Click the New Document button after you make this choice. Word creates a new document with a pageful of labels. Save and print this document on a sheet of labels.

   - **Single Label:** Select this option button to print one label. Then enter the row and column where the label is located and click the Print button.

FIGURE 7-6:
Printing labels.

Churning Out Letters, Envelopes, and Labels for Mass Mailings

Thanks to the miracle of computing, you can churn out form letters, labels, and envelopes for a mass mailing in the privacy of your home or office, just as the big companies do. Churning out form letters, envelopes, and labels is easy, as long as you take the time to prepare the source file. The *source file* is the file that the names and addresses come from. A Word table, an Excel worksheet, a Microsoft Access database table or query, or an Outlook Contacts list can serve as the source file. (Book 5 explains Outlook; Book 3 explains Excel; Book 6 explains Access.)

To generate form letters, envelopes, or labels, you merge the form letter, envelope, or label document with a source file. Word calls this process *merging*. During the merge, names and addresses from the source file are plugged into the appropriate places in the form letter, envelope, or label document. When the merge is complete, you can either save the form letters, envelopes, or labels in a new file or start printing right away.

The following pages explain how to prepare the source file and merge addresses from the source file with a document to create form letters, labels, or envelopes. Then you discover how to print the form letters, labels, or envelopes after you have generated them.

TIP

Word offers a mail-merge wizard (*wizard* is Microsoft's name for a step-by-step procedure you can follow to accomplish a task). If you want to try your hand at using the wizard to complete a mail merge, go to the Mailings tab, click the Start Mail Merge button, and choose Step by Step Mail Merge Wizard on the drop-down list. Good luck to you!

Preparing the source file

If you intend to get addresses for your form letters, labels, or envelopes from an Outlook Contact List on your computer, you're ready to go. However, if you haven't entered the addresses yet or you are keeping them in a Word table, Excel worksheet, Access database table, or Access query, make sure that the data is in good working order:

>> **Word table:** Save the table in its own file and enter a descriptive heading at the top of each column. In the merge, when you tell Word where to plug in address and other data, you will do so by choosing a heading name from the top of a column. In Figure 7-7, for example, the column headings are Last Name, First Name, Street, and so on. (Chapter 4 of this minibook explains how to construct a Word table.)

>> **Excel worksheet:** Arrange the worksheet in table format with a descriptive heading atop each column and no blank cells in any columns. Word will plug in addresses and other data by choosing heading names.

>> **Access database table or query:** Make sure that you know the field names in the database table or query where you keep the addresses. During the merge, you will be asked for field names. By the way, if you're comfortable in Access, query a database table for the records you will need. As you find out shortly, Word offers a technique for choosing only the records you want for your form letters, labels, or envelopes. However, by querying first in Access, you can start off with the records you need and spare yourself from having to choose records in Word.

FIGURE 7-7:
A Word source
table for a mail
merge.

Last Name	First Name	Street	City	State	ZIP	Birthday
Creed	Hank	443 Oak St.	Atherton	CA	93874	July 31
Daws	Leon	13 Spruce St.	Colma	CA	94044	April 1
Maves	Carlos	11 Guy St.	Reek	NV	89201	February 28
Ng	Winston	1444 Unger Ave.	Colma	CA	94404	November 12
Smith	Jane	121 First St.	Colma	CA	94044	January 10
Weiss	Shirley	441 Second St.	Poltroon	ID	49301	May 4

A Word table, Excel worksheet, or Access table or query can include more than address information. Don't worry about deleting information that isn't required for your form letters, labels, and envelopes. As you find out soon, you get to decide which information to take from the Word table, Excel worksheet, or Access table or query.

Merging the document with the source file

After you prepare the source file, the next step in generating form letters, labels, or envelopes for a mass mailing is to merge the document with the source file. Follow these general steps to do so:

1. Create or open a document.

- **Form letters:** Either create a new document and write your form letter, being careful to leave out the parts of the letter that differ from recipient to recipient, or open a letter you have already written and delete the address-ee's name, the address, and other parts of the letter that are particular to each recipient.

- **Envelopes:** Create a new document.

- **Labels:** Create a new document.

2. On the Mailings tab, click the Start Mail Merge button.

3. Choose Letters, Envelopes, or Labels on the drop-down list.

4. Prepare the groundwork for creating form letters, envelopes, or labels for a mass mailing.

What you do next depends on what kind of mass mailing you want to attempt:

- **Form letters:** You're ready to go. The text of your form letter already appears onscreen if you followed the directions for creating and writing it in Step 1.

- **Envelopes:** You see the Envelope Options dialog box, where, on the Envelope Options and Printing Options tabs, you tell Word what size envelope you will print on. See "Printing an Address on an Envelope," earlier in this chapter, for instructions about filling out these tabs (see Step 6). A sample envelope appears onscreen.

- **Labels:** You see the Label Options dialog box, where you tell Word what size labels to print on. See "Printing a Single Address Label (Or a Page of the Same Label)," earlier in this chapter, if you need advice for filling out this dialog box (refer to Steps 4 through 7).

5. Click the Select Recipients button and choose an option on the drop-down list to direct Word to your source file or the source of your address and data information.

Earlier in this chapter, "Preparing the source file" explains what a source file is. Your options are as follows:

- **Addresses from a Word table, Excel worksheet, Access database table, or Access query:** Choose Use an Existing List. You see the Select Data Source dialog box. Locate the Word file, the Excel worksheet, or the Access database, select it, and click Open.

  If you select an Excel worksheet or Access database, you see the Select Table dialog box. Select the worksheet, table, or query you want and click the OK button.

- **Addresses from Microsoft Outlook:** Choose the Choose from Outlook Contacts option (Outlook must be your default email program to get addresses from Outlook). Then, in the Select Contacts dialog box, choose Contacts and click OK. The Mail Merge Recipients dialog box appears (skip to Step 7).

6. Click the Edit Recipient List button.

The Mail Merge Recipients dialog box appears, as shown in Figure 7-8.

7. **In the Mail Merge Recipients dialog box, select the names of people to whom you will send mail; then click OK.**

To select recipients' names, check or uncheck the boxes on the left side of the dialog box.

8. **Enter the address block on your form letters, envelopes, or labels.**

The *address block* is the address, including the recipient's name, company, title, street address, city, and ZIP code. If you're creating form letters, click in the sample letter where the address block will go. If you're printing on envelopes, click in the middle of the envelope where the delivery address will go. Then follow these steps to enter the address block:

a. Click the Address Block button. The Insert Address Block dialog box appears, as shown in Figure 7-9.

b. Choose a format for entering the recipient's name in the address block. As you do so, watch the Preview window; it shows the actual names and addresses that you selected in Step 7.

c. Click the Match Fields button. You see the Match Fields dialog box, shown in Figure 7-9.

d. Using the drop-down lists on the right side of the dialog box, match the fields in your source file with the address block fields on the left side of the dialog box. In Figure 7-9, for example, the Street field is the equivalent of the Address 1 field on the left side of the dialog box, so Street is chosen from the drop-down list to match Address 1.

e. Click OK in the Match Fields dialog box and the Insert Address Block dialog box. The `<<AddressBlock>>` field appears in the document where the address will go. Later, when you merge your document with the data source, real data will appear where the field is now. Think of a field as a kind of placeholder for data.

9. **Click the Preview Results button on the Mailings tab to see real data rather than fields.**

Now you can see clearly whether you entered the address block correctly. If you didn't enter it correctly, click the Match Fields button (it's in the Write & Insert Fields group) to open the Match Fields dialog box and make new choices.

10. **Put the finishing touches on your form letters, labels, or envelopes:**

- **Form letters:** Click where the salutation ("Dear John") will go and then click the Greeting Line button. You see the Insert Greeting Line dialog box, shown in Figure 7-10. Make choices in this dialog box to determine how the letters' salutations will read.

The body of your form letter may well include other variable information such as names and birthdays. To enter that stuff, click in your letter where variable information goes, click the Insert Merge Field button. The Insert Merge Field dialog box appears and lists fields from the source file. Select a field, click the Insert button, and click the Close button. (You can also open the drop-down list on the Insert Merge Field button and choose a field from the source file.)

If you're editing your form letter and you need to see precisely where the variable information you entered is located, click the Highlight Merge Fields button. The variable information is highlighted in your document.

- **Envelopes:** To position the address block correctly, you may have to press the Enter key and tab keys to move it to the center of envelope. If you don't like the fonts or font sizes on the envelope, select an address, go to the Home tab, and change fonts and font sizes there.

  To enter a return address, click in the upper-left corner of the envelope and enter it there.

- **Labels:** Click the Update Labels button to enter all recipients' labels in the sample document.

11. **Make sure the Preview Results button is selected and then click the Next Record and Previous Record buttons on the Mailings tab to skip from recipient to recipient to see whether you have entered information correctly.**

The Next Record and Previous Record buttons are located in the Preview Results group. The items you see onscreen are the same form letters, envelopes, or labels you will see when you have finished printing.

Choose the names of recipients

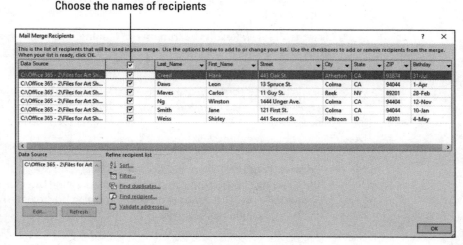

FIGURE 7-8:
Choosing who
gets mail.

202   BOOK 2 **Word 365**

Address block

FIGURE 7-9:
Creating the
address block
(left) and linking
it with address
fields (right).

FIGURE 7-10:
Entering the
greeting.

If an item is incorrect, open the source file and correct it there. When you save the source file, the correction is made in the sample document.

At last — you're ready to print the form letters, envelopes, or labels. Take a deep breath and keep reading.

Printing form letters, envelopes, and labels

After you have gone to the trouble to prepare the data file and merge it with the document, you're ready to print your form letters, envelopes, or labels. Start by loading paper, envelopes, or sheets of labels in your printer:

>> **Form letters:** Form letters are easiest to print. Just put the paper in the printer.

>> **Envelopes:** Not all printers are capable of printing envelopes one after the other. Sorry, but you probably have to consult the dreary manual that came with your printer to find out the correct way to load envelopes.

>> **Labels:** Load the label sheets in your printer.

Now, to print the form letters, envelopes, or labels, save the material in a new document or send it straight to the printer:

>> **Saving in a new document:** Click the Finish & Merge button and choose Edit Individual Documents (or press Alt+Shift+N). You see the Merge to New Document dialog box. Click OK. After Word creates the document, save it and print it. You can go into the document and make changes here and there before printing. In form letters, for example, you can write a sentence or two in different letters to personalize them.

>> **Printing right away:** Click the Finish & Merge button and choose Print Documents (or press Alt+Shift+M) to print the form letters, envelopes, or labels without saving them in a document. Click OK in the Merge to Printer dialog box and then negotiate the Print dialog box.

TIP

Save the form letters, labels, or envelopes in a new document if you intend to print them at a future date or ink is running low on your printer and you may have to print in two or more batches. Saving in a new document permits you to generate the mass mailing without having to start all over again with the merge process and all its tedium.

IN THIS CHAPTER

» Working in Outline view

» Creating a table of contents

» Indexing and cross-referencing
your work

» Managing footnotes and endnotes

Chapter 8

Tools for Reports and Scholarly Papers

This chapter is hereby dedicated to everyone who has had to delve into the unknown and write a report about it. Writing reports, manuals, and scholarly papers is not easy. You have to explore uncharted territory. You have to contemplate the ineffable. And you have to write bibliographies and footnotes and maybe an index, too. Word cannot take you directly to uncharted territory, but it can take some of the sting out of it.

This chapter explains how to construct an outline, handle footnotes and endnotes, generate a table of contents, index a document, include cross-references in documents, and stitch together a bibliography.

Alphabetizing a List

Which comes first in an alphabetical list, "San Jose, California" or "San José, Costa Rica"? You could research the matter on your own, delving into various dictionaries and online references, or you could rely on the Sort button for the answer. Follow these steps to quickly alphabetize a list:

1. **Select the list.**

2. **On the Home tab, click the Sort button.**

   You see the Sort Text dialog box. The Then By options are for sorting tables; they don't concern you, because you're sorting a list.

3. **Click OK.**

   That was easy.

Outlines for Organizing Your Work

Outline view is a great way to see at a glance how your document is organized and whether you need to organize it differently. To take advantage of this feature, you must have assigned heading styles to the headings in your document (Chapter 3 of this minibook explains styles). In Outline view, you can see all the headings in your document. If a section is in the wrong place, you can move it simply by dragging an icon or by clicking one of the buttons on the Outlining tab. To change the rank of a heading, simply click a button to promote or demote it.

To switch to Outline view, go to the View tab and click the Outline button (or press Alt+Ctrl+O). You see the Outlining tab, as shown in Figure 8-1. Rather than see text, you see the headings in your document, as well as the first line underneath each heading. Now you get a sense of what is in your document and whether it is organized well. By choosing an option from the Show Level drop-down list, you can decide which headings to see onscreen.

To leave Outline view when you're done reorganizing your document, click the Close Outline View button or a view button apart from Outline.

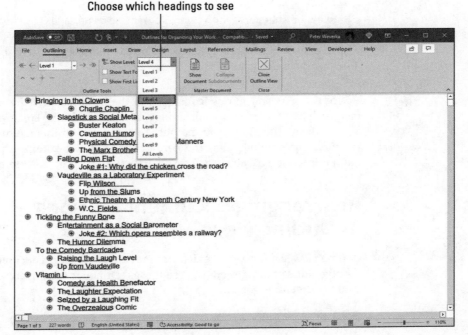

Choose which headings to see

FIGURE 8-1:
A document in
Outline view.

Viewing the outline in different ways

Before you start rearranging your document in Outline view, get a good look at it:

» **View some or all headings:** Choose an option from the Show Level drop-down list (refer to Figure 8-1). To see only first-level headings, for example, choose Level 1. To see first-, second-, and third-level headings, choose Level 3. Choose All Levels to see all the headings.

» **View heading formats:** Click the Show Text Formatting check box. When this check box is selected, you can see how headings were formatted and get a better idea of their ranking in your document.

» **View or hide the subheadings in one section:** To see or hide the subheadings and text in one section of a document, select that section by clicking the plus sign beside its heading; then, click the Expand button (or press Alt+Shift+plus sign) to see the subheadings, or click the Collapse button (or press Alt+Shift+minus sign) to hide the subheadings. You can also double-click the plus sign beside a heading to view or hide its subheadings. (Later in this chapter, "Collapsing and Expanding Parts of a Document" explains how to view or hide subheadings in Print Layout view.)

>> **View or hide paragraph text:** Click the Show First Line Only check box (or press Alt+Shift+L). When this check box is selected, you see only the first line in each paragraph. First lines are followed by an ellipsis (. . .) so that you know that more text follows.

REMEMBER

Notice the plus and minus icons next to the headings and the text. A plus icon means that the item has subheadings and text under it. For example, headings almost always have plus icons because text comes after them. A minus icon means that nothing is found below the item in question. For example, body text usually has a minus icon because body text is lowest on the Outline totem pole.

Rearranging document sections in Outline view

Outline view is mighty convenient for moving sections in a document and for promoting and demoting sections. Use these techniques to rearrange and reorganize your document:

>> **Move a section:** To move a section up or down in the document, select it and click the Move Up or Move Down button (or press Alt+Shift+↑ or Alt+Shift+↓). You can also drag the plus sign to a new location. If you want to move the subheadings and subordinate text along with the section, be sure to click the Collapse button to tuck all the subheadings and subtext into the heading before you move it.

>> **Promote and demote headings:** Click the heading and then click the Promote button or Demote button (or press Alt+Shift+← or Alt+Shift+→). For example, you can promote a Level 3 heading to Level 2 by clicking the Promote button. Click the Promote To Heading 1 button to promote any heading to a first-level heading; click the Demote To Body text button to turn a heading into prose.

>> **Choose a new level for a heading:** Click the heading and choose a new heading level from the Outline Level drop-down list.

Collapsing and Expanding Parts of a Document

As long as you apply heading styles (Heading 1, Heading 2, and so on) to headings, you can collapse and expand parts of a document. Click the Collapse button next to a heading to conceal its subheadings and subtext. Collapsing clears the screen of material that doesn't require your attention. Click the Expand button next to a heading to display its subheadings and subtext.

Figure 8-2 demonstrates expanding and collapsing. Use these techniques to collapse or expand the subheadings and subtext under a heading:

>> **Collapsing:** Click the Collapse button to the left of a heading.

>> **Expanding:** Move the pointer over a heading to display its Expand button; then click the Expand button.

TIP

You can collapse headings by default. On the Home tab, click the Paragraph group button to open the Paragraph dialog box. On the Indents and Spacing tab, choose an outline level and select the Collapsed by Default check box.

Click to expand

Click to collapse

FIGURE 8-2:
Collapse subheadings and subtext under a heading to keep the screen from getting crowded.

Generating a Table of Contents

A book-size document or long report isn't worth much without a table of contents (TOC). How else can readers find what they're looking for? Generating a table of contents with Word is easy, as long as you give the headings in the document different styles — Heading 1, Heading 2, and so on. (Chapter 3 of this minibook explains styles.) The beautiful thing about Word TOCs is the way they can be updated nearly instantly. If you add a new heading or erase a heading, you can update the TOC with a snap of your fingers. Moreover, you can quickly go from a TOC entry to its corresponding heading in a document by Ctrl+clicking the entry.

TIP

Before you create your TOC, create a new section in which to put it and number the pages in the new section with Roman numerals (Chapter 2 of this minibook explains sections and how to number pages). TOCs, including the TOC in this book, are usually numbered in this way. The first entry in the TOC should cite page number 1. If you don't heed my advice and create a new section, the TOC will occupy the first few numbered pages of your document, and the numbering scheme will be thrown off.

Creating a TOC

To create a table of contents, place the cursor where you want the TOC to go, visit the References tab, and click the Table of Contents button. On the drop-down list, choose one of Word's automatic TOC options or choose Custom Table of Contents to fashion a TOC on your own in the Table of Contents dialog box. (See "Customizing a TOC," later in this chapter, for information about fashioning a TOC in the Table of Contents dialog box.)

TIP

Suppose that you want to copy a TOC to another document. To copy a TOC, drag the pointer down its left margin to select it, and then press Ctrl+Shift+F9. Next, use the Copy and Paste commands to copy the TOC to the other document. Because Word gives the text of TOCs the Hyperlink character style, you have to change the color of the text in the TOC (it's blue) and remove the underlines. As for the original TOC, you "disconnected" it from the headings in your document when you pressed Ctrl+Shift+F9. Press the Undo button to undo the effects of pressing Ctrl+Shift+F9 and "disconnecting" your TOC from the headers to which it refers.

Updating and removing a TOC

Follow these instructions to update and remove a TOC:

>> **Updating a TOC:** If you add, remove, or edit a heading in your document, your TOC needs updating. To update it, go to the References tab and click the

Update Table button, or click in the TOC and press F9. A dialog box asks how to update the TOC. Either update the page numbers only or update the entire table, including all TOC entries and page numbers.

» **Removing a TOC:** On the References tab, click the Table of Contents button and choose Remove Table of Contents on the drop-down list.

Customizing a TOC

Want to tinker with your TOC? You can number the headings in different ways and tell Word to include or exclude certain headings.

To change around a TOC, click inside it, go to the References tab, click the Table of Contents button, and choose Custom Table of Contents on the drop-down list. You see the Table of Contents dialog box shown in Figure 8-3. Choose options to declare which headings you want for your TOC and how you want to format it:

» **Showing page numbers:** Deselect the Show Page Numbers box if you want your TOC to be a simple list that doesn't refer to headings by page.

» **Aligning the page numbers:** Select the Right Align Page Numbers check box if you want page numbers to line up along the right side of the TOC so that the ones and tens line up under each other.

» **Choosing a tab leader:** A *leader* is the punctuation mark that appears between the heading and the page number the heading is on. If you don't want periods as the leader, choose another leader or choose (None).

» **Choosing a format:** Choose a format from the Formats drop-down list if you don't care to use the one from the template. Just be sure to watch the Print Preview and Web Preview boxes to see the results of your choice.

WARNING

» **Choosing a TOC depth:** The Show Levels box determines how many heading levels are included in the TOC. Unless your document is a legal contract or other formal paper, enter a **2** or **3** here. A TOC is supposed to help readers find information quickly. Including lots of headings that take a long time to read through defeats the purpose of having a TOC.

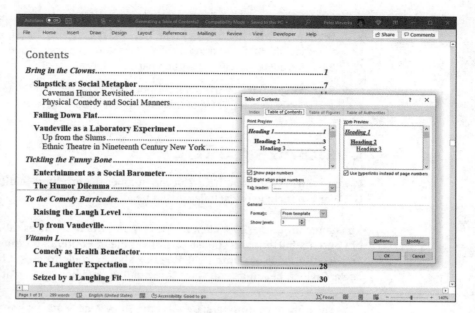

FIGURE 8-3:
You can decide for yourself which headings go in a TOC and how it's numbered.

Changing the structure of a TOC

Sometimes the conventional TOC that Word generates doesn't do the trick. Just because a heading has been given the Heading 1 style doesn't mean that it should receive first priority in the TOC. Suppose that you created another style called Chapter Title that should stand taller in the hierarchy than Heading 1. In that case, you need to rearrange the TOC so that Heading 1 headings rank second, not first, in the TOC hierarchy.

Use the Table of Contents Options and Style dialog boxes to tinker with a TOC. These dialog boxes are shown in Figure 8-4. To open them, click, respectively, the Options button or Modify button in the Table of Contents dialog box (refer to Figure 8-3).

>> **Assigning TOC levels to paragraph styles:** The Table of Contents Options dialog box lists each paragraph style in the document you're working in. For headings you want to appear in the TOC, enter a number in the TOC Level text box to determine the headings' rank. If headings assigned the Heading 1 style are to rank second in the TOC, for example, enter a 2 in Heading 1's TOC Level text box. You can exclude headings from a TOC by deleting a number in a TOC Level box.

>> **Including table entry fields:** To include text you marked for entry in the TOC, select the Table Entry Fields check box in the Table of Contents Options dialog box (later in this chapter, the sidebar "Marking oddball text for inclusion in the TOC" explains how TOC fields work).

>> **Changing the look of TOC entries:** The Style dialog box that you see when you click the Modify button gives you the chance to choose new fonts, character styles, and font sizes for TOC entries if you generated your TOC from a template. Click the Modify button. Then, in the Style dialog box, choose options to format the TOC style. For example, click the Bold button to boldface TOC entries. (Chapter 3 of this minibook explains modifying styles.)

FIGURE 8-4:
Changing a TOC's
structure and
formatting.

MARKING ODDBALL TEXT FOR INCLUSION IN THE TOC

Table of contents entries can refer to a particular place in a document, not just to headings that have been assigned heading styles. For example, you can include figure captions.

Use one of these techniques to mark an entry in your document for inclusion in the TOC:

- Click in the heading, figure caption, or whatnot. Next, click the Add Text button on the References tab and choose a TOC level on the drop-down list (the Do Not Show in Table of Contents option keeps text from being included in the TOC). If you choose Level 2, for example, the entry appears with other second-level headings.

(continued)

(continued)

- Click in a heading or text and press Alt+Shift+O. Then, in the Mark Table of Contents Entry dialog box, make sure that the words you want to appear in the TOC appear in the Entry text box (edit or enter the words if need be), and make sure that C (for Contents) appears in the Table Identifier box. In the Level box, enter a number to tell Word how to treat the entry when you generate the table of contents. For example, entering **1** tells Word to treat the entry like a first-level heading and give it top priority. A **3** places the entry with the third-level headings. Finally, click the Mark button.

When you generate the table of contents, be sure to include the oddball entries. To do that, click the Options button in the Table of Contents dialog box and, in the Table of Contents Options dialog box (refer to Figure 8-4), select the Table Entry Fields check box.

Indexing a Document

A good index is a thing of beauty. User manuals, reference works of any length, and reports that readers will refer to all require indexes. Except for the table of contents, the only way to find information in a long document is to look in the index. An index at the end of a company report reflects well on the person who wrote the report. It gives the appearance that the author put in a fair amount of time to complete the work, even if they didn't really do that.

An index entry can be formatted in many ways. You can cross-reference index entries, list a page range in an index entry, and break out an index entry into subentries and sub-subentries. To help you with your index, Figure 8-5 explains indexing terminology.

REMEMBER

Writing a good index entry is as hard as writing a good, descriptive heading. As you enter index entries in your document, ask yourself how you would look up information in the index, and enter your index entries accordingly.

Main entry   Cross-reference
            Page range

Sand Creek, Battle of *See* Indian Wars

Sioux City, 191

Sioux Indians, 149–157

    daily life, 151

    religious observances, 153

      shaman, 153

      Sun Dance, 155

    at Standing Rock Reservation, 150

Sitting Bull, 156, 159

Subentries   Sub-subentries

FIGURE 8-5:
Different ways of handling index entries.

Marking index items in the document

The first step in constructing an index is to mark index entries in your document. Marking index items yourself is easier than it seems. After you open the Mark Index Entry dialog box, it stays open so that you can scroll through your document and make entries.

1. **If you see a word or phrase in your document that you can use as a main, top-level entry, select it; otherwise, place the cursor in the paragraph or heading whose topic you want to include in the index.**

   You can save a little time by selecting a word, as I describe shortly.

2. **On the References tab, click the Mark Entry button (or press Alt+Shift+X).**

   The Mark Index Entry dialog box appears, as shown in Figure 8-6. If you selected a word or phrase, it appears in the Main Entry box.

3. **Choose how you want to handle this index entry (refer to Figure 8-5 to see the various ways to make index entries).**

WARNING

   When you enter the text, don't put a comma or period after it. Word does that when it generates the index. The text that you enter appears in your index.

   - **Main Entry:** If you're entering a main, top-level entry, leave the text in the Main Entry box (if it's already there), type new text to describe this entry, or edit the text that's already there. Leave the Subentry box blank.

   - **Subentry:** To create a subentry, enter text in the Subentry box. The subentry text will appear in the index below the main entry text, so make sure that some text is in the Main Entry box and that the subentry text fits under the main entry.

- **Sub-subentry:** A sub-subentry is the third level in the hierarchy. To create a sub-subentry, type the subentry in the Subentry box, enter a colon (:), and type the sub-subentry without entering a space, like so: **religious observances:shaman**.

4. **Decide how to handle the page reference in the entry.**

   Again, your choices are many:

   - **Cross-reference:** To go without a page reference and refer the reader to another index entry, click the Cross-Reference option button and type the other entry in the text box after the word *See.* What you type here appears in your index, so be sure that the topic you refer the reader to is really named in your index.

   - **Current Page:** Click this option to enter a single page number after the entry.

   - **Page Range:** Click this option if you're indexing a subject that covers several pages in your document. A page range index entry looks something like this: "Sioux Indians, 149–157." To make a page range entry, you must create a bookmark first. Leave the Mark Index Entry dialog box, select the text in the page range, and press Ctrl+Shift+F5 or click the Bookmark button on the Insert tab. In the Bookmark dialog box, enter a name in the Bookmark Name box, and click the Add button. (Chapter 1 of this minibook explains bookmarks.)

5. **You can boldface or italicize a page number or page range by clicking a Page Number Format check box.**

   In some indexes, the page or page range where the topic is explained in the most depth is italicized or boldfaced so that readers can get to the juiciest parts first.

6. **If you selected a single word or phrase in Step 1, you can click the Mark All button to have Word go through the document and mark all words that are identical to the one in the Main Entry box; click Mark to put this single entry in the index.**

   Click outside the Mark Index Entry dialog box and find the next topic or word that you want to mark for the index. Then click the Mark Entry button on the References tab and make another entry.

REMEMBER

A bunch of ugly field codes appear in your document after you mark an index entry. You can render them invisible by clicking the Show/Hide¶ button on the Home tab (or pressing Ctrl+Shift+8).

FIGURE 8-6:
Marking an index
entry.

Generating the index

After you mark all the index entries, it's time to generate the index:

1. **Place the cursor where you want the index to go, most likely at the end of the document.**

   You might type the word **Index** at the top of the page and format the word in a decorative way.

2. **On the References tab, click the Insert Index button.**

   You see the Index dialog box shown in Figure 8-7.

3. **Choose options in the dialog box and click OK.**

   As you make your choices, watch the Print Preview box to see what happens.

Here are the options in the Index dialog box:

» **Type:** Choose Run-in if you want subentries and sub-subentries to run together; choose Indented to indent subentries and sub-subentries below main entries (refer to Figure 8-5).

» **Columns:** Stick with 2, unless you don't have subentries or sub-subentries and you can squeeze three columns on the page or you are working on a landscape document.

FIGURE 8-7:
Generating an
index.

>> **Language:** Choose a language for the table, if necessary and if you have installed a foreign language dictionary. If you have installed the dictionary, you can run the spell checker over your index and make sure that the entries are spelled correctly. (Chapter 5 of this minibook explains foreign language dictionaries.)

>> **Right Align Page Numbers:** Normally, page numbers appear right after entries and are separated from entries by a comma, but you can right-align the entries so that they line up under one another with this option.

>> **Tab Leader:** Some index formats place a *leader* between the entry and the page number. A leader is a series of dots or dashes. If you're working with a format that has a leader, you can choose a leader from the drop-down list.

>> **Formats:** Word offers a number of attractive index layouts. You can choose one from the list.

>> **Modify:** Click this button if you're adventurous and want to create an index style of your own. (Chapter 3 of this minibook explains styles.)

To update an index after you create or delete entries, click it and then click the Update Index button on the References tab or right-click the index and then choose Update Field on the shortcut menu.

Editing an index

After you generate an index, read it carefully to make sure that all entries are useful to readers. Inevitably, something doesn't come out right, but you can edit index entries as you would the text in a document. Index field markers are enclosed in curly brackets with the letters *XE* and the text of the index entry in quotation marks, like so: { XE: "Wovoka: Ghost Dance" }. To edit an index marker, click the Show/Hide¶ button on the Home tab (or press Ctrl+Shift+8) to see the field markers and find the one you need to edit. Then delete letters or type letters as you would for normal text.

TIP

Here's a quick way to find index field markers: After clicking the Show/Hide¶ button, with the index fields showing, press Ctrl+G to open the Go To tab of the Find and Replace dialog box. In the Go To menu, choose Field; type **XE** in the Enter Field Name box, and click the Next button until you find the marker you want to edit. You can also use the Find command on the Home tab to look for index entries. Word finds index entries as well as text as long as you click the Show/Hide¶ button to display index fields in your document.

Putting Cross-References in a Document

Cross-references are very handy indeed. They tell readers where to go to find more information about a topic. The problem with cross-references, however, is that the thing being cross-referenced really has to be there. If you tell readers to go to a heading called "The Cat's Pajamas" on page 93, and neither the heading nor the page is really there, readers curse and tell you where to go, instead of the other way around.

Fortunately for you, Word lets you know when you make errant cross-references. You can refer readers to headings, page numbers, footnotes, endnotes, and plain old paragraphs. And as long you create captions for your cross-references with the Insert Caption button on the References tab, you can also make cross-references to equations, figures, graphs, listings, programs, and tables. If you delete the thing that a cross-reference refers to and render the cross-reference invalid, Word tells you about it the next time you update your cross-references. Best of all, if the page number, numbered item, or text that a cross-reference refers to changes, so does the cross-reference.

Follow these steps to create a cross–reference:

1. **Write the first part of the cross-reference text.**

   For example, you could write **To learn more about these cowboys of the pampas, see page** and then type a blank space. The blank space separates the word *page* from the page number in the cross-reference. If you are referring to a heading, write something like **For more information, see "**. Don't type a blank space this time because the cross-reference heading text will appear right after the double quotation mark.

2. **On the References tab, click the Cross-Reference button.**

   The Cross-Reference dialog box appears, as shown in Figure 8-8.

3. **Choose what type of item you're referring to in the Reference Type drop-down list.**

   If you're referring to a plain old paragraph, choose Bookmark. Then click outside the dialog box, scroll to the paragraph you're referring to, and place a bookmark there. (Chapter 1 of this minibook explains bookmarks.)

4. **Make a choice in the Insert Reference To box to refer to text, a page number, or a numbered item.**

   The options in this box are different, depending on your choice in Step 3.

   - **Text:** Choose this option (Heading Text, Entire Caption, and so on) to include text in the cross-reference. For example, choose Heading Text if your cross-reference is to a heading.

   - **Number:** Choose this option to insert a page number or other kind of number, such as a table number, in the cross-reference.

   - **Include Above/Below:** Check this box to include the word *above* or *below* to tell readers where, in relation to the cross-reference, the thing being referred to is located in your document.

5. **If you wish, leave the check mark in the Insert as Hyperlink check box to create a hyperlink as well as a cross-reference.**

   With a hyperlink, someone reading the document onscreen can Ctrl+click the cross-reference and go directly to what it refers to.

6. **In the For Which box, tell Word where the thing you're referring to is located.**

   To do so, select a heading, bookmark, footnote, endnote, equation, figure, graph, or whatnot. In long documents, you almost certainly have to click the scroll bar to find the one you want.

7. Click the Insert button and then click the Close button.

8. Back in your document, enter the rest of the cross-reference text, if necessary.

Choose what the reference refers to

Choose how to refer to the item

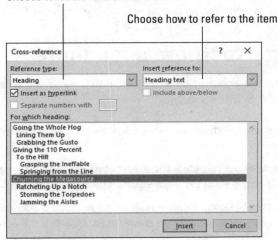

FIGURE 8-8:
Entering a
cross-reference.

When you finish creating your document, update all the cross-references. To do that, press Ctrl+A to select the entire document. Then press F9 or right-click in the document and choose Update Field on the shortcut menu.

TIP

If the thing referred to in a cross-reference is no longer in your document, you see `Error! Reference source not found` where the cross-reference should be. To find cross-reference errors in long documents, look for the word *Error!* with the Find command (press Ctrl+F). Investigate what went wrong, and repair or delete errant cross-references.

Putting Footnotes and Endnotes in Documents

A *footnote* is a bit of explanation, a comment, or a reference that appears at the bottom of the page and is referred to by a number or symbol in the text. An *endnote* is the same thing, except that it appears at the end of the section, chapter, or document. If you've written a scholarly paper of any kind, you know what a drag footnotes and endnotes are.

You will be glad to know that Word takes some of the drudgery out of footnotes and endnotes. For example, if you delete or add a note, all notes after the one you added or deleted are renumbered. And you don't have to worry about long footnotes because Word adjusts the page layout to make room for them. You can change the numbering scheme of footnotes and endnotes at will. When you are reviewing a document, all you have to do is move the pointer over a footnote or endnote citation. The note icon appears, as does a pop-up box with the text of the note.

Entering a footnote or endnote

You must be in Print Layout view to handle footnotes and endnotes. To enter a footnote or endnote in a document:

1. Place the cursor in the text where you want the note's number or symbol to appear.

2. On the References tab, click the Insert Footnote button (or press Ctrl+Alt+F) or the Insert Endnote button (or press Ctrl+Alt+D).

Word scrolls to the bottom of the page or the end of the document or section so that you can enter the note, as shown in Figure 8-9.

3. Enter your footnote or endnote.

4. Scroll upward to return to the main text.

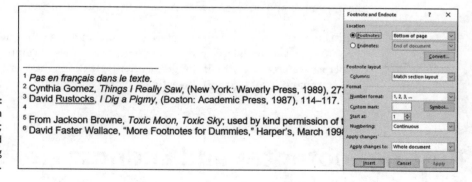

FIGURE 8-9: Entering a footnote (left); the Footnote and Endnote dialog box (right).

Click the Show Notes button at any time to see your notes at the bottom of the page or at the end of the section or document.

TIP

To quickly return from writing a note to the place in your document where the footnote or endnote number citation is located, double-click the number citation at the start of the note. For example, if you just finished entering footnote 3, double-click the number 3.

Choosing the numbering scheme and position of notes

Choosing the numbering scheme and positioning of endnotes and footnotes is quite easy. On the References tab, click the Footnotes group button. The Footnote and Endnote dialog box appears (refer to Figure 8-9). Tell Word where to place your notes:

» **Footnotes:** Choose Bottom of Page to put footnotes at the bottom of the page no matter where the text ends; choose Below Text to put footnotes directly below the last line of text on the page.

» **Endnotes:** Choose End of Section if your document is divided into sections (such as chapters) and you want endnotes to appear at the back of sections; choose End of Document to put all endnotes at the very back of the document.

» **Columns:** If you want to run footnotes or endnotes into columns, choose the number of columns you want.

In the Format area, tell Word how to number the notes:

» **Number Format:** Choose A B C, i ii iii, or another numbering scheme, if you want. You can also enter symbols by choosing the last option on this drop-down list.

» **Custom Mark:** You can mark the note with a symbol by clicking the Symbol button and choosing a symbol in the Symbol dialog box. If you go this route, you have to enter a symbol each time you insert a note. Not only that, you may have to enter two or three symbols for the second and third notes on each page or document because Word can't renumber symbols.

» **Start At:** To start numbering the notes at a place other than 1, A, or i, enter **2**, **B**, **ii**, or whatever in this box.

» **Numbering:** To number the notes continuously from the start of your document to the end, choose Continuous. Choose Restart Each Section to begin anew at each section of your document. For footnotes, you can begin anew on each page by choosing Restart Each Page.

By the way, the Convert button in the Footnote and Endnote dialog box is for fickle scholars who suddenly decide that their endnotes should be footnotes or vice versa. Click it and choose an option in the Convert Notes dialog box to turn footnotes into endnotes, turn endnotes into footnotes, or — in documents with both endnotes and footnotes — make the endnotes footnotes and the footnotes endnotes.

Deleting, moving, and editing notes

If a devious editor tells you that a footnote or endnote is in the wrong place, that you don't need a note, or that you need to change the text in a note, all is not lost:

» **Editing:** To edit a note, double-click its number or symbol in the text. You see the note onscreen. Edit the note at this point.

» **Moving:** To move a note, select its number or symbol in the text and drag it to a new location, or cut and paste it to a new location.

» **Deleting:** To delete a note, select its number or symbol and press the Delete key.

Footnotes and endnotes are renumbered when you move or delete one of them.

Compiling a Bibliography

A *bibliography* is a list, usually in alphabetical order by author name, of all the books, journal articles, websites, interviews, and other sources used in the writing of an article, report, or book. Writing a good bibliography is a chore. Besides keeping careful track of sources, you have to list them correctly. Does the author's name or work's name come first in the citation? How do you list a website or magazine article without an author's name?

Word's Bibliography feature is very nice in this regard: It solves the problem of how to enter citations for a bibliography. All you have to do is enter the bare facts about the citation — the author's name, title, publication date, publisher, and so on — and Word presents this information correctly in the bibliography. You can choose among several popular bibliographical styles (APA, Chicago, and others) from the Style drop-down list, as shown in Figure 8-10. After you make your choice, Word reformats all bibliography citations. You don't have to worry about whether titles should be underlined or italicized, or how authors' names should be listed in the bibliography.

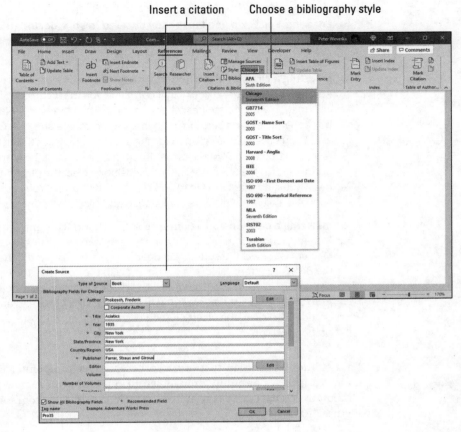

Insert a citation   Choose a bibliography style

FIGURE 8-10:
Adding a
citation (left)
and formatting
citations
(right) for a
bibliography.

Inserting a citation for your bibliography

An abbreviated citation appears in the text of your document in between parentheses where you enter a citation; the complete citation appears in the bibliography. After you enter the information about a citation, entering it a second time is
easy because Word keeps a master list of all citations you have used in your work,
both in the document you're working on and your other documents. To enter a
citation, click in your document at the place that refers to the source, go to the
References tab, and use one of these techniques to enter the citation:

>> **Creating a new citation:** Click the Insert Citation button and choose Add New
Source. You see the Create Source dialog box shown in Figure 8-10. Choose an
option on the Type of Source drop-down list and enter particulars about the
source. You can click the Show All Bibliography Fields check box to enlarge the
dialog box and enter all kinds of information about the source. Whether
clicking the check box is necessary depends on how detailed you want your
bibliography to be.

Tools for Reports and
Scholarly Papers

>> **Entering a citation you've already entered in your document:** Click the Insert Citation button and choose the citation on the drop-down list. The top of the drop-down list presents citations you've already entered.

>> **Inserting a citation placeholder:** Click the Insert Citation button and choose Add New Placeholder if you're in a hurry and you don't currently have all the information you need to describe the source. The Placeholder Name dialog box appears. Enter a placeholder name for the source and click OK. Later, when you have the information for the source, either click the citation in the text and choose Edit Source on its drop-down list or click the Manage Sources button, and in the Source Manager dialog box, select the placeholder name (it has a question mark next to it) and click the Edit button. You see the Edit Source dialog box. Enter the information and click OK.

>> **Inserting a citation you've entered in another document:** Click the Manage Sources button. You see the Source Manager dialog box. In the Master List, select the source you need if the source is listed; otherwise, click the Browse button, select the document with the source in the Open Source List dialog box, and click Open). Next, click the Copy button to copy sources from the Master List into your document. Then click Close and enter the citation by clicking the Insert Citation button and choosing the name of the citation you copied.

Your citation appears in text in parentheses. Move the pointer over the citation and click it to see an inline drop-down menu. From this menu, you can edit the citation as it appears in text as well as edit it in the bibliography, as shown in Figure 8-11.

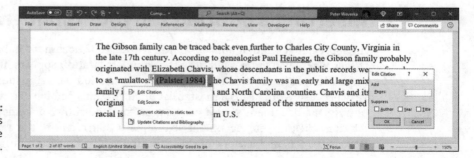

FIGURE 8-11:
In-text citations have inline drop-down lists.

Editing a citation

Use one of these techniques to edit a citation:

» Open the citation's inline drop-down menu (refer to Figure 8-11) and choose Edit Source. You see the Edit Source dialog box, where you can edit the citation.

» Click the Manage Sources button on the References tab. The Source Manager dialog box appears. Select the citation, click the Edit button, and change around the citation in the Edit Source dialog box.

Changing how citations appear in text

Citations appear in text enclosed in parentheses. Use one of these techniques to change how a citation appears in the text of your document:

» **Changing what's in parentheses:** Open the citation's drop-down menu and choose Edit Citation. You see the Edit Citation dialog box (refer to Figure 8-11). To suppress the author's name, year, or title from appearing inside parentheses, select the Author, Year, or Title check box (whether the citation in parentheses lists the author, year, or title depends on which citation style you choose). To make page numbers appear with the citation, enter page numbers in the Pages box.

» **Removing the in-text citation:** Swipe over the citation to select it and press Delete. Removing an in-text citation this way does not prevent the citation from appearing in the bibliography.

Generating the bibliography

Go to the References tab and follow these steps to generate your bibliography:

1. Click in your document where you want the bibliography to appear.

Probably that place is toward the end of the document.

2. On the References tab, open the Style drop-down list and choose a style.

If you're generating your bibliography for a paper you will submit to a journal or institution, ask the editors which style they prefer for bibliographies and choose that style from the list.

3. **Click the Manage Sources button.**

   You see the Source Manager dialog box. Citations in the Current List box will appear in your bibliography.

4. **If necessary, address citations in the Current List box.**

   If you entered any citation placeholders, their names appear in the list next to question marks. Select each placeholder, click the Edit button, and enter information in the Edit Source dialog box.

   To keep a citation from appearing in the bibliography, select it and click the Delete button.

5. **Click the Close button in the Source Manager dialog box.**

6. **Click the Bibliography button and choose a built-in bibliography or the Insert Bibliography command on the drop-down list.**

There it is — your bibliography.

Excel 365

Contents at a Glance

Chapter **1**

Up and Running with Excel

This chapter introduces *Microsoft Excel*, the official number cruncher of Office 365. The purpose of Excel is to track, analyze, and tabulate numbers. Use the program to project profits and losses, formulate a budget, or analyze Elvis sightings in North America. Doing the setup work takes time, but after you enter the numbers and tell Excel how to tabulate them, you're on Easy Street. Excel does the math for you. All you have to do is kick off your shoes, sit back, and see how the numbers stack up.

This chapter explains what a workbook and a worksheet is, and how rows and columns on a worksheet determine where cell addresses are. You also discover tips and tricks for entering data quickly in a worksheet and how to construct data-validation rules to make sure that data is entered accurately.

Creating a New Excel Workbook

Workbook is the Excel term for the files you create with Excel. When you create a workbook, you are given the choice of creating a blank workbook or creating a workbook from a template.

A *template* is a preformatted workbook designed for a specific purpose, such as budgeting, tracking inventories, or tracking purchase orders. Creating a workbook from a template is mighty convenient if you happen to find a template that suits your purposes, but in my experience, you almost always have to start from a generic, blank workbook because your data is your own. You need a workbook that you create yourself, not one created from a template by someone else.

To create a workbook, begin by going to the File tab and choosing New. You see the New window, shown in Figure 1-1. This window offers templates for creating workbooks and the means to search for templates online.

Create a blank workbook

Search online   Choose a template

FIGURE 1-1:
Create a
workbook by
starting in the
New window.

Create a workbook from a template

Use these techniques in the New window to choose a template and create a workbook:

TIP

» **Choose the blank workbook template:** Choose Blank Workbook to create a plain template.

Press Ctrl+N to create a new, blank workbook without opening the New window.

» **Choose a template:** Select a template to examine it in a preview window (refer to Figure 1-1). If you like what you see, click the Create button in the preview window to create a document from the template.

» **Search online for a template:** Enter a search term in the Search box and click the Start Searching button (or click a suggested search term). New templates appear in the New window. Click a template to preview it (see Figure 1-1). Click the Create button in the preview window to create a document from the template.

Book 1, Chapter 1 explains how to save files after you create them, as well as how to open a file, including an Excel workbook.

Getting Acquainted with Excel

If you've spent any time in an Office application, much of the Excel screen may look familiar to you. The buttons on the Home tab — the Bold and the Align buttons, for example — work the same in Excel as they do in Word. The Font and Font Size drop-down lists work the same as well. Any command in Excel that has to do with formatting text and numbers works the same in Excel and Word.

As mentioned earlier, an Excel file is a *workbook.* Each workbook comprises one or more worksheets. A *worksheet,* also known as a *spreadsheet,* is a table into which you enter data and data labels. Figure 1-2 shows a worksheet with data about rainfall in different counties.

A worksheet works like an accountant's ledger — only it's much easier to use. Notice how the worksheet is divided by gridlines into columns (A, B, C, and so on) and rows (1, 2, 3, and so on). The rectangles where columns and rows intersect are *cells,* and each cell can hold one data item, a formula for calculating data, or nothing at all.

Active cell address   Formula bar   Active cell

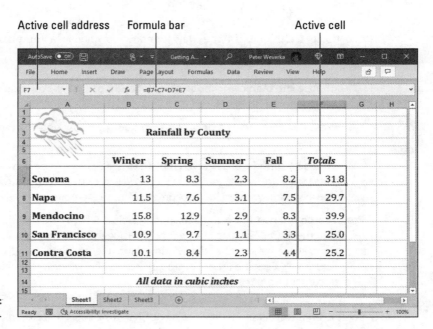

	A	B	C	D	E	F	G	H
1								
2								
3			Rainfall by County					
4								
5								
6		Winter	Spring	Summer	Fall	Totals		
7	Sonoma	13	8.3	2.3	8.2	31.8		
8	Napa	11.5	7.6	3.1	7.5	29.7		
9	Mendocino	15.8	12.9	2.9	8.3	39.9		
10	San Francisco	10.9	9.7	1.1	3.3	25.0		
11	Contra Costa	10.1	8.4	2.3	4.4	25.2		
12								
13								
14			All data in cubic inches					
15								

F7 ▾ : × ✓ fx =B7+C7+D7+E7

Sheet1   Sheet2   Sheet3   ⊕

FIGURE 1-2:
The Excel screen.

Each cell has a different cell address. In Figure 1-2, cell B7 holds 13, the number of inches of rain that fell in Sonoma County in the winter. Meanwhile, as the Formula bar at the top of the screen shows, cell F7, the *active cell,* holds the formula =B7+C7+D7+E7, the sum of the numbers in cells — you guessed it — B7, C7, D7, and E7.

REMEMBER

The beauty of Excel is that the program does all the calculations and recalculations for you after you enter the data. If I were to change the number in cell B7, Excel would instantly recalculate the total amount of rainfall in Sonoma County in cell F7. People like myself who struggled in math class will be glad to know that you don't have to worry about the math because Excel does it for you. All you have to do is make sure that the data and the formulas are entered correctly.

After you enter and label the data, enter the formulas, and turn your worksheet into a little masterpiece, you can start analyzing the data. For example, you can generate charts like the one in Figure 1-3. Do you notice any similarities between the worksheet in Figure 1-2 and the chart in Figure 1-3? The chart is fashioned from data in the worksheet, and it took me about half a minute to create that chart. (Book 8, Chapter 1 explains how to create charts in Excel, Word, and PowerPoint.)

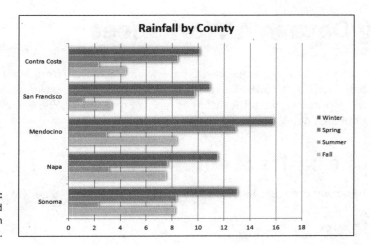

FIGURE 1-3:
A chart generated
from the data in
Figure 1-2.

Rows, columns, and cell addresses

Not that anyone needs them all, but an Excel worksheet has numerous columns and more than 1 million rows. The rows are numbered, and columns are labeled A to Z, then AA to AZ, then BA to BZ, and so on. The important thing to remember is that each cell has an address whose name comes from a column letter and a row number. The first cell in row 1 is A1, the second is B1, and so on. You need to enter cell addresses in formulas to tell Excel which numbers to compute.

To find a cell's address, either make note of which column and row it lies in or click the cell and glance at the Formula bar (refer to Figure 1-2). The left side of the Formula bar lists the address of the *active cell,* the cell that is selected in the worksheet. In Figure 1-2, cell F7 is the active cell.

Workbooks and worksheets

By default, each workbook includes one worksheet, called Sheet1, but you can add more worksheets (and rename worksheets, too). Think of a workbook as a stack of worksheets. Besides calculating the numbers in cells across the rows or down the columns of a worksheet, you can make calculations throughout a workbook by using numbers from different worksheets in a calculation. Chapter 2 of this minibook explains how to add worksheets, rename worksheets, and do all else that pertains to them.

Entering Data in a Worksheet

Entering data in a worksheet is an irksome activity. Fortunately, Excel offers a few shortcuts to take the sting out of it. These pages explain how to enter data in a worksheet, what the different types of data are, and how to enter text labels, numbers, dates, and times.

The basics of entering data

What you can enter in a worksheet cell falls into four categories:

>> Text

>> A value (numeric, date, or time)

>> A logical value (True or False)

>> A formula that returns a value, logical value, or text

Still, no matter what type of data you're entering, the basic steps are the same:

1. Click the cell where you want to enter the data or text label.

As shown in Figure 1-4, a square appears around the cell to tell you that the cell you clicked is now the active cell. Glance at the left side of the Formula bar if you're not sure of the address of the cell you're about to enter data in. The Formula bar lists the cell address.

2. Type the data in the cell.

If you find typing in the Formula bar easier, click and start typing there.

3. Press the Enter key to enter the number or label.

Besides pressing the Enter key, you can also press an arrow key (←, ↑, →, ↓), press Tab, click the Enter button (the check mark) on the Formula bar, or click elsewhere on the worksheet.

If you change your mind about entering data, click the Cancel button or press Esc to delete what you entered and start over. The Cancel button (an *X*) is located on the Formula bar next to the Enter button (a check mark) and the Insert Function button (labeled *fx*).

Chapter 3 of this minibook explains how to enter logical values and formulas. The next several pages describe how to enter text labels, numeric values, date values, and time values.

Enter the data here...   or here

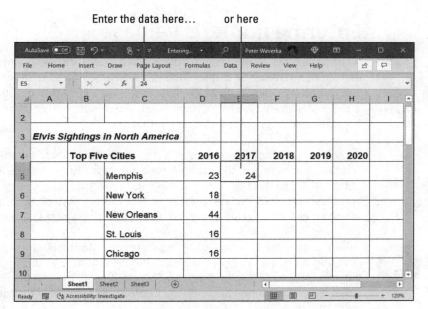

FIGURE 1-4:
Entering data.

Entering text labels

Sometimes a text entry is too long to fit in a cell. How Excel accommodates text entries that are too wide depends on whether data is in the cell to the right of the one you entered the text in:

>> If the cell to the right is empty, Excel lets the text spill into the next cell.

>> If the cell to the right contains data, the entry gets cut off. Nevertheless, the text you entered is in the cell. Nothing gets lost when it can't be displayed onscreen. You just can't see the text or numbers except by glancing at the Formula bar, where the contents of the active cell can be seen in their entirety.

Use these techniques to solve the problem of text that doesn't fit in a cell:

>> Widen the column to allow room for more text.

>> Shorten the text entry.

>> Reorient the text. (Chapter 4 of this minibook explains how to do it.)

>> Wrap the contents of the cell. *Wrapping* means to run the text down to the next line, much the same way as the text in a paragraph runs to the next line when it reaches the right margin. Excel makes rows taller to accommodate wrapped text in a cell. To wrap text in cells, select the cells, go to the Home tab, and click the Wrap Text button (found in the Alignment group).

Entering numeric values

REMEMBER

When a number is too large to fit in a cell, Excel displays pounds signs (###) instead of a number or displays the number in scientific notation (8.78979E+15). You can always glance at the Formula bar, however, to find out the number in the active cell. As well, you can always widen the column to display the entire number (as explained in Chapter 4 of this minibook).

To enter a fraction in a cell, enter a 0 or a whole number, a blank space, and the fraction. For example, to enter 3/8, type a **0**, press the spacebar, and type **3/8**. To enter 53/8, type **5**, press the spacebar, and type **3/8**. For its purposes, Excel converts fractions to decimal numbers, as you can see by looking in the Formula bar after you enter a fraction. For example, 53/8 displays as 5.375 in the Formula bar.

TIP

Here's a little trick for entering numbers with decimals quickly in all the Excel files you work on. To spare yourself the trouble of pressing the period key (.), you can tell Excel to enter the period automatically. Instead of entering **12.45**, for example, you can simply enter **1245**. Excel enters the period for you: 12.45. To perform this trick, go to the File tab, choose Options, visit the Advanced category in the Excel Options dialog box, click the Automatically Insert a Decimal Point check box, and in the Places text box, enter the number of decimal places you want for numbers. Deselect this option when you want to go back to entering numbers the normal way.

Entering date and time values

Dates and times can be used in calculations, but entering a date or time value in a cell can be problematic because these values must be entered in such a way that Excel can recognize them as dates or times, not text.

TECHNICAL STUFF

Not that you necessarily need to know it, but Excel converts dates and times to serial values for the purpose of being able to use dates and times in calculations. For example, July 31, 2004, is the number 38199. July 31, 2004, at noon is 38199.5. These serial values represent the number of whole days since January 1, 1900. The portion of the serial value to the right of the decimal point is the time, represented as a portion of a full day.

Entering date values

You can enter a date value in a cell in just about any format you choose, and Excel understands that you're entering a date. For example, enter a date in any of the following formats and you'll be all right:

m/d/yy	7/31/21
m-d-yyyy	7-31-2021
d-mmm-yy	31-Jul-21

Here are some basic things to remember about entering dates:

» **Date formats:** You can quickly apply a format to dates by selecting cells and using one of these techniques:

- On the Home tab, open the Number Format drop-down list and choose Short Date (*m/d/yyyy*; 7/31/2016) or Long Date (*day of the week, month, day, year;* Wednesday, July 31, 2016), as shown in Figure 1-5.

- On the Home tab, click the Number group button to open the Number tab of the Format Cells dialog box. As shown in Figure 1-5, choose the Date category and then choose a date format.

» **Current date:** Press Ctrl+; (semicolon) to enter the current date.

» **Current year's date:** If you don't enter the year as part of the date, Excel assumes that the date you entered is in the current year. For example, if you enter a date in the *m/d* (7/31) format during the year 2021, Excel enters the date as 7/31/21. As long as the date you want to enter is the current year, you can save a little time when entering dates by not entering the year because Excel enters it for you.

» **Dates on the Formula bar:** No matter which format you use for dates, dates are displayed in the Formula bar in the format that Excel prefers for dates: *m/d/yyyy* (7/31/2021). How dates are displayed in the worksheet is up to you.

REMEMBER

» **Twentieth and twenty-first century two-digit years:** When it comes to entering two-digit years in dates, the digits 30 through 99 belong to the twentieth century (1930–1999), but the digits 00 through 29 belong to the twenty-first century (2000–2029). For example, 7/31/13 refers to July 31, 2013, not July 31, 1913. To enter a date in 1929 or earlier, enter four digits instead of two to describe the year: **7-31-1929**. To enter a date in 2030 or later, enter four digits instead of two: **7-31-2030**.

REMEMBER

» **Dates in formulas:** To enter a date directly in a formula, enclose the date in quotation marks. (Make sure that the cell where the formula is entered has been given the Number format, not the Date format.) For example, the formula =TODAY( )–"1/1/2021" calculates the number of days that have elapsed since January 1, 2021. Formulas are the subject of Chapter 3 of this minibook.

Entering time values

Excel recognizes time values that you enter in the following ways:

h:mm AM/PM	3:31 AM
h:mm:ss AM/PM	3:31:45 PM

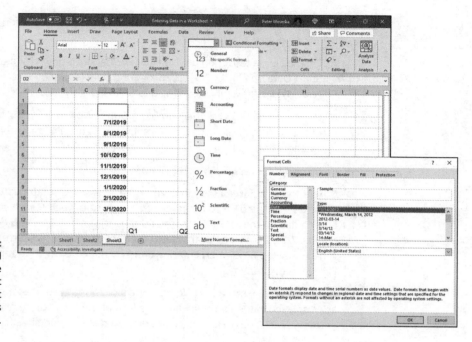

FIGURE 1-5:
Format dates and
numbers on the
Number Format
drop-down list
or Format Cells
dialog box.

Here are some things to remember when entering time values:

>> **Use colons:** Separate hours, minutes, and seconds with a colon (:).

>> **Time formats:** To change to the *h:mm:ss* AM/PM time format, select the cells, go to the Home tab, open the Number Format drop-down list, and choose Time (see Figure 1-5). You can also change time formats by clicking the Number group button on the Home tab and selecting a time format on the Number tab of the Format Cells dialog box.

>> **AM or PM time designations:** Unless you enter AM or PM with the time, Excel assumes that you're operating on military time. For example, 3:30 is considered 3:30 a.m.; 15:30 is 3:30 p.m. Don't enter periods after the letters *am* or *pm* (don't enter a.m. or p.m.).

>> **Current time:** Press Ctrl+Shift+; (semicolon) to enter the current time.

>> **Times on the Formula bar:** On the Formula bar, times are displayed in this format: *hours:minutes:seconds,* followed by the letters AM or PM. However, the time format used in cells is up to you.

Combining date and time values

You can combine dates and time values by entering the date, a blank space, and the time:

>> 7/31/21 3:31 am

>> 7-31-21 3:31:45 pm

ENTERING DATA WITH FLASH FILL

Don't look now, but Excel is peering over your shoulder to see whether it can enter data for you with Flash Fill, a mechanism whereby Excel recognizes the data you want to enter and offers to enter it on your behalf. When Excel recognizes a pattern in the data and thinks it can fill in a column for you, a ghostly image of the data Excel wants to enter appears in the column, as shown in the figure. Press Enter if you want to enter this data.

After you press Enter, the Flash Fill Options button appears. Click it to open a menu with options for Undoing Flash Fill and selecting cells.

Flash Fill is useful for cleaning up worksheets with data that you imported from a comma- or tab-delimited file. Often this data arrives in a mishmash with data from different categories in the same column.

Date	Transaction	Score	Name		
2/2/2013	Weverka-4971	48	Weverka		
2/2/2013	Johnson-891	42	Johnson		
2/3/2013	McKeil- 497	78	McKeil		
2/4/2013	Munoz-9071	23	Munoz		
2/4/2013	Hong-9781	12	Hong		
2/5/2013	Chester-9714	34	Chester		

Quickly Entering Lists and Serial Data with the AutoFill Command

Data that falls into the "serial" category — month names, days of the week, and consecutive numbers and dates, for example — can be entered quickly with the AutoFill command. Believe it or not, Excel recognizes certain kinds of serial data and enters it for you as part of the AutoFill feature. Instead of laboriously entering this data one piece at a time, you can enter it all at one time by dragging the mouse. Follow these steps to "autofill" cells:

1. **Click the cell that is to be first in the series.**

For example, if you intend to list the days of the week in consecutive cells, click where the first day is to go.

2. **Enter the first number, date, or list item in the series.**

3. **Move to the adjacent cell and enter the second number, date, or list item in the series.**

If you want to enter the same number or piece of text in adjacent cells, taking this step isn't necessary, but Excel needs the first and second items in the case of serial dates and numbers so that it can tell how much to increase or decrease the given amount or time period in each cell. For example, entering **5** and **10** tells Excel to increase the number by 5 each time so that the next serial entry is 15.

4. **Select the cell or cells you just entered data in.**

To select a single cell, click it; to select two, drag over the cells. Chapter 2 of this minibook describes all the ways to select cells in a worksheet.

5. **Click the AutoFill handle and start dragging in the direction in which you want the data series to appear on your worksheet.**

The *AutoFill handle* is the little green square in the lower-right corner of the cell or block of cells you selected. As you drag, the serial data appears in a pop-up box, as shown in Figure 1-6.

The AutoFill Options button appears after you enter the serial data. Click it and choose an option if you want to copy cells or fill the cells without carrying along their formats.

TIP

To enter the same number or text in several empty cells, drag over the cells to select them or select each cell by holding down the Ctrl key as you click. Then type a number or some text and press Ctrl+Enter.

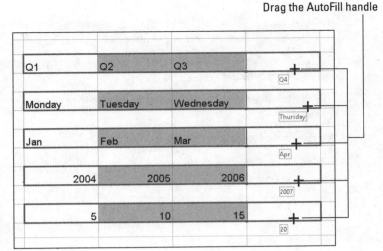

Drag the AutoFill handle

FIGURE 1-6:
Entering serial
data and text.

CREATING YOUR OWN AUTOFILL LIST

As you probably know, Excel is capable of completing lists on its own with the AutoFill feature. You can enter the days of the week or month names simply by entering one day or month and dragging the AutoFill handle to enter the others. Here's some good news: The AutoFill command can also reproduce the names of your coworkers, the roster of a softball team, street names, or any other list that you care to enter quickly and repeatedly in a worksheet.

Follow these steps to enter items for a list so that you can enter them in the future by dragging the AutoFill handle:

1. **If you've already entered items for the list on your worksheet, select the items.**

   If you haven't entered the items yet, skip to Step 2.

2. **On the File tab, choose Options to open the Excel Options dialog box.**

3. **Go to the Advanced category.**

4. **Click the Edit Custom Lists button (you have to scroll down to find it).**

   You see the Custom Lists dialog box.

(continued)

Up and Running with Excel

(continued)

5. **In the List Entries box, do one of the following:**

   If you selected the items in Step 1, click the Import button. The items you selected appear in the List Entries box.

   If you need to enter items for the list, enter them in the List Entries box, with one item on each line.

6. **Click the Add button.**

7. **Click OK.**

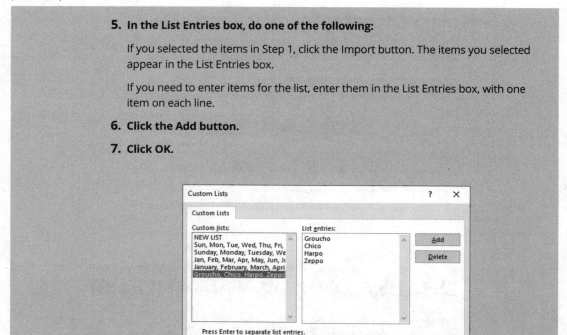

Formatting Numbers, Dates, and Time Values

When you enter a number that Excel recognizes as belonging to one of its formats, Excel assigns the number format automatically. Enter **45%**, for example, and Excel assigns the Percentage number format. Enter **$4.25**, and Excel assigns the Currency number format. Besides assigning formats by hand, however, you can assign them to cells from the get-go and spare yourself the trouble of entering dollar signs, commas, percent signs, and other extraneous punctuation. All you have to do is enter the raw numbers. Excel does the window dressing for you.

Excel offers five number-formatting buttons on the Home tab. Select cells with numbers in them and click one of these buttons to change how numbers are formatted:

>> **Accounting Number Format:** Places a dollar sign before the number and gives it two decimal places. You can open the drop-down list on this button and choose a currency symbol apart from the dollar sign.

>> **Percent Style:** Places a percent sign after the number and converts the number to a percentage.

>> **Comma Style:** Places commas in the number.

>> **Increase Decimal:** Increases the number of decimal places by one.

>> **Decrease Decimal:** Decreases the number of decimal places by one.

To choose among many formats and to format dates and time values as well as numbers, select the cells, go to the Home tab, and use one of these techniques:

>> Open the Number Format drop-down list and select an option.

>> Click the Number group button and make selections on the Number tab of the Format Cells dialog box. Figure 1-7 shows this dialog box. Choose a category and select options to describe how you want numbers or text to appear. You can also open the Format Cells dialog box by right-clicking and choosing Format Cells on the shortcut menu.

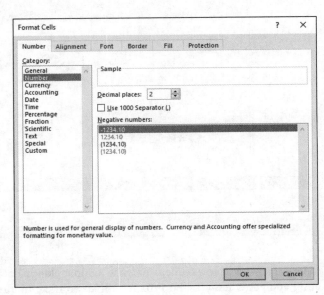

FIGURE 1-7: The Number category of the Format Cells dialog box.

To strip formats from the data in cells, select the cells, go to the Home tab, click the Clear button, and choose Clear Formats.

Entering ZIP codes can be problematic because Excel strips the initial zero from the number if it begins with a zero. To get around this problem, visit the Number tab of the Format Cells dialog box (see Figure 1-7), choose Special in the Category list, and select a ZIP code option.

Establishing Data-Validation Rules

By nature, people are prone to enter data incorrectly because the task of entering data is so dull. This is why data-validation rules are invaluable. A *data-validation rule* is a rule concerning what kind of data can be entered in a cell. When you select a cell that has been given a rule, an input message tells you what to enter, as shown in Figure 1-8. And if you enter the data incorrectly, an error alert tells you as much, also shown in Figure 1-8.

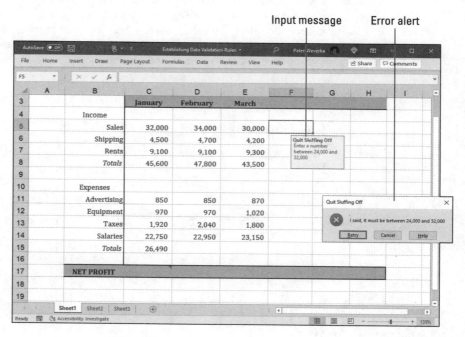

FIGURE 1-8:
A data-validation rule in action.

Data-validation rules are an excellent defense against sloppy data entry and that itchy feeling you get when you're in the middle of an irksome task. In a cell that records date entries, you can require dates to fall in a certain time frame. In a cell that records text entries, you can choose an item from a list instead of typing it yourself. In a cell that records numeric entries, you can require the number to fall within a certain range. Table 1-1 describes the different categories of data-validation rules.

TABLE 1-1   ## Data-Validation Rule Categories

Rule	What Can Be Entered
Any Value	Anything whatsoever. This is the default setting.
Whole Number	Whole numbers (no decimal points allowed). Choose an operator from the Data drop-down list and values to describe the range of numbers that can be entered.
Decimal	Same as the Whole Number rule except numbers with decimal points are permitted.
List	Items from a list. Enter the list items in cells on a worksheet, either the one you're working in or another. Then reopen the Data Validation dialog box, click the Range Selector button (you can find it on the right side of the Source text box), and select the cells that hold the list. The list items appear in a drop-down list on the worksheet.
Date	Date values. Choose an operator from the Data drop-down list and values to describe the date range. Earlier in this chapter, "Entering date and time values" describes the correct way to enter date values.
Time	Time values. Choose an operator from the Data drop-down list and values to describe the date and time range. Earlier in this chapter, "Entering date and time values" describes the correct way to enter a combination of date and time values.
Text Length	A certain number of characters. Choose an operator from the Data drop-down list and values to describe how many characters can be entered.
Custom	A logical value (True or False). Enter a formula that describes what constitutes a true or false data entry.

Follow these steps to establish a data-validation rule:

1. **Select the cell or cells that need a rule.**

2. **On the Data tab, click the Data Validation button.**

   As shown in Figure 1-9, you see the Settings tab of the Data Validation dialog box.

3. **On the Allow drop-down list, choose the category of rule you want.**

   Table 1-1, earlier in this chapter, describes these categories.

4. **Enter the criteria for the rule.**

   What the criteria is depends on what rule category you're working in. Table 1-1 describes how to enter the criteria for rules in each category. You can refer to cells in the worksheet by selecting them. To do that, either select them directly or click the Range Selector button and then select them.

5. **On the Input Message tab, enter a title and input message.**

You can see a title ("Quit sluffing off") and input message ("Enter a number between 24,000 and 32,000") in Figure 1-8. The title appears in boldface. Briefly describe what kind of data belongs in the cell or cells you selected.

6. **On the Error Alert tab, choose a style for the symbol in the Message Alert dialog box, enter a title for the dialog box, and enter a warning message.**

In the error message in Figure 1-8, shown previously, the Stop symbol was chosen. The title you enter appears across the top of the dialog box, and the message appears beside the symbol.

7. **Click OK.**

To remove data-validation rules from cells, select the cells, go to the Data tab, click the Data Validation button, and on the Settings tab of the Data Validation dialog box, click the Clear All button, and click OK.

FIGURE 1-9:
Creating a data-validation rule.

Chapter **2**

Refining Your Worksheet

This chapter delves into the workaday world of worksheets (say that three times fast). It explains how to edit worksheet data and move quickly here and there in a worksheet. For the purposes of collaboration, you find out how to make notes and comments on worksheets. You also discover techniques for entering data quickly, selecting cells, and copying and moving data in cells. This chapter describes how to move, delete, and rename worksheets as well as protect them from being edited or altered.

Editing Worksheet Data

Not everyone enters data correctly the first time. To edit data you entered in a cell, do one of the following:

» **Double-click the cell.** Doing so places the cursor squarely in the cell, where you can start deleting or entering numbers and text.

» **Click the cell and press F2.** This technique also lands the cursor in the cell.

» **Click the cell you want to edit.** With this technique, you edit the data on the Formula bar.

TIP

If nothing happens when you double-click, or if pressing F2 lands the cursor in the Formula bar rather than a cell, somebody has been fooling with the Options settings. On the File tab, choose Options, select the Advanced category in the Excel Options dialog box, and select the Allow Editing Directly in Cells check box.

Moving Around in a Worksheet

Going from place to place gets progressively more difficult as a worksheet gets larger. Luckily for you, Excel offers keyboard shortcuts for jumping around. Table 2-1 describes these keyboard shortcuts.

TABLE 2-1 **Keyboard Shortcuts for Getting Around in Worksheets**

Press . . .	To Move the Selection . . .
Home	To column A
Ctrl+Home	To cell A1, the first cell in the worksheet
Ctrl+End	To the last cell in the last row with data in it
←, →, ↑, ↓	To the next cell
Ctrl+←, →, ↑, ↓	In one direction toward the nearest cell with data in it or to the first or last cell in the column or row
PgUp or PgDn	Up or down one screen's worth of rows
Ctrl+PgUp or Ctrl+PgDn	Backward or forward through the workbook, from worksheet to worksheet

As well as pressing keys, you can use the following techniques to get from place to place in a worksheet:

>> **Scroll bars:** Use the vertical and horizontal scroll bars to move to different areas. Drag the scroll box to cover long distances. To cover long distances very quickly, hold down the Shift key as you drag the scroll box on the vertical scroll bar.

>> **Scroll wheel on the mouse:** If your mouse is equipped with a scroll wheel, turn the wheel to quickly scroll up and down.

>> **Name box:** Enter a cell address in the Name box and press Enter to go to the cell. The Name box is found to the left of the Formula bar.

GETTING WORKBOOK STATISTICS

To learn this and that about a worksheet or workbook, go to the Review tab and click the Workbook Statistics button (or press Ctrl+Shift+G). The Workbook Statistics dialog box opens. It tells you how many cells contain data and how many formulas you've created, among other juicy tidbits.

» **The Go To command:** On the Home tab, click the Find & Select button and choose Go To on the drop-down list (or press Ctrl+G or F5). You see the Go To dialog box. Enter a cell address in the Reference box and click OK. Cell addresses you've already visited with the Go To command are already listed in the dialog box. Click the Special button to open the Go To Special dialog box and visit a formula, comment, or other esoteric item.

» **The Find command:** On the Home tab, click the Find & Select button and choose Find on the drop-down list (or press Ctrl+F). Enter the data you seek in the Find What box and click the Find Next button. Click the Find All button to find all instances of the item you're looking for. A list of the items appears at the bottom of the dialog box; click an item to go to it.

To scroll to the active cell if you no longer see it onscreen, press Ctrl+Backspace.

TIP

Getting a Better Look at the Worksheet

Especially when you're entering data, it pays to get a good look at the worksheet. You need to know which column and row you're entering data in. These pages explain techniques for changing your view of a worksheet so that you always know where you are. Read on to discover how to freeze, split, and hide columns and rows. (On the subject of changing views, Book 1, Chapter 3 explains an essential technique for changing views: zooming in and zooming out.)

Freezing and splitting columns and rows

Sometimes your adventures in a worksheet take you to a faraway cell address, such as X31 or C39. Out there in the wilderness, it's hard to tell where to enter data because you can't see the data labels in the first column or first row that tell you where to enter data on the worksheet.

To see one part of a worksheet no matter how far you stray from it, you can *split* the worksheet or *freeze* columns and rows onscreen. In Figure 2-1, I split the worksheet so that column A (Property) always appears onscreen, no matter how far I scroll to the right; similarly, row 1 (Property, Management Fee, and so on) also appears at the top of the worksheet no matter how far I scroll down. Notice how the row numbers and column letters are interrupted in Figure 2-1. Because I split the screen, I always know what data to enter in a cell because I can clearly see property names in the first column and the column headings along the top of the worksheet.

FIGURE 2-1: Splitting a worksheet.

Freezing columns or rows on a worksheet works much like splitting except that lines instead of gray bars appear onscreen to show which columns and rows are frozen, and you can't adjust where the split occurs by dragging the boundary where the worksheet is split.

Giving the Split or Freeze Panes command

Follow these steps to split or freeze columns and rows onscreen:

1. **Click the cell that is directly below the row you want to freeze or split and is in the column to the right of the column that you want to freeze or split.**

In other words, click where you want the split to occur.

2. **On the View tab, split or freeze the columns and rows.**

Go to the View tab and use one of these techniques:

- **Splitting:** Click the Split button and then click and drag the split bars to split the screen horizontally or vertically (refer to Figure 2-1).

- **Freezing:** Click the Freeze Panes button and choose one of three Freeze options on the drop-down list. The second and third options, respectively, freeze the top row or first column. The first option, Freeze Panes, freezes the column(s) to the left and the row(s) above the cell you selected in Step 1.

Bars or lines appear onscreen to show which row(s) and column(s) have been frozen or split. Move where you will in the worksheet. The column(s) and row(s) you froze or split stay onscreen.

Unsplitting and unfreezing

Use one of these techniques to keep your worksheet from splitting or freezing to death:

- **Unsplitting:** Click the Split button again; double-click one of the split bars to remove it; or drag a split bar into the top or left side of the worksheet window.

- **Unfreezing:** On the View tab, click the Freeze Panes button and choose Unfreeze Panes on the drop-down list.

Hiding columns and rows

Another way to take the clutter out of a worksheet is to temporarily hide columns and rows:

>> **Hiding columns or rows:** Drag over the column letters or row numbers of the columns or rows that you want to hide. Dragging this way selects entire columns or rows. Then use one of these techniques:

- Right-click and choose Hide.

- Press Ctrl+0 (zero) to hide the columns or Ctrl+9 to hide the rows.

- On the Home tab, click the Format button, choose Hide & Unhide, and choose Hide Columns or Hide Rows.

>> **Unhiding columns and rows:** Select columns to the right and left of the hidden columns, or select rows above and below the hidden rows. To select columns or rows, drag over their letters or numbers. Then go to the Home tab, click the Format button, choose Hide & Unhide, and choose Unhide Columns or Unhide Rows. You can also right-click and choose Unhide.

TIP

It's easy to forget where you hid columns or rows. To make sure all columns and rows in your worksheet are displayed, click the Select All button (or press Ctrl+A) to select your entire worksheet. Then go to the Home tab, click the Format button and choose Hide & Unhide ⇨ Unhide Columns; click the Format button again and choose Hide & Unhide ⇨ Unhide Rows.

YOUR OWN CUSTOMIZED VIEWS

After you go to the trouble of freezing the screen or zooming in to a position you're comfortable with, you may as well save your view of the screen as a customized view. That way, you can call upon the customized view whenever you need it. View settings, the window size, the position of the grid onscreen, and cells that are selected can all be saved in a customized view.

Follow these steps to create a customized view:

1. **On the View tab, click the Custom Views button.**

   You see the Custom Views dialog box. It lists views you've already created, if you've created any.

2. **Click the Add button.**

   The Add View dialog box appears.

3. Enter a name for the view and click OK.

To switch to a customized view, click the Custom Views button, select a view in the Custom Views dialog box, and click the Show button.

Notes for Documenting Your Worksheet

It may happen that you return to your worksheet days or months from now and discover to your dismay that you don't know why certain numbers or formulas are there. For that matter, someone else may inherit your worksheet and be mystified as to what the heck is going on. To take the mystery out of a worksheet, document it by entering notes here and there.

A *note* is a little explanation that describes part of a worksheet. Each note is connected to a cell. You can tell where a note is because a small red triangle appears in the upper-right corner of cells to which notes are attached. Move the pointer over one of these triangles and you see the pop-up box, a note, and the name of the person who entered the note, as shown in Figure 2-2. Click the Notes button on the Review tab and choose Show All Notes to see every note in a worksheet.

Starting on the Review tab, follow these instructions to handle notes:

» **Entering a note:** Click the cell that deserves a note, click the Notes button, and choose the New Note on the drop-down list (or right-click and choose New Note). Enter your note in the pop-up box. Click in a different cell when you finish entering your note.

» **Reading a note:** Move the pointer over a cell with a small red triangle and read the note in the pop-up box (refer to Figure 2-2). You can also right-click a cell and choose Show/Hide Note.

» **Showing and hiding notes:** Click the Notes button and choose Show All Notes on the drop-down list to see or hide all the notes in a worksheet. To show or hide an individual note, right-click its cell and choose Show/Hide Note.

Click the Notes button to handle notes

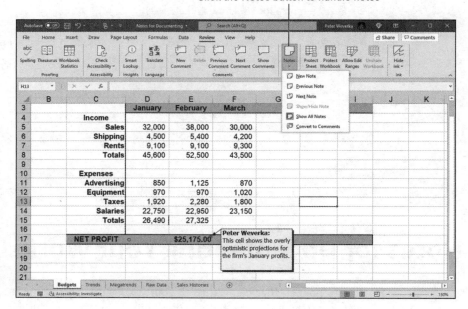

FIGURE 2-2:
Notes explain
what's what in a
worksheet.

» **Finding notes:** Click the Notes button and then choose the Previous Note or Next Note on the drop-down list to go from note to note.

» **Editing a note:** Select the cell with the comment, click the Notes button, and choose Edit Note. You can also right-click the cell and choose Edit Note.

» **Deleting notes:** Right-click the cell with the note and choose Delete Note. To delete several notes, select them by Ctrl+clicking and then right-click and choose Delete Note.

» **Deleting all notes (and comments):** Press Ctrl+A to select all cells in the worksheet. Then go to the Home tab, click the Clear button, and choose Clear Comments and Notes on the drop-down menu. Beware: This command deletes all comments as well as all notes. Don't select it if you want to keep the comments in your worksheet.

TIP

If your name doesn't appear in the pop-up box after you enter a note and you want it to appear there, go to the File tab, choose Options, select the General category in the Excel Options dialog box, and enter your name in the User Name text box.

Comments for Collaborating with Others on a Workbooks

When constructing a workbook is a team affair, consider writing comments to discuss with team members how to make the workbook better. Comments are meant for workbooks being shared. Each comment is attached to a cell. You can tell where a comment is because a purple comment icon appears in the upper-right corner of cells that have been commented on. Write comments to suggest ways to make a workbook better and to reply to others' suggestions.

Starting on the Review tab, follow these instructions to comment on a workbook you share with others:

>> **Entering a comment:** Click the cell that needs a comment and then click the New Comment button. A pop-up box appears for entering a comment. Enter your comment and click the Post Comment button. To edit a comment you made, click its icon, click the Edit button in the pop-up box, and make your edits.

>> **Displaying a single comment:** Move the pointer over the cell with the purple icon. The comment appears in a pop-up box.

>> **Displaying all comments**: Click the Show Comments button on the Review tab or the Comments button in the upper-right corner of the screen. The Comments pane opens, as shown in Figure 2-3. From there you can read, reply to, and enter comments.

>> **Replying to a comment:** Display the comment and enter your replay in the Reply text box. Click the Post button when you finish replying.

>> **Going from comment to comment:** Click the Previous Comment or Next Comment button. You can also scroll through comments in the Comments pane.

>> **Deleting comments:** Select the cell with the comment and click the Delete button on the Review tab. To delete a comment and all its replies, display it in the Comments pane, click the More Thread Actions button, and choose Delete Thread.

>> **Resolving a thread:** Display the comment in the Comments pane, click the More Thread Actions button, and choose Resolve Thread. A thread is a collection of comments all aimed at the same cell in a worksheet. Resolve a thread to signal that the discussion about the thread is closed.

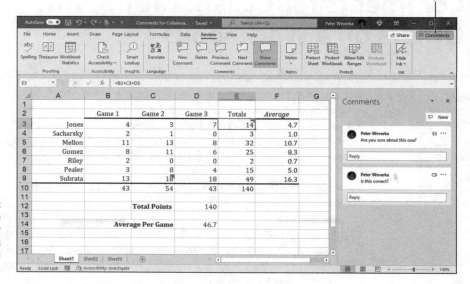

FIGURE 2-3:
Click the
Comments or
Show Comments
button to read
comments.

Selecting Cells in a Worksheet

To format, copy, move, delete, and format numbers and words in a worksheet, you have to select the cells in which the numbers and words are found. Here are ways to select cells and the data inside them:

>> **A block of cells:** Drag diagonally across the worksheet from one corner of the block of cells to the opposite corner. You can also click in one corner and Shift+click the opposite corner.

>> **Adjacent cells in a row or column:** Drag across the cells.

>> **Cells in various places:** While holding down the Ctrl key, click different cells.

>> **A row or rows:** Click a row number to select an entire row. Click and drag down the row numbers to select several adjacent rows.

>> **A column or columns:** Click a column letter to select an entire column. Click and drag across letters to select adjacent columns.

>> **Entire worksheet:** Click the Select All button, the triangle to the left of the column letters and above the row numbers; press Ctrl+A; or press Ctrl+Shift+Spacebar.

TIP

Press Ctrl+Spacebar to select the column that the active cell is in; press Shift+Spacebar to select the row where the active cell is.

After you select cells, you can deselect some of them by Ctrl+clicking the cells you want to deselect. You can select still more cells by Shift+clicking.

You can enter the same data item in several different cells by selecting cells and then entering the data in one cell and pressing Ctrl+Enter. This technique comes in very handy, for example, when you want to enter a placeholder zero (0) in several different cells.

Deleting, Copying, and Moving Data

In the course of putting together a worksheet, it is sometimes necessary to delete, copy, and move cell contents. Here are instructions for doing these chores:

» **Deleting cell contents:** Select the cells and then press the Delete key; on the Home tab, click the Clear button and choose Clear Contents; or right-click and choose Clear Contents.

» **Copying and moving cell contents:** Select the cells and use one of these techniques:

- **Cut or Copy and Paste commands:** When you paste the data, click where you want the first cell of the block of cells you're copying or moving to go. (Book 1, Chapter 2 explains copying and moving data in detail.) Be careful not to overwrite cells with data in them when you copy or move data. After you paste data, you see the Paste Options button. Click this button and choose an option from the drop-down list to format the data in different ways.

- **Drag and drop:** Move the pointer to the edge of the cell block, click when you see the four-headed arrow, and start dragging. Hold down the Ctrl key to copy the data.

Handling the Worksheets in a Workbook

A workbook can hold more than one worksheet. Keeping more than one worksheet in the same workbook has advantages. For example, in a workbook that tracks monthly income from rental properties, you can record monthly income on 12 worksheets, 1 for each month. By constructing formulas that calculate income data across the 12 worksheets, you can track annual income from the properties.

As Figure 2-4 shows, Excel places a tab at the bottom of the screen for each worksheet in a workbook. Initially, worksheets are named Sheet1, Sheet 2, and so on as you add them, but you can rename worksheets. Click a tab to go from worksheet to worksheet. Right-click a tab to open a shortcut menu with commands for handling worksheets.

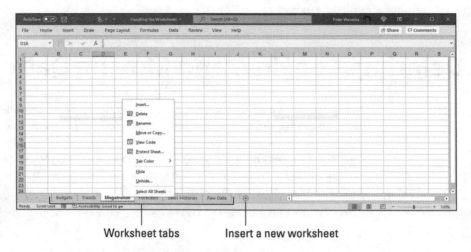

FIGURE 2-4:
You can have multiple worksheets in a workbook.

Worksheet tabs   Insert a new worksheet

Follow these instructions to move among, add, delete, rename, and change the order of worksheets:

>> **Inserting a new worksheet:** Click the New Sheet button (you can find it in the lower-left corner of the screen to the right of the worksheet tab); press Shift+F11; or on the Home tab, open the drop-down list on the Insert button and choose Insert Sheet.

>> **Moving among worksheets:** To go from one worksheet to another, click a worksheet tab along the bottom of the screen. If you can't see a tab, click one of the scroll arrows to the left of the worksheet tabs.

>> **Renaming a worksheet:** Right-click the worksheet tab, choose Rename on the shortcut menu, type a new name, and press Enter. You can also go to the Home tab, click the Format button, choose Rename Sheet on the drop-down list, and enter a new name.

>> **Selecting worksheets:** Click the worksheet's tab to select it. To select several worksheets, Ctrl+click their tabs or click the first tab and then Shift+click the last tab in the set. To select all the worksheets, right-click a tab and choose Select All Sheets on the shortcut menu.

>> **Rearranging worksheets:** Drag the worksheet tab to a new location. As you drag, a tiny black arrow and a page icon appear to show you where the worksheet will land after you release the mouse button. You can also select a sheet, go to the Home tab, click the Format button, and choose Move or Copy Sheet on the drop-down list. The Move or Copy dialog box appears, as shown in Figure 2-5. Select the sheet in the Before Sheet list where you want the worksheet to go and click OK.

>> **Deleting a worksheet:** Select the sheet, and on the Home tab, open the drop-down list on the Delete button and choose Delete Sheet. You can also right-click a worksheet tab and choose Delete. Be careful, because you can't restore your deleted worksheet by pressing the Undo button.

>> **Copying a worksheet:** Select the sheet, hold down the Ctrl key, and drag the worksheet tab to a new location.

>> **Moving a worksheet to another workbook:** Make sure that the other workbook is open, open the drop-down list on the Format button, and choose Move or Copy Sheet. Then select the other workbook's name in the Move or Copy dialog box and click OK.

>> **Color-coding a worksheet:** Right-click a worksheet tab and choose Tab Color. Then select a color in the submenu, or choose More Colors and select a color in the Colors dialog box.

FIGURE 2-5:
Besides dragging it, you can move a worksheet by using this dialog box.

TIP

You can change the size of columns or apply numeric formats to the same addresses in different worksheets by selecting all the sheets first and then formatting one worksheet. The formats apply to all the worksheets that you select. Being able to format several different worksheets simultaneously comes in handy, for example, when your workbook tracks monthly data and each worksheet pertains to one month. Another way to handle worksheets with similar data is to create the first worksheet and copy it to the second, third, and fourth worksheets with the Copy and Paste commands.

Keeping Others from Tampering with Worksheets

People with savvy and foresight sometimes set up workbooks so that one worksheet holds raw data and the other worksheets hold formulas that calculate the raw data. This technique prevents others from tampering with the raw data. Furthermore, if the worksheet with raw data is hidden, the chance that it will be tampered with is lower; and if the worksheet is protected, people can't tamper with it unless they have a password. These pages explain how to hide a worksheet so that others are less likely to find it. I also tell you how to protect a worksheet from being edited.

Hiding a worksheet

Follow these instructions to hide and unhide worksheets:

>> **Hiding a worksheet:** Right-click the worksheet's tab and choose Hide on the shortcut menu. You can also go to the Home tab, click the Format button, and choose Hide &Unhide ⇨ Hide Sheet.

>> **Unhiding a worksheet:** Right-click any worksheet tab and choose Unhide; or go to the Home tab, click the Format button, and choose Hide & Unhide ⇨ Unhide Sheet. Then, in the Unhide dialog box, select the sheet you want to unhide and click OK.

Protecting a worksheet

Protecting a worksheet means to restrict others from changing it — from formatting it, inserting new rows and columns, or deleting rows and columns, among other tasks. You can also prevent any editorial changes whatsoever from being made to a worksheet. Follow these steps to protect a worksheet from tampering by others:

1. **Select the worksheet that needs protection.**

2. **On the Review tab, click the Protect Sheet button.**

   You see the Protect Sheet dialog box, shown in Figure 2-6. You can also open this dialog box by going to the Home tab, clicking the Format button, and choosing Protect Sheet.

3. **Enter a password in the Password to Unprotect Sheet box if you want only people with the password to be able to unprotect the worksheet after you protect it.**

4. **On the Allow All Users of This Worksheet To list, select the check box next to the name of each task that you want to permit others to do.**

For example, select the Format Cells check box if you want others to be able to format cells.

TIP

Deselect the Select Locked Cells check box to prevent any changes from being made to the worksheet. By default, all worksheet cells are locked, and by preventing others from selecting locked cells, you effectively prevent them from editing any cells.

5. **Click OK.**

If you entered a password in Step 3, you must enter it again in the Confirm Password dialog box and click OK.

FIGURE 2-6:
Select what
you want others
to be able to do.

To unprotect a worksheet that you protected, go to the Review tab and click the Unprotect Sheet button. You must enter a password if you elected to require others to have a password before they can unprotect a worksheet.

Chapter **3**

Formulas and Functions for Crunching Numbers

Formulas are where it's at as far as Excel is concerned. After you know how to construct formulas and find constructing them to be pretty easy, you can put Excel to work. You can make the numbers speak to you. You can turn a bunch of unruly numbers into meaningful figures and statistics.

This chapter explains what a formula is, how to enter a formula, and how to enter a formula quickly. You also discover how to copy formulas from cell to cell and how to keep formula errors from creeping into your workbooks. Finally, this chapter explains how to make use of the hundred or so functions that Excel offers.

How Formulas Work

A *formula*, as you may recall from the sleepy hours you spent in math class, is a way to calculate numbers. For example, 2+3=5 is a formula. When you enter a formula in a cell, Excel computes the formula and displays its results in the cell. Click in cell A3 and enter =2+3, for example, and Excel displays the number 5 in cell A3.

Referring to cells in formulas

As well as numbers, Excel formulas can refer to the contents of different cells. When a formula refers to a cell, the number in the cell is used to compute the formula. In Figure 3-1, for example, cell A1 contains the number 2; cell A2 contains the number 3; and cell A3 contains the formula =A1+A2. As shown in cell A3, the result of the formula is 5. If I change the number in cell A1 from 2 to 3, the result of the formula in cell A3 (=A1+A2) becomes 6, not 5. When a formula refers to a cell and the number in the cell changes, the result of the formula changes as well.

Formula in the Formula bar

FIGURE 3-1:
A simple formula.

To see the value of using cell references in formulas, consider the worksheet shown in Figure 3-2. The purpose of this worksheet is to track the budget of a school's Parent Teacher Association (PTA):

» Column C, Actual Income, lists income from different sources.

» Column D, Projected Income, shows what the PTA members thought income from these sources would be.

» Column E, Over/Under Budget, shows how actual income compares to projected income from the different sources.

As the figures in the Actual Income column (column C) are updated, figures in the Over/Under Budget column (column E) and the Total Income row (row 8) change instantaneously. These figures change instantaneously because the formulas refer to the numbers in cells, not to unchanging numbers (known as *constants*).

FIGURE 3-2:
Using formulas in a worksheet.

Figure 3-3 shows the formulas used to calculate the data in the worksheet in Figure 3-2. In column E, formulas deduct the numbers in column D from the numbers in column C to show where the PTA over- or under-budgeted for the different sources of income. In row 8, you can see how the SUM function is used to total cells in rows 3 through 7. The end of this chapter explains how to use functions in formulas.

FIGURE 3-3:
The formulas used to generate the numbers in Figure 3-2.

REMEMBER

Excel is remarkably good about updating cell references in formulas when you move cells. To see how good Excel is, consider what happens to cell addresses in formulas when you delete a row in a worksheet. If a formula refers to cell C1 but you delete row B, row C becomes row B and the value in cell C1 changes addresses from C1 to B1. You would think that references in formulas to cell C1 would be out of date, but you would be wrong. Excel automatically adjusts all formulas that refer to cell C1. Those formulas now refer to cell B1 instead.

In case you're curious, you can display formulas in worksheet cells instead of the results of formulas, as was done in Figure 3-3, by pressing Ctrl+' (apostrophe) or clicking the Show Formulas button on the Formulas tab. (You may have to click the Formula Auditing button first, depending on the size of your screen.) Click the Show Formulas button a second time to see formula results again.

Referring to formula results in formulas

Besides referring to cells with numbers in them, you can refer to formula results in a cell. Consider the worksheet shown in Figure 3-4. The purpose of this worksheet is to track scoring by the players on a basketball team over three games:

>> The Totals column (column E) shows the total points each player scored in the three games.

>> The Average column (column F), using the formula results in the Totals column, determines how much each player has scored on average. The Average column does that by dividing the results in column E by 3, the number of games played.

In this case, Excel uses the results of the total-calculation formulas in column E to compute average points per game in column F.

Operators in formulas

Addition, subtraction, and division aren't the only operators you can use in formulas. Table 3-1 explains the arithmetic operators you can use and the key you press to enter each operator. In the table, operators are listed in the order of precedence (see the "The order of precedence" sidebar for an explanation of precedence).

Another way to compute a formula is to make use of a function. As "Working with Functions" explains, later in this chapter, a function is a built-in formula that comes with Excel. SUM, for example, adds the numbers in cells. AVERAGE finds the average of different numbers.

FIGURE 3-4:
Using formula
results as other
formulas.

Arithmetic Operators for Use in Formulas

TABLE 3-1

Precedence	Operator	Example Formula	Returns
1	% (Percent)	=50%	50 percent, or 0.5
2	^ (Exponentiation)	=50^2	50 to the second power, or 2500
3	* (Multiplication)	=E2*4	The value in cell E2 multiplied by 4
3	/ (Division)	=E2/3	The value in cell E2 divided by 3
4	+ (Addition)	=F1+F2+F3	The sum of the values in those cells
4	– (Subtraction)	=G5–8	The value in cell G5 minus 8

(continued)

TABLE 3-1 *(continued)*

Precedence	Operator	Example Formula	Returns
5	& (Concatenation)	="Part No. "&D4	The text *Part No.* and the value in cell D4
6	= (Equal to)	=C5=4	If the value in cell C5 is equal to 4, returns TRUE; returns FALSE otherwise
6	<> (Not equal to)	=F3<>9	If the value in cell F3 is *not* equal to 9, returns TRUE; returns FALSE otherwise
6	< (Less than)	=B9<E11	If the value in cell B9 is less than the value in cell E11, returns TRUE; returns FALSE otherwise
6	<= (Less than or equal to)	=A4<=9	If the value in cell A4 is less than or equal to 9, returns TRUE; returns FALSE otherwise
6	> (Greater than)	=E8>14	If the value in cell E8 is greater than 14, returns TRUE; returns FALSE otherwise
6	>= (Greater than or equal to)	=C3>=D3	If the value in cell C3 is greater than or equal to the value in cell D3, returns TRUE; returns FALSE otherwise

THE ORDER OF PRECEDENCE

When a formula includes more than one operator, the order in which the operators appear in the formula matters a lot. Consider this formula:

=2+3*4

Does this formula result in 14 (2+[3*4]) or 20 ([2+3]*4)? The answer is 14 because Excel performs multiplication before addition in formulas. In other words, multiplication takes precedence over addition.

The order in which calculations are made in a formula that includes different operators is called the *order of precedence.* Be sure to remember the order of precedence when you construct complex formulas with more than one operator:

1. Percent (%)

2. Exponentiation (^)

3. Multiplication (*) and division (/); leftmost operations are calculated first

4. Addition (+) and subtraction (-); leftmost operations are calculated first

5. Concatenation (&)

6. Comparison (<, <=, >,>=, and <>)

To get around the order-of-precedence problem, enclose parts of formulas in parentheses. Operations in parentheses are calculated before all other parts of a formula. For example, the formula =2+3*4 equals 20 when it is written this way: =(2+3)*4.

The Basics of Entering a Formula

No matter what kind of formula you enter, and no matter how complex the formula is, follow these basic steps to enter it:

1. **Click the cell where you want to enter the formula.**

2. **Click in the Formula bar if you want to enter the data there rather than the cell.**

3. **Enter the equals sign (=).**

   You must be sure to enter the equals sign before you enter a formula. Without it, Excel thinks you're entering text or a number, not a formula.

REMEMBER

4. **Enter the formula.**

   For example, enter **=B1*.06**. Make sure that you enter all cell addresses correctly. By the way, you can enter lowercase letters in cell references. Excel changes them to uppercase after you finish entering the formula. The next section in this chapter explains how to enter cell addresses quickly in formulas.

5. **Press Enter or click the Enter button (the check mark on the Formula bar).**

   The result of the formula appears in the cell.

Speed Techniques for Entering Formulas

Entering formulas and making sure that all cell references are correct is a tedious activity, but fortunately for you, Excel offers a few techniques to make entering formulas easier. Read on to find out how ranges make entering cell references easier and how you can enter cell references in formulas by pointing and clicking. You also find instructions here for copying formulas.

Clicking cells to enter cell references

The hardest part about entering a formula is entering the cell references correctly. You have to squint to see which row and column the cell you want to refer to is in. You have to carefully type the right column letter and row number. However, instead of typing a cell reference, you can click the cell you want to refer to in a formula.

In the course of entering a formula, click the cell on your worksheet that you want to reference. As shown in Figure 3-5, shimmering marquee lights appear around the cell that you clicked so that you can clearly see which cell you're referring to. The cell's reference address, meanwhile, appears in the Formula bar. In Figure 3-5, I clicked cell F3 instead of entering its reference address on the Formula bar. The reference F3 appears on the Formula bar, and the marquee lights appear around cell F3.

Click a cell to enter its cell reference address in a formula

FIGURE 3-5:
Clicking to enter a cell reference.

Get in the habit of pointing and clicking cells to enter cell references in formulas. Clicking cells is easier than typing cell addresses, and the cell references are entered more accurately.

Entering a cell range

A *cell range* is a line or block of cells in a worksheet. Instead of typing cell reference addresses one at a time, you can select cells on your worksheet. In Figure 3-6, I selected cells C3, D3, E3, and F3 to form cell range C3:F3. This spares me the trouble of entering one at a time the cell addresses that I want in the range.

The formula in Figure 3-6 uses the SUM function to total the numeric values in cell range C3:F3. Notice the marquee lights around the range C3:F3. The lights show precisely which range you're selecting. Cell ranges come in especially handy where functions are concerned (see "Working with Functions," later in this chapter).

FIGURE 3-6: Using a cell range in a formula.

To identify a cell range, Excel lists the outermost cells in the range and places a colon (:) between cell addresses:

>> A cell range comprising cells A1, A2, A3, and A4 is listed this way: A1:A4.

>> A cell range comprising a block of cells from A1 to D4 is listed this way: A1:D4.

You can enter cell ranges on your own without selecting cells. To do so, type the first cell in the range, enter a colon (:), and type the last cell.

Naming cell ranges so that you can use them in formulas

Whether you type cell addresses yourself or drag across cells to enter a cell range, entering cell address references is a chore. Entering =C1+C2+C3+C4, for example, can cause a finger cramp; entering =SUM(C1:C4) is no piece of cake, either.

To take the tedium out of entering cell ranges in formulas, you can name cell ranges. Then, to enter a cell range in a formula, all you have to do is select a name in the Paste Name dialog box or click the Use in Formula button on the Formulas tab, as shown in Figure 3-7. Naming cell ranges has an added benefit: You can choose a name from the Name Box drop-down list and go directly to the cell range whose name you choose, as shown in Figure 3-7.

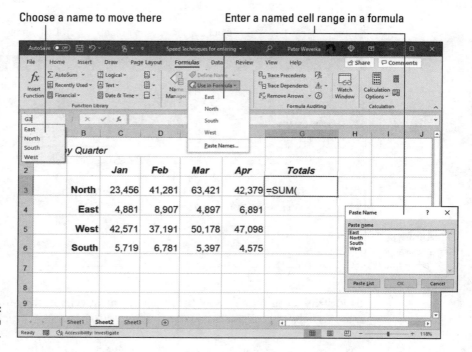

FIGURE 3-7:
Choosing a named cell range.

WARNING

Naming cell ranges has one disadvantage, and it's a big one. Excel doesn't adjust cell references when you copy a formula with a range name from one cell to another. A range name always refers to the same set of cells. Later in this chapter, "Copying Formulas from Cell to Cell" explains how to copy formulas.

Creating a cell range name

Follow these steps to create a cell range name:

1. **Select the cells that you want to name.**

2. **On the Formulas tab, click the Define Name button.**

You see the New Name dialog box.

3. **Enter a descriptive name in the Name box.**

Names can't begin with a number or include blank spaces.

4. **On the Scope drop-down list, choose Workbook or a worksheet name.**

Choose a worksheet name if you intend to use the range name you're creating only in formulas that you construct in a single worksheet. If your formulas will refer to cell range addresses in different worksheets, choose Workbook so that you can use the range name wherever you go in your workbook.

5. **Enter a comment to describe the range name, if you want.**

Enter a comment if doing so will help you remember where the cells you're naming are located or what type of information they hold. As I explain shortly, you can read comments in the Name Manager dialog box, the place where you go to edit and delete range names.

6. **Click OK.**

TIP

In case you're in a hurry, here's a fast way to enter a cell range name: Select the cells for the range, click in the Name Box (you can find it on the left side of the Formula bar, as shown in Figure 3-7), enter a name for the range, and press the Enter key.

Entering a range name as part of a formula

To include a cell range name in a formula, click in the Formula bar where you want to enter the range name, and then use one of these techniques to enter the name:

>> On the Formulas tab, click the Use in Formula button and choose a cell range name on the drop-down list (refer to Figure 3-7).

>> Press F3 or click the Use in Formula button and choose Paste Names on the drop-down list. You see the Paste Name dialog box (refer to Figure 3-7). Select a cell range name and click OK.

Quickly traveling to a cell range that you named

To go quickly to a cell range you named, open the drop-down list on the Name Box and choose a name (refer to Figure 3-7). The Name Box drop-down list is located on the left side of the Formula bar.

REMEMBER

To make this trick work, the cursor can't be in the Formula bar. The Name Box drop-down list isn't available when you're constructing a formula.

Managing cell range names

To rename, edit, or delete cell range names, go to the Formulas tab and click the Name Manager button. You see the Name Manager dialog box, as shown in Figure 3-8. This dialog box lists names, cell values in names, the worksheet on which the range name is found, and whether the range name can be applied throughout a workbook or only in one worksheet. To rename, edit, or delete a cell range name, select it in the dialog box and use these techniques:

>> **Renaming:** Click the Edit button and enter a new name in the Edit Name dialog box.

>> **Reassigning cells:** To assign different cells to a range name, click the Edit button. You see the Edit Name dialog box. To enter a new range of cells, either enter the cells' addresses in the Refers To text box or click the Range Selector button (it's to the right of the text box), drag across the cells on your worksheet that you want for the cell range, and click the Cell Selector button again to return to the Edit Name dialog box.

>> **Deleting:** Click the Delete button and click OK in the confirmation box.

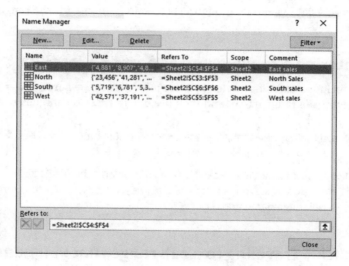

FIGURE 3-8:
The Name Manager dialog box.

Referring to cells in different worksheets

Excel gives you the opportunity to use data from different worksheets in a formula. If one worksheet lists sales figures from January and the next lists sales figures from February, you can construct a "grand total" formula in either worksheet to tabulate sales in the two-month period. A reference to a cell on a different worksheet is called a *3D reference*.

Construct the formula as you normally would, but when you want to refer to a cell or cell range in a different worksheet, click a worksheet tab to move to the other worksheet and select the cell or range of cells there. Without returning to the original worksheet, complete your formula in the Formula bar and press Enter. Excel returns you to the original worksheet, where you can see the results of your formula.

REMEMBER

The only odd thing about constructing formulas across worksheets is the cell references. As a glance at the Formula bar tells you, cell addresses in cross-worksheet formulas list the sheet name and an exclamation point (!) as well as the cell address itself. For example, this formula in Sheet 1 adds the number in cell A4 to the numbers in cells D5 and E5 in Sheet 2:

```
=A4+Sheet2!D5+Sheet2!E5
```

This formula in Sheet 2 multiplies the number in cell E18 by the number in cell C15 in Worksheet 1:

```
=E18*Sheet1!C15
```

This formula in Sheet 2 finds the average of the numbers in the cell range C7:F7 in Sheet 1:

```
=AVERAGE(Sheet1!C7:F7)
```

Copying Formulas from Cell to Cell

Often in worksheets, you use the same formula across a row or down a column, but different cell references are used. For example, in the worksheet shown in Figure 3-9, column F totals the rainfall figures in rows 7 through 11. To enter formulas for totaling the rainfall figures in column F, you could laboriously enter formulas in cells F7, F8, F9, F10, and F11. But a faster way is to enter the formula once in cell F7 and then copy the formula in F7 down the column to cells F8, F9, F10, and F11.

REMEMBER

When you copy a formula to a new cell, Excel adjusts the cell references in the formula so that the formula works in the cells to which it has been copied. Astounding! Opportunities to copy formulas abound on most worksheets. And copying formulas is the fastest and safest way to enter formulas in a worksheet.

Drag the AutoFill handle

FIGURE 3-9:
Copying a
formula.

Follow these steps to copy a formula:

1. **Select the cell with the formula you want to copy down a column or across a row.**

2. **Drag the AutoFill handle across the cells to which you want to copy the formula.**

    This is the same AutoFill handle you drag to enter serial data (see Chapter 1 of this minibook about entering lists and serial data with the AutoFill command). The AutoFill handle is the small green square in the lower-right corner of the cell. When you move the mouse pointer over it, it changes to a black cross. Figure 3-9 shows a formula being copied.

3. **Release the mouse button.**

> If I were you, I would click in the cells to which you copied the formula and glance at the Formula bar to make sure that the formula was copied correctly. I'd bet you it was.

You can also copy formulas with the Copy and Paste commands. Just make sure that cell references refer correctly to the surrounding cells.

Detecting and Correcting Errors in Formulas

It happens. Everyone makes an error from time to time when entering formulas in cells. Especially in a worksheet in which formula results are calculated into other formulas, a single error in one formula can spread like a virus and cause miscalculations throughout a worksheet. To prevent that calamity, Excel offers several ways to correct errors in formulas. You can correct them one at a time, run the error checker, and trace cell references, as the following pages explain.

TIP

By the way, if you want to see formulas in cells instead of formula results, go to the Formulas tab and click the Show Formulas button or press Ctrl+' (apostrophe). Sometimes seeing formulas this way helps to detect formula errors.

Correcting errors one at a time

When Excel detects what it thinks is a formula that has been entered incorrectly, a small green triangle appears in the upper-left corner of the cell where you entered the formula. And if the error is especially egregious, an *error message*, a cryptic three- or four-letter display preceded by a pound sign (#), appears in the cell. Table 3-2 explains common error messages.

To find out more about a formula error and perhaps correct it, select the cell with the green triangle and click the Error button. This small button appears beside a cell with a formula error after you click the cell, as shown in Figure 3-10. The drop-down list on the Error button offers opportunities for correcting formula errors and finding out more about them. Choose Help on This Error to open the Help task pane and examine why the error occurred (refer to Figure 3-10).

TABLE 3-2 **Common Formula Error Messages**

Message	What Went Wrong
#DIV/0!	You tried to divide a number by a zero (0) or an empty cell.
#NAME	You used a cell range name in the formula, but the name isn't defined. Sometimes this error occurs because you type the name incorrectly. (Earlier in this chapter, "Naming cell ranges so that you can use them in formulas" explains how to name cell ranges.)
#N/A	The formula refers to an empty cell, so no data is available for computing the formula. Sometimes people enter N/A in a cell as a placeholder to signal the fact that data isn't entered yet. Revise the formula or enter a number or formula in the empty cells.
#NULL	The formula refers to a cell range that Excel can't understand. Make sure that the range is entered correctly.
#NUM	An argument you use in your formula is invalid.
#REF	The cell or range of cells that the formula refers to isn't there.
#VALUE	The formula includes a function that was used incorrectly, takes an invalid argument, or is misspelled. Make sure that the function uses the right argument and is spelled correctly.

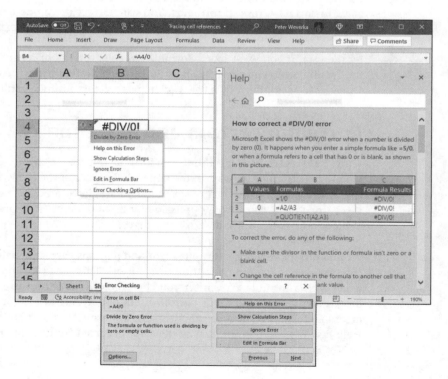

FIGURE 3-10:
Ways to detect and correct errors.

Running the error checker

Another way to tackle formula errors is to run the error checker. When the checker encounters what it thinks is an error, the Error Checking dialog box tells you what the error is (refer to Figure 3-10).

To run the error checker, go to the Formulas tab and click the Error Checking button. (You may have to click the Formula Auditing button first, depending on the size of your screen.)

If you see clearly what the error is, click the Edit in Formula Bar button, repair the error in the Formula bar, and click the Resume button in the dialog box (you find this button at the top of the dialog box). If the error isn't one that really needs correcting, either click the Ignore Error button or click the Next button to send the error checker in search of the next error in your worksheet.

Tracing cell references

In a complex worksheet in which formulas are piled on top of one another and the results of some formulas are computed into other formulas, it helps to be able to trace cell references. By tracing cell references, you can see how the data in a cell figures into a formula in another cell; or, if the cell contains a formula, you can see which cells the formula gathers data from to make its computation. You can get a better idea of how your worksheet is constructed, and in so doing, find structural errors more easily.

Figure 3-11 shows how cell tracers describe the relationships between cells. A *cell tracer* is a blue arrow that shows the relationships between cells used in formulas. You can trace two types of relationships:

>> **Tracing precedents:** Select a cell with a formula in it and trace the formula's *precedents* to find out which cells are computed to produce the results of the formula. Trace precedents when you want to find out where a formula gets its computation data. Cell tracer arrows point from the referenced cells to the cell with the formula results in it.

To trace precedents, go to the Formulas tab and click the Trace Precedents button. (You may have to click the Formula Auditing button first, depending on the size of your screen.)

>> **Tracing dependents:** Select a cell and trace its *dependents* to find out which cells contain formulas that use data from the cell you selected. Cell tracer arrows point from the cell you selected to cells with formula results in them.

Trace dependents when you want to find out how the data in a cell contributes to formulas elsewhere in the worksheet. The cell you select can contain a constant value or a formula in its own right (and contribute its results to another formula).

To trace dependents, go to the Formulas tab and click the Trace Dependents button. (You may have to click the Formula Auditing button first, depending on the size of your screen.)

FIGURE 3-11:
Tracing the relationships between cells.

To remove the cell tracer arrows from a worksheet, go to the Formulas tab and click the Remove Arrows button. You can open the drop-down list on this button and choose Remove Precedent Arrows or Remove Dependent Arrows to remove only cell-precedent or cell-dependent tracer arrows.

Working with Functions

A *function* is a canned formula that comes with Excel. Excel offers hundreds of functions, some of which are very obscure and fit for use only by rocket scientists or securities analysts. Other functions are very practical. For example, you can use the SUM function to quickly total the numbers in a range of cells. Rather than enter **=C2+C3+C4+C5** on the Formula bar, you can enter **=SUM(C2:C5)**, which tells Excel to total the numbers in cells C2, C3, C4, and C5. To obtain the product of the number in cell G4 and .06, you can use the PRODUCT function and enter **=PRODUCT(G4,.06)** on the Formula bar.

These pages explain how to use functions in formulas. You discover how to construct the arguments, enter function names, and get Excel's help with entering functions. Later in this chapter, "A Look at Some Very Useful Functions" examines how to use specific functions in formulas.

TIP

To get an idea of the numerous functions that Excel offers, go to the Formulas tab and click the Insert Function button. You see the Insert Function dialog box, shown in Figure 3-12. (Later in this chapter, I show you how this dialog box can help with using functions in formulas.) Choose a function category in the dialog box, choose a function name, and read the description. You can click the Help on This Function link to go online to a web page with a thorough description of the function and how it's used.

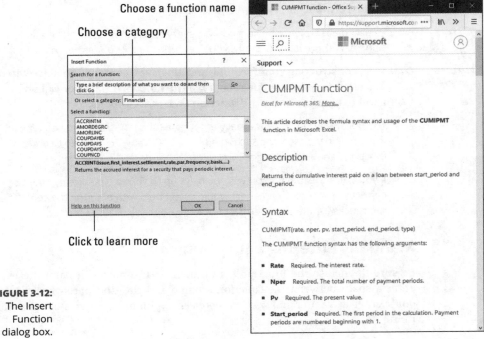

FIGURE 3-12:
The Insert Function dialog box.

Using arguments in functions

REMEMBER

Every function takes one or more *arguments*. Arguments are the cell references or numbers, enclosed in parentheses, that the function acts upon. For example, =AVERAGE(B1:B4) returns the average of the numbers in the cell range B1 through B4; =PRODUCT(6.5,C4) returns the product of multiplying the number 6.5 by the number in cell C4. When a function requires more than one argument, enter a comma between the arguments (enter a comma without a space).

Entering a function in a formula

To enter a function in a formula, you can enter the function name by typing it in the Formula bar, or you can rely on Excel to enter it for you. Enter function names yourself if you're well acquainted with a function and comfortable using it.

No matter how you want to enter a function as part of a formula, start this way:

1. **Select the cell where you want to enter the formula.**

2. **In the Formula bar, type an equals sign (=).**

Please, please, please be sure to start every formula by entering an equals sign (=). Without it, Excel thinks you're entering text or a number in the cell.

REMEMBER

3. **Start constructing your formula, and when you come to the place where you want to enter the function, type the function's name or call upon Excel to help you enter the function and its arguments.**

The upcoming section, "Manually entering a function" shows how to type in the function yourself; the section after that, "Getting Excel's help to enter a function," shows how to get Excel to do the work.

If you enter the function on your own, it's up to you to type the arguments correctly; if you get Excel's help, you also get help with entering the cell references for the arguments.

Manually entering a function

Be sure to enclose the function's argument or arguments in parentheses. Don't enter a space between the function's name and the first parenthesis. Likewise, don't enter a comma and a space between arguments; enter a comma, nothing more:

```
=SUM(F11,F14,23)
```

You can enter function names in lowercase. Excel converts function names to uppercase after you click the Enter button or press Enter to complete the formula. Entering function names in lowercase is recommended because doing so gives you a chance to find out whether you entered a function name correctly. If Excel doesn't convert your function name to uppercase, you made a typing error when you entered the function name.

When entering a formula with a function, you don't have to enter the closing parenthesis that encloses the function's arguments. After you press Enter, Excel enters the closing parenthesis for you.

Getting Excel's help to enter a function

Besides entering a function by typing it, you can do it by way of the Function Arguments dialog box, as shown in Figure 3-13. The beauty of using this dialog box is that it warns you if you enter arguments incorrectly. What's more, the Function Arguments dialog box shows you the results of the formula as you construct it so that you can tell whether you're using the function correctly.

Enter arguments

Function Arguments		? X
AVERAGE		
Number1	F3:F8	= {4.66666666666667;1;10.6666666666...
Number2		= number
		= 5.055555556

Returns the average (arithmetic mean) of its arguments, which can be numbers or names, arrays, or references that contain numbers.

Number1:   number1,number2,... are 1 to 255 numeric arguments for which you want the average.

Formula result =   5.1

Help on this function   OK   Cancel

FIGURE 3-13: The Function Arguments dialog box.

Formula result

Follow these steps to get Excel's help with entering a function as part of a formula:

1. **On the Formulas tab, tell Excel which function you want to use.**

You can do that with one of these techniques:

- **Click a Function Library button:** Click the button whose name describes what kind of function you want, and choose the function's name on the drop-down list. You can click the Financial, Logical, Text, Date & Time, Lookup & Reference, Math & Trig, or More Functions buttons.

- **Click the Recently Used button:** Click this button and choose the name of a function you used recently.

- **Click the Insert Function button:** Clicking this button opens the Insert Function dialog box (refer to Figure 3-12). Find and choose the name of a function. You can search for functions or choose a category and then scroll the names until you find the function you want.

   You see the Function Arguments dialog box (refer to Figure 3-13). It offers boxes for entering arguments for the function to compute.

2. **Enter arguments in the spaces provided by the Function Arguments dialog box.**

   To enter cell references or ranges, you can click or select cells in your worksheet. If necessary, click the Range Selector button (you can find it to the right of an argument text box) to shrink the Function Arguments dialog box and get a better look at your worksheet.

3. **Click OK when you finish entering arguments for your function.**

   I hope you didn't have to argue too strenuously with the Function Arguments dialog box.

QUICKLY ENTERING A FORMULA AND FUNCTION

Excel offers the AutoSum button and Quick Analysis button for quickly entering formulas that include a function.

Click the cell where you want the results of your formula to appear, and try these techniques for constructing formulas with the AutoSum button:

- On the Home or Formulas tab, click the AutoSum button to total nearby cells.

- On the Home or Formulas tab, open the drop-down list on the AutoSum button and choose Sum, Average, Count Numbers, Max, or Min. Respectively, these functions total, average, obtain the number of, obtain the highest value in, or obtain the lowest value in nearby cells.

Excel takes an educated guess as to which cells need totaling, averaging, or whatever, and quickly enters a formula for you.

Use the Quick Analysis button to construct a formula with the SUM, AVERAGE, or COUNT function, or one of their variations:

1. **Select the cells that will be used as arguments by the function.**

   The Quick Analysis button appears.

2. **Click the Quick Analysis button.**

3. **Choose Totals in the pop-up window.**

4. **Move the pointer over the various functions and glance at your worksheet to see the results of your formulas.**

5. **Select a function.**

A Look at Some Very Useful Functions

Starting with Table 3-3, the remainder of this chapter looks into functions that I consider especially useful or interesting. After you spend some time constructing formulas, you'll come up with your own list of useful or interesting functions.

AVERAGE for averaging data

Might as well start with an easy one. The AVERAGE function averages the values in a cell range. In Figure 3-14, for example, AVERAGE is used to compute the average rainfall in a three-month period in three different counties.

TABLE 3-3 **Common Functions and Their Use**

Function	Returns
AVERAGE(*number1,number2,...*)	The average of the numbers in the cells listed in the arguments
COUNT(*value1,value2,...*)	The number of cells that contain the numbers listed in the arguments
MAX(*number1,number2,...*)	The largest value in the cells listed in the arguments
MIN(*number1,number2,...*)	The smallest value in the cells listed in the arguments
PRODUCT(*number1,number2,...*)	The product of multiplying the cells listed in the arguments
STDEV(*number1,number2,...*)	An estimate of standard deviation based on the sample cells listed in the argument
STDEVP(*number1,number2,...*)	An estimate of standard deviation based on the entire sample cells listed in the arguments
SUM(*number1,number2,...*)	The total of the numbers in the arguments
VAR(*number1,number2,...*)	An estimate of the variance based on the sample cells listed in the arguments
VARP(*number1,number2,...*)	A variance calculation based on all cells listed in the arguments

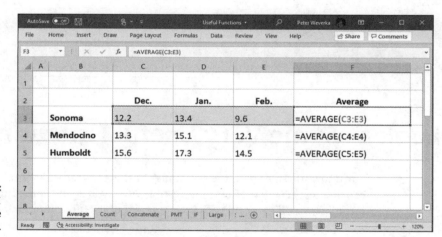

FIGURE 3-14: Using AVERAGE to find average rainfall data.

Use AVERAGE as follows:

```
AVERAGE(cell range)
```

Excel ignores empty cells and logical values in the cell range; cells with 0 are computed.

COUNT and COUNTIF for tabulating data items

Use COUNT, a statistical function, to count how many cells have data in them. Numbers and dates, not text entries, are counted. The COUNT function is useful for tabulating how many data items are in a range. In the spreadsheet at the top of Figure 3-15, for example, COUNT is used to compute the number of mountains listed in the data:

```
COUNT(C5:C9)
```

FIGURE 3-15:
The COUNT (above) and COUNTIF (below) function at work.

Use COUNT as follows:

```
COUNT(cell range)
```

Similar to COUNT is the COUNTIF function. It counts how many cells in a cell range have a specific value. To use COUNTIF, enter the cell range and a criterion in the argument, as follows. If the criterion is a text value, enclose it in quotation marks:

```
COUNTIF(cell range, criterion)
```

At the bottom of Figure 3-15, the formula determines how many of the mountains in the data are in Nepal:

```
=COUNTIF(D5:D9,"Nepal")
```

CONCAT for combining values

CONCAT, a text function, is useful for combining values from different cells into a single cell. In the spreadsheet at the top of Figure 3-16, for example, values from three columns are combined in a fourth column to list peoples' names in their entirety.

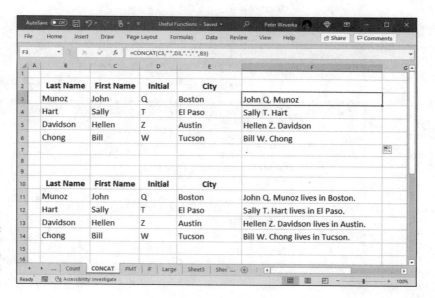

FIGURE 3-16:
Use the CONCAT function to combine values from cells.

Use CONCAT as follows:

```
CONCAT(text1, text2, text3...)
```

To include blank spaces in the text you're combining, enclose a blank space between quotation marks as an argument. Moreover, you can include original text in the concatenation formula as long as you enclose it in quotation marks and enter it as a separate argument. In Figure 3-16, I had to include a period after the middle initial, so in the formula, I entered a period in quotation marks as an argument:

```
=CONCAT(C3," ",D3,".","  ",B3)
```

In the spreadsheet shown at the bottom of Figure 3-16, I used the CONCATENATE function to write sentences ("John Q. Munoz lives in Boston."). I included the words "lives in" in the formula, as follows:

```
=CONCAT(C11," ",D11,".","  ",B11," ","lives in"," ",E11,".")
```

PMT for calculating how much you can borrow

If you're looking to buy a house, a car, or another expensive item for which you have to borrow money, the questions to ask yourself are, "How much can I borrow and still be able to make the monthly payment on the loan without stressing my budget unnecessarily? Can I safely make a monthly payment of $1,000, $1,500, $2,000?" How much you can afford to pay each month to service a loan determines how much you can realistically borrow.

Use the PMT (payment) function to explore how much you can borrow given different interest rates and different amounts. PMT determines how much you have to pay annually on different loans. After you determine how much you have to pay annually, you can divide this amount by 12 to see how much you have to pay monthly.

Use the PMT function as follows to determine how much you pay annually for a loan:

```
PMT(interest rate, number of payments, amount of loan)
```

As shown in Figure 3-17, set up a worksheet with five columns to explore loan scenarios:

>> **Interest rate (column A):** Because the interest rate on loans is expressed as a percentage, format this column to accept numbers as percentages (click the Percent Style button on the Home tab).

>> **No. of payments (column B):** Typically, loan payments are made monthly. For a 30-year home loan mortgage, enter 360 in this column (12 months × 30 years); for a 15-year mortgage, enter 180 (12 months × 15 years). Enter the total number of loan payments you will make during the life of the loan.

>> **Amount of loan (column C):** Enter the amount of the loan.

>> **Annual payment (column D):** Enter a formula with the PMT function in this column to determine how much you have to pay annually for the loan. In Figure 3-17, the formula is

```
=PMT(A3,B3,C3)
```

>> **Monthly payment (column E):** Divide the annual payment in column D by 12 to determine the monthly payment:

```
=D3/12
```

FIGURE 3-17:
Exploring loan scenarios with the PMT function.

After you set up the worksheet, you can start playing with different loan scenarios — different interest rates and amounts — to find out how much you can comfortably borrow and comfortably pay each month to pay back the loan.

IF for identifying data

The IF function examines data and returns a value based on criteria you enter. Use the IF function to locate data that meets a certain threshold. In the worksheet shown in Figure 3-18, for example, the IF function is used to identify teams that are eligible for the playoffs. To be eligible, a team must have won more than six games. The IF function identifies whether a team has won more than six games and, in the Playoffs column, enters the word *Yes* or *No* accordingly.

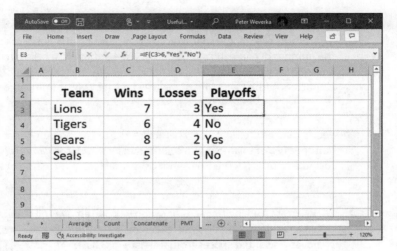

FIGURE 3-18: Exploring data with the IF function.

Use the IF function as follows:

```
IF(logical true-false test, value if true, value if false)
```

Instructing Excel to enter a value if the logical true-false test comes up false is optional; you must supply a value to enter if the test is true. Enclose the value in quotation marks if it is a text value such as the word *Yes* or *No*.

In Figure 3-18, the formula for determining whether a team made the playoffs is as follows:

```
=IF(C3>6,"Yes","No")
```

If the false "No" value was absent from the formula, teams that didn't make the playoffs would not show a value in the Playoffs column; these teams' Playoffs column would be empty.

LEFT, MID, and RIGHT for cleaning up data

Sometimes when you import data from another software application, especially if it's a database application, the data arrives with unneeded characters. You can use the LEFT, MID, RIGHT, and TRIM functions to remove these characters:

» LEFT returns the leftmost characters in a cell to the number of characters you specify. For example, in a cell with CA_State, this formula returns CA, the two leftmost characters in the text:

```
=LEFT(A1,2)
```

» MID returns the middle characters in a cell starting at a position you specify to the number of characters you specify. For example, in a cell with http://www.dummies.com, this formula uses MID to remove the extraneous seven characters at the beginning of the URL and get www.dummies.com:

```
=MID(A1,7,50)
```

» RIGHT returns the rightmost characters in a cell to the number of characters you specify. For example, in a cell containing the words *Vitamin B1*, this formula returns B1, the two rightmost characters in the name of the vitamin:

```
=RIGHT(A1,2)
```

» TRIM, except for single spaces between words, removes all blank spaces from inside a cell. Use TRIM to remove leading and trailing spaces. This formula removes unwanted spaces from the data in cell A1:

```
=TRIM(A1)
```

PROPER for capitalizing words

The PROPER function makes the first letter of each word in a cell uppercase. As are LEFT and RIGHT, it is useful for cleaning up data you imported from elsewhere. Use PROPER as follows:

```
PROPER(cell address)
```

LARGE and SMALL for comparing values

Use the LARGE and SMALL functions, as well as their cousins MIN, MAX, and RANK, to find out where a value stands in a list of values. For example, use LARGE to locate the ninth oldest man in a list, or MAX to find the oldest man. Use MIN to find the smallest city by population in a list, or SMALL to find the fourth smallest. The RANK function finds the rank of a value in a list of values.

Use these functions as follows:

» MIN returns the smallest value in a list of values. For the argument, enter a cell range or cell array. In the worksheet shown in Figure 3-19, the following formula finds the fewest number of fish caught at any lake on any day:

```
=MIN(C3:G7)
```

» SMALL returns the *n*th smallest value in a list of values. This function takes two arguments: first, the cell range or cell array, and next, the position, expressed as a number, from the smallest of all values in the range or array. In the worksheet shown in Figure 3-19, this formula finds the second smallest number of fish caught in any lake:

```
=SMALL(C3:G7,2)
```

» MAX returns the largest value in a list of values. Enter a cell range or cell array as the argument. In the worksheet shown in Figure 3-19, this formula finds the most number of fish caught in any lake:

```
=MAX(C3:G7)
```

» LARGE returns the *n*th largest value in a list of values. This function takes two arguments: first, the cell range or cell array, and next, the position, expressed as a number, from the largest of all values in the range or array. In the worksheet shown in Figure 3-19, this formula finds the second largest number of fish caught in any lake:

```
=LARGE(C3:G7,2)
```

» RANK returns the rank of a value in a list of values. This function takes three arguments:

- The cell with the value used for ranking

- The cell range or cell array with the comparison values for determining rank

- Whether to rank in order from top to bottom (enter 0 for descending) or bottom to top (enter 1 for ascending)

In the worksheet shown in Figure 3-19, this formula ranks the total number of fish caught in Lake Temescal against the total number of fish caught in all five lakes:

```
=RANK(H3,H3:H7,0)
```

FIGURE 3-19: Using functions to compare values.

NETWORKDAY and TODAY for measuring time in days

Excel offers a couple of date functions for scheduling, project planning, and measuring time periods in days.

NETWORKDAYS measures the number of workdays between two dates (the function excludes Saturdays and Sundays from its calculations). Use this function for scheduling purposes to determine the number of workdays needed to complete a project. Use NETWORKDAYS as follows:

```
NETWORKDAYS(start date, end date)
```

TODAY gives you today's date, whatever it happens to be. Use this function to compute today's date in a formula. The TODAY function takes no arguments and is entered like so, parentheses included:

```
TODAY()
```

To measure the number of days between two dates, use the minus operator and subtract the latest date from the earlier one. For example, this formula measures the number of days between 1/1/2021 and 6/1/2021:

```
="6/1/2021"-"1/1/2021"
```

The dates are enclosed in quotation marks to make Excel recognize them as dates. Make sure that the cell where the formula is located is formatted to show numbers, not dates.

LEN for Counting Characters in Cells

Use the LEN (length) function to obtain the number of characters in a cell. This function is useful for making sure that characters remain under a certain limit. The LEN function counts blank spaces as well as characters. Use the LEN function as follows:

```
LEN(cell address)
```

Chapter **4**

Making a Worksheet Easier to Read and Understand

This short and pithy chapter explains how to dress a worksheet in its Sunday best in case you want to print and present it to others. It explains how to align numbers and text, insert rows and columns, and change the size of rows and columns. You find out how to decorate a worksheet with colors and borders as well as create and apply styles to make formatting tasks go more quickly. Finally, this chapter describes everything you need to know before you print a worksheet, including how to make it fit on one page and repeat row labels and column names on all pages.

Laying Out a Worksheet

Especially if you intend to print your worksheet, you may as well make it look sharp. And you can do a number of things to make worksheets easier to read and understand. You can change character fonts. You can draw borders around or shade important cells. You can also format the numbers so that readers know, for example, whether they're staring at dollar figures or percentages. This part of Chapter 4 is dedicated to the proposition that a worksheet doesn't have to look drab and solemn.

Aligning numbers and text in columns and rows

To start with, numbers in worksheets are right-aligned in cells, and text is left-aligned. Numbers and text sit squarely on the bottom of cells. You can, however, change the way that data is aligned. For example, you can make data float at the top of cells rather than rest at the bottom, and you can center or justify data in cells. Figure 4-1 illustrates different ways to align text and numbers. How text is aligned helps people make sense of your worksheets. In Figure 4-1, for example, Income and Expenses are left-aligned so that they stand out and clarify what the right-aligned column labels below are all about.

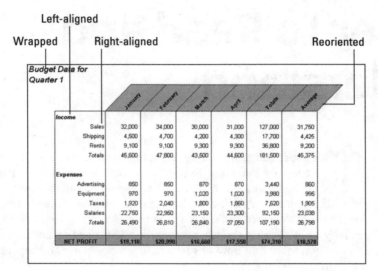

FIGURE 4-1:
Ways to align data.

Select the cells whose alignment needs changing and follow these instructions to realign data in the cells:

>> **Changing the horizontal (side-to-side) alignment:** On the Home tab, click the Align Left, Center, or Align Right button. You can also click the Alignment group button, and on the Alignment tab of the Format Cells dialog box, choose an option on the Horizontal drop-down list. Figure 4-2 shows the Format Cells dialog box.

>> **Changing the vertical (top-to-bottom) alignment:** On the Home tab, click the Top Align, Middle Align, or Bottom Align button. You can also click the Alignment group button to open the Format Cells dialog box (refer to Figure 4-2) and choose an option on the Vertical drop-down list. The Justify option makes all the letters or numbers fit in a cell, even if it means wrapping text to two or more lines.

>> **Reorienting the cells:** On the Home tab, click the Orientation button and choose an option on the drop-down list. (For Figure 4-2, I chose the Angle Counterclockwise option.) You can also click the Alignment group button, and on the Alignment tab of the Format Cells dialog box (refer to Figure 4-2), drag the diamond in the Orientation box or enter a number in the Degrees text box.

FIGURE 4-2:
The Alignment tab of the Format Cells dialog box.

TIP

Changing the orientation of text in cells is an elegant solution to the problem of keeping a worksheet from getting too wide. Numbers are usually a few characters wide, but heading labels can be much wider than that. By changing the orientation of a heading label, you make columns narrower and keep worksheets from growing too wide to fit on the screen or page.

MERGING AND CENTERING TEXT ACROSS SEVERAL CELLS

In the illustration shown here, "Sales Totals by Regional Office" is centered across four different cells. Normally, text is left-aligned, but if you want to center it across several cells, drag across the cells to select them, go to the Home tab, and click the Merge & Center button. Merging and centering allows you to display text across several columns.

To "unmerge and uncenter" cells, select the text that you merged and centered, open the drop-down list on the Merge & Center button, and choose Unmerge Cells. You can also deselect the Merge Cells check box in the Format Cells dialog box (refer to Figure 4-2).

B	C	D	E	F	G
		Sales Totals by Regional Office			
	North	West	East	South	

Inserting and deleting rows and columns

At some point, everybody has to insert new columns and rows and delete ones that are no longer needed. Make sure before you delete a row or column that you don't delete data that you really need. Do the following to insert and delete rows and columns:

» **Deleting rows or columns:** Drag across the row numbers or column letters of the rows or columns you want to delete; then right-click and choose Delete, or, on the Home tab, open the drop-down list on the Delete button and select Delete Sheet Rows or Delete Sheet Columns.

» **Inserting rows:** Select the row below the row you want to insert; then, on the Home tab, open the drop-down list on the Insert button and choose Insert Sheet Rows, or right-click the row you selected and choose Insert on the shortcut menu. For example, to insert a new row above row 11, select the current row 11 before choosing Insert Sheet Rows. You can insert more than one row at a time by selecting more than one row before giving the Insert Sheet Rows command.

>> **Inserting columns:** Select the column to the right of where you want the new column to be; then, on the Home tab, open the drop-down list on the Insert button and choose Insert Sheet Columns, or right-click the column you selected and choose Insert on the shortcut menu. You can insert more than one column this way by selecting more than one column before giving the Insert command.

A fast way to insert several rows or columns is to insert one and keep pressing F4 or press Ctrl+Y (the Repeat command) until you insert all the rows or columns you need.

After you insert rows or columns, the Insert Options button appears. Click it and choose an option from the drop-down list if you want your new row or column to have the same or different formats as the row or column you selected to start the Insert operation.

To insert more than one row or column at a time, select more than one row number or column letter before giving the Insert command.

Changing the size of columns and rows

By default, columns are 8.43 characters wide. To make columns wider, you have to widen them yourself. Rows are 15 points high, but Excel makes them higher when you enter letters or numbers that are taller than 15 points (72 points equals one inch). Excel offers a bunch of different ways to change the size of columns and rows. You can start on the Home tab and choose options on the Format button drop-down list, as shown in Figure 4-3, or you can rely on your wits and change sizes manually by dragging or double-clicking the boundaries between row numbers or column letters.

Before you change the size of columns or rows, select them (Chapter 2 of this minibook explains how). Click or drag across row numbers to select rows; click or drag across column letters to select columns.

Adjusting the height of rows

Here are ways to change the height of rows:

>> **One at a time:** Move the mouse pointer onto the boundary between row numbers and, when the pointer changes to a cross, drag the boundary between rows up or down. A pop-up box tells you how tall the row will be after you release the mouse button.

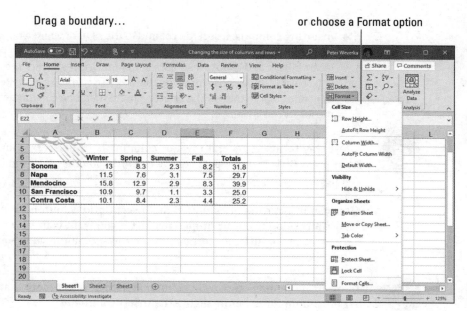

Drag a boundary...   or choose a Format option

FIGURE 4-3:
Ways to
change the
size of columns
and rows.

>> **Several at a time:** Select several rows and drag the boundary between one of the rows. When you do so, all rows change height. You can also go to the Home tab, click the Format button, choose Row Height, and enter a measurement in the Row Height dialog box.

>> **Tall as the tallest entry:** To make a row as tall as its tallest cell entry, double-click the border below a row number (after you've selected a row) or go to the Home tab, click the Format button, and choose AutoFit Row Height.

Adjusting the width of columns

Here are ways to make columns wider or narrower:

>> **One at a time:** Move the mouse pointer onto the boundary between column letters, and when the pointer changes to a cross, drag the border between the columns. A pop-up box tells you what size the column is.

>> **Several at a time:** Select several columns and drag the boundary between one of the columns; all columns adjust to the same width. You can also go to the Home tab, click the Format button, choose Column Width, and enter a measurement in the Column Width dialog box.

>> **As wide as their entries:** To make columns as wide as their widest entries, select the columns, go to the Home tab, click the Format button, and choose AutoFit Column Width on the drop-down list. You can also double-click the right border of a column letter. By "auto-fitting" columns, you can be certain that the data in each cell in a column appears onscreen.

TIP

To change the 8.43-character standard width for columns in a worksheet, go to the Home tab, click the Format button, choose Default Width on the drop-down list, and enter a new measurement in the Standard Width dialog box.

Decorating a Worksheet with Borders and Colors

The job of gridlines is simply to help you line up numbers and letters in cells. By default, gridlines aren't printed, and because gridlines aren't printed, drawing borders on worksheets is absolutely necessary if you intend to print your worksheet. Use borders to steer the reader's eye to the most important parts of your worksheet — the totals, column labels, and heading labels. You can also decorate worksheets with colors. This part of the chapter explains how to put borders and colors on worksheets.

Cell styles for quickly formatting a worksheet

A *style* is a collection of formats — boldface text, a background color, or a border around cells — that can be applied all at one time to cells without having to visit a bunch of different dialog boxes or give a bunch of different commands. Styles save time. If you find yourself choosing the same formatting commands time and time again, consider creating a style. That way, you can apply all the formats simultaneously and go to lunch earlier. Excel comes with many built-in styles, and you can create styles of your own, as the following pages explain.

Applying a built-in cell style

By way of the Cell Styles gallery on the Home tab, you can choose from any number of attractive styles for cells in a worksheet. Excel offers styles for titles and headings, styles for calling attention to what kind of data is in cells, and styles to accent cells. Follow these steps to reformat cells by choosing a cell style:

1. **Select the cells that need a new look.**

2. **On the Home tab, click the Cell Styles button.**

   As shown in Figure 4-4, the Cell Styles gallery opens.

3. **Select a cell style.**

   The Cell Styles gallery is divided into categories. Find a style that suits your purposes.

FIGURE 4-4: Choosing a new style from the Cell Styles gallery.

TIP

To remove a style from cells, select the cells, open the Cell Styles gallery, and choose Normal. (You find Normal in the "Good, Bad and Neutral" category.)

Creating your own cell style

The names of cell styles you create on your own are placed at the top of the Styles gallery under the Custom heading. Create a cell style if you're the creative type or if no built-in style meets your high standards. Follow these steps to create a cell style:

1. **Apply the formatting commands you want for your style to a single cell.**

   For example, left-align cell data. Or apply a fill color to the cells (see "Decorating worksheets with colors," later in this chapter). Or change fonts and font sizes. Knock yourself out. Choose all the formatting commands you want for your new style.

2. **On the Home tab, open the Styles gallery.**

Depending on the size of your screen, you may have to click the Styles button and then click the More button first.

3. **Choose New Cell Style at the bottom of the gallery.**

You see the Style dialog box shown in Figure 4-5. It lists formatting specifications that you chose for the cell you selected in Step 1. If these specifications aren't what you're after, or if you want to change a specification, you can click the Format button and construct your new style in the Format Cells dialog box.

4. **Enter a descriptive name for your style in the Style Name text box.**

5. **Click OK.**

Next time you open the Cell Styles gallery, you see the name of your style at the top, under Custom.

FIGURE 4-5:
Creating a new style for the Cell Styles gallery.

To remove a style you created from the Styles gallery, right-click its name in the gallery and choose Delete on the shortcut menu.

Formatting cells with table styles

Especially if your worksheet data is arranged neatly into columns and rows so that it looks like a conventional table, one of the easiest ways to decorate cells is to take advantage of table styles. Excel offers many preformatted table styles that you can apply to columns and rows on a worksheet.

Follow these steps to experiment with table styles:

1. **Select the cells you want to format as a table.**

2. **On the Home tab, click the Format As Table button and select a table style in the gallery.**

   The Create Table dialog box appears.

3. **If the cells you want to format include headers, the labels at the top of column rows that describe the data in the columns below, select the My Table Has Headers check box.**

4. **Click OK in the Create Table dialog box.**

   You can go to the Table Design tab to refine your table. Choose a different table style in the gallery if you don't care for the style you chose.

To remove a table style from cells, select the cells, go to the Table Design tab, open the Table Styles gallery, and choose Clear.

As Chapter 5 of this minibook explains, choosing the Format As Table command can be a way to filter and sort table data. This is why the Format As Table command places filter buttons in the first row of tables. To remove these filter buttons, deselect the Filter Button check box on the Table Design tab.

Slapping borders on worksheet cells

Put borders on worksheet cells to box in cells, draw lines beneath cells, or draw lines along the side of cells. Borders can direct people who review your worksheet to its important parts. Typically, for example, a line appears above the Totals row of a worksheet to separate the Totals row from the rows above and help readers locate cumulative totals.

To draw borders on a worksheet, start by selecting the cells around which or through which you want to place borders. Then do one of the following to draw the borders:

>> **Borders button:** On the Home tab, open the drop-down list on the Borders button (it's in the Font group) and choose a border, as shown in Figure 4-6.

>> **Drawing:** On the Home tab, open the drop-down list on the Borders button and choose Draw Border or Draw Border Grid. Then drag on the screen to draw the borders. Press Esc when you finish drawing.

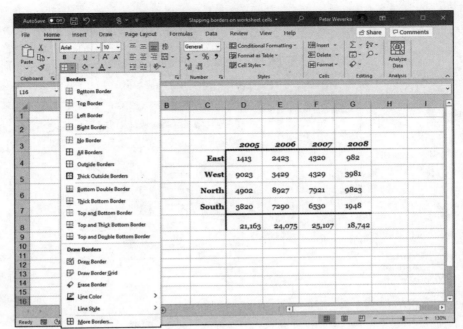

FIGURE 4-6:
Drawing a
border with
the Borders
button.

>> **Format Cells dialog box:** On the Home tab, click the Format button and choose Format Cells, or choose More Borders on the Borders button drop-down list. The Format Cells dialog box opens, as shown in Figure 4-7. On the Border tab, select a border style and either click in the Border box to tell Excel where to draw the border or click a Presets button. The Border tab offers different lines for borders and colors for borderlines as well.

To remove the border from cells, select the cells, open the drop-down list on the Borders button, and choose No Border.

Decorating worksheets with colors

Apply background colors to cells to make them stand out or help the people who review your worksheets understand how they are laid out. Select the cells that need a background color and use these techniques to splash color on your worksheet:

>> On the Home tab, click the Format button and choose Format Cells on the drop-down list. You see the Format Cells dialog box. On the Fill tab, select a color and click OK. Figure 4-7 shows what the Fill tab looks like.

>> On the Home tab, open the drop-down list on the Fill Color button and select a color.

FIGURE 4-7:
Go to the Format Cells dialog box to apply color (left) or draw borders (right).

Getting Ready to Print a Worksheet

Printing a worksheet isn't simply a matter of giving the Print command. A worksheet is a vast piece of computerized sprawl. Most worksheets don't fit neatly on a single page. If you simply click the Print button to print your worksheet, you wind up with page breaks in unexpected places, both on the right side of the page and the bottom. Read on to discover how to set up a worksheet so that the people you hand it to can read and understand it.

Making a worksheet fit on a page

Unless you tell it otherwise, Excel prints everything from cell A1 to the last cell with data in it in the southeast corner of the worksheet. Usually, it isn't necessary to print all those cells because some of them are blank. And printing an entire worksheet often means breaking the page up in all kinds of awkward places. To keep that from happening, following are some techniques for making a worksheet fit tidily on one or two pages.

TIP

As you experiment with the techniques described here, switch occasionally to Page Layout view. In this view, you get a better idea of what your worksheet will look like when you print it. To switch to Page Layout view, click the Page Layout button on the status bar or View tab.

Printing part of a worksheet

To print part of a worksheet, select the cells you want to print, go to the Page Layout tab, click the Print Area button, and choose Set Print Area on the drop-down list. This command tells Excel to print only the cells you selected. On the worksheet, a box appears around cells in the print area. To remove the box from your worksheet, click the Print Area button and choose Clear Print Area on the drop-down list.

Printing a landscape worksheet

If your worksheet is too wide to fit on one page, try turning the page on its side and printing in landscape mode. In landscape mode, pages are wider than they are tall. Landscape mode is often the easiest way to fit a worksheet on a page.

To make yours a landscape worksheet instead of a portrait worksheet, go to the Page Layout tab, click the Orientation button, and choose Landscape on the drop-down list.

Seeing and adjusting the page breaks

Reading a worksheet is extremely difficult when it's broken awkwardly across pages. Where one page ends and the next begins is a *page break*. Use these techniques to see where page breaks occur, adjust the position of page breaks, and insert and remove page breaks:

>> **Viewing where page breaks occur:** Click the Page Break Preview button on the status bar or View tab. As shown in Figure 4-8, you switch to Page Break Preview view. In this view, page numbers appear clearly on the worksheet and dashed lines show you where Excel wants to break the pages.

>> **Adjusting page break positions:** In Page Break Preview view, drag a dashed line to adjust the position of a page break. After you drag a dashed line, it ceases being a default page break and becomes a manual page break. Manual page breaks are marked by solid lines, not dashed lines (see Figure 4-8). You can drag them, too. Excel shrinks the numbers and letters on your worksheet if you try to squeeze too much data on a worksheet by dragging a page break.

» **Inserting a page break:** Select the cell directly below where you want the horizontal break to occur and directly to the right of where you want the vertical break to be, go to the Page Layout tab, click the Breaks button, and choose Insert Page Break. Drag a page break to adjust its position.

» **Removing a page break:** Select a cell directly below or directly to the right of the page break, go to the Page Layout tab, click the Breaks button, and choose Remove Page Break.

» **Removing all manual page breaks:** To remove all manual page breaks you inserted, go to the Page Layout tab, click the Breaks button, and choose Reset All Page Breaks.

Insert and remove page breaks

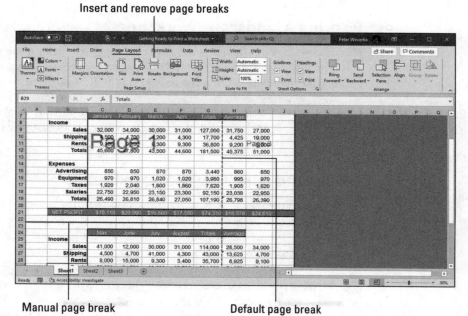

FIGURE 4-8:
Deciding where
pages break.

Manual page break   Default page break

Switch to Page Layout or Normal view after you're done fooling with page breaks. You can clearly see page breaks in Page Layout view. In Normal view, page breaks are marked by a dotted line.

"Scaling to fit" a worksheet

To scale the numbers and letters in a worksheet and make them a bit smaller so that they fit on a page, you can experiment with the Scale to Fit options. These options are located on the Page Layout tab. Starting in Page Layout view, go to the Page Layout tab and test-drive these options to make your worksheet fit on a single page or a certain number of pages:

>> **Scaling by width:** Open the Width drop-down list and choose an option to make your worksheet fit across one or more pages. Choose the 1 Page option, for example, to squeeze a worksheet horizontally so that it fits on one page.

>> **Scaling by height:** Open the Height drop-down list and choose an option to make your worksheet fit across a select number of pages. For example, choose the 2 Pages option to shrink a worksheet vertically so that it fits on two pages.

>> **Scaling by percentage:** Enter a percentage measurement in the Scale box to shrink a worksheet vertically and horizontally. To scale this way, you must choose Automatic in the Width and Height drop-down

TIP

You can also fit a worksheet on a select number of pages by going to the Page Setup dialog box shown in Figure 4-9. With this technique, you get a chance to "print-preview" your worksheet and get a better look at it after you change the scale. On the Page Layout tab, click the Page Setup group button to open the Page Setup dialog box. On the Page tab of the dialog box, select the Fit To option button and enter the ideal number of pages you want for your worksheet in the Page(s) Wide By and Tall text boxes. Excel shrinks the data as much as is necessary to make it fit on the number of pages you asked for. Click the Print Preview button to preview your worksheet in the Print window and find out whether shrinking your worksheet this way helps.

Adjusting the margins

Another way to stuff all the data onto one page is to narrow the margins a bit. Go to the Page Layout tab and use either of these techniques to adjust the size of the margins:

>> Click the Margins button and choose Narrow on the drop-down list.

>> Click the Page Setup group button, and on the Margins tab of the Page Setup dialog box, change the size of the margins, as shown in Figure 4-9. By clicking the Print Preview button, you can preview your worksheet in the Print window and adjust margins there by dragging them. Select the Show Margins button to display the margins. (This little button is in the lower-right corner of the Print window.)

FIGURE 4-9:
The Page (left) and Margins tab (right) of the Page Setup dialog box.

Making a worksheet more presentable

Before you print a worksheet, visit the Page Setup dialog box and see what you can do to make your worksheet easier for others to read and understand. To open the Page Setup dialog box, go to the Page Layout tab and click the Page Setup group button. Here are your options:

>> **Including page numbers on worksheets:** On the Page tab of the Page Setup dialog box (refer to Figure 4-9), enter **1** in the First Page Number text box. Then, on the Header/Footer tab, open the Header or Footer drop-down list and choose an option that includes a page number. Choosing the Page 1 of ? option, for example, enters the page number and the total number of pages in the worksheet in your header or footer.

>> **Putting headers and footers on pages:** On the Header/Footer tab of the Page Setup dialog box, choose options from the Header and Footer drop-down lists. You can find options for listing the filename, page numbers, the date, and your name. By clicking the Custom Header or Custom Footer button, you can open the Header or Footer dialog box and construct a header or footer there. Figure 4-10 shows the Header dialog box.

>> **Centering worksheet data on the page:** On the Margins tab of the page Setup dialog box, select Horizontally or Vertically to center the worksheet relative to the top or bottom or sides of the page. You can select both check boxes. The preview screen shows what your choices mean in real terms.

>> **Printing gridlines, column letters, and row numbers:** By default, the gridlines, column letters, and row numbers that you know and love in a worksheet aren't printed, but you can print them by going to the Sheet tab of the Page Setup dialog box and selecting the Gridlines check box as well as the Row and Column Headings check box.

FIGURE 4-10:
Constructing a fancy header.

Repeating row and column headings on each page

If your worksheet is a big one that stretches beyond one page, you owe it to the people who view your worksheet to repeat row and column headings from page to page. Without these headings, no one can tell what the data in the worksheet means. Follow these steps to repeat row and column headings from page to page:

1. **On the Page Layout tab, click the Print Titles button.**

You see the Sheet tab of the Page Setup dialog box.

2. **Select the Row and Column Headings check box.**

You can find this check box under Print.

3. **To repeat rows, click the Range Selector button next to the Rows to Repeat at Top text box; to repeat columns, click the Range Selector button next to the Columns to Repeat at Left text box.**

These buttons are located on the right side of the dialog box. The dialog box shrinks so that you can get a better look at your worksheet.

4. **Select the row or column with the labels or names you need.**

As long as they're next to each other, you can select more than one row or column by dragging over the row numbers or column letters.

5. **Click the Range Selector button to enlarge the dialog box and see it again.**

The text box now lists a cell range address.

6. **Repeat Steps 3 through 5 to select column or row headings.**

7. **Click OK to close the Page Setup dialog box.**

If I were you, I would click the Print Preview button in the Page Setup dialog box first to make sure that row and column headings are indeed repeating from page to page.

To remove row and column headings, return to the Sheet tab of the Page Setup dialog box and delete the cell references in the Rows to Repeat at Top text box and the Columns to Repeat at Left text box. You can also press Ctrl+F3 and delete Print_Titles in the Name Manager dialog box.

Chapter **5**

Advanced Techniques for Analyzing Data

This chapter offers a handful of tricks for analyzing the data that you so carefully and lovingly enter in a worksheet. Delve into this chapter to find out how to get insights into your data and how to manage, sort, and filter data in lists. You also discover how conditional formats can help data stand out, how the Goal Seek command can help you target values in different kinds of analyses, and how you can map out different scenarios with data by using one- and two-input data tables. Finally, this chapter explains how a PivotTable can help turn an indiscriminate list into a meaningful source of information.

Getting Quick Analyses from Excel

When you're in a hurry to analyze data in a worksheet, take advantage of the Analyze Data command, sparklines, and forecast sheets. These tools can help you examine data closely, recognize trends, and foretell the future. Better keep reading.

Running a rough-and-ready data analysis

When you choose the Analyze Data command, Excel peers into your worksheet and comes up with tables and charts it thinks are insightful. The tables and charts appear in the Analyze Data task pane, as shown in Figure 5-1.

Narrow the analysis   Refine the analysis

Insert an item

FIGURE 5-1:
Examining data in the Analyze Data task pane.

To run a data analysis, start by clicking in a worksheet column or row with data that deserves more attention. Then go to the Home tab and click the Analyze Data button.

You're invited to scroll through items in the Analyze Data task pane to see worksheet data in a new light. While you're at it, you can take advantage of these amenities in the task pane:

» **Pinpoint one area for analysis:** Enter a question in the text box (or click a suggested question) to rerun the analysis and aim it at a narrower subject.

» **Refine the analysis:** Click the Which Fields Interest You the Most? link. A new window opens in the task pane so that you can choose which columns or rows to analyze and whether you want to total or average data. Click the Update button after you make your choices.

» **Insert a table or chart in your worksheet:** Click the Insert link below a table or chart to place it on a new worksheet in your workbook.pk

TIP

Scroll to the bottom of the Analyze Data task pane and click the Show All Results link to see the numerous tables and charts Excel is capable of generating.

Seeing what the sparklines say

Maybe the easiest way to analyze information in a worksheet is to see what the sparklines say. Figure 5-2 shows examples of sparklines. In the form of a tiny line or bar chart, sparklines tell you about the data in a row or column.

Choose a sparkline

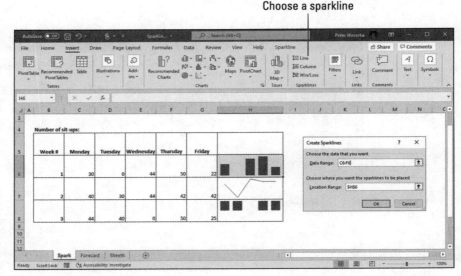

FIGURE 5-2:
Sparklines in action (top to bottom): Column, Line, and Win/Loss.

Follow these steps to create a sparkline chart:

1. **Select the cell where you want the chart to appear.**

2. **On the Insert tab, click the Line, Column, or Win/Loss button.**

   The Create Sparklines dialog box appears.

3. **Drag in a row or column of your worksheet to select the cells with the data you want to analyze.**

4. **Click OK in the Create Sparklines dialog box.**

To change the look of a sparkline chart, go to the Sparkline tab. There you will find commands for changing the color of the line or bars, choosing a different sparkline type, and doing one or two other things to pass the time on a rainy day. Click the Clear button to remove a sparkline chart.

TIP

You can also create a sparkline chart with the Quick Analysis button. Drag over the cells with the data you want to analyze. When the Quick Analysis button appears, click it, choose Sparklines in the pop-up window, and then choose Line, Column, or Win/Loss.

Generating a forecast sheet

A *forecast sheet* is a worksheet and chart that aim to predict the future. Excel generates forecast sheets from historical data — that is, from cells with date values or time values. Figure 5-3 shows a forecast sheet. Forecast sheets tell you, in theory at least, what the future holds.

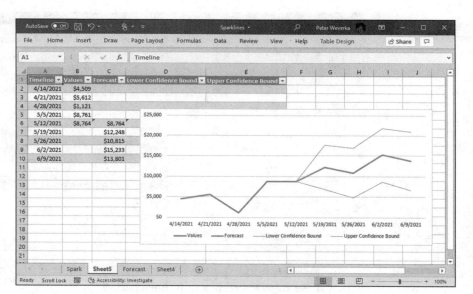

FIGURE 5-3:
A forecast sheet.

Follow these steps to create a forecast sheet and add it to your workbook:

1. **Select the data Excel needs for forecasting purposes.**

Select data in two corresponding columns or rows. One column or row must contain date or time values. Moreover, the date or time values must be recorded at regular intervals. For example, date value cells could record dates on the first of each month; time value cells could record times at the top of each hour.

2. **On the Data tab, click the Forecast Sheet button.**

   The Create Forecast Worksheet window appears. It shows what the chart portion of the forecast sheet will look like after you create it.

3. **Click the Create button.**

   Excel adds a worksheet to your workbook. It forecasts future trends in the form of a worksheet and a chart. I hope you like what you see.

Conditional Formats for Calling Attention to Data

A *conditional format* is one that applies when data meets certain conditions. To call attention to numbers greater than 10,000, for example, you can tell Excel to highlight those numbers automatically. To highlight negative numbers, you can tell Excel to display them in bright red. Conditional formats help you analyze and understand data better.

Select the cells that are candidates for conditional formatting and follow these steps to tell Excel when and how to format the cells:

1. **On the Home tab, click the Conditional Formatting button (you may have to click the Styles button first, depending on the size of your screen).**

2. **Choose Highlight Cells Rules or Top/Bottom Rules on the drop-down list.**

   You see a submenu with choices about establishing the rule for whether values in the cells are highlighted or otherwise made more prominent:

   - **Highlight Cells Rules:** These rules are for calling attention to data if it falls in a numerical or date range, or it's greater or lesser than a specific value. For example, you can highlight cells that are greater than 400.

   - **Top/Bottom Rules:** These rules are for calling attention to data if it falls within a percentage range relative to all the cells you selected. For example, you can highlight cells with data that falls in the bottom 10-percent range.

3. **Choose an option on the submenu.**

   You see a dialog box similar to the ones in Figure 5-4.

4. On the left side of the dialog box, establish the rule for flagging data.

5. On the With drop-down list, choose how you want to call attention to the data.

For example, you can display the data in red or yellow. You can choose Custom Format on the drop-down list to open the Format Cells dialog box and choose a font style or color for the text.

6. Click OK.

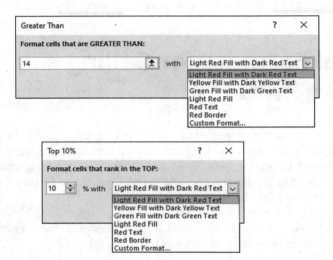

FIGURE 5-4:
Establishing a condition format for data.

To remove conditional formats, select the cells with the formats, go to the Home tab, click the Conditional Formatting button, and choose Clear Rules⇨ Clear Rules from Selected Cells.

You can also establish conditional formats by selecting cells and pressing Ctrl+Q or clicking the Quick Analysis button (which appears next to cells after you select them). In the pop-up window, choose the Formatting tab and then click Greater Than or Top 10% to create a highlight-cell or top/bottom rule.

Managing Information in Lists

Although Excel is a spreadsheet program, many people use it to keep and maintain lists, such as the list shown in Figure 5-5. Addresses, inventories, and employee data are examples of information that typically is kept in lists. These pages explain how to sort and filter a list to make it yield more information. Sort a list to put it in alphabetical or numeric order; filter a list to isolate the information you need.

FIGURE 5-5:
A list in a worksheet.

REMEMBER

Before you attempt a sort or filter operation, use the Format As Table command to capture the data you want to sort or filter in a list. Chapter 4 of this mini-book explains how to format cells so that they form a table. (*Hint:* Select the cells, click the Format As Table button on the Home tab, and select a table style in the gallery.)

Sorting a list

Sorting means to rearrange the rows in a list on the basis of data in one or more columns. Sort a list on the Last Name column, for example, to arrange the list in alphabetical order by last name. Sort a list on the ZIP Code column to arrange the rows in numerical order by ZIP code. Sort a list on the Birthday column to arrange it chronologically from earliest born to latest born.

Here are all the ways to sort a list:

>> **Sorting on a single column:** Click any cell in the column you want to use as the basis for the sort. For example, to sort item numbers from smallest to largest, click in the Item Number column. Then use one of these techniques to conduct the sort operation:

- On the Data tab, click the Sort Smallest to Largest or Sort Largest to Smallest button. These buttons are located in the Sort & Filter group.

- Open the drop-down menu on the column heading and choose Sort Smallest to Largest or Sort Largest to Smallest on the drop-down menu (see Figure 5-5). Click the Filter button on the Data tab if you don't see the drop-down menus.

>> **Sorting on more than one column:** Click the Sort button on the Data tab. You see the Sort dialog box, as shown in Figure 5-6. Choose which columns you want to sort with and the order in which you want to sort. To add a second or third column for sorting, click the Add Level button.

FIGURE 5-6:
Sort to arrange the list data in different ways.

Filtering a list

Filtering means to scour a worksheet list for certain kinds of data. To filter, you tell Excel what kind of data you're looking for, and the program assembles rows with that data to the exclusion of rows that don't have the data. You end up with a shorter list with only the rows that match your filter criteria. Filtering is similar to using the Find command except that you get more than one row in the results of the filtering operation. For example, in a list of addresses, you can filter for addresses in California. In a price list, you can filter for items that fall within a certain price range.

WARNING

To filter data, your list needs column headers, the descriptive labels in the first row that describe what is in the columns below. Excel needs column headers to identify and be able to filter the data in the rows. Each column header must have a different name.

To filter a list, start by going to the Data tab and clicking the Filter button. As shown in Figure 5-7, a drop-down list appears beside each column header.

Your next task is to open a drop-down list in the column that holds the criteria you want to use to filter the list. For example, if you want to filter the list to show items that cost more than $100, open the Cost column drop-down list; if you want to filter the list so that only the names of employees who make less than $30,000 annually appear, open the Salary drop-down list.

Click the Filter button

FIGURE 5-7:
Filter a worksheet to isolate data.

Filter by exclusion   Filter with criteria

After you open the correct column drop-down list, tell Excel how you want to filter the list:

>> **Filter by exclusion:** On the drop-down list, deselect the Select All check box and then select the check box next to each item you *don't* want to filter out. For example, to filter an Address list for addresses in Boston, Chicago, and Miami, deselect the Select All check box and then select the check boxes next to Boston, Chicago, and Miami on the drop-down list. Your filter operation turns up only addresses in those three cities.

>> **Filter with criteria:** On the drop-down list, choose Number Filters, and then choose a filter operation on the submenu (or simply choose Custom Filter). You see the Custom AutoFilter dialog box, as shown in Figure 5-7.

Choose an operator (equals, is greater than, or another) from the drop-down list, and either enter or choose a target criterion from the list on the right side of the dialog box. You can search by more than one criterion. Select the And option button if a row must meet both criteria to be selected, or select the Or option button if a row can meet either criterion to be selected.

Click the OK button on the column's drop-down list or the Custom AutoFilter dialog box to filter your list.

REMEMBER

To see all the data in the list again — to *unfilter* the list — click the Clear button on the Data tab.

Forecasting with the Goal Seek Command

In a conventional formula, you provide the raw data, and Excel produces the results. With the Goal Seek command, you declare what you want the results to be, and Excel tells you the raw data that you need to produce those results. The Goal Seek command is useful in analyses when you want the outcome to be a certain way and you need to know which raw numbers will produce the outcome that you want.

Figure 5-8 shows a worksheet designed to find out the monthly payment on a mortgage. With the PMT function, the worksheet determines that the monthly payment on a $250,000 loan with an interest rate of 6.5 percent and to be paid over a 30-year period is $1,580.17. Suppose, however, that after calculating this monthly payment, you determine that you could pay more than $1,580.17 per month. Suppose that you could pay $1,750 or $2,000 per month. Instead of an outcome of $1,580.17, you want to know how much you could borrow if monthly payments — the outcome of the formula — were increased to $1,750 or $2,000.

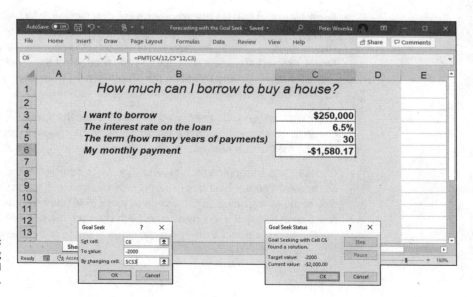

FIGURE 5-8:
Experimenting with the Goal Seek command.

To make determinations such as these, you can use the Goal Seek command. This command lets you experiment with the arguments in a formula to achieve the results you want. In the case of the worksheet in Figure 5-8, you can use the Goal Seek command to change the argument in cell C3, the total amount you can borrow, given the outcome you want in cell C6, $1,750 or $2,000, the monthly payment on the total amount.

Follow these steps to use the Goal Seek command to change the inputs in a formula to achieve the results you want:

1. **Select the cell with the formula whose arguments you want to experiment with.**

2. **On the Data tab, click the What-If Analysis button and choose Goal Seek on the drop-down list.**

   You see the Goal Seek dialog box, shown in Figure 5-8. The address of the cell you selected in Step 1 appears in the Set Cell box.

3. **In the To Value text box, enter the target results you want from the formula.**

   In the example in Figure 5-8, you enter **-2000**, the monthly payment you can afford for the 30-year mortgage.

4. **In the By Changing Cell text box, enter the address of the cell whose value is unknown.**

   To enter a cell address, go outside the Goal Seek dialog box and click a cell on your worksheet. In Figure 5-8, you select the address of the cell that shows the total amount you want to borrow.

5. **Click OK.**

   The Goal Seek Status dialog box appears, as shown in Figure 5-8. It lists the target value that you entered in Step 3.

6. **Click OK.**

   On your worksheet, the cell with the argument you wanted to alter now shows the target you're seeking. In the case of the example worksheet in Figure 5-6, you can borrow $316,422 at 6.5 percent, not $250,000, by raising your monthly mortgage payments from $1,580.17 to $2,000.

Performing What-If Analyses with Data Tables

For something a little more sophisticated than the Goal Seek command (which I describe in the preceding section), try performing what-if analyses with data tables. With this technique, you change the data in input cells and observe what effect changing the data has on the results of a formula. The difference between the Goal Seek command and a data table is that with a data table, you can experiment simultaneously with many different input cells and in so doing experiment with many different scenarios.

Using a one-input table for analysis

In a *one-input table*, you find out what the different results of a formula would be if you changed one *input cell* in the formula. In Figure 5-9, that input cell is the interest rate on a loan. The purpose of this data table is to find out how monthly payments on a $250,000, 30-year mortgage are different, given different interest rates. The interest rate in cell B4 is the input cell.

FIGURE 5-9: A one-input data table.

Follow these steps to create a one-input table:

1. **On your worksheet, enter values that you want to substitute for the value in the input cell.**

REMEMBER

To make the input table work, you have to enter the substitute values in the right location:

- **In a column:** Enter the values in the column starting one cell below and one cell to the left of the cell where the formula is located. In Figure 5-9, for example, the formula is in cell E4 and the values are in the cell range D5:D15.

- **In a row:** Enter the values in the row starting one cell above and one cell to the right of the cell where the formula is.

2. **Select the block of cells with the formula and substitute values.**

Select a rectangle of cells that encompasses the formula cell, the cell beside it, all the substitute values, and the empty cells where the new calculations will soon appear.

- **In a column:** Select the formula cell, the cell to its left, all the substitute-value cells, and the cells below the formula cell.

- **In a row:** Select the formula cell, the cell above it, the substitute values in the cells directly to the right, and the now-empty cells where the new calculations will appear.

3. **On the Data tab, click the What-If Analysis button and choose Data Table on the drop-down list.**

You see the Data Table dialog box (refer to Figure 5-9).

4. **In the Row Input Cell or Column Input Cell text box, enter the address of the cell where the input value is located.**

To enter this cell address, go outside the Data Table dialog box and click the cell. The input value is the value you're experimenting with in your analysis. In the case of the worksheet shown in Figure 5-9, the input value is located in cell B4, the cell that holds the interest rate.

If the new calculations appear in rows, enter the address of the input cell in the Row Input Cell text box; if the calculations appear in columns (refer to Figure 5-9), enter the input cell address in the Column Input Cell text box.

5. **Click OK.**

Excel performs the calculations and fills in the table.

To generate the one-input table, Excel constructs an array formula with the TABLE function. If you change the cell references in the first row or plug in different values in the first column, Excel updates the one-input table automatically.

Using a two-input table for analysis

In a two-input table, you can experiment with two input cells rather than one. Getting back to the example of the loan payment in Figure 5-9, you can calculate not only how loan payments change as interest rates change but also how payments change if the life of the loan changes. Figure 5-10 shows a two-input table for examining monthly loan payments given different interest rates and two different terms for the loan: 15 years (180 months) and 30 years (360 months).

FIGURE 5-10:
A two-input
data table.

Follow these steps to create a two-input data table:

1. **Enter one set of substitute values below the formula in the same column as the formula.**

In Figure 5-10, different interest rates are entered in the cell range D5:D15.

2. **Enter the second set of substitute values in the row to the right of the formula.**

In Figure 5-10, 180 and 360 are entered. These numbers represent the number of months of the life of the loan.

3. **Select the formula and all substitute values.**

Do this correctly and you select three columns, including the formula, the substitute values below it, and the two columns to the right of the formula. You select a big block of cells (the range D4:F15, in this example).

4. **On the Data tab, click the What-If Analysis button and choose Data Table on the drop-down list.**

The Data Table dialog box appears (refer to Figure 5-10).

5. **In the Row Input Cell text box, enter the address of the cell referred to in the original formula where substitute values to the right of the formula can be plugged in.**

Enter the cell address by going outside the dialog box and selecting a cell. In Figure 5-10, for example, the rows to the right of the formula are for length-of-loan substitute values. Therefore, I select cell B5, the cell referred to in the original formula where the length of the loan is listed.

6. **In the Column Input Cell text box, enter the address of the cell referred to in the original formula where substitute values below the formula are.**

In Figure 5-10, the substitute values below the formula cell are interest rates. Therefore, I select cell B4, the cell referred to in the original formula where the interest rate is entered.

7. **Click OK.**

Excel performs the calculations and fills in the table.

Analyzing Data with PivotTables

PivotTables give you the opportunity to reorganize data in a long worksheet list and in so doing analyze the data in new ways. You can display data such that you focus on one aspect of the list. You can turn the list inside out and perhaps discover things you didn't know before.

When you create a PivotTable, what you really do is turn a multicolumn list into a table for the purpose of analysis. For example, the four-column list in Figure 5-11 records items purchased in two grocery stores over a four-week period. The four columns are

>> **Item:** The items purchased

>> **Store:** The grocery store (Safepath or Wholewallet) where the items were purchased

>> **Cost:** The cost of the items

>> **Week:** When the items were purchased (Week 1, 2, 3, or 4)

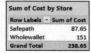

FIGURE 5-11: A raw multicolumn list (left) turned into meaningful PivotTables (right).

This raw list doesn't reveal anything; it's hardly more than a data dump. However, as Figure 5-11 shows, by turning the list into PivotTables, you can tease the list to find out, among other things:

>> How much was spent item by item in each grocery store, with the total spent for each item (Sum of Cost by Item and Store)

>> How much was spent on each item (Sum of Cost by Item)

>> How much was spent at each grocery store (Sum of Cost by Store)

>> How much was spent each week (Sum of Cost by Week)

REMEMBER

Make sure that the list you want to analyze with a PivotTable has column headers. Column headers are the descriptive labels that appear across the top of columns in a list. Excel needs column headers to construct PivotTables.

Getting a PivotTable recommendation from Excel

The easiest way to create a PivotTable is to let Excel do the work. Follow these steps:

1. Select a cell anywhere in your data list.

2. On the Insert tab, click the Recommended PivotTables button.

The Recommended PivotTables dialog box appears, as shown in Figure 5-12. This dialog box presents a number of PivotTables.

3. Scroll the list of PivotTables on the left side of the dialog box, selecting each one and examining it on the right side of the dialog box.

4. Select a PivotTable and click OK.

The PivotTable appears on a new worksheet.

FIGURE 5-12: These PivotTables come highly recommended.

Advanced Techniques
for Analyzing Data

Creating a PivotTable from scratch

Follow these steps to create a PivotTable on your own:

1. **Select a cell anywhere in your data list.**

2. **On the Insert tab, click the PivotTable button.**

   Excel selects what it believes is your entire list, and you see the PivotTable from Table or Range dialog box. If the list isn't correctly selected, click outside the dialog box and select the data you

3. **Choose the New Worksheet option and click OK.**

   You can choose the Existing Worksheet option and select cells on your worksheet to show Excel where you want to place the PivotTable, but in my experience, creating it on a new worksheet and moving it later is the easier way to go.

   The PivotTable Analyze tab and PivotTable Fields task pane appear, as shown in Figure 5-13. The task pane lists the names of fields, or column headings, from your table.

4. **In the PivotTable Fields task pane, drag field names into the four areas (Filters, Columns, Rows, and Values) to construct your PivotTable.**

   As you construct your table, you see it take shape onscreen. You can drag fields in and out of areas as you please. Drag one field name into each of these areas:

   - **Rows:** The field whose data you want to analyze.

   - **Columns:** The field by which you want to measure and compare data.

   - **Values:** The field with the values used for comparison.

   - **Filters (optional):** A field you want to use to sort table data. (This field's name appears in the upper-left corner of the PivotTable. You can open its drop-down list to sort the table; see "Sorting a list," earlier in this chapter.)

Putting the finishing touches on a PivotTable

Go to the PivotTable Design tab to put the finishing touches on a PivotTable:

» **Grand Totals:** Excel totals columns and rows in PivotTables. If you prefer not to see these "grand totals," click the Grand Totals button and choose an option to remove them from rows, columns, or both.

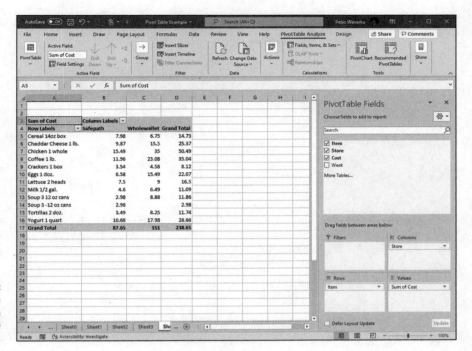

FIGURE 5-13:
Constructing a
PivotTable on
the PivotTable
Analyze tab.

>> **Report Layout:** Click the Report Layout button and choose a PivotTable layout on the drop-down list.

>> **PivotTable Styles:** Choose a PivotTable style to breathe a little color into your PivotTable.

TIP

To construct a chart from a PivotTable, go to the PivotTable Analyze tab and click the PivotChart button. The Insert Chart dialog box opens. Book 8, Chapter 1 explains how to navigate this dialog box.

Advanced Techniques
for Analyzing Data

4

PowerPoint 365

Contents at a Glance

IN THIS CHAPTER

» Finding your way around the screen

» Creating a presentation

» Changing views of the screen

» Manipulating slides

Chapter **1**

Getting Started in PowerPoint

It's impossible to sit through a conference, seminar, or trade show without seeing at least one PowerPoint presentation. PowerPoint has found its way into nearly every office and boardroom. I've heard of a man (a very unromantic man) who proposed to his wife by way of a PowerPoint presentation.

As nice as PowerPoint can be, it has its detractors. If the software isn't used properly, it can come between the speaker and the audience. In a *New Yorker* article titled "Absolute PowerPoint: Can a Software Package Edit Our Thoughts?," Ian Parker argued that PowerPoint may actually be more of a hindrance than a help in communicating. PowerPoint, Parker wrote, is "a social instrument, turning middle managers into bullet-point dandies." The software, he added, "has a private, interior influence. It edits ideas . . . . It helps you make a case, but also makes its own case about how to organize information, how to look at the world."

To make sure that you use PowerPoint wisely, this chapter shows what creating a PowerPoint presentation entails. After a brief tour of PowerPoint, you find out how to create presentations, get a better view of your work, insert slides, put together a photo album, and hide slides.

Getting Acquainted with PowerPoint

Figure 1-1 (top) shows the PowerPoint window. That thing in the middle of the window is a *slide*, the PowerPoint word for an image that you show your audience. Surrounding the slide are many tools for entering text and decorating slides. When the time comes to show your slides to an audience, you dispense with the tools and make the slide fill the screen, as shown in Figure 1-1 (bottom).

FIGURE 1-1:
The PowerPoint window (top) and a slide as it looks in a presentation (bottom).

To make PowerPoint do your bidding, you need to know a little jargon:

>> **Presentation:** All the slides, from start to finish, that you show your audience. Sometimes presentations are called *slide shows.*

>> **Slides:** The images you create with PowerPoint. During a presentation, slides appear onscreen one after the other.

>> **Notes:** Printed pages that you, the speaker, write and print so that you know what to say during a presentation. Only the speaker sees notes. Chapter 5 in this minibook explains notes.

>> **Handout:** Printed pages that you may give to the audience along with a presentation. A handout shows the slides in the presentation. Handouts are also known by the somewhat derogatory term *leave-behinds.* Chapter 5 of this minibook explains handouts.

A Brief Geography Lesson

Figure 1-2 shows the different parts of the PowerPoint screen. I'd hate for you to get lost in PowerPoint Land. Fold down the corner of this page so that you can return here if screen terminology confuses you:

FIGURE 1-2: The different parts of the PowerPoint screen.

Quick Access toolbar · Slide · The Ribbon

Slides pane · Notes pane · View buttons · Zoom controls

>> **Quick Access toolbar:** A toolbar with four buttons — Save, Undo, Repeat, and Start From Beginning (as well as Touch/Mouse Mode if your computer has a touchscreen). You see this toolbar wherever you go in PowerPoint.

>> **Ribbon:** The place where the tabs are located. Click a tab — Home, Insert, Draw, Design, Transitions, Animations, Slide Show, Review, or View — to start a task.

>> **Slides pane:** In Normal view, the place on the left side of the screen where you can see the slides or the text on the slides in your presentation. Scroll in the Slides pane to move backward and forward in a presentation.

>> **Slide window:** Where a slide (in Normal view) or slides (in Slide Sorter view) are displayed. Scroll to move backward or forward in your presentation.

>> **Notes pane:** Where you type notes (in Normal view) that you can refer to when giving your presentation. The audience can't see these notes — they're for you and you alone. See Chapter 5 of this minibook for details.

>> **View buttons:** Buttons you can click to switch to (from left to right) Normal, Slide Sorter, Reading View, and Slide Show. See "Getting a Better View of Your Work," later in this chapter.

>> **Zoom controls:** Tools for enlarging or shrinking a slide (in Normal and Slide Sorter view).

A Whirlwind Tour of PowerPoint

To help you understand what you're getting into, you're invited on a whirlwind tour of PowerPoint. Creating a PowerPoint presentation entails completing these basic tasks:

>> **Creating the slides:** After you create a new presentation, your next task is to create the slides. PowerPoint offers many preformatted slide layouts, each designed for presenting information a certain way.

>> **Notes:** As you create slides, you can jot down notes in the Notes pane. You can use these notes later to formulate your presentation and decide what to say to your audience while each slide is onscreen (see Chapter 5 of this minibook).

>> **Designing your presentation:** After you create a presentation, the next step is to think about its appearance. You can change slides' colors and backgrounds, as well as choose a *theme* for your presentation, an all-encompassing design that applies to all (or most of) the slides (see Chapter 2 of this minibook).

>> **Inserting tables, charts, diagrams, and shapes:** A PowerPoint presentation should be more than a loose collection of bulleted lists. Starting on the Insert tab, you can place tables, charts, and diagrams on slides, as well as adorn your slides with text boxes, WordArt images, and shapes (see Book 8, Chapter 4 for more about WordArt and other ways to embellish your slides).

>> **"Animating" your slides:** PowerPoint slides can play video and sound, as well as be "animated" (see Chapter 4 of this minibook). You can make the items on a slide move on the screen. As a slide arrives, you can make it spin or flash.

>> **Delivering your presentation:** During a presentation, you can draw on the slides. You can also blank the screen and show slides out of order. In case you can't be there in person, PowerPoint gives you the opportunity to create self-running presentations and presentations that others can run on their own. You can also distribute presentations as videos (see Chapter 5 of this minibook).

Creating a New Presentation

All PowerPoint presentations are created using a template, A *template* is a blue-print for creating slides. Each template comes with its own particular slide layouts, colors, and fonts. When you create a presentation, you are invited to choose the template best suited for your audience. Figure 1-3 shows examples of templates.

FIGURE 1-3: Examples of PowerPoint templates.

PowerPoint offers these templates for creating presentations:

» **The Blank Presentation template:** A bare-bones template that you can use as the starting point for designing a presentation on your own.

» **Office templates:** Sophisticated templates designed by Microsoft artists. Figure 1-4 shows some of these templates in the New window, the window where you create presentations.

» **Personal templates:** Templates that you or someone apart from Microsoft designed and created. Many companies provide templates with their company colors and fonts for employees to use when creating PowerPoint presentations.

Blank Presentation template

Enter a search term to find an online template

Choose a template

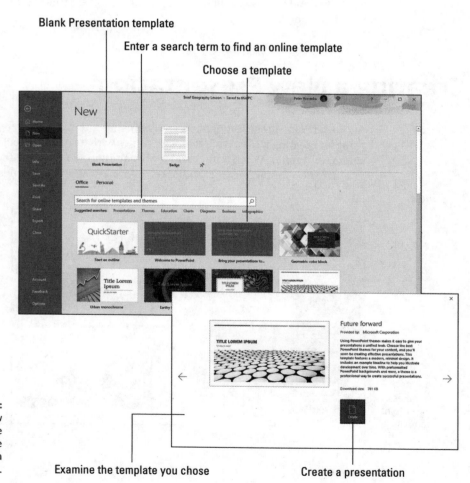

FIGURE 1-4:
In the New window, choose a template for creating a presentation.

Examine the template you chose

Create a presentation

WARNING

Office templates are a mixed blessing. They're designed by artists and they look very good. Some templates come with *boilerplate text* — already written material that you can recycle into your presentation. However, presentations made from templates are harder to modify. Sometimes the design gets in the way. As well, a loud or intricate background may overwhelm a diagram or chart you want to put on a slide.

Follow these steps to create a PowerPoint presentation:

1. Click the File tab.

2. Choose New.

The New window opens (refer to Figure 1-4).

3. Choose a template.

Choose the template that is best suited for the audience who will see your presentation.

- **Blank Presentation:** Click the Blank Presentation icon. A new presentation is created. (By pressing Ctrl+N, you can create a new, blank presentation without even opening the New window.)

- **Office template:** Select an Office template in the New window. A preview window opens so that you can examine the slide layouts and themes that the template offers (refer to Figure 1-4). You can search for a template by entering a search term in the Search box. Click the Close button to return to the New window; click the Create button to create a presentation with the template you selected.

- **Personal template:** Click the Personal tab to go to the folder where your personal templates are stored. Then select a template and click the Create button. The Personal tab appears in the New window only if you've created templates or copied them to your computer.

WARNING

Where personal templates are stored on your computer depends on whether you upgraded from an earlier version of Office. To tell PowerPoint where your personal templates are stored, click the File tab and choose Options. In the PowerPoint Options dialog box, go to the Save category, and in the Default Personal Templates Location text box, enter the path to the folder where you keep personal templates. Your personal templates are likely stored in one of these folders:

```
C:\Users\Your Name\AppData\Roaming\Microsoft\PowerPoint
```

```
C:\Users\Your Name\Documents\Custom Office Templates
```

Advice for Building Persuasive Presentations

TIP

Before you create any slides, think about what you want to communicate to your audience. Your goal isn't to dazzle the audience with your PowerPoint skills, but communicate something — a company policy, the merits of a product, the virtues of a strategic plan. Your goal is to bring the audience around to your side. To that end, here is some practical advice for building persuasive presentations:

» **Start by writing the text in Word.** Start in Microsoft Word, not PowerPoint, so that you can focus on the words. In Word, you can clearly see how a presentation develops. You can make sure that your presentation builds to its rightful conclusion. PowerPoint has a special command for getting headings from a Word file. (See "Conjuring slides from Word document headings," later in this chapter.)

» **When choosing a design, consider the audience.** A presentation to the American Casketmakers Association calls for a mute, quiet design; a presentation to the Cheerleaders of Tomorrow calls for something bright and splashy. Select a slide design that sets the tone for your presentation and wins the sympathy of the audience.

» **Keep it simple.** To make sure that PowerPoint doesn't upstage you, keep it simple. Make use of the PowerPoint features, but do so judiciously. An animation in the right place at the right time can serve a valuable purpose. It can highlight an important part of a presentation and grab the audience's attention. But stuffing a presentation with too many gizmos turns a presentation into a carnival sideshow and distracts from your message.

» **Follow the one-slide-per-minute rule.** At the very minimum, a slide should stay onscreen for at least one minute. If you have 15 minutes to speak, you're allotted no more than 15 slides for your presentation, according to the rule.

» **Beware the bullet point.** Terse bullet points have their place in a presentation, but if you put them there strictly to remind yourself what to say next, you're doing your audience a disfavor. Bullet points can cause drowsiness. They can be a distraction. The audience skims the bullets when it should be attending to your voice and the argument you're making. When you're tempted to use a bulleted list, consider using a table, chart, or diagram instead. Figure 1-5 demonstrates how a bulleted list can be presented instead in a table, chart, or diagram.

>> **Take control from the start.** Spend the first minute introducing yourself to the audience without running PowerPoint (or, if you do run PowerPoint, put a simple slide with your company name or logo onscreen). Make eye contact with the audience. This way, you establish your credibility. You give the audience a chance to get to know you.

>> **Make clear what you're about.** In the early going, state very clearly what your presentation is about and what you intend to prove with your presentation. In other words, state the conclusion at the beginning as well as the end. This way, your audience knows exactly what you're driving at and can judge your presentation according to how well you build your case.

>> **Personalize the presentation.** Make the presentation a personal one. Tell the audience what *your* personal reason for being there is or why *you* work for the company you work for. Knowing that you have a personal stake in the presentation, the audience is more likely to trust you. The audience understands that you're not a spokesperson, but a *speaker* — someone who has come before them to make a case for something that you believe in.

>> **Tell a story.** Include an anecdote in the presentation. Everybody loves a pertinent and well-delivered story. This piece of advice is akin to the previous one about personalizing your presentation. Typically, a story illustrates a problem for *people* and how *people* solve the problem. Even if your presentation concerns technology or an abstract subject, make it about people. "The people in Shaker Heights needed faster Internet access," not "the data switches in Shaker Heights just weren't performing fast enough."

>> **Rehearse and then rehearse some more.** The better you know your material, the less nervous you will be. To keep from getting nervous, rehearse your presentation until you know it backward and forward. Rehearse it out loud. Rehearse it while imagining you're in the presence of an audience.

>> **Use visuals, not only words, to make your point.** You really owe it to your audience to take advantage of the table, chart, diagram, and picture capabilities of PowerPoint. People understand more from words and pictures than they do from words alone. It's up to you — not the slides — as the speaker to describe topics in detail with words.

Want to see how PowerPoint can suck the life and drama out of a dramatic presentation? Try visiting the Gettysburg PowerPoint Presentation, a rendering of Lincoln's Gettysburg Address in PowerPoint. Yikes! You can find it here: http://vimeo.com/7849863.

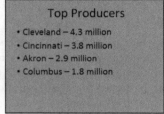

FIGURE 1-5:
List information presented in a table (top), chart (middle), and diagram (bottom).

Creating New Slides for Your Presentation

After you create a presentation, your next step on the path to glory is to start adding the slides. To create a new slide, you start by choosing a slide layout. *Slide layouts* are the preformatted slide designs that help you enter text, graphics, and other things. Some slide layouts have *text placeholder frames* for entering titles and text; some come with *content placeholder frames* designed especially for inserting a table, chart, diagram, picture, image, or media clip.

When you add a slide, select the slide layout that best approximates the slide you have in mind for your presentation. Figure 1-6 shows the slide layouts that are available when you create a presentation with the Blank Presentation template. These pages explain how to insert slides and harvest them from Word document headings.

FIGURE 1-6:
Slides available
in the Blank
Presentation
template.

Inserting a new slide

Follow these steps to insert a new slide in your presentation:

1. **Select the slide that you want the new slide to go after.**

In Normal view, select the slide on the Slides pane. In Slide Sorter view, select the slide in the main window.

2. **On the Home or Insert tab, click the bottom half of the New Slide button.**

You see a drop-down list of slide layouts. (If you click the top half of the New Slide button, you insert a slide with the same layout as the one you selected in Step 1.)

3. **Select the slide layout that best approximates the slide you want to create.**

Don't worry too much about selecting the right layout. You can change slide layouts later on, as "Selecting a different layout for a slide" explains later in this chapter.

Speed techniques for inserting slides

TIP

When you're in a hurry, use these techniques to insert a slide:

>> **Creating a duplicate slide:** Select the slide or slides you want to duplicate, and on the Home or Insert tab, open the drop-down list on the New Slide button and choose Duplicate Selected Slides. You can also open the drop-down list on the Copy button and choose Duplicate.

>> **Copying and pasting slides:** Click the slide you want to copy (or Ctrl+click to select more than one slide) and then click the Copy button on the Home tab (or press Ctrl+C). Next, click to select the slide that you want the copied slide (or slides) to appear after and click the Paste button (or press Ctrl+V).

>> **Recycling slides from other presentations:** Select the slide that you want the recycled slides to follow in your presentation, and on the Home or Insert tab, open the drop-down list on the New Slide button and choose Reuse Slides. The Reuse Slides task pane opens. Click the Browse button, select a presentation in the Browse dialog box, and click Open. The Reuse Slides task pane shows thumbnail versions of slides in the presentation you selected. One at a time, click slides to add them to your presentation. You can right-click a slide and choose Insert All Slides to grab all the slides in the presentation.

Conjuring slides from Word document headings

If you think about it, Word headings are similar to slide titles. Headings, like slide titles, introduce a new topic. If you know your way around Word and you want to get a head start creating a PowerPoint presentation, you can borrow the headings in a Word document for your PowerPoint slides.

After you import the headings from Word, you get one slide for each Level 1 heading (headings given the Heading 1 style). Level 1 headings form the title of the slides, Level 2 headings form first-level bullets, Level 3 headings form second-level bullets, and so on. Paragraph text isn't imported. Figure 1-7 shows what headings from a Word document look like after they land in a PowerPoint presentation.

Follow these steps to use headings in a Word document to create slides in a PowerPoint presentation:

1. **On the View tab, click the Outline View button.**

The Outline tab displays slide text (see Figure 1-7). You get a better sense of how headings from the Word document land in your presentation by viewing your presentation from the Outline tab.

Each level-1 heading in the Word document becomes a slide title in PowerPoint

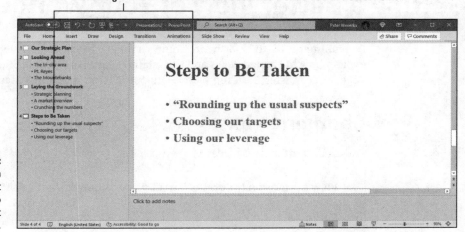

FIGURE 1-7:
Headings from a
Word document
imported into
a PowerPoint
presentation.

2. **Select the slide that the new slides from the Word document will follow.**

3. **On the Home or Insert tab, open the drop-down list on the New Slide button and choose Slides from Outline.**

You see the Insert Outline dialog box.

4. **Select the Word document with the headings you want for your presentation and click the Insert button.**

Depending on how many first-level headings are in the Word document, you get a certain number of new slides. These slides probably need work. The Word text may need tweaking to make it suitable for a PowerPoint presentation.

Selecting a different layout for a slide

If you mistakenly choose the wrong layout for a slide, all is not lost. You can start all over. You can graft a new layout onto your slide with one of these techniques:

» On the Home tab, click the Layout button and choose a layout on the drop-down list.

» Right-click the slide (being careful not to right-click a frame or object), choose Layout, and choose a layout on the submenu.

TIP

PowerPoint also offers the Reset command for giving a slide its original layout after you've fiddled with it. If you push a slide all out of shape and you regret doing so, select your slide, go to the Home tab, and click the Reset button.

Getting a Better View of Your Work

Depending on the task at hand, some views are better than others. These pages explain how to change views and the relative merits of Normal, Slide Sorter, Notes Page, Slide Master, Reading View, Handout Master, and Notes Master view.

Changing views

PowerPoint offers two places to change views:

>> **View buttons on the status bar:** Click a View button — Normal, Slide Sorter, Reading View, or Slide Show — on the status bar to change views, as shown in Figure 1-8.

>> **View tab:** On the View tab, click a button in the Presentation Views or Master Views group, as shown in Figure 1-8.

Click a View button on the View tab…

FIGURE 1-8: Techniques for changing views.

or click a View button on the status bar

Looking at the different views

Here is a survey of the different views with suggestions about using each one:

- » **Normal view for examining slides:** Switch to Normal view and select a slide in the Slides pane when you want to examine a slide. In this view, thumbnail slides appear in the Slides pane, and you can see your slide in all its glory in the middle of the screen.

- » **Outline view for fiddling with text:** Switch to Outline view when you want to enter or read text (refer to Figure 1-7). The words appear in outline form on the left side of the screen. Outline view is ideal for editing the text in a presentation.

- » **Slide Sorter view for moving and deleting slides:** In Slide Sorter view, you see thumbnails of all the slides in the presentation (use the Zoom slider to change the size of thumbnails). From here, moving slides around is easy, and seeing many slides simultaneously gives you a sense of whether the different slides are consistent with one another and how the whole presentation is shaping up. The slides are numbered so that you can see where they appear in a presentation.

- » **Notes Page view for reading your speaker notes:** In Notes Page view, you see notes you've written to aid you in your presentation, if you've written any. You can write notes in this view as well as in the Notes pane in Normal view. Chapter 5 of this minibook explains Notes pages.

- » **Reading View view for focusing on slides' appearance:** In Reading View view, you also see a single slide, but it appears onscreen with the View buttons and with buttons for moving quickly from slide to slide. Switch to Reading View view to proofread slides and put the final touches on a presentation.

- » **The Master views for a consistent presentation:** The Master views — Slide Master, Handout Master, and Notes Master — are for handling *master styles,* the formatting commands that pertain to all the slides in a presentation, handouts, and notes. To switch to these views, go to the View tab and click the appropriate button. Chapter 2 of this minibook looks into master slides and master styles.

TIP

PowerPoint offers a button called Fit Slide to Current Window that you can click to make the slide fill the window. This little button is located in the lower-right corner of the screen, to the right of the Zoom controls.

Hiding and Displaying the Slides Pane and Notes Pane

In Normal view, the Slides pane with its slide thumbnails appears on the left side of the screen, and the Notes pane appears on the bottom of the screen so that you can scribble notes about slides. Sometimes these panes just take up valuable space. They clutter the screen and occupy real estate that could be better used for formatting slides. Follow these instructions to temporarily close the Slides and Notes panes:

>> **Hiding and displaying the Notes pane:** Click the Notes button on the status bar or View tab. To change the size of the Notes pane, move the pointer over the border between the pane and the rest of the screen, and after the pointer changes to a two-headed arrow, drag the border.

>> **Hiding and displaying the Slides pane:** To hide the Slides pane, move the pointer over the border between the pane and the middle of the screen, and when the pointer changes to a two-headed arrow, drag the border to the left. To display the Slides pane, click the Thumbnails button (located at the top of the Slides pane).

REMEMBER

You can change the size of either pane by moving the pointer over its border and then clicking and dragging.

Selecting, Moving, and Deleting Slides

As a presentation takes shape, you have to move slides forward and backward. Sometimes you have to delete a slide. And you can't move or delete slides until you select them first. Herewith are instructions for selecting, moving, and deleting slides.

Selecting slides

The best place to select slides is Slide Sorter view (if you want to select several at a time). Use one of these techniques to select slides:

>> **Select one slide:** Click the slide.

>> **Select several different slides:** Hold down the Ctrl key and click each slide in the Slides pane or in Slide Sorter view.

>> **Select several slides in succession:** Hold down the Shift key and click the first slide and then the last one.

>> **Select a block of slides:** In Slide Sorter view, drag across the slides you want to select. Be sure when you click and start dragging that you don't click a slide.

>> **Selecting all the slides:** On the Home tab, click the Select button and choose Select All on the drop-down list (or press Ctrl+A).

Moving slides

To move or rearrange slides, you're advised to go to Slide Sorter view. Select the slide or slides that you want to move and use one of these techniques to move slides:

>> **Dragging and dropping:** Click the slides you selected and drag them to a new location.

>> **Cutting and pasting:** On the Home tab, cut the slide or slides to the Windows Clipboard (click the Cut button, press Ctrl+X, or right-click and choose Cut). Then select the slide that you want the slide or slides to appear after and give the Paste command (click the Paste button, press Ctrl+V, or right-click and choose Paste). You can right-click between slides to paste with precision.

Deleting slides

Before you delete a slide, think twice about deleting. Short of using the Undo command, you can't resuscitate a deleted slide. Select the slide or slides you want to delete and use one of these techniques to delete slides:

>> Press the Delete key.

>> Right-click and choose Delete Slide on the shortcut menu.

Putting Together a Photo Album

Photo album is just PowerPoint's term for inserting many photographs into a presentation all at one time. You don't necessarily have to stuff the photo album with travel or baby pictures for it to be a proper photo album. The Photo Album is a wonderful feature because you can use it to dump a bunch of photos in a

PowerPoint presentation without having to create slides one at a time, insert the photos, and endure the rest of the rigmarole. Create a photo album to quickly place a bunch of photos on PowerPoint slides.

Creating your photo album

PowerPoint creates a new presentation for you when you create a photo album. To start, take note of where on your computer the photos you want for the album are. Then go to the Insert tab and click the Photo Album button. You see the Photo Album dialog box, as shown in Figure 1-9. For such a little thing, the Photo Album dialog box offers many opportunities for constructing a PowerPoint presentation. Your first task is to decide which pictures you want for your album. Then you choose a slide layout for the pictures.

Choose a layout

Insert photos   Change the order of slides

FIGURE 1-9:
Create a photo album in this dialog box.

Inserting pictures and creating slides

Here is the lowdown on choosing pictures for a photo album:

>> **Inserting photos:** Click the File/Disk button, select photos in the Insert New Pictures dialog box, and click the Insert button. You can select more than one photo at a time by Ctrl+clicking. The filenames of photos you selected appear in the Pictures in Album box. Slide numbers appear as well so that you know which photos are on which slides.

>> **Deciding how photos are framed:** Open the Frame Shape drop-down list and choose an option for placing borders or rounded corners on your photos. (This option isn't available if you choose Fit to Slide on the Picture Layout drop-down list.)

>> **Inserting a text box:** Insert a text box if you want to enter commentary in your photo album. In the Pictures in Album box, select the picture or text box that you want your new text box to go after; then click the New Text Box button. Later, you can go into your presentation and edit the placeholder text, which PowerPoint aptly enters as *Text Box*.

>> **Providing captions for all pictures:** To place a caption below all the pictures in your photo album, select the Captions Below ALL Pictures check box. PowerPoint initially places the picture filename in the caption, but you can delete this caption and enter one of your own. (To select this option, you must choose a picture layout option besides Fit to Slide.)

>> **Changing the order of pictures:** Select a picture in the Pictures in Album box and then click an arrow button to move it forward or backward in the presentation.

>> **Changing the order of slides:** Ctrl+click to select each picture on a slide. Then click an arrow as many times as necessary to move the slide forward or backward in the presentation.

>> **Removing a picture:** Select a picture in the Pictures in Album box and click the Remove button to remove it from your photo album. You can Ctrl+click pictures to select more than one.

Choosing a layout for slides

Your next task is to go to the bottom of the Photo Album dialog box (refer to Figure 1-9) and choose a layout for the slides in the presentation. Open the Picture Layout drop-down list to choose one of the seven picture layouts:

>> Choose Fit to Slide for a presentation in which each picture occupies an entire slide.

>> Choose a "pictures" option to fit 1, 2, or 4 pictures on each slide.

>> Choose a "pictures with" option to fit 1, 2, or 4 pictures as well as a text title frame on each slide.

Changing the look of pictures

The Photo Album dialog box (refer to Figure 1-9) offers a handful of tools for changing the look of the pictures. When you use these tools, keep your eye on the Preview box — it shows you what you're doing to your picture.

>> **Making all photos black and white:** Select the ALL Pictures Black and White check box.

>> **Rotating pictures:** Click a Rotate button to rotate a picture clockwise or counterclockwise.

>> **Changing the contrast:** Click a Contrast button as many times as necessary to sharpen or mute the light and dark colors or shades in the picture.

>> **Changing the brightness:** Click a Brightness button as many times as necessary to make a picture brighter or more somber.

>> **Choosing a frame shape for pictures:** If you opted for a "picture" or "picture with" slide layout, you can choose a shape — Soft Edge Rectangle, Compound Frame, or others — for your pictures on the Frame Shape drop-down list.

>> **Choosing a theme for your photo album:** If you selected a "picture" or "picture with" slide layout, you can choose a theme for your slide presentation. Click the Browse button and choose a theme in the Choose Theme dialog box.

At last, click the Create button when you're ready to create the photo album. PowerPoint attaches a title slide to the start of the album that says *Photo Album* with your name below.

Putting on the final touches

Depending on the options you chose for your photo album, it needs all or some of these final touches:

>> **Fix the title slide:** Your title slide should probably say more than the words *Photo Album* and your name.

>> **Fill in the text boxes:** If you asked for text boxes with your photo album, by all means, replace PowerPoint's generic text with meaningful words of your own.

>> **Write the captions:** If you asked for photo captions, PowerPoint entered photo filenames below photos. Replace these filenames with something more descriptive.

Editing a photo album

To go back into the Photo Album dialog box and rearrange the photos in your album, go to the Insert tab, open the drop-down list on the Photo Album button, and choose Edit Photo Album on the drop-down list. You see the Edit Photo Album dialog box. It looks and works exactly like the Photo Album dialog box (refer to Figure 1-9). Of course, you can also edit your photo album by treating it like any other PowerPoint presentation. Change the theme, fiddle with the slides, and do what you will to torture your photo album into shape.

Hidden Slides for All Contingencies

Hide a slide when you want to keep it on hand "just in case" during a presentation. Hidden slides don't appear in slide shows unless you shout *Ollie ollie oxen free!* and bring them out of hiding. Although you, the presenter, can see hidden slides in Normal view and Slide Sorter view, where their slide numbers are crossed through, the audience doesn't see them in the course of a presentation unless you decide to show them. Create hidden slides if you anticipate having to steer your presentation in a different direction — to answer a question from the audience, prove your point more thoroughly, or revisit a topic in more depth. Merely by right-clicking and choosing a couple of commands, you can display a hidden slide in the course of a slide show.

Hiding a slide

TIP

The best place to put hidden slides is at the end of a presentation, where you know you can find them. Follow these steps to hide slides:

1. **Select the slide or slides that you want to hide.**

2. **On the Slide Show tab, click the Hide Slide button.**

   You can also right-click a slide in the Slides pane or Slide Sorter view and choose Hide Slide. Hidden slides' numbers are crossed through in the Slides pane and the Slide Sorter window.

To unhide a slide, click the Hide Slide button again or right-click the slide and choose Hide Slide.

Showing a hidden slide during a presentation

Hidden slides don't appear during the course of a presentation, but suppose that the need arises to show one. Before showing a hidden slide, take careful note of which slide you're viewing now. You have to return to this slide after viewing the hidden slide. (Chapter 5 of this minibook describes the ins and outs of giving slide presentations.)

Follow these steps to view a hidden slide during a presentation:

1. **Click the Slides button (located in the lower-left corner of the screen).**

   You see a screen with thumbnail versions of the slides in your presentation. You can also open this screen by right-clicking and choosing See All Slides.

2. **Select a hidden slide so that the audience can view it.**

   You can tell which slides are hidden because their slide numbers are enclosed in parentheses.

How do you resume your presentation after viewing a hidden slide? If you look at only one hidden slide, you can right-click and choose Last Viewed on the shortcut menu to return to the slide you saw before the hidden slide. If you've viewed several hidden slides, right-click the screen, choose See All Slides, and select a slide to pick up where you left off.

Chapter **2**

Fashioning a Look for Your Presentation

From the audience's point of view, this chapter is the most important in this minibook. What your presentation looks like — which theme and background style you select for the slides in your presentation — sets the tone. From the very first slide, the audience judges your presentation on its appearance. When you create a look for your presentation, what you're really doing is declaring what you want to communicate to your audience.

This chapter explains how to handle slide backgrounds. It examines what you need to consider when you select colors and designs for backgrounds. You also discover how to select and customize a theme, and how to create your own slide backgrounds. This chapter looks into how to change the background of some but not all of the slides in a presentation. It also explains how to use master slides and master styles to make sure that slides throughout your presentation are consistent with one another.

Looking at Themes and Slide Backgrounds

What a presentation looks like is mostly a matter of the theme you choose and the slide backgrounds you make for the slides in your presentation. A *theme* is a "canned" slide design. Themes are designed by graphic artists. Most themes include sophisticated background patterns and colors. As well, you can create a background of your own from a single color, a gradient mixture of two colors, or a picture.

Figure 2-1 shows examples of themes. When you installed PowerPoint on your computer, you also installed a dozen or more themes, and you can acquire more themes online from Office.com and other places. After you select a theme, you can select a theme variant — a slight variation on the theme you selected.

FIGURE 2-1:
Examples of themes.

Figure 2-2 shows examples of backgrounds you can create yourself. Self-made backgrounds are not as intrusive as themes. The risk of the background overwhelming the lists, tables, charts, and other items in the forefront of slides is less when you fashion a background style yourself. You can apply a background that you create to a single slide or all the slides in your presentation.

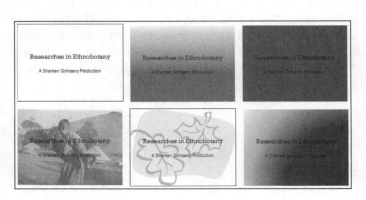

FIGURE 2-2:
Examples of background styles (clockwise from upper left): plain style, gradient, solid color, customized radial gradient, picture, and photo.

To choose a theme or create slide backgrounds, start on the Design tab, as shown in Figure 2-3. The Design tab offers themes, theme variants, and the Format Background pane, the place to go when you want to fashion a fashionable background for slides.

Choose fill effects and picture settings

Click to open the Format Background pane

Choose a theme   Choose a variant on a theme

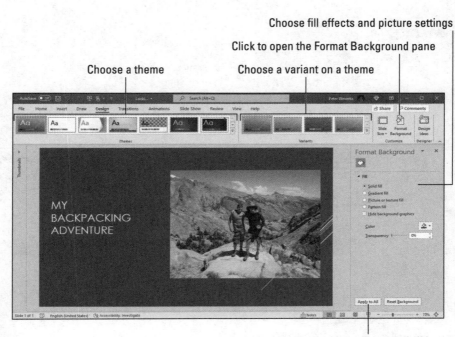

Apply the settings to all slides

FIGURE 2-3:
Decide what your presentation looks like on the Design tab.

TIP

More than any other design decision, what sets the tone for a presentation are the colors you select for slide backgrounds. If the purpose of your presentation is to show photographs you took on a vacation to Arizona's Painted Desert, select light-tone, hot colors for the slide backgrounds. If your presentation is an aggressive sales pitch, consider a black background. There is no universal color theory for selecting the right colors in a design because everyone is different. Follow your intuition. It will guide you to the right background color choices.

GETTING DESIGN IDEAS FROM POWERPOINT

PowerPoint may be able to help you with design ideas for a slide in your presentation. To take your cue from PowerPoint and change the look of a slide:

1. Select the slide.

2. On the Home tab or Design tab, click the Design Ideas button.

   If PowerPoint can be of assistance, slide designs appear in the Design Ideas tab, as shown on the right side of the figure.

3. Select a design to apply it to the slide you selected.

   If the design doesn't appeal to you after all, click the Undo button (or press Ctrl+Z).

PowerPoint suggests designs that are appropriate based on your history with designing slides in presentations. The designs are available only if you trust Microsoft to examine your presentations and the content of all your Office files. For more information about this topic, see Book 1, Chapter 1.

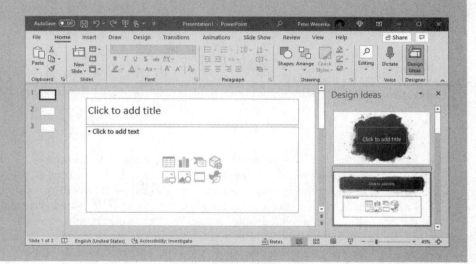

Choosing a Theme for Your Presentation

PowerPoint offers many different themes in the Themes gallery, and if you happen to have PowerPoint presentations at hand, you can borrow a theme from another presentation. Experimenting with themes is easy. You are hereby encouraged to test different themes until you find the right one.

Starting on the Design tab, use one of these techniques to select a new theme for your presentation:

>> **Selecting a theme in the Themes gallery:** Open the Themes gallery and move the pointer over different themes to "live-preview" them. Click a theme to select it.

>> **Borrowing a theme from another presentation:** On the Design tab, open the Themes gallery and click Browse for Themes. You see the Choose Theme or Themed Document dialog box. Locate and select a presentation with a theme you can commandeer for your presentation and then click the Apply button.

To refine your theme, choose an option in the Variants gallery on the Design tab (refer to Figure 2-3).

Creating Slide Backgrounds on Your Own

Besides a theme, your other option for creating slide backgrounds is to do it on your own. For a background, you can have a solid color, a transparent color, a gradient blend of colors, a picture, or an image.

>> **Solid color:** A single, uniform color. You can adjust a color's transparency and in effect "bleach out" the color to push it farther into the background.

>> **Gradient:** A mixture of different colors with the colors blending into one another.

>> **Picture:** A picture you get from the Internet or store on your computer.

>> **Pattern:** A pattern such as stripes or diamonds.

>> **Texture:** A uniform pattern that gives the impression that the slide is displayed on a material such as cloth or stone.

How to create these kinds of slide backgrounds on your own is the subject of the next several pages.

Using a solid (or transparent) color for the slide background

Using a solid or transparent color for the background gives your slides a straightforward, honest look. Because all the slides are the same color or transparent color, the audience can focus better on the presentation itself rather than the razzle-dazzle. Follow these steps to use a solid or transparent color as the background for slides:

1. **On the Design tab, click the Format Background button.**

   The Format Background pane opens.

2. **Click the Solid Fill option button.**

3. **Click the Color button and choose a color on the drop-down list.**

   The muted theme colors are recommended because they look better in the background, but you can select a standard color or click the More Colors button to select a color in the Colors dialog box. In the Colors dialog box, either choose a color on the Standard tab or enter a color's RGB setting on the Custom tab.

4. **Drag the Transparency slider if you want a "bleached out" color rather than a slide color.**

   At 0% transparency, you get a solid color; at 100%, you get no color at all.

5. **Click the Apply to All button and then the Close button (the X) to close the Format Background pane.**

   I sincerely hope you like your choice of colors, but if you don't, try, try, try again.

Creating a gradient color blend for slide backgrounds

Gradient refers to how and where two or more colors grade, or blend, into one another on a slide. As well as the standard linear gradient direction, you can opt for a radial, rectangular, or path gradient direction. Figure 2-4 shows examples of gradient fill backgrounds. These backgrounds look terribly elegant. Using a gradient is an excellent way to create an original background that looks different from all the other presenter's slide backgrounds.

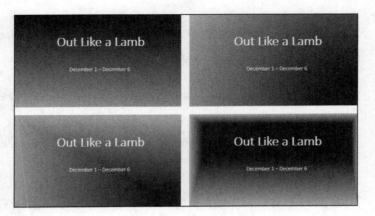

Follow these steps to create a gradient background for slides:

1. **On the Design tab, click the Format Background button to open the Format Background pane.**

2. **Click the Gradient Fill option button.**

TIP

Before you experiment with gradients, try opening the Preset Gradients drop-down list to see whether one of the ready-made gradient options does the job for you.

3. **On the Type drop-down list, choose what type of gradient you want — Linear, Radial, Rectangular, Path, or Shade from Title (see Figure 2-4).**

If you choose Linear, you can enter a degree measurement in the Angle box to change the angle at which the colors blend. At 90 degrees, for example, colors blend horizontally across the slide; at 180 degrees, they blend vertically.

4. **Create a gradient stop for each color transition you want on your slides.**

Gradient stops determine where colors are, how colors transition from one to the next, and which colors are used. You can create as many gradient stops as you want. Here are techniques for handling gradient stops:

- **Adding a gradient stop:** Click the Add Gradient Stop button. A new gradient stop appears on the slider. Drag it to where you want the color blend to occur.

- **Removing a gradient stop:** Select a gradient stop on the slider and click the Remove Gradient Stop button.

- **Choosing a color for a gradient stop:** Select a gradient stop on the slider, click the Color button, and choose a color on the drop-down list.

- **Positioning a gradient stop:** Drag a gradient stop on the slider or use the Position box to move it to a different location.

5. **Drag the Brightness slider to make the colors dimmer or brighter.**

6. **Drag the Transparency slider to make the colors on the slides more or less transparent.**

   At 0% transparency, you get solid colors; at 100%, you get no color at all.

7. **Click the Apply to All button.**

   Very likely, you have to experiment with stop colors and stop positions until you blend the colors to your satisfaction. Good luck.

Placing a picture in the slide background

As long as they're on the pale side or you've made them semitransparent, pictures from Office.com or the Internet do fine for slide backgrounds. They look especially good in title slides. Figure 2-5 shows examples of pictures as backgrounds. As Book 8, Chapter 3 explains, Office.com offers numerous photos and pictures. You're invited to place one in the background of your slides by following these steps:

1. **On the Design tab, click the Format Background button to open the Format Background pane.**

2. **Click the Picture or Texture Fill option button.**

3. **Click the Insert button.**

   You see the Insert Pictures dialog box.

4. **Search for and select a picture that you can use in the background of your slides.**

   Book 8, Chapter 3 explains the ins and outs of trolling for pictures.

5. **In the Format Background pane, enter a Transparency measurement.**

   Drag the Transparency slider or enter a measurement in the box. The higher the measurement, the more transparent the image is (see Figure 2-5).

6. **Enter measurements in the Offsets boxes to make your picture fill the slide.**

7. **Click the Apply to All button and then click the Close button in the Format Background pane.**

   There you have it. The picture you selected lands in the slides' backgrounds.

FIGURE 2-5:
For backgrounds,
a picture usually
has to be at
least somewhat
transparent.
These slides
are (from left to
right) 0%, 40%,
65%, and 85%
transparent.

Using a photo of your own for a slide background

Figure 2-6 shows examples of photos being used as slide backgrounds. Besides getting a photo from the Internet, you can use one of your own photos.

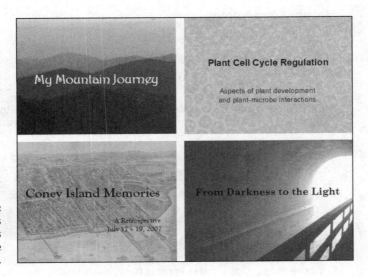

FIGURE 2-6:
Examples
of pictures
used as slide
backgrounds.

Select your photo carefully. A photo with too many colors — and that includes the majority of color photographs — obscures the text and makes it difficult to read. You can get around this problem by "recoloring" a photo to give it a uniform color tint; selecting a grayscale photograph; selecting a photo with colors of a similar hue; or making the photo semitransparent; but all in all, the best way to solve the problem of a photo that obscures the text is to start with a quiet, subdued photo. (Book 8, Chapter 3 explains all the ins and outs of using photos in Office 365.)

One more thing: Select a landscape-style photo that is wider than it is tall. Power-Point expands photos to make them fill the entire slide background. If you select a skinny, portrait-style photo, PowerPoint has to do a lot of expanding to make it fit on the slide, and you end up with a distorted background image.

Yet one more thing: Most photos that can be obtained on the Internet are copyrighted. If you plan to use a photo from the Internet, find out whether someone owns the copyright, and if the photo does have an owner, obtain permission to use the photo.

Follow these steps to use a picture as a slide background:

1. **On the Design tab, click the Format Background button to open the Format Background pane.**

2. **Click the Picture or Texture Fill option button.**

3. **Click the Insert button.**

   A pop-up box asks where to get the picture.

4. **Click the From a File button.**

   The Insert Picture dialog box appears.

5. **Locate the photo you want, select it, and click the Insert button.**

   The picture lands on your slide.

6. **Enter a Transparency measurement to make the photo fade a bit into the background.**

   Drag the slider or enter a measurement in the Transparency box. The higher percentage measurement you enter, the more "bleached out" the picture is.

7. **Using the Offsets text boxes, enter measurements to make your picture fit on the slides.**

8. **Click the Picture icon in the Format Background pane.**

   This icon, one of three, is located at the top of the Format Background pane.

9. Experiment with the Picture Corrections and Picture Color options to make your picture more suitable for a background.

10. Click the Apply to All button.

How do you like your slide background? You may have to open the Format Background pane again and play with the transparency setting. Only the very lucky and the permanently blessed get it right the first time.

Using a texture for a slide background

Yet another option for slide backgrounds is to use a texture. As shown in Figure 2-7, a *texture* gives the impression that the slide is displayed on a material such as marble or parchment. A texture can make for a very elegant slide background. Follow these steps to use a texture as a slide background:

1. On the Design tab, click the Format Background button to open the Format Background pane.

2. Click the Picture or Texture Fill option button.

3. Click the Texture button and choose a texture on the drop-down list.

4. Enter a Transparency measurement to make the texture less imposing.

Drag the slider or enter a measurement in the Transparency box.

5. Click the Apply to All button and then click Close.

FIGURE 2-7: Different textures (clockwise from upper left): Papyrus, Canvas, Newsprint, and Cork.

Changing the Background of a Single or Handful of Slides

To make a single slide (or a handful of slides) stand out in a presentation, change their background or theme. A different background tells your audience that the slide being presented is a little different from the one before it. Maybe it imparts important information. Maybe it introduces another segment of the presentation. Use a different background or theme to mark a transition, indicate that your presentation has shifted gears, or mark a milestone in your presentation.

Follow these steps to change the background of one or several slides in your presentation:

1. **In Slide Sorter view, select the slide or slides that need a different look.**

   You can select more than one slide by Ctrl+clicking slides.

2. **On the Design tab, choose a different theme or background for the slides you selected.**

   How you do this depends on whether you're working with a theme or a slide background:

   - **Theme:** In the Themes gallery, right-click a theme and choose Apply To Selected Slides.

   - **Slide background:** Make like you're creating a background style for all the slides (see "Creating Slide Backgrounds on Your Own," earlier in this chapter) but don't click the Apply to All button.

REMEMBER

When you assign a different theme to some of the slides in a presentation, PowerPoint creates another Slide Master. You may be surprised to discover that when you add a new slide to your presentation, a second, third, or fourth set of slide layouts appears on the New Slide drop-down list. These extra layouts appear because your presentation has more than one Slide Master. Later in this chapter, "Using Master Slides and Master Styles for a Consistent Design" explains what Slide Masters are.

Choosing the Slide Size

By default, slides in PowerPoint presentations are 16:9 ratio widescreen slides. In versions of PowerPoint prior to 2013, slides were 4:3 ratio standard size. The widescreen slide size is meant to accommodate modern letterbox computer screens, which are wider than they were in the past.

To change the size of the slides in a presentation, go to the Design tab and click the Slide Size button. Then, on the drop-down list, choose Standard (4:3), choose Widescreen (16:9), or choose Custom Slide Size and choose a different size in the Slide Size dialog box.

REMEMBER

All slides in a presentation must be the same size. Sorry, you can't mix and match slides of different sizes.

Using Master Slides and Master Styles for a Consistent Design

Consistency is everything in a PowerPoint design. Consistency of design is a sign of professionalism and care. In a consistent design, the fonts and font sizes on slides are consistent from one slide to the next, the placeholder text frames are in the same positions, and the text is aligned the same way across different slides. In the bulleted lists, each entry is marked with the same bullet character. If the corner of each slide shows a company logo, the logo appears in the same position.

It would be torture to have to examine every slide to make sure it is consistent with the others. In the interest of consistency, PowerPoint offers master styles and master slides. A *master slide* is a model slide from which the slides in a presentation inherit their formats. A *master style* is a format that applies to many different slides. Starting from a master slide, you can change a master style and in so doing, reformat many slides the same way. These pages explain how master slides can help you quickly redesign a presentation.

Switching to Slide Master view

To work with master slides, switch to *Slide Master view,* as shown in Figure 2-8. From this view, you can start working with master slides:

1. Go to the View tab.

2. Click the Slide Master button.

In Slide Master view, you can select a master slide in the Slides pane, format styles on a master slide, and in this way reformat many different slides. (Click the Close Master View button or a view button such as Normal or Slide Sorter to leave Slide Master view.)

Select the Slide Master...

or a layout   Change a master style

FIGURE 2-8:
In Slide Master
view, you can
reformat many
different slides
simultaneously.

Understanding master slides and master styles

Master slides are special, high-powered slides. Use master slides to deliver the same formatting commands to many different slides. Whether the commands affect all the slides in your presentation or merely a handful of slides depends on whether you format the Slide Master (the topmost slide in Slide Master view) or a layout (one of the other slides):

>> **The Slide Master:** The *Slide Master* is the first slide in the Slides pane in Slide Master view (refer to Figure 2-8). It's a little bigger than the master slides, as befits its status as Emperor of All Slides. Formatting changes you make to the Slide Master affect all the slides in your presentation. When you select a theme for your presentation, what you're really doing is assigning a theme to the Slide Master. Because formatting commands given to the Slide Master apply throughout a presentation, the theme design and colors are applied to all slides. If you want a company logo to appear on all your slides, place the logo on the Slide Master.

>> **Layouts:** As you know, you choose a slide layout — Title and Content, for example — on the New Slide drop-down list to create a new slide. In Slide Master view, PowerPoint provides one *layout* for each type of slide layout in your presentation. By selecting and reformatting a layout in Slide Master view, you can reformat all slides in your presentation that were created with the same slide layout. For example, to change fonts, alignments, and other

formats on all slides that you created with the Title layout, select the Title layout in Slide Master view and change master styles on the Title layout. Each layout controls its own little fiefdom in a PowerPoint presentation — a fiefdom comprised of slides created with the same slide layout.

>> **Master styles:** Each master slide — the Slide Master and each layout — offers you the opportunity to click to edit master styles (refer to Figure 2-8). The master style governs how text is formatted on slides. By changing a master style on a master slide, you can change the look of slides throughout a presentation. For example, by changing the Master Title Style font, you can change fonts in all the slide titles in your presentation.

PowerPoint's Slide Master–layouts–slides system is designed on the "trickle down" theory. When you format a master style on the Slide Master, formats trickle down to layouts and then to slides. When you format a master style on a layout, the formats trickle down to slides you created using the same slide layout. This chain-of-command relationship is designed to work from the top down, with the master slide and layouts barking orders to the slides below. In the interest of design consistency, slides take orders from layouts, and layouts take orders from the Slide Master.

REMEMBER

In Slide Master view, you can move the pointer over a layout thumbnail in the Slides pane to see a pop-up box that tells you the layout's name and which slides in your presentation "use" the layout. For example, a pop-up box that reads "Title and Content Layout: used by slide(s) 2–3, 8" tells you that slides 2 through 3 and 8 in your presentation are governed by the Title and Content layout.

Editing a master slide

Now that you know the relationship among the Slide Master, layouts, and slides, you're ready to start editing master slides. To edit a master slide, switch to Slide Master view, select a master slide, and change a master style. To insert a picture on a master slide, visit the Insert tab.

Changing a master slide layout

Changing the layout of a master slide entails changing the position and size of text frames and content frames as well as removing these frames:

>> **Changing size of frames:** Select the frame you want to change, and then move the pointer over a frame handle on the corner, side, top or bottom of the frame and drag when you see the double-headed arrow.

» **Moving frames:** Move the pointer over the perimeter of a frame, click when you see the four-headed arrow, and drag.

» **Removing a frame from the Slide Master:** Click the perimeter of the frame to select it and then press Delete.

» **Adding a frame to the Slide Master:** Select the slide master, and on the Slide Master tab, click the Master Layout button. You see the Master Layout dialog box. Select the check box beside the name of each frame you want to add and click OK.

Chapter **3**

Entering the Text

This chapter explains how to change the appearance of text, create text boxes, and create text box shapes. I solve the riddle of what to do when text doesn't fit in a text box or text placeholder frame. You also discover how to align text, handle bulleted and numbered lists, and put footers and headers on all or some of the slides in your presentation.

By the time you finish reading this chapter, if you read it all the way through, you will be one of those people others turn to when they have a PowerPoint question about entering text on slides. You'll become a little guru in your own right.

Entering Text

No presentation is complete without a word or two, which is why the first thing you see when you add a new slide to a presentation are the words "Click to add text." As soon as you "click," the words of instruction disappear, and you're free to enter a title or text of your own. Most slides include a text placeholder frame at the top for entering a slide title; many slides also have another, larger text place-holder frame for entering a bulleted list.

As shown in Figure 3-1, the easiest way to enter text on slides is to click in a text placeholder frame and start typing. The other way is to switch to Outline view and enter text in the Slides pane (see Figure 3-1).

On the Slides pane in Outline view   In a text placeholder frame

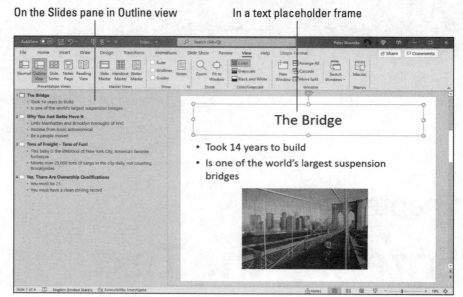

FIGURE 3-1:
Ways of
entering text.

Enter text on slides the same way you enter text in a Word document — by wiggling your fingers over the keyboard. While you're at it, you can change fonts, the font size of text, and the color of text, as the following pages explain. (Chapter 1 of this minibook describes how to get the text for slides from the headings in a Word document; Book 1, Chapter 2 explains everything a sane person needs to know about handling fonts.)

Choosing fonts for text

If you aren't happy with the fonts in your presentation, you have two ways to remedy the problem:

» **Dig in and choose new fonts on a slide-by-slide basis.** Select the text, go to the Home tab, and choose a font from the Font drop-down list or the Font dialog box. You can also change fonts in the mini-toolbar that appears when you select text.

» **Choose a new font on a master slide to change fonts throughout your presentation.** Chapter 2 of this minibook explains master slides and how you can use them to change formats simultaneously on many slides. In Slide Master view, select a master slide and change its fonts on the Home tab.

TIP

Embed the fonts in your presentation if you intend to share it with others and you want to preserve the fonts you chose. To embed fonts, go to the File tab and choose Options. On the Save tab of the Options dialog box, select Embed Fonts in File. As well, select Embed All Characters if others co-edit your file and you don't want them to override your font selections.

Changing the font size of text

For someone in the back row of an audience to be able to read text in a PowerPoint presentation, the text should be no smaller than 28 points. Try this simple test to see whether text in your presentation is large enough to read: Stand five or so feet from your computer and see whether you can read the text. If you can't read it, make it larger.

Go to the Home tab and select the text whose size you want to change. Then use one of these techniques to change font sizes:

>> **Font Size drop-down list:** Open this list and choose a point size. To choose a point size that isn't on the list, click in the Font Size text box, enter a point size, and press Enter. You can also change font sizes in the mini-toolbar that appears when you select text.

>> **Font dialog box:** Click the Font group button to open the Font dialog box. Then either choose a point size from the Size drop-down list or enter a point size in the Size text box and click OK.

TIP

>> **Increase Font Size and Decrease Font Size buttons:** Click these buttons (or press Ctrl+Shift+> or Ctrl+Shift+<) to increase or decrease the point size by the next interval on the Font Size drop-down list. Watch the Font Size list or your text and note how the text changes size. This is an excellent technique when you want to "eyeball it" and you don't care to fool with the Font Size list or Font dialog box.

Changing the look of text

For the daring and experimental, PowerPoint offers about a hundred different ways to change the look of text. You can change colors, make the text glow, and make the text cast a shadow, among other things.

Use one of these techniques to give text a makeover:

>> **Changing color:** Select the text, and on the Home tab, open the drop-down list on the Font Color button and choose a color. You can also click the Font group button to open the Font dialog box and choose a color there.

>> **Choosing text fills, outlines, and effects:** On the Design tab, click the Format Background button. Then select the text and click the Text Options tab in the Format Shape pane. As shown in Figure 3-2, the Text Options tab in the Format Shape pane offers many ways to change the appearance of text:

- **Fill:** Show the text in gradients, textures, or patterns. You can assign a transparent color to text by choosing a color and dragging the Transparency slider.

- **Outline:** Change the text outline — the outermost lines that form the letters and numbers. Try this: Under Fill, choose the No Fill option, and then choose a solid line as the outline (refer to Figure 3-2).

- **Effects:** Give the letters and numbers a shadow, a reflection, a glow, a softer edge, or another dimension. Before you experiment with these commands, try choosing an option on the Presets menu. Preset options demonstrate what these text effects can do and give you a head start in fashioning a text effect.

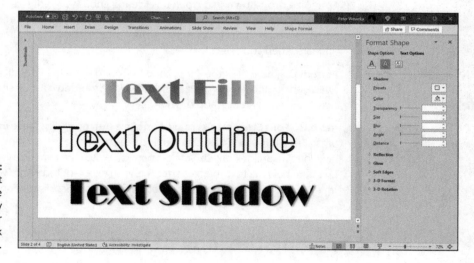

FIGURE 3-2:
The Format Shape pane offers many commands for changing the look of text.

TIP

Before you change the look of text, peer into your computer screen and examine the background theme or color you selected for your slides. Unless the text is a different color from the background, the audience can't read the text. As you experiment with changing the look of text, make sure that your audience can still read it.

FIXING A TOP-HEAVY TITLE

In typesetting terminology, a *top-heavy title* is a title in which the first line is much longer than the second. Whenever a title extends to two lines, it runs the risk of being top-heavy. Unsightly top-heavy titles look especially bad on PowerPoint slides, where text is blown up to 40 points or more.

To fix a top-heavy title, click where you prefer the lines to break and then press Shift+Enter. Pressing Shift+Enter creates a *hard line break*, a forced break at the end of one line. (To remove a hard line break, click where the break occurs and then press the Delete key.)

The only drawback of hard line breaks is remembering where you made them. In effect, the line breaks are invisible. When you edit a title with a line break, the line break remains, and unless you know it's there, you discover the line breaking in an odd place. The moral is: If you're editing a title and the text keeps moving to the next line, you may have entered a hard line break and forgotten about it.

Fun with Text Boxes and Text Box Shapes

Text boxes give you an opportunity to exercise your creativity. They add another element to slides. Use them to position text wherever you want, annotate a chart or equation, or place an announcement on a slide. You can even create a vertical text box in which the text reads from top to bottom instead of left to right, or turn a text box into a circle, arrow, or other shape. Figure 3-3 shows examples of text boxes and text box shapes.

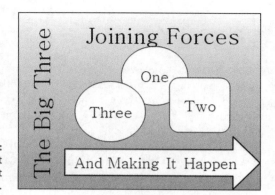

In Office terminology, a PowerPoint text box is an object. Book 8, Chapter 4 explains all the different techniques for handling objects, including how to make them overlap and change their sizes. Here are the basics of handling text boxes in PowerPoint:

>> **Creating a text box:** On the Insert tab, click the Text Box button and move the pointer to a part of the slide where you can see the *text box pointer,* a downward-pointing arrow. Then click and start dragging to create your text box, and enter the text.

>> **Filling a text box with color:** On the Shape Format tab, choose a style on the Shape Styles gallery or click the Shape Fill button and select a color. You can also go to the Design tab, click the Format Background button, and select a color, picture, pattern, or gradient in the Format Shape pane.

>> **Rotating a text box (text included):** Use one of these techniques to rotate a text box along with the text inside it:

- Drag the rotation handle, the circle above the text box.

- On the Shape Format tab, click the Rotate button and choose a Rotate or Flip command on the drop-down list.

- On the (Drawing Tools) Format tab, click the Size group button (you may have to click the Size button first) and, in the Format Shape pane, enter a measurement in the Rotation box.

>> **Changing the direction of text:** On the Home tab, click the Text Direction button and choose a Rotate or Stacked option.

>> **Turning a shape into a text box:** Create a shape, and then click in the shape and start typing. (Book 8, Chapter 4 explains how to create a shape.)

TIP

Many people object to the small text boxes that appear initially when you create a text box. If you prefer to establish the size of text boxes when you create them, not when you enter text, change the AutoFit setting and then create a default text box with the new setting. The next section in this chapter explains how to change the AutoFit settings.

Controlling How Text Fits in Text Frames and Text Boxes

When text doesn't fit in a text placeholder frame or text box, PowerPoint takes measures to make it fit. In a text placeholder frame, PowerPoint shrinks the amount of space between lines and then it shrinks the text itself. When text doesn't fit in a text box, PowerPoint enlarges the text box to fit more text. PowerPoint handles overflow text as part of its AutoFit mechanism.

How AutoFit works is up to you. If, like me, you don't care for how PowerPoint enlarges text boxes when you enter the text, you can tell PowerPoint not to "auto-fit" text, but instead to make text boxes large from the get-go. And if you don't care for how PowerPoint shrinks text in text placeholder frames, you can tell PowerPoint not to shrink text. These pages explain how to choose AutoFit options for overflow text in your text frames and text boxes.

Choosing how AutoFit works in text frames

When text doesn't fit in a text placeholder frame and PowerPoint has to "auto-fit" the text, the AutoFit Options button appears beside the text box. Click this button to open a drop-down list with options for handling overflow text, as shown in Figure 3-4. The AutoFit options — along with a couple of other techniques, as I explain shortly — represent the "one at a time" way of handling overflow text. You can also change the default AutoFit options for handling overflow text, as I also explain if you'll bear with me a while longer and quit your yawning.

FIGURE 3-4:
The laundry list of AutoFit options.

Auto-fitting the text one frame at a time

WARNING

When text doesn't fit in a text placeholder frame, especially a title frame, the first question to ask is, "Do I want to fool with the integrity of the slide design?" Making the text fit usually means shrinking the text, enlarging the text frame, or compromising the slide design in some way, but audiences notice design inconsistencies. Slides are shown on large screens where design flaws are easy to see.

Making text fit in a text frame usually means making a compromise. Here are different ways to handle the problem of text not fitting in a text frame. Be prepared to click the Undo button when you experiment with these techniques:

>> **Edit the text:** Usually when text doesn't fit in a frame, the text needs editing. It needs to be made shorter. A slide is not a place for a treatise. Editing the text is the only way to make it fit in the frame without compromising the design.

>> **Enlarge the frame:** Click the AutoFit Options button and choose Stop Fitting Text to This Placeholder on the shortcut menu (see Figure 3-4). Then select the frame and drag the bottom or top selection handle to enlarge it.

>> **Decrease the font size:** Select the text, go to the Home tab, and choose a smaller Font Size measurement. You can also click the Decrease Font Size button (or press Ctrl+<) to decrease the font size.

>> **Decrease the amount of spacing between lines:** On the Home tab, click the Paragraph group button to open the Paragraph dialog box and decrease the After measurement under Spacing.

>> **Change the frame's internal margins:** Similar to a page, text frames have internal margins to keep text from getting too close to a frame border. By shrinking these margins, you can make more room for text. Right-click the text frame and choose Format Shape. Then, in the Format Shape pane, go to the Size & Properties tab, and under the Text Box settings, enter smaller margin measurements.

>> **Create a new slide for the text:** If you're dealing with a list or paragraph text in a body text frame, the AutoFit Options drop-down list offers two ways to create a new slide (refer to Figure 3-4). Choose Continue on a New Slide to run the text onto another slide; choose Split Text Between Two Slides to divide the text evenly between two slides. I don't recommend either option, though. If you need to make a new slide, do it on your own and then rethink how to present the material. Inserting a new slide to accommodate a long list throws a presentation off track.

Choosing default AutoFit options for text frames

Unless you change the default AutoFit options, PowerPoint shrinks the amount of space between lines and then shrinks the text itself to make text fit in text placeholder frames. Follow these steps if you want to decide for yourself whether PowerPoint "auto-fits" text in text frames:

1. **Open the AutoFormat As You Type tab in the AutoCorrect dialog box.**

   Here are the two ways to get there:

   - Click the AutoFit Options button (refer to Figure 3-4) and choose Control AutoCorrect Options on the drop-down list.

   - On the File tab, choose Options to open the PowerPoint Options dialog box. In the Proofing category, click the AutoCorrect Options button.

2. **Deselect the AutoFit Title Text to Placeholder check box to prevent auto-fitting in title text placeholder frames.**

3. **Deselect the AutoFit Body Text to Placeholder check box to prevent auto-fitting in text placeholder frames apart from title frames.**

4. **Click OK.**

Choosing how AutoFits works in text boxes

PowerPoint offers three options for handling overflow text in text boxes:

» **Do Not AutoFit:** Doesn't fit text in the text box but lets text spill out

» **Shrink Text on Overflow:** Shrinks the text to make it fit in the text box

» **Resize Shape to Fit Text:** Enlarges the text box to make the text fit inside it

Follow these steps to tell PowerPoint how or whether to fit text in text boxes:

1. **Select the text box.**

2. **Right-click the text box and choose Format Shape.**

   The Format Shape task pane opens.

3. **Go to the Size & Properties tab.**

4. **Display the Text Box options.**

5. **Choose an AutoFit option: Do Not AutoFit, Shrink Text on Overflow, or Resize Shape to Fit Text.**

Positioning Text in Frames and Text Boxes

How text is positioned in text frames and text boxes is governed by two sets of commands: the Align Text commands and the Align commands. These commands are located on the Home tab. By choosing combinations of Align and Align Text commands, you can land text where you want it in a text frame or text box. With the cursor inside a text frame or text box, wrestle with these two commands until you land your text where you want it to be in a text frame or box:

» **Align commands control horizontal (left-to-right) alignments.** On the Home tab, click the Align Left (press Ctrl+L), Center (press Ctrl+E), Align Right (press Ctrl+R), or Justify button (press Ctrl+J).

» **Align Text commands control vertical (up-and-down) alignments.** On the Home tab, click the Align Text button and choose Top, Middle, or Bottom on the drop-down list, as shown in Figure 3-5.

FIGURE 3-5: Choose an Align Text and an Align command to position text in text frames and boxes.

Handling Bulleted and Numbered Lists

What is a PowerPoint presentation without a list or two? It's like an emperor without any clothes on. This part of the chapter explains everything there is to know about bulleted and numbered lists.

Lists can be as simple or complex as you want them to be. PowerPoint offers a bunch of different ways to format lists, but if you're in a hurry or you don't care whether your lists look like everyone else's, you can take advantage of the Numbering and Bullets buttons and go with standard lists. Nonconformists and people with nothing else to do, however, can try their hand at making fancy lists. The following pages cover that topic, too.

Creating a standard bulleted or numbered list

In typesetting terms, a *bullet* is a black, filled-in circle or other character that marks an item on a list. Many slide layouts include text frames that are formatted already for bulleted lists. All you have to do in these text frames is "Click to add text" and keep pressing the Enter key while you enter items for your bulleted list. Each time you press Enter, PowerPoint adds another bullet to the list. Bulleted lists are useful when you want to present the audience with alternatives or present a list in which the items aren't ranked in any order. Use a numbered list to rank items in a list or present step-by-step instructions.

Follow these instructions to create a standard bulleted or numbered list:

>> **Creating a bulleted list:** Select the list if you've already entered the list items, go to the Home tab, and click the Bullets button. You can also right-click, choose Bullets on the shortcut menu, and choose a bullet character on the submenu if you don't care for the standard, black, filled-in circle.

>> **Creating a numbered list:** Select the list if you've already entered the list items, go to the Home tab, and click the Numbering button. You can also right-click, choose Numbering on the shortcut menu, and select a numbering style on the submenu.

>> **Converting a numbered to a bulleted list (or vice versa):** Drag over the list to select it, go to the Home tab, and then click the Bullets or Numbering button.

To remove the bullets or numbers from a list, select the list, open the drop-down list on the Bullets or Numbering button, and choose None.

Choosing a different bullet character, size, and color

As Figure 3-6 demonstrates, the black filled-in circle isn't the only character you can use to mark items in a bulleted list. You can also opt for what PowerPoint calls *pictures* (colorful bullets of many sizes and shapes) or symbols from the Symbol dialog box. While you're at it, you can change the bullets' color and size.

WARNING

If you decide to change the bullet character in your lists, be consistent from slide to slide. Unless you want to be goofy, select the same bullet character throughout the lists in your presentation for the sake of consistency. You don't want to turn your slide presentation into a showcase for bullets, do you?

Entering the Text

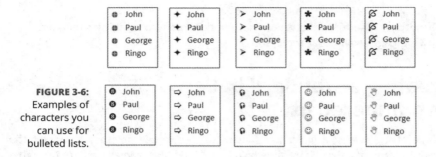

To use pictures or unusual symbols for bullets, start by selecting your bulleted list, going to the Home tab, and opening the drop-down list on the Bullets button. Do any of the bullets on the drop-down list tickle your fancy? If one does, select it; otherwise, click the Bullets and Numbering option at the bottom of the drop-down list. You see the Bulleted tab of the Bullets and Numbering dialog box, as shown in Figure 3-7. Starting there, you can customize your bullets:

>> **Use a picture for bullets:** Click the Picture button and search for a bullet in the Insert Pictures dialog box.

>> **Use a symbol for bullets:** Click the Customize button and select a symbol in the Symbol dialog box.

>> **Change bullets' size:** Enter a percentage figure in the Size % of Text box. For example, if you enter **200**, the bullets are twice as large as the font size you choose for the items in your bulleted list.

>> **Change bullets' color:** Click the Color button in the Bullets and Numbering dialog box and choose an option on the drop-down list. Theme colors are considered most compatible with the theme design you chose for your presentation.

FIGURE 3-7:
The Bullets
and Numbering
dialog box.

Choosing a different list-numbering style, size, and color

PowerPoint offers seven different ways of numbering lists. As well as choosing a different numbering style, you can change the size of numbers relative to the text and change the color of numbers. To select a different list-numbering style, size, or color, begin by selecting your list, going to the Home tab, and opening the drop-down list on the Numbering button. If you like one of the numbering-scheme choices, select it; otherwise choose Bullets and Numbering to open the Numbered tab of the Bullets and Numbering dialog box (refer to Figure 3-7). In this dialog box, you can customize list numbers:

>> **Choose a numbering scheme:** Select a numbering scheme and click OK.

>> **Change the numbers' size:** Enter a percentage figure in the Size % of Text box. For example, if you enter 50, the numbers are half as big as the font size you choose for the items in your numbered list.

>> **Change the numbers' color:** Click the Color button and choose a color on the drop-down list. Theme colors are more compatible with the theme design you chose than the other colors are.

Putting Footers (and Headers) on Slides

A *footer* is a line of text that appears at the foot, or bottom, of a slide. Figure 3-8 shows a footer. Typically, a footer includes the date, a company name, and/or a slide number, and footers appear on every slide in a presentation if they appear at all. That doesn't mean you can't exclude a footer from a slide or put footers on some slides, as I explain shortly. For that matter, you can move slide numbers, company names, and dates to the top of slides, in which case they become *headers.* When I was a kid, "header" meant crashing your bike and falling headfirst over the handlebars. How times change.

These pages explain everything a body needs to know about footers and headers — how to enter them, make them appear on all or some slides, and exclude them from slides.

Some background on footers and headers

PowerPoint provides the Header & Footer command to enter the date, a word or two, and a slide number on the bottom of all slides in your presentation. This command is really just a convenient way to enter a footer on the Slide Master without having to switch to Slide Master view. As Chapter 2 of this minibook explains, the Slide Master governs the formatting and layout of all slides in your presentation. The Slide Master includes text placeholder frames for a date, some text, and a slide number. Anything you enter on the Slide Master, including a footer, appears on all your slides.

5/17/2009   What's Underfoot?   3

FIGURE 3-8:
An example
of a footer.

If a date, some text, and a slide number along the bottom of all the slides in your presentation is precisely what you want, you've got it made. You can enter a footer on every slide in your presentation with no trouble at all by using the Header & Footer command. However, if you're a maverick and you want your footers and headers to be a little different from the next person's — if you want the date, for example, to be in the upper-right corner of slides or you want footers to appear on some slides but not others — you have some tweaking to do. You may have to create a nonstandard footer or remove the footer from some of the slides.

Putting a standard footer on all your slides

A standard footer includes the date, some text, and the page number. To put a standard footer on all the slides in your presentation, go to the Insert tab and click the Header & Footer button. You see the Header and Footer dialog box, as shown in Figure 3-9. Choose some or all of these options and click the Apply to All button:

>> **Date and Time:** Select this check box to make the date appear in the lower-left corner of all your slides. Then tell PowerPoint whether you want a current or fixed date:

- **Update Automatically:** Select this option button to make the day's date (or date and time) appear in the footer, and then open the drop-down list to choose a date (or date and time) format. With this option, the date you give your presentation always appears on slides.

- **Fixed:** Select this option button and enter a date in the text box. For example, enter the date you created the presentation. With this option, the date remains fixed no matter when or where you give the presentation.

» **Slide Number:** Select this check box to make slide numbers appear in the lower-right corner of all slides.

» **Footer:** Select this check box, and in the text box, enter the words that you want to appear in the bottom, middle of all the slides.

» **Don't Show on Title Slide:** Keeps the footer from appearing on the title slide, usually the first slide in a presentation.

FIGURE 3-9:
Entering a standard footer.

Creating a nonstandard footer

As "Some background on footers and headers" explains, earlier in this chapter, you have to look elsewhere than the Header and Footer dialog box if you want to create something besides the standard footer. Suppose you want to move the slide number from the lower-right corner of slides to another position? Or you want to fool with the fonts in headers and footers?

Follow these steps to create a nonstandard footer:

1. **Create a standard footer if you want your nonstandard footer to include today's date and/or a slide number.**

   If you want to move the slide number into the upper-right corner of slides, for example, create a standard footer first (see the preceding topic in this chapter). Later, you can move the slide number text frame into the upper-right corner of slides.

2. **On the View tab, click the Slide Master button.**

   You switch to Slide Master view. Chapter 2 of this minibook explains this view and how to format many slides simultaneously with master slides.

3. **Select the Slide Master, the topmost slide in the Slides pane (if necessary).**

4. **Adjust and format the footer text boxes to taste (as they say in cookbooks).**

   For example, move the slide number text frame into the upper-right corner to put slide numbers there. Or change the font in the footer text boxes. Or place a company logo on the Slide Master to make the logo appear on all your slides.

5. **Click the Close Master View button to leave Slide Master view.**

   You can always return to Slide Master view and adjust your footer.

Removing a footer from a single slide

On a crowded slide, the date, footer text, page number, and other items in the footer can get in the way or be a distraction. Fortunately, removing one or all of the footer text frames from a slide is easy:

1. **Switch to Normal view and display the slide with the footer that needs removing.**

2. **On the Insert tab, click the Header & Footer button.**

   The Header and Footer dialog box appears.

3. **Deselect check boxes — Date and Time, Slide Number, and Footer — to tell PowerPoint which parts of the footer you want to remove.**

4. **Click the Apply button.**

   Be careful not to click the Apply to All button. Clicking this button removes footers throughout your slide presentation.

Chapter **4**

Making Your Presentations Livelier

The purpose of this chapter is to make your presentation stand out in a crowd. It suggests ways to enliven your presentation with pictures, charts, slides, and tables. It shows how transitions and animations can make a presentation livelier. Finally, you discover how to play sound and video during a presentation.

Suggestions for Enlivening Your Presentation

Starting on the Insert tab, you can do a lot to make a presentation livelier. The Insert tab offers buttons for putting pictures, tables, charts, diagrams, and shapes on slides:

» **Pictures:** Everyone likes a good graphic or photo, but more than that, audiences understand more from words and pictures than they do from words alone. A well-chosen photo or image reinforces the ideas that you're trying to put across in your presentation. (See Book 8, Chapter 3 for how to work with graphics and insert them into a slide.)

» **Tables:** A table is a great way to plead your case or defend your position. Raw table data is irrefutable — well, most of the time, anyway. Create a table when you want to demonstrate how the numbers back you up. (See "Presenting Information in a Table," later in this chapter.)

» **Charts:** Nothing is more persuasive than a chart. The bars, pie slices, or columns show the audience instantaneously that production is up or down, or that sector A is outperforming sector B. The audience can compare the data and see what's what. (See Book 8, Chapter 1.)

» **Diagrams:** A diagram is an excellent marriage of images and words. Diagrams allow an audience to literally visualize a concept, idea, or relationship. You can present an abstract idea such that the audience understands it better. (See Book 8, Chapter 2.)

» **Shapes:** Lines and shapes can also illustrate ideas and concepts. You can also use them as slide decorations. (See Book 8, Chapter 4.)

Presenting Information in a Table

The purpose of a table is to present information for comparison purposes — to see which car gets the best gas mileage, which company made the most money, or who shucked the most corn. Tables on slides can't be used for reference purposes because they appear briefly onscreen; viewers can't refer to them later on. Nevertheless, a table is a great way to present a quick summary of the bare facts.

PowerPoint offers no fewer than four ways to create a table. The best slide layout for creating tables is Title and Content because it offers space for a title and provides the Table icon, which you can click to create a table. Create your table with one of these techniques:

» **Dragging on the Table menu:** On the Insert tab, click the Table button, point on the drop-down list to the number of columns and rows you want, and click, as shown in Figure 4-1.

» **Clicking the Table icon:** Click the Table icon in a content placeholder frame. You see the Insert Table dialog box, shown in Figure 4-1. Enter the

>> **Using the Insert Table dialog box:** On the Insert tab, click the Table button and choose Insert Table on the drop-down list. The Insert Table dialog box shown in Figure 4-1 appears. Enter the number of columns and rows you want and click OK.

>> **Drawing a table:** On the Insert tab, click the Table button and choose Draw Table on the drop-down list. The pointer changes into a pencil. Use the pencil to draw the table borders. On the Table Design tab, you can click the Draw Table button and draw the columns and rows for the table. Click the Eraser button to erase parts of the table.

Point to how many columns and rows you want...   or enter how many you want

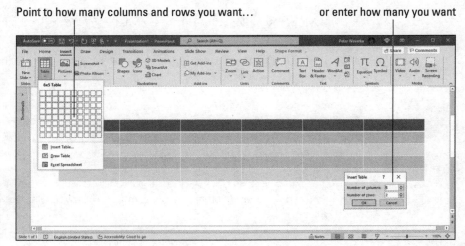

FIGURE 4-1: Declare how many columns and rows you want for your table.

REMEMBER

After you create a table, PowerPoint places two new tabs on the Ribbon, one called Table Design and one called Layout. The Table Design tab offers commands for changing the look of the table; the Layout tab is for changing around the rows and columns.

The techniques for working with tables in Word and PowerPoint are terribly similar. I suggest going to Book 2, Chapter 4 if your aim is to create a really, really nice table.

THE GRID AND DRAWING GUIDES

The *grid* is an invisible set of horizontal and vertical lines to which objects — images, pictures, and shapes — cling when you move them on a slide. The grid is meant to help you line up objects squarely with one another. When you drag an object, it sticks to the nearest point on the grid.

PowerPoint also offers the *drawing guides* for aligning objects. You can drag these vertical and horizontal lines onscreen and use them to align objects with precision.

To display the grid and the drawing guides:

- **Displaying (and hiding) the grid:** Press Shift+F9 or go to the View tab and select the Gridlines check box.

- **Displaying (and hiding) the drawing guides:** Press Alt+F9 or go to the View tab and select the Guides check box.

By default, objects "snap to the grid" when you move them. That means objects stick to the nearest grid line when you move them across a slide. To control whether objects snap to the grid, right-click (but not on an object or frame), choose Grid and Guides, and in the Grid and Guides dialog box, deselect the Snap Objects to Grid check box.

Even if the Snap Objects to Grid check box in the Grid and Guides dialog box is selected, you can move objects without them snapping to a gridline by holding down the Alt key while you drag.

Exploring Transitions and Animations

In PowerPoint-speak, a *transition* is a little bit of excitement that occurs as one slide leaves the screen and the next slide climbs aboard. An *animation* is movement on the slide. For example, you can animate bulleted lists such that the bullet points appear on a slide one at a time when you click the mouse rather than all at one time.

WARNING

Before you know anything about transitions and animations, you should know that they can be distracting. The purpose of a presentation is to communicate with the audience, not display the latest, busiest, most dazzling presentation technology. For user-run, kiosk-style presentations, however, eye-catching transitions and animations can be useful because they draw an audience. (A user-run presentation plays on its own, as I explain in Chapter 5 of this minibook.) For audiences that enjoy high-tech wizardry, transitions and animations can be a lot of fun and add to a presentation.

Showing transitions between slides

Transitions include the Morph, Fade, and Push. Figure 4-2 shows how a transition works. For the figure, I chose the Clock transition. This slide doesn't so much arrive onscreen as it does sweep onto the screen in a clockwise fashion. You get a chance to test-drive these transitions before you attach them to slides.

FIGURE 4-2: The Clock transition in action.

Assigning transitions to slides

To show transitions between slides, select the slide or slides that need transitions, go to the Transitions tab, and select a transition in the Transition to This Slide gallery. (To apply the same transition to all the slides in a presentation, click the Apply To All button after you select a transition.) The names and images in the gallery give you an idea of what the transitions are, and you can click the Preview button on the Transitions tab at any time to watch a transition you chose.

The Transitions tab offers these tools for tweaking a transition:

» **Effect Options:** Click the Effect Options button and choose an effect on the drop-down list. For example, choose From Top or From Bottom to make a transition arrive from the top or bottom of the screen. Not all transitions offer effect options.

» **Sound:** Open the Sound drop-down list and choose a sound to accompany the transition. The Loop Until Next Sound option at the bottom of the drop-down list plays a sound continuously until the next slide in the presentation appears.

» **Duration:** Enter a time period in the Duration box to declare how quickly or slowly you want the transition to occur.

As I mention earlier, you can click the Apply To All button to assign the same transition to all the slides in your presentation.

Altering and removing slide transitions

In Slide Sorter view and in the Slides pane in Normal view, the transition symbol, a flying star, appears next to slides that have been assigned a transition. Select the slides that need a transition change, go to the Transitions tab, and follow these instructions to alter or remove transitions:

» **Altering a transition:** Choose a different transition in the Transition to This Slide gallery. You can also choose different effect options and sounds, and change the duration of the transition.

» **Removing a transition:** Choose None in the Transition to This Slide gallery.

Animating parts of a slide

When it comes to animations, you can choose between *animation schemes*, the pre-built special effects made by the elves of Microsoft, or customized animations that you build on your own. Only fans of animation and people with a lot of time on their hands go the second route.

Choosing a ready-made animation scheme

Follow these steps to preview and choose an animation scheme for slides:

1. **Go to the Animations tab.**

2. **Click to select the element on the slide that you want to animate.**

   For example, select a text frame with a bulleted list. You can tell when you've selected an element because a selection box appears around it.

3. **In the Animation Styles gallery, choose an animation effect, as shown in Figure 4-3.**

   You can choose Entrance, Emphasis, Motion Paths, and Exit animation effects. As soon as you make your choice, the animation springs to life, and you can click the Preview button at any time to see your animation in all its glory.

4. **Click the Effect Options button and experiment with choices on the drop-down list to tweak your animation.**

   Which options are available depends on the animation you chose.

5. **If you choose a text-box or text-frame element with more than one paragraph in Step 2, click the Effect Options button and tell PowerPoint whether to animate all the text or animate each paragraph separately from the others.**

   - **As One Object or All at Once:** All the text is animated at the same time.

   - **By Paragraph:** Each paragraph is treated separately and is animated on its own. For example, each item in a bulleted list is treated as a separate element — each item fades, wipes, or flies in after the one before it, not at the same time as the one before it.

   Very briefly, you see a preview of the animation choice you made. To get a good look at the animation you just chose for your slide, click the Preview button on the Animations tab.

To remove an animation, return to the Animation Styles gallery and choose None.

Choose an animation   How elements are animated

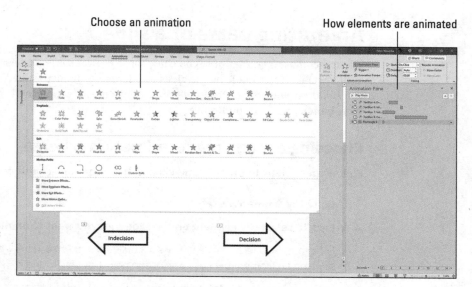

FIGURE 4-3:
Apply effects in
the Animation
gallery.

Fashioning your own animation schemes

To fashion your own animation scheme, go to the Animations tab and click the Animation Pane button. You see the Animation pane, as shown in Figure 4-3. It lists, in order, each animation that occurs on your slide (if animations occur). Select an element on the slide and follow these general instructions to animate it:

>> Click the Add Animation button and choose an animation.

>> On the Start drop-down list, declare whether the animation begins when you click your slide (On Click), at the same time as the previous animation (With Previous), or after the previous animation (After Previous).

>> In the Duration box, enter how long you want the animation to last.

>> In the Delay box, enter a time period to declare how soon after the previous animation in the Animation pane you want your animation to occur.

>> Select an animation in the task pane and click a Re-Order button to change the order in which animations occur, if more than one element is animated on your slide.

Making Audio Part of Your Presentation

Especially in user-run, kiosk-style presentations, audio can be a welcome addition. Audio gives presentations an extra dimension. It attracts an audience. PowerPoint offers two ways to make audio part of a presentation:

>> **As part of slide transitions:** A sound is heard as a new slide arrives onscreen. On the Transitions tab, open the Sound drop-down list and choose a sound. (See "Showing transitions between slides," earlier in this chapter.)

>> **On the slide itself:** The means of playing audio appears on the slide in the form of an Audio icon, as shown in Figure 4-4. By moving the mouse over this icon, you can display audio controls, and you can use these controls to play audio. You can also make audio play as soon as the slide arrives onscreen.

FIGURE 4-4: Making audio part of a presentation.

Inserting an audio file on a slide

Follow these steps to insert an audio file in a slide:

1. Go to the Insert tab.

2. Click the Audio button.

3. Choose Audio on My PC.

The Insert Audio dialog box appears.

4. Locate and select a sound file.

5. Click Insert.

An Audio icon appears on the slide to remind you that audio is supposed to play when your slide is onscreen. You can change the size of this icon by selecting it and dragging a corner handle or going to the Audio Format tab and entering new Height and Width measurements. You can also drag the icon into an out-of-the-way corner of your slide.

To quit playing a sound file on a slide, select its Audio icon and then press the Delete key.

Telling PowerPoint when and how to play an audio file

To tell PowerPoint when and how to play an audio file, start by selecting the Audio icon and going to the Playback tab, as shown in Figure 4-5. From there, you can control when and how audio files play:

>> **Controlling the volume:** Click the Volume button and choose an option on the drop-down list to control how loud the audio plays.

>> **Playing the audio file automatically in the background:** Click the Play in Background button. Clicking this button tells PowerPoint to play the audio automatically, across slides, until you or another presenter clicks the Pause button to stop the audio from playing.

>> **Deciding when and how to play audio:** Click the No Style button. Then select these options:

- **Start:** Choose Automatically to make the audio play as soon as the slide appears; choose When Clicked On to play the audio when you click the Audio icon on your slide. (The In Click Sequence option is for playing an audio as part of an animation.)

- **Play Across Slides:** Play the audio file throughout a presentation, not just when the slide with the audio file appears.

- **Loop Until Stopped:** Play the audio file continuously until you or another presenter clicks the Pause button.

>> **Hiding and unhiding the Audio icon:** Select the Hide During Show check box. If you hide the Audio icon, the file must play automatically; otherwise, you won't see the icon and be able to click it and view the audio controls.

>> **Rewind After Playing:** Starts replaying the audio file from the beginning after it is finished playing.

Click the Play button on the Playback tab to play an audio file

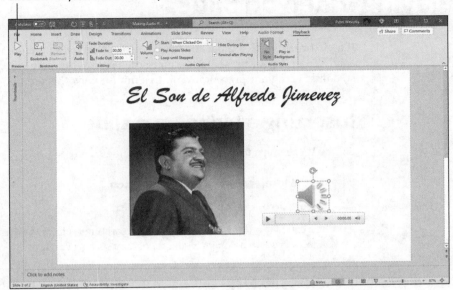

FIGURE 4-5:
Visit the Playback tab to control when and how sounds play.

To play an audio file, click the Play button on the audio icon or click the Play button on the Playback tab.

Playing audio during a presentation

While an audio file is playing during a presentation, controls for starting, pausing, and controlling the volume appear onscreen (refer to Figure 4-4). They appear onscreen, I should say, if the Audio icon appears on your slide. (If you've hidden the Audio icon, you're out of luck because you can't see the Audio icon or use its audio controls.)

Follow these instructions to start, pause, and control the volume of an audio recording during a presentation:

>> **Starting an audio file:** Move the pointer over the Audio icon, and when you see the Audio controls, click the Play/Pause button (or press Alt+P).

>> **Pausing an audio file:** Click the Play/Pause button (or press Alt+P). Click the button again to resume playing the audio file.

>> **Muting the volume:** Click the Mute/Unmute icon (or press Alt+U).

>> **Controlling the volume:** Move the pointer over the Mute/Unmute icon to display the volume slider and then drag the volume control on the slider.

Playing Video on Slides

If a picture is worth a thousand words, what is a moving picture worth? Ten thousand? To give your presentation more cachet, you can play video on slides and in so doing, turn your presentation into a mini-movie theater.

Inserting a video on a slide

Follow these steps to insert a video on a slide:

1. **On the Insert tab, click the Video button.**

2. **Choose an option on the drop-down list.**

   You can play a video file stored on your computer, play a stock video, or play a video stored on an online video repository such as YouTube.

   - **This Device:** You see the Insert Video dialog box. (You can also open this dialog box by clicking the Insert Video icon on some slide layouts.) Select a video stored on your computer and click Insert.

   - **Stock Videos:** The Media dialog box appears, as shown in Figure 4-6. Go to the Videos tab, search for and select a video, and click Insert.

   - **Online Video:** A dialog box for inserting videos appears. Paste the URL (the Internet address) of the video you want to show into the dialog box and click Insert.

   The video appears on your slide. If I were you, I would find out how (or whether) the video plays. To do that, click the Play/Pause button (or press Alt+P) or click the Play button on the Playback or Video Format tab.

REMEMBER

The Online Video command establishes a connection between your slide and an online video. To use computer terminology, it *embeds* the video in your slide. Your video plays from the web page where it is located, not from your computer, so your computer must be connected to the Internet to play an online video.

Fine-tuning a video presentation

As shown in Figure 4-7, select the video and go to the Playback tab to fine-tune a video presentation. The Playback tab offers all kinds of commands for making a video play the way you want it to play. Here are different ways to fine-tune a video presentation:

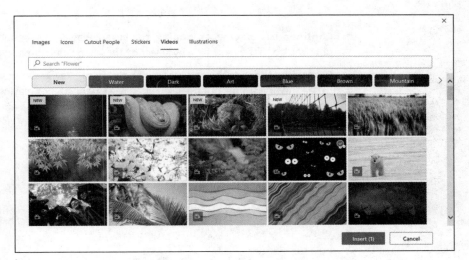

FIGURE 4-6:
Choosing a stock video for a presentation.

>> **Adding a bookmark:** Add a bookmark to be able to skip ahead or backward to a place in the video when you play it. To add a bookmark, play the video to the place where you want the book mark to be and then stop playing the video. Next, click the Add Bookmark button. The bookmark appears in the form of a circle. You can click this circle to go to the bookmark while you play the video. To remove a bookmark, select it on the timeline and click the Remove Bookmark button.

>> **Trimming the video:** To trim from the start or end of a video, click the Trim Video button. Then, in the Trim Video dialog box, drag the green slider to trim from the start of the video; drag the red slider to trim from the end.

>> **Fading in and out:** Enter time measurements in the Fade In and Fade Out text boxes to make the video fade in or out.

>> **Controlling the volume:** Click the Volume button and choose Low, Medium, High, or Mute to control how loud the video sound is.

>> **Playing the video automatically or when you click the Play/Pause button:** Open the Start drop-down list and choose Automatically or When Clicked On to tell PowerPoint when to start playing the video.

>> **Playing the video at full screen:** Make a video fill the entire screen by selecting the Play Full Screen check box. Be careful of this one. Videos can look terribly grainy when they appear on the big screen.

>> **Hiding the video when it isn't playing:** You can hide the video until you start playing it by selecting the Hide While Not Playing check box. Be sure to choose Automatically on the Start drop-down list if you select this check box.

Making Your
Presentations Livelier

>> **Continuously playing, or looping, the video:** Play a video continuously or until you go to the next slide by selecting the Loop Until Stopped check box.

>> **Rewinding the video when it's finished playing:** Rewind a video if you want to see the first frame, not the last, when the video finishes playing. Select the Rewind After Playing check box to make the start of the video appear after the video plays; deselect this option to freeze-frame on the end of the video when it finishes playing.

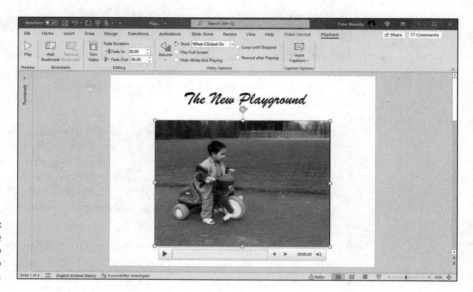

FIGURE 4-7:
Visit the Playback tab to fine-tune a video presentation.

Experimenting with the look of the video

Want to make your video look a little sharper? If so, you are hereby invited to experiment with the commands on the Format tab and Format Video pane shown in Figure 4-8.

To open the Format Video pane, go to Format tab and do one of the following:

>> Click the Corrections button and choose Video Corrections Options on the drop-down list.

>> Click the Video Styles group button.

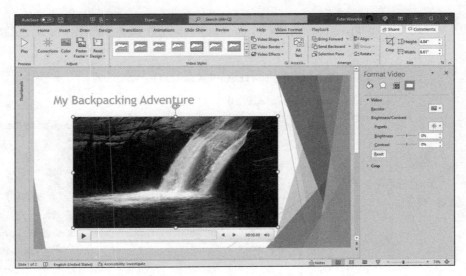

FIGURE 4-8:
You can change
the look of a
video.

When you're in an experimental mood, select your video and try these techniques for changing its appearance:

>> **Recolor the video:** Click the Color button (on the Format tab) or the Recolor button (in the Format Video pane) and select a color or black-and-white option.

>> **Change the brightness and contrast:** Click the Corrections button and choose a setting in the gallery, or change the Brightness and Contrast settings in the Format Video pane.

Recording a Voice Narration for Slides

A voice narration in a PowerPoint presentation is sophisticated indeed. A self-playing, kiosk-style presentation can be accompanied by a human voice such that the narrator gives the presentation without actually being there. To narrate a presentation, a working microphone must be attached or built in to your computer. You record the narration for slides one slide at a time or all at one time, and the recording is stored in the PowerPoint file, not in a separate audio file.

The best way to record voice narrations is to do it on a slide-by-slide basis. You can record across several slides, but getting your voice narration and slides to be in sync with one another can be a lot of trouble.

Place your script on your desk and follow these steps to record a voice narration for a slide:

1. **Select the slide that needs a voice narration.**

2. **Go to the Insert tab.**

3. **Open the drop-down list on the Audio button and choose Record Audio.**

You see the Record Sound dialog box shown in Figure 4-9.

4. **Click the Record button and start reading your script.**

Click the Stop button when you want to pause recording; click the Record button to resume recording.

You can click the Play button at any time to play back what you have recorded so far. Notice that the dialog box notes how many seconds your recording lasts.

5. **Click the OK button in the Record Sound dialog box when you have finished recording the narration for your slide.**

The Audio icon appears on your slide to show that your slide is accompanied by an audio file.

FIGURE 4-9:
Recording in
PowerPoint.

Play   Stop   Record

Your next task is to select the Audio icon, go to the Playback tab, and tell Power-Point when to play the audio recording, at what volume to play it, and whether you want it to loop. See "Telling PowerPoint when and how to play an audio file," earlier in this chapter.

WARNING

To play voice narrations during a presentation, make sure that the Play Narrations check box is selected on the Slide Show tab.

Chapter **5**

Delivering a Presentation

At last, the big day has arrived. It's time to give the presentation. "Break a leg," as actors say before they go on stage. This chapter explains how to rehearse your presentation to find out how long it is and how to show your presentation. You discover some techniques to make your presentation livelier, including how to draw on slides with a pen or highlighter and blank out the screen to get the audience's full attention. The chapter describes how to handle the speaker notes and print handouts for your audience. In case you can't be there in person to deliver your presentation, this chapter shows you how to create a user-run presentation, a self-running presentation, and video of a presentation.

All about Notes

Notes are strictly for the speaker. The unwashed masses can't see them. Don't hesitate to write notes to yourself when you put together your presentation. The notes will come in handy when you're rehearsing and giving your presentation.

They give you ideas for what to say and help you communicate better. Here are instructions for entering, editing, and printing notes:

» **Entering a note:** To enter a note, start in Normal or Outline view and enter the note in the Notes pane. If the Notes pane isn't displayed, click the Notes button on the status bar or View tab. Treat the Notes pane like a page in a word processor. For example, press Enter to start a new paragraph and press the Tab key to indent text. You can drag the border above the Notes pane up or down to make the pane larger or smaller.

» **Editing notes in Notes Page view:** After you've jotted down a bunch of notes, switch to Notes Page view and edit them. To switch to Notes Page view, visit the View tab and click the Notes Page button. Notes appear in a text frame below a picture of the slide to which they refer. You may have to zoom in to read them.

» **Printing your notes:** On the File tab, choose Print (or press Ctrl+P). You see the Print window. Under Settings, open the second drop-down list and choose Note Pages on the pop-up menu. Then click the Print button.

Rehearsing with a Robot Coach

How'd you like a coach to help you perfect your PowerPoint presentation? Power-Point can't provide a flesh-and-blood coach, but it can critique presentations and generate reports like the one shown in Figure 5-1. These reports tell you whether your pacing, pitch, and speech are up to snuff. They offer advice for giving better presentations.

Open the presentation you have worked so hard to create and follow these steps to see whether PowerPoint's robot coach can be of help:

1. **On the Slide Show tab, click the Rehearse with Coach button.**

The Welcome screen appears.

2. **Click the Start Rehearsing button and give your presentation.**

Pretend you're giving your presentation before a real audience. Go from slide to slide, keeping the pace you expect to keep. As you go along, PowerPoint offers the occasional tip or word of encouragement in the box in the lower-right corner of the screen.

When your presentation is complete, the Your Rehearsal Report screen appears (see Figure 5-1).

3. **Examine the rehearsal report and take note of where PowerPoint says you can do better.**

I hope you didn't "umm" and "uhh" as much as I did.

PowerPoint can critique a presentation only if you trust Microsoft to examine PowerPoint presentations and the content of all your Office files. For more information about this topic, see Book 1, Chapter 1.

FIGURE 5-1:
A Rehearsal Report with advice for improving a presentation.

Rehearsing and Timing Your Presentation

Slide presentations and theatrical presentations have this in common: They are as good as the number of times you rehearse them. Be sure to rehearse your presentation many times over. The more you rehearse, the more comfortable you are giving a presentation. Follow these steps to rehearse a presentation, record its length, and record how long each slide is displayed:

1. **Select the first slide in your presentation.**

2. **Go to the Slide Show tab.**

3. **Click the Rehearse Timings button.**

The Recording toolbar appears, as shown in Figure 5-2, and you switch to Slide Show view.

4. **Give your presentation one slide at a time, and click the Next button on the Recording toolbar to go from slide to slide.**

When each slide appears, imagine that you're presenting it to an audience. Say what you intend to say during the real presentation. If you anticipate questions from the audience, allot time for questions and answers.

The Recording toolbar tells you how long each slide has been displayed and how long your presentation is so far. You can do these tasks from the Recording toolbar:

- **Go to the next slide:** Click the Next button.

- **Pause recording:** Click the Pause Recording button to temporarily stop the recording so that you can feed the dog or take a phone call. Click the Resume Recording button to resume recording.

- **Repeat a slide:** Click the Repeat button if you get befuddled and want to start over with a slide. The slide timing returns to 0:00:00.

5. **In the dialog box that asks whether you want to keep the slide timings, note how long your presentation is (refer to Figure 5-2).**

Is your presentation too long or too short? I hope, like Baby Bear's porridge, your presentation is "just right." But if it's too long or short, you have some work to do. You have to figure out how to shorten or lengthen it.

6. **In the dialog box that asks whether you want to keep the new slide timings, click Yes if you want to see how long each slide stayed onscreen during the rehearsal.**

By clicking Yes, you can go to Slide Sorter view and see how long each slide remained onscreen.

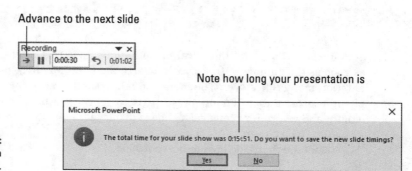

Advance to the next slide

Note how long your presentation is

FIGURE 5-2:
Timing a rehearsal.

WARNING

If you save the slide timings, PowerPoint assumes that, during a presentation, you want to advance to the next slide manually or after the recorded time, whichever comes first. For example, suppose the first slide in your presentation remained onscreen for a minute during the rehearsal. During your presentation, the first slide will remain onscreen for a minute and automatically yield to the second slide unless you click to advance to the second slide before the minute has elapsed. If you recorded slide timings strictly to find out how long your presentation is, you need to tell PowerPoint not to advance automatically to the next slide during a presentation after the recorded time period elapses. On the Slide Show tab, deselect the Use Timings check box.

Showing Your Presentation

Compared to the preliminary work, giving a presentation can seem kind of anti-climactic. All you have to do is go from slide to slide and woo your audience with your smooth-as-silk voice and powerful oratory skills. Well, at least the move-from-slide-to-slide part is pretty easy. These pages explain how to start and end a presentation, all the different ways to advance or retreat from slide to slide, and how to jump to different slides.

Starting and ending a presentation

Here are the different ways to start a presentation from the beginning:

>> On the Quick Access toolbar or Slide Show tab, click the From Beginning button (or press F5).

>> Select the first slide and then click the Slide Show view button on the status bar.

You can start a presentation in the middle by selecting a slide in the middle and then clicking the Slide Show view button, or by going to the Slide Show tab and clicking the From Current Slide button.

Here are the different ways to end a presentation prematurely:

>> Press Esc or – (the Hyphen key).

>> Click the Slide Control button and choose End Show on the pop-up menu. The Slide Control button is located in the lower-left corner of the screen, as shown in Figure 5-3.

>> Right-click and choose End Show in the shortcut menu.

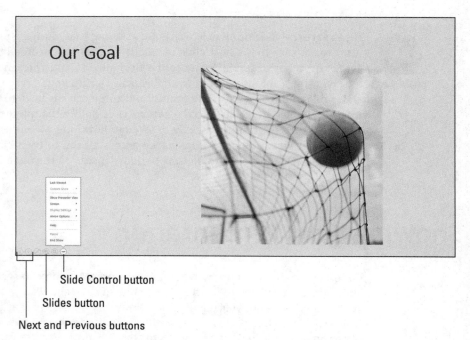

FIGURE 5-3:
Besides using keyboard shortcuts, you can move from slide to slide by clicking onscreen.

Slide Control button

Slides button

Next and Previous buttons

Going from slide to slide

In a nutshell, PowerPoint offers four ways to move from slide to slide in a presentation. Table 5-1 describes techniques for navigating a presentation using the four different ways:

» **Click the Next or Previous button:** These buttons are located in the lower-left corner of the screen (refer to Figure 5-3). If you don't see them, jiggle the mouse.

» **Click the Slides button and choose a slide:** Clicking the Slides button displays thumbnail versions of all the slides in the presentation. Click a thumbnail to go to a specific slide. (To return to the slide you saw previously, right-click and choose Last Viewed on the shortcut menu.)

» **Right-click onscreen:** Right-click and choose a navigation option at the top of the shortcut menu.

» **Press a keyboard shortcut:** Press one of the numerous keyboard shortcuts that PowerPoint offers for going from slide to slide (see Table 5-1).

TABLE 5-1   **Techniques for Getting from Slide to Slide**

To Go Here	Button	Right-Click and Choose...	Keyboard Shortcut
Next slide*	Next	Next	Enter, spacebar, N, PgDn, ↓, or →
Previous slide	Previous	Previous	Backspace, P, PgUp, ↑, or ←
Specific slide	Slides	See All Slides	*Slide number*+Enter; Ctrl+S and then select *Slide number and title*
Last viewed slide	Slide Control	Last Viewed	
First slide			Home
Last slide			End

If animations are on a slide, commands for going to the next slide instead make animations play in sequence. To bypass animations and go to the next slide, use a command for going forward across several slides. (See "Jumping forward or backward to a specific slide.")

Going forward (or backward) from slide to slide

To go forward from one slide to the following slide in a presentation, click onscreen. After you click, the next slide appears. If all goes well, clicking is the only technique you need to know when giving a presentation to go from slide to slide, but Table 5-1 lists other ways to go to the next slide in a presentation as well as techniques for going backward to the previous slide.

TIP

To go to the first slide in a presentation, press Home; to go to the last slide, press End.

Jumping forward or backward to a specific slide

If you find it necessary to jump forward or backward across several slides in your presentation to get to the slide you want to show, it can be done with these techniques:

» Click the Slides button in the lower-left corner of the screen (refer to Figure 5-3). Thumbnail versions of the slides in the presentation appear. Click a thumbnail to view a slide.

» Press Ctrl+S. You see the All Slides dialog box. It lists all slides in your presentation. Select the slide you want to show and click the Go To button (or double-click the slide).

PRESENTER VIEW FOR DUAL MONITORS

If two monitors are connected to your computer, you have the option of using Presenter view to give presentations. In Presenter view, the full-screen slide appears on one monitor and a special screen for showing your presentation appears in the other. In this screen, speaker notes are easier to read, and the buttons and other controls for getting from slide to slide are larger. Moreover, a timer shows you how long each slide has been onscreen.

Regardless of whether two monitors are connected to your computer, you can test-drive Presenter view by pressing Alt+F5.

To give presentations in Presenter view, go to the Slide Show tab and select Use Presenter View. On the Monitor drop-down list, choose Automatic to allow PowerPoint to choose which monitor the audience sees, or choose a monitor name to select the monitor yourself.

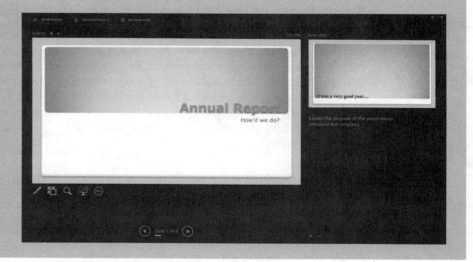

Tricks for Making Presentations a Little Livelier

Herewith are a few tricks to make your presentations a little livelier. I explain how to draw on slides, highlight parts of slides, blank the screen, and zoom in. Take this bag of tricks to your next PowerPoint presentation to make your presentation stand out.

Wielding a pen or highlighter in a presentation

Drawing on slides is an excellent way to add a little something to a presentation. Whip out a pen and draw on a slide to get the audience's attention. Draw to underline words or draw check marks as you hit the key points, as shown in Figure 5-4.

FIGURE 5-4: Choose a pen and ink color on the Pen pop-up list.

Select a color

Choose a pen or highlighter

Drawing or highlighting on a slide

Follow these steps during a presentation to draw or highlight on a slide:

1. **Click the Pen button and choose a color on the pop-up menu.**

The Pen button is located in the lower-left corner of the screen (refer to Figure 5-4).

2. **Click the Pen button again and choose Pen (to draw on slides) or Highlighter (to highlight parts of a slide).**

PowerPoint also offers the Laser Pointer, which you can use to call out important parts of a slide during a presentation.

3. **Drag the mouse to draw or highlight on the slide.**

4. **Press Esc when you're finished using the pen or highlighter.**

WARNING

Be careful not to press Esc twice because the second press tells PowerPoint to end the presentation.

You can also right-click, choose Pointer Options, and make selections on the submenu to draw or highlight (choose Ink Color to choose a color).

Hiding and erasing pen and highlighter markings

Follow these instructions to hide and erase pen and highlighter markings during a slide presentation:

>> **Temporarily showing or hiding markings:** Right-click and choose Screen ➪ Show/Hide Ink.

>> **Permanently erasing markings one at a time:** Click the Pen button and choose Eraser (or right-click and choose Pointer Options ➪ Eraser). The Eraser appears. Click a line to erase it. Press Esc after you're finished using the Eraser.

>> **Permanently erasing all the markings on a slide:** Press E or click the Pen button and choose Erase All Ink on Slide (refer to Figure 5-4).

REMEMBER

At the end of a presentation in which you marked on slides, the Want to Keep Ink Annotations? dialog box asks whether you want to keep or discard your markings. Click the Keep or Discard button. If you elect to keep them, the markings become part of your presentation, and you can't delete them with the Eraser or by choosing the Erase All Ink on Slide command.

Follow these instructions to erase or hide pen and highlighter markings *after* a slide presentation:

>> **Erase the markings:** On the Review tab, open the drop-down list on the Hide Ink button and choose one of these options:

  • **Delete All Ink on this Slide:** Deletes markings you made on a slide you selected.

  • **Delete All Ink in This Presentation:** Deletes markings you made on all the slides in your presentation.

>> **Hide the markings:** On the Review tab, click the Hide Ink button.

If you prefer not to see the Want to Keep Ink Annotations? dialog box because you intend never to keep your markings, go to the File tab and choose Options. In the PowerPoint Options dialog box, select the Advanced category and deselect the Prompt to Keep Ink Annotations When Exiting check box.

Blanking the screen

TIP

Here's a technique for adding a little drama to a presentation: When you want the audience to focus on you, not the PowerPoint screen, blank the screen. Make an all-black or all-white screen appear where a PowerPoint slide used to be. Every head in the audience will turn your way and listen keenly to what you have to say next. I sure hope you have something important to say.

Follow these instructions to blank out the screen during a presentation:

>> **Black screen:** Press B, the period key, or right-click and choose Screen ⇨ Black Screen.

>> **White screen:** Press W, the comma key, or right-click and choose Screen ⇨ White Screen.

To see a PowerPoint slide again, click onscreen or press any key on the keyboard.

Zooming in

Yet another way to add pizazz to a presentation is to zoom in on slides. To draw the audience's attention to part of a slide, you can magnify it by following these steps:

1. **Click the Zoom button in the lower-left corner of the screen.**

You can also right-click and choose Zoom In. The pointer changes to a magnifying glass.

2. **Move to and click the part of a slide you want the audience to focus on.**

The pointer changes to hand. At this point, you can drag onscreen to move the zoomed-in slide to a different position.

3. **Press Esc.**

Delivering a Presentation When You Can't Be There in Person

Let me count the ways that you can deliver a presentation without being there in person:

>> Deliver your presentation in the form of a *handout,* a printed version of the presentation with thumbnail slides.

- » Create a self-running presentation.

- » Create a user-run presentation with action buttons that others can click to get from slide to slide.

- » Show your presentation over the Internet.

- » Make a video of your presentation.

- » Show a presentation as an animated GIF.

The rest of this chapter explains these techniques for delivering a presentation when you can't be there in the flesh.

Providing handouts for your audience

Handouts are thumbnail versions of slides that you print and distribute to the audience. Figure 5-5 shows examples of handouts. Handouts come in one, two, three, four, six, or nine slides per page. If you select three slides per page, the handout includes lines that your audience can take notes on (see Figure 5-5); the other sizes don't offer these lines.

FIGURE 5-5:
Examples of handouts (from left to right) at one, three, six, and nine slides per page.

To tell PowerPoint how to construct handouts, go to the View tab and click the Handout Master button. In Handout Master view, on the Handout Master tab, you can do a number of things to make your handouts more useful and attractive. As you make your choices, keep your eye on the sample handout page; it shows what your choices mean in real terms.

- » **Handout Orientation:** Select Portrait or Landscape. In landscape mode, the page is turned on its side and is longer than it is tall.

- » **Slide Size:** Select Standard or Widescreen.

- » **Slides-Per-Page:** Open the drop-down list and choose how many slides appear on each page. Refer to Figure 5-5 to see some of the choices.

>> **Header:** Select the Header check box and enter a header in the text frame to make a header appear in the upper-left corner of all handout pages. Candidates for headers include your name, your company name, and the location of a conference or seminar. The point is to help your audience identify the handout.

>> **Footer:** Select the Footer check box and enter a footer in the text frame in the lower-left corner of handout pages. Candidates for footers are the same as candidates for headers.

>> **Date:** Select this check box if you want the date you print the handout to appear on the handout pages.

>> **Page Number:** Select this check box if you want page numbers to appear on the handout pages.

>> **Background Styles:** Open the Background Styles drop-down list and select a gradient or color, if you're so inclined. Chapter 2 of this minibook explains background styles. Make sure that the background doesn't obscure the slide thumbnails or put too much of a burden on your printer.

To print handouts, go to the File tab and choose Print (or press Ctrl+P). You see the Print window. Under Settings, open the second drop-down list, and under Handouts, choose how many slides to print on each page. Then click the Print button.

Creating a self-running, kiosk-style presentation

A self-running, kiosk-style presentation is one that plays on its own. You can make it play from a kiosk or simply send it to coworkers so that they can play it. In a self-running presentation, slides appear onscreen one after the other without you or anyone else having to advance the presentation from slide to slide. When the presentation finishes, it starts all over again from Slide 1.

Telling PowerPoint how long to keep slides onscreen

PowerPoint offers two ways to indicate how long you want each slide to stay onscreen:

>> **Entering the time periods yourself:** Switch to Slide Sorter view and go to the Transitions tab. Then deselect the On Mouse Click check box and select the After check box, as shown in Figure 5-6. Next, tell PowerPoint to keep all slides

onscreen the same amount of time, or choose a different time period for each slide:

- **All slides the same time:** Enter a time period in the After text box and click the Apply to All button.

- **Each slide a different time:** One by one, select each slide and enter a time period in the After text box.

>> **Rehearsing the presentation:** Rehearse the presentation and save the timings. (See "Rehearsing and Timing Your Presentation," earlier in this chapter.) Be sure to save the slide timings after you're finished rehearsing. In Slide Sorter view, you can see how long each slide will stay onscreen (see Figure 5-6).

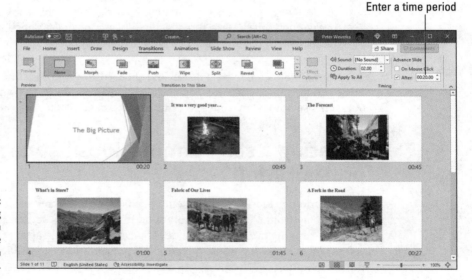

Enter a time period

FIGURE 5-6:
Enter how long you want each slide or all the slides to remain onscreen.

Telling PowerPoint that your presentation is self-running

Before you can "self-run" a presentation, you have to tell PowerPoint that you want it to do that. Self-running presentations don't have the control buttons in the lower-left corner. You can't click the screen or press a key to move forward or backward to the next or previous slide. The only control you have over a self-running presentation is pressing the Esc key (pressing Esc ends the presentation).

Follow these steps to make yours a kiosk-style, self-running presentation:

1. **Go to the Slide Show tab.**

2. **Click the Set Up Slide Show button.**

   You see the Set Up Slide Show dialog box.

3. **Under Show Type, choose the Browsed at a Kiosk (Full Screen) option.**

   When you select this option, PowerPoint automatically selects the Loop Continuously Until 'Esc' check box.

4. **Click OK.**

   That's all there is to it.

Creating a user-run presentation

A *user-run*, or *interactive*, presentation is one that the viewer gets to control. The viewer decides which slide appears next and how long each slide remains onscreen. User-run presentations are similar to websites. Users can browse from slide to slide at their own speed. They can pick and choose what they want to investigate. They can backtrack and view slides they saw previously or return to the first slide and start anew.

Self-run presentations are shown in Reading view (click the Reading View button on the status bar to see what self-run presentations look like). A taskbar appears along the bottom of the screen. On the right side of the taskbar, viewers can click the Previous button or Next button to go from slide to slide. They can also click the Menu button to open a pop-up menu with commands for navigating slides.

Another way to help readers get from slide to slide is to create action buttons. An *action button* is a button that you can click to go to another slide in your presentation or the previous slide you viewed, whatever that slide was. PowerPoint provides 12 action buttons in the Shapes gallery. Figure 5-7 shows some action buttons and the dialog box you use to create them.

Drawing an action button

After you draw an action button from the Shapes gallery, the Action Settings dialog box shown in Figure 5-7 appears so that you can tell PowerPoint which slide to go to when the button is clicked. Select the slide (or master slide) that needs action and follow these steps to adorn it with an action button:

1. **Starting in Normal view on the Home or Insert tab, open the Shapes gallery and scroll to the Action Buttons category at the bottom.**

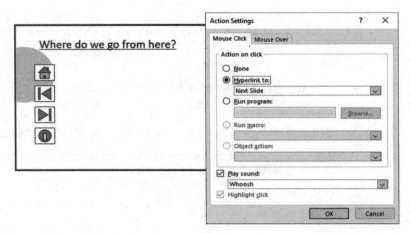

FIGURE 5-7:
Action buttons.

2. **Click an action button to select it.**

   Choose the button that best illustrates which slide will appear when the button is clicked.

3. **Draw the button on the slide.**

   To do so, drag the pointer in a diagonal fashion. (As far as drawing them is concerned, action buttons work the same as all other shapes and other objects. Book 8, Chapter 4 explains how to manipulate objects.) The Action Settings dialog box shown previously in Figure 5-7 appears after you finish drawing your button.

4. **Go to the Mouse Over tab if you want users to activate the button by moving the mouse pointer over it, not clicking it.**

5. **Select the Hyperlink To option button.**

6. **On the Hyperlink To drop-down list, choose an action for the button.**

   You can go to the next slide, the previous slide, the first or last slide in a presentation, the last slide you viewed, or a specific slide.

   To make clicking the action button take users to a specific slide, choose Slide on the list. You see the Hyperlink to Slide dialog box, which lists each slide in your presentation. Select a slide and click OK.

7. **To play a sound when your action button is activated, select the Play Sound check box and select a sound on the drop-down list.**

TIP

   "Mouse-over" hyperlinks require sound accompaniment so that users understand when they've activated an action button.

8. **Click OK in the Actions Settings dialog box.**

   To test your button, you can right-click it and choose Open Link.

To change a button's action, select it and then click the Action button on the Insert tab, or right-click your action button and choose Edit Link. In the Action Settings dialog box, choose a new action (or None) and click OK.

Making yours a user-run presentation

Follow these steps to declare yours a user-run presentation:

1. **Go to the Slide Show tab.**

2. **Click the Set Up Slide Show button.**

You see the Set Up Show dialog box.

3. **Select the Browsed by an Individual (Window) option button.**

4. **Click OK.**

Your presentation is no longer quite yours. It also belongs to all the people who view it in your absence.

Presenting a presentation online

Presenting online means to play a presentation on your computer for others who watch it over the Internet. As you go from slide to slide, audience members see the slides on their web browsers. Presenting online is an excellent way to show a presentation to others during a conference call or to others who don't have PowerPoint.

Office 365 creates a temporary web address for you to show your presentation. Before showing it, you send audience members a link to this web address. Audience members, in turn, click the link to open and watch your presentation in their web browsers.

WARNING

Before presenting online, make sure you know the email addresses of the people who will view your presentation. Make sure as well that they are available to view it. Online presentations are shown in real time. After you close a presentation, its link is broken and the audience can no longer watch it in their web browsers.

Follow these steps to show a presentation online:

1. **On the Slide Show tab, click the Present Online button.**

The Present Online dialog box appears.

2. **Select Enable Remote Viewers to Download the Presentation if you want audience members to have a copy of the presentation as well as view it.**

3. **Click the Connect button.**

Office 365 generates a URL link for you to send to the people who will view your presentation, as shown in Figure 5-8.

4. **Send the link to your audience.**

You can send the link with Outlook or another email software.

- **Copy and send the link by email:** Click Copy Link to copy the link to the Clipboard. Then, in your email software, paste the link into invitations you send to audience members.

- **Send the link with Outlook:** Click the Send in Email link. An Outlook message window appears. Address and send the message.

5. **Make sure that audience members have received the email invitation and are ready to watch your presentation.**

6. **Click the Start Presentation button.**

Audience members see the presentation in their browsers.

7. **Give the presentation.**

Use the same techniques to advance or retreat from slide to slide as you use in any presentation.

When the presentation ends, you land in the Present Online tab.

8. **On the Present Online tab, click the End Online Presentation button; click End Online Presentation in the confirmation dialog box.**

Your audience sees this notice: "The presentation has ended."

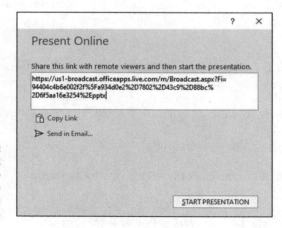

FIGURE 5-8:
Others can click the URL link to view an online presentation in a browser window.

Creating a presentation video

Yet another way to distribute a video is to record it in an MPEG-4 file and distribute the file to others. PowerPoint offers a command for creating an MPEG-4 version of a presentation. Every aspect of a PowerPoint presentation, including transitions, animations, sound, video itself, and voice narrations, is recorded in the presentation video.

Figure 5-9 shows an MPEG-4 version of a PowerPoint presentation being played in Windows Media Player.

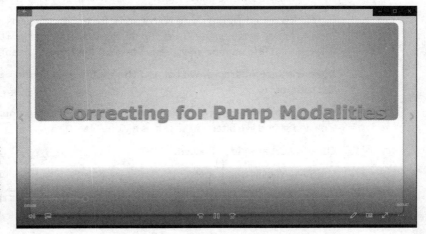

FIGURE 5-9:
Viewing an MPEG-4 version of a PowerPoint presentation in Windows Media Player.

TIP

Before creating your presentation video, consider how long you want each slide to appear onscreen. You can make each slide appear for a specific length of time or make all slides appear for the same length of time. To decide for yourself how long each slide appears, switch to Slide Sorter view, go to the Transitions tab, and for each slide, select the After check box and enter a measurement in the After text box. (Earlier in this chapter, "Creating a self-running, kiosk-style presentation" explains in detail how to establish how long each slide stays onscreen.)

Follow these steps to create an MPEG-4 version of a PowerPoint presentation:

1. **On the File tab, choose Export.**

2. **Choose Create a Video.**

   You see the Create a Video window.

3. **Open the first drop-down list and choose a display resolution for your video.**

4. **Open the second drop-down list and choose whether to use recorded timings and narrations.**

Your choices are twofold. If you recorded a voice narration for your PowerPoint presentation, choose the second option if you want to preserve the voice narration in the video.

- **Don't Use Recorded Timings and Narrations:** Each slide stays onscreen for the same amount of time. Enter a time period in the Seconds to Spend on Each Slide box to declare how long each slide stays onscreen.

- **Use Recorded Timings and Narrations:** Each slide stays onscreen for the time period listed on the Transition tab (see the Tip at the start of this section to find out how to list slide times on the Transition tab).

5. **Open the second drop-down list and choose Preview Timings and Narrations.**

Your presentation video plays. How do you like it? This is what your video will look and sound like after you save it as a video file.

6. **Click the Create Video button.**

The Save As dialog box opens.

7. **Choose a folder for storing the MPEG-4 file, enter a name for the file, and click the Save button.**

The status bar along the bottom of the PowerPoint screen shows the progress of the video as it is being created. Creating a video can take several minutes, depending on how large your PowerPoint presentation is and how many fancy gizmos, such as sound and animation, it contains.

Showing a presentation as an animated GIF

Yet another way to show a presentation without being there is to save it as an animated GIF (graphic interface format) file. An *animated GIF* is series of graphic images appearing one after the other. In the case of a PowerPoint presentation, each slide is made into a GIF image, and the images play consecutively from the first slide in your presentation to the last. All you need is a web browser to view an animated GIF. Saving a PowerPoint presentation as an animated GIF is a way to distribute presentations to people who don't have PowerPoint.

In my experience, only the most rudimentary PowerPoint presentations can be saved as animated GIFs. Follow these steps to save a presentation as an animated GIF:

1. **On the File tab, choose Export.**

   The Export window opens.

2. **Choose Create an Animated GIF.**

   You see the Create an Animated GIF window.

3. **Open the first drop-down list and choose a file size.**

4. **Select the Make Background Transparent check box if you want to remove themes and backgrounds from slide images.**

5. **Enter how many seconds you want each slide to appear.**

   Sorry, all slides in the presentation appear for the same length of time.

6. **If you want only a handful of slides, not all slides, to appear, enter slide numbers in the Slides text boxes.**

7. **Click the Create GIF button.**

   The Save As dialog box opens.

8. **Choose a folder for storing the animated GIF, enter a name, and click the Save button.**

   Double-click the animated GIF file to open and play it in a photo application.

5

Outlook 365

Contents at a Glance

IN THIS CHAPTER

» **Getting around in Outlook**

» **Searching in folders**

» **Deleting items**

» **Archiving old-and-in-the-way items**

Chapter **1**

Outlook Basics

This chapter pulls back the curtain and gives you a first glimpse of *Outlook*, the emailer, calendar, and personal organizer in the Office 365 suite of applications. Read on to find out once and for all what Outlook does, how to get from folder to folder, and the different ways to view the stuff in folders. You can find advice about keeping folders well organized, deleting stuff, and cleaning out items in folders that you no longer need.

What Is Outlook, Anyway?

Outlook isn't in character with the rest of the Office applications. It's a little different in that what you see onscreen changes when you click an App button. Click an App button in Outlook — Mail, Calendar, People, Tasks — and you go to a different Outlook window altogether. The App buttons are located on the left side of the screen.

Outlook serves many purposes. To wit, Outlook is all this:

» **An emailer:** You can use it to send and receive email messages and files, as well as organize email messages in different folders so that you can keep track of them. (See Chapter 3 of this minibook.)

>> **An appointment scheduler:** Outlook is a calendar for scheduling appointments and meetings, including online meetings managed by way of Microsoft Teams. You can tell at a glance when and where you're expected, be alerted to upcoming appointments and meetings, and invite coworkers to meetings. (See Chapter 4 of this minibook, and if you use Microsoft Teams, Book 10.)

>> **An address book:** Outlook is an address book for storing the addresses, phone numbers, and email addresses of friends, foes, clients, and family members. (See Chapter 2 of this minibook.)

>> **A task reminder:** Outlook is a means of planning projects. You can tell when deadlines fall and plan your workload accordingly. (See Chapter 4 of this minibook.)

>> **A notes receptacle:** Outlook is a place to jot down notes and reminders.

Navigating the Outlook Apps

The first thing you should know about Outlook is this: Outlook offers several different apps and they are available from the app bar, as shown in Figure 1-1.

App bar

Folder pane

Selected folder

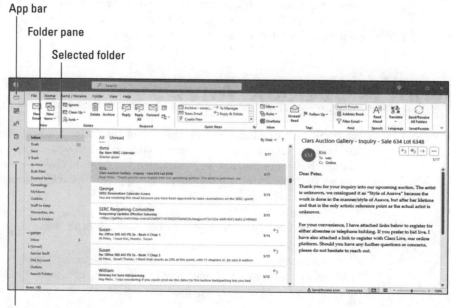

FIGURE 1-1:
The Mail app with the Inbox folder selected.

Click to see more app names

When you want to undertake a new task, click an App button on the app bar — Mail, Calendar, People, and so on (see Figure 1-1). Clicking one of these buttons displays folders that have to do, respectively, with your Mail, Calendar, Contacts, and so on. These folders appear on the Folder pane (see Figure 1-1).

REMEMBER

If you don't see the Folder pane, go to the View tab, click the Folder Pane button, and choose Normal on the drop-down list.

TIP

You can open a folder in a new window. To do so, right-click a app bar button or folder name and choose Open in New Window.

Categorizing Items

One of your biggest tasks in Outlook, if you choose to accept it, is to categorize items in folders so that you can find and deal with them. Finding items can be a chore in a folder with a lot of items, but by categorizing items, you can find the ones you're looking for. Categories are color-coded to make identifying them easier. After you assign a category to an item, you can arrange items in folders by category, and in so doing, find items. Categorizing is a great way to stay on top of all the chores you have to do.

TECHNICAL STUFF

Categories aren't available for some kinds of email. To get technical about it, if yours is an IMAP-type email account, you can't categorize your email messages.

Creating a category

Follow these steps to create a category for organizing folder items:

1. **Select an item in a folder to which you want to assign your new category.**

   For example, select a contact or an email message.

2. **On the Home tab, click the Categorize button and choose All Categories on the drop-down list.**

   You see the Color Categories dialog box, as shown in Figure 1-2. At this point, you can create a category from scratch or revamp one of Outlook's color-named categories:

   - **Creating your own category:** Click the New button to open the Add New Category dialog box, as shown in Figure 1-2. Then enter a name for your category and choose a color on the drop-down list. While you're at it, you can open the Shortcut Key drop-down list and choose a shortcut key combination for assigning your new category to items. Click the OK button in the Color Categories dialog box.

- **Renaming a category:** In the Color Categories dialog box (see Figure 1-2), select a color category and click the Rename button. Then enter a new name in place of the old one. You can choose a different color for your category by choosing a color in the Color drop-down list. To assign it a shortcut key, open the Shortcut Key drop-down list and choose a shortcut key combination.

To delete a category, return to the Color Categories dialog box, select the category's name, and click the Delete button. Although the category is deceased, items to which you assigned the category keep their category assignments.

Assigning items to categories

Follow these steps to assign a category to a folder item:

1. **Select the item.**

2. **On the Home tab, click the Categorize button and choose a category on the drop-down list.**

You can also right-click, choose Categorize, and select a category on the shortcut menu, or press a Ctrl+key combination if you assigned one to the category. An item can be assigned more than one category.

To remove a category assignment, select the item, click the Categorize button, and choose Clear All Categories.

Arranging items by category in folders

To arrange items by category in a folder, select the folder in the Folder pane and use one of these techniques:

» On the View tab, choose Categories in the Arrangement gallery.

» In a list, click the Categories column heading to sort items by category.

Searching for Stray Folder Items

If you can't locate an item in a folder by scrolling, changing views, or any other means, run a search. To start a search, go to the folder you want to search, click in the Search box (or press Ctrl+E), enter a search term, and press Enter. You can find the Search box above the Ribbon. As soon as you click in the Search box, Outlook opens the Search tab so that you can describe what you're seeking, as shown in Figure 1-3.

Search box

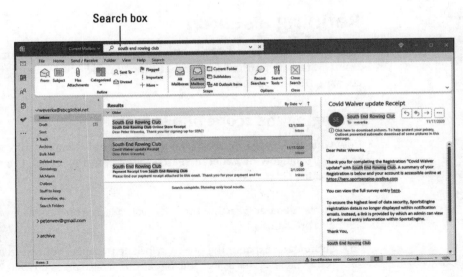

FIGURE 1-3: Describe what you're searching for in the Search box.

As the following pages explain, you can conduct an instant search, narrow your search by choosing Refine options, or conduct an advanced search starting from the Search tab. To close the search and go back to seeing the contents of your folder, click the Close Search button on the Search tab.

Here's a fast way to run a search: Click the Recent Searches button on the Search tab and choose a search on the drop-down list to rerun one of the last six searches you conducted.

Conducting an instant search

What Microsoft calls an "instant search" is a keyword search of the folder you're viewing. If a keyword you enter in the Search box is found in an email message, calendar appointment, contact, or other item, the item appears in the search results and the keyword is highlighted (refer to Figure 1-3).

As you type in the Search box, Outlook suggests search terms on a drop-down list. You can click one of these terms to undertake a search.

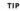

To change how instant searches are conducted, click the Search Tools button on the Search tab and choose Search Options on the drop-down list. You go to the Search category in the Outlook Options dialog box. From there, you can choose which folders are searched and how search results are displayed when you conduct an instant search.

Refining a search

Refine a search when an instant search brings up too many or too few search results. Starting on the Search tab, refine your search by changing its scope and choosing Refine options.

Changing the scope of a search

How wide the scope of a search is determines how many results are found in the search. To narrow or widen a search, click a button in the Scope group on the Search tab:

>> **Current Folder:** Searches the folder you selected on the Folder pane. You can also press Ctrl+Alt+K.

>> **Subfolders:** Expands the search to include the folder you selected on the Folder pane as well as its subfolders. You can also press Ctrl+Alt+Z.

- » **All Mailboxes (for email searching only):** If you receive email through Outlook from more than one address (Outlook calls different addresses "mailboxes"), this option expands a search to include email from all addresses. You can also press Ctrl+Alt+A.

- » **Current Mailbox (for email searching only):** Expands the search of email from one address (one "mailbox") to include all folders that contain email, including, for example, the Draft and Sent folders,

- » **All Outlook Items:** Expands the search to all Outlook folders. Move the pointer over the search results to see a pop-up box that lists which folder an item is stored in.

Choosing Refine options

To narrow a search, click buttons in the Refine group on the Search tab. After you click a button, Outlook provides a place in the Search box for you to enter a keyword. Which buttons appear in the Refine group depends on which folder you search.

In a folder that contains email, for example, you can click the From button and enter a sender name in the Search box to search for emails you received from a particular person. You can click the Subject button and enter a keyword to search the subject descriptions in email you received.

Conducting an advanced search

If, woe is me, you can't find what you're looking for with an instant search or a refined search, you can try your luck with an advanced search.

On the Search tab, click the Search Tools button and choose Advanced Find on the drop-down list. You see the Advanced Find dialog box, as shown in Figure 1-4. In the Look drop-down list, choose what you want to search for. Click the Browse button to open the Select Folder(s) dialog box, where you can select more than one folder to search in. Then choose options in the three tabs to formulate your search. Which options are available depends on which folder you're searching. Click Find Now to start your search.

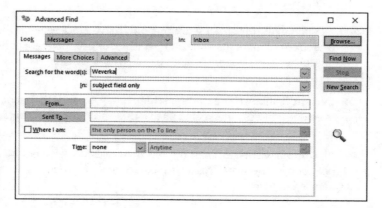

FIGURE 1-4:
Pinpoint what you're searching for in the Advanced Find dialog box.

Deleting Email Messages, Contacts, Tasks, and Other Items

Outlook folders are notorious for filling quickly. Email messages, contacts, and tasks soon clog the folders if you spend any time in Outlook. From time to time, go through the email folders, Contacts window, Task window, and Calendar to delete items you no longer need. To delete items, select them and do one of the following:

» On the Home tab, click the Delete button.

» Press the Delete key.

» Right-click and choose Delete.

REMEMBER

Deleted items — email messages, calendar appointments, contacts, and tasks — land in the Deleted Items folder in case you want to recover them. To delete items once and for all, open the Deleted Items folder and start deleting like a madman.

To empty the Delete Items folder altogether, right-click the folder and choose Empty Folder. You can also visit the File tab, choose Info, click the Tools button, and choose Empty Deleted Items Folder on the drop-down list.

TIP

To recover a deleted item, open the Deleted Items folder, right-click the item, choose Move, and select the location where the item came from.

Be sure to check out "Running the Mailbox Cleanup command" at the end of this chapter. It explains a quick way to delete unwanted Inbox messages.

Cleaning Out Your Folders

Getting rid of unneeded items in folders is essential for good mental health. All that clutter can be distressing. Earlier in this chapter, "Deleting Email Messages, Contacts, Tasks, and Other Items," explains how to muck out folders by emptying them. These pages explain two more techniques for removing detritus from folders — archiving and the Mailbox Cleanup command.

Archiving the old stuff

In some cases, Outlook puts email messages, tasks, and appointments older than six months in the *Archive folder,* a special folder for items that Outlook thinks are stale and not worth keeping anymore. Outlook calls sending these items to the Archive folder "autoarchiving." Items that have been archived aren't lost forever. You can visit them by opening the Archive Folders folder and its subfolders on the Folder pane. These folders and subfolders are created automatically the first time you archive items.

Archiving is a way of stripping your mail folders, tasks lists, and calendar of items that aren't necessarily important anymore, but you still want to keep. How and when items are archived is up to you. To archive items, you can archive them on your own, establish a default set of archiving rules that apply to all folders, or, if a folder needs individual attention and shouldn't be subject to the default archiving rules, establish special rules for that folder. Each folder can have its own set of archiving rules or be subject to the default rules.

To tell Outlook how to archive old stuff:

>> **Establishing default archiving rules:** On the File tab, choose Options to open the Outlook Options dialog box. Then, on the Advanced tab, click the AutoArchive Settings button. You see the AutoArchive dialog box shown in Figure 1-5. See the upcoming section "Default archiving rules."

>> **Establishing rules for a specific folder:** Select the folder, go to the Folder tab, and click the AutoArchive Settings button. You see the AutoArchive tab of the Properties dialog box, as shown in Figure 1-5. See "Archiving rules for a folder."

FIGURE 1-5:
Making the
default archiving
rules (left) and
rules for a folder
(right).

Default archiving rules

Negotiate these options in the AutoArchive dialog box to establish default archiving rules (see Figure 1-5):

>> **Run AutoArchive Every:** Enter a number to tell Outlook how often to archive items.

>> **Prompt Before AutoArchive Runs:** If this check box is selected, you see a message box before archiving begins, and you can decline to archive if you want by selecting No in the message box.

>> **Delete Expired Items (Email Folders Only):** Select this check box to delete all email messages when the time period has expired.

>> **Archive or Delete Old Items:** Deselect this option if you *don't* want to archive items.

>> **Show Archive Folder in Folder List:** Select this option if you want to keep the archived version of the folder in the Folder pane. Archived items are kept in this folder so that you can review them.

>> **Clean Out Items Older Than:** Choose a cut-off time period after which to archive items.

>> **Move Old Items To:** Click the Browse button and select a folder if you want to store the Archive file in a certain location.

>> **Permanently Delete Old Items:** Select this option if you want to delete, not archive, old items.

Archiving rules for a folder

Choose among these options in the Properties dialog box to establish archiving rules for a specific folder (refer to Figure 1-5):

>> **Do Not Archive Items in This Folder:** Select this option if items in the folder aren't worth archiving.

>> **Archive Items in This Folder Using the Default Settings:** Select this option to defer to the default archiving rules for the folder.

>> **Archive This Folder Using These Settings:** Select this option to establish archiving rules for the folder.

>> **Clean Out Items Older Than:** Choose a cut-off time period after which to archive the items in the folder.

>> **Move Old Items to the Default Archive Folder:** Select this option to move items to the folder you selected as the default.

>> **Move Old Items To:** Click the Browse button and select a folder if you want to store the archived items in a specific location.

>> **Permanently Delete Old Items:** Select this option if you want to delete, not archive, items in this folder.

TIP

Besides archiving, another way to remove bric-a-brac automatically is to take advantage of the Rules Wizard to delete certain kinds of email messages when they arrive. See Chapter 3 of this minibook for more information.

Running the Mailbox Cleanup command

The Mailbox Cleanup command is an all-purpose command for finding email messages, archiving items, deleting items, and deleting alternate versions of items. To use the command, go to the File tab, choose Info, click the Tools button, and choose Mailbox Cleanup. You see the Mailbox Cleanup dialog box, shown in Figure 1-6. The dialog box offers a speedy entrée into these different Outlook tasks:

>> **Seeing how much disk space folders occupy:** Click the View Mailbox Size button and then take note of folder sizes in the Folder Size dialog box.

>> **Finding items:** Select an option button to find items older than a certain number of days or larger than a certain number of kilobytes, enter a days or kilobytes number, and click the Find button. You land in the Advanced Find dialog box. Earlier in this chapter, "Conducting an advanced search" explains this dialog box. Use it to select items and delete them.

» **Archiving items:** Click the AutoArchive button to archive items in your folders. See "Archiving the old stuff," earlier in this chapter, for details.

» **Emptying the deleted items folder:** Click the Empty button to empty the Deleted Items folder. See "Deleting Email Messages, Contacts, Tasks, and Other Items," earlier in this chapter.

» **Delete all alternative versions of items:** Click Delete if you conduct emailing through a Exchange Server account and you want to delete alternative versions of items that were created during synchronization.

FIGURE 1-6:
Mucking out the mailboxes.

IN THIS CHAPTER

» Recording information about a person

» Creating a contact group

» Locating a person's information in the People app

» Sharing your information with coworkers

Chapter **2**

Maintaining the People App

O utlook includes the People app for storing information about friends, family, and coworkers. The People app is a super-powered address book. It offers folders for storing people's names, addresses, phone numbers, email addresses, web pages, birthdays, anniversaries, nicknames, and other stuff besides. When you address an email message, you can get it straight from a contact list in the People app and thereby be sure that the address is entered correctly.

This short but happy chapter explains how to use the People app to maintain information about people, create contact groups to make sending the same message to many people easier, find information about a person, and print information about a person. The chapter also describes how to share information about people with others in a work environment.

To open the People app, click the People button in the app bar on the left side of the screen.

Entering and Editing Contact Information

In the People app, each person about whom you keep information is called a *contact*, and information about contacts is kept in the *Contacts folder*. To open the People app, click the People button on the app bar.

These pages explain how to enter information about a person and update the information if it happens to change.

Entering information about a new contact

To enter information about a contact in the Contacts folder, start by doing one of the following:

>> On the Home tab, click the New Contact button (or click the New Items button and choose Contact on the drop-down list).

>> Press Ctrl+N (in the Contacts window) or Ctrl+Shift+C (in another window).

You see the Contact form, as shown in Figure 2-1. In this form are places for entering just about everything there is to know about a person except his or her favorite ice cream flavor. Enter all the information you care to record, keeping in mind these rules of the road as you go along:

WARNING

>> **Full names, addresses, and so on:** Although you may be tempted to simply enter addresses, phone numbers, names, and so on in the text boxes, don't do it! Click the Full Name button, for example, to enter a name (refer to Figure 2-1). Click the Business or Home button to enter an address in the Check Address dialog box (refer to Figure 2-1). By clicking these buttons and entering data in dialog boxes, you permit Outlook to separate the component parts of names, addresses, and phone numbers. This way, Outlook can use names and addresses as a source for mass mailings and mass emailings.

When entering information about a company, not a person, leave the Full Name field blank and enter the company's name in the Company field.

>> **Information that matters to you:** If the form doesn't appear to have a place for entering a certain kind of information, try clicking a triangle button and choosing a new information category from the pop-up menu. Click the triangle button next to the Business button and choose Home, for example, if you want to enter a home address rather than a business address.

FIGURE 2-1:
A Contact form.

» **File As:** Open the File As drop-down list and choose an option for filing the contact in the People app. Contacts are filed alphabetically by last name, first name, company name, or combinations of the three. Choose the option that best describes how you expect to find the contact in the Contacts folder.

» **Mailing addresses:** If you keep more than one address for a contact, display the address to which you want to send mail and select the This Is the Mailing Address check box. This way, in a mass mailing, letters are sent to the correct address.

» **Email addresses:** You can enter up to three email addresses for each contact. (Click the triangle button next to the Email button and choose Email 2 or Email 3 to enter a second or third address.) In the Display As text box, Outlook shows you what the To: line of email messages looks like when you send email to a contact. By default, the To: line shows the contact's name followed by his or her email address in parentheses. However, you can enter whatever you wish in the Display As text box, and if entering something different helps you distinguish between email addresses, enter something different. For example, enter Lydia – Personal so that you can tell when you send email to Lydia's personal address as opposed to her business address.

» **Photos:** To put a digital photo in a Contact form, click the Add Contact Picture placeholder, and in the Add Contact Picture dialog box, select a picture and click OK.

>> **Details:** To keep a detailed dossier on a contact, click the Details button (you may have to click the Show button first, depending on the size of your Contact form) and enter information in the Details window. This window offers places for recording birthdays and other minutia. Click the General button when you finish entering details.

TIP

Be sure to write a few words in the Notes box to describe how and where you met the contact. When the time comes to weed out contacts, reading these descriptions can help you decide who gets weeded and who doesn't.

When you finish entering information, click the Save & Close button. If you're in a hurry to enter contacts, click the Save & New button. Doing so opens an empty form so that you can record information about another contact.

TIP

Want to add the name of someone who sent you an email message to the Contacts folder? Right-click the sender's name in the message window and choose Add to Outlook Contacts on the shortcut menu.

Changing a contact's information

To change a contact's information, double-click a contact name to open the Contact window, make your changes, and click the Save & Close button.

TIP

While you're in the Contact window, try clicking the All Fields button and entering information in the All Fields window. As shown in Figure 2-2, the All Fields window lists fields in a line-by-line fashion. Choose an option on the Select From drop-down list, scroll in the form, and update fields as necessary.

MAPPING OUT AN ADDRESS

To find your way to a contact's home or place of business, click the Map It button in the Contact window. As long as your computer is connected to the Internet and an address is on file for the contact, your web browser opens to the Bing.com website, where you find a map with the address at its center. You can get driving directions from this map. Good luck getting there!

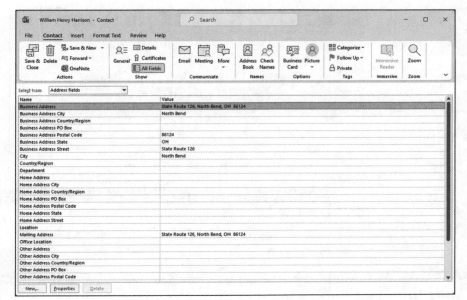

FIGURE 2-2:
Editing contact
data in the All
Fields window.

Contact Groups for Sending Messages to Groups

The captain of the volleyball team and the secretary of the PTA are examples of people who have to send email messages to the same group of people on a regular basis. You might be in the same boat. You might have to send email messages to the same 10 or 12 people from time to time. Entering email addresses for that many people each time you want to send email is a drag. To keep from having to enter so many email addresses, you can create a *contact group,* a list with multiple email addresses. To address your email message, you simply enter the name of the contact group, not the individual names, as shown in Figure 2-3.

Creating a contact group

Follow these steps to bundle email addresses into a contact group:

1. **On the Home tab, click the New Contact Group button (or press Ctrl+Shift+L).**

   You see the Contact Group window, as shown in Figure 2-4.

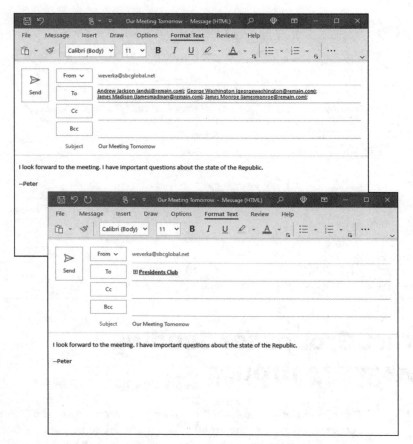

FIGURE 2-3:
Instead of
entering many
addresses (top),
enter a contact
group name
(bottom).

2. **Enter a descriptive name in the Name text box.**

3. **Click the Add Members button and choose an option on the drop-down list to tell Outlook where you store the addresses of friends and colleagues.**

If you're a loyal user of Outlook, you likely choose From Outlook Contacts. You see the Select Members dialog box.

4. **Hold down the Ctrl key and select the name of each person you want to include in the contact group.**

5. **Click the Members button and click OK.**

You can find the Members button in the lower-left corner of the dialog box. The names you chose appear in the Contact Group window.

You can add the names of people who aren't in your Contacts folder by clicking the Add Members button, choosing New Email Contact on the drop-down list, and filling out the Add New Member dialog box.

6. **Click the Save & Close button in the Contact Group window.**

In the Contacts folder, contact group names are marked with the Contact group icon.

Click to send an email to a group

FIGURE 2-4:
Entering
addresses for a
contact group.

Addressing email to a contact group

To address an email message to a contact group, start in the Inbox folder and click the New Email button on the Home tab. A Message window opens. Click the To button to open the Select Names dialog box and then select a contact group name and click the To button. Contact group names appear in boldface and are marked with a Contact Group icon.

TIP

The fastest way to address email to a contact group is to start in the Contacts folder, double-click the group's name to open the Contact Group window (refer to Figure 2-4), and then click the Email button.

Editing a contact group

The names of contact groups appear in the Contracts folder, You can treat contact groups like other contacts. In the Contacts folder, double-click a contact group name to open the Contact Group window (refer to Figure 2-4). From there, you can add names to a group, remove names from a group, and delete a group.

Maintaining the
People App

Finding a Contact

The number of contacts can grow very large, so Outlook offers various ways to locate contacts. Here are some techniques for locating a contact:

>> **Use the scroll bar:** Click the arrows or drag the scroll box to move through the list.

>> **Click a letter button:** Click a letter button on the left side of the window to move in the list to names beginning with a specific letter.

>> **Change views:** On the Home tab, go to the Current View gallery and choose a view option: People, Business Card, Card, Phone, or List. Changing views often helps in a search.

>> **Search Contacts text box:** Enter a keyword in the Search box. (See Chapter 1 of this minibook for instructions about searching for items in folders.)

Sharing Contacts with Coworkers

In the Outlook, all contacts are stored in a single folder called, not suprisingly, Contacts. What if you want to share your contacts with a colleague? You can do it as long as you and your colleague are in the same Office 365 organization. You can do it, in other words, if you and your colleague are in the same workplace.

Contacts you share with others (and contacts others share with you) are "read only." That means that you can view the contact information but not alter it in any way. Only the person who shared the contacts initially can alter contact information. Of course, anyone can use shared contacts to address email messages and to create appointments, as usual.

WARNING

Contact folders you create apart from the default Contacts folder can't be shared with colleagues. Only the default Contacts folder can be shared.

Sharing your Contacts folder

Some organizations don't allow contacts to be shared. Bearing that in mind, follow these steps to share the default Contacts folder with a coworker:

1. **Click People on the navigation bar, if necessary.**

2. **Make sure the Contacts folder is selected.**

   Unless you created contact folders apart from the default folder, the built-in Contacts folder is selected automatically.

3. **On the Folder tab, click the Share Contacts button.**

   This button is located in the Share group. A new email message appears. The message invites your coworker to view your Contacts folder, as shown in Figure 2-5.

4. **Address and send the email message.**

   While you're at it, you might tell the recipient that you are sharing the contacts in your Contacts folder.

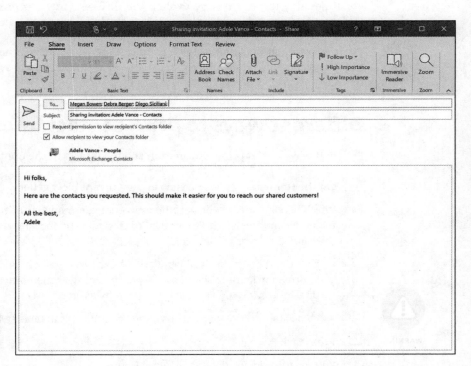

FIGURE 2-5: An invitation to share a Contacts folder.

TIP

To "unshare" a Contacts folder you regret sharing with a colleague, select the Contacts folder if necessary, visit the Folder tab, and click the Folder Properties button. The Contacts Properties dialog box opens. On the Permissions tab, select your colleague's name and click Remove.

Sharing someone else's contacts

You can tell which contacts in your Contacts folder were shared with you — and are "read only" — because they show up in the Shared Contacts listing. Contacts that colleagues have shared with you are like other contacts. You can send email to these contacts, for example. A shared contact is different only insofar as you can't edit or alter it in any way.

Printing the Contacts Folder

The paperless office hasn't arrived yet in spite of numerous predictions to the contrary, and sometimes you need to print your contacts on old-fashioned paper. For times like these, I hereby explain the different ways to print the Contacts folder and how to fiddle with the look of the printed pages.

TIP

To print information about a single contact, double-click his or her name to open the Contact folder. Then press Ctrl+P, and in the Print window, click the Print button.

Different ways to print contact information

Follow these steps to print information about contacts in the Contacts folder:

1. **On the Home tab, choose a view in the Current View gallery.**

Which printing options you get when you print information from the Contacts folder depends on which view of the Contacts folder is showing when you give the command to print:

- If you start in People, Business Card, or Card view, you can print Contacts information in these styles: card style, booklet style, memo style, or phone directory style. (You find out what these styles are shortly.)

- If you start in Phone or List view, you can print only in table style.

2. **Press Ctrl+P.**

You see the Print window, as shown in Figure 2-6.

3. **Under Settings, choose an option.**

TIP

Glance at the right side of the window to see what the option choices are and choose the option that suits you best.

4. **Click the Print Options button if you want to change the number of columns that are printed, change fonts, change headers and footers, or otherwise fiddle with the printed pages.**

   The next section in this chapter explains these options.

5. **Click the Print button to start printing.**

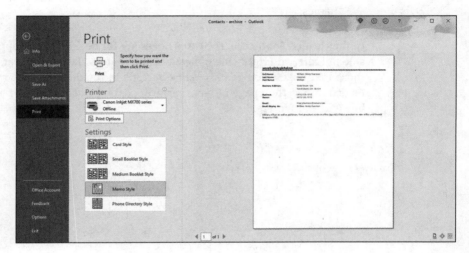

FIGURE 2-6:
Printing contact
information.

Changing the look of printed pages

To determine what Contact folder information looks like when you print it, click the Print Options button in the Print window (refer to Figure 2-6). You see the Print dialog box. In this dialog box, click the Page Setup button and choose options on the Format tab of the Page Setup dialog box to change the look of the printed pages:

>> **Where contact information is printed:** Contact information is printed alphabetically, with a letter heading to mark where the *A*s, *B*s, *C*s, and so on begin. To place contacts that begin with each letter on separate pages, select the Start on a New Page option button.

>> **Number of columns:** Choose a number in the Number of Columns drop-down list to tell Outlook how many columns you want.

>> **Blank forms at end:** Choose a number (or None) on the drop-down list to place forms at the end of the pages for people to write down more addresses.

>> **Contact index on side:** Select the Contact Index on Side check box to print thumbnail letter headings on the sides of pages.

>> **Letter headings for each letter:** To remove the letter headings that mark where contacts starting with a certain letter begin, deselect the Headings for Each letter check box.

>> **Fonts and font sizes:** Click a Font button and choose a different font or font size for headings and body text.

>> **Gray shades:** Choose this option to make gray shades appear behind contact names.

In the Header/Footer tab, the three boxes are for deciding what appears on the left side, middle, and right side of headers and footers. Type whatever you please into these text boxes. You can also click buttons in the dialog box to enter fields — a page number, total page number, printing date, printing time, or your name — in headers and footers.

Chapter **3**

Handling Your Email

"Neither snow nor rain nor heat nor gloom of night stays these couriers from the swift completion of their appointed rounds," reads the inscription on the Eighth Avenue New York Post Office Building. Emailers face a different set of difficulties. Instead of snow, rain, or gloomy nights, they face the task of having to manage volumes of email.

This chapter explains the basics of sending and receiving email, but it also goes a step further to help you organize and manage your email messages. It shows you how to send files and pictures with email messages. You also find out how to reorganize email in the Inbox window and be alerted to incoming messages from certain people or from people writing about certain subjects. This chapter shows you how to create folders for storing email and explains how to prevent junk email from arriving on your digital doorstep.

Setting Up an Email Account

Before you can send and receive email, you must provide Outlook with connection information about your email service. You can use Outlook to manage email from an Outlook account, Google Mail account, Yahoo mail, and just about any other email service. Outlook needs your name, your email address, and the password with which you log on to the email service.

You can configure Outlook to send and retrieve email from more than one account. For each email account you configure, Outlook places a new folder profile (Outlook calls it a "mailbox") in the Folder pane.

Follow these steps to configure an email account with Outlook:

1. On the File tab, choose Info (if Info isn't already chosen).

The Account Information window opens.

2. Click the Add Account button.

You see the Add Account dialog box.

3. Enter your email address and click Connect.

4. Enter your password and click Connect.

If all goes well, the connection is made and Outlook places a new folder profile in the Folder pane.

If Outlook can't configure your account, you are asked to configure the account manually. To do so, you likely need the following, which you can obtain by seeking help online from your email service provider:

>> **POP3 (Post Office Protocol version 3),** the protocol for retrieving messages from your email provider's incoming mail server. Outlook needs an IP address or domain name system (DNS) name, something like *inbound.att.net*.

>> **SMTP (Simple Mail Transfer Protocol),** the protocol for sending messages through your provider's outgoing mail server. Outlook needs an IP address or DNS name, something like *outbound.attn.net*.

>> **IMAP (Internet Message Access Protocol),** the protocol for reading and managing messages stored on a server, not on the user's computer. Outlook needs your password.

To cease managing an email account with Outlook, go to the File tab and choose Info. Then click the Account Settings button and choose Account Settings on the drop-down list. In the Account Settings dialog box, select the account and click the Remove button.

Addressing and Sending Email Messages

Sadly, you can't send chocolates or locks of hair by email, but you can send digital pictures and computer files. These pages explain how to do it. You also discover how to send copies and blind copies of email messages, reply to and forward email, send email from different accounts, and postpone sending a message. Better keep reading.

The basics: Sending an email message

The first half of this chapter addresses everything you need to know about sending email messages. Here are the basics:

1. **In any mail folder, click the New Email button on the Home tab (or press Ctrl+N).**

A Message window like the one in Figure 3-1 appears. You can open this window in a folder apart from mail folders by clicking the New Items button and choosing Email Message on the drop-down list (or by pressing Ctrl+Shift+M). The New Items button is located on the Home tab.

2. **Enter the recipient's email address in the To text box.**

The next topic in this chapter, "Addressing an email message," explains the numerous ways to address an email message. You can address the same message to more than one person by entering more than one address in the To text box. For that matter, you can send copies of the message and blind copies of the message to others (see "Sending copies and blind copies of messages," later in this chapter).

3. **In the Subject text box, enter a descriptive title for the message.**

When your message arrives on the other end, the recipient sees the subject first. Enter a descriptive subject that helps the recipient prioritize the message. After you enter the subject, it appears in the title bar of the Message window.

4. **Type the message.**

Whatever you do, don't forget to enter the message itself!

5. **Click the Send button (or press Alt+S).**

Messages remain in the Outbox folder if you postpone sending them or if Outlook can't send them right away because your computer isn't connected to the Internet.

TIP

If you decide in the middle of writing a message to write the rest of it later, go to the File tab and choose Save (or press Ctrl+S) and close the Message window. The message lands in the Drafts folder. When you're ready to finish writing the message, open the Drafts folder and double-click your unfinished message to resume writing it.

Copies of the email messages you send are kept in the Sent Items folder, where you can review messages you sent.

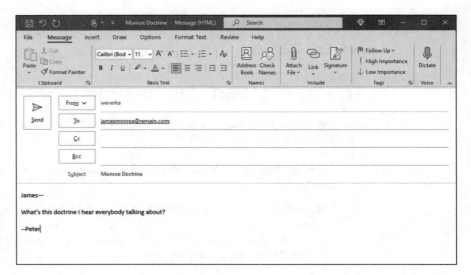

FIGURE 3-1:
Addressing and composing an email message.

MAKING OUTLOOK YOUR DEFAULT EMAIL PROGRAM

The default email program is the one that opens when you click an email hyperlink on a web page or give the order to send an Office file from inside an Office program. Follow these steps in Windows 10 or Windows 11 if you want to make Outlook the default email program on your computer:

1. **Click the Start button and choose Settings to open the Settings window.**

2. **Select Apps to open the Apps & Features window.**

3. Select Default Apps.

   In the Default Apps window, the application listed under Email tells you what your default email program is.

4. **Click to select the default program that is currently listed and then choose Outlook from the Choose an App pop-up menu.**

Addressing an email message

How do you address an email message in the To text box of the Message window (to see the Message window, refer to Figure 3-1)? Let me count the ways:

>> **Type the name of a contact from the People app:** Simply type a person's name, as shown in Figure 3-2. If you entered the person's name in the People app, a drop-down list with the name appears, and you can select the name on the drop-down list.(Chapter 2 of this minibook describes the People app.)

>> **Get the address (or addresses) from the People app:** Click the To (or Cc or Bcc) button to send a message to someone whose name is on file in the People app. You see the Select Names dialog box, as shown in Figure 3-2. Click or Ctrl+click to select the names of people to whom you want to send the message. Then click the To button (or the Cc or Bcc button) to enter addresses in the To text box (or the Cc or Bcc text box) of the Message window. Click OK to return to the Message window.

>> **Type the address:** Type the address if you know it offhand. You can paste an address into the Message window by right-clicking and choosing the Paste command.

>> **Reply to a message sent to you:** Select the message in the Inbox folder and click the Reply button. The Message window opens with the address of the person to whom you're replying already entered in the To text box. You can also click the Reply All button to reply to enter the email addresses of all the people to whom the original message was sent.

TIP

You can create contact groups for sending the same email message to a group of people without having to enter an address for each recipient. For information about contact groups, see Chapter 2 of this minibook.

Sending copies and blind copies of messages

When you send a copy of a message, the person who receives the message knows that copies have been sent because the names of people to whom copies were sent appear at the top of the email message. But when you send blind copies, the person who receives the message doesn't know that others received it. Send a blind copy when you prefer the recipient *not* to know that others also received the message.

To send copies and blind copies of messages, enter email addresses in the Cc or Bcc text box of the Message window, or in the Select Names dialog box (refer to Figure 3-2), select names and then click the Cc or Bcc button.

Click To (or Cc or Bcc) and choose names

Type and choose a name

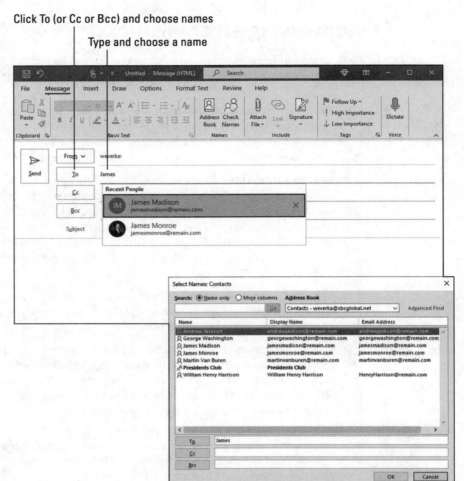

FIGURE 3-2:
Getting addresses
from the
People app.

TECHNICAL STUFF

Why are these buttons called Cc and Bcc? The Cc stands for "carbon copy" and the Bcc stands for "blind carbon copy." These terms originated in the Mesozoic era when letters were composed on the typewriter, and to make a copy of a letter, you inserted carbon paper between two paper sheets and typed away.

Replying to and forwarding email messages

Replying to and forwarding messages is as easy as pie. For one thing, you don't need to know the recipient's email address to reply to a message. In the Inbox, select or open the message you want to reply to or forward and do the following on the Home tab, Message tab, or Reading pane:

>> **Reply to author:** Click the Reply button (or press Ctrl+R). The Message window or Reading pane opens with the sender's name already entered in the To box and the original message in the text box below. Write a reply and click the Send button.

>> **Reply to all parties who received the message:** Click the Reply All button (or press Ctrl+Shift+R). The Message window or Reading pane opens with the names of all parties who received the message in the To and Cc boxes and the original message in the text box. Type your reply and click the Send button.

>> **Forward a message:** Click the Forward button (or press Ctrl+F). The Message window or Reading pane opens with the text of the original message. Either enter an email address in the To text box or click the To button to open the Select Names dialog box and then select the names of the parties to whom the message will be forwarded. Add a word or two to the original message if you like; then click the Send button.

WARNING

Forwarding a message to a third party without the permission of the original author is a breach of etiquette and very bad manners. I could tell you a story about an email message of mine that an unwitting editor forwarded to a cantankerous publisher, but I'm saving that story for the soap opera edition of this book.

TIP

To add a sender's name to the People app, right-click the name in the Message window and choose Add to Outlook Contacts.

Sending Files and Photos

Yes, it can be done. You can send files and photos along with your email messages. As long as you know where the file or photo is stored on your computer or OneDrive, you can send it lickety–split.

Sending a file along with a message

Sending a file along with an email message is called *attaching* a file in Outlook lingo. You can send a file or several files along with an email message by following these steps:

1. **In the Message window, go to the Message or Insert tab and click the Attach File button.**

   A drop-down list appears with the names of files you opened recently. If the file you want to send is on the list, select its name and be done with it; if the file's name isn't on the list, keep reading.

2. **Choose Browse This PC (or if you keep files in Teams, SharePoint, or OneDrive, choose Browse Web Locations and select the location on the submenu).**

   You see the Insert File dialog box.

3. **Locate and select the file that you want to send along with your email message.**

   Ctrl+click filenames to select more than one file. When you send a file by way of OneDrive or SharePoint, the file itself isn't sent; instead, recipients get a link they can click to open the file.

4. **Click the Insert button.**

   The name of the file (or files) appears in the Attachments box in the Message window. Address the message and type a note to send along with the file. You can open the drop-down list on a filename in the Attachments box and choose Open to open a file you're about to send. Or, if you change your mind about sending the file, you can choose Remove Attachment.

TIP

Here's a fast way to attach a file to a message: Find the file in File Explorer and drag it into the Message window. The file's name appears in the Attachments box as though you placed it there by clicking the Attach File button.

Including a photo in an email message

As shown in Figure 3-3, you can include a photo in the body of an email message. Follow these steps:

1. **In the Message window, go to the Insert tab.**

2. **Click in the body of the email message where you want the picture to go.**

3. **Click the Pictures button and choose This Device on the drop-down menu.**

   You see the Insert Picture dialog box. If the Pictures button is grayed out and you can't click it, go to the Format Text tab and click the Aa HTML button. Choosing Aa HTML as the format for email messages enables you to send photos in the body of email messages.

Handling Your Email

4. **Locate and select the digital picture you want to send; then click the Insert button.**

   The picture lands in the Message window. Book 8, Chapter 3 explains how to manipulate graphic images in Outlook and the other Office applications.

   Want to remove a picture from an email message? Select it and press the Delete key.

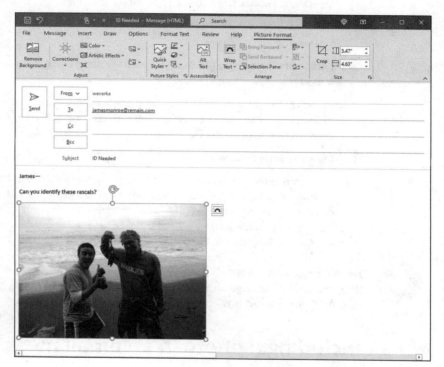

FIGURE 3-3:
Inserting a photo
in an email
message.

Receiving Email Messages

I hope that all the email messages you receive carry good news. These pages explain how to collect your email and all the different ways that Outlook notifies you when email has arrived. You can find several tried-and-true techniques for reading email messages in the Inbox window. Outlook offers a bunch of different ways to rearrange the window as well as the messages inside it.

Getting your email

Starting in the Inbox folder on the Send/Receive tab, here are all the different ways to collect email messages that were sent to you:

- ›› **Collect all email:** Click the Send/Receive All Folders button (or press F9). Mail is sent from and delivered to all your email accounts.

- ›› **Collect mail for the Inbox folder only:** Click the Update Folder button (or press Shift+F9).

- ›› **Send all unsent mail:** Click the Send All button.

- ›› **Collect email from a single account (if you have more than one):** Click the Send/Receive Groups button, and on the drop-down list, choose the name of a group or an email account.

Being notified that email has arrived

Take the email arrival quiz. Winners get the displeasure of knowing that they understand far more than is healthy about Outlook. How can you tell when email has arrived in the Inbox folder?

A) You hear this sound: *ding*.

B) The mouse cursor briefly changes to a little envelope.

C) A little envelope appears in the notification area to the left of the Windows clock. (You can double-click the envelope to open the Inbox folder.)

D) A pop-up *desktop alert* with the sender's name, the message's subject, and the text of the message appears briefly on your desktop.

E) All of the above.

The answer is E, "All of the above," but if four arrival notices strike you as excessive, you can eliminate one or two. On the File tab, choose Options, and in the Mail category of the Options dialog box, go the Message Arrival area and change the settings.

Reading Your Email in the Inbox Window

Messages arrive in the Inbox window, as shown in Figure 3-4. You can tell a thing or two about messages by glancing in the window:

>> Unread messages are shown in boldface type.

>> Messages that you've read (or at least opened to view) are shown in Roman type, not bold type.

>> In the Folder pane, a number beside a folder tells you how many unread messages are in those folders. (The number in square brackets beside the Drafts and Junk Email folders tells you how many items, read and unread, are in those folders.)

To read a message, select it and look in the Reading pane, or to focus more closely on a message, double-click it to open it in a Message window, as shown in Figure 3-4.

Reading pane

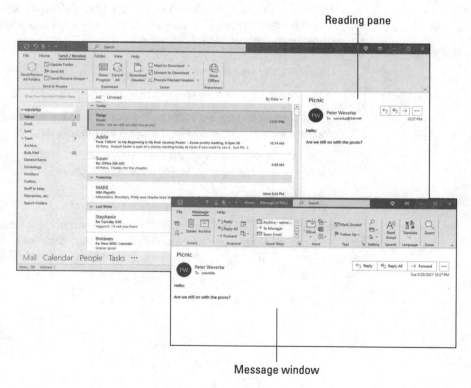

FIGURE 3-4:
Reading a message in the Reading pane and Message window.

Message window

Later in this chapter, "Techniques for Organizing Email Messages" explains how to organize messages in the Inbox folder. Meanwhile, here are some simple techniques you can use on the View tab to unclutter the Inbox folder and make messages easier to read:

» **Rearranging messages:** In the Arrangement gallery, choose an option. For example, choose Date to arrange messages according to the date and time they were received. Choose From to arrange messages by sender name in alphabetical order. Click the Reverse Sort button to reverse the way the messages are arranged.

» **Hiding and displaying the Reading pane:** Click the Reading Pane button and choose Off, Right, or Bottom on the drop-down list to make the Reading pane appear or disappear. The Reading pane gives you an opportunity to read messages without opening them in a Message window.

  The Reading pane offers a Reply, Reply All, and Forward button for quickly replying to and forwarding email messages.

» **Hiding and displaying the Folder pane:** Click the Folder Pane button and choose Normal or Minimized (or press Alt+F1 or click the Minimize the Folder Pane button on the Folder pane itself). By hiding the Folder pane, you get even more room to display messages.

TIP

Suppose you open an email message but regret doing so because you want the boldface text to appear on the message's name. In other words, you want to handle the message later on. To make a message in the Inbox window appear as if it has never been opened, right-click it and choose Mark As Unread.

Handling Files That Were Sent to You

You can tell when someone sends you files along with an email message because the paper clip icon appears in the Attachment column of the Inbox window (if column headings are displayed). Moreover, the name of the file or files appears in the Reading pane (if the Reading pane is open). When you double-click to open the message in a window, the names of files sent to you appear across the top of the message window, as shown in Figure 3-5.

Attached files   Save files

Handle individual files

FIGURE 3-5:
Receiving a file.

Opening a file you received

Follow these instructions to open a file that was sent to you:

>> Double-click the filename.

>> Click to select the filename, and on the Attachments tab, click the Open button.

>> Open the drop-down list on the filename and choose Open on the shortcut menu (see Figure 3-5).

TIP

As long as the file being sent to you is a Word, PowerPoint, Excel, or Publisher file, you can preview it inside the Message window or Reading pane. To do so, click the filename (or choose Preview on the file's drop-down list). Click the Show Message button to see the message again, not the file preview.

Saving a file you received

Follow these instructions to save a file that was sent to you in a folder of your choice:

>> Click to select the filename, and on the Attachments tab, click the Save As button and save the file using the Save Attachment dialog box. Click the Save All Attachments button to save more than one file.

>> Click to select the filename, and on the Attachments tab, click the Upload button and save the file to OneDrive or SharePoint. Click the Upload All Attachments button to save more than one file.

>> Open the filename's drop-down list (see Figure 3-5), choose Save As, and save the file in the Save Attachment dialog box. Choose Save All Attachments to save more than one file.

Techniques for Organizing Email Messages

If you're one of those unfortunate souls who receives 100, 150, 200 or more email messages daily, you owe it to yourself and your sanity to figure out a way to organize email messages such that you keep the ones you want, you can find email messages easily, and you can quickly eradicate the email messages that don't matter to you. Outlook offers numerous ways to manage and organize email messages. Pick and choose the techniques that work for you.

In a nutshell, here are all the techniques for organizing email messages:

>> **Re-sort messages in the Inbox window:** On the View tab, choose an Arrangement option to change how messages are listed. Earlier in this chapter, "Reading Your Email in the Inbox Window" explains the Arrangement options.

>> **Delete the messages that you don't need:** Before they clutter the Inbox, delete messages that you're sure you don't need as soon as you get them. To delete a message, select it and click the Delete button on the Home tab, press the Delete key, or right-click and choose Delete.

>> **Move messages to different folders:** Create a folder for each project you're involved with, and when an email message about a project arrives, move it to a folder. See "All about Email Folders," later in this chapter.

>> **Move messages automatically to different folders as they arrive:** Instead of moving messages yourself after they arrive, you can tell Outlook to move messages automatically to different folders. See "Rules for earmarking messages as they arrive," later in this chapter.

>> **Delete junk mail as it arrives:** You can delete junk mail automatically. See "Yes, You Can Prevent Junk Mail (Sort Of)," later in this chapter.

>> **Ignore messages from pesky senders:** On the Home tab, select a message and click the Ignore button to prevent messages from a sender from appearing in the Inbox. Ignored messages go straight to the Deleted Items folder.

>> **Flag messages:** Flag a message with a color-coded flag to let you know to follow up on it. See "Flagging email messages," the next section in this chapter.

>> **Categorize messages:** Assign email messages to categories; then, arrange email messages by category in the Inbox window. See Chapter 1 of this minibook for info about categorizing items in a folder.

>> **Make liberal use of the Search commands:** You can always find a stray message with the Search commands. (See Chapter 1 of this minibook to know more about searching for items in folders.)

>> **Archive messages you no longer need:** Archiving is a good way to strip the Inbox folder of items that you don't need. See Chapter 1 of this minibook for more about archiving.

>> **Use the Mailbox Cleanup command:** This handy command archives messages, deletes them, and deletes alternative versions of messages. See Chapter 1 of this minibook for more about the Mailbox Cleanup command.

Flagging email messages

One way to call attention to email messages is to flag them. Flag a message, for example, to mark it as urgent. After you flag a message, you can arrange messages by their flag status in the Inbox folder. Follow these instructions to flag an email message:

>> **Starting in the Message window:** Click the Follow Up button and choose Flag Message on the drop-down list, as shown in Figure 3-6.

>> **Starting in the Inbox folder:** Select the message, and on the Home tab, click the Follow Up button and choose a flag. You can also right-click and choose Follow Up.

To "unflag" a message, click the Follow Up button and choose Clear Flag, or right-click and choose Clear Flag. Later in this chapter, "Rules for earmarking messages as they arrive" explains how you can flag messages automatically as they arrive.

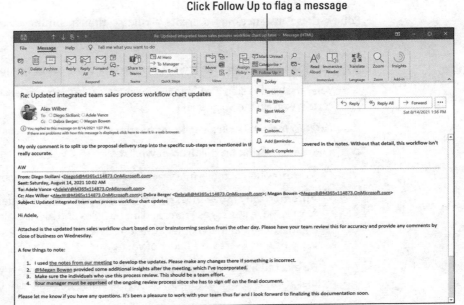

FIGURE 3-6:
Flagging a
message in the
Message window.

Rules for earmarking messages as they arrive

To help you organize messages better, Outlook gives you the opportunity to earmark messages in various ways and even move messages as they arrive automatically to folders apart from the Inbox folder. Being able to move messages immediately to a folder is a great way to keep email concerning different projects separate. For example, you can move email messages from a colleague to a specific folder as the messages arrive.

To earmark messages for special treatment, Outlook has you create so-called rules. You can create a rule to

» Move email from a particular person automatically to a folder.

» Be alerted when email arrives from a certain person or the Subject line of a message includes a certain word.

Handling Your Email

Follow these instructions to create a rule so that incoming email messages are given special treatment:

1. **Select an email message from a person whose messages require a rule.**

   You can skip this step if your goal is to create a rule for messages that contain a certain word in the Subject line.

2. **On the Home tab, click the Rules button.**

3. **Choose an option on the drop-down list.**

   Choose an option to move messages to a folder or be alerted about messages.

   - **Automatically move messages from this person to a folder:** Choose Always Move Messages From, and in the Rules and Alerts dialog box, select a folder. (Later in this chapter, "Creating a new folder for storing email" explains how to create a folder of your own.)

   - **Be alerted about messages:** Choose Create Rule. You see the Create Rule dialog box shown in Figure 3-7. Fill in the dialog box and click OK.

TIP

To change or delete a rule, go to the Home tab, click the Rules button, and choose Manage Rules & Alerts. On the Email Rules tab of the Rules and Alerts dialog box, select a rule and change, copy, or delete it.

FIGURE 3-7:
The Create Rule
dialog box.

All about Email Folders

Where Outlook email is concerned, everything has its place and everything has its folder. Email messages land in the Inbox folder when they arrive. Messages you write go to the Outbox folder until you send them. Copies of email messages you send are kept in the Sent Items folder. And you can create folders of your own for storing email.

If you're one of those unlucky people who receive numerous email messages each day, you owe it to yourself to create folders in which to organize email messages. Create one folder for each project you're working on. That way, you know where to find email messages when you want to reply to or delete them. These pages explain how to move email messages between folders and create folders of your own for storing email.

Moving email messages to different folders

Open or select the message you want to move and use one of these techniques to move an email message to a different folder:

- >> On the Home tab or a Message window, click the Move button and choose a folder name on the drop-down list. If the folder's name isn't on the list, choose Other Folder and select a folder in the Move Items dialog box.

- >> Right-click, choose Move, and select a folder name or choose Other Folder and select a folder in the Move Items dialog box.

- >> Display the folder you want to receive the message in the Folder pane. Then drag the message from the Inbox to the folder in the Folder pane.

Earlier in this chapter, "Rules for earmarking messages as they arrive" explains how to move email messages automatically to folders as email is sent to you.

Creating a new folder for storing email

Follow these steps to create a new folder:

1. **On the Folder tab, click the New Folder button.**

You see the Create New Folder dialog box, as shown in Figure 3-8. You can also open this dialog box by pressing Ctrl+Shift+E or right-clicking a folder in the Folder list and choosing New Folder.

2. **Select the folder that the new folder will go inside.**

To create a first-level folder, select the name of the topmost folder in the hierarchy.

3. **Enter a name for the folder.**

4. **Click OK.**

Handling Your Email

To delete a folder you created, open it, go to the Folder tab, and click the Delete Folder button. Items in the folder are deleted along with the folder itself. To rename a folder, open it, go to the Folder tab, click the Rename Folder button, and enter a new name.

You can't rename or delete default folders such as Inbox, Sent, and Deleted.

Yes, You Can Prevent Junk Mail (Sort of)

Outlook maintains a folder called Junk Email especially for storing junk email, or *spam* as the digital variety is sometimes called. Email messages with certain words or phrases in the Subject line — *for free!*, *money-back guarantee*, *order now* — are routed automatically to the Junk Email folder, where they needn't bother you. What's more, you can add senders' names to the Blocked Senders list and route mail from those senders straight into the Junk Email folder.

WARNING

As nice as it is, the Junk Email folder has one fatal flaw: Sometimes a legitimate email message finds its way into the folder. From time to time, you have to look in the Junk Email folder to see whether something of value is in there — and that sort of defeats the purpose of routing messages automatically to the Junk Email folder. You still have to look through all that junk email!

Realistically, the only way to prevent getting junk email is to safeguard your email address. These pages explain how to help stamp out junk email in your lifetime by using features inside Outlook and taking preventative measures.

Defining what constitutes junk email

Outlook maintains a Safe Senders and a Blocked Senders list to help distinguish email from junk email. To help Outlook recognize junk email and route it to the Junk Email folder, you can take these measures to add addresses to the lists:

>> **Add a sender to the Safe Senders list:** Senders on this list are deemed legitimate, and their email messages are always routed to the Inbox folder. In the Message window or Home tab of a mail folder, click the Junk button and choose Never Block Sender. Choose this option if you find a legitimate email message in the Junk Email folder.

>> **Add an address to the Blocked Senders list:** Email from senders on the Blocked Senders list goes straight to the Junk Email folder. In the Message window or Home tab of a mail folder, click the Junk button and choose Block Sender.

>> **Editing the Safe Senders and Blocked Senders lists:** Click the Junk button and choose Junk E-mail Options. The Junk E-mail Options dialog box opens. On the Safe Senders and Blocked Senders tab, select email addresses as necessary and click the Remove button.

To quickly move an email message from the Junk Email folder to the Inbox folder, click the Junk button and choose Not Junk on the drop-down list. The Mark As Not Junk dialog box appears. Click the Always Trust E-mail From check box and click OK.

Preventative medicine for junk email

TIP

As zealous as Outlook is about preventing junk email, the program can't really do the job. Junk emailers change addresses frequently. They are clever about putting words in the subject lines of their messages so that the messages aren't recognized as spam. The only foolproof way to keep your email address free of junk email is to follow these suggestions:

>> **Use a secondary email address:** Create a secondary email account and give its email address to businesses and merchants on the Internet who might sell your address to spammers or might themselves be spammers. The Internet offers many places to create free web-based email accounts. For example, check out Gmail (http://gmail.com) and Yahoo Mail (http://mail.yahoo.com). Never give your primary email address to strangers.

» **Don't reply to spam:** Don't reply to junk email messages under any circumstances. By replying, all you do is alert the spammer to the fact that your email address is legitimate, and that makes you a target of even more spam.

» **Don't unsubscribe to junk email messages:** Some spam messages contain an Unsubscribe link that you can click to prevent more messages from coming. The links are a ruse. All you do by clicking them is make spammers aware that your email address is live and therefore worth targeting with more spam.

» **Don't buy anything advertised by spam:** Even if the message is selling what looks to be a terrific bargain, resist the temptation. By buying, you expose yourself to all the risks of replying to junk email.

Chapter **4**

Managing Your Time and Schedule

The purpose of the Outlook Calendar is to keep you from arriving a day late and a dollar short. Use the Calendar to schedule meetings and appointments. Use it to make the most of your time. This chapter explains how to go from day to day, week to week, and month to month in the Calendar window. It shows you how to schedule and reschedule appointments and meetings, look at your schedule in different ways, and schedule and handle meetings with coworkers.

Introducing the Calendar

Use the Calendar to juggle appointments and meetings, remind yourself where you're supposed to be, and get there on time. Surveying your schedule in the Calendar window is easy. Merely by clicking a button, you can tell where you're supposed to be today, any given day, this week, this work week, this month, or any month.

Figure 4-1 shows, for example, someone's schedule during the work week of August 22 – August 26 (a work week comprises Monday through Friday, not Monday through Sunday). All you have to do to find out how busy you are on a particular day, week, or month is gaze at the Calendar window. When someone invites you to a meeting or wants to schedule an appointment, you can open the Calendar and see right away whether your schedule permits you to attend the meeting or make the appointment.

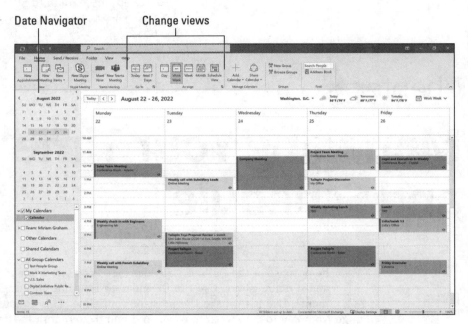

FIGURE 4-1:
The Calendar in
Work Week view.

Outlook gives you opportunities to categorize meetings and appointments so that you can tell at a glance what they're all about. Moving a meeting or appointment is simply a matter of dragging it elsewhere in the Calendar window. By double-clicking a meeting or appointment in the Calendar window, you can open a window to find out where the meeting takes place or read notes you jotted down about the meeting. You can even make a bell ring and the Reminder message box appear when a meeting or appointment is forthcoming.

The Different Kinds of Activities

REMEMBER

For scheduling purposes, Outlook makes a distinction between appointments and meetings. You can schedule the following activities:

» **Appointment:** An activity that occupies a certain day or a certain time period on a certain day. For example, a meeting that takes place between 11 a.m. and 12 p.m. is an appointment. An all-day event such as a retreat is also considered an appointment. An appointment is just for you; it has no invitees.

» **Meeting:** Same as an appointment except that you can invite others to attend. You can make an online video call part of a meeting. As you choose a time for a meeting, you can view others' calendars to find the optimal time.

HOW'S THE WEATHER?

The Calendar window gives a weather report with temperature readings or projections for today, tomorrow, and the day after that.

To get temperature readings for your hometown, click the down arrow and choose Add Location on the drop-down menu. Then enter the name of your town or your town's ZIP code.

| San Francisco, California ▾ | ☀ Today 64° F /51° F | ☀ Tomorrow 64° F /52° F | ☀ Thursday 66° F /53° F |

Seeing Your Schedule

Days on which meetings or appointments are scheduled appear in boldface in the Date Navigator, the calendar located in the Folder pane. Following are techniques for getting around in the Calendar window and viewing your schedule in different ways.

Going to a different day, week, or month

Use these techniques to go to different days, weeks, or months in the Calendar window:

>> **To today:** On the Home tab, click the Today button. Clicking this button selects today's date on your calendar in whatever view you happen to be in.

>> **To the next seven days:** On the Home tab, click the Next 7 Days button to see the next seven days starting with today's date.

>> **To a specific day:** Click a day in the Date Navigator (located on the Folder pane). You can also press Ctrl+G and select a day in the Go To Date dialog box. If you don't see the Date Navigator, go to the View tab, click the Folder Pane button, and choose Normal on the drop-down list.

>> **To the previous or next day, work week, week, or month:** Click a Back or Forward arrow. These arrows are in the upper-left corner of the Calendar window and on either side of the month name in the Date Navigator.

TIP

Here's a quick way to go from month to month in the Date Navigator: Click the month name in the Date Navigator and hold down the mouse button. You see a list of month names. Drag the pointer to the name of the month you want to go to.

Use the scroll bar on the right side of the window to travel from hour to hour in Day, Work Week, and Week view. In Month view, manipulating the scroll bar takes you from month to month.

Rearranging the Calendar window

To get a sense of what is expected of you and where you're supposed to be, go to the Home or View tab and click one of these buttons to rearrange your view of the Calendar window:

>> **Day:** Shows today's date only (press Ctrl+Alt+1).

>> **Work Week:** Shows Monday through Friday of this week (press Ctrl+Alt+2).

>> **Week:** Shows the entire week, Sunday through Saturday (press Ctrl+Alt+3).

>> **Month:** Shows the entire month (press Ctrl+Alt+4).

TIP

What constitutes a work week and which day is the first day of the week differs from place to place. If the Calendar doesn't conform to your notions of what a week is, go to the File tab and choose Options. Then, in the Outlook Options dialog box, go to the Calendar category and choose different Work Time options.

Scheduling Appointments and Meetings

Now that you know how the Calendar window works, the next step is to fill the pages of the Calendar with all kinds of busywork. These pages explain how to schedule events, schedule recurring events, and magically transform an email message into an event. You can find many intriguing shortcuts on these pages.

Scheduling an event: The basics

Follow these basic steps to schedule an appointment, recurring appointment, meeting, or recurring meeting:

1. Select the day in which you want to schedule the event.

TIP

If the event occupies a certain time period, you can select the time period in Day, Work Week, or Week view and save yourself the trouble of entering a time period in the Appointment window. To select a time period, drag downward in the Calendar window. To create a half-hour appointment, simply double-click a half-hour slot in Day, Work Week, or Week view. The Appointment dialog box opens with the Start and End time entered already.

2. On the Home tab, click the New Appointment button (or press Ctrl+N).

As shown in Figure 4-2, you see the Appointment window for naming the event, stating its starting and ending time, and choosing whether you want to be alerted to its occurrence. In a folder apart from the Calendar, you can display this window by going to the Home tab, clicking the New Items button, and choosing Appointment on the drop-down list.

3. Enter information in the Appointment tab.

Enter a subject, location (you can open the drop-down list and choose one you've entered before, start date and time, and end date and time. To enter a recurring meeting or appointment, click the Recurrence button. A recurring event is one that takes place weekly, monthly, or yearly.

4. **Open the Reminder drop-down list (located in the Options group) and choose an option if you want to be reminded when the event is imminent (or choose None if you don't care to be reminded).**

   Choose an option from the drop-down list to make the Reminder message box appear before the event begins.

5. **Click the Save & Close or Send button when you finish describing the appointment.**

   The appointment is entered in the Calendar window.

Click to schedule an event

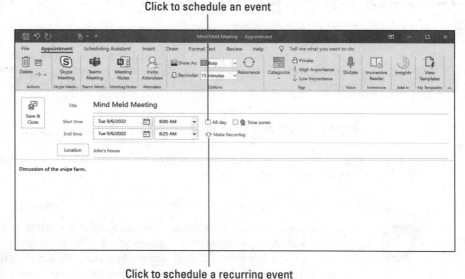

FIGURE 4-2:
The window
for scheduling
activities.

Click to schedule a recurring event

Scheduling a recurring appointment

To enter a recurring appointment, click the Recurrence button in the Appointment window (refer to Figure 4-2). You see the Appointment Recurrence dialog box, as shown in Figure 4-3. Describe how persistent the activity is and click OK:

>> **Appointment Time:** Enter the starting and ending time, if you didn't do so already in the Appointment form.

>> **Recurrence Pattern:** Use the options to describe how often the activity recurs.

>> **Range of Recurrence:** Describe when the recurring events will cease recurring. Choose the No End Date option button if the activity occurs *ad infinitum, ad nauseam* (that's Latin for "unto infinity, most nauseously").

FIGURE 4-3:
My, this
appointment is
persistent!

In the Calendar window, recurring activities are marked by the arrow chasing its tail icon.

Scheduling an all-day appointment

Select the All Day check box in the Appointment window (refer to Figure 4-2) to schedule an all-day appointment. In the Calendar, all-day appointments are listed at the start of the day before appointments and meetings.

USING AN EMAIL MESSAGE TO SCHEDULE AN APPOINTMENT

Here's a neat little trick that can save you time when email correspondence has to do with scheduling an appointment. To get a head start on scheduling, drag the email message from the Inbox folder to the Calendar folder on the Navigation bar. On the theory that you want to schedule an appointment around the information in the email message, the Appointment window appears onscreen. For the subject of the appointment, Outlook enters the subject of the email message. The text of the email message appears in the window as well. Fiddle with the particulars of the appointment and click the Save & Close button.

Canceling, Rescheduling, and Altering Activities

Canceling, rescheduling, and altering appointments is pretty easy. You can always double-click an activity to open an Appointment window and change the particulars there. And you can take advantage of these shortcuts:

>> **Canceling:** Select an activity, go to the Appointment tab, and click the Delete button. When you click the Delete button to cancel a recurring activity, a drop-down list appears on the Delete button so that you can delete one occurrence of the activity or the entire series.

>> **Rescheduling:** Drag the activity to a new location in the schedule. Release the mouse button when the activity is in the new time slot.

>> **Changing start and end times:** In Day, Work Week, or Week view, move the pointer over the top or bottom of the activity and start dragging when you see the double arrow.

>> **Changing the description:** Click in the activity's box and start typing or editing.

Managing Meetings with the Calendar

As mentioned earlier in this chapter, a meeting is similar to an appointment, but meetings involve more than one person. Starting in Outlook, you can send meeting invitations to colleagues; in turn, colleagues can accept or decline invitations. When a colleague accepts an invitation to a meeting, the meeting is scheduled automatically on the colleague's calendar. People who have an Office 365 work or school account can see their colleagues' calendars, determine when colleagues have free time to attend a meeting, and schedule meetings accordingly.

These pages explain how to schedule and invite colleagues to meetings, accept or decline a meeting invitation, and reschedule or cancel a meeting.

Scheduling and inviting colleagues to a meeting

Schedule and invite colleagues to meetings starting in the Inbox folder by sending them an email message:

1. **On the Home tab, click the New Items button and choose Meeting on the drop-down menu.**

   A message window opens.

2. **Address the email message to colleagues you want to invite to the meeting.**

3. **Enter a meeting name in the Subject field.**

4. **Enter a preferred Start Time and End Time for the meeting.**

5. **If you want to schedule a Skype meeting or a meeting by way of Microsoft Teams, click the Add Skype Meeting or Add Teams Meeting link.**

   Invitees will be able to join the meeting by clicking the meeting link in the invitation (Book 10, Chapter 5 explains online meetings.)

6. **On the Meeting tab, click the Scheduling Assistant button.**

   This button is located in the Show group. The Scheduling Assistant window opens, as shown in Figure 4-4. This window lists colleagues you invited to the meeting; it shows whether their schedules conflict with the meeting time you proposed.

   If all is well and there are no scheduling conflicts, skip to Step 8. Otherwise, read on.

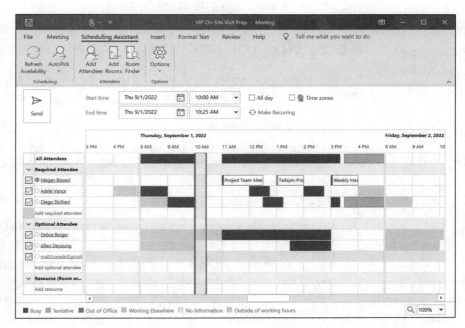

FIGURE 4-4:
The Scheduling Assistant window shows whether a time slot is available for a meeting.

7. Use the hourly calendar view to select a time block that is available to all parties.

Use your mouse to drag and drop a time range. If you make a mistake, click outside your selected area and start over. Color codes in the Scheduling Assistant window tell you whether colleagues have free time, are busy, or are otherwise occupied and can't attend a meeting.

8. Click the Appointment button to return to the message window.

9. If your organization lets you book rooms and other resources through Outlook, enter the name of the room where you want to hold the meeting in the Location box.

You can also click the Rooms button to open a list of rooms and select a name there.

10. Click Send.

If you didn't enter or choose a location for the meeting, Outlook asks whether you want to send the invitation without saying where the meeting is to be held. Click Send to proceed.

The meeting organizer can track all attendees' responses by opening the meeting in their Calendar, going to the Meeting tab, and clicking the Tracking button. The organizer can see at a glance which recipients responded to the meeting request and how they replied to the meeting invitation.

Accepting (or declining) meeting invitations

Meeting invitations arrive by email. Follow these steps to accept or decline a coworker's meeting invitation:

1. Open the email message.

As shown in Figure 4-5, the invitation comes with options for accepting, tentatively accepting, and declining the invitation. Choosing Tentative tells your coworker you aren't sure whether you can make it to the meeting.

2. Click Accept, Tentative, or Decline.

3. On the drop-down list that appears, choose how to respond to the invitation.

As Figure 4-5 shows, you can edit your response, send the response straightaway, or elect not to respond to the invitation by email. Unless you choose Do Not Send a Response, a notification is sent to the meeting organizer after you

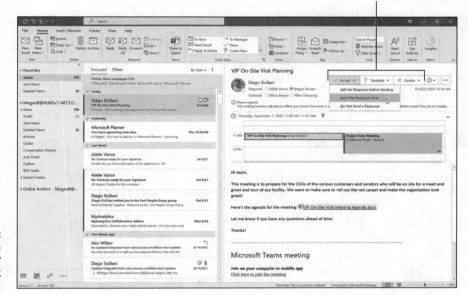

Accept or decline the meeting

FIGURE 4-5:
Choose an option to reply to a meeting invitation.

TIP

Click the Propose New Time button in the Invitation window (refer to Figure 4-5) if you want to propose a different time for the meeting. Clicking this button opens the Scheduling Assistant so that you can propose a different time to the meeting organizer.

Canceling and rescheduling meetings

Only the person who proposed a meeting can cancel it. Follow these steps to cancel a meeting:

1. In the Outlook Calendar, double-click the meeting that needs canceling or rescheduling.

The Meeting window opens.

2. On the Meeting tab, click Cancel Meeting.

3. Click Send Cancellation.

The meeting is removed from invitees' calendars.

To reschedule a meeting, open the meeting request and start the Scheduling Assistant. After you've proposed a new date and time for the meeting, click Send Update to send the modified meeting request to coworkers.

Access 365

Contents at a Glance

Chapter **1**

Introducing Access

The word *database* is prone to making most people feel kind of queasy. Can you blame them? Database terminology — record, field, and filter — is the worst of the worst. It even puts other computer terminology to shame. Databases intimidate most people. Even brave souls with a considerable amount of experience in Word and Excel shy away from *Access*, the Office 365 database program. However, Access can be invaluable for storing and organizing customer lists, inventories, addresses, payment histories, donor lists, and volunteer lists.

This chapter introduces databases and the concepts behind databases. It shows you how to create a database and database tables for storing information. The second half of this chapter explains how to design databases. Sorry, but you have to know about database design before you can start fooling with databases. You can't jump right in as you can with the other Office programs.

TIP

Access offers a practice database called Northwind that you can experiment with as you get to know your way around databases. To open this database, click the File tab and choose New. Then, in the New window, enter **Northwind** in the Search box and click the Start Searching button.

What Is a Database, Anyway?

You may not know this, but you're no stranger to databases. The address book on your computer is a database. The telephone directory in the desk drawer is, too. A recipe book is also a database, in that recipes are categorized under different headings. Any place where information is stored in a systematic way can be considered a *database*. The only difference between a computerized database and a conventional database, such as a cookbook or dictionary, is that storing, finding, and manipulating data is easier in a computerized database.

Imagine how long it would take to find all the New York addresses in an address list with 10,000 entries. In Access, you can query a 10,000-entry database and find all New York addresses in a matter of seconds. For that matter, you can query to find all the addresses in a certain ZIP code. You can put the list in alphabetical order by last name or in numerical order by ZIP code. Doing these chores without a computer requires many hours of dreary, monotonous labor.

Tables, Queries, Forms, and Other Objects

One problem with getting to know a database program — and the primary reason that people are intimidated by databases — is that you can't jump right in. You have to know how data is stored in a database and how it is extracted, to use database terminology. You have to know about *objects*, Access's bland word for database tables, queries, forms, and all else that makes a database a database. To help you get going, these pages offer a crash course in databases. They explain the different *objects* — tables, queries, forms, and reports — that make up a database. Fasten your seat belt. If you complete the crash course without crashing, you're ready to create your first database.

Database tables for storing information

Information in databases is stored in *database tables* like the one in Figure 1-1. In a database table, you include one field for each category of information you want to keep on hand. *Fields* are the equivalent of columns in a table. Your first duty when you create a database table is to name the fields and tell Access what kind of information you propose to store in each field. The database table in Figure 1-1 is for storing employee information. It has ten fields: ID, Company, Last Name, First Name, E-mail Address, Job Title, Business Phone, Home Phone, Mobile Phone, and Fax Number.

A record   A field   Cells

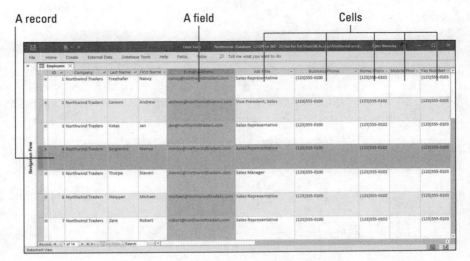

FIGURE 1-1:
A database table.

A database can comprise one database table or many different tables that are linked together. If you're dealing with a lot of information, storing data in more than one table is to your advantage. Later in this chapter, "Separating information into different database tables" explains why storing data across several database tables is advantageous.

ACCESS DATABASE TERMINOLOGY

Stumbling over database terminology is easy. To keep yourself from stumbling, fold back the corner of this page and return here if one of these database terms puzzles you:

- **Cell:** In a database table, a place for entering one piece of data. Cells appear in a database table where a field and record intersect.

- **Database:** A systematic way of organizing information so that it can be retrieved and manipulated easily.

- **Database table:** A collection of data records arranged into well-defined categories, or fields. Most relational databases have more than one table.

- **Dynaset:** The results of a search for data in a database. (This term is short for dynamic set.) A dynaset is not to be confused with a dinosaur.

(continued)

(continued)

- **Field:** One category of information in a database table. Fields are the equivalent of columns in a conventional table.

- **Filtering:** Finding the records in a database table that have the same or nearly the same field value. Filtering is a more convenient but not as sophisticated means of querying a database.

- **Foreign key field:** In a relationship between two database tables, the field that is on the "many" side of a one-to-many relationship. The primary key field is on the "one" side.

- **Form:** Similar to a dialog box, a place with text boxes and drop-down lists for entering records in a database table.

- **Module:** A Visual Basic procedure whose job is to perform a certain task in Access.

- **Object:** The catch-all term for the tables, queries, forms, and reports that you create and open starting in the Navigation pane.

- **Primary key field:** The field in a database table where unique, one-of-a-kind data is stored. To query more than one database table at a time, the tables must have primary key fields.

- **Query:** A question asked of a database that yields information. Queries can be made of a single database table, several tables, or even other queries.

- **Record:** In a database table, all the data that has been recorded about one person or thing. A record is the equivalent of a row in a conventional table.

- **Relational database:** A database program in which data is kept in more than one database table, relationships are established between tables, and queries can be conducted and reports made by assembling data from different tables. Access is a relational database. A database that permits only one table is a *flat-file database*.

- **Report:** Information gathered from a database and laid out in such a way that it's easy to read and understand. Reports are meant to be printed and distributed.

- **Sort:** To rearrange records in a database table so that the records appear in alphabetical, numerical, or date order in one field.

Forms for entering data

After you create the fields in the database table, you can start entering the records. A *record* describes all the data concerning one person or thing. Although you can enter records straight into a database table, the easiest way to enter a record is with a *form*. Similar to a dialog box, a form has convenient text boxes and drop-down lists for entering information, as shown in Figure 1-2. On a form, you can see clearly what kind of information needs entering in each field.

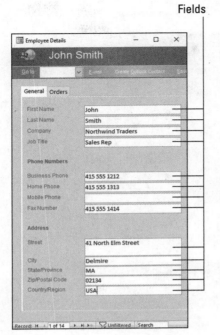

FIGURE 1-2:
A form for
entering data.

Queries for getting the data out

Figure 1-3 shows a simple query for finding out which employees in the database table shown in Figure 1-1 are Sales Representatives. A *query* is a question you ask of a database. The question here is, "Who is a Sales Representative?" Notice the criterion "Sales Representative" in the Job Title field on the Query grid.

In an address database, you can use a query to find all the people in a particular ZIP code or state. If information about contributions is stored in the database, you can find out who contributed more than $500 last year. Queries can get very complex. For example, you can find all the people in a particular city who contributed between $50 and $500 and volunteered more than eight hours in the past year. You can construct the query so that it produces each person's name and telephone number, or you can construct it so that all the information you have concerning each person appears in the query results.

When you get junk mail, it likely comes to your mailbox as the result of a database query. Companies routinely buy and sell customer databases. They query these databases to gather the names of people who they believe are well-disposed to purchasing the products they sell. Next time you get junk mail solicitation, study the letter and ask yourself, "How did I get in this database, and which database query produced my name?" The junk mailer is probably targeting extraordinarily beautiful, intelligent people.

Table being queried   Query criteria

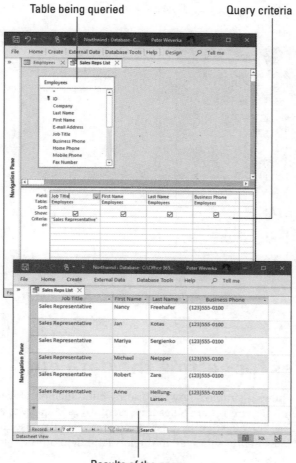

FIGURE 1-3:
Querying a
database.

Results of the query

After you create a query, you can save it and run it again. You can use it as the basis for constructing new queries. The information in database tables usually changes over time. Customers change addresses. New products come online, and others are discontinued. But no matter how much the data changes, you can find out exactly what you want to know from a database by running a well-crafted query.

Reports for presenting and examining data

Figure 1-4 shows a *report*. Reports can be made from database tables or from the results of queries. Reports are usually read by managers and others who don't get their hands dirty in databases. They're meant to be printed and distributed so that the information can be scrutinized and analyzed. Access offers many attractive reports. Don't worry: The program does most of the layout work for you, and exporting reports to a Word file is easy.

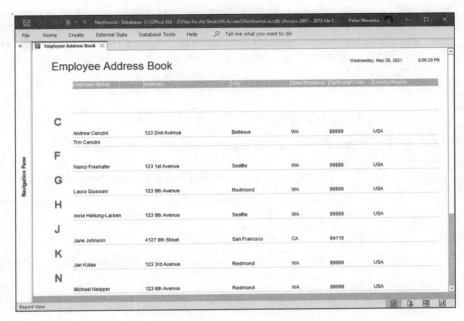

FIGURE 1-4:
A report gathers data for scrutiny and analysis.

Macros and modules

Macros and modules aren't covered in this minibook, but they are also database objects. A *macro* is a series of commands. You can store macros for running queries and doing other Access tasks. A *module* is a collection of Visual Basic procedures and declarations for performing tasks in Access.

Creating a Database File

Creating a database is a lot of work, at least in the beginning. You have to design the database (a subject that I explain shortly). You have to enter the raw information into the tables. You have to construct queries that allow yourself and others to read meaning into the data (see Chapter 4 of this minibook). By contrast, creating a database file for storing the information is the easy part.

Access offers two ways to create a new database file. You can do it from scratch or get the help of a template. With a template, some of the work is done for you. The template comes with prefabricated queries, forms, and reports. However, templates are for people who already know their way around Access databases. To make use of a template, you have to know how to modify a preexisting database.

REMEMBER

Before you create a database file, start by deciding where in your computer to store it. Unlike other Office programs, Access requires you to save and name a new database file as soon as you create it.

Creating a blank database file

Follow these instructions to create a blank database file:

1. **On the File tab or Access opening screen, choose New.**

   If you just started Access, you see the opening screen. The New window appears.

2. **Click the Blank Database icon.**

   A dialog box appears for choosing the folder where you will store your new database.

3. **Click the Browse button.**

   The Browse button is located to the right of the File Name text box. You see the File New Database dialog box.

4. **Select the folder where you want to keep the database file, enter a name in the File Name text box, and click OK.**

5. **Click the Create button.**

   The Navigation pane and a blank table appear. Later in this chapter, "Finding Your Way Around the Navigation Pane" explains what this pane is all about. I suggest you go there without delay or deferral.

Getting the help of a template

As I explain earlier, templates are wonderful if you have the wherewithal to modify them. Access offers prefabricated databases for tracking assets, keeping inventory, scheduling resources, and doing other things. Unfortunately, the only way to find out whether one of the templates is worthwhile is to go to the trouble to create a database from a template, open the database file, and look around.

Follow these steps to create a database file from a template:

1. **On the File tab or Access opening screen, choose New.**

The New window opens. Templates are located on the bottom half of the window.

2. **Select a template or use the Search box to obtain a template online from Microsoft.**

Templates showing the globe icon are applications, not databases. Access applications are designed for use with web browsers.

3. **Click the Browse button.**

The Browse button is located to the right of the File Name text box. The File New Database dialog box opens.

4. **Select the folder where you want to keep the database file, enter a name in the File Name text box, and click OK.**

5. **Click the Create button.**

The Navigation pane and a blank table appear. Read on to find out how to find your way around the Navigation pane.

Finding Your Way Around the Navigation Pane

The first thing you see when you open most database files is a Navigation pane like the one in Figure 1-5. This is the starting point for doing all your work in Access. From here, you can select an object — that horrible word again! — and begin working. Tables, queries, and other objects you create are added to the Navigation pane when you create them.

Here are shorthand instructions for doing this, that, and the other thing in the Navigation pane:

>> **Choosing an object type:** Select a group (Tables, Queries, Forms, Reports, and so on) from the Object Type drop-down list at the top of the Navigation pane, or select All Access Objects to see all the groups, as shown in Figure 1-5.

>> **Creating a new object:** Go to the Create tab and choose what type of object you want to create. When creating new forms and reports, click a table or query in the Navigation pane to base the new form or report on a table or query.

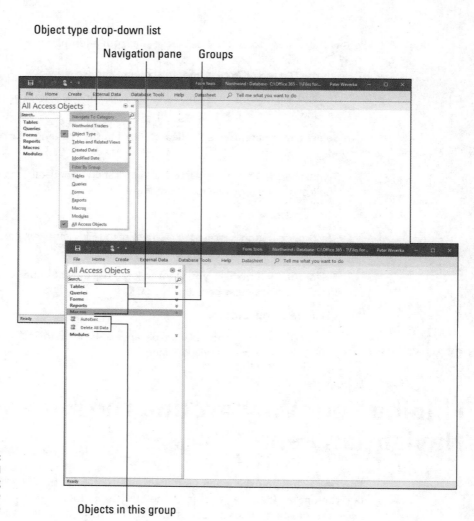

Object type drop-down list

Navigation pane   Groups

FIGURE 1-5:
Finding and
selecting
objects with the
Navigation pane

Objects in this group

>> **Opening an object:** To open a database table, query, form, or report, do one of the following: Double-click it; select it and press Enter; or right-click it and choose Open on the shortcut menu.

>> **Opening an object in Design view:** The task of formulating database tables, forms, and queries is done in Design view. If an object needs reformulating, right-click it and choose Design View on the shortcut menu or click the Design View button in the lower-right corner of the screen.

>> **Finding objects:** Use the Search bar (located at the top of the Navigation pane) to search for objects.

>> **Opening and closing the Navigation pane:** Click the Shutter Bar Open/Close button on upper-right corner of the Navigation pane (or press F11) when you want to shrink it and get it out of the way. You can also resize this pane by clicking the far-right edge and dragging it left or right.

Designing a Database

Introducing Access

Being a database designer isn't nearly as glamorous as being a fashion designer, but it has its rewards. If you design your database carefully and correctly, it can be very useful to you and others. You can enter information accurately. When the time comes to draw information from the database, you get precisely the information you need. These pages explain everything you need to consider when designing a database. Pay close attention to "Separating information into different database tables," later in this chapter, because the hardest part about designing a database is deciding how to distribute information across database tables and how many database tables to have.

Deciding what information you need

The first question to ask yourself is about the kind of information you want to get out of the database. Customer names and addresses? Sales information? Information for inventory tracking? Interview your coworkers to find out what information could be helpful to them. Give this matter some serious thought. Your goal is to set up the database so that every tidbit of information your organization needs can be recorded.

TIP

A good way to find out what kind of information matters to an organization is to examine the forms that the organization uses to solicit or record information. These forms show precisely what the organization deems worthy of tracking in a database. Figure 1-6, for example, shows the paper form that players fill out to sign up for a baseball league whose database tables appear in Figure 1-7. Compare Figure 1-6 with Figure 1-7 and you can see that the Players, Teams, and Divisions database tables all have fields for entering information from this form.

FIGURE 1-6:
Paper forms also have fields.

FIGURE 1-7:
Plans for database tables and field names.

Separating information into different database tables

After you know the information you want to record in the database, think about how to separate the information into database tables. Many are tempted to put all the information into a single database table, but because Access is a *relational database*, you can query more than one table at a time, and in so doing, assemble information from different tables.

To see how it works, consider the simple database, as shown in Figure 1-7. The purpose of this little database and its four tables is to store information about the players, coaches, and teams in a baseball league. The Team Name field appears in three tables. It serves as the link among the tables and permits more than one to be queried. By querying individual tables or combinations of tables in this database, I can assemble team rosters, make a list of coaches and their contact information, list teams by division, put together a mailing list of all players, find out which players have paid their fee, and list players by age group, among other things. This database comprises four tables:

>> **Players:** Includes fields for tracking players' names, addresses, birthdays, which teams they're on, and whether they paid their fees

>> **Coaches:** Includes fields for tracking coaches' names, addresses, and the names of the teams they coach

>> **Teams:** Includes fields for tracking team names and which division each team is in

>> **Divisions:** Includes fields for tracking division numbers and names

Deciding how many database tables you need and how to separate data across the different tables is the hardest part of designing a database. To make the task a little easier, do it the old-fashioned way with a pencil and eraser. Here are the basic rules for separating data into different tables:

>> **Restrict a table to one subject only:** Each database table should hold information about one subject only — customers, employees, products, and so on. This way, you can maintain data in one table independently from data in another table. Consider what would happen in the Little League database (refer to Figure 1-7) if coach and team data were kept in a single table, and one team's coach was replaced by someone new. You would have to delete the old coach's record, delete information about the team, enter information about the new coach, and reenter information about the team that you just deleted. But by keeping team information separate from coach information, you can update coach information and still maintain the team information.

>> **Avoid duplicate information:** Try not to keep duplicate information in the same database table or duplicate information across different tables. By keeping the information in one place, you have to enter it only once, and if you have to update it, you can do so in one database table, not several.

Entire books have been written about database design, and this book can't do the subject justice. You can, however, store all your data in a single table if the data you want to store isn't very complex. The time you lose entering all the data in a single table is made up by the time you save not having to design a complex database with more than one table.

Choosing fields for database tables

As I explain earlier, *fields* are categories of information. Each database table needs at least one field. If the table itself is a subject, you could say that its fields are facts about the subject. An Address database table needs fields for recording street addresses, cities, states, and ZIP codes. A Products database table needs fields for product ID numbers, product names, and unit prices. Just the facts, ma'am. Within the confines of the subject, the database table needs one field for each piece of information that is useful to your organization.

When you're planning which fields to include in a database table, follow these guidelines:

>> Break up the information into small elements. For example, instead of a Name field, create a First Name field and a Last Name field. This way, you can sort database tables by last name more easily.

>> Give descriptive names to fields so that you know what they are later. A more descriptive name, such as *Serial Number,* is clearer than *SN.*

>> Think ahead and include a field for each piece of information your organization needs. Adding a field to a database table late in the game is a chore. You have to return to each record, look up the information, and enter it.

>> Don't include information that can be derived from a calculation. As I explain in Chapter 4 of this minibook, calculations can be performed as part of a query or be made part of a table. For example, you can total the numbers in two fields in the same record or perform mathematical calculations on values in fields.

Deciding on a primary key field for each database table

REMEMBER

Each database table must have a *primary key field.* This field, also known as the *primary key,* is the field in the database table where unique, one-of-a-kind data is stored. Data entered in this field — an employee ID number, a part number, a bid number — must be different in each record. If you try to enter the same data in the primary key field of two different records, a dialog box warns you not to do that. Primary key fields prevent you from entering duplicate records. They also make queries more efficient. In a query, you tell Access what to look for in database tables, Access searches through the tables, and the program assembles information that meets the criteria. Primary key fields help Access recognize records and not collect the same information more than once in a query.

Social security numbers make good primary key fields because no two people have the same social security number. Invoice numbers and serial numbers also make excellent primary key fields. Returning to the sample baseball league database (refer to Figure 1-7), which fields in the Little League database tables are primary key fields? In the Teams table, Team Name can be the primary key field because no two teams have the same name. Division Number can also be a primary key field because divisions in the league are numbered and no two divisions have the same number.

The Players and Coaches database tables, however, present a problem when it comes to choosing a primary key field. Two players might have the same last name, which rules out Last Name as a primary key field. A brother and sister might have the same telephone number, which rules out a Telephone No. field. Because no field holds values that are certain to be different from record to record, I introduce fields called Player Number and Coach Number. For the purpose of this database, players and coaches are assigned numbers. (Chapter 2 in this minibook explains how Access can assign sequential numbers for you in a database table.)

Mapping the relationships between tables

If your database includes more than one table, you have to map how the tables relate to one another. Usually, relationships are formed between the primary key field in one table and the corresponding field in another, called the *foreign key*. Figure 1-8 shows the relationships between the tables in the Little League database. Because these tables are linked by common fields, I can gather information from more than one table for a query or report. Chapter 2 in this minibook takes up the subject of linking tables in more detail. For now, when you design your database, consider how to connect the various tables with common fields.

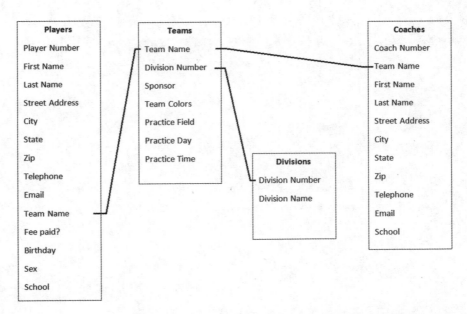

FIGURE 1-8:
Table
relationships.

Chapter **2**

Building Your Database Tables

D atabase tables are the building blocks of a database. They hold the raw data. Relationships among the tables permit you to query and generate reports from several different tables. How well your database tables are put together and how accurately data is entered in the tables determine whether your database is a thing of beauty or a wilted flower.

This chapter explains how to create database tables and fields for the tables. It explains what primary key fields are and how primary key fields and indexed fields make it easier for Access to sort, search, and query a database. This chapter describes how to forge relationships among tables. Fasten your seatbelts. In this chapter, you find numerous tips and tricks for making sure that data is entered accurately in your database tables.

Creating a Database Table

Raw data is stored in database tables (or in a single table, if you decide to keep all the data in one place). The first and most important part of setting up a database is creating the tables and entering the data. After you enter the data, you can harass your database for information about the things and people your database keeps track of. If you haven't done so already, read the sections in Chapter 1 of this minibook that pertain to storing information and designing a database before you create a database table. Chapter 1 of this minibook explains what database tables are and how to fashion a splendid one.

The business of creating a database table starts on the Create tab. As I explain in detail in the next few pages, Access offers three ways to create a database table:

>> **Create the database table from scratch:** Enter and format the fields one at a time on your own.

>> **Get the help of a template:** Get prefabricated fields assembled in a table. This is the way to go if you know Access well and you can modify database tables and table fields.

>> **Import the database table from another database:** This technique can be an enormous timesaver if you can recycle data that has already been entered in a database table in another Access database.

Creating a database table from scratch

Creating a table from scratch entails creating the table and then entering the fields one by one. After open or create a database file, follow these steps to create a database table from scratch: you

1. **Go to the Create tab.**

2. **Click the Table Design button.**

   The Design window appears. From here, you enter fields for your database table. I hate to be like a City Hall bureaucrat who gives everybody the runaround, but I can't help myself. Turn to "Entering and Altering Table Fields," later in this chapter, to find out how to enter fields in a database table.

3. **Click the Save button on the Quick Access toolbar.**

   The Save As dialog box appears.

4. **Enter a descriptive name for your table and click OK.**

   Return to the Navigation pane and you see the name of the table you created. If you don't believe me, click the Tables group to see the names of tables in your database.

Creating a database table from a template

If you know your way around Access and know how to modify database tables, you can do worse than create a database table with a template. Access offers four template types: Contacts (for storing contact addresses and phone numbers); Issues (for prioritizing issues); Tasks (for tracking projects, their status, and when they are due); and Users (for storing email addresses). As well as creating a table, Access creates ready-made queries, forms, and reports to go along with the table. After you create a table with a template, you can remove fields that you don't want. Deleting fields is always easier than adding new ones.

Follow these steps to use a template to create a table (and accompanying queries, forms, and reports):

1. Close all objects if any objects are open.

To close an object, click its Close button or right-click its tab and choose Close on the shortcut menu.

2. On the Create tab, click the Application Parts button.

A drop-down list with options for creating forms and tables appears. (The tables are listed under "Quick Start.")

3. Choose Contacts, Issues, Tasks, or Users.

If you have other tables in your database, a dialog box asks whether you want to create a relationship between the table you're creating and another table.

4. Select the There Is No Relationship option button and click Create.

Later in this chapter, "Establishing Relationships among Database Tables" explains how to create relationships on your own. If you want to create these relationships now and you have the wherewithal to do it, select an option besides There Is No Relationship, choose a table on the drop-down list, and click the Next button to choose which field to forge the relationship with.

5. On the Navigation pane, right-click the name of the table you created and choose Design View (or click the Design View button in the lower-right corner of the screen).

In Design view, you can see the names of the fields in the table. If the table contains fields you don't want, or you want to change the names of the fields, turn to "Entering and Altering Table Fields," later in this chapter.

Importing a table from another database

Few things are more tedious than entering records in a database table. If the records you need were already entered elsewhere, more power to you. Follow these steps to get a database table from another Access database:

1. **Go to the External Data tab.**

2. **Click the New Data Source button, choose From Database on the drop-down list, and choose Access on the sublist.**

The Get External Data – Access Database dialog box opens.

3. **Click the Browse button, and in the File Open dialog box, select the Access database with the table you need and click Open.**

You return to the Get External Data – Access Database dialog box.

4. **Select the first option button (Import Tables, Queries, Forms, Reports, Macros, and Modules into the Current Database) and click OK.**

You see the Import Objects dialog box, as shown in Figure 2-1.

5. **On the Tables tab, select the database table you want.**

You can import more than one database table by clicking several table names or clicking the Select All button.

TIP

You can import a table structure — its field names and formats — without importing the data in the table. To do so, click the Options button in the Import Objects dialog box, and under Import Tables, select the Definition Only option button (refer to Figure 2-1).

6. **Click OK.**

FIGURE 2-1:
Fetching a table from another database.

WARNING

If the table you want to import includes lookup fields, import the tables or queries that the lookup fields refer to as well as the table itself. Without those tables or queries, the lookup fields won't be able to obtain any values. Later in this chapter, "Creating a lookup data-entry list" explains what lookup fields are.

Opening and Viewing Tables

To open a table, start in the Navigation pane and select the Tables group to view the names of database tables you created. How you open a table depends on whether you want to open it in Datasheet view or Design view. Here's the difference between these views (see Figure 2-2):

» Design view is for creating fields and describing their parameters.

» Datasheet view is for entering and examining data in a table.

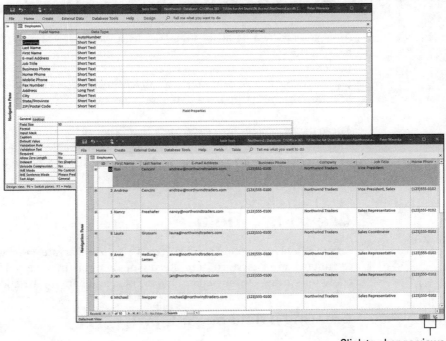

FIGURE 2-2:
A table in Design view (top) and Datasheet view (bottom).

Click to change views

Select a table on the Navigation pane and use one of these techniques to open and view it:

>> **Opening in Design view:** Right-click the table's name in the Navigation pane and choose Design View on the shortcut menu.

>> **Opening in Datasheet view:** On the Navigation pane, double-click the table's name or right-click its name and choose Open on the shortcut menu.

>> **Switching between views with the View button:** On the Home tab, click the View button and choose Datasheet View or Design View.

>> **Switching between views on the status bar:** Click the Datasheet View or Design View button on the right side of the status bar (refer to Figure 2-2).

>> **Switching between views by right-clicking:** Right-click the table's tab and choose Datasheet View or Design View.

Entering and Altering Table Fields

After you create a database table, the next task is to enter the fields, or if Access created the table for you, alter the fields to your liking. As Chapter 1 of this mini-book explains, fields represent categories of information in a database table. They are the equivalent of columns in a conventional table. Fields determine what kind of information is stored in a database table.

These pages explain how to create a field, choose the right data type, display data in fields, and designate the primary key field in a table. While I'm on the subject of fields, W.C. Fields said, "Horse sense is the thing a horse has which keeps it from betting on people."

Creating a field

Create a field on your own or get Access's help and create a ready-made field. Both techniques are described here. Ready-made fields include fields designed especially for storing currency data, hyperlinks, and date information.

Creating a field on your own

To create a field on your own, open the table that needs a new field and follow these steps on the (Table Tools) Table Design tab:

1. Switch to Design view if you aren't already there.

To switch to Design view, click the Design View button on the status bar.

2. If necessary, insert a new row for the field.

To do so, click in the field that is to go after the new field, and then click the Insert Rows button on the (Table Tools) Table Design tab.

3. Enter a name in the Field Name column.

Names can't include periods or be longer than 64 letters, but you don't want to enter a long name anyway because it won't fit very well along the top of the table.

WARNING

Some database programs don't permit spaces in field names. If you intend to export Access data to other database programs, don't include spaces in field names. Instead, run the words together or separate words with an underscore character, like this: underscore_character.

4. Press the Tab key or click in the Data Type column, and choose a data type from the drop-down list, as shown in Figure 2-3.

Data types classify what kind of information is kept in the field. The next topic in this chapter, "All about data types," explains data types.

5. If you want, enter a description in the Description column.

These descriptions can be very helpful when you need to reacquaint yourself with a field and find out what it's meant to do.

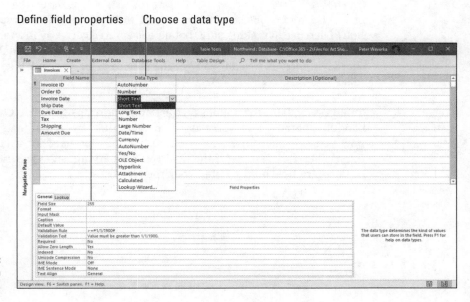

Define field properties   Choose a data type

FIGURE 2-3:
Choosing a
data type.

TIP

In case the name you choose for your field isn't descriptive enough, you can give the field a second name. The name appears in Datasheet view, on forms, and on reports. To enter a second, descriptive field name, enter the name in the Caption field on the General tab of the Design view window.

Later in this chapter, "Field Properties for Making Sure That Data Entries Are Accurate" demonstrates how to define field properties in the Design view window to make it easier for data-entry clerks to enter the data.

Taking advantage of ready-made fields

You can get a head start creating a field by using a ready-made field and then modifying it, if necessary. To create a ready-made field, switch to Datasheet view and select the field that you want your new field to go after. Then, on the (Table Tools) Table Fields tab, click a field button or click the More Fields button and choose the name of a field on the drop-down list.

Look for field buttons in the Add & Delete group. Field buttons include Short Text, Number, and Currency. After you create your new field, switch to Design view and examine its field properties. Some of these properties may need modifying. See "Field Properties for Making Sure That Data Entries Are Accurate" for information about field properties.

All about data types

To choose a data type for a field, start in Design view, open the Data Type drop-down list, and choose a data type (refer to Figure 2-3). Data types are the first line of defense in making sure that data is entered correctly in a table. Try to enter text in a field assigned the Currency or Number data type, and Access tells you that your entry is invalid. You get the chance to fix your mistake as soon as you make it.

Table 2-1 explains the options on the Data Type drop-down list. Choose data types carefully, because how you classify the data that is entered in a field determines how you can query the field for information. Querying for a number range is impossible, for example, if the field you're querying isn't classified as a Number or Currency field on the Data Type drop-down list.

TABLE 2-1 **Data Types for Fields**

Data Type	What It's For
Short Text	For storing text (city names, for example), combinations of text and numbers (street addresses, for example), and numbers that won't be calculated or used in expressions (telephone numbers, ZIP codes, and social security numbers, for example). A Short Text field can be no longer than 255 characters.
Long Text	For storing long descriptions. Fields assigned this data type can hold 65,535 characters, not that anyone needs that many.
Number	For storing numbers to be used in calculations or sorting. (If you're dealing with monetary figures, choose the Currency data type.)
Large Number	For importing and linking to BigInt (big integer) data. This data type is for working with calculations involving extremely large numbers.
Date/Time	For storing dates and times and being able to sort data chronologically or use dates and times in calculations.
Date/ Time Extended	For storing dates and times such that they are compatible with the SQL Server datatime2 data type.
Currency	For storing monetary figures for use in calculations and sorting.
AutoNumber	For entering numbers in sequence that will be different from record to record. Use the AutoNumber data type for the primary key field if no other field stores unique, one-of-a-kind data. (See "Designating the primary key field," later in this chapter.)
Yes/No	For storing True/False, Yes/No, On/Off type data. Choose this data type to enter data with a check box in the field. When the box is selected, the data in the field is True, Yes, or On, for example.
OLE Object	For embedding an OLE link in your Access table to another object — an Excel worksheet or Word document. (Consider using the Attachment data type as well.)
Hyperlink	For storing hyperlinks to other locations on the Internet or on the company intranet.
Attachment	For storing an image, spreadsheet, document, chart, or other file. Attaching a file to a database table is similar to attaching a file to an email message. Attachments do not require as much disk space as OLE objects because they don't require Access to store a bitmap image of the original file.
Calculated	For entering a mathematical expression that uses data from other fields in the database table.
Lookup Wizard	For creating a drop-down list with choices that a data-entry clerk can choose from when entering data. See "Creating a lookup data-entry list," later in this chapter.

Building Your
Database Tables

DECIDING HOW THE DATA IN FIELDS IS DISPLAYED

To decide how numbers, times, dates, currency values, and Yes/No data are displayed in fields, go to the General tab in the Field Properties part of the Design view and choose an option on the Format drop-down list. The display options are useful indeed. Choose the Currency format, for example, and you don't have to enter the dollar signs or commas when you enter a dollar figure in the field because the dollar sign and commas are entered for you.

Moreover, you can create a format of your own by entering these placeholder symbols in the Format text box:

- @ (at symbol): A character or space is required. For example, @@@@-@@ inserts a hyphen between the first set of numbers and the second. You don't have to enter the hyphen, only the text or numbers.

- & (ampersand): A character or space is optional. For example, @@@@@-&&&& in a ZIP Code field tells Access that either entry is correct, a five-character ZIP code or the ZIP code that has five characters plus the four extra characters.

- > (right bracket): Displays all characters in the field as uppercase. Merely by entering this symbol in the Format text box, you can display all entries in the field as uppercase without the data-entry clerk's having to hold down the Shift or Caps Lock key.

- < (left bracket): Displays all characters in the field as lowercase.

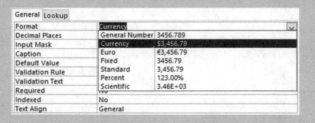

Designating the primary key field

As I explain in Chapter 1 of this minibook, no database table is complete without a primary key field. The *primary key field* identifies which field in the table is unique and contains data that differs from record to record. Duplicate values and null values can't be entered in the primary key field. (A *null value* indicates a missing or unknown value.) Choosing a primary key field is so important that Access doesn't let you close a table unless you choose one.

TIP

If no field in your table holds one-of-a-kind data that is different from record to record, get around the problem with one of these techniques:

» **The AutoNumber data type:** Create a new field, give it a name, choose AutoNumber from the Data Type drop-down list (refer to Figure 2-3), and make your new field the primary key field. This way, when you enter data, Access enters a unique number to identify each record in the field. (To generate random numbers instead of sequential numbers in an AutoNumber field, go the General tab of the Design view window, open the New Values drop-down list, and choose Random instead of Increment.)

» **A multiple-field primary key:** Combine two or more fields and designate them as the primary key. For example, if you're absolutely certain that no two people whose names will be entered in your database table have the same name, you can make the First Name and Last Name fields the primary key. The problem with multiple-field primary keys, however, is that it takes Access longer to process them, and you run the risk of entering duplicate records.

Follow these steps on the (Table Tools) Table Design tab to designate a field in a database table as the primary key field:

1. **In Design view, select the field or fields you want to be the primary key.**

To select a field, click its *row selector,* the small box to its left; Ctrl+click row selectors to select more than one field.

2. **Click the Primary Key button.**

A small key symbol appears on the row selector to let you know which field or fields are the primary key fields.

To remove a primary key, click its row selector and then click the Primary Key button all over again.

Moving, renaming, and deleting fields

Suppose that you need to move, rename, or delete a field. To do so, switch to Design view and follow these instructions:

» **Moving a field:** Select the field's row selector (the box to its left) and release the mouse button. Then click again and drag the selector up or down to a new location.

» **Renaming a field:** Click in the Field Name box where the name is, delete the name that's there, and type a new name.

>> **Deleting a field:** Click in the Field Name box, go to the (Table Tools) Table Design tab, and click the Delete Rows button. You can also right-click the field and choose Delete Rows on the shortcut menu.

Field Properties for Making Sure That Data Entries Are Accurate

Unfortunately, entering the data in a database table is one of the most tedious activities known to humankind. And because the activity is so dull, people are prone to make mistakes when they enter data in a database table. One way to cut down on mistakes is to take advantage of the Field Properties settings on the General tab in the Design view window. Figure 2-4 shows the General tab.

Field properties

Description of the property

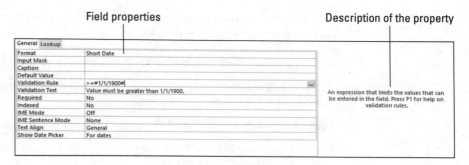

FIGURE 2-4: Establishing field properties.

These properties determine what can and can't be entered in the different fields of a database table. Some of the settings are invaluable. The Field Size property, for example, determines how many characters can be entered in a field. In a State field where two-letter state abbreviations are to be entered, make the Field Size property 2 to be certain that no one enters more than two characters. If the majority of people you're tracking in an address database live in New York, enter NY in the Default Value property. That way, you spare data-entry clerks from having to enter NY the majority of the time. They won't have to enter it because NY is already there.

The Lookup tab in the Field Properties part of the Design view window is for creating a data-entry drop-down list. It, too, is invaluable. If you happen to know that only four items can be entered in a field, create a drop-down list with the four items. That way, data-entry clerks can choose from a list of four valid items instead of having to enter the data themselves and perhaps enter it incorrectly. (See "Creating a lookup data-entry list," later in this chapter.)

A look at the Field Properties settings

Especially if yours is a large database, you're encouraged to study the field properties carefully and make liberal use of them. The Field Properties settings safeguard data from being entered incorrectly. Following is a description of the different properties (listed here in the order in which they appear in the Design view window) and instructions for using them wisely. Which properties you can assign to a field depends on which data type the field was assigned.

Field Size

In the Field Size box for Text fields, enter the maximum number of characters that can be entered in the field. Suppose that the field you're dealing with is ZIP Code, and you want to enter five-number ZIP codes. By entering **5** in the Field Size text box, only five characters can be entered in the field. A sleepy data-entry clerk couldn't enter a six-character ZIP code by accident.

For Number fields, select a value for the field size from the drop-down list. Table 2-2 describes these field sizes.

TABLE 2-2   ## Numeric Field Sizes

Field Size	Description
Byte	An integer that holds values from 0–255.
Integer	An integer that holds values from –32,768– +32,767.
Long Integer	An integer that holds values from –2,147,483,648– +2,147,483,647.
Single	A floating-point number that holds large values up to 7 significant digits.
Double	A floating-point number that holds large values up to 15 significant digits.
Replication ID*	A globally unique identifier (GUID) required for replication; this number is generated randomly.
Decimal	A number with defined decimal precision. The default precision is 0, but you can set the scale up to 28.

Not supported by the .accdb file format.

TECHNICAL STUFF

The Single, Double, and Decimal field size options hold different ranges of numbers. For now, if you need to store numbers after the decimal point, choose the Double field size so that you cover most situations.

Format

Earlier in this chapter, "Deciding how the data in fields is displayed" (a sidebar) explains the Format property. Click the drop-down list and choose the format in which text, numbers, and dates and times are displayed.

Decimal Places

For a field that holds numbers, open the Decimal Places drop-down list and choose how many numbers can appear to the right of the decimal point. This property affects how numbers and currency values are displayed, not their real value. Numbers are rounded to the nearest decimal point. The Auto option displays the number of decimal places permitted by the format you chose on the Format drop-down list.

Input Mask

For Text and Date field types, this feature provides a template with punctuation marks to make entering the data easier. Telephone numbers, social security numbers, and other numbers that typically are entered along with dashes and parentheses are ideal candidates for an input mask (another ridiculous database term!). On the datasheet, blank spaces appear where the numbers go, and the punctuation marks stand at the ready to receive numbers, as shown in Figure 2-5.

Job Title	Business Phone	Home Phone
Sales Representative	(123)555-0100	(123)555-0102
Vice President, Sales	(123)555-0100	(123)555-0102
Sales Representative	(___)___-____	(123)555-0102

FIGURE 2-5: Input masks make data entry easier.

In the Input Mask text box, enter a **0** where numbers go and enter the punctuation marks where they go. For example, enter (000) 000-0000 or 000/000-0000 to enter an input mask for a telephone number like the one shown in Figure 2-5. You can also create input masks by clicking the three dots beside the Input Mask text box. Doing so opens the Input Mask Wizard dialog box, where you can fashion a very sophisticated input mask.

Caption

If the field you're working on has a cryptic or hard-to-understand name, enter a more descriptive name in the Caption text box. The value in the Caption property appears as the column heading in Datasheet view, as a label on forms, and on reports in place of the field name. People entering data understand what to enter after reading the descriptive caption.

Default Value

When you know that the majority of records require a certain value, number, or abbreviation, enter it in the Default Value text box. That way, you save yourself the trouble of entering the value, number, or abbreviation most of the time because the default value appears already in each record when you enter it. You can always override the default value by entering something different.

Validation Rule

As long as you know your way around operators and Boolean expressions, you can establish a rule for entering data in a field. For example, you can enter an expression that requires dates to be entered in a certain time frame. Or you can require currency figures to be above or below a certain value. To establish a validation rule, enter an expression in the Validation Rule text box. To use dates in an expression, the dates must be enclosed by number signs (#). Here are some examples of validation rules:

>1000	The value you enter must be over 1,000.
<1000	The value you enter must be less than 1,000.
>=10	The value you enter must be greater than or equal to ten.
<>0	The value you enter cannot be zero.
>=#1/1/2021#	The date you enter must be January 1, 2021, or later.
>=#1/1/2021# And <#1/1/2022#	The date you enter must be in the year 2021.

To get help forming expressions, click the three dots beside the Validation Rule text box to open the Expression Builder, as shown in Figure 2-6, and build an expression there. Try clicking the Help button in the Expression Builder dialog box. Doing so opens the Access Help program, where you can get advice about building expressions.

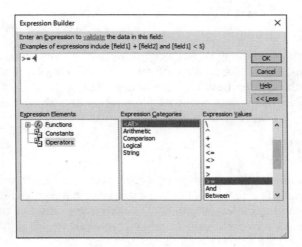

FIGURE 2-6:
Creating a
validation rule.

Validation Text

If someone enters data that violates a validation rule that you enter in the Validation Rule text box, Access displays a standard error message. The message reads,
"One or more values are prohibited by the validation rule set for [this field]. Enter
a value that the expression for this field can accept." If this message is too cold
and impersonal for you, you can create a message of your own for the error message dialog box. Enter your friendly message in the Validation Text text box.

Required

By default, no entry has to be made in a field, but if you choose Yes instead of No
in the Required box and you fail to make an entry in the field, a message box tells
you to be sure to make an entry.

Allow Zero Length

This property allows you to enter zero-length strings in a field. A *zero-length
string* — two quotation marks with no text or spaces between them ("") —
indicates that no value exists for a field. To see how zero-length strings work,
suppose that your database table calls for entering email addresses. If you
didn't know whether one person has an email address, you would leave the E-Mail
Address field blank. If, however, you knew that the person didn't have an email
address, you could indicate as much by entering a zero-length string. Choose Yes
on the drop-down list to permit zero-length strings to be entered in the field.

Indexed

This property indicates whether the field has been indexed. As "Indexing for
Faster Sorts, Searches, and Queries" explains, later in this chapter, indexes make

sorting a field and searching through a field go faster. The word *No* appears in this text box if the field has not been indexed.

Unicode Expression

Choose Yes from the Unicode Expression drop-down list if you want to compress data that is now stored in Unicode format, which is a standardized encoding scheme. Storing data this way saves on disk space, and you probably don't want to change this property.

Smart Tags

If you intend to enter Smart Tags in the field, indicate which kind you enter by clicking the three dots next to the Smart Tags box and choosing an option in the Action Tags dialog box.

Text Align

This property determines how the text is aligned in a column or on a form or report. Select General to let Access determine the alignment, or select Left, Right, Center, or Distribute.

Text Format

Available on Long Text fields, this drop-down list lets you choose to allow rich text in the field. With this property set to Rich Text, you can make different words bold, italic, underline, and change font sizes and colors. Set it to Plain Text for plain, boring text with no formatting. I wonder why that isn't the setting's name.

Append Only

Available on Long Text fields, this property lets you add data only to a Long Text field to collect a history of comments.

Show Date Picker

This property is available on Date/Time fields. Choose For Dates to place a button next to the column that data-entry clerks can click to open a calendar and select a date instead of typing numbers.

IME Mode/IME Sentence mode

These options are for converting characters and sentences from East Asian versions of Access.

Creating a lookup data-entry list

Perhaps the best way to make sure that data is entered correctly is to create a data-entry drop-down list. That way, anyone entering the data in your database table can do so by choosing an item from the list, not by typing it in, as shown in Figure 2-7. This method saves time and prevents invalid data from being entered. Access offers two ways to create the drop-down list:

>> **Create the list by entering the items yourself:** Go this route when you're dealing with a finite list of items that never change.

>> **Get the items from another database table:** Go this route to get items from a column in another database table. This way, you can choose from an ever-expanding list of items. When the number of items in the other database table changes, so does the number of items in the drop-down list, because the items come from the other database table. This is a great way to get items from a primary key field in another table.

FIGURE 2-7: A so-called lookup list.

Creating a drop-down list on your own

Follow these steps to create a drop-down, or *lookup*, list with entries you type:

1. **In Design view, click the field that needs a drop-down list.**

2. **Open the Data Type drop-down list and choose Lookup Wizard, the last option in the list.**

   The Lookup Wizard dialog box appears.

3. **Select the second option, I Will Type in the Values That I Want, and click the Next button.**

4. **Under Col1 in the next dialog box, enter each item you want to appear in the drop-down list; then click the Next button.**

You can create a multicolumn list by entering a number in the Number of Columns text box and then entering items for the list.

5. **Enter a name for the field, if necessary, and click the Finish button.**

Switch to Datasheet view and open the drop-down list in the field to make sure that it displays properly.

To remove a lookup list from a field, select the field, go to the Lookup tab in the Design view window, open the Display Control drop-down list, and choose Text Box.

TIP

To see what's on a drop-down list, select the field for which you created the list, switch to Design view, and select the Lookup tab in the Field Properties pane. As shown in Figure 2-8, you can edit the list by editing or removing items in the Row Source text box. Be sure that a semicolon (;) appears between each item.

General	Lookup	
Display Control	Combo Box	⌄
Row Source Type	Value List	
Row Source	"King";"Queen";"Prince";"Knave"	
Bound Column	1	
Column Count	1	
Column Heads	No	
Column Widths	1"	
List Rows	16	
List Width	1"	
Limit To List	No	
Allow Multiple Values	No	
Allow Value List Edits	No	
List Items Edit Form		
Show Only Row Source V	No	

FIGURE 2-8:
Lookup field
properties.

Getting list items from a database table

Before you can get list items from another database table, you might want to define a relationship between the tables; it's not required, but it's recommended. Later in this chapter, "Establishing Relationships among Database Tables" explains how to do that. Follow these steps to get items in a drop-down list from another database table:

1. **In Design view, click the field that needs a list, open the Data Type drop-down list, and choose Lookup Wizard.**

The Lookup Wizard dialog box appears.

2. **Select the first option, I Want the Lookup Field to Get the Values from Another Table or Query, and click Next.**

   You see a list of tables in your database.

3. **Select the table with the data you need and click the Next button.**

   The dialog box shows you a list of available fields in the table.

4. **Select the field where the data for your list is stored.**

5. **Click the > button.**

   The name of the list appears on the right side of the dialog box, under Selected Fields.

6. **Click the Next button.**

   Normally, lists are displayed in ascending order, but you can select a field and click the Ascending button to reverse the order of the list. (Note that the button turns into the Descending button.)

7. **Click the Finish button.**

   If you're so inclined, you can change the width of the list before clicking Finish, but you can always do that on the datasheet, as Chapter 3 of this minibook explains.

TIP

Suppose that you obtain the items from the wrong field or wrong database table. To fix that problem, select the field for which you created the list, and in Design view, select the Lookup tab (refer to Figure 2-8). Choose Text Box instead of Combo Box on the Display Control drop-down list and start all over.

Indexing for Faster Sorts, Searches, and Queries

Indexing means to instruct Access to keep information about the data in a field or combination of fields. Because Access keeps this information on hand, it doesn't have to actually search through every record in a database table to sort data, search for data, or run a query. In a large database table, indexes make sorting, searching, and querying go considerably faster because Access looks through its own data rather than the data in tables. The performance difference between querying a database table that has and has not been indexed is astonishing. That's the good news. The bad news is that indexes inflate the size of Access files.

TIP

By default, the field you choose as the primary key field is indexed. I recommend choosing other fields, in addition to the primary key field, for indexing if you often conduct queries and searches. When you choose a field to index, choose one with data that varies from record to record and is likely to be the subject of searches, sorts, and queries. That way, the index means something. However, a field with data that is mostly the same from record to record is a waste of a good index, not to mention disk space. By the way, Access automatically indexes fields whose names include the words *ID, Code, Num,* and *Key,* the idea being that these fields are likely to store essential information worthy of indexing.

Indexing a field

To index a field, switch to Design view, select the field you want to index, and on the General tab of the Field Properties part of the Design window, open the Indexed drop-down list and choose one of these options:

>> **Yes (Duplicates OK):** Indexes the field and allows duplicate values to be entered in the field.

>> **Yes (No Duplicates):** Indexes the field and disallows duplicate values. If you choose this option, the field works something like a primary key field in that Access does not permit you to enter the same value in two different records.

Indexing based on more than one field

An index created on more than one field is called a *multifield index.* Multifield indexes make sorting, querying, and searching the database table go faster. They are especially valuable in sorting operations where records in one field are usually the same but records in a companion field are different. In a large database table that stores names and addresses, for example, many names in the Last Name field are the same, so indexing on the Last Name field isn't worthwhile, but indexing the First Name and Last Name fields helps Access distinguish records from one another.

Follow these steps to generate a multifield index:

1. **Switch to Design view, and on the (Table Tools) Table Design tab, click the Indexes button.**

You see the Indexes dialog box, as shown in Figure 2-9. The dialog box lists the primary key field already because it's indexed by default. You also see any fields to which you set the Indexed property to Yes.

2. **On a blank line in the dialog box, enter a name for the index in the Index Name column.**

3. **In the Field Name column, open the drop-down list and choose the first field you want for the multifield index.**

Access sorts the records first on this field and then on the second field you choose.

4. **In the next row, leave the Index Name blank and choose another field name from the drop-down list.**

This field is the second field in the index. You can use as many as ten different fields in a multifield index. In Figure 2-9, two fields are in a multifield index: First Name and Last Name.

5. **Choose Descending in the Sort Order column if you want the field sorted in descending order.**

Most of the time, you want to leave the Sort Order set to Ascending because most people read from A to Z.

6. **Click the Close button.**

Click the Indexes button in Design view if you need to return to the Indexes dialog box and change how fields are indexed.

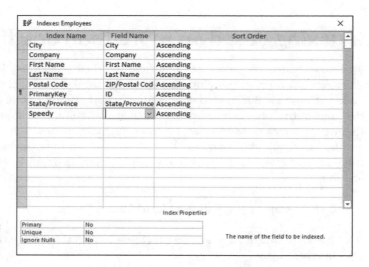

FIGURE 2-9: The Indexes dialog box.

Establishing Relationships among Database Tables

As Chapter 1 of this minibook explains, you have to establish relationships among tables if you want to query or generate reports with data from more than one database table. Relationships define the field that two or more different tables have in common. To understand why relationships among tables are necessary, consider the query shown in Figure 2-10. The purpose of this query is to list all companies that ordered items in 2021, list the companies by name, and list the city where each company is located.

FIGURE 2-10:
To conduct a query with more than one table, the tables must have a relationship.

Consider what Access does to run this query:

» Access deals with two database tables, Customers and Orders.

» In the Orders table, Access looks in the Order Date field to isolate all records that describe orders made in the year 2021. The expression for finding these records is shown on the Criteria line in Figure 2-10: Between #1/1/2021# And #12/31/2021#.

» Because a relationship exists between the ID field in the Customers table and the Customer ID field in the Orders table — that is, the two fields hold the same type of information — Access can match the 2021 records it finds in the Orders table with corresponding records in the Customers table. Where the Customer ID of a 2021 record in the Orders table and an ID in the Customers table match, Access assembles a new record and places it in the query results.

» Data for determining which records appear in the query results is found in the Order Date field in the Orders table. But the information compiled in the query results — customer IDs, company names, and cities — comes from fields in the Customers table. Thanks to the relationship between the ID and Customer ID fields in these tables, Access can draw upon information from both tables.

Types of relationships

The vast majority of relationships between tables are *one-to-many relationships* between the primary key field in one database table and a field in another. Table relationships fall in these categories:

» **One-to-many relationship:** Each record in one table is linked to many records in another table. The relationship in Figure 2-10 is a one-to-many relationship. Each ID number appears only once in the ID field of the Customers table, but in the Orders table, the same Customer ID number can appear in many records because the same customer can order many different products. When you link tables, Access creates a one-to-many relationship when one of the fields being linked is either a primary key field or an indexed field that has been assigned the No (No Duplicates) setting. (See "Indexing for Faster Sorts, Searches, and Queries," earlier in this chapter.)

» **One-to-one relationship:** Two fields are linked. This relationship is rare and is sometimes used for security purposes.

» **Many-to-many relationship:** This complex relationship actually describes crisscrossing relationships in which the linking field is not the primary key field in either table. To create a many-to-many relationship, an intermediary table called a *junction table* is needed. This relationship is rare.

REMEMBER

Sometimes, fields in separate tables that hold the same data also have the same name, but that isn't necessary. For example, a field called ZIP Code in one table might be called Postal Code in another. What matters is that fields that are linked have the same data type. For example, you can't create a relationship between a text field and a number field.

Handling tables in the Relationships window

Open the Relationships window to manage database tables and their relationships to each other. To open this window, go to the Database Tools tab and click the Relationships button. After you click this button, Access opens the (Relationship Tools) Relationships Design tab so that you can handle table relationships, as shown in Figure 2-11.

Read on to see how to add tables to the Relationships Design window, manage the tables, and forge links between tables.

Right-click to edit or delete a relationship

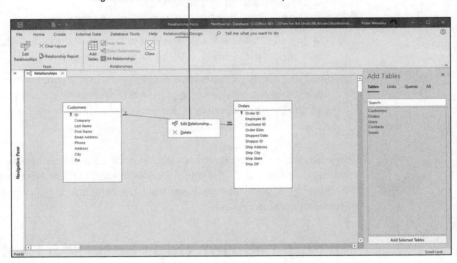

Adding tables to the Relationships window

Before you can forge relationships between tables, you have to place tables in the Relationships Design window. Follow these steps to add a table to the window:

1. **In the (Relationships Tools) Relationships Design tab, click the Add Tables button.**

   The Add Tables task pane opens (refer to Figure 2-11). It lists the tables in your database.

2. **Drag a table name from the task pane into the window.**

   If Access recognizes what it thinks is a relationship between the new table and a table that is already in the Relationships window, it creates a relationship between the tables.

Managing the tables

Apart from linking tables in the Relationships Design window (a subject I explain shortly), use these techniques on the Relationships Design tab to handle tables:

>> **Repositioning and resizing the tables:** Each table appears in its own window. Drag tables from place to place, drag a border to change a window's size, and scroll to see field names.

>> **Removing a table from the window:** Select the table and click the Hide Table button.

>> **Removing all tables from the window:** Click the Clear Layout button and choose Yes in the confirmation box.

>> **Placing tables back on the window:** Click the Add Table button and drag table names from the Add Tables task pane to the window.

>> **Placing all tables back in the window:** To put all the tables with relationships back in the window, click the All Relationships button.

>> **Studying a table's relationships:** Click the Clear Layout button to remove all tables from the window; then place the table back in the window, select it, and click the Direct Relationships button. All tables that are related to the selected table are added to the layout.

TIP

To generate and print an Access report that shows how tables in your database are linked, go to the (Relationship Tools) Relationships Design tab and click the Relationship Report button. Then save the report and print it. Chapter 5 of this minibook explains reports.

Forging relationships between tables

On the (Relationship Tools) Relationships Design tab (refer to Figure 2-11), make sure that both tables are on display and then follow these steps to forge a relationship between them:

1. **Click to select the field in one table; then hold down the mouse button, drag the pointer to the field in the other table where you want to forge the link, and release the mouse button.**

You see the Edit Relationships dialog box, as shown in Figure 2-12. The names of the two fields appear in the Edit Relationships dialog box.

Notice the Relationship Type at the bottom of the dialog box. If you accidentally create a link to the wrong field, choose the correct field from the drop-down list in the dialog box.

2. **Select the Enforce Referential Integrity check box.**

   If you don't select this box, the relationship between the tables is indeterminate, instead of being a one-to-many relationship. *Referential integrity* (another hideous database term!) has to do with whether values in the two different fields corroborate each other.

3. **Select Cascade options if you so choose.**

   One of these options is excellent; the other is dangerous:

   - **Cascade Update Related Fields:** If you change a value on the "one" side of the relationship, a matching value on the "many" side changes as well to preserve referential integrity. For example, if you create a multifield primary key of First Name and Last Name and then change the name of someone, the related fields in the other table change automatically to preserve referential integrity. This is a great way to make sure that information is up to date.

   - **Cascade Delete Related Records:** If you delete a record in the "one" table, all records in the "many" table to which the deleted record is linked are also deleted. For example, if you delete an employee from the "one" table, all records in the "many" table that include that employee are deleted! Access warns you before making the deletion, but still! This option is dangerous, and I don't recommend selecting it.

4. **Click the Create button to forge the relationship.**

   In the Relationships window (refer to Figure 2-11), a line is drawn between the table fields. The number 1 appears on the "one" side of the relationship and the infinity symbol (∞) appears on the "many" side.

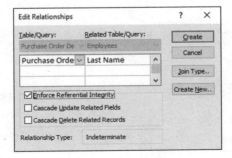

FIGURE 2-12:
Creating a table relationship.

WARNING

After you create a one-to-many relationship between tables with the Enforce Referential Integrity check box selected, you can't enter a value in the "many" table unless it's already in the "one" table. For example, suppose that the "one" table includes a primary key field called Employee Number, and this field is linked to a field in the "many" table that is also called Employee Number. If you enter an Employee Number in the "many" table that isn't in the "one" table, Access warns you that it can't be done without violating referential integrity. The best way to solve this problem is to create a lookup data-entry list in the "many" table with values from the primary key field in the "one" table. See "Creating a lookup data-entry list," later in this chapter.

Editing table relationships

In the Relationships window (refer to Figure 2-11), select the line that represents the relationship between two database tables and follow these instructions to edit or remove the relationship:

» **Editing the relationship:** Click the Edit Relationships button, right-click and choose Edit Relationship, or double-click the line. You see the Edit Relationships dialog box, where you can overhaul the relationship. (The previous topic in this chapter explains how.)

» **Deleting the relationship:** Press the Delete key or right-click and choose Delete. Then select Yes in the confirmation box.

Chapter **3**

Entering the Data

A t last — you can start entering the data. If you set up your database tables, named the fields, and established relationships between the tables, you're ready to go. This short chapter explains how to enter the data in a database table. It shows you how to enter data on a datasheet or enter data by way of a form. This chapter also describes how to find missing records in case one goes astray.

There's no getting around it: Entering data is truly a tedious activity. But if you set up the fields well and take advantage of input masks and other field properties, it isn't so bad. It's better than stepping on a shovel blade, anyway.

The Two Ways to Enter Data

When it comes to entering data in a database table, you can take your pick between Datasheet view and a form. Figure 3-1 compares and contrasts the two. Here are the advantages of entering data in Datasheet view:

>> Many records appear simultaneously.

>> You can compare data easily between records.

>> You can sort by column with the commands in the Sort and Filter group on the Home tab (as discussed in Chapter 4 of this minibook).

>> You can scroll up or down to locate records.

FIGURE 3-1:
Entering records
in Datasheet view
(left) and in a
form (right).

Here are the advantages of entering the data in a form:

>> You don't have to scroll left or right to see all the fields.

>> Getting from field to field is easier.

>> Fields are clearly labeled so that you always know what to enter.

Entering the Data in Datasheet View

Entering data in Datasheet view is like entering data in a conventional table. As with a table, a datasheet has columns and rows. Records are entered in rows, and each column represents a field. Fans of Datasheet view like being able to look at a dozen records simultaneously. For fans of Datasheet view, these pages explain how to enter data in a datasheet and change a datasheet's appearance.

Database tables open in Datasheet view when you double-click their names in the Navigation pane. But if you happen to be gazing at a table in Design view, click the View button on the Home tab or the Datasheet View button on the status bar.

Entering data

In Datasheet view, the bottom of the window tells you how many records are entered in the database table and which record the cursor is in. To enter a new record, move to a new, empty row and start entering the data. To create a new row, do one of the following:

» On the Home tab, click the New button.

» Click the New (Blank) Record button in the Datasheet navigation buttons. These buttons are located in the bottom-left corner of the Datasheet view window.

» Scroll to the bottom of the Datasheet view window and begin typing in the row with an asterisk (*) next to it.

» Press Ctrl++ (the plus key).

A pencil icon appears on the row selector to let you know which record you're dealing with. To get from field to field, click in a field, press the Tab key, or press Enter. Table 3-1 lists keyboard shortcuts for getting around in a datasheet.

TABLE 3-1 **Datasheet Shortcuts**

Press . . .	To Move . . .
↑	To the previous record. You can also press the Previous button on the Navigation buttons.
↓	To the next record. You can also press the Next button.
Tab or Enter	To the next field in the record.
Shift+Tab	To the previous field in the record.
Home	To the first field in the record.
End	To the last field in the record.
Ctrl+Home	To the first field in the first record. You can also press the First button.
Ctrl+End	To the last field in the last record. You can also press the Last button.
Page Up	Up one screen.
Page Down	Down one screen.

To delete a record, click its row selector and press the Delete key or the Delete button (located on the Home tab). You can also click in a record, go to the (Table Tools) Table Fields tab, and click the Delete button there. After you delete a record, it is gone forever. You can't resuscitate it.

ENTERING DATA IN THE ZOOM BOX

To make putting a long entry in a field a little easier, Access offers the Zoom box. Instead of having to stay within the narrow confines of a datasheet field, you can press Shift+F2 to open the Zoom box and enter the data there. After you click OK, the data is entered in the field.

The Zoom box is especially convenient for entering data in a Memo field. Memo fields can hold a whopping 65,535 characters. Move the cursor into a field and press Shift+F2 to open the Zoom box and read all the text in the field.

Two tricks for entering data quicker

In a database table with many fields, it's sometimes hard to tell what data to enter. When the pointer is in the sixth or seventh field, for example, you can lose sight of the first field, the one on the left side of the datasheet that usually identifies the person or item whose record you're entering.

TIP

To freeze a field so that it appears onscreen no matter how far you travel toward the right side of the datasheet, right-click the field's column heading and choose Freeze Fields on the shortcut menu. To unfreeze the fields, right-click the column heading and choose Unfreeze All Fields on the shortcut menu. You can freeze more than one field by dragging across field names at the top of the datasheet before choosing to freeze the columns. Is it getting cold in here?

Another way to handle the problem of not being able to identify where data is supposed to be entered is to hide columns in the datasheet. To perform this trick, select the columns you want to hide by dragging the pointer across their names; then right-click the column heading and choose Hide Fields on the shortcut menu. To see the columns again, right-click any column heading and choose Unhide Fields on the shortcut menu. You see the Unhide Columns dialog box. Select the fields that you want to see on the datasheet.

TIP

The fastest way to hide a column is to drag the border between it and the next column to the left until the column disappears.

Changing the appearance of the datasheet

To make the datasheet a little less cluttered and unwieldy, try experimenting with its appearance. Access offers a few handy shortcuts for doing just that:

» **Rearranging columns:** To move a column to a different location, click its name at the top of the datasheet and drag it to the left or right.

» **Resizing columns:** Move the pointer between column names at the top of the datasheet, and when you see the double-headed arrow, click and start dragging. To make a column just large enough to fit its widest entry, move the pointer between column names and double-click when you see the double-headed arrow.

» **Changing fonts:** The default font for a datasheet is Calibri 11-point, but the Home tab offers commands for changing fonts and font sizes. Look for these commands in the Text Formatting group.

» **Changing the look of gridlines:** On the Home tab, open the drop-down list on the Gridlines button and choose options to change the number and thickness of gridlines.

» **Alternate row colors:** On the Home tab, open the drop-down list on the Alternate Row Color button and choose a color for alternating rows on the datasheet.

TIP

To experiment all at one time with the many options for changing a datasheet's appearance, go to the Home tab and click the Text Formatting group button. You see the Datasheet Formatting dialog box, as shown in Figure 3-2. If you want a customized look for all the datasheets you work on, visit the File tab and select Options. Then go to the Datasheet category in the Options dialog box and go to town.

Entering the Data

FIGURE 3-2:
The Datasheet
Formatting
dialog box.

Entering the Data in a Form

Forms like the one shown in Figure 3-3 are very convenient for entering data. The labels tell you exactly what to enter. Personally, I prefer entering data in a form to entering data on a datasheet. On a form, you take it one step — make that one record — at a time. Not looking at a dozen records makes the task of entering data a little easier. These pages explain how to create a form for entering information in a database table. You also get advice for moving around with the Navigation buttons.

Creating a form

Fortunately, the Form Wizard makes it easy to create a form for entering information in a database table. All you have to do is start the wizard, choose the table, and make a couple of design decisions. To create a form, go to the Create tab and click the Form Wizard button. You see the first of several Form Wizard dialog boxes. Answer these questions and keep clicking the Next button until the time comes to click Finish:

>> **Tables/Queries:** From the drop-down list, choose the name of the database table you need to enter data in.

>> **Selected Fields:** Click the >> button to enter all the field names in the Select Fields box.

>> **Layout:** Select the Columnar option button. The other layouts aren't much good for entering data in a table. If you choose Tabular or Datasheet, you may as well enter data straight into the datasheet rather than rely on a form.

>> **Title:** Name your form after the table you created it for so that you can identify the form easily in the Navigation pane.

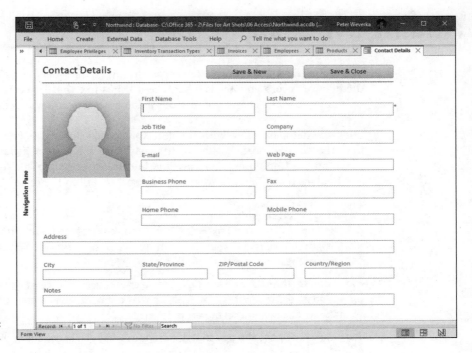

FIGURE 3-3:
A form.

To delete a form, right-click its name in the Navigation pane and choose Delete on the shortcut menu.

Entering the data

To open a form and begin entering data in its database table, display the form's name in the Navigation pane and then double-click the form's name. You can also right-click the name of the form and choose Open.

REMEMBER

To enter data in a form, click the New (Blank) Record button. This button is located with the Navigation buttons at the bottom of the form window. A new, empty form appears. Start typing. Press the Tab key, press the Enter key, or click to move from field to field. You can move backward through the fields by pressing Shift+Tab. If you enter half a record and want to start over, press the Esc key to empty the current field. Press Esc again to empty all the fields.

The Navigation buttons at the bottom of the form window tell you how many records are in the database table and which record you're looking at. From left to right, the Navigation buttons take you to the first record, previous record, next record, and last record.

Finding a Missing Record

Sometimes data goes astray. You scroll through a datasheet but simply can't find the item or record you need so badly. For times like those, Access offers the Find command. Use the command to scour a database for errant information.

Open the database table with the data that needs finding. If you know in which field the data is located, click in the field. You can save a little time that way. Then, on the Home tab, click the Find button (or press Ctrl+F). You see the Find and Replace dialog box, as shown in Figure 3-4. Fill in the dialog box as follows:

>> **Find What:** Enter the item you're looking for. If you're looking for a null value, enter **null** in this text box. Enter "" (two double quotation marks) to find zero-length strings. Table 3-2 describes the wildcard characters you can use in searches.

>> **Look In:** If you clicked in a field before choosing the Find command, Current Field is selected in this box. To search the entire database table, choose Current Document on the drop-down list.

>> **Match:** Choose the option that describes what you know about the item. Choosing the Any Part of Field option can make for a long search. For example, a search for the letters *chin* finds, among others, China, Ching, and itching — any word with the consecutive letters *chin*.

>> **Search:** Choose an option — All, Up, or Down — that describes which direction to start searching.

>> **Match Case:** If you know the combination of upper- and lowercase letters you're after and you enter the combination in the Find What text box, select this check box.

>> **Search Fields As Formatted:** If you're searching for a field that has been formatted a certain way, select this check box and make sure that the text or numbers you enter in the Find What text box are formatted correctly. For example, if you're searching for a record with the date July 31, 1958, and you choose the *mm/dd/yyyy* format, enter the date as 07/31/1958.

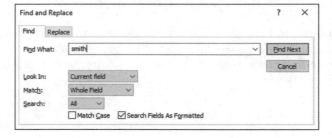

FIGURE 3-4:
Finding data.

TABLE 3-2　　　**Wildcard Characters for Searches**

Character	Description	Example
?	A single character	**b?t** finds *bat, bet, bit,* and *but.*
#	A single numeric digit	**9411#** finds *94111, 94112, 94113,* and so on.
*	Any group of consecutive characters	**t*o** finds *to, two,* and *tattoo.*
[xyz]	Any character in the brackets	**t[aio]pper** finds *tapper, tipper,* and *topper,* but not *tupper.*
[!xy]	Any character not in the brackets	**p[!io]t** finds *pat* and *pet,* but not *pit* and *pot.*
x–z	Any character in a range of characters	**[1–4]000** finds *1000, 2000, 3000,* and *4000,* but not *5000.* The range must be in ascending order.

Click the Find Next button to conduct the search. The item might be found in more than one location. Keep clicking Find Next (or pressing Alt+F) until you find the item or you die of thirst on the hot sands of the digital desert.

TIP

To quickly find the first value of a search term, start typing in the Search box in the form window or in Datasheet view. As soon as you start typing, the cursor moves to the first instance of the data you enter. The Search box is located at the bottom of the screen.

Finding and Replacing Data

Finding and replacing data is remarkably similar to finding data. The difference is that you enter data in the Replace With text box as well as the familiar Find What text box and other option boxes. Figure 3-5 shows the Replace tab of the Find and Replace dialog box. Does it look familiar? If it doesn't, read the preceding topic in this chapter, "Finding a Missing Record."

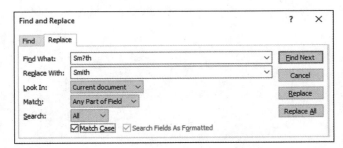

FIGURE 3-5:
Replacing data.

To find and replace data, go to the Home tab and click the Replace button (or press Ctrl+H). You see the Replace tab of the Find and Replace dialog box. After you enter the replacement data in the Replace With text box, make sure that Whole Field is selected in the Match drop-down list. Conducting a find-and-replace operation with Any Part of Field or Start of Field selected in the Match drop-down list can have unintended consequences. For example, a search for *Brook* also finds *Brooklyn, Middlebrook,* and other words that include *brook.* Blindly replacing the *brook* text string with *stream* produces, for example, *Streamlyn* and *Middlestream.*

WARNING

Unless you're as confident as a gambler with four aces, don't click the Replace All button to replace all instances of the text or numbers in the database table or field you're searching in. Instead, click the Replace button to find and replace text or numbers one instance at a time.

By the way, you can also find and replace data with an update query. Chapter 4 of this minibook covers update queries.

IN THIS CHAPTER

» Sorting, or rearranging, records in a database table

» Filtering records in a table to see only the records you need

» Querying to collect and examine information stored in a database

» Looking at different kinds of queries

Chapter **4**

Sorting, Querying, and Filtering for Data

N ow that you've laid the groundwork, you can put your database through its paces and make it do what databases are meant to do: provide information of one kind or another. This chapter explains how to pester an Access database for names, addresses, dates, statistical averages, and whatnot. It shows how to sort records and filter a database table to see records of a certain kind. You also find out how to query a database to get it to yield its dark secrets and invaluable information.

Sorting Records in a Database Table

Sorting rearranges records in a database table so that the records appear in alphabetical, numerical, or date order in one field. By sorting the records in a database, you can locate records faster. What's more, being able to sort data means that you don't have to bother about the order in which you enter records because you can always sort them later to put them in a particular order.

Ascending vs. descending sorts

Records can be sorted in ascending or descending order:

» **Ascending order:** Arranges records in alphabetical order from A to Z, numbers from smallest to largest, and dates chronologically from earliest to latest.

» **Descending order:** Arranges text from Z to A, numbers from largest to smallest, and dates chronologically from latest to earliest.

Sorting records

Follow these steps to sort the records in a database table:

1. In Datasheet view, click anywhere in the field by which you want to sort the records.

2. On the Home tab, click the Ascending or Descending button.

You can also right-click a field name at the top of a column and choose Sort A to Z or Sort Z to A on the shortcut menu. The menu choices change based on the type of data. For Number fields, you can sort smallest to largest and vice versa; for Date fields, choose to sort oldest to newest, or vice versa.

TIP

You can sort on more than one field by clicking a field and sorting it, and then clicking a second field and sorting it. Just make sure you sort the fields in reverse order. For example, to sort the database by the Employee, Customer, and Order ID fields, click in Order ID and sort it in ascending order; click in Customer and sort it in ascending order; click in Employee and sort it in ascending order. If you mess up and forget how the table is sorted, click the Remove Sort button. This button is located on the Home tab underneath the Ascending and Descending buttons.

Filtering to Find Information

Filtering isolates all the records in a database table that have the same field values or nearly the same field values. Instead of all the records in the table appearing on the datasheet, only records that meet the filtering criteria appear, as shown in Figure 4-1.

Remove (toggle) the filter

Filter indicator

FIGURE 4-1:
Results of a filtering operation.

The basic idea behind filtering is to choose a field value in the database table and use it as the standard for finding or excluding records. For example, you can find all the orders for a particular customer, all orders taken in the month of April, or all the orders that a particular customer placed in April. For that matter, you can filter by exclusion and see the records of all the orders in a database table *not* taken in April and *not* for a particular customer. Filtering is useful when you need to find records with specific information in a single database table.

Different ways to filter a database table

For comparison purposes, here are shorthand descriptions of the four ways to filter a database table. All filtering operations begin in Datasheet view on the Home tab. These techniques are described in detail in the upcoming pages.

>> **Filter by Selection:** Select all or part of a field in the database table, click the Selection button, and choose a filtering option. Access isolates all records with the data you select. This method works best when you can't quite decide what you're looking for. It's the only filtering method that permits you to look for data found in a whole field or part of a field. You can also filter data that doesn't match the selection.

>> **Filter for Input:** Select the field you want to filter with and click the Filter button. A dialog box appears so that you can choose values in the field or enter comparison operators to describe the numeric or date values you are filtering for. With this technique, you can filter for data ranges.

THE DIFFERENCE BETWEEN A FILTER AND A QUERY

The biggest difference between filtering and querying is that you can save a query and call upon it more than once. Queries are kept at the ready in the Navigation pane. A filter, on the other hand, is as good as the first time you use it, although you can save and run it as a query. Filters apply to a single database table, whereas you can query to assemble information from more than one table. In the results of a query, you can include as many fields as you want, but the results of a filtering operation show all the fields in the database table, regardless of whether you want them.

When it comes to examining data, a query is more sophisticated than a filter. Although you can use standard comparison operators to find records by filtering, querying gives you the opportunity to use complex expressions as well as comparison operators. You can filter, for example, to find people whose income is greater than or less than a certain amount. However, because you can write expressions in queries, you can query to find people whose income falls within a certain range.

>> **Filter by Form:** Click the Advanced button and choose Filter by Form. You see a form with one drop-down list for each field in your table. From the drop-down lists, make choices to describe the records you're looking for and then click the Toggle Filter button. This method is more flexible than the others because you can conduct OR as well as AND filtering operations. For example, you can isolate the records of people named Smith who also live in California, or the people who live in California or New York.

>> **Advanced Filter/Sort:** Click the Advanced button and choose Advanced Filter/Sort. The Filter window opens. Drag the name of the field you want to filter onto the grid. Then choose a Sort option and enter a search criterion. This filtering technique has more in common with queries than filters. Truth be told, the Advanced Filter/Sort command is merely a way to query a single table.

TIP

After you filter a database table, you can run a second (or third or fourth) filter operation to filter the data even more and further isolate the data you are looking for.

"Unfiltering" a database table

REMEMBER

You can tell when you're looking at a database table that has been filtered rather than a database table with all its records because the word *Filtered* appears at the bottom of the window next to the Navigation buttons (refer to Figure 4-1). Moreover, the filter icon appears in the field names of columns used in the filter operation, and the Toggle Filter button on the Ribbon is highlighted.

When you finish filtering a database table, use one of these techniques to "unfilter" it and see all the records in the table again:

>> Click the word *Filtered* at the bottom of the window. You can click this word again or click the Toggle Filter button to repeat the filter operation.

>> On the Home tab, click the Toggle Filter button. You can click this button again to repeat the filter operation.

>> On the Home tab, click the Advanced button and choose Clear All Filters on the drop-down list. Choosing this option kills the filter operation; you can't repeat it except by reconstructing it in the Datasheet window.

Filtering by selection

Filtering by selection is the fastest way to filter a database table. It's also the best way when you're not sure what you're looking for, because you can search for partial words and phrases. Follow these steps to filter by selection:

1. **Display the database table that needs filtering in Datasheet view.**

2. **Tell Access how to filter the records.**

To find all records with the same value or text in a particular field, simply click in a field with the value or text. If you aren't quite sure what to look for, select part of a field. For example, to find all names that start with the letters *St,* select St in one of the name fields.

3. **On the Home tab, click the Selection button and choose a filtering option.**

The options you see are specific to the cell you clicked or the data you selected in Step 2. For example, if you click a Last Name field that contains the name *Smith,* your options include Equals "Smith" and Does Not Equal "Smith." Select an option to include or exclude records in the filter operation.

Filtering for input

Filtering for input gives you the advantage of being able to filter for data ranges. Use this technique to isolate records that fall within a numerical or date range. Follow these steps to filter for input:

1. **Display the database table that you want to filter in Datasheet view.**

2. **Select the field with the data you want to use for the filter operation.**

To select a field, click its name along the top of the datasheet.

3. **On the Home tab, click the Filter button.**

As shown in Figure 4-2, a dialog box appears so that you can describe records that you want to filter for. You can also open this dialog box by clicking the button to the right of a field name.

4. **Tell Access how to filter the database table.**

You can choose values or describe a data range:

- **Choose values in the field:** The dialog box lists all values in the field. Deselect the Select All check box and then click to select the values you want to filter with.

- **Describe a numeric or date range:** Choose Number Filters or Date Filters and select a comparison operator on the submenu (refer to Figure 4-2). The Custom Filter dialog box appears. Enter a comparison value and click OK.

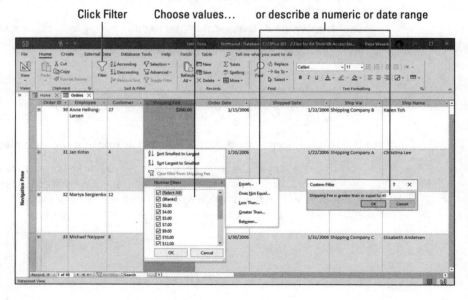

FIGURE 4-2:
Filtering by input for numeric data values.

You can repeat Steps 2 through 4 to filter the database table even further.

Filtering by form

Filtering by form is a sophisticated filtering method. It permits you to filter in more than one field using an *OR search*. For example, you can tell Access to look in the Last Name field for people named *Hernandez*, as well as look in the City field for *Hernandezes* who live in Los Angeles *or* San Francisco. Moreover, you can use comparison operators in the filter operation. Follow these steps to filter by form:

1. **In Datasheet view, go to the Home tab, click the Advanced button, and choose Filter by Form on the drop-down list.**

   Only field names appear on the datasheet, as shown in Figure 4-3.

2. **Click in a field, open its drop-down list, and enter a comparison value or select a value on the drop-down list.**

   You can choose a value on the drop-down list or, in Number and Currency fields, enter a comparison operator and a value. Table 4-1 explains the comparison operators.

3. **If you want, enter more criteria for the filtering operation.**

   You can enter values in other fields as well as filter more than once in the same field.

   - **Enter values in other fields:** Open the drop-down list in a field and enter a comparison value or select a value on the drop-down list.

   - **Filter more than once in the same field:** Select a field in which you already entered a search criterion. Then click the Or tab and either enter a comparison value or choose a value from the drop-down list.

     When you click the Or tab, the search choices you made previously disappear from the screen. Don't worry — Access remembers them on the Look For tab. You can click the Or tab again if you want to enter more criteria for Or searching.

4. **Click the Toggle Filter button.**

   The results of the filtering operation appear in the datasheet.

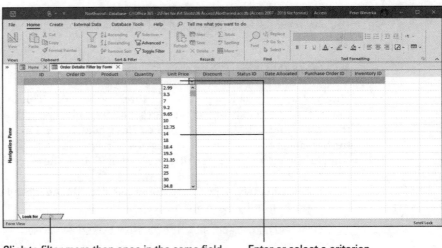

FIGURE 4-3:
Filtering by form.

Click to filter more than once in the same field   Enter or select a criterion

TABLE 4-1   **Comparison Operators for Filtering and Querying**

Operator	Name	Example
<	Less than	<10, any number smaller than ten
<=	Less than or equal to	<=10, ten as well as any number smaller than ten
>	Greater than	>10, any number larger than ten
>=	Greater than or equal to	>=10, ten as well as any number equal to or larger than ten
=	Equal to	=10, ten — not any other number
<>	Not equal to	<>10; all numbers except ten (instead of <>, you can enter the word *not*)
Between . . . And . . .	Between	Between 10 And 15, a number between 10 and 15 or equal to 10 or 15

Querying: The Basics

Querying means to ask a question of a database and get an answer in the form of records that meet the query criteria. Query when you want to ask a detailed question of a database. "Who lives in Los Angeles and donated more than $500 last year?" is an example of a query. So is, "Which orders were purchased by people who live in California and therefore have to pay sales tax, and how much sales tax was charged with these orders?" A query can search for information in more than one database table. For that matter, you can query other queries for information.

A query can be as sophisticated or as simple as you need it to be. In the results of the query, you can show all the fields in a database table or only a few necessary fields.

Access offers several different ways to query a database (the different techniques are described later in this chapter, in "Six Kinds of Queries"). Still, no matter which kind of query you're dealing with, the basics of creating and running a query are the same. You start on the Create tab to build new queries. To open a query you already created, double-click its name on the Navigation pane. The following pages introduce you to queries, how to create them, and how to modify them.

Creating a new query

To create a new query, start on the Create tab and click the Query Design or Query Wizard button.

» **Create the query in Design view:** Click the Query Design button to see the Query Design window, as shown in Figure 4-4, as well as the Add Tables task pane for telling Access which database tables to query. Construct your query in the Design window (the following pages explain how).

» **Create the query with a wizard:** Click the Query Wizard button to display the New Query dialog box and then choose a wizard option (four possible Query Wizards are available) and answer the questions that the Query Wizard asks. You're asked which table or tables to query, which fields to include in the query, and which fields to include in the query results. (The following pages explain these issues.)

To run a query, open the query in the Query window, go to the (Query Tools) Query Design tab, and click the Run button. The results of the query appear in Datasheet view.

Viewing queries in Datasheet and Design views

Select a query on the Navigation pane and use these techniques to view it in Datasheet or Design view. Datasheet view shows the results of running a query. Create and modify queries in Design view.

» **Opening in Design view:** Right-click the query's name in the Navigation pane and choose Design View on the shortcut menu.

» **Opening in Datasheet view:** On the Navigation pane, double-click the query's name or right-click its name and choose Open on the shortcut menu.

Table pane

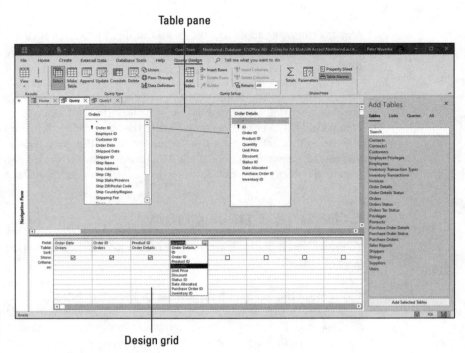

FIGURE 4-4:
The Query Design
window.

Design grid

>> **Switching between views with the View button:** On the Home tab, open
the drop-down list on the View button. Then choose Design View or Datasheet
View on the drop-down list.

>> **Switching between views on the status bar:** Click the Datasheet View or
Design View button on the right side of the status bar.

>> **Switching between views by right-clicking:** Right-click the query's title bar
and choose Datasheet View or Design View.

Finding your way around the Query Design window

The Query Design window (refer to Figure 4-4) is where you construct a query
or retool a query you constructed already. Switch to Design view to see the Query
Design window. You see this window straightaway after you click the Query Design
button to construct a new query. The Query Design window is divided into halves:

>> **Table pane:** Lists the database tables you're querying as well as the fields in
each table. You can drag the tables to new locations or drag a table border to
change its size and view more fields.

>> **Design grid:** Lists which fields to query from the tables, how to sort the query results, which fields to show in the query results, and criteria for locating records in fields.

Choosing which database tables to query

Follow these steps to choose which database tables to get information from in a query:

1. **Go to the (Query Tools) Query Design tab and click the Add Tables button.**

The Add Tables task pane opens (refer to Figure 4-4). It lists all the tables in your database.

2. **Place the names of tables you want to query in the Table pane.**

You can use these techniques to place a table in the Table pane:

- Double-click a table name in the Add Tables task pane.
- Drag a table name from the Add Tables task pane to the Table pane.
- Ctrl+click table names to select more than one table, and then drag the tables names onto the Table pane.

If you don't see the Add Tables task pane, click the Add Tables button on the (Query Tools) Query Design tab.

The tables you chose for your query appear in the Table pane of the Query Design window (refer to Figure 4-4). To remove a table from a query, right-click it in the Table pane and choose Remove Table on the shortcut menu.

REMEMBER

To query more than one table, you need to establish relationships among tables. (Chapter 2 of this minibook has information about establishing relationships among database tables.) So-called *join lines* in the Query Design window show how the tables are related to one another.

TIP

If you haven't defined relationships between the tables, you can still join them together by dragging a field from one table onto a field in another table. This is the same method used to create relationships between tables. Joining tables in a query doesn't create an actual relationship; it's just a temporary join for the sake of the query.

Choosing which fields to query

After you choose which tables to query, the next step is to choose which fields to query from the tables you selected. The object is to list fields from the Table pane in the first row of the Design grid, as shown in Figure 4-5. Data from fields listed in the first row of the Design grid is used to produce query results.

Fields are listed here

FIGURE 4-5:
Determining which fields to query.

Access offers these techniques for listing field names in the first row of the Design grid:

>> **Dragging a field name:** Drag a field name into a column on the Design grid. The field name appears on the grid, as does the name of the table that you drag the field name from.

>> **Double-clicking a field name:** Double-click a field name to place it in the next available column in the Design grid.

>> **Choosing a table and field name:** Click in the Table row, open the drop-down list, and choose the name of a table. Then, in the Field box directly above, open the drop-down list and choose a field name.

>> **Selecting all the fields in a table:** In the unlikely event that you want all the fields from a table to appear in the query results, either double-click the asterisk (*) at the top of the list of field names or drag the asterisk into the Design grid. Access places the name of the table followed by an asterisk in the Field text box. The asterisk signifies that all the fields from the table are included in the query.

To remove a field name from the Design grid, select it and press the Delete key or go to the (Query Tools) Query Design tab and click the Delete Columns button.

Sorting the query results

At the start of this chapter, "Sorting Records in a Database Table" explains what sorting is. The Sort row of the Design grid — directly underneath the Table name — contains a drop-down list. To sort the query, click the drop-down list in a field and choose Ascending or Descending to sort the results of a query on a particular field. To sort the results on more than one field, make sure that the first field to be sorted appears to the left of the other fields. Access reads the sort order from left to right.

MOVING FIELD COLUMNS ON THE QUERY GRID

The order in which field names appear in the Query grid is also the order in which they appear in the query results. Follow these steps to put field columns in the right order in the Query grid:

1. **Click a column's selector button to select a column.**

   This button is the narrow gray box directly above the field name. The pointer turns into a downward-pointing arrow when you move it over the selector button.

2. **Click the selector button again and drag the column to the left or right.**

Choosing which fields appear in query results

Although a field is part of a query and is listed in the Query grid, displaying information from the field in the query results isn't always necessary. Consider the Query grid shown in Figure 4-6. The object of this query is to get a list of customers by ZIP code that ordered products in the year 2018. To that end, the query criteria cell in the Order Date field is Between #1/1/2018# And #12/31/2018#. However, when the query results are generated, listing the precise dates when the orders shipped isn't necessary because the object of the query is to get a list of customers by ZIP code who ordered products in 2018.

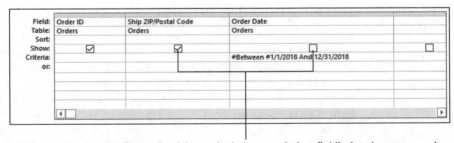

FIGURE 4-6: Choosing what appears in the query results.

Select or deselect the Show check box to include or exclude a field's data in query results

REMEMBER

Whether a field's Show check box is selected in the Query grid determines whether its results are part of the query results. Deselect the Show box if a field is necessary for producing records in a query but not necessary in the query results.

By the way, after you save and reopen a query, Access moves deselected Show fields to the right side of the Query grid, where you usually have to scroll to see them.

Entering criteria for a query

What separates a run-of-the-mill query from a supercharged query is a *criterion*, an expression or value you enter on the Criteria line under a field. Enter criteria on the Criteria line of the Query grid. By entering criteria, you can pinpoint records in the database with great accuracy. In Figure 4-7, the Query grid instructs Access to retrieve orders with invoices due before January 1, 2009 that charged more than $2,000 and were shipped to Massachusetts (MA), Connecticut (CT), or New York (NY).

Field:	Customer ID	Order ID	Invoice ID	Due Date	Amount Due	Ship State/Province		
Table:	Orders	Orders	Invoices	Invoices	Invoices	Orders		
Sort:	Ascending							
Show:	☑	☑	☑	☑	☑	☑	☐	
Criteria:				<#1/1/2009#	>2000			
or:						"MA"		
						"CT"		
						"NY"		

FIGURE 4-7: Including criteria in a query.

REMEMBER

As Figure 4-7 shows, Access places double quotation marks ("") around text criteria and number signs (#) around date criteria. When you enter text or date criteria, don't enter the double quotation marks or number signs. Access enters them for you.

TIP

When you need help writing an expression for a query, try clicking the Builder button to construct your query in the Expression Builder dialog box. This button is located on the (Query Tools) Query Design tab.

Entering numeric criteria

Enter numeric criteria in Number and Currency fields when you want to isolate records with specific values. Earlier in this chapter, Table 4-1 describes comparison operators that you can use for querying and filtering. These operators are invaluable when it comes to mining a database for information. Use the greater than (>) and less than (<) operators to find values higher or lower than a target value. Use the Between operator to find values between two numbers. For example, *Between 62 And 55* in a Currency field isolates records with all items that sell for between $62.00 and $55.00.

WARNING

Do not include commas in numbers when you enter them as criteria. For example, enter 3200, not 3,200. Enter a comma and you get a "The expression you entered contains invalid syntax. . ." error message.

Entering text criteria

To enter a text criterion, type it in the Criteria text box. For example, to find students who attended the Ohio State University, enter Ohio State in the Criteria text box of the University field. Access places double quotation marks ("") around the text you enter when you move the pointer out of the Criteria text box.

Wildcards and the Not operator can come in very handy when entering text criteria:

>> **Wildcards:** Wildcards enable you to query for data whose spelling you aren't quite sure of. (In Chapter 3 of this minibook, Table 3-2 explains what the wildcard characters are and how to use them.) For example, entering Sm?th in the Criteria box of the Last Name field finds all Smiths and Smyths. Entering E* in the Company field finds all company names that begin with the letter *E*.

>> **Not operator:** Use the Not operator to exclude records from query results. For example, to exclude records with Belgium in the Shipped To field, enter Not Belgium in the Criteria text box. This is a great way to strip unneeded records from a query.

Entering date criteria

All the operators that work for numeric data (see Table 4-1, earlier in this chapter) also work for data entered in a Date field. For example, you would enter **>7/31/1958** in a Birth Date field to find all people born after (greater than) July 31, 1958. You would enter **Between 1/1/1920 And 12/31/1929** to retrieve data about people born in the Roaring Twenties.

Access places number signs (#) around date criteria after you enter it. You can enter dates in the following formats:

>> 11/22/21

>> 11/22/2021

>> 22-Nov-21

>> November 22, 2021

REMEMBER

For the purpose of entering two-digit years in dates, the digits 30 through 99 belong to the twentieth century (1930–1999), but the digits 00 through 29 belong to the twenty-first century (2000–2029). For example, >4/1/24 refers to April 1, 2024, not April 1, 1924. To enter a date in 1929 or earlier, enter four digits instead of two to describe the year: **>4/1/1929**. To enter a date in 2030, or later, enter four digits instead of two: **>4/1/2038**. To avoid any confusion, enter four-digit years all the time.

TIP

The Date() function can come in very handy when you want to retrieve data relative to today's date, whatever it happens to be. For example, to retrieve purchase orders made between January 1, 2019 and today's date, enter this expression: **Between 1/1/2019 And Date().**

At last — saving and running a query

To save a query and inscribe its name forever in the Navigation pane, click the Save button on the Quick Access toolbar and enter a descriptive name in the Save As dialog box. The name you enter appears in the Queries group in the Navigation pane.

After you laboriously construct your query, take it for a test drive. To run a query:

>> **Starting from the Query Design window:** Click the Run button on the (Query Tools) Query Design tab.

>> **Starting from the Navigation pane:** Double-click an existing query's name, or right-click its name and choose Open on the shortcut menu.

Six Kinds of Queries

For your pleasure and entertainment, the rest of this chapter describes six useful types of queries. Access offers a handful of other queries, but I don't go there. Those queries are pretty complicated. If you become adept at querying, however, you're invited to look into the Help system for advice about running the query types that aren't explained here.

Select query

A *select query* is the standard kind of query, which I explain earlier in this chapter. A select query gathers information from one or more database tables and displays the information in a datasheet. A select query is the most common query, the primal query, the starting point for most other queries.

Top-value query

A *top-value query* is an easy way to find out, in a Number or Currency field, the highest or lowest values. On the Query grid, enter the name of the Number or

Currency field you want to know more about; then choose Ascending in the Sort drop-down list to rank values from lowest to highest, or choose Descending in the Sort drop-down list to rank values from highest to lowest. Finally, on the (Query Tools) Query Design tab, enter a value in the Return text box or choose a value on the Return drop-down list:

>> **Highest or lowest by percentage:** Enter or choose a percentage to find, for example, the highest or lowest 25 percent of the values. To enter a percentage, type a percent sign (%) after your entry and press the Enter key.

>> **Highest or lowest by ranking number:** Enter or choose a number to find, for example, the top-ten or lowest-ten values. Press the Enter key after you enter a number.

REMEMBER

This may seem counterintuitive, but to see the top values, you have to sort the field you're ranking in descending order. For example, if you sort employees by number of sales in descending order, the employees with the top sales appear at the top. To see the bottom values, sort in ascending order.

Summary query

Similar to a top-value query, a *summary query* is a way of getting cumulative information about all the data in a field. In a field that stores data about sales in Kentucky, for example, you can find the average amount of each sale, the total amount of all the sales, the total number of all the sales, and other data.

To run a summary query, go to the (Query Tools) Query Design tab and click the Totals button. A new row called Total appears on the Query grid. Open the Total drop-down list in the field whose contents you want to summarize and choose a function. Table 4-2 describes the functions.

The Group By, Expression, and Where choices in the Totals drop-down list are for including fields you're not performing a function on:

>> **Group By:** For choosing which fields to show totals for

>> **Expression:** For creating a calculated field

>> **Where:** For setting criteria (you can't include the field in the query)

TABLE 4-2

Summary Query Functions

Function	Returns
Sum	The total of all values in the field
Avg	The average of all values
Min	The lowest value
Max	The highest value
Count	The number of values
StDev	The standard deviation of the values
Var	The variance of the values
First	The first value
Last	The last value

Calculation query

A *calculation query* is one in which calculations are performed as part of the query. For example, you can calculate the sales tax on items sold or total the numbers in two fields in the same record. The beauty of a calculation query is that the data is recomputed each time you run the query. If the data used to make a calculation changes, so does the result of the calculation. If you were to include the calculation in a database table, you would have to recalculate the data yourself each time one of the values changed. With a calculation query, Access does the math for you.

To construct a calculation query, you create a new field in the Query grid for storing the results of the calculation; then enter a name for the field and a formula for the calculation. Follow these steps to create a calculation query:

1. **Create a query as you normally would and be sure to include the fields you want to use for calculation purposes in the Query grid.**

2. **In the Field box of a blank field, enter a name for the Calculation field and follow it with a colon.**

   In Figure 4-8, I entered **Subtotal:**. The purpose of the new Subtotal field is to multiply, for each product, the Unit Price by the Quantity to find out how much profit was earned from each product.

3. **After the colon, in square brackets ([]), enter the name of a field whose data you use for the calculation.**

   In Figure 4-8, data from the Unit Price and Quantity fields are used in the calculation, so their names appear in square brackets: [Unit Price] and [Quantity]. Be sure to spell field names correctly so that Access can recognize them.

4. Complete the calculation.

How you do this depends on what kind of calculation you're making. In Figure 4-8, I entered an asterisk (*) to multiply one field by another. The equation multiplies the values in the Unit Price and Quantity fields. You can add the data from two different fields — including calculated fields — by putting their names in brackets and joining them with a plus sign, like so: [SubTotal]+[Shipping Cost].

5. Click the Run button to run your calculation query.

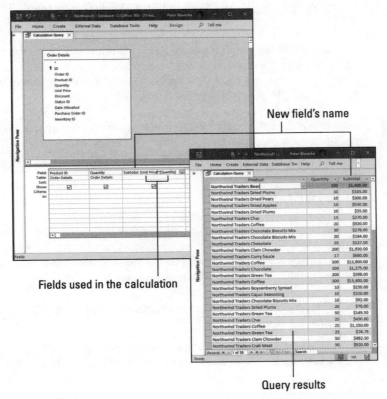

New field's name

Fields used in the calculation

Query results

FIGURE 4-8:
A calculation query.

TIP

Sometimes the results of the query aren't formatted correctly on the datasheet. To assign a new format to a field that you create for the purposes of making a calculation query, right-click the field on the Query grid and choose Properties. The Property Sheet appears. On the General tab, click the Format drop-down list and choose the correct format for your new, hand-crafted field.

Delete query

Be careful about running delete queries. A *delete query* deletes records and doesn't give you the opportunity to get the records back if you change your mind about deleting them. If used skillfully, however, a delete query is a good way to purge records from more than one database table at one time. Back up your database file before running a delete query.

To run a delete query, start a new query, and on the (Query Tools) Query Design tab, click the Delete button. Then make as though you were running a select query but target the records you want to delete. Finally, click the Run button to run the query.

You can delete records from more than one table as long as the tables are related and you chose the Cascade Delete Related Records option in the Edit Relationships dialog box when you linked the tables. (See Chapter 2 of this minibook for advice about forging relationships between tables.)

To preview the records that will be deleted before you run the delete query, switch to Datasheet view (click the View button). Those records you see? The delete query will delete them if you click the Run button.

Update query

An *update query* is a way to reach into a database and update records in several different tables all at one time. Update queries can be invaluable, but as with delete queries, they can have untoward consequences. Back up your database before you run an update query; then follow these steps to run it:

1. **Starting in Design view, go to the (Query Tools) Query Design tab and click the Update button.**

2. **In the field with the data that needs updating, enter text or a value in the Update To line. You can even enter another field name in square brackets ([]).**

   What you enter in the Update To line replaces what's in the field of the records you collect.

3. **Click the Run button.**

To update records in more than one table, you must have chosen the Cascade Update Related Fields option in the Edit Relationships dialog box when you linked the tables. (See the section in Chapter 2 of this minibook about forging relationships between tables.)

Chapter **5**

Presenting Data in a Report

The prettiest way to present data in a database table or query is to present it in a report. Even people who are allergic to databases can put up with database material in a report. Reports are easy to read and understand. They succinctly present the data so that you and others can interpret it. This brief chapter explains how to create reports, open them, and edit them.

Creating a Report

Access comes with all kinds of complicated tools for fashioning your own report — for laying out the pages in different ways and making data fields show up in different parts of the page. If ever a task called for relying on a wizard, creating a report is it. You can save yourself a lot of trouble, and fashion sophisticated-looking reports as well, by dispensing with the fancy report-making tools and letting the wizard do the job.

TIP

What's more, the easiest and best way to make a report is to base your report on a query. As part of fashioning a report with a wizard, you can tell Access which database tables and which fields to get the data from. In other words, you can query your database from inside the Report Wizard. However, doing that requires turning somersaults and cartwheels. Far easier is to run a query to produce the results you want in your report, save your query, and then fashion a report from the query results. Chapter 4 in this minibook explains how to create a query.

Figure 5-1 shows a report created with the Report Wizard. To create a report with the Report Wizard, go to the Create tab and click the Report Wizard button. You see the first of several Report Wizard dialog boxes. Negotiate the dialog boxes as follows, clicking the Next button as you go along:

>> **Tables/Queries:** Open the Table/Queries drop-down list and choose the query where the information in the report will come from. A list of fields in the query appears in the Available Fields box.

>> **Available Fields and Selected Fields:** Select the fields whose data you want in the report by selecting the fields one at a time and clicking the > button. Doing so moves field names from the Available Fields box to the Selected Fields box. Add all the fields by clicking the >> button.

>> **Do You Want to Add Any Grouping Levels?:** Include subheadings in your report by selecting a field name and clicking the > button to make it a subheading. If you're building your report on a query that includes related tables, the Report Wizard automatically adds subheadings.

>> **What Sort Order Do You Want?:** Select up to four fields to sort the data in your report. Even if you sort the fields in a query, the report handles sorting on its own. If you include grouping levels, the report already sorts on these fields.

>> **How Would You Like to Lay Out Your Report?:** Experiment with the options, and watch the Preview box, to choose a layout for your report. If your report has a lot of fields, you may want to print it in Landscape view.

>> **What Title Do You Want for Your Report?:** Enter a descriptive title. The name you choose appears in the Reports group in the Navigation pane. From there, you double-click the name when you want to see the report.

>> **Preview the Report:** Select this option button and click Finish.

The report appears in the Preview window. How do you like it? Later in this chapter, "Tweaking a Report" offers some tips for making a report look spiffier.

Top Ten Orders by Sales Amount				
Order Date	Order ID	SaleAmount	CompanyName	Shipped Date
2/23/2006	36	$1,930.00	Company C	2/25/2006
3/10/2006	38	$13,800.00	Company BB	3/11/2006
3/24/2006	44	$1,674.75	Company A	
3/24/2006	41	$13,800.00	Company G	
4/5/2006	46	$3,690.00	Company I	4/5/2006
4/8/2006	47	$4,200.00	Company F	4/8/2006
4/22/2006	58	$3,520.00	Company D	4/22/2006
6/5/2006	78	$1,560.00	Company CC	6/5/2006
6/5/2006	77	$2,250.00	Company Z	6/5/2006
6/23/2006	79	$2,490.00	Company F	6/23/2006

Wednesday, July 18, 2018   Page 1 of 1

FIGURE 5-1:
An example
of a report.

Opening and Viewing Reports

If you've spent any time whatsoever in Access, you know the drill for opening a so-called object. Follow these steps to open a report:

1. **In the Navigation pane, select the Reports group.**

   You see the names of reports you created.

2. **Double-click a report name or right-click a name and choose Open from the shortcut menu.**

   The report appears in Report view.

TIP

To update a report so that it includes recently added data, go to the Home tab and click the Refresh All button.

Tweaking a Report

As I mention at the start of this chapter, Access offers a bunch of complex tools for changing the layout and appearance of a report. If you're courageous and have lots of time on your hands, you're invited to take these tools in hand and go to it. In the Reports group of the Navigation pane, right-click a report and choose Layout View on the shortcut menu. Your report appears in Layout view, as shown in Figure 5-2. In this view, using tools on the (Report Layout Tools) Report Layout Design, Arrange, Format, and Page Setup tabs, you can tweak your report's appearance.

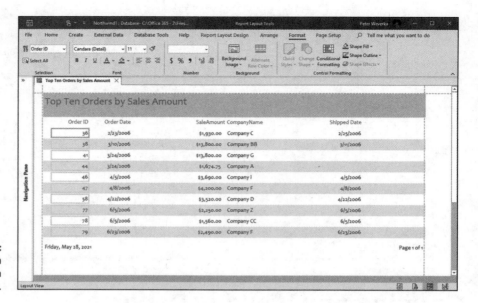

FIGURE 5-2:
The report in
Figure 5-1 in
Layout view.

I tell you how to create a report with the Report Wizard in order to avoid having
to visit this imposing window. However, you can change a report's appearance
in Report Layout View without going to very much trouble if you follow these
instructions:

>> **Choosing a new layout:** On the (Report Layout Tools) Arrange tab, click the
Stacked or Tabular button, or click the Gridlines button and choose an option
on the drop-down list, to change your report's layout.

>> **Including page numbers:** To include page numbers on the report, go
to the (Report Layout Tools) Report Layout Design tab and click the Page
Numbers button. You see the Page Numbers dialog box, shown in
Figure 5-3. Choose the Page N option button to display a page number
only, or select the Page N of M option button to display a page number as
well as the total number of pages in the report (as in "Page 2 of 4"). Choose
Position and Alignment options to describe where on the page to put the
page number.

>> **Changing the margins:** On the (Report Layout Tools) Page Setup tab, click the
Margins button and select Normal, Wide, or Narrow on the drop-down list.

FIGURE 5-3:
Putting on the
page numbers.

AN EASIER WAY TO TWEAK A REPORT — IN WORD

An easier way to tweak a report is to transfer your report to Microsoft Word and edit it there. Follow these steps to turn an Access report into a Word document:

1. **On the External Data tab, click the More button in the Export group and choose Word on the drop-down list.**

   You see the Export - RTF File dialog box.

2. **Click the Browse button, and in the File Save dialog box, choose a folder for storing the Word document; then click the Save button.**

3. **In the Export - RTF File dialog box, choose Open the Destination File After the Export Operation Is Complete.**

4. **Click the OK button.**

In a moment, your Access report appears in Word. The file is an RTF (rich text format) file. To save it as a Word file, go to the File tab, choose Save As, click the Browse button, and in the Save As dialog box, open the Save As Type drop-down list and choose Word Document. Books 1 and 2 describe how to work with files in Word.

7

Publisher 365

Contents at a Glance

Chapter **1**

Introducing Publisher

N ot long ago, creating professional publications like the kind you can create with Publisher 365 required sophisticated printing equipment and a background in graphic design. However, even a novice can now create professional-looking publications with Publisher. As long as you rely on a publication design — a template that comes with Publisher — most of the layout work is done for you. All you have to do is enter the text and the other particulars.

"A Print Shop in a Can"

Publisher has been called "a print shop in a can" because the application is great for creating prefabricated brochures, business cards, calendars, newsletters, resumes, posters, and the like. To make these publications without going to a great deal of trouble, however, you have to stick to the template. Each *template* provides you with a ready-made brochure, calendar, and so on.

Chances are, you can find a suitable template for whatever kind of publication you want to create. Figure 1-1 shows examples of newsletter templates. Templates include placeholders for graphics and text. To create a publication, you choose a template, choose a design, enter graphics and text in the publication where the placeholders are, and tweak the publication to your liking.

Choose a template   Customize the design

FIGURE 1-1:
Creating a
publication in the
Built-In
Templates
window.

Striking out on your own and designing publications like those in Figure 1-1 can be done, but you need a thorough knowledge of Publisher and a full head of hair. You need the hair because much of it will have been pulled out in frustration by the time you finish your design. I venture to say that the people who invented Publisher expect everyone to work from ready-made templates. Designing publications from scratch is simply too difficult. Don't be discouraged, however, because you can usually find a publication design for whatever you want to communicate.

Introducing Frames

The publications that you make with Publisher are composed of frames. A *frame* is a placeholder for text, a graphic, or a table. Complex publications have dozens of frames; simple publications have only a few. Frames keep text and graphics from overlapping. They make sure that everything stays on the page where it should be. As you create a publication, you enter text or graphics in frames.

The publication in Figure 1-2 is made up of several frames that were stitched together to form a poster. On the left side of the figure, I selected the frames, and you can see the frame boundaries; the right side of the figure shows what the poster looks like after it is printed. Frames make laying out publications easier. When you want to move text, a picture, a table, or an image, you simply drag its frame to a new location. After you select a frame, the commands you give apply to the text or graphic in the frame. Frames do not appear in the finished product; they are meant strictly to help with laying out text and graphics.

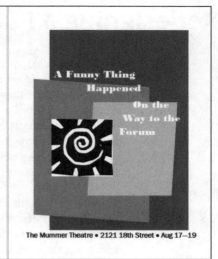

FIGURE 1-2:
A poster with frames showing (left); the poster as it looks when printed (right).

Creating a Publication

To create a new publication, go to the File tab and choose New (or press Ctrl+N). You see the New window, where you create a publication with any of these techniques:

>> **Search online for a template:** On the Office tab, in the Search for Online Templates text box, enter the name of a publication type and click the Start Searching button (or press Enter). Select a category and click a template to examine it in a preview screen. Click the Create button to create a publication.

>> **Choose a built-in template:** On the Built-In tab (refer to Figure 1-1), select the icon representing a category (Brochures, Business Cards, and so on). You see a dozen or more templates. Scroll through the list, select a template, and click Create.

REMEMBER

As you search for a template, you can click the Back or Home button to retrace your search in the New window.

TIP

After you select a built-in template in the New window, you can choose a color scheme, a font scheme for your publication, and other options on the right side of the window. But I suggest waiting until you've created your publication before choosing colors and fonts. You can study your publication more closely after you create it. You can look through it and decide what you want it to look like. What's more, choosing new colors and fonts for a publication isn't as hard as all that, as I explain shortly.

Redesigning a Publication

WARNING

Make your design choices carefully. In theory, you can change publication designs, color schemes, and design options when you are well along in a project, but in practice, changing these designs can have unforeseen consequences. If you change the color of a headline, for example, and then choose a new color scheme, the headline might be swallowed or rendered invisible by a background color in the new scheme. If you enter a bunch of text, change the size of a few frames, and then choose a new template for your publication, you may turn your publication into corned-beef hash and have to start over.

To redesign a publication, go to the Page Design tab. As shown in Figure 1-3, this tab offers opportunities for changing templates, the orientation and size of pages, color schemes, and font schemes. If your publication has more than one page, click page thumbnails in the Pages pane to visit different pages and see what they look like. (If you don't see the Pages pane, go to the View tab and select the Page Navigation check box.)

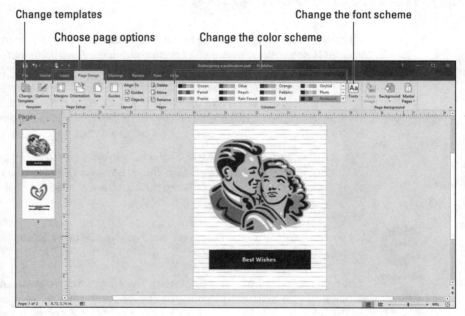

FIGURE 1-3: Go to the Page Design tab to change templates, color schemes, font schemes, color schemes, and page options.

Choosing a different template

Not happy with the template you chose when you created your publication? To exchange it for a new one, go to the Page Design tab and click the Change Template button. You see the Change Template window, where you can select a different template (refer to Figure 1-1).

Choosing a color scheme

To choose a different color scheme for your publication, go to the Page Design tab and select a scheme in the Schemes gallery (refer to Figure 1-3). If you're daring, choose Create New Color Scheme at the bottom of the gallery and fashion your own color scheme in the Create New Color Scheme dialog box.

Choosing a font scheme

You will be glad to know that most of the text formats that are available in Word are also available in Publisher on the Home tab. To boldface text, select it and click the Bold button. To change font sizes, choose an option on the Font Size drop-down list.

To avoid going to the trouble of formatting text, you can choose a *font scheme*, a pair of fonts for the headings and body text in a publication. Font schemes spare you the trouble of having to format the text on your own. The schemes were designed by people who know what they're doing. They look good.

To choose a font scheme, go to the Page Design tab, click the Fonts button, and select a scheme on the drop-down list. If you really know what you're doing, you can choose Create New Font Scheme on the drop-down list and select fonts for heading text and body text in the dialog box that appears.

Setting up your pages

Go to the Page Design tab to determine the margin size, orientation, and page size of your publication:

- » **Margins:** Click the Margins button and choose an option on the drop-down list or click Custom Margins to enter margin measurements in the Layout Guides dialog box.

- » **Orientation:** Click the Orientation button and choose Portrait or Landscape on the drop-down list to stand your publication upright or turn it on its side.

- » **Size:** Click the Size button and select a page size on the drop-down list. You can choose Create New Page Size in the list to open the Create New Page Size dialog box and declare a page size of your own. Decide right away which page size to use for your publication. How large or small the page is determines how the headings, graphics, and text fit on the pages.

Getting a Better View of Your Work

Because seeing the little details as well as the big picture matters so much in a publication, Publisher offers many tools for changing views of your work. Figure 1-4 shows what these tools are. They are described in the following pages.

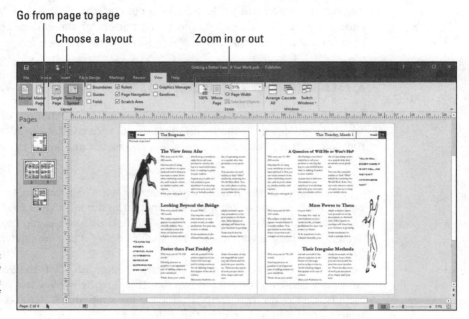

FIGURE 1-4:
Go to the View tab to change views of your work.

Zooming in and out

Apart from the standard Zoom controls found in most Office programs (Book 1, Chapter 3 describes the Zoom controls that appear in the lower-right corner of the screen), Publisher offers a handful of other commands for zooming in or out. Go to the View tab and take advantage of these techniques as you refine your publication:

>> **Make the page fit squarely in the window:** Click the Whole Page button (or press Ctrl+Shift+L) to make the entire page fit in the window. The lower-right corner of the window also offers a Whole Page button; you can click it when you're not working in the View tab.

>> **Make the width of the page fit in the window:** Click the Page Width button.

> » **Focus on objects:** Select an object (a text frame or graphic, for example) or a handful of objects and click the Selected Objects button to zoom in on what you selected. Being able to focus this way is very helpful when you're working on a publication that is crowded with words and images.
>
> » **View your publication at its actual size:** Click the 100% button.

Viewing single pages and two-page spreads

On the View tab, click the Two-Page Spread button to see facing pages in newsletters, brochures, and other publications with more than one page (refer to Figure 1-4). Choose this command early and often. It permits you to see what readers of your publication will see when they view facing pages. Click the Single Page button to see a single page in the window.

Going from page to page

Use these techniques to get from page to page in a publication:

> » **Pages pane:** In a publication with more than one page, go from page to page by clicking thumbnail pages in the Pages pane (refer to Figure 1-4). To display this pane, visit the View tab and click the Page Navigation check box.
>
> » **The Go To Page dialog box:** On the Home tab, open the drop-down list on the Find button and choose Go To Page (or press Ctrl+G). Then enter a page number in the Go To Page dialog box.

TIP

To help you identify pages, you can name them. When you move the pointer over a page thumbnail in the Pages pane, the name appears in a pop-up box. To name a page, right-click its thumbnail in the Pages pane and choose Rename on the shortcut menu. In the Rename Page dialog box, enter a descriptive name.

Understanding and Using the Layout Guides

Making frames, graphics, and lines of text line up squarely on the page is essential if your publication is to look smart and snappy. Readers tend to go cock-eyed when they see side-by-side columns with the text in one column slightly askew of the text in the column beside it. A graphic or text frame that spills into the margin is a breach of etiquette punishable by death. A row of graphics has to be just that — a row, not a crooked line. To keep pages neat and tidy, Publisher offers several types of layout guides, as the following pages explain.

Making use of layout guides

As shown in Figure 1-5, Publisher offers margin guides, grid guides, ruler guides, and baselines to help you lay out frames, graphics, and other objects on the pages of your publications. Use these layout guides early and often.

FIGURE 1-5:
Layout guides
(left to right):
margin guides,
grid guides,
ruler guides, and
baselines.

Margin guides

Margin guides are blue lines that clearly show where page margins begin and end (refer to Figure 1-5). Use the margin guides to make sure that objects don't stray too far into the margin.

Margin guides appear on the page as long as the Guides check box on the View tab is selected. Where the margin guides appear depends on the Margin setting you chose for your publication. (On the Page Design tab, click the Margins button and select a setting.)

Grid guides

Grid guides are blue lines that appear in grid form across the page (refer to Figure 1-5). Frames and objects can be made to "snap to the grid" (see "Aligning objects to ruler and grid lines," later in this chapter). Because the objects snap, you're spared the trouble of aligning them because they line up on grid guides.

To determine where gridlines are and display them on pages, go to the Page Design tab, click the Guides button, and choose Grid and Baseline Guides on the drop-down list. You see the Grid Guides tab of the Layout Guides dialog box, as shown in Figure 1-6. Do the following and click OK:

>> Enter numbers to determine how many rows and columns form the grid.

>> Enter Spacing measurements to determine how close objects can come to grid guides. Think carefully about entering a number less than .2 in the Spacing boxes. If you enter 0, for example, objects and frames will touch each other when they snap to the grid.

>> Select the Add Center Guide between Columns and Rows check box if you want to draw a line between the lines formed by columns and rows in the grid.

FIGURE 1-6:
Creating grid
guides and
baselines in the
Layout Guides
dialog box.

To remove grid guides, return to the Grid Guides tab of the Layout Guides dialog box and enter **1** in the Columns text box and **1** in the Rows text box. You can also go to the View tab and deselect the Guides check box to temporarily remove grid guides.

Ruler guides

Ruler guides are green horizontal and vertical lines that you can place on the page for assistance in aligning frames and objects (refer to Figure 1-5). You can draw ruler guides where you need them and remove the guides very easily when they get in the way. Whereas grid guides appear on every page in a publication, ruler guides appear on one page. You can, however, place the same ruler guides on every page by drawing the ruler guides on the master page. (Chapter 3 of this minibook describes master pages.)

Go to the Page Design tab and use one of these techniques to place ruler guides on a page:

>> **Built-in ruler guides:** Click the Guides button and choose a built-in ruler guide option on the drop-down list to place many ruler guides on a page.

>> **Drawn ruler guides:** Click the Guides button and choose Add Horizontal Ruler Guide or Add Vertical Ruler Guide. A ruler guide appears horizontally or vertically across the center of the page. Click and drag the ruler guide across the page to a new location.

>> **Ruler Guides dialog box:** Click the Guides button and choose Ruler Guides. You see the Ruler Guides dialog box. Enter horizontal or vertical measurements for the guides and click OK.

TIP

You can also place a ruler guide on a page by copying a ruler guide that is already there. Hold down the Ctrl key and drag an existing ruler guide to create a new guide.

To remove ruler guides from a page, go to the Page Design tab, click the Guides button, and choose No Ruler Guides on the drop-down list. You can temporarily remove ruler guides by deselecting the Guides check box on the View tab.

Baselines

Baselines are brown, dotted, horizontal lines that appear on the page to help with aligning frames, objects, and lines of text (refer to Figure 1-5). To make baselines appear, go to the View tab and select the Baselines check box.

To decide the frequency of baselines, go to the Page Design tab, click the Guides button, and choose Grid and Baseline Guides on the drop-down list. The Layout Guides dialog box appears. On the Baseline Guides tab, enter Spacing measurements to determine how tight or loose the lines are, and enter Offset measurements to determine how far off the margin settings the lines are. Figure 1-6 shows the Baseline Guides tab of the Layout Guides dialog box.

Aligning objects to ruler and grid lines

On the Page Design tab, the commands in the Layout group make frames and objects align to ruler guides or grid guides. Aligning helps to make objects line up squarely. On the Page Design tab, select the Guides check box to make objects align to the guides; select the Objects check box to make objects align to other objects on the page.

HANDLING THE RULERS

Rulers, when they aren't coming in very handy, get in the way. To display or hide rulers, go to the View tab and select or deselect the Rulers check box.

For precision work, you can drag a ruler into the middle of the window and use it as an aid for lining up frames and other objects, as shown in the figure. Hold down the Shift key, click a ruler, and drag it into the middle of the window. To move it back to where it came from, Shift+drag all over again.

Chapter **2**

Refining a Publication

This chapter picks up where the previous chapter left off. In Chapter 1 of this minibook, you discover how to create a publication, find your way around the screen, and use the different guides. In this chapter, you explore how to make a publication your own. This chapter offers speed techniques for entering and editing text. It explains how to handle frames, make text "flow" from frame to frame, and put graphics and other kinds of art in a publication. *Bon voyage!*

Entering Text on the Pages

The placeholder text that appears in publication designs has to go, of course. One of your first tasks is to replace the placeholder text with your own words. If you're putting together a sign or greeting card, you have only a handful of words to write, and you can write them in Publisher. But if you're working on a story (*story* is Publisher's term for an article that reaches across several text frames), the easiest way to handle the text is to write it in Word and import it.

If you have to replace more than two dozen words, follow these steps to replace the placeholder text in a text frame with text from a Word document:

1. **In Word, write the text and save the text in a file.**

   You can call on all of the Word commands to edit the text. Book 2 covers Word.

2. **In Publisher, click in the placeholder text, go to the Home tab, click the Styles button, and note on the Styles drop-down list which style has been assigned to the placeholder text.**

   You can tell which style has been assigned to the text because it is selected on the Styles drop-down list. In Step 6, you will assign the style that is currently applied to the text to the replacement text you insert into the text frame.

3. **If necessary, press Ctrl+A to select the text in the story.**

4. **On the Insert tab, click the Insert File button.**

   You see the Insert Text dialog box. You can also open this dialog box by right-clicking and choosing Change Text⇨ Text File.

5. **Select the Word file with the replacement text and click the OK button.**

   Replacement text from the Word file "flows" into the text frame or frames. If the replacement text doesn't fit in the text frames allotted to the story, you see the Autoflow dialog box. You can click the Yes button to tell Publisher to flow the text into different text frames in the publication, but I recommend clicking No in the Autoflow dialog box. Later in this chapter, "Making text flow from frame to frame" explains how to decide on your own where to put overflow text from a story.

   The replacement text maintains the styles assigned to it in the Word document. In the next step, you reassign a style to the text.

WARNING

6. **Press Ctrl+A to select the text in the story, go to the Home tab, click the Styles button, and choose the style that was assigned to the placeholder text.**

   In Step 2, you noted which style this was.

Making Text Fit in Text Frames

When text doesn't fit in a text frame, red selection handles appear around the frame, and if the text frame holds a story, the Text In Overflow icon appears in the lower-right corner of the text frame, as shown in Figure 2-1. When you see this icon and the red selection handles, it means that you must make decisions about how to fit stray text into text frames. You can either fit the text into an existing frame, or, if you're dealing with a story, flow the text to other frames. These pages explain strategies for handling text that doesn't fit in text frames.

Buttons for managing text flow   Go to Previous Text button

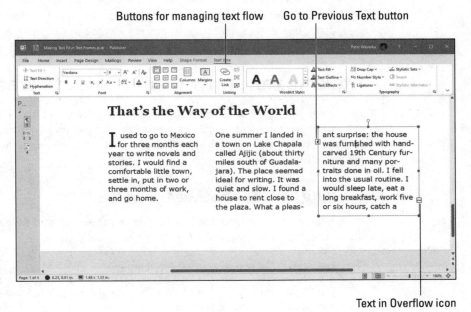

Text in Overflow icon

FIGURE 2-1:
"Flowing" text
from frame
to frame.

Fitting overflow text in a single frame

To fit a heading or paragraph into a single text frame, try one of these techniques:

>> **Shrink the text automatically:** On the Text Box tab, click the Text Fit button and choose Shrink Text On Overflow on the drop-down list. This command shrinks the point size of text so that all text fits in the frame. Sometimes, however, shrinking the text this way makes the heading or paragraph hard to read.

Refining a Publication

- » **Edit the text:** Snip out a word or sentence here and there to make the text fit. Have you ever wondered why magazine articles always fill the page and never end in the middle? That's because skillful editors and typesetters remove and add words here and there to make the story fit the page.

- » **Make the text frame larger:** Click the frame to display the selection handles; then, drag a handle.

- » **Make the text frame margins smaller:** Like a page, text frames have internal margins to keep text from getting too close to the frame border. To shrink these margins and make more room for text, go to the Text Box tab, click the Margins button, and choose Narrow on the drop-down list. You can also choose Custom Margins, and on the Text Box tab of the Format Text Box dialog box, enter smaller measurements for the text-box margins.

Making text flow from frame to frame

As shown in Figure 2-1, the Text In Overflow icon and red selection handles appear when story text overflows a text frame. How do you flow story text from frame to frame and handle a story that is spread across several frames? Better keep reading.

Flowing text to another frame

If necessary, create a new text box for the overflow text and follow these steps to direct text from one frame to another in your publication:

1. **Select the text frame with overflowing text.**

    You can tell when text is overflowing because the Text in Overflow icon appears in the lower-right corner of the frame (refer to Figure 2-1).

2. **On the Text Box tab, click the Create Link button.**

    The pointer turns into an overflowing pitcher (or is that a beer stein?) after you click the button.

3. **Move the pointer over the box that you want the text to flow into.**

    You may have to click a page navigation button to go to another page.

4. **Click in the target text box to make the text flow there.**

Handling text frames in a story

As I mention earlier, text frames that are linked are known as a story in Publisher–speak. Here are techniques for handling text frames that are linked in a story:

- » **Going from text frame to text frame:** On the Text Box tab, click the Next or Previous button to go from frame to frame. You can also select a text frame and click its Go to Next Text Box or Go to Previous Text Box icon.

- » **Selecting the text in all the text frames:** Press Ctrl+A; or go to the Home tab, click the Select button, and choose Select All Text in Text Box on the drop-down list.

- » **Breaking the link between frames:** Select the frame that you want to be the last one in the chain, and on the Text Box tab, click the Break button.

TIP

In a crowded publication, you can easily overlook a text frame with overflowing text. To find these text frames, go to the File tab, and on the Info page, click the Run Design Checker button. Then, in the Design Checker task pane, look for "Story with Text in Overflow Area."

Filling out a text frame

The opposite of an overflow problem is a text frame with too much blank space. Here are some techniques for handling semi–vacant text frames:

- » **Use the Best Fit option:** On the Text Box tab, click the Text Fit button and choose Best Fit on the drop-down list. This command enlarges the text so that it fills the frame. Sometimes, however, the command makes text too big.

- » **Edit the text:** Add a word or sentence here or there. In the case of headings, write a subheading as well.

- » **Insert a graphic, page part, or advertisement:** Placing a small graphic, page part, or advertisement on the page makes the page livelier and fills the dead space. Chapter 3 of this minibook explains techniques for decorating dead space on pages.

CONTINUATION SLUGS

A *continuation slug* is a notice that tells the reader where to turn to continue reading an article or where an article is continued from. Publisher offers a nifty command for entering continuation slugs at the bottom or top of text frames:

1. **Right-click the text frame that needs a slug and choose Format Text Box.**

2. **On the Text Box tab of the Format Text Box dialog box, select the Include "Continued on Page" or Include "Continued from Page" check box and click OK.**

Formatting Text

Use these techniques to format the text in a publication:

>> **Home tab font and paragraph commands:** The commands on the Home tab for changing the look of text and paragraphs are nearly identical to the Home tab commands in Word and PowerPoint. Book 1, Chapter 2 explains these commands.

>> **Styles:** Select text, and on the Home tab, click the Styles button and choose a style on the drop-down list to format text. Each template comes with many different styles. Beware, however, because you can get lost on the Style drop-down list. Be prepared to click the Undo button often as you experiment with styles.

Making Text Wrap around a Frame or Graphic

Wrap text around a frame, an image, a picture, or a WordArt image and you get a very elegant layout. Figure 2-2 shows text that has been wrapped around an image. Looks nice, doesn't it? Wrapping text may be the easiest way to impress innocent bystanders with your layout prowess. As Figure 2-2 shows, text wrapped tightly follows the contours of the picture, whereas text wrapped squarely runs flush with the picture's frame.

FIGURE 2-2:
Text wrapped tightly (left) and squarely (right).

TIP

Here are shorthand instructions for wrapping text:

1. **Select the item that text is to wrap around.**

In Figure 2-2, you would select the image.

2. **On the Format tab, click the Wrap Text button and choose a wrapping option on the drop-down list.**

For Figure 2-2, I chose Tight for the picture on the left and Square for the picture on the right.

The Wrap Text commands are identical in Word and Publisher. Book 2, Chapter 6 (about wrapping objects in Word) explains the wrapping commands in detail.

Replacing the Placeholder Pictures

As you must have noticed by now, publication designs are littered with generic pictures and graphics. Besides writing your own words where the placeholder ones are, replace the generic pictures with pictures of your own. Well, do it if you please. You are welcome to pass off the generic pictures as your own. I won't tell anybody.

Follow these steps to put a picture of your own where a placeholder picture is now:

1. **Click the placeholder picture to select it.**

TIP

You can also select a picture by clicking its name in the Graphics Manager. To use the Graphics Manager, go to the View tab and select the Graphics Manager check box. The Graphics Manager opens on the right side of the screen.

2. **On the Picture Format tab, click the Change Picture button and choose Change Picture on the drop-down list.**

The Insert Pictures screen appears.

3. **Choose From a File.**

You see the Insert Picture dialog box.

4. **Select a picture and click the Insert button.**

Book 8, Chapter 3 describes how to handle graphics in all the Office programs. You'll be delighted to discover that graphics are handled the same way, no matter which program you're toiling in.

TIP

You can postpone choosing a picture to replace a placeholder picture. Right-click the picture in question and choose Change Picture⇨ Remove Picture on the drop-down list. Publisher places a picture icon in the frame to remind you to insert a picture later on. You can click this picture icon to open the Insert Pictures screen.

Inserting Frames on the Pages

Publications are made of frames — text-box frames, table frames, and picture frames. Nothing appears on the pages of a publication unless it appears within the confines of a frame. These pages explain everything you need to know about frames. You can find out how to insert a new frame, adjust the size of a frame, align frames, and place borders around frames. You can also see how to make frames and the words or images inside them overlap.

Inserting a new frame

How you insert a new frame depends on what you want to insert: a text box, table, picture, or WordArt image. Start by clicking the page roughly where you want the frame to go. Then insert the new frame by using the techniques described here. (See "Making Text Wrap around a Frame or Graphic," earlier in this chapter, for information about wrapping text around a frame. See "Changing the size and position of frames," later in this chapter, to find out how to change a frame's shape.)

To delete a frame, all you have to do is select it and press the Delete key or right-click and choose Delete Object. You can tell when a frame is selected because selection handles appear on the corners and sides. Deleting a frame also deletes the text or objects inside it.

Inserting a text-box frame

To insert a text-box frame, go to the Insert or Home tab and click the Draw Text Box button. Then click the page and drag to create the text box. Book 8, Chapter 4 explains how to change the background color and border of a text box.

Inserting a table

To insert a table, go to the Insert or Home tab and use one of these techniques:

>> Click the Table button and move the pointer in the drop-down list to the number of columns and rows you want, click, and let go of the mouse button.

>> Click the Table button and choose Insert Table on the drop-down list. The Create Table dialog box appears. Enter the number of rows and columns you want and click OK.

Inserting a picture

Follow these steps to insert a picture:

1. **On the Insert tab, click the Picture Placeholder button.**

A picture placeholder frame appears.

2. **As best you can, make the frame the size you want your picture to be.**

The next section in this chapter, "Changing the size and position of frames," describes how to do this.

3. **Click the picture icon in the placeholder frame.**

The Insert Pictures screen appears.

4. **Click From a File.**

You see the Insert Pictures dialog box.

5. **Select a picture and click the Insert button.**

Book 8, Chapter 3 explains all there is to know about the Insert Picture dialog box.

6. **On the Picture Format tab, click the Fit button to make a picture that is too large for the frame fit inside the frame, or click the Fill button to make a picture that is too small for the frame fill the frame.**

Changing the size and position of frames

After you click a frame and see the selection handles, you're ready to change the size of the frame or adjust its position on the page. Use these standard techniques for resizing and moving frames:

» **Changing the size of a frame:** Move the pointer over a selection handle and start dragging. If you're dealing with anything but a text frame, be careful about dragging a selection handle on the side of the frame. Dragging a side handle changes the frame's size as well as its proportions. Images can blur or become distorted when you change their proportions. To change the size of a frame but keep its proportions, hold down the Shift key while dragging a corner handle.

» **Changing the position of a frame:** Move the pointer onto the frame (or the perimeter of a frame, if you're dealing with a text box), and click and drag when you see the four-headed arrow. To move more than one frame simultaneously, Ctrl+click the frames you want to move.

As explained in Chapter 1 of this minibook, frames snap to the grid as you move them, but you can hold down the Alt key as you drag to adjust frames with precision. You can also press an arrow key to move them ever so slightly.

Making Frames Overlap

When frames overlap, you have to tell Publisher which frame goes in front of the other. And you are hereby invited to overlap frames because overlapping frames are artful and look good on the page. Figure 2-3 shows a portion of a newsletter. If you look closely, you can see where frames overlap in the figure. Overlapping frames like these make for a sophisticated layout.

FIGURE 2-3:
Examples of overlapping frames.

Making frames overlap like the ones in Figure 2-3 requires a delicate balancing act using these commands:

>> **Text wrapping:** On the Format tab, click the Wrap Text button and choose None on the drop-down list.

>> **Fill Color:** For frames and objects on the bottom of the stack to show through, the frames and objects above them cannot have a fill color that would obscure other objects. To remove the fill color, select the object, and on the Format tab, open the drop-down list on the Shape Fill button and choose No Fill.

>> **Object and frame order:** To tell Publisher which object goes where in the stack, go to the Format tab and click the Bring Forward or Send Backward button as necessary. Book 8, Chapter 4 explains all the techniques for handling overlapping objects.

Inserting, Removing, and Moving Pages

Suppose that you have too many pages or you need to add a page or two. On the Pages pane (select the Page Navigation check box on the View tab), click a thumbnail to select the page where you want to insert, remove, or move pages. Then follow these instructions:

» **Inserting a new page:** On the Insert tab, click the Page button and choose an option on the drop-down list:

   ● **Insert Blank Page:** Inserts an empty page.

   ● **Insert Duplicate Page:** Inserts a page identical to the thumbnail page you selected.

   ● **Insert Page:** Opens the Insert Pages dialog box, shown in Figure 2-4, where you can enter the number of pages you want to insert and click the More button to put the new pages before or after the page you selected. You can also tell Publisher what to put on the new page or pages.

» **Removing a page:** On the Page Design tab, click the Delete button. You can also right-click a page thumbnail and choose Delete.

» **Moving a page:** On the Page Design tab, click the Move button. Give instructions for moving the page in the Move Page dialog box and click OK.

FIGURE 2-4:
Inserting a
new page.

Refining a Publication

Chapter **3**

Putting on the Finishing Touches

This final chapter in Book 7 is devoted to the Project to Beautify Publications, a joint effort of the publisher and the author to try to make publications less bland and more original. The author has noticed, on the bulletin boards and lampposts in his neighborhood, that the rummage sale and lost-pet notices look a little rough around the edges. The neighbors are using sophisticated software to produce their notices, but they're not using it well. They are relying solely on templates, which make the publications look alike. These pages explain a few simple tricks for making publications more sophisticated.

This chapter explores drop caps and horizontal rules, page backgrounds and borders, borders and backgrounds for frames, and how to place a logo in the same place on each page in a publication. It shows you Publisher's excellent Design Checker. Finally, this chapter offers advice for printing publications at a commercial print shop.

Decorating the Text

Here are a couple of tricks to amaze your friends and intimidate your enemies. These pages explain how horizontal rules and drop caps can make a publication a little livelier. Don't worry — horizontal rules have nothing to do with which side of the bed to sleep on, and drop caps don't explode when you unroll them on the sidewalk and strike them with a hammer.

Drawing a horizontal rule on a frame

A *horizontal rule* is a horizontal line that divides one part of a page from another and directs the reader's eye on the page. There are two horizontal rules in Figure 3-1. By varying the width of the lines and placing lines in strategic places, you can make a publication look more elegant and graceful.

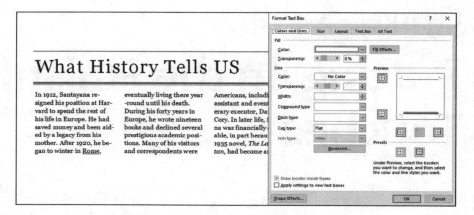

FIGURE 3-1:
Examples of
horizontal rules.

TIP

Usually where horizontal rules come in pairs, the bottommost rule is thicker than its twin. The thicker bottom line encourages the reader's eye to move down the page and find an article to read.

Select the frame and follow these steps to draw a horizontal rule on a frame:

1. **On the Format tab, click the Text or Size group button.**

   You can also select the frame, right-click it, and choose Format (the Format command has different names depending on what type of frame or object you're working with). You see the Format dialog box (refer to Figure 3-1).

2. **Visit the Color and Lines tab.**

3. **In the Preview box, click the top of the box to draw a rule above the frame or the bottom of the box to draw a rule below.**

   By clicking part of the Preview box, you tell Publisher where you want to draw the rule.

4. **On the Width menu, enter how wide you want the line to be in points.**

   Watch the Preview box to see how wide the line is.

5. **On the Compound Type menu, choose the kind of line you want.**

If you want a dashed line, select it from the Dashed drop-down list. You can adjust the thickness of the line in the Weight text box.

6. **To draw a second rule on the frame, click again in the Preview box and repeat Steps 4 and 5.**

7. **Click OK.**

To remove a horizontal rule from a frame, select the frame, open the Format dialog box, open the Color drop-down list, and choose No Line.

Dropping in a drop cap

A *drop cap* is a large capital letter that "drops" into the text. Drop caps are usually found in the first paragraph of an article or chapter. Pound for pound, considering how little effort is required, a drop cap yields the most reward for the least amount of work. Follow these steps to place a drop cap in a publication:

1. **Click the paragraph that is to receive the drop cap.**

2. **On the Text Box tab, click the Drop Cap button and choose a drop cap on the drop-down list or choose Custom Drop cap to open the Drop Cap dialog box.**

Figure 3-2 shows the Drop Cap dialog box. From here, you can choose how far to drop the capital letter or select a font and color for the letter.

To remove a drop cap, click the Drop Cap button and choose No Drop Cap (the first option on the drop-down list).

FIGURE 3-2:
Fashioning a drop cap.

Techniques for Decorating Pages

No one likes a dull publication. Following are some simple techniques to make pages a little bit livelier. Read on to find out how to take advantage of page parts, borders, accents, and advertisements. You will also find instructions for painting an entire page with a background color or gray shade.

Plugging in a page part

"Page part" is Publisher's word for a page element that you can quickly plug into a page. Use a page part to fill in empty space on a page or get a head start in formatting part of a page. As shown in Figure 3-3, page parts include the following:

>> **Headings:** A ready-made title for a page or story. Headings often include a subheading.

>> **Pull quotes:** A preformatted text-box frame for displaying a quotation from a story.

>> **Sidebars:** A preformatted text-box frame for a companion story. Sidebars usually appear on a side of the page in a smaller font.

>> **Stories:** A preformatted story, including a heading and a subheading.

Follow these steps to put a page part on a page:

1. **On the Insert tab, click the Page Parts button.**

2. **Choose a heading, pull quote, sidebar, or story on the drop-down list.**

   Choose More Page Parts to open the Building Block Library and choose from many more page parts.

After the element lands on the page, you can change its size or shift its position by using the same techniques you use with other objects. (Book 8, Chapter 4 explains how to manipulate objects.)

Experimenting with borders and accents

Publisher offers what it calls "borders and accents" to make pages a little livelier. Borders and accents are page decorations that also serve a purpose:

>> **Bars:** Decorative patterns for filling empty page space.

>> **Emphasis:** Two-sided text-box frames to make text boxes stand out on the page.

>> **Frames:** Four-sided text-box frames to make text boxes stand out.

Heading   Sidebar

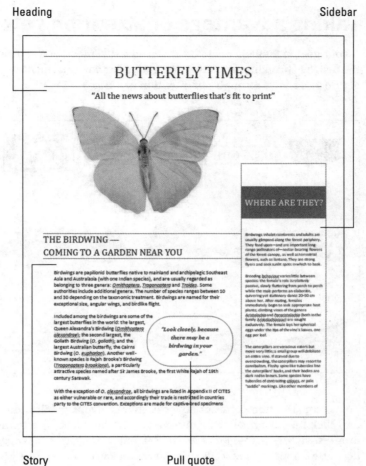

FIGURE 3-3:
Examples of
page parts.

Story   Pull quote

>> **Lines:** Unusual lines.

>> **Patterns:** Checkerboard and other patterns for filling empty page space.

Follow these steps to place a border or accent on a publication page:

1. **On the Insert tab, click the Borders & Accents button.**

2. **Choose a border or accent on the drop-down list.**

Choose More Borders and Accents and make a selection in the Building Block
Library if you want to place a line or pattern on a page.

The border or accent lands on the page. (Book 8, Chapter 4 explains how to manipulate objects such as borders and accents.)

Taking advantage of attention getters

If your goal in Publisher is to create an advertisement, you can get a head start on the task by sprinkling an "attention getter" or advertisement in your publication. Figure 3-4 shows examples of attention getters.

FIGURE 3-4: Examples of "attention getters."

To use an attention getter or advertisement in your publication, go to the Insert tab, click the Advertisements button, and choose an ad or attention getter on the drop-down list. Choose More Advertisements on the drop-down list to open a dialog box with many, many advertisements and attention getters. (Book 8, Chapter 4 explains how to change the size and position of objects such as advertisements and attention getters.)

Backgrounds for pages

Yet another nifty trick is to put a color, gray-shade, or other type of background on the page. Be sure to choose a background that doesn't get in the way of your publication or render it impossible to read. Shrink the publication to 40 percent so that you can see what backgrounds really look like; then follow these steps to give a page or all the pages in your publication a background:

1. **On the Page Design tab, click the Background button.**

    A drop-down list opens.

2. **Move the pointer over the options on the drop-down list to "live-preview" the choices.**

You can choose More Backgrounds on the drop-down list to open the Format Background dialog box and choose or create a page background there. The dialog box gives you the opportunity to use a gradient, texture, pattern, or picture for a page background.

3. **Apply your choice to a single page or all pages in your publication.**

You have the option of changing the page background on one page or all the pages:

- **One page:** On the Background button drop-down list, right-click your choice and choose Apply to Current Page.

- **All pages:** On the Background button drop-down list, right-click your choice and choose Apply to All Pages.

To remove the background from a page, click the Background button and choose No Background on the drop–down list.

TIP

To apply a page background from the Format Background dialog box to all the pages in a publication, switch to Master Page view, go to the Page Design tab, click the Background button, and create or choose a page background in the Format Background dialog box. Because it is on the master page, your page background choice applies to all pages. Master pages is the next topic in this chapter.

Master Pages for Handling Page Backgrounds

In a publication with many pages, the same object sometimes goes on every page. A company logo on the corner of each page looks mighty elegant. Page numbers and copyright information are also found on all the pages of some publications. The good news is that you don't have to place the objects on each page individually. Instead, you can place the objects on the *master page.* Whatever is on the master page appears on all pages in a publication (unless you decide that the master page shouldn't apply to a particular page). Forthwith are instructions for handling master pages.

Switching to Master Page view

To change the appearance of the master page, place an object on the master page, or see precisely what is on the master page, start by switching to Master Page view:

- ❯❯ On the View tab, click the Master Page button.

- ❯❯ On the Page Design tab, click the Master Pages button and choose Edit Master Pages on the drop-down list.

You can tell when you're looking at a master page because you see the Master Page tab on the Ribbon, and the page thumbnails in the Pages pane show letters instead of numbers.

To leave Master Page view, go to the Master Page tab and click the Close Master Page button.

Changing the look of a master page

All commands for changing the look of run-of-the-mill pages also apply to master pages. Place objects and frames on the master page as if you were putting them on run-of-the-mill pages. Change the page background as if you were changing the background of a normal page.

To edit a master page, switch to Master Page (see the earlier section "Switching to Master Page view"), select the master page you want to work with in the Pages pane (if you've created more than one master page), and get to work.

Applying (or unapplying) a master page to publication pages

By default, the master page applies to all pages, but sometimes unapplying a master page is necessary because objects on the master page get in the way. And if you created more than one master page, you have to tell Publisher which master page to apply to which publication page.

Follow these instructions to unapply or apply master pages to pages in a publication:

>> **Unapplying a master page:** In Normal view, go to the Page Design tab, display the page you want to unattach from the master page, click the Master Pages button, and choose None on the drop-down list.

>> **Applying a different master page:** Use one of these techniques to apply a different master page to pages in your publication:

- In Normal view, display a page, go to the Page Design tab, click the Master Pages button, and choose a different master page on the drop-down list.

- In Master Page view, go to the Master Page tab, select a master page in the Pages pane, and click the Apply To button. On the Apply To drop-down list, choose Apply to All Pages to apply a different master page to all the pages in your publication. Choose Apply Master Page on the drop-down list and enter page-range numbers in the Apply Master Page dialog box to apply the master page to a select group of pages.

Running the Design Checker

When at last your publication is ready for printing, be sure to run the Design Checker. This helpful tool can alert you to frames that fall on nonprinting parts of the page, stories that "overflow" without finding a text frame to go to, invisible objects, and a host of other problems.

On the File tab, choose Info, and click the Run Design Checker button to run the Design Checker. As shown in Figure 3-5, the Design Checker task pane opens and lists items that need your attention. Open an item's drop-down list and choose Go to This Item to locate it in your publication. Sometimes the drop-down list offers a quick fix as well.

FIGURE 3-5:
Running the
Design Checker.

TIP

To see which design flaws the Design Checker looks for, click the Design Checker Options hyperlink in the Design Checker task pane. Then, in the Design Checker Options dialog box, select the Checks tab and read the list.

Commercially Printing a Publication

You know the routine for printing a publication on your computer: Go to the File tab, choose Print, negotiate the Print window, and click the Print button. To print a publication with a commercial printer, Publisher offers the Save for a Commercial Printer command. This command creates a PDF file for use by print shops. PDF is now the standard file format for print shops.

Follow these steps to save your publication as a PDF that you can hand off to a printer:

1. **On the File tab, choose Export.**

   The Export window opens.

2. **Choose Save for a Commercial Printer.**

3. **On the first drop-down list, choose Commercial Press.**

4. **On the second drop-down list, choose Both PDF and Publisher .pub Files.**

5. **Click the Pack and Go Wizard button.**

   The Pack and Go Wizard dialog box opens.

6. **Choose a location for your publication file or choose to burn it to a CD.**

7. **Click Next and follow the instructions for creating the PDF and** .pub **file.**

8

Working with Charts and Graphics

Contents at a Glance

Chapter **1**

Creating a Chart

Nothing is more persuasive than a chart. The bars, pie slices, lines, or columns show immediately whether production is up or down, cats are better than dogs or dogs better than cats, or catsup tastes better than ketchup. Fans of charts and graphs will be glad to know that putting a chart in a Word document, Excel worksheet, or PowerPoint slide is fairly easy.

This chapter explains how to create a chart. It looks at which charts are best for presenting different kinds of data, how to change a chart's appearance, and how to save charts in a template that you can use again. You discover some nice chart tricks, including how to make a picture the backdrop for a chart and how to annotate a chart. This chapter also addresses common chart problems.

The Basics: Creating a Chart

Throughout this chapter, I explain the whys, wherefores, and whatnots of creating a chart. Before going into details, here are the basic steps that everyone needs to know to create a chart in Word, Excel, and PowerPoint:

1. **Go to the Insert tab.**

2. **If you're working in Excel, select the data you'll use to generate the chart (in Word and PowerPoint, skip to Step 3).**

In Excel, you select the data on a worksheet before creating the chart, but in Word and PowerPoint, you enter the data for the chart after you create the chart.

3. **Select the kind of chart you want.**

   How you select a chart type depends on which program you're working in:

   - **Excel:** On the Insert tab, open the drop-down list on one of the buttons in the Charts group (Column, Bar, and so on) and select a chart type; or click the Recommended Charts button or Charts group button to open the Insert Chart dialog box and select a chart there. As shown in Figure 1-1, the Insert Chart dialog box shows all the kinds of charts you can create. Go to the Recommended Charts tab to see which charts Excel recommends.

   - **Word and PowerPoint:** Click the Chart button. You see the Insert Chart dialog box, shown in Figure 1-1. Select a chart type, select a variation, and click OK. A data grid opens on your screen. (In PowerPoint, you can also click the Chart icon on a placeholder frame to open the Insert Chart dialog box.)

   The next topic in this chapter, "Choosing the Right Chart," describes all the chart types and advises you which to choose.

4. **In Word and PowerPoint, replace the sample data in the data grid with the data you need for generating your chart.**

   Later in this chapter, "Providing the Raw Data for Your Chart" explains how to enter data in the data grid, and the sidebar "Getting chart data from a table (Word and PowerPoint)" explains how to copy the data from a table.

   After you finish entering the data, click the Close button in the data grid.

5. **Modify your chart, if you desire.**

   The Chart Design and Format tabs and the buttons to the right of the chart offer commands for making a chart look just-so (see "Changing a Chart's Appearance," later in this chapter).

TIP

Click the Recent button in the Insert Chart dialog box to see all the charts you examined in your search for the right chart.

And if you decide to delete the chart you created? Click its perimeter to select it and then press the Delete key.

Choose a chart type   Choose a variant

FIGURE 1-1:
Which chart
do you want?

Choosing the Right Chart

If you're a fan of charts, the huge selection of charts can make you feel like a kid in a candy store, but if charts aren't your *forté,* the wealth of charts you can choose from can be daunting. You can choose among charts in 17 categories (refer to Figure 1-1). Which chart is best? The golden rule for choosing a chart type is to choose the one that presents information in the brightest possible light. The purpose of a chart is to compare information across different categories. Select a chart that draws out the comparison so that others can clearly make comparisons. Table 1-1 describes the 17 chart types and explains in brief when to use each type of chart.

TABLE 1-1   ## Chart Types

Chart Type	Best Use/Description
Area	Examine how values in different categories fluctuate over time, and see the cumulative change in values. (Same as a line chart except that the area between trend lines is colored in.)
Bar	Compare values in different categories against one another, usually over time. Data is displayed in horizontal bars. (Same as a column chart except that the bars are horizontal.)
Box & Whisker	Examine how data is distributed (the whiskers define the range of data and the boxes define the median).
Column	Compare values in different categories against one another, usually over time. Data is displayed in vertical columns. (Same as a bar chart except that the bars are vertical.)
Combo	Contrast two sets of data, with one chart overlying the other to draw out the contrast. Data is displayed in lines, bars, and stacks.
Funnel	Compare data items as the proportion of a whole. Data is displayed in bars of progressively decreasing size. This chart is used to show data loss at each stage of a process
Histogram	Measure the frequency of data. Data is displayed in bars, with the width of each bar representing a data range and the height of each bar representing the frequency of data within the range.
Line	Examine how values fluctuate over time. Data is displayed in a set of points connected by a line.
Map	Compare data across geographical regions. One data axis must contain countries, regions, or postal codes that Office recognizes as geographical regions.
Pie	See how values compare as percentages of a whole. Data from categories is displayed as a percentage of a whole.
Radar	Examine data as it relates to one central point. Data is plotted on radial points from the central point. This kind of chart is used to make subjective performance analyses.
Stock	See how the value of an item fluctuates as well as its daily, weekly, or yearly high, low, and closing price. This chart is used to track stock prices, but it can also be used to track air temperature and other variable quantities.
Surface	Examine color-coded data on a 3-D surface to explore relationships between data values.
Sunburst	Compare values at different levels of a hierarchy. This chart is a stacked, or multilevel, pie chart.
Treemap	Evaluate data in nested rectangles that show the relative size of data and the relationship between data items.
Waterfall	See how positive and negative values contribute to a cumulative value.
XY (Scatter)	Compare different numeric data point sets in space to reveal patterns and trends in data. (Similar to a bubble chart except that the data appears as points instead of bubbles.)

Providing the Raw Data for Your Chart

Every chart is constructed from *raw data* — the numbers and labels you select in an Excel worksheet (in Excel) or enter in the data grid (in Word and PowerPoint). If you're operating in Word or PowerPoint, you see, in the data grid, sample data in a *data range,* as shown in Figure 1-2. The information inside the data range is used to generate the chart. You can tell where the data range begins and ends because it is enclosed in a blue border. Your job is to replace the sample data in the data range with data of your own. As you enter your data, the chart on your slide or page takes shape.

FIGURE 1-2:
To create a chart in Word or PowerPoint, enter data in the data grid.

GETTING CHART DATA FROM A TABLE (WORD AND POWERPOINT)

Rather than painstakingly enter data in the data grid, you can get the data you need for a chart from a Word or PowerPoint table. In fact, entering the data in a Word or PowerPoint table and copying it to the data grid is easier than entering data in the narrow confines of the data grid.

Follow these steps to generate a chart from data in a table you created in Word or PowerPoint:

1. **Click the table to select it.**

2. **On the (Table) Layout tab, click the Select button and choose Select Table on the drop-down list.**

3. **Press Ctrl+C to copy the table data to the Clipboard.**

4. **Click your chart to select it.**

5. **On the Chart Design tab, click the Edit Data button to open the data grid.**

6. **Click the Select All button in the data grid (or press Ctrl+A). Clicking the Select All button selects all cells in the grid. The button is located above 1 in the first row and to the left of the A in the first column.**

7. **Press Delete to erase the data in the grid.**

8. **Press Ctrl+V to copy the data from the table into the data grid.**

If the table you copied into the data grid is larger than the sample data that was there before, you're done. You can breathe easy. But if the table is smaller than the sample data, you have to make the data range smaller so that it encompasses only the data you copied from your table. Move the pointer to the lower-right corner of the data range and then drag in a northwesterly direction until the blue box encloses the data from your Word or PowerPoint table.

As you enter numbers and labels in the data grid, watch your chart take shape. Here are the basics of entering data in the data grid:

>> **Entering the data in a cell:** A cell is the box in a data grid where a column and row intersect; each cell can contain one data item. To enter data in a cell, click the cell and start typing. When you're finished, press Enter, press Tab, or click a different cell.

>> **Deleting the data in a cell:** To delete the data in a cell, including the sample data, click the cell and press Delete.

REMEMBER

>> **Displaying the numbers:** When a number is too large to fit in a cell, the number is displayed in scientific notation (you can double-click the number to enlarge the cell in which it is located). Don't worry — the number is still recorded and is used to generate your chart. You can display large numbers by widening the columns in which the numbers are found. Move the pointer between column letters (A, B, and so on at the top of the worksheet) and when you see the double-headed arrow, click and drag to the right.

>> **Changing the size of the data range:** To enclose more or fewer cells in the data range, move the pointer to the lower-right corner of the data range, and when the pointer changes into a two-headed arrow, click and drag so that the blue box encloses only the data you want for your chart (refer to Figure 1-2).

TIP

The data grid offers the Edit Data in Microsoft Excel button in case you want to enter data for your chart in Excel. Click this button and enter data in Excel if you're comfortable working there.

In Word and PowerPoint, click the Edit Data button on the Chart Design tab at any time to open the data grid and fiddle with the numbers and data from which your chart is generated.

Positioning Your Chart in a Workbook, Page, or Slide

To change the position of a chart, click to select it, click its perimeter, and when you see the four-headed arrow, start dragging. Otherwise, follow these instructions to land your chart where you want it to be:

>> **Excel:** To move your chart to a different worksheet or create a new worksheet to hold your chart, go to the Chart Design tab and click the Move Chart button. You see the Move Chart dialog box.

- To move your chart to a different worksheet, click the Object In option button, choose the worksheet in the drop-down list, and click OK.

- To create a new worksheet for a chart, click the New Sheet option button, enter a name for the new worksheet, and click OK.

>> **Word:** Starting in Print Layout view, select your chart, and in the Layout or Format tab, click the Position button (you may have to click the Arrange

button first, depending on the size of your screen). You see a drop-down list with text-wrapping options. Choose the option that describes how you want surrounding text to behave when it crashes into your chart. Book 2, Chapter 6 looks in detail at wrapping text around charts and other objects in Word.

TIP

You can also position a chart by selecting it, clicking the Layout Options button, and choosing an option on the Layout Options drop-down menu. The Layout Options button appears to the right of a chart after you select a chart.

>> **PowerPoint:** Select the chart and drag it on the slide to the right position.

Changing a Chart's Appearance

Charts are awfully nice already, but perhaps you want to redesign one. Perhaps you're an interior decorator type and you want to give charts your own personal touch. Office presents many different ways to refine a chart. As shown in Figure 1-3, you can click one of the three buttons — Chart Elements, Chart Styles, or Chart Filters — that appear beside a chart when you select it. You can also go to Chart Design tab and the Format tab. Your opportunities for tinkering with a chart are many.

These pages explain how to change a chart's appearance and layout, starting with the biggest change you can make — exchanging one type of chart for another.

Changing the chart type

The biggest way to overhaul a chart is to ditch it in favor of a different chart type. Luckily for you, Office makes this task simple. I wish that changing jobs was this easy. Follow these steps to change a pumpkin into a carriage or an existing chart into a different kind of chart:

1. Click your chart to select it.

2. On the ChartDesign tab, click the Change Chart Type button, or right-click your chart and choose Change Chart Type on the shortcut menu.

The Change Chart Type dialog box appears. Does it look familiar? This is the same dialog box you used to create your chart in the first place.

3. Select a new chart type and click OK.

Not all chart types can be converted successfully to other chart types. You may well have created a monster, in which case go back to Step 1 and start all over or click the Undo button.

FIGURE 1-3:
Click a button to the right of a chart or go to the ChartDesign or Format tab to change the look of a chart.

Changing the size and shape of a chart

To make a chart taller or wider, follow these instructions:

» Click the perimeter of the chart to select it and then drag a handle on the side to make it wider, or a handle on the top or bottom to make it taller. You can hold down the Shift key and drag a corner handle to change a chart's size but keep its proportions.

» Go to the Format tab and enter measurements in the Height and Width boxes. You can find these boxes in the Size group (you may have to click the Size button to see them, depending on the size of your screen).

Choosing a new look for your chart

Select your chart and experiment with these different ways to change its look:

» **Select a chart style:** On the ChartDesign tab, choose an option in the Chart Styles gallery. Or click the Chart Styles button and select a style on the drop-down menu (refer to Figure 1-3).These gallery options are quite sophisticated. You would have a hard time fashioning these charts on your own.

» **Change the color scheme:** On the ChartDesign tab, click the Change Colors button and select a color on the drop-down list. Or click the Chart Styles button and select a color on the drop-down menu (refer to Figure 1-3).

Later in this chapter, "Changing a chart element's color, font, or other particular" explains how to dig down deep and change one particular aspect of a chart — its legend, plot area, or vertical axis, for example.

WARNING

If your file includes more than one chart, make the charts consistent with one another. Give them a similar appearance so that your file doesn't turn into a chart fashion show. You can make charts consistent with one another by choosing similar options for charts in the Chart Styles gallery.

Changing the layout of a chart

Charts are composed of different elements — the legend, the labels, and the titles. Figure 1-4 identifies chart elements. Where these elements appear is up to you. Whether to include them is up to you as well. You can, for example, place the legend on the right side of your chart or go without a legend. By choosing which elements to include and where to put elements, you fashion a layout for your chart.

Select your chart and experiment with these techniques to decide on a layout:

» On the ChartDesign tab, click the Quick Layout button and select an option in the gallery.

» On the ChartDesign tab, click the Add Chart Element button. Then choose an element on the drop-down list, and on the submenu, choose whether to place the element (the None option) or where to place it.

» Click the Chart Elements button and choose an element on the drop-down menu. Then either deselect an element to remove it or select an element and choose where to place it on the submenu. Figure 1-5, for example, shows how to choose where to place the legend.

Vertical axis title   Title   Legend

FIGURE 1-4:
The layout
elements
of a chart.

Vertical axis labels   Horizontal axis labels

Horizontal axis title   Data labels

FIGURE 1-5:
Clicking the Chart
Elements button
is one way to
handle chart
layouts.

TIP

Hover the pointer over the options on the Chart Elements menus and glance at
your chart. You can see right away what each option does to your chart.

TIP

To remove series or category names from a chart, click the Chart Filters button and, on the drop-down menu, deselect a column or row option button (see
Figure 1-3).

Handling the gridlines

Gridlines are lines that cross a chart and indicate value measurements. Most charts include major gridlines to show where bars or columns meet or surpass a major unit of measurement, and you can also include fainter, minor gridlines that mark less significant measurements.

Use these techniques to handle gridlines:

>> On the ChartDesign tab, click the Add Chart Element button, choose Gridlines on the drop-down list, and select or deselect an option on the submenu.

>> Click the Chart Elements button, choose Gridlines, and select or deselect a check box on the submenu, as shown in Figure 1-6.

FIGURE 1-6:
Choosing a
Gridlines option
by way of the
Chart Elements
button.

Deselecting all the gridline options removes the gridlines from a chart. Choose More Options on the submenu to open the Format Major Gridlines task pane, where you can change the color of gridlines, make gridlines semitransparent, and make gridlines wider or narrower.

WARNING

Gridlines are essential for helping read charts, but be very, very careful about displaying minor gridlines on charts. These lines can make your chart unreadable. They can turn a perfectly good chart into a gaudy pinstripe suit.

Changing a chart element's color, font, or other particular

The Format tab is the place to go to change the color, line width, font, or font size of a chart element. Go to the Format tab, for example, to change the color of the bars in a bar chart, the color of text, or the chart background color.

Follow these basic steps to change a color, line width, font, or font size in part of a chart:

1. **Go to the Format tab.**

2. **In the Chart Elements drop-down list, select the chart element that needs a facelift.**

   You can find this list in the upper-left corner of the screen, as shown in Figure 1-7.

3. **Click the Format Selection button.**

   The Format task pane opens (see Figure 1-7).

4. **Format the chart element you selected.**

   In the Format task pane, you can find all the tools you need to change the color, outline, and size of a chart element. These tools are explained in detail in Chapter 4 of this minibook.

Select the chart element

Choose Format Selection

Format the element

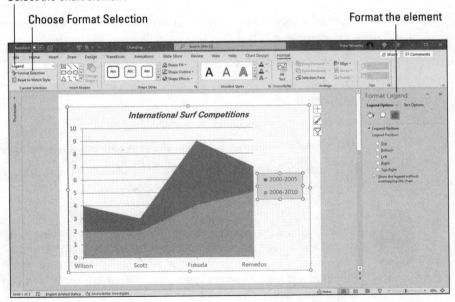

FIGURE 1-7: Choose what you want to format on the Chart Elements drop-down list.

TIP

If your experiments with retouching a chart go awry and you want to start over, click the Reset to Match Style button on the Format tab.

Saving a Chart as a Template So That You Can Use It Again

If you go to the significant trouble of redecorating a chart and you expect to do it again the same way in the future, save your chart as a template. This way, you can call on the template in the future to create the same chart and not have to decorate it again. Perhaps you've created charts with your company's colors or you've created a chart that you're especially proud of. Save it as a template to spare yourself the work of reconstructing it.

A chart template holds data series colors, gridline settings, plot area colors, font settings, and the like. It doesn't hold data. These pages explain how to save a chart as a template and how to create a chart with a template you created.

Saving a chart as a template

Follow these steps to make a template out of a chart:

1. **Save your file to make sure the chart settings are saved on your computer.**

2. **Select your chart.**

3. **Right-click your chart and choose Save As Template on the shortcut menu.**

   You see the Save Chart Template dialog box.

4. **Enter a descriptive name for the template and click the Save button.**

   Include the type of chart you're dealing with in the name. This will help you understand which template you're selecting when the time comes to choose a chart template.

TECHNICAL STUFF

By default, chart templates are saved in this folder: `C:\Users\Username\AppData\Roaming\Microsoft\Templates\Charts`. The templates have the `.ctrx` extension. If you want to delete or rename a template, open the Charts folder in File Explorer and do your deleting and renaming there. You can open the Charts folder very quickly by clicking the Manage Templates button in the Insert Chart dialog box (this button appears after you choose the Templates category).

Creating a chart from a template

To create a chart from your own customized template, open the Create Chart dialog box (click the Chart button on the Insert tab) and go to the Templates category. The dialog box shows a list of templates you created. Move the pointer over a template to read its name in a pop-up box. Select a template and click OK.

Chart Tricks for the Daring and Heroic

This chapter wouldn't be complete without a handful of chart tricks to impress your friends and intimidate your enemies. In the pages that follow, you discover how to make charts roll over and play dead. You also find out how to decorate a chart with a picture, annotate a chart, and place a trendline on a chart.

Decorating a chart with a picture

As shown in Figure 1-8, a picture looks mighty nice on the plot area of a chart — especially a column chart. If you have a picture in your computer that would serve well to decorate a chart, you are hereby encouraged to start decorating. Follow these steps to place a picture in the plot area of a chart:

1. **Select your chart.**

2. **On the Format tab, open the Chart Elements drop-down list and choose Plot Area.**

3. **Click the Format Selection button.**

   The Format Plot Area task pane opens.

4. **If necessary, click Fill & Line to display the Fill and Border options, and under Fill, click the Picture or Texture Fill option button.**

5. **Click the Insert button.**

   You see the Insert Pictures dialog box.

6. **Select and insert a picture from a file on your computer, a stock image, or an online picture**

TIP

   Try to select a light-colored picture that will serve as a background. Chapter 3 of this minibook explains how you can recolor a picture to make it lighter.

   You may need to change the color of the *data markers* — the columns, bars, lines, or pie slices — on your chart to make them stand out against the picture. See "Changing a chart element's color, font, or other particular," earlier in this chapter.

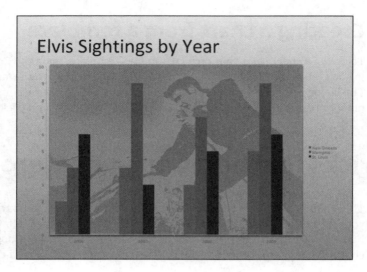

FIGURE 1-8:
Using a picture
as the backdrop
of a chart.

Annotating a chart

To highlight part of a chart — an especially large pie slice, a tall column, or a bar showing miniscule sales figures — annotate it with a callout text box and place the text box beside the pie slice, column, or bar. Figure 1-9 shows an example of an annotated chart. The annotation tells you that one sector isn't performing especially well and somebody ought to get on the ball.

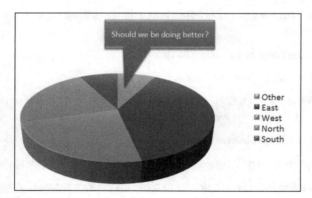

FIGURE 1-9:
Annotations point
out a chart's
salient features.

To annotate a chart, select a callout shape, enter text in the callout shape, and connect the shape to part of your chart. Follow these steps to annotate a chart:

1. **Select your chart and go to the Format tab.**

2. **Open the Shapes gallery, scroll to the Callouts section of the drop-down list, and choose a callout.**

   Depending on the size of your screen, you may have to click the Insert button to get to the Shapes button.

3. **Drag on the page or slide to draw the callout shape.**

   Chapter 4 of this minibook explains drawing shapes in gory detail.

4. **Type the annotation inside the callout shape.**

   After you type the text, you can select it, go to the Home tab, and choose a font and font size for it.

5. **Resize the callout shape as necessary to make it fit with the chart.**

6. **Drag the orange circle on the callout shape to attach the callout to the chart.**

   You probably have to do some interior decorating to make the callout color fit with the chart. Chapter 4 of this minibook explains how to change an object's color.

Placing a trendline on a chart

Especially on column charts, a *trendline* can help viewers more clearly see changes in data. Viewers can see, for example, that sales are going up or down, income is rising or falling, or annual rainfall is increasing or decreasing. Figure 1-10 shows an example of a trendline on a chart. In this case, the trendline shows that the deer population in Sacramento County is rising.

Follow these steps to put a trendline on a chart:

1. **On the ChartDesign tab, click the Add Chart Element button.**

2. **Choose Trendline on the drop-down list and select a trendline option on the submenu.**

   The Add Trendline dialog box appears.

3. **Choose the data series that you want to highlight with a trendline and click OK.**

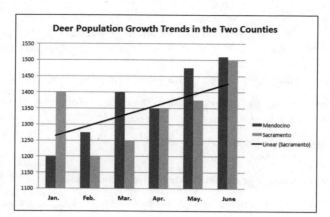

FIGURE 1-10:
A trendline helps viewers recognize changes in data.

To remove a trendline from a chart, go to the ChartDesign tab, click the Add Chart Element button, choose Trendline on the drop-down list, and choose None on the submenu.

Troubleshooting a Chart

Sometimes tinkering with a chart opens a Pandora's Box of problems. You find yourself having to correct little errors that appear in charts. Here are some short-hand instructions for fixing common chart problems:

» **The dates in the chart aren't formatted right.** To change the way in which dates are formatted on a chart, go to the Format tab, open the Chart Elements drop-down list, and choose Horizontal (Value) Axis or Vertical (Value) Axis. Then click the Format Selection button, and in the Format Axis task pane, go to the Number category, select Date in the Category menu, and choose a date format.

» **The numbers in the chart aren't formatted right.** To change the number of decimal places, include comma separators in numbers, display currency symbols, or do all else that pertains to numbers, go to the Format tab, open the Chart Elements drop-down list, and choose Horizontal (Value) Axis or Vertical (Value) Axis. Then click the Format Selection button. You see the Format Axis task pane. Visit the Number category and select options for displaying numbers.

» **"Category 1" or "Series 1" appears in the chart legend.** To direct you to the right place to enter data in the data grid, phantom names such as "Category 1" and "Series 1" appear in worksheets. Sometimes these phantoms wind up in chart legends as well. To remove them, go to the ChartDesign tab and click the Edit Data button. You see the data grid, where the data range used to generate the chart is enclosed in a blue box. Drag the lower-right corner of the box so that the box encloses only the data you want for your chart.

» **In 3-D charts, small markers are obscured by large markers in the foreground.** For all the data markers to be shown in a 3-D chart, the smaller ones have to be in the foreground. To rearrange data markers, go to the ChartDesign tab and click the Select Data button to open the Select Data Source dialog box. Then select a series and click the Up or Down button to rearrange the series in your chart. Series that are high on the list go to the back of the chart; series that are low on the list go to the front.

» **The chart doesn't gather all data from the worksheet.** On the Chart Design tab, click the Edit Data button, and in the data grid that stores data for your chart, enlarge the blue data-range box so that it encloses all your data. You can enlarge the box by dragging its lower-right corner.

Chapter **2**

Making a SmartArt Diagram

long with charts and tables, diagrams are the best way to present your ideas. Diagrams clearly show, for example, employees' relationships with one another, product cycles, workflow processes, and spheres of influence. A diagram is an excellent marriage of images and words. Diagrams allow an audience to literally visualize a concept, idea, or relationship.

This chapter explains how to construct diagrams from SmartArt graphics and how to create a diagram. It shows how to customize diagrams by changing the size of diagrams and diagram shapes, adding and removing shapes, and changing shapes' colors. You also discover how to change the direction of a diagram and enter the text. Finally, this chapter demonstrates how to create a diagram from scratch with shapes and connectors.

The Basics: Creating SmartArt Diagrams

In Word, PowerPoint, and Excel, diagrams are made from *SmartArt graphics*. These diagram graphics are "interactive" in the sense that you can move, alter, and write text on them. In other words, you can use them to construct diagrams. You can alter these diagrams to your liking. You can make a diagram portray precisely what you want it to portray, although you usually have to wrestle with the diagram a bit.

Choosing a diagram

The first step in creating a diagram is to select a layout in the Choose a SmartArt Graphic dialog box, shown in Figure 2-1. To open this dialog box, go to the Insert tab and click the SmartArt button. After you create the initial diagram, you customize it to create a diagram of your own. About 160 diagrams are in the dialog box. They fall into these nine categories:

Diagram Type	Use
List	For describing blocks of related information as well as sequential steps in a task, process, or workflow
Process	For describing how a concept or physical process changes over time or is modified
Cycle	For illustrating a circular progression without a beginning or end, or a relationship in which the components are in balance
Hierarchy	For describing hierarchical relationships between people, departments, and other entities, as well as portraying branchlike relationships in which one decision or action leads to another
Relationship	For describing the relationship between different components (but not hierarchical relationships)
Matrix	For showing the relationship between quadrants
Pyramid	For showing proportional or hierarchical relationships
Picture	For creating diagrams that include photographs and pictures (This catch-all category presents picture diagrams from the other categories.)
Office.com	For presenting data in tabbed arcs, radials, block processes, and other unusual ways

WARNING

If you intend to construct a "flow chart type" diagram with many branches and levels, go to the Hierarchy category and select the Organization Chart or one of the hierarchy diagrams. As "Laying Out the Diagram Shapes" explains later in this chapter, only these choices permit you to make a diagram with many different branches and levels.

Diagram types   Select a diagram   Diagram explanation

Making the diagram your own

After you select a generic diagram in the Choose a SmartArt Graphic dialog box and click OK, the next step is to make the diagram your own by completing these tasks:

>> **Change the diagram's size and position:** Change the size and position of a diagram to make it fit squarely on your page or slide. See "Changing the Size and Position of a Diagram," later in this chapter.

>> **Add shapes to (or remove shapes from) the diagram:** Adding a shape involves declaring where to add the shape, promoting or demoting the shape with respect to other shapes, and declaring how the new shape connects to another shape. See "Laying Out the Diagram Shapes," later in this chapter.

>> **Enter text:** Enter text on each shape, or component, of the diagram. See "Handling the Text on Diagram Shapes," later in this chapter.

If you so desire, you can also customize your diagram by taking on some or all of these tasks:

>> **Changing its overall appearance:** Choose a different color scheme or 3-D variation for your diagram. See "Choosing a Look for Your Diagram," later in this chapter.

>> **Changing shapes:** Select a new shape for part of your diagram, change the size of a shape, or assign different colors to shapes to make shapes stand out. See "Changing the Appearance of Diagram Shapes," later in this chapter.

If you're comfortable creating a diagram of your own by drawing shapes and lines, no law says you have to begin in the Choose a SmartArt Graphic dialog box. Later in this chapter, "Creating a Diagram from Scratch" looks into creating a diagram by making use of text boxes, lines, and shapes.

Creating the Initial Diagram

The first step in fashioning a diagram is to choose a SmartArt graphic in the Choose a SmartArt Graphic dialog box. After that, you roll up your sleeves, change the diagram's size and shape, and enter the text. If you select the wrong diagram to start with, all is not lost. You can choose another diagram in its place, although how successful swapping one diagram for another is depends on how lucky you are and how far along you are in creating your diagram. These pages explain how to create an initial diagram and swap one diagram for another.

Creating a diagram

Follow these steps to create a diagram:

1. **On the Insert tab, click the SmartArt button.**

You see the Choose a SmartArt Graphic dialog box (refer to Figure 2-1). In PowerPoint, you can also open the dialog box by clicking the SmartArt icon in a content placeholder frame.

STARTING FROM A SKETCH

You can spare yourself a lot of trouble by starting from a sketch when you create a diagram. Find a pencil with a good eraser, grab a blank piece of paper, and start drawing. Imagine what your ideal diagram looks like. Draw the arrows or lines connecting the different parts of the diagram. Write the text. Draw the diagram that best illustrates what you want to communicate.

Later, in the Choose a SmartArt Graphic dialog box (refer to Figure 2-1), you can select the diagram that most resembles the one you sketched. The dialog box offers more than 200 types of diagrams. Unless you start from a sketch and have a solid idea of the diagram you want, you can get lost in the dialog box. Also, if you don't start from a sketch, adding shapes to the diagram and landing shapes in the right places can be a chore.

2. **Select a diagram in the Choose a SmartArt Graphic dialog box.**

Diagrams are divided into nine categories, as I explain earlier in this chapter. The dialog box offers a description of each diagram. Either select a type on the left side of the dialog box or scroll the entire list to find the graphic that most resembles the diagram you want.

TIP

If you want to create a graph with many levels and branches, go to the Hierarchy category and select one of these charts: Organization Chart or Name and Title Organization Chart (move the pointer over a chart in the SmartArt Graphic dialog box to see a pop-up listing the chart's name). These two diagrams are much more complex than the others and allow for branching. See "Laying Out the Diagram Shapes," later in this chapter, for details.

3. **Click OK.**

The next topic in this chapter explains how to swap one diagram for another, in case you chose wrongly in the Choose a SmartArt Graphic dialog box.

Swapping one diagram for another

If the diagram you chose initially doesn't do the job, you can swap it for a different diagram. How successful the swap is depends on how far along you are in creating your diagram and whether your diagram is simple or complex. Follow these steps to swap one diagram for another:

1. **Click your diagram to select it.**

2. **Go to the SmartArt Design tab.**

3. **Open the Layouts gallery.**

You see a gallery with diagrams of the same type as the diagram you're working with.

4. **Select a new diagram or choose More Layouts to open the Choose a SmartArt Graphic dialog box and select a diagram there.**

You may have to click the trusty Undo button and start all over if the diagram you selected for the swap didn't do the job.

TIP

To break a diagram into its component parts, select the diagram, go to the Format tab, click the Group button, and choose Ungroup on the drop-down list. (Book 8, Chapter 4 describes grouping and ungrouping in detail.)

Changing the Size and Position of a Diagram

To make a diagram fit squarely on a page or slide, you have to change its size and position. Resizing and positioning diagrams and other objects is the subject of Chapter 4 of this minibook, but in case you don't care to travel that far to get instructions, here are shorthand instructions for resizing and positioning diagrams:

>> **Resizing a diagram:** Select the diagram, move the pointer over a selection handle on the corner or side, and start dragging after the pointer changes into a two-headed arrow. You can also go to the Format tab and enter new measurements in the Height and Width boxes. (You may have to click the Size button to see these text boxes, depending on the size of your screen.)

>> **Repositioning a diagram:** Select the diagram, move the pointer over its perimeter, and when you see the four-headed arrow, click and start dragging.

REMEMBER

Notice when you resize a diagram that the shapes in the diagram change size proportionally. Most diagrams are designed so that shapes fill out the diagram. When you change the size of a diagram, remove a shape from a diagram, or add a shape, shapes change size within the diagram.

Laying Out the Diagram Shapes

At the heart of every diagram are the rectangles, circles, arrows, and whatnots that make the diagram what it is. These shapes illustrate the concept or idea you want to express. Your biggest challenge when creating a diagram is laying out the diagram shapes.

The following pages explain how to select diagram shapes, add shapes, reposition shapes, and remove shapes from diagrams. They also offer instructions specific to working with hierarchy diagrams.

Selecting a diagram shape

Before you can remove a shape from a diagram or indicate where you want to add a new shape, you have to select a diagram shape. To select a diagram shape, move the pointer over its perimeter and click when you see the four-headed arrow appear on your pointer.

You can tell when a diagram shape is selected because a solid line, not a dotted line, appears around the shape and the cursor changes into an I-beam, as shown in Figure 2-2. When you see dotted lines around a shape, you're expected to enter text.

Selected diagram shape

Removing a shape from a diagram

Removing a shape from a diagram is as easy as falling off a turnip truck as long as you correctly select the shape before you remove it. To remove a shape, select it and press Delete. Other shapes grow larger when you remove a shape, in keeping with the "fill out the diagram by any means necessary" philosophy.

Moving diagram shapes to different positions

If a shape in a diagram isn't in the right position, don't fret, because you can change the order of shapes very easily by going to the SmartArt Design tab and clicking the Move Up or Move Down button.

Select the diagram shape that needs repositioning and click the Move Up or Move Down button as many times as necessary to land the shape in the right place.

Adding shapes to diagrams apart from hierarchy diagrams

Unlike hierarchy diagrams, list, process, cycle, relationship, and matrix diagrams don't have branches. They always travel in one direction only. This makes adding shapes to these diagrams fairly straightforward. To add a shape, you select a shape in the diagram and then add the new shape so that it appears before or after the shape you selected, as shown in Figure 2-3.

Select a shape and choose an Add Shape option   The new shape

FIGURE 2-3:
To add a shape,
start by selecting
the shape that
your new shape
will go before
or after.

Follow these steps to add a shape to a list, process, cycle, relationship, matrix, or pyramid diagram:

1. **In your diagram, select the shape that your new shape will appear before or after.**

    Earlier in this chapter, "Selecting a diagram shape" explains how to select diagram shapes.

2. **Choose the Add Shape After or Add Shape Before command.**

    To get to these commands, use one of these techniques:

    - On the SmartArt Design tab, open the drop-down list on the Add Shape button and choose Add Shape After or Add Shape Before, as shown in Figure 2-3.

    - Right-click the shape you selected, choose Add Shape on the shortcut menu, and then choose Add Shape After or Add Shape Before on the submenu.

Adding shapes to hierarchy diagrams

Hierarchy diagrams are more complex than other diagrams because they branch out such that shapes are found on different levels. This branching out makes add-ing shapes to hierarchy diagrams problematic.

As shown in Figure 2-4, Office offers four Add Shape commands for adding shapes to hierarchy diagrams: Add Shape After, Add Shape Before, Add Shape Above, and

Add Shape Below. What these commands do depends on whether the diagram is horizontally or vertically oriented, because what constitutes after, before, above, and below is different in vertical and horizontal diagrams. Suffice it to say that when you add shapes to hierarchy diagrams, you often have to try different commands, clicking the Undo button and starting all over until you get it right.

Select a shape and choose one of four Add Shape commands

FIGURE 2-4:
You can add a shape after, before, above, or below a shape in a hierarchy diagram.

Follow these steps to add a shape to a hierarchy diagram:

1. **In your diagram, select the shape to which your new shape will be connected.**

Earlier in this chapter, "Selecting a diagram shape" describes how to select a shape.

2. **Choose an Add Shape command.**

Figure 2-4 shows what Add Shape commands do. You can choose Add Shape commands with one of these techniques:

- On the SmartArt Design tab, open the drop-down list on the Add Shape button and choose an Add Shape command (refer to Figure 2-4).

- Right-click the shape you selected, choose Add Shape on the shortcut menu, and choose an Add Shape command on the submenu.

Adding shapes to Organization charts

An Organization chart diagram offers many opportunities for connecting shapes. The shapes can branch out from one another in four directions as well as appear to the side in the "assistant" position. When you place one shape below another shape, you can make the new shape *hang* so that it is joined to a line that drops, or hangs, from another shape. These pages explain how to add shapes and create hanging relationships between one shape and the shapes subordinate to it.

Adding an Organization Chart shape

Besides adding a shape after, before, above, or below a shape, you can add an assistant shape to an Organization Chart diagram, as shown in Figure 2-5. An assistant shape is an intermediary shape between two levels. Follow these steps to add a shape to an Organization Chart diagram:

1. **Select the shape to which you will add a new shape.**

Earlier in this chapter, "Selecting a diagram shape" explains how to select shapes. As shown in Figure 2-5, shapes are surrounded by solid lines, not dotted lines, when you select them properly.

2. **Choose an Add Shape command.**

You can choose Add Shape commands in two ways:

- On the SmartArt Design tab, open the drop-down list on the Add Shape button and choose an Add Shape (or Add Assistant) command (see Figure 2-5).

- Right-click the shape you selected, choose Add Shape on the shortcut menu, and then choose an Add Shape (or Add Assistant) command on the submenu.

Figure 2-5 demonstrates what the Add Shape commands do to a vertically oriented diagram. Notice that Add Shape Before places a new shape to the left of the shape you selected; Add Shape After places a new shape to the right.

WARNING

Be careful about choosing the Add Shape Above command. This command effectively bumps the shape you selected to a lower level in order to make room for the new shape. In effect, you demote one shape when you place a new shape above it.

TIP

Shapes created with the Add Assistant command land on the left side of the line to which they're attached, but if you prefer the assistant shape to be on the right side of the line, you can drag it to the right.

Select a shape and choose one of the five Add Shape commands

FIGURE 2-5:
Adding a shape to
an Organization
Chart diagram.

Hanging a shape below another shape in an Organization Chart

Besides the standard relationship between shapes above and below one another, you can create a *hanging relationship* in an Organization Chart diagram. Figure 2-6 shows the four kinds of hanging relationships — Standard, Both, Left Hanging, and Right Hanging. In a hanging relationship, the line hangs from a shape, and subordinate shapes are connected to the line.

FIGURE 2-6:
Ways that shapes
can hang in
Organization
Chart diagrams.

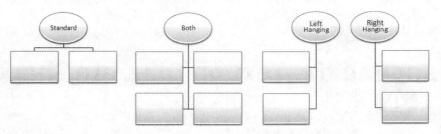

Making a SmartArt Diagram

You can create a hanging relationship between shapes before or after you create the subordinate shapes. Follow these steps to create a hanging relationship:

1. **Select the shape to which other shapes will hang or are hanging.**

2. **On the SmartArt Design tab, click the Layout button.**

3. **On the drop-down list, choose Standard, Both, Left Hanging, or Right Hanging.**

Promoting and demoting shapes in hierarchy diagrams

Shapes in hierarchy diagrams are ranked by level. If a shape is on the wrong level, you can move it higher or lower in the diagram by clicking the Promote or Demote button on the SmartArt Design tab. Promoting and demoting shapes can turn into a donnybrook if you aren't careful. If the shapes being promoted or demoted are attached to subordinate shapes, the subordinate shapes are promoted or demoted as well. This can have unforeseen and sometimes horrendous consequences.

Follow these steps to promote or demote a shape (and its subordinates) in a hierarchy diagram:

1. **Select the shape that needs a change of rank.**

   You can select more than one shape by Ctrl+clicking.

2. **Go to the SmartArt Design tab.**

3. **Click the Promote or Demote button.**

   Do you like what you see? If not, you may have to click the Undo button and start all over.

Handling the Text on Diagram Shapes

When you create a new diagram, "[Text]" (the word *Text* enclosed in brackets) appears on shapes. Your job is to replace this generic placeholder with something more meaningful and less bland. These sections explain how to enter text and bulleted lists on shapes.

Entering text on a diagram shape

Use one of these techniques to enter text on a diagram shape:

>> **Click in the shape and start typing:** The words you type appear in the shape, as shown in Figure 2-7.

>> **Enter text in the Text pane:** Enter the text by typing it in the Text pane, as shown in Figure 2-7. The text pane opens to the left of the diagram. To open the text pane, go to the SmartArt Design tab and click the Text Pane button or click the arrow button to the left of the diagram.

FIGURE 2-7: Type directly on diagram shapes or enter text on the Text pane.

The text in diagrams shrinks as you enter more text so that all text is the same size. If you want to make the text larger or smaller in one shape, see "Changing fonts and font sizes on shapes," later in this chapter.

Entering bulleted lists on diagram shapes

Some diagram shapes have built-in bulleted lists, but no matter. Whether or not a shape is prepared to be bulleted, you can enter bullets in a diagram shape. Here are instructions for entering and removing bullets:

>> **Entering a bulleted list:** Select the shape that needs bullets, and on the SmartArt Design tab, click the Add Bullet button. Either enter the bulleted items directly into the shape (pressing Enter as you type each entry) or click the Text Pane button to open the Text pane (refer to Figure 2-7) and enter bullets there.

>> **Removing bulleted items:** Click before the first bulleted entry and keep pressing the Delete key until you have removed all the bulleted items. You can also start in the Text pane (refer to Figure 2-7) and press the Delete key there until you've removed the bulleted items, or drag to select several bulleted items and then press Delete.

TURNING A BULLETED LIST INTO A DIAGRAM (POWERPOINT)

Suppose you're working along in PowerPoint when suddenly the realization strikes you that a bulleted list in a text frame or text box would work much better as a diagram. For those occasions, you can click the Convert to SmartArt button. By clicking this button, you can turn the text in a text frame or text box into a diagram. If the text frame or box contains a bulleted list, each bulleted item becomes a diagram shape.

Follow these steps to turn a text frame or text box into a diagram:

1. **Select the text frame or text box.**

2. **On the Home tab, click the Convert to SmartArt Graphic button.**

   You see a drop-down list with basic diagram choices.

3. **Either select a diagram on the list or choose More SmartArt Graphics to open the Choose a SmartArt Graphic dialog box and select a diagram there.**

Changing a Diagram's Direction

As long as your diagram is horizontally oriented, you can change its direction. As shown in Figure 2-8, you can flip it over such that the rightmost shape in your diagram becomes the leftmost shape, and what was the leftmost shape becomes the rightmost shape. If arrows are in your diagram, the arrows point the opposite direction after you flip the diagram. You can't flip vertically oriented diagrams this way. Sorry, but diagrams that run north to south, not west to east, can't be rolled over.

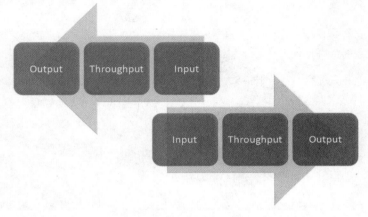

FIGURE 2-8: You can flip horizontal diagrams so that they run the opposite direction.

Follow these steps to flip a horizontally oriented diagram:

1. **Select the diagram.**

2. **On the SmartArt Design tab, click the Right to Left button.**

    If you don't like what you see, click the button again or click the Undo button.

Choosing a Look for Your Diagram

Decide how a diagram looks by starting on the SmartArt Design tab. Starting there, you can choose a color scheme for your diagram and a different style. Between the Change Colors drop-down list and the SmartArt Styles gallery, you can find a combination of options that presents your diagram in the best light:

>> **Change Colors button:** Click the Change Colors button to see color schemes for your diagram on the drop-down list, as shown in Figure 2-9. Point at a few options to live-preview them.

>> **SmartArt Styles gallery:** Open the SmartArt Styles gallery to choose simple and 3-D variations on the diagram.

Select a color scheme   Select a diagram style

TIP

If you experiment too freely and want to backpedal, click the Reset Graphic button on the SmartArt Design tab. Clicking this button reverses all the formatting changes you made to your diagram.

TIP

If your Word document, Excel worksheet, or PowerPoint presentation includes many diagrams, make sure your diagrams are consistent in appearance. Choose similar colors for diagrams. If you like 3-D diagrams, make the majority of your diagrams 3-D. Don't let the diagrams overwhelm the ideas they are meant to express. The point is to present ideas in diagrams, not turn your work into a SmartArt diagram showcase.

Changing the Appearance of Diagram Shapes

To call attention to one part of a diagram, you can change the appearance of a shape and make it stand out. Any part of a diagram that is different from the other parts naturally gets more attention. To change the appearance of a shape, consider changing its size or color, exchanging one shape for another, or changing the font and font size of the text. These topics are covered in the following pages.

Changing the size of a diagram shape

A shape that is larger than other shapes in a diagram gets the attention of the audience. Select your shape and use one of these techniques to enlarge or shrink it:

>> On the Format tab, click the Larger or Smaller button as many times as necessary to make the shape the right size.

>> Move the pointer over a corner selection handle, and when the pointer changes to a two-headed arrow, click and start dragging.

Notice that the text inside the shape remains the same size although the shape is larger. To change the size of the text in a shape, see "Changing fonts and font sizes on shapes," later in this chapter.

TIP

To return a diagram shape to its original size after you've fooled with it, right-click the shape and choose Reset Shape.

Exchanging one shape for another

Another way to call attention to an important part of a diagram is to change shapes, as shown in Figure 2-10. Rather than a conventional shape, use an oval, block arrow, or star. You can substitute a shape in the Shapes gallery for any diagram shape (Chapter 4 of this minibook explores the Shapes gallery). To exchange one shape for another in a diagram, select the shape and use one of these techniques:

>> On the Format tab, click the Change Shape button and select a shape in the Shapes gallery.

>> Right-click the shape, choose Change Shape on the shortcut menu, and select a shape on the submenu.

FIGURE 2-10: Using different shapes and different-sized shapes in a diagram.

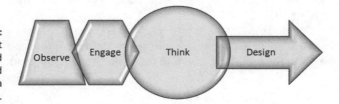

Observe   Engage   Think   Design

Changing a shape's color, fill, or outline

Yet another way to call attention to a shape is to change its color, fill, or outline border, as shown in Figure 2-11. Select a shape and go to the Format tab to change a shape's color, fill, or outline.

>> **Restyling a shape:** Select an option in the Shape Styles gallery to give a shape a makeover.

>> **Filling a shape with a new color:** Click the Shape Fill button and make a choice from the drop-down list to select a color, picture, two-color gradient, or texture for the shape.

>> **Changing the outline:** Click the Shape Outline button and choose a color and weight for the shape's border on the drop-down list.

>> **Applying a shape effect:** Click the Shape Effects button to select a shape effect for your shape.

FIGURE 2-11: Ways to make a diagram shape stand out.

Changing fonts and font sizes on shapes

To make a diagram shape stand out, try changing the font and font size of the text on the shape. Before you change fonts and font sizes, however, you should know that changing fonts in a shape effectively disconnects the shape from the other shapes in the diagram. Normally text changes size throughout a diagram when you add or remove shapes, but when you change the font or font size in one shape, it is no longer associated with the other shapes; its letters don't change their size or appearance when shapes are added or removed from the diagram of which it is a part.

To alter the text on a diagram shape, select the text, go to the Home tab, and choose a different font, font size, and font color, too, if you want.

Creating a Diagram from Scratch

If you have the skill and the wherewithal, you can create a diagram from scratch by piecing together shapes, arrows, and connectors. The diagram in Figure 2-12, for example, was made not from SmartArt graphics but from shapes, arrows, and connectors. Chapter 4 of this minibook explains how to draw shapes and lines between shapes. You can enter text on any shape merely by clicking inside it and wiggling your fingers over the keyboard.

Making a diagram from scratch has some advantages. You can draw the connectors any which way. Lines can cross the diagram chaotically. You can include text boxes as well as shapes (the diagram in Figure 2-12 has four text boxes). Don't hesitate to fashion your own diagrams when a presentation or document calls for it.

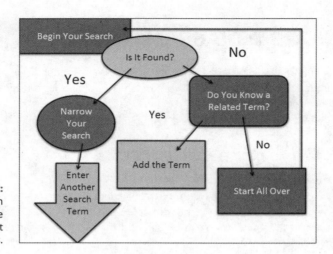

FIGURE 2-12:
A homegrown
diagram made
without SmartArt
graphics.

Chapter **3**

Handling Graphics and Photos

A picture, so they say, is worth a thousand words. Whether it's worth a thousand words or merely 950 is debatable. What is certain is that visuals help people remember things. A carefully chosen image in a PowerPoint presentation, Word document, or Excel worksheet helps others understand you better. The image reinforces the ideas or information that you're trying to put across.

This chapter explains how you can make pictures — photographs and graphics — part of your Word documents, PowerPoint presentations, and Excel worksheets. It looks into graphic file formats and other issues pertaining to graphics as well as how to touch up graphics in an Office application.

All about Picture File Formats

Graphics and photographs come in many different file formats, and as far as Office is concerned, some are better than others. These pages explain what you need to know about graphic files to use them wisely in Office files. Here, you find out what bitmap and vector graphics are, what resolution and color depth are, and how graphic files are compressed.

Bitmap and vector graphics

All graphic images fall into either the bitmap or vector category:

>> A *bitmap graphic* is composed of many thousands of tiny dots called *pixels* that, taken together, form an image (the term *pixel* comes from "picture element"). A photograph is a bitmap graphic.

>> A *vector graphic* is drawn with the aid of computer instructions that describe the shape and dimension of each line, curve, circle, and so on.

The difference between the two formats is that vector graphics do not distort when you enlarge or shrink them, whereas bitmap graphics lose clarity when their size is changed. Furthermore, vector images do not require nearly as much disk space as bitmap graphics. Drop a few bitmap graphics in a file and soon you're dealing with a file that is close to 750K in size.

Resolution

Resolution refers to how many pixels comprise a bitmap image. The higher the resolution, the clearer the image. Resolution is measured in *dots per inch* (dpi), sometimes called *pixels per inch* (ppi). Images with more dots — or pixels — per inch are clearer and display more fineness of detail. When you scan an image, the scanner permits you to choose a dots-per-inch setting.

High-resolution images look better but require more disk space than low-resolution images. Figure 3-1 illustrates the difference between a high-resolution and low-resolution photograph.

FIGURE 3-1:
A high-resolution photo (left) and the same photo at low resolution (right).

Compression

TECHNICAL STUFF

Compression refers to an algorithm by which bitmap graphic files can be made smaller. In effect, compression enables your computer to store a bitmap graphic with less disk space. Some bitmap graphic types can't be compressed; other bitmap graphic types are compressed using either lossless or lossy compression:

>> **Lossless compression:** To maintain the picture's integrity, the same number of pixels are stored in the compressed file as in the original. Because the pixels remain intact, you can change the size of a file that has undergone lossless compression without losing picture quality.

>> **Lossy compression:** Without regard for the picture's integrity, pixel data in the original picture is lost during compression. Therefore, if you try to enlarge a picture that has undergone lossy compression, the picture loses quality.

Color depth

TECHNICAL STUFF

Color depth refers to the number of colors that can be displayed in a graphics file. The larger the color depth, the larger the number of colors that can be displayed, the richer the graphic looks, and the larger its file size is. Color depth is measured in bits. To get technical on you, color depth is measured in the number of bits that are needed to describe each pixel's color in the image. A bit, or "binary digit," is the smallest unit of data measurement in computing. These are the color-depth measurements:

Bit Size	Color Depth
1-bit	Black and white only
8-bit	256 colors
16-bit	65,536 colors
24-bit	16,777,216 colors
32-bit	4,294,967,296 colors

To look like photographs and not cartoons, photographs require a color depth of at least 16-bits. Sometimes color depth is described in terms of a color palette. For example, a graphic format with an 8-bit color depth is said to have a 256-color palette.

Choosing file formats for graphics

WARNING

One of the challenges of using photographs and graphics in Office files is keeping file sizes to a minimum. A file that is loaded down with many photographs can take a long time to load and send over the Internet.

The trick is to find a balance between high-quality, high-resolution graphics and the need to keep file sizes low. Here are some tips for choosing graphic file formats:

>> Consider sticking with vector graphics if you're including graphics in your file strictly for decoration purposes. Vector images are easy to come by, don't require very much disk space, and can be edited in Office.

>> For photographs, make PNG your first choice for graphics. PNG images have a fairly high resolution and don't require very much disk space.

>> If you're dealing with black-and-white photos, logos, or simple graphics for when resolution doesn't matter, use GIF files. These files eat up the least amount of disk space.

Inserting a Picture in an Office File

After you've weighed the merits of different kinds of graphics and decided which one is best for you, you can insert it. To insert a picture, either use one stored on your computer or get one from the Internet.

REMEMBER

After a picture lands in a file, it becomes an object. Chapter 4 of this minibook explains how to manipulate objects — how to move them, change their size, and change their borders. Later in this chapter, "Touching Up a Picture" looks into various ways to change the appearance of graphics.

Inserting a picture of your own

Inserting a picture stored on your computer (or computer network) is as simple as choosing it in the Insert Picture dialog box. Follow these steps to insert a picture on a PowerPoint slide, Word document, or Excel worksheet:

1. Go to the Insert tab.

2. Click the Pictures button.

3. **Choose This Device on the drop-down menu.**

You see the Insert Picture dialog box, as shown in Figure 3-2. In PowerPoint, you can also open this dialog box by clicking the Pictures icon in a content placeholder frame.

4. **Select a file in the Insert Picture dialog box.**

As Figure 3-2 shows, you can choose a View option to see what a graphic looks like.

TIP

You can click the File Types button to open a drop-down list and choose a file type to locate files of a certain type in the dialog box. This button is located above the Insert and Cancel buttons.

5. **Click the Insert button.**

Go to the Picture Format tab to see all the different ways you can manipulate a picture after you insert it.

Select a picture   Choose a View option

FIGURE 3-2:
You can preview a picture file before you insert it.

If you chose the wrong picture, don't fret because you can exchange one picture for another. On the Picture Format tab, click the Change Picture button, choose From a File, and select a different picture in the Insert Picture dialog box.

Handling Graphics and Photos

Obtaining a picture online

Don't have a suitable picture on your computer? You can obtain a picture online. As shown in Figure 3-3, you can obtain a picture from these places:

>> **Office.com:** Search for stock images available from Office.com.

>> **The Internet:** Search the Internet for pictures using the Bing search engine.

FIGURE 3-3:
Searching for
stock images
(top) and online
pictures (bottom).

Follow these steps to obtain a picture from the Internet or a stock image from Office.com:

1. **Go to the Insert tab.**

2. **Click the Pictures button.**

3. **Choose Stock Images or Online Pictures on the drop-down menu.**

   A dialog box opens so that you can search for images (see Figure 3-3). In PowerPoint, you can search for stock images by clicking the Stock Images icon in a content placeholder frame.

4. **Enter a search term in the text box (and press Enter as well if you're searching the Internet for a picture).**

5. **Select the picture you want and click the Insert button.**

   Your next task is to move the image into position and perhaps change its size. Chapter 4 of this minibook explains how to manipulate pictures and other objects.

Be careful about taking images indiscriminately from the Internet. Permission is required to use copyrighted images.

SHOOTING A SCREENSHOT

Word, PowerPoint, Excel, and Outlook make it easier than ever to take a picture of a screen on your computer and insert it in a document, slide, worksheet, or email message. Follow these steps to take a picture of a screen:

1. **If you want to capture a portion of one screen, open the screen.**

2. **On the Insert tab, click the Screenshot button.**

   A drop-down list shows you thumbnail images of each screen that is open on your computer.

3. **Choose a thumbnail image to shoot an entire screen, or choose Screen Clipping and drag onscreen to shoot a portion of a screen.**

A picture of the screen or a portion of the screen lands in your document, slide, worksheet, or email message.

Here are a couple of other tried-and-true techniques for capturing screens:

- Press PrtScn to capture an entire screen to the Clipboard.

- Press Alt+PrtScn to capture the active part of the screen to the Clipboard. For example, to capture a dialog box, select the dialog box and press Alt+PrtScn.

After the screen capture is on the Clipboard, you can paste it where you will.

Touching Up a Picture

Every picture can be a collaboration. You can do the following to make a picture your own as well as the work of the original artist:

>> **Softening and sharpening:** Mute or polish a picture. See "Softening and sharpening pictures," later in this chapter.

>> **Changing the brightness and contrast**: Adjust a picture's tone. See "Correcting a picture's brightness and contrast."

>> **Recoloring:** Give your picture a brand-new set of colors or gray shades. See "Recoloring a picture."

>> **Choosing an artistic effect:** Take your picture for a walk on the wild side. See "Choosing an artistic effect."

>> **Choosing a picture style:** Present your picture in an oval fame, soft-edged frame, or other type of frame. See "Selecting a picture style."

>> **Cropping:** Cut out the parts of a picture that you don't want. See "Cropping off part of a picture."

>> **Removing picture areas:** Keep the essentials of a picture and remove the rest. See "Removing the background."

If you regret experimenting with your picture and you want to start all over, go to the Picture Format tab and click the Reset Picture button. Then, on the drop-down list, choose Reset Picture to restore the picture to its original appearance, or choose Reset Picture & Size to restore the picture to its original appearance and size.

Softening and sharpening pictures

Figure 3-4 shows the effects of the softening/sharpening settings. These settings mute a picture or make it look more succinct. To soften or sharpen a picture, select it and use one of these techniques:

>> On the Picture Format tab, click the Corrections button and choose a Sharpen and Soften option on the drop-down list.

>> Open the Format Picture task pane and drag the Sharpness slider or enter a negative or positive number in the text box. Negative numbers soften the picture; positive numbers sharpen it. To open the Format Picture task pane, click the Corrections button and choose Picture Corrections Options on the drop-down list.

FIGURE 3-4:
Effects of the
Sharpen/Soften
settings.

Correcting a picture's brightness and contrast

Figure 3–5 shows a picture that has been made over several times with the Bright–ness and Contrast settings. Brightness settings govern the overall brightness of a picture; contrast settings determine how distinguishable the different parts of the picture are from one another. Change a picture's brightness and contrast to make it fit better on a page or slide. Select your picture and use one of these techniques:

>> On the Picture Format tab, click the Corrections button and choose a Brightness and Contrast option on the drop-down list.

>> Open the Format Picture task pane and change the Brightness and Contrast settings. Negative Brightness settings make a picture darker; positive settings make it brighter. Negative Contrast settings mute the differences between the parts of a picture; positive settings heighten the differences. To open the Format Picture task pane, click the Corrections button and choose Picture Corrections Options on the drop-down list.

FIGURE 3-5:
Effects of the
Brightness and
Contrast settings.

Handling Graphics
and Photos

Recoloring a picture

Recolor a picture to give it a makeover. Figure 3-6 shows examples of Recolor options. As well as recoloring a picture, you can change its color saturation and color tone settings. *Color saturation* refers to the purity and intensity of the colors; *color tone* determines the degree of lightness and darkness. Recoloring is useful for giving a picture a uniform appearance. Select your picture and use these techniques to recolor it:

>> On the Picture Format tab, click the Color button and choose a Color Saturation, Color Tone, or Recolor option on the drop-down list. You can choose More Variations at the bottom of the list and choose a color on the sublist.

>> Open the Format Picture task pane and change the Color Saturation and Color Tone settings. Change the Saturation setting to mute or bring out the colors; change the Temperature setting to make the color tones darker or lighter. To open the Format Picture task pane, click the Color button and choose Picture Color Options.

FIGURE 3-6:
Examples of
Recolor options.

TIP

Live-previewing really comes in handy when you're recoloring a graphic. As you change Color Saturation and Color Tone settings, you can see the effect of your choices on the picture.

MAKING A COLOR TRANSPARENT

The Picture Format tab offers the Set Transparent Color command for making one color in a picture transparent and thereby allowing the background to show through in certain parts of a picture. The Set Transparent Color command works by making all the pixels in a picture that are the same color transparent. In a picture in which one color predominates, you can make this color transparent and get some interesting effects.

To experiment with the Set Transparent Color command:

1. **Select the picture.**

2. **On the Picture Format tab, click the Color button and choose Set Transparent Color on the drop-down list.**

3. **Click in your picture on the color that you want to be transparent.**

You can choose the Set Transparent Color command again and make another color in your picture transparent.

Choosing an artistic effect

Figure 3-7 demonstrates four of the 23 artistic effects that you can apply to a picture: Pencil Sketch, Glow Diffused, Glass, and Glow Edges. To experiment with the artistic effects and maybe find one to your liking, select your picture and use one of these techniques:

>> Go to the Picture Format tab, click the Artistic Effects button, and choose an effect on the drop-down list.

>> Open the Format Picture task pane and choose an artistic effect. To open the Format Picture dialog box, click the Artistic Effects button and choose Artistic Effects Options.

FIGURE 3-7:
Examples of
artistic effects.

Selecting a picture style

A *picture style* is way of presenting or framing a picture. Figure 3-8 shows examples of picture styles. Picture styles include Simple Frame, Soft Edge Rectangle, Perspective Shadow, and Reflected Bevel. To choose a picture style for a picture, select it, go to the Picture Format tab, open the Picture Styles gallery, and choose a style.

FIGURE 3-8:
Examples of
picture styles.

REMEMBER

If you don't like the picture style you chose (or you don't care for any change you made to a picture), click the Reset Picture button to reverse all your format changes and start over.

If you like the picture styles, you may be enamored as well with the picture effects. On the Picture Format tab, click the Picture Effects button and experiment with the options on the drop-down list and sublists.

Cropping off part of a picture

Cropping means to cut off part of a picture. I'm afraid you can't use the Office cropping tool like a pair of scissors or an Xacto knife to zigzag cut around the edges of a picture or cut a hole in the middle. You can, however, cut strips from the side, top, or bottom. In Figure 3-9, the cropping tool is being used to cut off extraneous parts of a picture.

FIGURE 3-9:
Cropping off parts of a picture.

Select your picture, go to the Picture Format tab, and use one of these techniques to crop it:

>> **Crop manually:** Crop the picture by dragging its cropping handles. Click the Crop button. Cropping handles appear around the picture, as in Figure 3-9. Drag cropping handles to lop off a part or parts of the picture. Click the Crop button again or press Esc after you finish cropping.

>> **Crop to a shape:** Crop the picture to a rectangle, circle, or other shape. Open the drop-down list on the Crop button, choose Crop to Shape, and select a shape in the Shapes gallery.

>> **Crop to proportions:** Crop the picture to a proportional size setting. Open the drop-down list on the Crop button, choose Aspect Ratio, and choose a ratio. For example, choose 1:1 to crop to a perfect square with the width and height the same size.

>> **Crop by filling:** For placing an image in a picture placeholder, crop the image to make it fit in the placeholder box. Open the drop-down list on the Crop button and choose Fill.

>> **Crop by fitting:** For placing an image in a picture placeholder, shrink the picture to make it fit. Open the drop-down list on the Crop button and choose Fit.

TIP

With the cropping handles showing, you can drag the picture left, right, up, or down to determine where it is cropped.

When you crop a picture, you don't cut off a part of it — not as far as your computer is concerned. All you do is tell Office not to display part of a graphic. The graphic is still whole. You can, however, compress a graphic after you crop it, and in so doing truly shave off a part of the graphic and thereby decrease the size of the file you're working with, as "Compressing Pictures to Save Disk Space" explains, later in this chapter.

Removing the background

Yet another way to diddle with pictures is to use the Remove Background command. This command endeavors to locate the unessential parts of a picture so that you can remove them. In Figure 3-10, I removed the sky and then placed a rainbow image behind the skyline.

FIGURE 3-10:
Removing parts of a picture (in this case the sky).

Select a picture and follow these steps to test-drive the Remove Background command:

1. **On the Picture Format tab, click the Remove Background button.**

   The Background Removal tab opens and the parts of your picture that Office wants to remove turn a lurid shade of magenta, which you could see in Figure 3-10 if this book were in color.

2. **On the Background Removal tab, indicate what you want to keep and remove.**

   Keep your eye on what's magenta and what's not as you use these techniques, and consider zooming to 200 percent or more so that you can get a good look at your picture:

   • **Changing the size of the box:** Drag the side and corner handles of the box to capture what you want to keep or remove.

- **Marking what you want to keep:** Click the Mark Areas to Keep button. The pointer changes into a pencil. Drag the pencil to indicate what you want to keep.

- **Marking what you want to remove:** Click the Mark Areas to Remove button. The pointer changes to a pencil. Drag the pencil to indicate what you want to remove.

Of course, you can click the Undo button to backtrack as you work. If you get thoroughly lost on the Background Removal tab, click the Discard All Changes button and start all over.

3. **Click the Keep Changes button when you finish marking what you want to keep and remove.**

How do you like your picture now? If it needs more work, click the Remove Background button again and diddle some more on the Background Removal tab. Click the Discard All Changes button if you want your original picture without the background removed.

Compressing Pictures to Save Disk Space

By compressing pictures, you reduce their file size and consequently the size of the file you're working on. Not all pictures can be compressed, as the "Compression" section explains, earlier in this chapter, and some types of graphics lose their integrity when they're compressed. You can't resize lossy-compressed graphics without their looking odd.

Compress pictures to make files load faster and make email messages with file attachments travel faster over the Internet. Compressing a picture file reduces its pixels per inch (ppi) setting. Follow these steps to compress pictures:

1. **Optionally, select the picture or pictures you want to compress if you want to compress only one or two; otherwise, select any picture.**

The Compress Pictures command compresses all the graphics in a file unless you select graphics first.

2. **Go to the Picture Format tab.**

3. **Click the Compress Pictures button.**

You see the Compress Pictures dialog box, as shown in Figure 3-11.

4. **Select the Apply Only to This Picture check box if you selected graphics in Step 1 that you want to compress.**

5. **Click the Delete Cropped Areas of Pictures check box if you want to delete the unused portions of pictures you cropped.**

As "Cropping off part of a picture" explains, earlier in this chapter, Office crops graphics in name only. It retains the cropped part of the graphic in case you want it back, but you can remove the cropped part as well by selecting this check box.

6. **Choose a target output for the pictures.**

These options tell Office which pixels per inch (ppi) setting to use when compressing graphics. Which setting you choose depends on where you intend to show your graphics.

7. **Click OK.**

FIGURE 3-11:
Compress
pictures to
reduce file sizes.

Chapter **4**

Drawing and Manipulating Lines, Shapes, and Other Objects

Office 365 comes with drawing commands for drawing lines, arrows, shapes, block arrows, stars, banners, and callout shapes. And Office provides numerous ways to manipulate these objects after you draw them. The drawing commands are meant to bring out the artist in you. Use them to make diagrams, fashion your own ideagrams, and illustrate difficult concepts and ideas. Lines and shapes give you a wonderful opportunity to exercise your creativity. A picture is worth a thousand words, so they say, and the drawing commands give you a chance to express yourself without having to write a thousand words.

In this chapter, you discover the many ways to manipulate lines, shapes, text boxes, icons, 3-D model images, WordArt images, and graphics. You discover how to lay out these objects on a page or slide, flip them, change their colors, resize them, move them, and otherwise torture them until they look just right. You discover how to make lines and arrows, draw by freehand, draw connections between shapes, and draw ovals, squares, other shapes, and WordArt images.

Use the techniques I describe in this chapter to bring something more to your Word documents, PowerPoint presentations, and Excel worksheets: originality. With the techniques I describe in this chapter, you can bring the visual element into your work. You can communicate with images as well as words and numbers.

The Basics: Making Lines, Arrows, and Shapes

Figure 4-1 demonstrates how you can use lines, arrows, and shapes (not to mention text boxes) to illustrate ideas and concepts. Sometimes, saying it with lines and shapes is easier and more informative than saying it with words. Even in Excel worksheets, you can find opportunities to use lines, arrows, and shapes. For example, draw arrows and lines on worksheets to illustrate which cells are used to compute formulas.

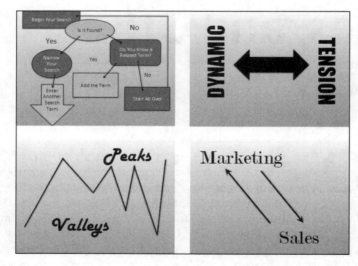

FIGURE 4-1: Exercise your creativity by including lines, arrows, and shapes in your work.

Follow these basic steps to make a line, arrow, or shape:

1. **Go to the Insert tab.**

   In Word, you must be in Print Layout view to draw and see lines and shapes.

2. **Click the Shapes button to open the Insert Shapes gallery.**

   As shown in Figure 4-2, the Shapes gallery appears. The shapes are divided into several categories, including Lines, Basic Shapes, and Block Arrows, as well as a category at the top of the gallery where shapes you chose recently are shown. (PowerPoint also offers a Shapes gallery on the Home tab.)

3. **Select a line, arrow, or shape in the Shapes gallery.**

4. **Drag on your page, slide, or worksheet.**

   As you drag, the line, arrow, or shape appears before your eyes.

5. **To alter your line, arrow, or shape — that is, to change its size, color, or outline — go to the Shape Format tab.**

   This tab offers many commands for manipulating lines and shapes. (Those commands are explained throughout this chapter.) You must select a line or shape to make the Shape Format tab appear.

   In the upper-left corner of the Shape Format tab is another Shapes gallery for creating new shapes to go along with the one you created.

FIGURE 4-2: To make a line, arrow, or shape, choose it in the Shapes gallery.

Handling Lines, Arrows, and Connectors

Earlier in this chapter, Figure 4-1 shows examples of how you can use lines and arrows to present ideas. As well as lines and arrows, the Shapes gallery offers *connectors*, the special lines that link shapes and can bend and stretch as you move shapes around. Use connectors along with lines and arrows to describe the relationships between the people or things in a diagram. These pages explain how to handle lines, arrows, and connectors.

Changing the length and position of a line or arrow

To change anything about a line or arrow, start by clicking to select it. You can tell when a line has been selected because round selection handles appear at either end. Follow these instructions to move a line or adjust its length or angle:

>> **Changing the angle of a line:** Drag a selection handle up, down, or sideways. You can see where your line will be when you release the mouse button.

>> **Changing the length:** Drag a selection handle away from or toward the opposite selection handle.

>> **Changing the position:** Move the pointer over the line itself and click when you see the four-headed arrow. Then drag the line to a new location.

Changing the appearance of a line, arrow, or connector

What a line looks like is a matter of its color, its *weight* (how wide it is), its *dash status* (it can be filled out or dashed), and its *cap* (its ends can be rounded, square, or flat). To change the appearance of a line, start by selecting it, going to the Shape Format tab, and opening the drop-down list on the Shape Outline button (this button is in the Shape Styles group). As shown in Figure 4-3, you see a drop-down list with commands for handling the appearance of lines, arrows, and connectors:

>> **Color:** Select a color on the drop-down list (refer to Figure 4-3).

>> **Width:** Choose Weight on the drop-down list (refer to Figure 4-3) and then choose a line width on the submenu. You can also choose More Lines on the submenu to open the Format Shape task pane and change the width there. Enter a Width setting in points to make the line heavier or thinner.

>> **Dotted or dashed lines:** Choose Dashes on the drop-down list and then choose an option on the submenu. Again, you can choose More Lines to open the Format Shape task pane and choose from many dash types and compound lines (refer to Figure 4-3).

>> **Line caps:** Click the Shape Styles group button to open the Format Shape task pane (refer to Figure 4-3). Then select a cap type (Square, Round, or Flat).

FIGURE 4-3:
Change the appearance of lines on the Shape Outline drop-down list and Format Shape task pane.

TIP

You can also change the appearance of a line on the Shape Format tab by opening the Shape Styles gallery and selecting a style.

Attaching and handling arrowheads on lines and connectors

Arrows, of course, have arrowheads, and arrowheads on lines and connectors can go on either side or both sides of a line. What's more, arrowheads come in different sizes and shapes. To handle arrowheads on lines and connectors, select your line or connector and go to the Shape Format tab. Then use one of these techniques to handle the arrowheads:

>> Open the drop-down list on the Shape Outline button, choose Arrows (refer to Figure 4-3), and select an arrow on the submenu.

>> Click the Shape Styles group button to open the Format Shape task pane. Then choose Arrow settings to describe where you want the arrowheads to be, what you want them to look like, and what size you want them to be.

TIP

To attach an arrowhead or arrowheads to a line or connector you've already drawn, select the line and proceed as though you were attaching arrowheads to a line that already has an arrow.

Connecting shapes by using connectors

Under Lines, the Shapes gallery offers six different connectors. Use *connectors* to link shapes and text boxes to form a diagram. Connectors differ from conventional lines in an important way: After you attach one to a shape, it stays with the shape when you move the shape. You don't have to worry about remaking all the connections after you move a shape. You can move shapes at will and let the connectors between shapes take care of themselves.

Figure 4-4 shows three types of connectors in action. (By the way, if you came here to explore how to make a diagram, be sure to check out Chapter 2 of this minibook as well. It explains Office SmartArt diagramming.)

WARNING

To connect shapes in Word, the shapes must be on the drawing canvas. Book 2, Chapter 6 describes the Word drawing canvas. (On the Insert tab, click the Shapes button and choose New Drawing Canvas to create one.)

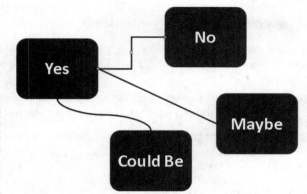

FIGURE 4-4:
The three types of connectors (from top to bottom): elbow, straight, and curved.

Making the connection

Before you draw the connections, draw the shapes and arrange them on the slide where you want them to be in your diagram. Then follow these steps to connect two shapes with a connector:

1. **Select the two shapes that you want to connect.**

   To select the shapes, hold down the Ctrl key and click each one.

2. **On the Shape Format tab, open the Shapes gallery.**

3. **Under Lines, select the connector that will best fit between the two shapes you want to link together.**

4. **Move the pointer over a selection handle on one of the shapes you want to connect.**

5. **Click and drag the pointer over a selection handle on the other shape, and when you see selection handles on that shape, release the mouse button.**

When you click a connector, you see round, green selection handles on the shapes that are joined by the connector. These round handles tell you that the two shapes are connected and will remain connected when you move them.

REMEMBER

To delete a connector, click to select it and press Delete.

If your connector is attached to the wrong shape, don't despair. Select the connector, and on the Shape Format tab, click the Edit Shape button and choose Reroute Connectors. Then move the pointer over the green handle on the side of the connector that needs to be attached elsewhere, click, drag the connector elsewhere on the other shape, and release the mouse button when you see the green selection handles.

TIP

Adjusting a connector

Chances are, your connector needs adjusting to make it fit correctly between the two shapes. Click to select your connector and follow these techniques to adjust it:

>> **Changing the shape of a connector:** Drag the circle (or circles) on the connector. As you drag, the connector assumes different shapes.

>> **Changing the connector type:** Right-click the connector, choose Connector Types on the drop-down menu, and choose Straight Connector, Elbow Connector, or Curved Connector on the submenu.

>> **Handling arrows on connectors:** If the arrows on the connector aren't there, are pointing in the wrong direction, or shouldn't be there, change the arrowheads around using the same techniques you use with standard arrows. See "Attaching and handling arrowheads on lines and connectors," earlier in this chapter.

WARNING

Make sure that the connector lines in your diagram are consistent with one another. Give them the same style and appearance, or else it will be hard to make sense of your diagram.

Handling Rectangles, Ovals, Stars, and Other Shapes

Figure 4-5 illustrates how shapes can come in very handy for illustrating concepts and ideas. You can combine shapes to make your own illustrations. Apart from the standard rectangle and oval, you can draw octagons and various other "–agons," arrows, stars, and banners. You are hereby encouraged to make shapes a part of your work, and you'll be glad to know that drawing shapes is not difficult. These pages explain how to draw a shape, exchange one shape for another, change a shape's symmetry, and enter words on a shape.

FIGURE 4-5:
An example of using shapes (and connectors) to convey an idea.

WARNING

In Word, you must be in Print Layout view to draw and handle shapes. If you intend to draw more than one shape in Word, create a drawing canvas to hold the shapes (on the Insert tab, click the Shapes button and choose New Drawing Canvas). Book 2, Chapter 6 describes the drawing canvas in Word.

Drawing a shape

Follow these steps to draw a shape:

1. On the Insert tab, click the Shapes button to open the Shapes gallery.

You can also insert shapes from the Shapes gallery on the Shape Format tab.

2. Select a shape in the gallery.

If you've drawn the shape recently, you may be able to find it at the top of the gallery under Recently Used Shapes.

3. Click and drag diagonally to draw the shape, as shown at the top of Figure 4-6.

TIP

Hold down the Shift key as you drag if you want the shape to retain its proportions. For example, to draw a circle, select the Oval shape and hold down the Shift key as you draw.

Changing a shape's size and shape

Selection handles appear on the corners and sides of a shape after you select it. With the selection handles showing, you can change a shape's size and shape:

» Hold down the Shift key and drag a corner handle to change a shape's size and retain its symmetry.

» Drag a side, top, or bottom handle to stretch or scrunch a shape.

Choosing a different shape

To exchange one shape for another, select the shape and follow these steps:

1. On the Shape Format tab, click the Edit Shape button.

You can find this button in the Insert Shapes group.

2. Choose Change Shape on the drop-down list.

3. Select a new shape in the Shapes gallery.

Drag to draw a shape

Drag a yellow circle to change a shape's symmetry

FIGURE 4-6:
Drag to draw
a shape (top);
drag a yellow
circle to change a
shape's symmetry
(bottom).

Changing a shape's symmetry

A yellow circle, sometimes more than one, appears on some shapes. By dragging a circle, you can change a shape's symmetry. Figure 4-6 (shown previously), for example, shows the same shape (the Sun shape) altered to show different symmetries. Notice where the yellow circles are. By dragging a yellow circle even a short distance, you can do a lot to change a shape's symmetry.

Using a shape as a text box

Here's a neat trick: Rather than use the conventional rectangle as a text box, you can use a shape. Figure 4-7 shows examples of shapes being used as text boxes. By placing words on shapes, you can make the shapes illustrate ideas and concepts.

Follow these instructions to handle text box shapes:

>> **Entering the text:** Click in the shape and start typing. In Word, you can right-click and choose Add Text if you have trouble typing in the shape.

>> **Editing the text:** Click in the text and start editing. That's all there is to it. If you have trouble getting inside the shape to edit the text, select the shape, right-click it, and choose Edit Text on the shortcut menu.

>> **Changing the font, color, and size of text:** Select the text, right-click the text, and choose Font. Then, in the Font dialog box, choose a font, font color, and a font size for the text.

>> **Allowing the shape to enlarge for text:** You can allow the shape to enlarge and receive more text. On the Shape Format tab, click the Shape Styles group button, and in the Text Options/Text Box category of the Format Shape task pane, select the Resize Shape to Fit Text option button.

FIGURE 4-7:
Shapes can do double duty as text boxes.

TURNING A TEXT BOX INTO A TEXT BOX SHAPE

To turn a conventional text box into a text box shape, follow these instructions:

1. **Select the text box by clicking its perimeter.**

2. **On the Shape Format tab, click the Edit Shape button, choose Change Shape, and then select a shape in the Shapes gallery.**

After the conversion, you usually have to enlarge the shape to accommodate the text.

Drawing by Freehand

Visit the Draw tab in Word, PowerPoint, or Excel to draw by freehand. If you have a steady hand, you can draw on a page, slide, or worksheet. If you have a touchscreen, so much the better, because you can draw with your hand. And if your computer is equipped with a tablet and stylus, you can do some real drawing.

These pages explain how to draw lines, erase lines, and otherwise fool with a drawing until it is just so. They also explain how to draw math equations. The Draw tools work much better on a touchscreen, but if yours isn't a touchscreen, you can still draw by dragging the mouse.

WARNING

To draw by freehand in Word, you must be in Print Layout view and you must draw on a drawing canvas. Click the Drawing Canvas button on the Draw tab to create a drawing canvas. Book 2, Chapter 6 describes the drawing canvas in Word.

Freehand drawing with a pen or highlighter

Follow these steps to draw on a page, slide, or worksheet with a pen, pencil, or highlighter:

1. Go to the Draw tab.

2. In the Pens gallery, choose a pen, pencil, or highlighter.

As shown in Figure 4-8, use one of these techniques:

- Tap or click the pen or highlighter you want.

- Tap or click the down arrow on a pen or highlighter. From the menu that appears, choose a line thickness and line color.

3. Drag onscreen with your finger or the mouse.

As you make your drawing, you can return to the Pens gallery and choose different drawing tools, colors, and lines types.

4. Press Esc when you finish drawing by freehand.

Changing the look of freehand drawings

Not that you necessarily want to open this can of worms, but you can edit drawings. Starting on the Draw tab, here are instructions for changing the look and appearance of drawings:

Choose a pen, pencil, or highlighter

FIGURE 4-8:
Visit the Draw tab to make freehand drawings.

>> **Selecting a line:** Click the Select button (the arrow) and tap or click the line. Round selection handles appear to show the line is selected.

>> **Selecting more than one line:** Hold down the Ctrl key and tap or click lines. You can also tap or click the Lasso Select button and drag slantwise across the drawing.

>> **Erasing a line:** Tap or click the Eraser button and then tap or click Eraser or Point Eraser on the drop-down menu. Then tap or click to erase. Use the Eraser command to erase complete lines; use the Point Eraser command to erase part of a line. When you finish erasing, tap or click the Eraser button again (or press Esc). In Word and PowerPoint, you can open the drop-down list on the Eraser button to choose erasers of different sizes.

>> **Resizing:** After you select a line, use one of these techniques to resize it:

   ● Drag a corner handle to change a shape's size and retain its symmetry.

   ● Drag a side, top, or bottom handle to stretch or scrunch it.

>> **Moving:** After you select a line, move the pointer on top of it. When you see the four-headed arrow, start dragging.

>> **Rotating:** Select a line and drag its Rotate button.

>> **Deleting:** Select a line and press Delete.

Drawing a math expression

The Insert tab offers the Equation Editor (click the Equation button) for writing mathematical equations, and you're welcome to give it a spin, but much more useful than the Equation Editor is another tool on the Draw tab called Math Input Control. As shown in Figure 4-9, you can use it to construct mathematical expressions.

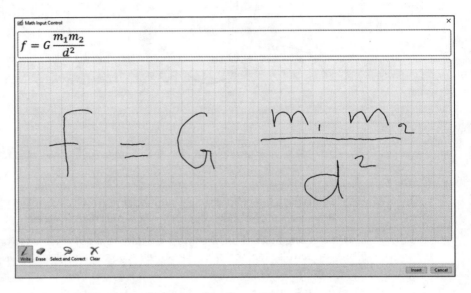

FIGURE 4-9: Writing a math expression.

To write a math expression, go to the Draw tab, tap or click the Ink to Math button, and choose Open Ink Equation Editor on the submenu. The Math Input Control dialog box appears (refer to Figure 4-9). Keep your eye on the Preview area while you follow these instructions to construct your equation:

» **Writing:** Tap or click the Write button and drag onscreen to write your expression.

» **Erasing numbers and symbols:** Tap or the Erase button and drag to erase a number or symbol.

» **Correcting errors:** If the Ink Equation Editor enters the wrong number or symbol, tap or click the Select and Correct button and then tap or click the part of the expression that is incorrect. A drop-down menu appears. If the correct number or symbol is on the menu, select it.

» **Erasing the expression:** Tap or click the Clear button to wipe the slate clean and start anew.

Click the Insert button to land the equation on an Excel worksheet, Word page, or PowerPoint slide.

Decorating Your Work with Icons

Does your Word page, PowerPoint slide, or Excel worksheet need decorating? If it does, consider tossing in a decorative icon like the ones shown in Figure 4-10. Office offers dozens of them.

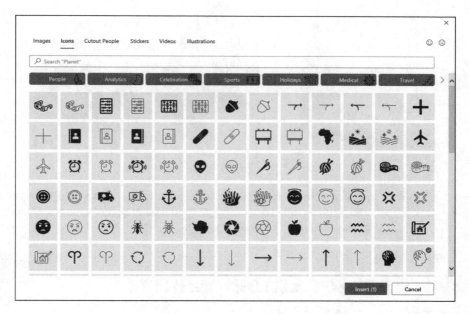

FIGURE 4-10:
Icons aplenty in the Insert Icons dialog box.

To insert an icon, go to the Insert tab and click the Icons button. A dialog box appears so you can choose an icon (refer to Figure 4-10). Select an icon and click the Insert button.

Treat your icon as you would any other object — a shape, a photo, or a graphic. Later in this chapter, "Manipulating Lines, Shapes, Art, Text Boxes, and Other Objects" explains how to resize, reshape, and reposition objects, icons included.

Inserting a 3-D Model

In Office lingo a 3-D model is a kind of graphic that you can rotate, turn, and present from different angles. Figure 4-11 shows an example of a 3-D model. By dragging the rotation icon, you can view the 3-D model in different ways.

Drag the rotation icon to view the model differently

FIGURE 4-11:
An example of a
3-D model.

If you want to experiment with 3-D models, go to the Insert tab and click the 3D Models button. The Online 3D Models dialog box appears. Select a 3-D model and click the Insert button.

WordArt for Embellishing Letters and Words

WordArt gives you the opportunity to decorate letters and words like letters and words on a birthday cake. Figure 4-12 shows the WordArt gallery, where WordArt is made, and an example of WordArt in action. After you insert WordArt, you can fool with the WordArt Styles buttons on the (Drawing Tools) Format tab and embellish the word or phrase even further.

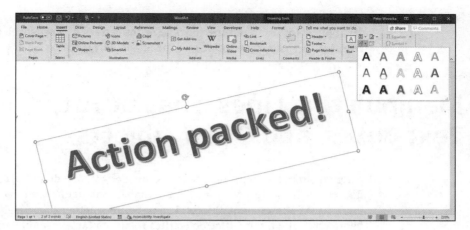

FIGURE 4-12:
A WordArt image.

Creating WordArt

Follow these steps to create WordArt:

1. On the Insert tab, click the WordArt button.

In Excel, the button is called Insert WordArt. A drop-down list with WordArt styles appears.

2. Select a WordArt style.

Don't worry about selecting the right style; you can choose a different one later on.

3. Enter text in the WordArt text box.

Congratulations. You just created WordArt.

Editing WordArt

Usually, you have to wrestle with WordArt before it comes out right. Select the words, go to the Shape Format tab, and use these techniques to win the wrestling match:

>> **Editing the words:** Click in the WordArt text box and edit the text there.

>> **Choosing a new WordArt style:** Open the WordArt Styles gallery and choose a style.

>> **Changing the letters' color:** Click the Text Fill button and choose a color on the drop-down list.

>> **Changing the letters' outline:** Click the Text Outline button and make choices to change the letters' outline.

TIP

To apply color or an outline to some of the letters or words, select the letters or words before choosing options on the Shape Format tab.

Manipulating Lines, Shapes, Art, Text Boxes, and Other Objects

After you insert a shape, line, text box, image, graphic, diagram, chart, or embedded object in a file, it ceases being what it was before and becomes an *object.* Figure 4-13 shows eight objects. I'm not sure whether these eight objects resent being objectified, but Office objectifies them. As far as manipulating these items in Office is concerned, these are just objects.

FIGURE 4-13: Examples of objects.

The techniques for manipulating objects are the same whether you're dealing with a line, shape, graphic, diagram, or text box. The good news from your end is that you have to master only one set of techniques for handling these objects. Whether you want to move, change the size of, change the color of, or change the outline of a text box, graphic, or shape, the techniques are the same.

In the remainder of this chapter are instructions for doing these tasks with objects:

» **Selecting:** Before you can do anything to objects, you have to select them. See "Selecting objects so that you can manipulate them."

» **Making use of the rulers and grid:** Rulers (in Word, PowerPoint, Excel, and Publisher) and the grid (in Word and PowerPoint) can be very helpful for aligning and placing objects. See "Hiding and displaying the rulers and grid."

» **Changing an object's size and shape:** You can enlarge, shrink, stretch, and scrunch objects to make them wider or taller. See "Changing an object's size and shape."

>> **Applying color:** Changing an object's color makes it stand out. You can apply patterns to some objects. See "Changing an Object's Color, Outline Color, and Transparency."

>> **Moving and positioning:** You can land objects with precision in a Word document, PowerPoint slide, or Excel worksheet. See "Moving and Positioning Objects."

>> **Aligning and distributing:** Another way to move and position objects is to realign or redistribute them across a page, slide, or worksheet. See "Tricks for aligning and distributing objects."

>> **Overlapping:** When you're dealing with several objects, they're bound to overlap — and sometimes overlapping objects make for an interesting effect. On the right side of Figure 4-13, for example, several objects overlap and give the impression that they were "dropped there." See "When objects overlap: Choosing which appears above the other," later in this chapter, to handle overlapping objects.

>> **Rotating and flipping:** Viewers turn their heads when they see an object that has been flipped or rotated. You can rotate and flip shapes, lines, text boxes, graphics, and WordArt images. See "Rotating and flipping Objects."

>> **Grouping:** To make working with several different objects easier, you can *group* them so that they become a single object. After objects have been grouped, manipulating them — manipulating it, I should say — is easier. See "Grouping objects to make working with them easier," later in this chapter.

If you sighed after you finished reading this long list, I don't blame you. But be of good cheer: Most of these commands are easy to pick up, and including lines, shapes, text boxes, WordArt images, and graphics in your work is a good way to impress your friends and intimidate your enemies.

Selecting objects so that you can manipulate them

Before you can move or change the border of a graphic, text box, or other object, you have to select it. To select an object, simply click it. Sometimes, to align or decorate several objects simultaneously, you have to select more than one object at the same time. To select more than one object:

>> Ctrl+click them. In other words, hold down the Ctrl key as you click the objects.

>> On the Home tab, click the Select button and choose Select Objects on the drop-down list. Then click on one side of the objects you want to select and drag the pointer across the other objects.

>> Display the Selection pane. It lists objects on the drawing canvas (Word), slide (PowerPoint), or worksheet (Excel). You can click or Ctrl+click object names in the pane to select objects. Figure 4-14 shows the Selection pane. Select an object and use one of these techniques to open the Selection pane:

- On the Shape Format tab or Picture Format tab, click the Selection Pane button.

- On the Home tab, click the Select button and choose Selection Pane on the drop-down list. (You may have to click the Editing button first, depending on the size of your screen.)

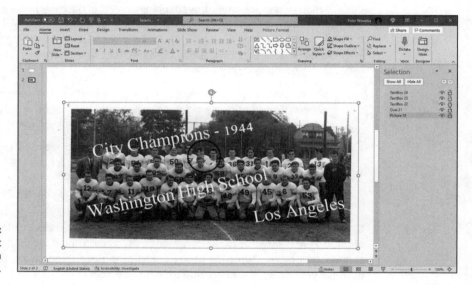

FIGURE 4-14:
Click an object in the Selection pane to select it.

REMEMBER

After you select an object, its selection handles appear. Objects have eight selection handles, one at each corner and one at each side. To tell whether an object is selected, look for its selection handles.

Hiding and displaying the rulers and grid

Word, PowerPoint, and Excel offer two rulers, one along the top of the window and one along the left side. Use the rulers to help place and align objects. To display or hide these rulers, use one of these techniques:

>> On the View tab, click the Ruler check box. (You may have to click the Show button first, depending on the size of your screen.) To see the rulers, you must be in Print Layout view In Word and Page Layout view in Excel.

>> In PowerPoint, you can also hide or display rulers by right-clicking a slide (but not an object or frame) and choosing Ruler on the shortcut menu.

The grid can come in very handy for aligning objects. On the View tab, click the Gridlines check box to see the grid. (You may have to click the Show button first.) The grid settings in PowerPoint are quite sophisticated (see Book 4, Chapter 4 for details).

TIP

By the way, fans of the metric system will be pleased to know that you can display centimeters (or millimeters, points, or picas) on the ruler instead of inches. On the File tab, choose Options. In the Options dialog box, go to the Advanced category, open the Show Measurements in Units Of drop-down list, and choose a unit of measurement.

Changing an Object's Size and Shape

Usually when an object arrives onscreen, you have to wrestle with it. You have to change its size (and sometimes its shape as well). Figure 4-15 demonstrates how to resize an object. Select your object and use one of these methods to change its size and shape:

>> **"Eyeball it":** Hold down the Shift key and drag a *corner* selection handle to make the object larger or smaller but maintain its proportions. Drag a selection handle on the *side* to stretch or crimp an object and change its shape as well as its size.

>> **Enter height and width measurements:** On the Format tab, enter measurements in the Height and Width boxes (see Figure 4-15). Depending on the size of your screen, you may have to click the Size button before you can see these boxes.

>> **Open the Format task pane or Layout dialog box:** Click the Size group button on the Format tab to open the Format task pane (in PowerPoint and Excel) or the Layout dialog box (in Word). Then change the Height and Width settings (see Figure 4-15).

TIP

Whether you can change an object's shape as well as its size depends on whether the object's aspect ratio is *locked.* If you're wrestling with an object and it won't do your bidding — if it refuses to change shape or it changes shape, and you don't want it to do that — unlock its aspect ratio setting. Click the Size group button, and in the task pane or dialog box that appears, select or deselect the Lock Aspect Ratio check box. When an object's aspect ratio is *locked,* it maintains its shape as you change its size, but when it's *unlocked,* you can change its shape as well as its size.

Drag a selection handle...   or enter measurements

FIGURE 4-15:
Ways to resize
an object.

TIP

You can change the size and shape of several objects at one time by selecting all the objects before giving a command to change sizes. Being able to change objects' size this way is convenient when you want to change the size of many objects but maintain their relationships to one another.

Changing an Object's Color, Outline Color, and Transparency

If an object's color doesn't suit you, you have the right to change colors. For that matter, you can opt for a "blank" object with no color or make the object semi-transparent. As the saying goes, "It's a free country."

Office has its own lingo when it comes to an object's color. Remember these terms when you make like Picasso with your shapes, text boxes, and graphics:

>> **Fill colors:** The color that fills in an object is called the *fill*. You can apply fill color to shapes, text boxes, and WordArt, but not pictures. Besides colors, you can use a picture, gradient, or texture as the fill. (See the next topic in this chapter, "Filling an object with color, a picture, or a texture.")

>> **Outline colors:** The line that goes around the perimeter of an object is called the *outline*. You can choose a color, style, and line width for outlines. (See "Putting the outline around an object," later in this chapter.)

REMEMBER

The easiest way to decorate a shape, text box, or WordArt image is to visit the Format tab and make a selection in the Styles gallery. These ready-made gallery selections can spare you the work of dealing with fill color and, outlines. Just remember not to mix and match different Style options; use them with consistency.

Filling an object with color, a picture, or a texture

Shapes, text boxes, and WordArt images are empty when you first create them, but you can fill them with a color, picture, gradient, or texture by following these basic steps:

1. Select the object that needs a facelift.

2. Apply a color, picture, gradient, or texture to the object.

Use one of these application techniques:

- On the Format tab, click the Shape Fill button. Then, on the drop-down list, choose a color, picture, gradient, or texture.

- Click the Shape Styles group button to open the Format task pane, as shown in Figure 4-16. Then choose a color, picture, gradient, or texture.

Click the Shape Fill button and choose No Fill to remove the color, picture, gradient, or texture from an object.

Click the Shape Styles group button...   to open the Format task pane

FIGURE 4-16:
Shape fills (from left to right): color, picture, gradient, and texture.

Figure 4-16 shows the same object filled with a color, picture, gradient, and texture. Which do you prefer? Your choices are as follows:

>> **Color:** Applies a single color to the object.

>> **Picture:** Places a picture in the object. You see the Insert Pictures dialog box, where you can search for and select a picture.

>> **Gradient:** Applies gradient color shading to the object. You can choose between various shading styles.

>> **Texture:** Offers 24 patterns meant to simulate various surfaces. The choices include Granite, Paper Bag, and Pink Tissue Paper. Be sure to use the scroll bar to see all the choices.

>> **Pattern:** Applies a pattern to the object. Select Pattern Fill in the Format task pane and then choose a pattern.

Making a color transparent

TIP

A transparent color is like gauze because instead of being solid, it shows what's behind it. Transparent colors are especially useful in text boxes because the text shows through and can be read easily. Follow these steps to make the fill color in a text box, shape, or WordArt image transparent or semi-transparent:

1. **Right-click the object and choose Format.**

The Format task pane opens (see Figure 4-16).

2. **In the Fill category, drag the Transparency slider to choose how transparent a color you want.**

At 100%, the color is completely transparent and, in fact, not there; at 1%, the color is hardly transparent at all.

You can also make a graphic transparent by recoloring it. See Chapter 3 of this minibook.

USING THE EYEDROPPER TO SELECT AN ONSCREEN COLOR (POWERPOINT ONLY)

Suppose you become enamored of a color that you see on your screen and you want to apply this color to an object. For example, suppose you want to apply the particular shade of yellow in your company logo to a shape. Using the eyedropper, you can select the color you like so well and apply it to an object on a page or slide. Follow these steps:

1. **Select the text box, shape, slide, WordArt image, or other object that needs recoloring.**

2. **On the Format tab, click the Shape Fill button and choose Eyedropper on the drop-down list.**

   The pointer changes to an eyedropper.

3. **Move the eyedropper over the onscreen color that you want for the object you selected in Step 1.**

   How you move the eyedropper depends on where the color you want is located on the screen.

   If the onscreen color is on a PowerPoint slide, simply move the eyedropper over the color.

   If the onscreen color is outside your PowerPoint application — if it's on a web page, for example — hold down the left mouse button as you drag the eyedropper outside the PowerPoint window. Drag the eyedropper until it is over the color you want.

   A pop-up color box shows the color that the eyedropper is on, the name of the color, and the color's RGB (red green blue) settings.

4. **Click when the pop-up color box shows you the color you want for the object you selected in Step 1.**

   The object you selected in Step 1 gets the new color.

Putting the outline around an object

The *outline* is the line that runs around the perimeter of an object. Put an outline color around an object to give it more definition or make it stand out. Figure 4-17 shows examples of outlines. What a shape outline looks like has to do with the color, width, and dash style you choose for it.

FIGURE 4-17:
An object's outline has to do with its color, width, and dash type.

Follow these steps to change an object's outline:

1. **Select the object.**

2. **Change the outline.**

Use one of these techniques to change the outline:

- On the Format tab, click the Shape Outline button. Then, on the drop-down list, choose a color, weight, and dash type.

- Click the Shape Styles group button to open the Format task pane (see Figure 4-17). Then, under Line, choose a color, width, and dash type.

To remove the outline from an object, click the Shape Outline button and choose No Outline or choose No Line in the Format task pane.

Moving and Positioning Objects

Moving objects is considerably easier than moving furniture. Select the object you want to reposition and use one of these techniques to land it in the right place:

- **Dragging:** Move the pointer over the perimeter of the object, click when you see the four-headed arrow, and drag the object to a new location. Hold down the Shift key as you drag to move an object either horizontally or vertically in a straight line.

- **Using a task pane or dialog box (in PowerPoint and Word):** On the Format tab, click the Size group button. (Depending on the size of your screen, you may have to click the Size button first.) You see the Format task pane or Layout dialog box. On the Position category or tab, enter Horizontal and Vertical position measurements to place the object on the slide or page.

- **Nudging:** If you can't quite fit an object in the right place, try using a Nudge command. Nudge commands move objects up, down, left, or right. Press one of the arrow keys ($\uparrow$, $\downarrow$, $\leftarrow$, $\rightarrow$) to move the object a little bit. Hold down the Ctrl key as you press an arrow key to make the object move by tiny increments.

TIP

Use the task pane or dialog box method of positioning objects when you want objects to be in the exact same position on different pages or slides.

Tricks for aligning and distributing objects

When several objects appear in the same place, use the Align and Distribute commands to give the objects an orderly appearance. You can make your Word page, PowerPoint slide, or Excel worksheet look tidier by aligning the objects or by distributing them so that they are equidistant from one another. Office offers special commands for doing these tasks.

Aligning objects

The Align commands come in handy when you want objects to line up with one another. Suppose you need to align several shapes. As shown in Figure 4-18, you can use an Align command to line up the shapes with precision. You don't have to tug and pull, tug and pull until the shapes are aligned with one another. In the figure, I used the Align Top command to line up the shapes along the top. In Word and PowerPoint, besides aligning objects with respect to one another, you can align objects or with respect to the page (in Word) or the slide (in PowerPoint). For example, you can line up objects along the top of a slide.

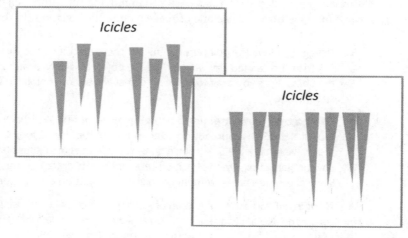

FIGURE 4-18:
Use the Align commands to align objects. These objects are aligned along the top.

Follow these steps to line up objects:

1. **Move the objects where you roughly want them to be, and if you want to align objects with respect to one another, move one object to a point that the others will align to.**

When Office aligns objects with respect to one another, it aligns them to the object in the leftmost, centermost, rightmost, topmost, middlemost, or bottommost position, depending on which Align command you choose.

2. **Select the objects you want to align.**

Earlier in this chapter, "Selecting objects so that you can manipulate them" looks at selection techniques.

3. **Go to the Format tab.**

   You can also go to the Layout tab in Word.

4. **Click the Align button, and on the drop-down list, choose whether to align the objects with respect to one another or with respect to the page or page margin (in Word) or a slide (in PowerPoint).**

   Depending on the size of your screen, you may have to click the Arrange button to get to the Align button.

5. **Click the Align button again and choose an Align command — Left, Center, Right, Top, Middle, or Bottom.**

6. **If necessary, drag the objects on the page.**

   That's right — drag them. After you give an Align command, the objects are still selected, and you can drag to adjust their positions.

Distributing objects so that they are equidistant

The Distribute commands — Distribute Horizontally and Distribute Vertically — come in handy for laying out objects on a page or slide. These commands arrange objects so that the same amount of space appears between each one. Rather than go to the trouble of pushing and pulling objects until they are distributed evenly, you can simply select the objects and choose a Distribute command.

Figure 4-19 demonstrates how the Distribute commands work. In the figure, I chose the Distribute Horizontally command so that the same amount of horizontal (side-by-side) space appears between the objects. Distributing objects such as these on your own is a waste of time when you can use a Distribute command.

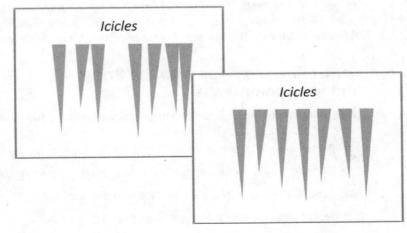

FIGURE 4-19:
The Distribute commands rearrange objects so that the same amount of space is between them.

Follow these steps to distribute objects horizontally or vertically on a page or slide:

1. **Arrange the objects so that the outermost objects — the ones that will go on the top and bottom or left side and right side — are where you want them to be.**

   In other words, if you want to distribute objects horizontally across a page, place the leftmost object and rightmost object where you want them to be. Office will distribute the other objects equally between the leftmost and rightmost object.

2. **Select the objects.**

3. **Go to the Format tab.**

   You can also go to the Layout tab in Word.

4. **Click the Align button and choose a Distribute option on the drop-down list.**

   To find the Align button, you may have to click the Arrange button first, depending on the size of your screen.

When objects overlap: Choosing which appears above the other

On a page or slide that is crowded with text boxes, shapes, and graphics, objects inevitably overlap, and you have to decide which object goes on top of the stack and which on the bottom. In a Word document, you have to decide as well whether text appears above or below objects.

Objects that deliberately overlap can be interesting and attractive to look at. On the right side of Figure 4-20, for example, a graphic image and text box appear in front of a shape. Makes for a nice effect, no? These pages explain controlling how objects overlap with the Bring and Send commands and the Selection pane.

Controlling overlaps with the Bring and Send commands

Word, PowerPoint, and Excel offer these commands for handling objects in a stack:

>> **Bring Forward:** Moves the object higher in the stack

>> **Bring to Front:** Moves the object in front of all other objects in the stack

>> **Send Backward:** Moves the object lower in the stack

>> **Send to Back:** Moves the object behind all other objects

Select an object   Choose a Bring or Send command

FIGURE 4-20:
An example
of objects
overlapping.

Word offers these additional commands:

>> **Bring in Front of Text:** Moves the object in front of text on the page

>> **Send Behind Text:** Moves the object behind text on the page so that the text
appears over the object

Select an object and use one of these techniques to give a Bring or Send command:

>> On the Format tab, click the Bring Forward or Send Backward button, or open
the drop-down list on one of these buttons and choose a Bring or Send
command (refer to Figure 4-20). Depending on the size of your screen, you
may have to click the Arrange button before you can get to a Bring or
Send command.

In Word, the Bring and Send commands are also available on the Layout tab;
in Excel, they are available on the Page Layout tab; in PowerPoint, they are
also available on the Home tab, although you may have to click the Arrange
button first, depending on the size of your screen.

>> Right-click an object and choose a Bring or Send command on the shortcut
menu.

WARNING

In Word, you can't choose a Bring or Send command unless you've chosen a text-
wrapping option apart from In Line with Text for the object. Select your object, go
to the Format tab, click the Text Wrap button, and choose an option on the drop-
down list apart from In Line with Text. Book 2, Chapter 6 looks at text wrapping
in Word.

If an object on the bottom of the stack shows through after you place it on the bottom, the object on the top of the stack is transparent or semi-transparent. Transparent objects are like gauze curtains — they reveal what's behind them. If you want to make the object on the top of the stack less transparent, see "Making a color transparent," earlier in this chapter.

Controlling overlaps with the Selection pane

Another way to control how objects overlap is to open the Selection pane, select an object, and click the Bring Forward or Send Backward button as necessary to move the object up or down in the stack. Earlier in this chapter, "Selecting objects so that you can manipulate them" explains the Selection pane. (On the Format tab, click the Selection Pane button to open it.)

Rotating and flipping objects

Rotating and flipping objects — that is, changing their orientation — is a neat way to spruce up a page or slide, as Figure 4-21 demonstrates. You can rotate and flip these kinds of objects: lines, shapes, text boxes, graphics, and WordArt images. To flip or rotate an object, select it and do one of the following:

>> **Roll your own:** Drag the object's *rotation handle,* the semicircle that appears after you select it. Hold down the Shift key as you drag to rotate the shape by 15-degree increments.

>> **Choose a Rotate or Flip command:** On the Format tab, click the Rotate button and choose an option on the drop-down list (refer to Figure 4-21). The Rotate commands rotate objects by 90 degrees; the Flip commands flip objects over. The Rotate button is also found on the Layout tab (in Word), the Page Layout tab (in Excel), and the Home tab (in PowerPoint). You may have to click the Arrange button to see the Rotate button, depending on the size of your screen.

>> **Open the Format task pane or Layout dialog box:** On the Rotate drop-down list, choose More Rotation Options to open the Format task pane or Layout dialog box. Enter a degree measurement in the Rotation text box.

To rotate several objects simultaneously, Ctrl+click to select each object and then give a rotation command.

Drag the rotation handle...   or choose a Rotate or Flip command

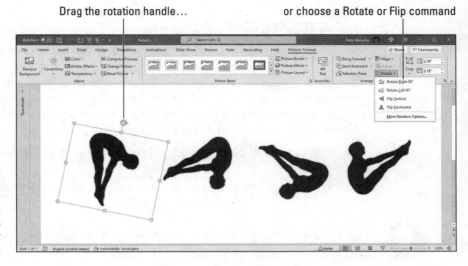

FIGURE 4-21:
Members of an
audience turn
their heads
when objects
are rotated or
flipped.

Grouping objects to make working with them easier

Consider the graphic image, shape, and text box in Figure 4-22. To move, resize, or reshape these objects, I would have to laboriously move them one at a time — that is, I would have to do that if it weren't for the Group command.

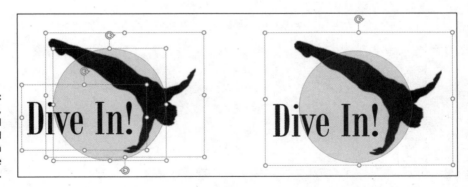

FIGURE 4-22:
You can move,
resize, and
reshape grouped
objects as though
they were a single
object.

The Group command assembles different objects into a single object to make moving, resizing, and reshaping objects easier. With the Group command, you select the objects that you want to "group" and then you wrap them into a bundle so that they become easier to work with.

Grouping objects

Select the objects and do one of the following to group them into one happy family:

» On the Format tab (or the Layout tab in Word, the Page Layout tab in Excel, and the Home tab in PowerPoint), click the Group button and choose Group on the drop-down list. Depending on the size of your screen, you may have to click the Arrange button to get to the Group button.

» Right-click one of the objects you selected and choose Group⇨Group.

After objects are grouped, they form a single object with the eight selection handles.

TIP

To add an object to a group, select the object and the grouped objects by Ctrl+clicking and then choose the Group command.

Ungrouping objects

To ungroup an object and break it into its components parts, perhaps to fiddle with one of the objects in the group, select the object, go to the Format tab, click the Group button, and choose Ungroup. You can also right-click and choose Group⇨Ungroup.

9

Office 365: One Step Beyond

Contents at a Glance

Chapter **1**

Customizing an Office Program

This short chapter describes a handful of things you can do to customize Office 365 programs. Don't be afraid to make like a software developer and change a program to your liking. Many people are wary of retooling Office programs, but you can always reverse the changes you make if you don't like them, as I explain throughout this chapter.

This chapter shows how to put your favorite button commands on the Ribbon and Quick Access toolbar. Instead of fishing around for your favorite commands, you can assemble them on the Ribbon or Quick Access toolbar and locate them right away. You also discover how to change around the status bar, dress up an Office program in a new set of clothes, and designate your own keyboard shortcuts in Word.

Customizing the Ribbon

As you surely know by now, the Ribbon is the stretch of ground across the top of all Office programs. The Ribbon is composed of tabs. On each tab, commands are arranged by group. To undertake a task, you visit a tab on the Ribbon, find the group with the command you want, and choose the command. If you are so inclined, you can customize the Ribbon. You can place the tabs and commands you know and love where you want to find them on the Ribbon. And you can remove tabs and commands that aren't useful to you.

To customize the Ribbon, open the Customize Ribbon tab of the Options dialog box with one of these techniques:

» On the File tab, choose Options, and select the Customize Ribbon category in the Options dialog box.

» Right-click a tab or button and choose Customize the Ribbon.

You see commands for customizing the Ribbon, as shown in Figure 1-1. The right side of the dialog box ("Customize the Ribbon") lists the names of tabs, groups within tabs, and commands within groups that are currently on the Ribbon. To customize the Ribbon, you arrange the right side of the dialog box to your liking. You display the tabs, groups, and commands that you want for the Ribbon on the right side of the dialog box.

Display tab, group, and command names   Tab name   Group name

Add or remove tabs, groups, and commands   Command names

Restore the original settings

Change the order of tabs

FIGURE 1-1: Starting in the Customize Ribbon category of the Options dialog box, you can customize the Ribbon.

The left side of the dialog box ("Choose Commands From") presents every tab, group, and command in your Office program. To customize the Ribbon, you select a tab, group, or command on the left side of the dialog box and move it to the right side by clicking the Add button.

Keep reading to find out how to display tabs, groups, and commands in the Options dialog box and how to do all else that pertains to customizing the Ribbon. In case you make a hash of the Ribbon, you also find instructions for restoring the Ribbon to its original state.

Displaying and selecting tab, group, and command names

To customize the Ribbon, you need to display and select tab names, group names, and command names in the Options dialog box (refer to Figure 1-1). Start by opening the drop-down lists and choosing a display option:

>> **Choose Commands From (left side of dialog box):** Choose an option to locate the tab, group, or command you want to add to the Ribbon. For example, choose All Commands to see an alphabetical list of all the commands in the Office program you're working in; choose Main Tabs to see a list of tabs.

>> **Customize the Ribbon (right side of dialog box):** Choose an option to display the names of all tabs, main tabs, or tool tabs. Tool tabs are the context-sensitive tabs that appear after you insert or click something. For example, the Table Tools tabs appear when you construct tables in Word.

After you choose display options on the drop-down lists, you can display the names of groups and commands (refer to Figure 1-1):

>> **Displaying group names:** Click a plus sign icon next to a tab name to see the names of its groups. You can click the minus sign icon to fold group names back into a tab name.

>> **Displaying command names in groups**: Click the plus sign icon next to a group name to see the names of its commands. You can click the minus sign icon to collapse command names.

After you display the tab, group, or command name, click to select it.

Moving tabs and groups on the Ribbon

To change the order of tabs on the Ribbon or groups on a tab, go to the Customize Ribbon category of the Options dialog box (refer to Figure 1-1) and select the name of a tab or group on the right side of the dialog box. Then drag the name or click the Move Up or Move Down button (the arrow buttons located on the right side of the dialog box). Drag or click the buttons as necessary until tabs or groups are in the order that you see fit.

WARNING

Be careful when moving groups. Move a group too far and you run the risk of moving it to a different tab on the Ribbon.

Adding, removing, and renaming tabs, groups, and commands

In the Options dialog box (refer to Figure 1-1), display and select the tab, group, or command you want to add, remove, or rename. Then proceed to add, remove, or rename it. (Earlier in this chapter, "Displaying and selecting tab, group, and command names" explains how to display items in the Options dialog box.)

Adding items to the Ribbon

Follow these steps to add a tab, group, or command to the Ribbon:

1. **On the left side of the Customize Ribbon category of the Options dialog box, select the tab, group, or command you want to add.**

For example, to add the Tables group to the Home tab, select the Tables group.

WARNING

Commands can be added only to custom groups. To add a command to the Ribbon, create a new group for the command (see "Creating new tabs and groups," later in this chapter).

2. **On the right side of the dialog box, select the tab or custom group where you want to place the item.**

If you're adding a tab to the Ribbon, select a tab. The tab you add will go after the tab you select.

3. **Click the Add button.**

Removing items from the Ribbon

Follow these steps to remove a tab, group, or command from the Ribbon:

1. **On the right side of the Customize Ribbon category of the Options dialog box, select the tab, group, or command you want to remove.**

2. **Click the Remove button.**

Except for tabs you create yourself, you can't remove tabs from the Ribbon. And you can't remove a command unless you remove it from a group you created yourself.

Renaming tabs and groups

Sorry, you can't rename a command. Follow these steps to rename a tab or group:

1. **On the right side of the Customize Ribbon category of the Options dialog box, select the tab or group you want to rename.**

2. **Click the Rename button.**

You see the Rename dialog box, as shown in Figure 1-2.

3. **Enter a new name and click OK.**

When renaming a group that you created yourself, you can choose a symbol for the group in the Rename dialog box (see Figure 1-2).

FIGURE 1-2:
Renaming a tab (left) and a group (right).

Creating new tabs and groups

Create new tabs and groups on the Ribbon for commands that are especially useful to you. Follow these steps on the Customize Ribbon category of the Options dialog box (refer to Figure 1-1) to create a new tab or group:

1. **On the right side of the dialog box, display and select the name of a tab or group.**

Earlier in this chapter, "Displaying and selecting tab, group, and command names" explains how to select items in the Options dialog box.

- **Tab:** If you're creating a tab, select a tab name. The tab you create will appear after the tab you select.

- **Group:** If you're creating a group, select a group name. The group you create will appear after the group you select.

2. **Click the New Tab or New Group button.**

Your Office program creates a new tab or group called "New Tab (Custom)" or "New Group (Custom)." If you created a tab, Office also creates a new group inside your new tab.

3. **Click the Rename button to give the tab, group, or both a name.**

In the Rename dialog box, enter a descriptive name and click OK. If you're naming a group, the Rename dialog box gives you the opportunity to select an icon to help identify the group (see Figure 1-2).

4. **Add groups, commands, or both to your newly made tab or group.**

For instructions, see "Adding items to the Ribbon," earlier in this chapter.

Resetting your Ribbon customizations

If you make a hash of the Ribbon, all is not lost because you can restore the original settings. In the Options dialog box, click the Reset button (refer to Figure 1-1) and choose one of these commands on the drop-down list:

» **Reset Only Selected Ribbon Tab:** Select a tab name on the right side of the Options dialog box and choose this command to restore a tab to its original state.

» **Reset All Customizations:** Choose this command to restore the Ribbon in its entirety. All changes you made are reversed.

You can also remove tabs and groups you created if you discover you don't need them. See "Removing items from the Ribbon," earlier in this chapter.

EXPORTING AND IMPORTING PROGRAM CUSTOMIZATIONS

You can preserve your Ribbon and Quick Access toolbar customizations for posterity in a special file called an Import Customization file; these files have the `.exportedUI` file extension. Keep the file on hand for when you need it, or distribute the file to coworkers. For that matter, a coworker who is proud of his or her customizations can send them to you in a file and you can load the customizations into your Office program.

To save your Ribbon and Quick Access toolbar customization settings in a file, go to the File tab, choose Options, and visit to the Customize Ribbon or Quick Access toolbar category of the Options dialog box. Then click the Import/Export button and choose Export All Customizations on the drop-down list. The File Save dialog box opens. Give the customizations file a name and click the Save button.

To load customizations from a file into your Office program, return to the Customize Ribbon or Quick Access toolbar category of the Options dialog box, click the Import/Export button, and choose Import Customization File. You see the File Open dialog box. Select the file and click the Open button.

Customizing the Quick Access Toolbar

No matter where you go in Office, you see the Quick Access toolbar in the upper-left corner of the screen. This toolbar offers the AutoSave and Save buttons. However, which buttons appear on the Quick Access toolbar is entirely up to you. You can put your favorite buttons on the toolbar to keep them within reach. And if the Quick Access toolbar gets too big, you can move it below the Ribbon, as shown in Figure 1-3. Adding buttons to and removing buttons from the Quick Access toolbar is, I'm happy to report, a piece of cake. And moving the toolbar below the Ribbon is as easy as pie.

Adding buttons to the Quick Access toolbar

Use one of these techniques to add buttons to the Quick Access toolbar:

>> Right-click a button you want to see on the toolbar and choose Add to Quick Access toolbar on the shortcut menu (refer to Figure 1-3). You can add all the commands in a group to the Quick Access toolbar by right-clicking the group name and choosing Add to Quick Access toolbar.

Right-click a button to add it to the Quick Access toolbar

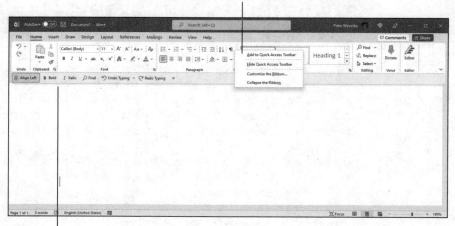

FIGURE 1-3:
Merely by right-clicking, you can add a button to the Quick Access toolbar.

The Quick Access toolbar below the Ribbon

> » Click the Customize Quick Access toolbar button (located to the right of the Quick Access toolbar) and choose a button on the drop-down list. The list offers buttons deemed most likely to be placed on the Quick Access toolbar by the makers of Office.

> » On the File tab, choose Options, and go to the Quick Access toolbar category in the Options dialog box (or right-click any button or tab and choose Customize Quick Access toolbar on the shortcut menu). You see the Quick Access toolbar category of the Options dialog box, as shown in Figure 1-4. On the Choose Commands From drop-down list, select the name of the button you want to add to the Quick Access toolbar. Then click the Add button.

TIP

To restore the Quick Access toolbar to its original buttons, click the Reset button in the Options dialog box (refer to Figure 1-4) and choose Reset Only Quick Access toolbar on the drop-down list. Choosing Reset All Customizations resets Ribbon customizations as well as Quick Access toolbar customizations.

Changing the order of buttons on the Quick Access toolbar

Follow these steps to change the order of buttons on the Quick Access toolbar:

1. **Click the Customize Quick Access toolbar button and choose More Commands on the drop-down list.**

Select a button   Click Add

FIGURE 1-4:
Add, remove,
and reorder
Quick Access
toolbar buttons
in the Options
dialog box.

The Quick Access toolbar category of the Options dialog box appears (refer to Figure 1-4). You can also open this dialog box by right-clicking any button or tab and choosing Customize Quick Access toolbar.

2. Select the name of a button on the right side of the dialog box and click the Move Up or Move Down button.

These arrow buttons are located on the right side of the dialog box.

3. Repeat Step 2 until the buttons are in the right order.

4. Click OK.

Removing buttons from the Quick Access toolbar

Use one of these techniques to remove buttons from the Quick Access toolbar:

» Right-click a button and choose Remove from Quick Access toolbar on the shortcut menu.

>> Right-click any button or tab and choose Customize Quick Access toolbar. You see the Quick Access toolbar category of the Options dialog box (refer to Figure 1-4). Select the button you want to remove on the right side of the dialog box and click the Remove button.

REMEMBER

You can click the Reset button in the Options dialog box (refer to Figure 1-4) to remove all the buttons you placed on the Quick Access toolbar.

Placing the Quick Access toolbar above or below the Ribbon

The Ribbon is the stretch of ground along the top of the screen where the tabs and buttons are found. If your Quick Access toolbar contains many buttons, consider placing it below the Ribbon, not above it (refer to Figure 1-3). Follow these instructions to place the Quick Access toolbar above or below the Ribbon:

>> **Quick Access toolbar below the Ribbon:** Right-click the toolbar, and on the shortcut menu, choose Show Quick Access toolbar Below the Ribbon.

>> **Quick Access toolbar above the Ribbon:** Right-click the toolbar, and on the shortcut menu, choose Show Quick Access toolbar Above the Ribbon.

TIP

You can hide the Quick Access toolbar altogether. To do so, right-click a button on the toolbar and choose Hide Quick Access Toolbar. To see the toolbar again, right-click and choose Show Quick Access toolbar.

Customizing the Status Bar

The status bar along the bottom of the window gives you information about the file you're working on. The Word status bar, for example, tells you which page you're on, how many pages are in your document, and several other things. In PowerPoint, the status bar tells you which slide you're looking at. It also presents the view buttons and zoom controls.

To choose what appears on the status bar, right-click the status bar. You see a drop-down list similar to the one in Figure 1-5. By selecting and deselecting items in this list, you can decide what appears on the status bar.

FIGURE 1-5:
Right-click the status bar to customize it.

Changing the Screen Background and Office Theme

Starting on the Accounts screen, you can change the screen background and Office theme. The *screen background* is the fluff that appears along the top of Office application windows. The *Office theme* is the color (or lack thereof) that appears around the perimeter of Office application windows. You are encouraged to experiment with screen backgrounds and Office themes until you find a combination that works for you.

Follow these steps to choose a screen background and Office theme:

1. **On the File tab, choose Account.**

You see the Account screen, as shown in Figure 1-6.

2. **Open the Office Background drop-down list and choose an option.**

3. **Open the Office Theme drop-down menu and choose an option.**

Choosing the Black theme changes Office screens to so-called *dark mode.* Some people believe dark mode prevents eyestrain. In dark mode, text is white; it appears against a black background.

4. **Click the Back button.**

How do you like your new get-up? If you don't like it, repeat these steps until you get it right.

A screen background and Office theme you apply in one Office program applies to all the other programs as well.

REMEMBER

Customizing Keyboard Shortcuts in Word

In Microsoft Word, you can change the keyboard shortcuts. A *keyboard shortcut* is a combination of keys that you press to give a command. For example, pressing Ctrl+P opens the Print window; pressing Ctrl+S gives the Save command. If you don't like a keyboard shortcut in Word, you can change it and invent a keyboard shortcut of your own. You can also assign keyboard shortcuts to symbols, macros, fonts, building blocks, and styles.

Follow these steps to choose keyboard shortcuts of your own in Microsoft Word:

1. **On the File tab, choose Options.**

   You see the Word Options dialog box.

2. **Go to the Customize Ribbon category.**

3. **Click the Customize button (you can find it at the bottom of the dialog box next to the words "Keyboard Shortcuts").**

   You see the Customize Keyboard dialog box, as shown in Figure 1-7.

4. **In the Categories list, choose the category with the command to which you want to assign the keyboard shortcut.**

   At the bottom of the list are the Macros, Fonts, Building Blocks, Styles, and Common Symbols categories.

5. **Choose the command name, macro, font, building block, style, or symbol name in the Commands list.**

6. **In the Press New Shortcut Key box, type the keyboard shortcut.**

   Press the actual keys. For example, if the shortcut is Ctrl+8, press the Ctrl key and the 8 key — don't type C-t-r-l-+8.

   If you try to assign a shortcut that has already been assigned, the words "Currently assigned to" and a command name appear below the Current Keys box. You can override the preassigned keyboard assignment by entering a keyboard assignment of your own.

7. **If you want the keyboard shortcut changes you make to apply to the document you're working on, not to all documents created with the template you're working with, open the Save Changes In drop-down list and choose your document's name.**

8. **Click the Assign button.**

9. **When you finish assigning keyboard shortcuts, close the Customize Keyboard dialog box.**

To delete a keyboard shortcut, display it in the Current Keys box, select it, and click the Remove button.

REMEMBER

You can always get the old keyboard shortcuts back by clicking the Reset All button in the Customize Keyboard dialog box.

Select a command

FIGURE 1-7:
Assigning
keyboard
shortcuts to Word
commands.

Enter a shortcut

Chapter **2**

Ways of Distributing Your Work

This chapter explains how to distribute your work to coworkers and friends. You'll be glad to know that people who don't have Office 365 can still read and review an Office file you created. You can print it for them, save it so that it can be read in Adobe Acrobat Reader, or save it as a web page. This chapter explains all that as well as how to send a file right away by email. By the way, Book 4, Chapter 5 describes other ways to distribute PowerPoint presentations. You can provide audience handouts, save presentations as video files, and show your presentation online.

Printing — the Old Standby

As much as I wish my clunky printer didn't occupy so much space on my desk, I need it from time to time. Sometimes I have to print letters, for example. The printer is not yet obsolete. The day when all work is done digitally and is sent or viewed over the Internet is fast upon us, but it's not quite here.

To print a file, preview a file before you print it, and do all else that pertains to printing, go to the File tab and choose Print (or press Ctrl+P). You land in the Print window, as shown in Figure 2-1. From here, you can choose how many copies to print, choose a part of a file to print, and get a look at your file before you print it. Notice that the Print window offers zoom controls buttons and buttons for going from page to page (or slide to slide).

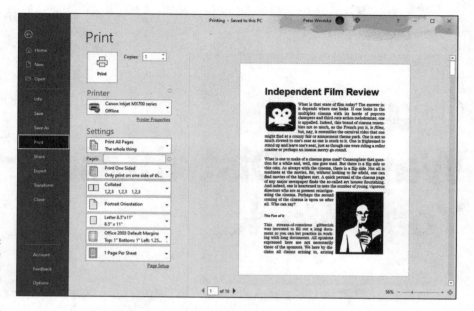

FIGURE 2-1:
Starting in the Print window, you can preview and print files.

- **Page number slider (Publisher only):** Drag this slider to make page numbers appear so that you know which page or pages you're viewing. The further you drag to the right, the more visible page numbers are. The Page number slider is located at the top of the Print window.

- **Ruler button (Publisher only):** Click the Ruler button to make page-size measurements appear. This button is located at the top of the window.

- **View Multiple Sheets button (Publisher only):** Click this button and choose an option on the drop-down list to view more than one page at a time.

Distributing a File in PDF Format

Figure 2-2 shows a PDF file in Adobe Reader, the application designed for viewing PDF (portable document format) files. The Adobe Reader application is free and easy to obtain on the Internet.

Starting in any Office application, you can save a file as a PDF. Saving an Office file as a PDF is a great way to show files to people who don't have Office 365 software. For example, someone who doesn't have Excel can view your Excel file after you save it as a PDF. Moreover, you can post PDF files on the Internet so that others can view them there.

About PDF files

PDF files are designed to be viewed and printed in web browsers and in Adobe Reader. Nearly every computer has Adobe Reader. If someone to whom you sent a PDF file doesn't have the application, they can download it for free at this web page:

```
http://get.adobe.com/reader/
```

Book 2, Chapter 2 explains how you can open and edit PDF files in Word 365.

Saving an Office file as a PDF

Follow these steps to save an Office file as a PDF file:

1. **Go to the File tab and choose Export to open the Export window.**

2. **Choose Create PDF/XPS Document.**

3. **Click the Create PDF/XPS button.**

The Publish as PDF or XPS dialog box appears. If your goal is to create an XPS file, not a PDF file, open the Save As Type drop-down list and choose XPS Document (*.xps). Microsoft created the XPS format to compete with the PDF format. As are PDF files, XPS files are meant to present data from different programs. However, the XPS format is not nearly as well known or frequently used as the PDF format.

4. **Select a folder for storing your PDF (or XPS) file, give it a name, and click the Publish button.**

Your file opens in the Edge browser application (or whatever your computer's default web browser is). You can also open it in Adobe Acrobat Reader.

Later in this chapter, "Saving an Office File as a Web Page" explains another way to distribute Office files to people who don't have Office — by saving the files as web pages.

Sending Your File in an Email Message

As long as you handle your email with Outlook, you can send the file you're working on to a friend or coworker without having to open Outlook. Moreover, you can send a PDF or XPS version of the file. You simply choose a command and send the thing over the Internet. Follow these steps to send an open file you're working on to a friend or coworker:

1. **Go to the File tab and choose Share.**

The Share window opens.

2. **Under Attach a Copy Instead, choose an Email option.**

How do you want to send your file? Click one of these buttons:

- **Send as a file:** Send the file as an attachment to an email message.

- **Send as a PDF:** Send a PDF version of the file as an attachment to an email message.

An Outlook message window appears with the name of your file on the subject line and the file itself in the Attached box. Your file is ready to send along with the email message.

3. **Enter the recipient's address in the To box and a message in the Message box.**

    Book 5, Chapter 3 explains how to address, compose, and send email messages with Outlook.

4. **Click the Send button.**

    That was fast! It was faster than opening Outlook and attaching the file to the email message on your own.

Saving an Office File as a Web Page

Figure 2-3 shows what a Word document looks like after it is saved as a web page and displayed in a web browser. Looks like a normal Word document, doesn't it? Anyone with a web browser can view a Word document or other Office file after it's saved as a web page. Save an Office file as a web page and post it on the Internet so that people who don't have Office can view it.

These pages explain how to save an Office file as a web page and open a web page you created in a web browser.

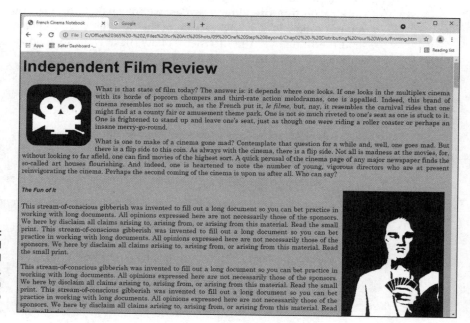

FIGURE 2-3:
A Word document saved as a web page, as seen through the eyes of a web browser.

Turning a file into a web page

Follow these steps to save an Office file as a web page:

1. **Go to the File tab and choose Export.**

   The Export window opens.

2. **Choose Change File Type.**

   Change File Type options appear, as shown in Figure 2-4.

3. **Choose the Single File Web Page option and click the Save As button.**

   The Save As dialog box opens.

4. **Click the Change Title button, enter a descriptive title in the Enter Text dialog box, and click OK.**

   The title you enter will appear in the title bar along the top of the web browser window.

5. **Choose a folder for storing your new web page.**

6. **Click the Save button.**

   If your file includes features that can't be displayed in a web browser, the Compatibility Checker dialog box tells you what those features are. Click the Continue button to create your web page.

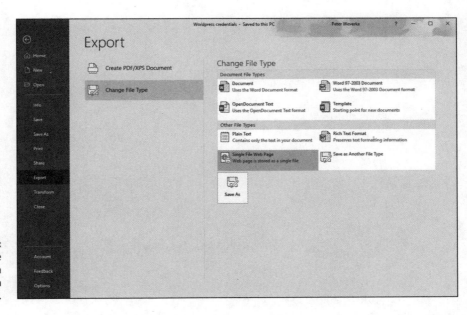

FIGURE 2-4: Change the file type to turn an Office file into a web page.

Opening a web page in your browser

To open a web page that you fashioned from an Office file, open the folder where you stored the web page in File Explorer and double-click the `.htm` file. For example, if your file is called Sales Projections, double-click the `Sales Projections.htm` file to open the web page.

10

Microsoft Teams

Contents at a Glance

Chapter **1**

Getting around in Teams

Microsoft Teams is the newest major addition to Office 365, having been introduced in 2017 as a response to the success of chat and collaboration apps like Slack and a need to modernize the online meetings experience in Skype for Business.

Initially a slow grower, Teams became popular in 2018 and 2019 and skyrocketed upon the arrival of the Covid-19 pandemic in 2020. The pandemic forced huge numbers of people to work and study remotely for an extended period. In mid-2021, Microsoft reported nearly 150 million people worldwide using the app every day.

There are differences in features and settings among the desktop, browser, and mobile apps. Differences also exist among the business, education, and government versions of Office 365. This minibook covers features that are available in the desktop app, unless otherwise specified for typical enterprise or business customers. Education and government customers have a bit different experience, but not a big one; for government, the biggest difference is the timing of feature rollouts, which are typically delayed because of compliance reviews that Microsoft must go through to meet U.S. government standards.

There is also a personal version of Teams built right into Windows 11, which is Microsoft's answer to the success of apps like iMessage and FaceTime in the Apple ecosystem. Many features of the business version of Teams are available in the personal app as well. Because things change so frequently, exact steps and screenshots in this minibook may vary from your experience or may lack the newest features, but the main principles should continue to apply.

In this chapter, you find out how to access all the major features in Teams, update and share your status, use apps and plug-ins, and find people, messages, and files.

Viva la Teams!

Welcome to Microsoft Teams, the central collaboration hub of Office 365. Although you may interact with various applications in Office 365, all of them somehow work with Teams in a way to let you communicate and collaborate centrally through Teams so that you don't have to app-hop nearly as much as you used to. With Teams, you can centralize your work while also using the tried-and-true Office 365 tools you're used to.

Taking a quick tour of Teams

Teams brings together communication, collaboration, and online meetings into a single app, complete with strong integration with most of the other Office 365 apps. Teams also has an App store that enables you to connect to additional Microsoft-created features as well as third-party tools like Evernote, Trello, YouTube, and even Zoom. Teams is fully supported on all major operating systems — Windows, macOS, iOS, iPadOS, and Android — through a dedicated app for each. You can also use a browser version of Teams on almost any desktop computer. You can easily hop between a PC at work, a Mac at home, a browser in a hotel, and an iPhone — all from the same account.

Teams provides the following features:

>> **Teams and their channels:** The namesake of the app provides a permission-protected online workspace for threaded conversations, file sharing and editing, and channel meetings. A *channel* is a subcategory of a Team, used to divide a Team into pertinent subtopics. A Team and its channels are meant to help move clunky communication and collaboration processes from your email Inbox into a centralized location, with the goal of reducing notifications overall and keeping work better organized. Chapter 2 of this minibook focuses on Teams and channels.

>> **Chat:** You use the Chat app to have one-on-one and group private chats with both colleagues and external users of Teams and Skype. Teams chat is similar to other chat apps like WhatsApp, IRC, and Skype (or even AOL Instant Messenger, if you remember that), but it has many more features than most of those other tools. Chapter 3 of this minibook focuses on how to Chat.

- » **Calls and meetings:** You can host interactive video conferences within Teams and include anyone inside or outside your organization, or simply start an audio call with a single person. Chat, share your screen, upload files, record meetings, lead webinars, and interact from your desktop or mobile device. This feature compares to Zoom but provides a lot more capabilities thanks to its deep integration with the rest of Office 365. Chapter 5 of this minibook tells you much more about meetings.

- » **Files:** Access your OneDrive, SharePoint, and Teams files right in the Files app in Teams. You can even bring in files from other services, like Dropbox and Google Drive. Chapter 4 of this minibook covers the Files app.

Introducing Microsoft Viva

If you use a personal Microsoft account (such as an outlook.com, hotmail.com, or xbox.com account), feel free to skip this section. If you're an Office 365 work or school user, you'll likely hear the term *Microsoft Viva* tossed around, so I cover it briefly. Working with Viva can be confusing, but boiled down, it consists of four modules, each of which bundles existing Office 365 tools into groupings that sell well with management, HR, training, and other internal service teams (as opposed to the typical Microsoft customer: your IT team).

Some Viva modules require additional licenses, but most do not. Most Viva experiences are built into Teams, so Teams itself is essentially the platform for Viva. Here are the four modules:

- » **Viva Connections:** Connections aims to be the "employee portal" for Office 365. Connections brings together SharePoint communication sites (your intranet) and Yammer communities into Teams through the Home and Communities app in the Teams app bar (see Figure 1-1). Talk to your IT team for more information if you're interested. Most Office 365 licenses include Connections for free.

- » **Viva Insights:** Insights provides, well, insight into how you spend your time while working and promotes a healthier mental state through break scheduling, virtual commutes, suggested focus time, and other well-being tools right in Teams. It's well-intended, but it remains to be seen whether people actually take time for something like a virtual commute. Most Office 365 licenses include Insights for free.

- » **Viva Learning:** Learning serves as a central learning center in Teams, merging internal training videos and resources with third-party tools and learning-management systems like LinkedIn Learning, Microsoft Learn, Blackboard, Coursera, and Cornerstone. Most Office 365 licenses include Learning for free, but many integrated learning platforms require their own licenses.

>> **Viva Topics:** Topics is an artificial intelligence (AI) knowledge-management tool for 1) automatically tagging content to improve search; and 2) creating topic pages about internal concepts, projects, and tools. You can think of Topics as an automatically generated internal information source. Topics is built on SharePoint Syntex, which requires an additional per-user license.

REMEMBER

Microsoft Viva is simply an additional way to group related apps and tools in Office 365. It's important to at least be aware of Viva because Viva experiences are built almost exclusively into Microsoft Teams. But it likely won't directly change how you use Teams in a big-picture sense, so don't let it confuse you.

Navigating in Teams

This section demystifies the Teams interface. Along the far-left side of the window is the *app bar*, which is the vertical pane that holds your basic Teams apps: Activity, Chat, Teams, Calendar, Calls, and Files. You can pin other Teams apps that you install to this bar as well; see "Enhancing Your Teams Experience with Helpful Extras," later in this chapter, for details.

When you click any of the apps on the app bar, Teams opens to a window showing the rail and the main area for that app. The *rail* is the jumping-off point for which app is open and typically lists the most recent or important information in that app. The *main area* contains the actual content for the app you're in. Each app in Teams deals with these areas differently, but the setup stays relatively constant. The Calendar app is the exception; it has no rail but instead takes up the whole space and displays your Office 365 calendar, which is the same calendar you use in Outlook 365. See Figure 1-1 for an overview of the areas in Teams.

REMEMBER

As you begin to move around in Teams, keep these navigation tips in mind:

>> To switch among Teams apps, click the app name in the app bar. The rail may have a title in bold type at the top, such as Teams, Feed, or Chat, depending on the app. If you see a downward-pointing caret next to the title, clicking the title opens a drop-down menu, which lets you switch views or see more information if you want.

>> If you're using the desktop app, use the Back and Forward navigation buttons just as you do when browsing the Internet. These buttons are incredibly useful but often forgotten. They show up only in the desktop app, directly above the app bar. If you're using Teams in the browser, use the browser's navigation buttons.

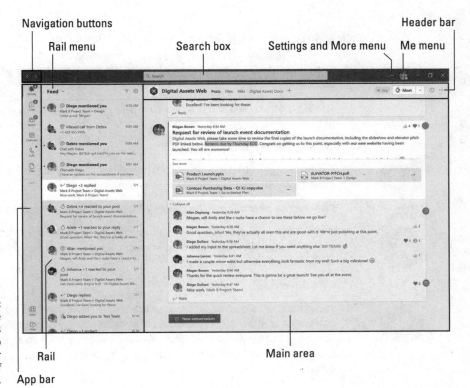

Navigation buttons

Rail menu

Search box

Settings and More menu

Header bar

Me menu

Rail

App bar

Main area

FIGURE 1-1:
You find the
various Teams
apps in the app
bar and a similar
layout in most of
the Teams apps.

Personalizing Teams to Use It Effectively

You can configure Teams to better meet your needs by choosing among the built-in settings and personalization options. The following pages cover how to add or update a profile photo, manage your status and notifications, enable dark mode, and configure your audio and video devices for meetings.

Adding a profile photo

The first thing any good Teams user should do is add a profile photo so that your peers and colleagues can attach a face to a name. Adding or updating your photo in Teams updates your profile in all Office 365 apps (though the update can take hours or days to work its way through all the apps).Your photo should be a straight-on view of your face, well lighted and with a clear contrast between your face and the background. Do not upload photos of your pets or favorite sports teams or characters, and definitely don't include family or other people. The photo should clearly be you and only you.

Getting around
in Teams

Follow these steps to upload a new or updated profile photo:

1. Click your profile photo or initials near the top-right corner of the suite bar.

The Me menu opens and displays your photo or initials, status, and other options.

2. Click Upload Picture.

A window opens to your computer's file system. Note that your profile photo must be 4MB or smaller, and I recommend 648 x 648 pixels.

3. Choose the photo from the folder where it resides on your computer.

It's best if your photo is cropped square or as close to square as possible before you upload. You can't crop or rearrange non-square photos, so do the image work before uploading.

4. Click Save.

Your face should take up as much of the profile photo circle as possible. You don't need to show off your blouse or tie, or anything that might be in the background. Many areas within the Office 365 apps where your photo will show up are small, so the more tightly the image is cropped to your face, the better.

Setting your status

After people know who you are with your new profile photo, they're probably going to want to reach out to you. You may not always be available to take their chat or call, though. That's where your Teams status comes in.

Your status appears anywhere your profile photo does in Teams, like your Me menu, a chat, or a conversation. If you do nothing with your status, it automatically shows you as available (green), away (yellow), or busy (red), depending on what you're doing. If you have an appointment on your calendar (Outlook or Teams) that lists you as busy, your status in Teams shows as busy throughout that appointment. If you're actively using your computer or mobile device in Teams and you're not booked in an appointment, you are shown as available. If you've let your computer go into idle or sleep mode, your status changes to away. See Figure 1-2 for an example.

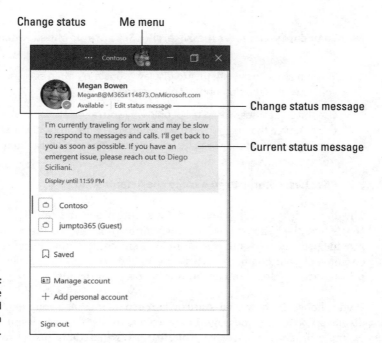

Change status   Me menu

Change status message

Current status message

FIGURE 1-2:
You can change
your status and
status message in
the Me menu.

However, you can manage your status to let people know whether you're truly free or not. You can also include a status message, which can help direct people who want to reach out to you. Follow these steps to change your status and status message:

1. **Click your profile photo or initials in the top-right corner.**

Your Me menu opens.

2. **Click your current status under your email address.**

A drop-down menu with status choices appears.

3. **Choose the status you prefer or click Duration to set a status for a certain period of time.**

The Do Not Disturb status automatically turns on when you share your screen in a meeting, so you don't have to set it during those situations. You cannot set your status as Available for a duration (probably so that people can't appear to be working when they're not).

4. **To update your status message, click Set a Status Message next to your status.**

You can also choose whether to display your status when someone messages you, as well as the duration of your message.

Use the status message to tell people why you're not available or to point them to a resource that might help them when you're not around. The status message automatically displays your out-of-office message (automatic reply) from Outlook when it's set.

5. **Click Reset Status to go back to the default setting.**

TIP

The do not disturb status blocks most notifications and calls from bothering you, so it's useful when you need a some uninterrupted focus time. However, you can provide priority access to certain individuals (maybe your boss?) so that they can circumvent your do not disturb status and get through to you. See the "Setting up priority access" section, later in this chapter, for details.

REMEMBER

If you choose to show your status when people message you, your status message displays above any message box a colleague uses to send you a message (for example, in chat or a Team). This feature is incredibly useful for ensuring that people know what to expect when they send you a message.

TIP

You can quickly set your status using slash commands. In the Teams Search box (refer to Figure 1-2), type **/available**, **/away**, **/brb**, **/busy**, **/dnd**, or **/offline** (using a forward slash mark before each word) and then press Enter. See the "Using slash commands" section, later in this chapter, for details.

Enabling Quiet Hours on the mobile app

Work-life balance is an important concern for the modern worker. Unfortunately, tools like email and Teams have encouraged people to message each other at all hours, and quick response times beget even quicker response-time expectations. It's a vicious cycle. You can walk away from your desktop, but your phone is usually always in your pocket. To give you a respite, the Teams mobile app offers an option to disable notifications during the hours and days of your choosing. The feature is called Quiet Hours.

REMEMBER

Quiet Hours suppresses only message notifications. It does not disable Teams calls from coming through to your phone. Feel free to not answer those calls.

Follow these steps to enable Quiet Hours:

1. **From the Teams mobile app, tap your profile photo or initials in the top-left corner.**

2. **In the menu that appears, tap Notifications, and then tap During Quiet Time.**

3. **Tap the toggle next to Quiet Hours to select the hours of workdays to disable notifications.**

   Typically you would choose the hours you do not work, like 5:00 p.m. until 9:00 a.m. (as opposed to your work hours, such as 9:00 a.m. to 5:00 p.m.).

4. **Tap the toggle next to Quiet Days to select the days of the week to disable notifications completely.**

   If you normally work Monday through Friday and you want quiet weekends, choose Saturday and Sunday.

5. **Tap the back arrow to return to Teams.**

   Your selections are saved automatically.

REMEMBER

People on your priority access list cannot circumvent your Quiet Hours settings. See the next section for details about priority access.

Setting up priority access

Priority access allows you to provide people you choose the ability to bypass the do not disturb status if you've enabled it (or you're sharing your screen in a meeting or call). Priority access is useful when you want key people to be able to get hold of you — such as your boss — even when everyone else can't. Note that your priority access list cannot circumvent your Quiet Hours settings; see the previous section for details.

Follow these steps to manage your priority access list:

1. **Click the ellipsis near the top-right corner of the suite bar to open the Settings and More menu.**

2. **Click Settings to open the Settings pane and then click Privacy.**

   The Privacy settings appear.

3. **Click the Manage Priority Access button and then, under Add People, type the name of the person you want to give access to.**

   Select the name from the drop-down list that appears as you start typing.

   You can also remove people from your list by clicking *X* next to their name.

   Your updates are saved automatically. You can leave the menu when you're done by clicking the *X* in the top-right corner of the pane.

Managing settings

Teams comes with a lot of settings options, but they're not obvious or easy to find. Still, you might find it worthwhile to take advantage of all the toggles, tick boxes, and features available to configure Teams in a way that works best for you.

To access your settings, click the ellipsis near the top-right corner of the desktop app to open the Settings and More drop-down menu. In the mobile app, tap your profile picture or initials and then tap Settings on the menu that appears. You will have more settings options in the desktop app than the mobile app.

You should take some time to review the available options. A little time now can save you a lot of time in the future. Options range from choosing how Teams starts up and whether spell check is enabled to managing notifications in other organizations. You can also manage privacy features, read receipt settings, device settings for video calls, and app permissions, just to mention some (as shown in Figure 1-3).

FIGURE 1-3:
The Settings pane on the desktop Teams app.

Choosing notification settings

Notifications are likely to be the first thing you want to configure. The move to Teams can lead to more total notifications across Outlook and Teams and, well, it doesn't have to be that way. Figure 1-4 shows the notifications settings. Follow these steps to manage these notification settings:

1. **Click the ellipsis to open the Settings and More drop-down menu near the top-right corner of the desktop app, or tap your profile photo or initials in the mobile app.**

2. **Click or tap Settings.**

3. **In the Settings pane that appears, click or tap Notifications.**

   Various types of notification options appear, depending on whether you're in the desktop or mobile app. Figure 1-4 shows these options in the desktop app.

4. **Choose how you want to be notified concerning chat, meetings, channels, and people.**

   Again, the available choices depend on whether you're in the desktop or mobile app.

Some of the key items that you can manage on the desktop app include the "missed message" emails, which you can disable entirely if you don't need them; the notification style you want (native Windows or macOS notifications versus the proprietary Teams notification style); whether Teams displays a message preview; whether you get a notification when a meeting starts; and an option to get notified when a specific person becomes available.

On the mobile app, you have similar, though fewer, options as what you find on the desktop app. As explained in the earlier section "Enabling Quiet Hours on the mobile app," you can manage Quiet Hours, disable mobile notifications when you're active on the desktop app, and limit notifications when you're in meetings. Plus you can always control your device's notifications overall using the built-in options in iOS or Android.

WARNING

Your notification settings do not sync between desktop and mobile. If you want your notifications configured, you need to set them on both desktop and mobile devices. If you access Teams in the web browser, it should use your settings from the desktop app.

TIP

You can manage notifications for specific channels and conversations in each channel. This can help you pare down the notifications that are relevant to you, hopefully reducing your overall notification count in a way that you could never do if you continued working in Outlook exclusively. See Chapter 2 of this minibook for details about channel and conversation options.

Getting around in Teams

FIGURE 1-4:
Choose the notification settings that will help you home in on the good stuff.

Enabling dark mode or high-contrast mode

Dark mode is one of the most popular features for apps in the modern world, and an app like Teams wouldn't be complete without it. Teams offers both dark mode and high-contrast options in the form of a theme. Follow these steps to manage your theme in Teams:

1. **Click the ellipsis near the top-right corner of the desktop app to open the Settings and More menu.**

2. **In the drop-down menu, click Settings.**

   The Settings pane opens.

3. **Click General.**

   You see the various General settings (refer to Figure 1-3).

4. **Under Theme, click Default, Dark, or High Contrast.**

   When you've settled on one, click *X* to close the Settings pane. Your settings are saved automatically.

Setting up and testing your audio and video devices

Another critical area in your settings is your device listing. Meetings are an essential element of Microsoft Teams, and you want to ensure that your audio and video work correctly before you join a meeting, not *as* you join it. Not only can you use your settings to select your devices, you can also run a test call to ensure that the audio and video are working as expected. Follow these steps to manage your devices:

1. Click the ellipsis near the top-right corner of the desktop app to open the Settings and More menu.

2. In the drop-down menu, click Settings.

The Settings pane opens.

3. Click Devices to open the Devices settings list.

4. Under Audio Devices, select your speaker and microphone.

TIP

If you select from the first drop-down menu, it sets both the speaker and microphone on the same device. However, you can use different speakers or microphones if you have multiple ones. For example, you can use Bluetooth headphones to listen while using a separate USB microphone for sending your voice.

5. Under Camera, select the camera you want to use.

If your computer has a built-in webcam (like most laptops), Teams will likely default to that choice. If you have an external camera, you can choose that.

6. Scroll back up the screen to find the Make a Test Call button and click it to run your devices through a mock call.

This feature starts a call with Teams Echo. You hear a request to record a message. The request shows you how well your speakers sound. Your recording indicates how good your microphone sounds to someone else. Listen for background noises or other distracting sounds and do your best to minimize them for the best experience in meetings.

TIP

Whenever you need to run a test call again, you can do so quickly by using a slash command. In the Teams Search box, type **/testcall** and then press Enter. (The "Using slash commands" section, later in this chapter, tells you more about slash commands.)

Getting around in Teams

Filtering and Searching

Sometimes it pays to cut down on "noise" and drill into content that is relevant to your interests. Starting from the Activity app, you can filter your feed to see only what interests you. A red badge on the Activity icon indicates that you have unread or missed notifications. The Activity app is a one-stop shop for pinpointing what is pertinent to you — channels, conversations, chats, files, and so on. You can also conduct powerful filters and searches using the Activity app or the Teams Search box.

Filtering your Activity feed

The Activity feed presents actions that you can take in the channels in which you participate. Many people start their workday by seeing what's up on the Activity feed, where you find mentions, replies, and other notifications. Think of it as your Teams Inbox.

Follow these steps to filter your activity feed to focus on the information you need:

1. **Click Activity in the app bar.**

   Your activity feed displays in the rail.

2. **Click the Activity selector to choose Feed (if your Feed isn't already showing).**

   The Activity selector is located at the top of the Activity rail, as shown in Figure 1-5. The selector offers two choices:

   - **Feed:** Shows all your mentions and post replies.

   - **My Activity:** Shows posts you initiated.

3. **Click the Filter icon (the icon with three lines at the top right on the Activity rail) and enter a term to search by.**

   You can also click the ellipsis to the right of the Search field to open the More Options drop-down menu, which lets you filter further by activity type. You can filter your Activity feed using different criteria, such as Unread, Mentions, and others, as shown in Figure 1-5.

FIGURE 1-5:
Filtering your
Activity feed.

Searching for a post, message, or other content

How do you find the file your manager mentioned in passing last week? Or recall the name of the movie a colleague suggested during a private chat three months ago? Follow these steps to search Teams for a specific post, message, or file:

1. **Click the Search box at the top and start typing a search term.**

The Search box immediately suggests results. You may not even need to perform a formal search! An example of a search term might be *Revenue projection reports* or simply *reports*.

2. **Click the search term you want or press Enter to see more results.**

Search results appear across multiple tabs, as shown in Figure 1-6: All, Messages, People, and Files.

3. **Select a tab to steer your search in the right direction.**

Use the filter options below the tabs to pare down your results. Each tab has different filter options, but most let you filter by date ranges and people. (Fingers crossed that you find what you're searching for.)

Using slash commands

Everyone loves a shortcut, and Teams provides a list of unique ones called *slash commands*. Enter a slash command into the Teams Search box and you can directly kick off the action for that command. For example, you can set your status by typing **/brb** (for be right back), **/dnd** (for do not disturb), or **/offline** (meaning you can't be reached). Or you can quickly call someone by entering **/call** and providing a name. Slash commands are especially popular with computer programmers who use Teams, but everyday people can equally benefit.

The Search box will suggest results   View result types   Filter your results

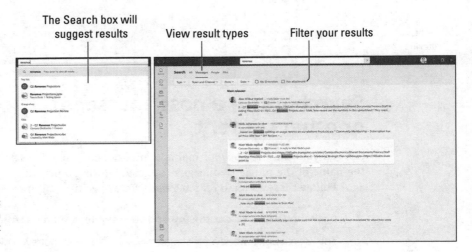

FIGURE 1-6:
Filter your search results to cut out extraneous stuff.

Follow these steps to use a slash command:

1. **Click the Search box in the top bar of Teams and type / (forward slash).**

A list of available slash commands appears, as shown in Figure 1-7.

2. **Type / and type the command you want to use and press Enter.**

You can also click the command in the menu.

3. **Enter any additional information needed, depending on the slash command you use.**

For example, if you want to send a private chat message to someone, after you type **/chat** and press Enter (Steps 1 and 2), a drop-down list of names appears. If the person you want isn't in the last, enter the name in the Person Search box above the drop-down list. Then you can enter the message and press Enter to send it.

SEARCH TIPS FOR TEAMS AND OFFICE 365

Search is a major topic of discussion, if not a bone of contention, in many organizations. But you can get better results by knowing some key search skills. These tips aren't just for Teams, either — you can use them in the Office 365 home page Search box, any SharePoint Search box, and pretty much anywhere you see a Search box in any app in Office 365. Oh, and they work in Google, too:

- **Filter your results:** Use refiners when available to remove extraneous and irrelevant content. In Teams search, you can filter messages and files using various filters below the Search box including date, Team, channels, and who was involved. If you know a message you want from last year is in a certain channel, don't waste your time looking at results from all Teams and channels.

- **Use quotation marks:** Add quotation marks around a phrase to return results with exactly that phrase. Without quotes, your results will include the terms, but not necessarily together in the document or message where it was found. For example, *"laptop sales"* will return different results than *laptop sales* with no quotation marks.

- **Use - or NOT:** Filter your results by removing a certain term using a hyphen or the word *NOT* in all caps. If you search *revenue projections q1*, you may get results for Q2, Q3, and Q4. Instead, search *revenue projections q1 -q2 -q3* or search *revenue projections q1 NOT q2 NOT q3*. Hyphens and *NOT* can be used interchangeably, even in the same search query, but you can't use a space after a hyphen whereas you must use a space after *NOT*.

- **Use *:** An asterisk — in this context, called a *wildcard* — at the end of a portion of a word will return results with various forms of the word. *Proj** returns *project, projection, projections*, and other variations on that word. You can use the asterisk only at the end of the word, not the beginning or middle.

- **Put them together:** Go searching for *revenue proj* "laptop sales" q1 -q2 -q3 -q4* and then filter your results using the available refiners. You should notice better or more appropriate results.

To learn more advanced searching tips and tricks, search *keyword query language* in your favorite search engine to learn more about this easy-to-use search protocol that works across all Microsoft search experiences.

FIGURE 1-7:
Choose from a bunch of slash commands to quickly take an action.

Command	Action
/activity	See someone's activity
/available	Set your status to available
/away	Set your status to away
/brb	Set your status to be right back
/busy	Set your status to busy
/call	Call someone
/chat	Send quick message to a person
/dnd	Set your status to do not disturb
/files	See your recent files
/find	Search the page
/goto	Go right to a team or channel
/help	Get help with Teams
/join	Join a team
/keys	See keyboard shortcuts
/mentions	See all your @mentions
/offline	Set your status to appear offline
/org	See someone's org chart
/pop	Pop out a chat into a new window
/saved	See your saved list
/testcall	Make a test call
/unread	See all your unread activity
/whatsnew	See what's new in Teams
/who	Ask Who a question about someone

Using Teams to Know Your Colleagues Better

Teams is all about interacting with others, so when you need to know about someone else, the app has your back. The following pages cover how to view a person's profile card and how to see where they sit in the organization chart (if you have one).

Viewing a person's profile card

Profile cards abound in Office 365. You can hover over someone's profile photo or initials in almost every app and get more information about them, and Teams is no exception. Teams offers a lot of shortcuts actions through its profile card, too. Figure 1-8 provides a view of the profile card.

The Teams profile card shows a number of standard facts about the person (as long as the information is provided), including name, job title, organization, phone number, email address, manager, profile photo, and status. Additional information might be included by your organization. But that's not all: Through a profile card, you can also send a private chat message, open an email draft, and start an audio or video call to the person.

Start or open chat   Start a call

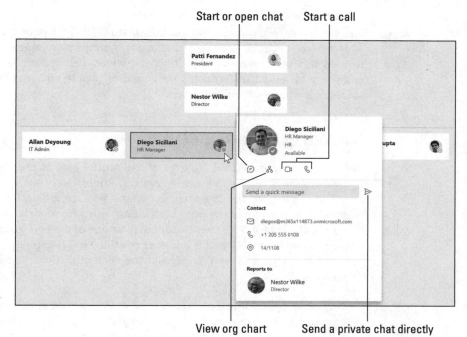

View org chart   Send a private chat directly

FIGURE 1-8:
You can
garner lots of
information
about a person
from their
profile card.

Follow these steps to access and use the profile card:

1. **Hover your cursor over another person's photo or initials.**

When you hover over one of these items, the person's contact information is
displayed in the card that pops up.

2. **To send a chat message, enter your message in the Send a Quick Message
box and press Send.**

This feature allows you to send a message without leaving the screen
you're on.

TIP

3. **To go to your ongoing chat with that person, click the Chat icon.**

4. **To open an email draft addressed to that person, click the Email icon.**

5. **To call that person, click the Audio or Video call button to start the
respective call type.**

Audio and Video both make a call, but the latter starts with your video on. You
can disable your video after connecting a video call; likewise you can enable
your video if you start an audio call.

Getting around
in Teams

TIP

You can hover over various contact information (such as phone number or email address) and click the Copy icon that appears on the right side of the profile card to copy this information and paste it elsewhere. This feature is useful if you're authoring an email in Outlook to a bunch of people and want to quickly grab someone's email address to include.

Viewing the org chart

One of the most beneficial features of the profile card is the org chart. Simply by hovering over a person's name, you can immediately see whom that person reports to. But click the Org Chart icon, and you see a hierarchal tree showing where the person sits in the org chart, along with who reports to the same manager (refer to Figure 1-8). This feature may be one of the best graphical organization representations Microsoft has ever provided in an app out of the box. (Past versions of SharePoint have tried, and the current Outlook still hasn't matched Teams.)

WARNING

The org chart works only if each employee's manager is identified in the directory. If you don't see an org chart or the connections appear incorrect, reach out to your IT team and suggest that they manage who reports to whom, because it's an incredibly useful piece of information to have in one click.

Enhancing Your Teams Experience with Helpful Extras

A unique feature of Microsoft Teams is the ability to add plug-ins to Teams, chats, meetings, and elsewhere. A *plug-in* is a connection to another app or service, whether it's provided by Microsoft or a third-party tool. An added plug-in in Teams can be a tab in a channel or chat, an app in the Teams app bar, and even bots (automated virtual assistants) that interact through natural language chat with you.

A deep dive of Teams apps is beyond the scope of this minibook, but you should be aware of some of the best apps available out of the box and take some time to investigate whether they'd be useful to you. Available apps include Microsoft-provided ones (to add to the built-in features of Teams) and third-party tools, which bring non-Microsoft tools right into Teams, minimizing the app-jumping fatigue you're likely familiar with.

Using built-in apps

Teams provides apps out of the box that you can make use of without any installation, as long as your IT team has enabled them for your use. If you don't see them after following the steps that follow, reach out to your IT team and ask for access. Some of these tools are super handy.

Follow these steps to open and use an existing app:

1. **Below your apps in the app bar, click the ellipsis to open the More Added Apps menu.**

2. **In the Apps menu that opens, click the app you want to select it.**

TIP

The app is temporarily added to the app bar. To have it show up there each time you open Teams, you can pin it to the app bar by right-clicking the app's icon and then clicking Pin. (You unpin it using the same steps.)

3. **Click the app's name in the app bar to open and use the app.**

Some of the key apps to consider using include:

» **Approvals:** You can send a request or file through an automated approval request right in Teams. Approvals can be sent to an individual or multiple people, and you can manage all sent and received approval requests right in the Approvals app. Templates and built-in connections to Adobe Sign and Docusign are available, and you can customize your approval processes using Microsoft Power Automate, which is likely included with your Office 365 subscription.

» **Insights:** The Insights app opens Viva Insights, which provides, well, insight into how you spend your time while working and is intended to promote a healthier mental state through break scheduling, virtual commutes, suggested focus time, and other well-being tools. See the "Introducing Microsoft Viva" section, earlier in this chapter, for more details about Viva.

» **Shifts:** Manage schedules, reservations, and other aspects of your work with this hourly scheduling feature built into Teams. (Shifts used to be a separate Office 365 app called StaffHub.)

» **Tasks by Planner and To Do:** Manage team and personal tasks from Microsoft Planner and Microsoft To Do, the team and individual task apps in Office 365. Tasks by Planner and To Do is among the more popular Teams apps because it centralizes your tasks from two major task tools into one place, as shown in Figure 1-9.

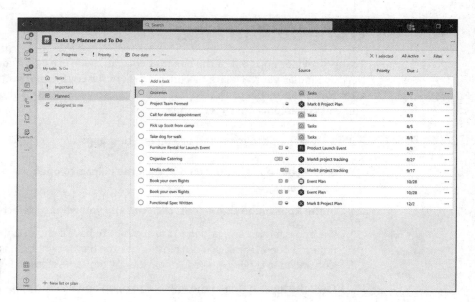

FIGURE 1-9:
The Tasks by
Planner and
To Do app.

REMEMBER

You can also find built-in apps available in the toolbar under channel and chat message boxes. For example, when you send a message in a channel or private chat, you can click an app icon under the message box to add content from a given app. Click the ellipsis for more app options. From here, you can send an approval request, link directly to a YouTube video, send a praise badge, and create a poll using Microsoft Forms (included with your Office 365 account).

Using tabs

Apps are useful, but tabs can be even more so because they're so easy to integrate into channels, chats, and meetings. Technically, tabs are also apps, but you typically use the best ones just as tabs, so that's the nomenclature I use here.

Each channel, chat, and calendar appointment includes tabs at the top. You typically see a Posts or Chat tab, a Files tab, a Wiki or Meeting Notes tab, and a big + (plus sign) icon. The + icon is what you want to look for. By clicking this button, you can add an app as a tab so that it's directly accessible in your channel, chat, and meeting with one click.

Teams offers hundreds of tab options for chat and channels. So when would you use a tab? Consider a channel that's being used by a sales team. The team wants to follow their revenue and sales dashboard. They can add a Power BI or Excel tab to display that information from merely one click away (of course, you need to have the dashboard already created).

Or perhaps you have a group chat going with three people with whom you'll be presenting a PowerPoint presentation at a big partner meeting. You can share the PowerPoint file in the chat and then add it as a tab for quick access to edit it right in the chat area. And for your meetings, you can add the agenda as a Word tab so that everyone has quick access; better yet, add the Forms app to create live polls during your meeting.

Follow these steps to add a tab to a channel, chat, or meeting:

1. **In the Channel, Chat, or Meeting Details pane, click the + (plus sign) icon at the right end of the tab listing at the top of the main area.**

   The Add a Tab pane appears, as shown in Figure 1-10.

2. **Click the app you want to add as a tab.**

   If you add a Word, Excel, PowerPoint, OneNote, or PDF file as a tab, the file must already exist in the channel or chat's Files tab. (See Chapter 4 of this minibook for more about how to create, organize, and share files in Teams.)

3. **If the app isn't already installed in Teams, follow the prompts to add the app to your Team or chat (depending on where you're adding the tab).**

4. **In the Tab Name text box, give the tab a name.**

   Keep it short and sweet. The shorter the name, the more tabs you can display at once.

5. **Click Add or Install.**

   Your new tab is now in the tab listing.

6. **Click the tab to open it.**

   You can click and drag the tab name left or right to rearrange your tabs.

REMEMBER

Your IT team controls whether you have access to and can add tabs. If you don't see many apps available to add as tabs, reach out to IT and ask how the tabs can be made available. Also, if you have guests in your Teams, they cannot add tabs to channels.

When it comes to tabs, some key apps are more useful than others. Consider the following list when adding tabs to your channel, chat, or meeting:

» **Office apps:** Word, Excel, PowerPoint, or OneNote files can all be added as tabs. When you open the tab for one of these files, it opens in the web version of the app so that you can edit directly in that tab. Key files can be one click away! See Chapter 1 of Book 11 for more on the differences between the desktop and web version of the Office apps.

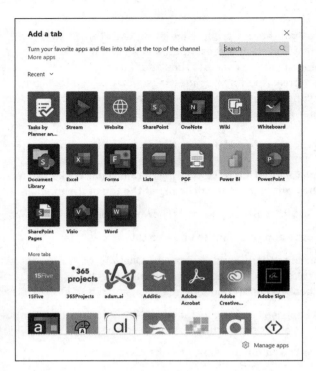

FIGURE 1-10:
Tab options for
a channel (there
are more options
here than
in a chat).

>> **PDF:** As with the Office apps, a PDF can be added as a tab as well. Adding a PDF tab is a useful way to have key information at your fingertips. ***Note:*** PDFs with form fields cannot be edited in a tab; the contents of the tab are view only.

>> **Website:** Add any website as a tab for quick access to critical information like stock tickers, weather maps, social media feeds, and more. If the website requires you to log in, Teams can't remember that, but in the experience of one of the authors, it asks for your password only about once per day. You can add only websites whose URLs start with https://.

>> **Lists:** Microsoft Lists is a list and tracking app included with Office 365. This tab provides direct access to a status, tracking, itinerary, and asset management lists right from your channel. (You can't use Lists in chat.) See Book 11, Chapter 3 for more about Lists.

>> **SharePoint:** Add any SharePoint page or document library to a channel (not chat, unfortunately) for quick access to the organization home page, a team home page, or other useful web pages in your network. And if the Files tab isn't enough for you, add another document library to your channel. See Chapter 4 of this minibook for more details on adding a library as a tab, and see Book 11 for more on SharePoint.

>> **Other Microsoft apps:** If you use other Microsoft apps like Dynamics 365, Planner, Power Apps, Power Automate, Power BI, Project, Whiteboard, Visio, or Yammer, you can have quick access to these through a dedicated tab. Note that some of the apps or features therein come with an additional licensing fee.

>> **Third-party apps:** Be on the lookout for any non-Microsoft apps you may already subscribe to. Some of the big ones include Adobe Sign, Asana, Box, Evernote, Intercom, Jira, SurveyMonkey, Trello, YouTube, and Zendesk. Some integrate better than others. Don't buy licenses to one of these apps just because there's a tab; test it by itself first to make sure it gives you what you need.

Using the Teams App store

The Teams App store is the central place to find all the apps that are available to you. This is helpful because you can experience apps as tabs, connectors, bots, or apps in the app bar. But the App store shows you all the apps available in one place.

To access the App store, click the Apps icon in the app bar. From here you can view new, featured, and popular apps as well as dozens of app categories and capabilities, as shown in Figure 1-11. If your organization has created custom apps, you find them under a section called Built for Your Org. The Search box is your friend, so make sure to use it! You never know what you might find that could help make you more productive and efficient.

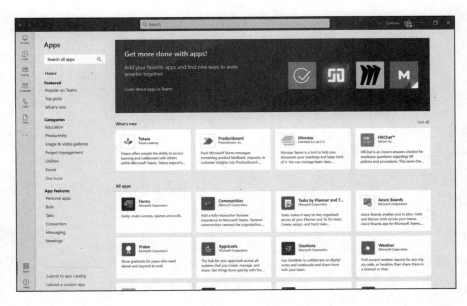

FIGURE 1-11: The Teams App store is the central place to find useful apps and install them for your use.

Chapter **2**

Getting Up to Speed with Teams and Channels

The namesake of this app is the Team, and it's time to delve into what a Team is. A *Team* is a permission-protected online workspace that comes with topic-specific channels that allow for threaded conversations, file sharing and editing, and in-channel Team meetings. Transparency is the name of the game: Every member of a Team has access to pretty much everything in the Team, including edit access to all files. For the most part, this access applies to external guests you may invite, too.

For many organizations, the use of Teams represents a paradigm shift in their working culture. Siloes and private messaging in email and chat — not to mention email attachments that make configuration control a nightmare — have been the norm since, well, the last millennium. Now's your chance to join the future of work with a typically better, more efficient, more secure way to communicate and collaborate both with people inside and outside of your organization. This chapter helps you confidently navigate individual Teams and channels.

Diving in to Microsoft Teams

The progression from ad hoc email messages to more strategic, group-based workspaces was inevitable when you take into account the recent history of communication and collaboration. Email is easy and cheap, but by the early 2000s, workers everywhere were already complaining about being overwhelmed by too much email. Adding the smartphone to the mix later that decade meant that notifications began to take over people's lives. Teams is the better alternative to email. This section explains all the ways in which this app can streamline communication and make you and your coworkers more productive.

Seeing the benefits of using a Team

Teams offers an alternative to the arbitrary ping pong of emails with multiple copies of attachments flying around that someone needs to spend hours merging. Teams also reduces the number of disconnected chat messages that you have to deal with from various chat apps like Skype for Business, WhatsApp, and even text messaging.

With a Team, you have a dedicated membership within that Team, whether it consists of a small working group of six members or an organization-wide Team of 9,000.

REMEMBER

When someone joins a Team, they receive access to everything in the Team: all conversations, all files, and all apps. When someone leaves, they lose access. The content is secure and accessible only to those it should be. Anyone who joins a Team can review the content and get caught up in the manner they prefer, as opposed to getting dozens of emails dumped on them from each teammate.

A Team is made up of *channels*, which are subgroups organized by topic (see Figure 2-1). You can follow or ignore various channels based on your preferences. With email, someone can easily over-CC "just in case," which can be detrimental to the recipients. But within a Team, the recipient, not the sender, decides what to read and follow. If you care only about the Budget and Finance channel, you don't have to regularly follow the Engineering, Marketing, and Project Management channels. Turn off the notifications for those channels and pop in once in a while to check in.

Conversations in a Team can be cleaner than what you encounter with email. Many of the emails you receive are acknowledgements, internal communications, marketing, and spam. All those "got it," "thanks," "see you then," and "okay" emails are replaced in Teams with a simple thumbs-up reaction. Your internal communications can remain in email, allowing you to ignore your Inbox longer. Marketing and spam messages are unlikely or even impossible to wind up in Teams (thank goodness!).

Channels

Team

Pin your favorite channels here

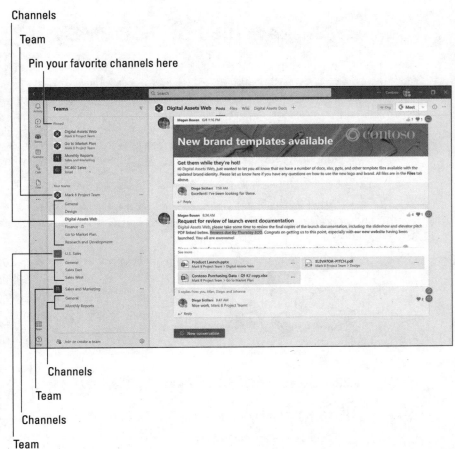

FIGURE 2-1:
Separate your
Team into topics
using channels
to help organize
things and keep
your notifications
under control.

Channels

Team

Channels

Team

Ultimately, being part of a Team helps you to stay more focused on the work and your time management by keeping the extraneous and unimportant items out of your regular email Inbox. See the "Choosing notification settings" section in Chapter 1 of this minibook for more details on effectively managing your work messages.

Creating a Team

Before creating a Team, check to make sure that one doesn't already exist that could meet the need. Having multiple Teams for basically the same use makes it tough to track what content is in which Team.

BEST PRACTICES OF TEAM MEMBERSHIP

For all the advantages offered by being on a Team, the Teams app can still have its downsides when people don't use it well. No collaborative app is perfect, after all. Here are some common issues to keep in mind to avoid contributing to the typical pitfalls of collaborative tools:

- Private chat can be distracting from getting work done in a Team. Setting your status to Do Not Disturb for blocks of focus time can really help with that.

- Avoid overusing @messages, especially to channels and Teams.

- Try not to upload files when sending a message. Instead, store and organize the file in an appropriate place ahead of time, and reference that file in the message as a link.

- Always use a subject line in a new channel conversation; otherwise, you make it difficult to find when scrolling. Every email needs a subject line; so too should every Teams conversation.

- Avoid posting new conversations to multiple channels very often. Doing so creates internal spam.

Follow these steps to create a Team:

1. Click Teams in the app bar.

Your Teams appear in a list in the rail.

2. At the bottom of the rail, click Join or Create a Team and then click Create a Team.

The Create a Team listing opens in the main area.

3. Choose whether to create a Team from scratch, from an existing Team, or from a provided template.

Your organization may provide custom templates specific to your business processes. If you're not sure whether you should use a template, ask your IT team.

4. Choose the sensitivity (if applicable) and privacy of your Team.

Choose among these options, if available:

- **Sensitivity:** Select from the drop-down menu at the top. This option appears if your organization is using sensitivity labels; ask your IT team for help picking.

- **Privacy:** Choose Private, Public, or Org Wide by clicking the respective button (if applicable). Public teams are searchable by anyone in the organization, even those who aren't members of the Team.

5. **Give your Team a name and description in the provided text boxes; then click Create.**

   Names should never include acronyms. Your organization may have a naming convention. Ask your IT team for help on that if you're not sure. Don't skimp on the description; it sets the stage for the intended use of the Team.

6. **Add members by searching for individuals or groups in the Start Typing a Name or Group box; then click Add.**

   This is one place where you can add people to the Team. You can skip this step and do it later if you want (click the Skip button if so). If your organization allows it, you can add external people by adding their email address.

REMEMBER

When you create a Team, you become the owner. You can add more owners and members. Owners can manage the Team; members generally take part only in the conversations and content.

TIP

The ability to create a Team may be limited to certain people or a request process managed by your IT team. If you don't see the ability to create a Team, reach out to your IT team for help.

Joining a Team

Follow these steps to join a Team:

1. **Click Teams in the app bar.**

   Your Teams appear in a list in the rail.

2. **At the bottom of the rail, click Join or Create a Team.**

   The main area lists all the public Teams in your organization if there are any. You can scroll through or use the Search box to find Teams by keyword.

3. **When you've found a Team to join, click the Join Team button under the Team name.**

   You can't see the content of a Team — or even the description — until you've joined. You can always leave if you're not satisfied with what you find. See "Leaving a Team," later in this chapter, for details.

TIP

You can also join a Team using a Join code provided by a Team owner or member. The Team owner can provide you with a special code that you can enter in the text box of the Join a Team with a Code box you'll see in the Team listing area referenced in Step 2.

If your organization has opted to use organization-wide Teams, you'll be included in all of them by default, along with everyone else in the organization.

Opening a Team and viewing its channels

Follow these steps to go to a team and visit its channels:

1. Click Teams in the app bar.

Your Teams appear in a list in the rail.

2. Click the name of a Team to which you're assigned.

Each Team consists of one or more channels, whose names appear on the rail under the Team name.

3. Click a channel name and browse its content.

Each channel starts off with the following tabs at the top of the main area:

- **Posts:** This is for announcements and channel conversations. See Chapter 3 of this minibook for details.

- **Files:** Upload and edit files within your Team. See Chapter 4 of this minibook for details.

- **Wiki:** Track meeting notes in a collaborative, multi-editing environment. Beware, though, that wikis don't have an Undo or Restore option, nor do they show up in search results.

- **+ (plus sign) icon for Add a Tab:** Add new tabs to the channel if you have permission. See the "Using Tabs" section in Chapter 1 of this minibook for details.

4. When you've finished reviewing your Teams and channels, click Teams in the app bar to return to the Teams list.

Adding people to a Team

If you're the owner of a Team, you can manage the membership of that Team, including other owners. Members can suggest additional members to a Team as well. Follow these steps to add someone to a Team (if you're an owner) or suggest someone for a Team (if you're a member):

1. Click Teams in the app bar.

Your Teams appear in a list in the rail.

2. **Click the ellipsis next to a Team name to open the More Options drop-down menu; then click Add Member.**

   The Add Members to *(Team Name)* pane appears.

3. **In the Search box, enter the name of a person or group and, when the name appears, click the Add button.**

   The person or members of a group are added to a list on this pane.

   If your organization allows it, you can invite external guests by adding their email address in the Search box.

4. **(Optional) For each person in the list, click the Member drop-down menu to the right of their name to change their role to Owner if they need added permissions.**

   Owners have full control of a Team. Members have fewer rights. Three owners per Team is a sweet spot. Fewer, and there aren't enough backups if someone is out; more, and accountability is difficult to rely upon.

5. **Click the Close button.**

TIP

You have multiple other ways to invite people to a Team or share a Team with them. See the next section for details.

Sharing a Team

You can share a Team with someone other than by adding a member directly (described in the preceding section, "Adding people to a Team"). Sometimes you want to share an open invitation to join a Team, or you may want to be able to approve someone's addition.

Follow these steps to share an invitation to a Team with someone:

1. **Click Teams in the app bar.**

   Your Teams appear in a list in the rail.

2. **Click the ellipsis next to a Team name to open the More Options drop-down menu; then click Get Link to Team.**

   The Get a Link to the Team pane opens.

3. **Click Copy.**

   The link is copied to your Clipboard. Share the link with an internal person however you prefer (paste it in an email, private chat, or text message). This method requires you to approve someone's request to join after the recipient clicks the link. If you prefer to invite someone to the Team without the need to approve the request, continue on to the next step.

4. **Click the ellipsis next to the Team name to open the More Options drop-down menu; then click Manage Team**

   The Team settings open in the main area.

5. **Click the Settings tab at the top of the main area and then click Join Code to expand that section.**

   You see the option to copy or create a Team code.

6. **In the Join Code section, click the Copy button under the code. If a code doesn't already exist, click the Generate button.**

   Share the code with an internal person however you prefer (for example, through an email, private chat, or text message). The invitee should follow the guidance in the "Joining a Team" section, earlier in this chapter. This method does not require approval to join; after the code is entered, the invitee automatically becomes a member.

Managing Team settings

Team ownership is a big responsibility. You hold the keys to the kingdom. You can manage membership, determine whether members can create channels respond to posts in certain channels, decide which members can use the @mention feature (see the "@mentioning in a conversation message" section, in Chapter 3 of this minibook), whether guests are allowed, and a lot more. Although a full overview of ownership best practices is beyond the scope of this minibook, you should know where to find the various tools.

Follow these steps to manage settings at the Team level:

1. **Click Teams in the app bar.**

   Your Teams appear in a list in the rail.

2. **Click the ellipsis next to the Team name to open the More Options drop-down-menu.**

3. **Click Manage Team.**

   The Team settings open in the main area.

4. **Click the Settings tab at the top of the main area.**

   You find many options on this page, as shown in Figure 2-2. Again, the space allotted here does not allow coverage of all these options, but most are self-explanatory.

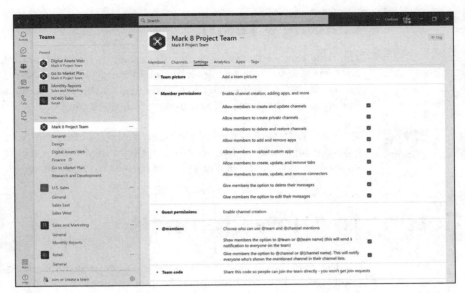

FIGURE 2-2:
If you're the
owner of a Team,
you should
become familiar
with these
options.

You can also manage settings at a channel level. To get to those settings, click
Teams in the app bar, click a Team name, and then click the ellipsis next to a
channel name. In the More Options drop-down menu that appears, click Manage
Channel and then click the Settings tab. As with the Team settings, you find some
options that you can manage here. The General channel and any private channels
have more options than other channels.

Here's a brief overview of the other tabs with management options on the Manage
Team page shown in Figure 2-2:

» **Members:** Add and remove members of your Team and change the roles of
existing members.

» **Pending Requests:** A person who is not a member who has received a link to
a Team and requested access or has been nominated to join a Team by an
existing member will be listed here for an owner to approve or deny.

» **Channels:** View a list of all channels in a Team, with access to various
channel-specific management options.

» **Analytics:** View usage metrics of the Team, including active participants,
meeting information, and inactive channels.

» **Apps:** Manage the apps and tabs that have been added to your Team.

» **Tags:** Create and organize subgroups of Team members so that it's easier to
@mention them without having to @mention a number of individuals or
channels.

Leaving a Team

The time may come when you you're ready to leave a team. Maybe the project has ended, or you're moving on to a new Team. To leave a Team, you simply click Teams in the app bar, click the ellipsis next to the Team name to open the More Options drop-down menu, and then click Leave Team.

WARNING

You can't automatically re-join a Team yourself unless the Team is public or you have the Join code. If neither is an option and you want to get back in, ask an owner to add you, or ask a member to request that you be added.

Getting to Know Channels

Use the channels in your Team to separate conversations and files by topic in an organized and efficient manner. Think of channels as next-generation folders in a network shared drive. Don't go haywire with how many channels you create, though. Most people using Teams do best with 10 to 15 active channels at a time. Fewer than that and you may end up overwhelming the few channels you have; more than that and it's hard to keep up with them all. The following sections take you deeper into channels.

Creating a channel

Both owners and members of a Team can create channels as long as the owners haven't disabled the setting for members to create channels. If you're an owner of a large Team, you may not want to let members create channels, because it can get out of hand. See "Managing Team settings," earlier in this chapter, for more about Team settings.

Follow these steps to create a channel:

1. **Click Teams in the app bar.**

   Your Teams appear in a list in the rail.

2. **Click the ellipsis next to the Team name and then, in the More Options drop-down menu, click Add channel.**

   The Create a Channel pane opens, where you provide information about your channel.

3. **Give the channel a name and description, select the channel type, and then click Add.**

Enter your channel name and description in the appropriate text boxes. Keep channel names short but descriptive, avoiding acronyms and jargon. Don't skimp on the description. The description sets the tone for how members should use the channel.

Choose the channel type from the drop-down box. Select from the following options:

- **Standard:** All members of your Team will have access to conversations, files, and apps.

- **Private:** Protect the permissions of the channel by only giving a subset of your Team membership access.

- **Shared:** Add Teams users from outside your organization so that they have easy access to collaborate with you.

If you choose Standard, your channel is listed under the Team name in the rail after you click Add. See the remaining steps for the other choices.

4. **If you select Private Channel, in the Add Members to the (Channel Name) Channel pane, add channel members by searching for individuals or groups in the Start Typing a Name or Group box; then click Add. Click Done when you've finished.**

You can only add members to a private channel who are already members of the Team.

5. **If you selected Shared Channel, in the Share (Channel Name) Channel pane, share with people by searching for individuals or entering the email address of an external Office 365 user in the Start Typing a Name box; then click Add. Click Done when you've finished.**

The recipient will receive an invitation to the shared channel, which they can access directly in their Teams app.

WARNING

You cannot switch the privacy of a channel after it has been created. Be strategic with your choice from the start, because if you determine that you need to change a standard channel to a private one, you will need to create a new channel and then move files. But you can't move conversations without expensive third-party tools.

TIP

At the time of publishing, the maximum number of channels per Team was 200 (including deleted channels). That said, for the sanity of your Team members, you should never come close to approaching this number.

Using private channels

A private channel offers a protected space inside your Team. Although a channel may seem like a tempting feature to jump into immediately, think through how you want to use any private channel first. It's a complex feature, and creating and owning a private channel is a responsibility that rises almost to the level of owning the Team itself. Typical reasons for private channels include:

>> To give managers in the Team a place to discuss sensitive topics

>> To give finance and budget professionals a place to discuss financial information

Here are important details to keep in mind about creating a private channel:

>> All members of the private channel must already be members or owners of the parent Team.

>> If the Team owners are not members of the private channel, they cannot see inside the channel (though they do see the channel name and description), which means that you can't rely on them for support or ownership responsibility.

>> Files in the private channel are stored in a SharePoint site separate from the parent Team, which can confuse people if they're not used to the concept (see more about how SharePoint and Teams interact in Chapter 4 of this minibook).

>> Many features of standard channels don't work in private channels, including channel meetings and various apps and tabs.

>> Owning a private channel is a similar responsibility to owning a whole Team, and often the people who request or create private channels are not really qualified for the role yet.

REMEMBER

Before you create a private channel, truly convince yourself that you need one. Also, prepare for the eccentricities that come with it, and communicate those issues with members before you create one. A new Team is often a better option. You can pin the important channels to the top of the rail so that your list of Teams isn't completely overwhelming. (See the upcoming section for details on pinning a channel.)

TIP

At the time of publishing, the maximum number of private channels per Team was 30 and the maximum number of members of a private channel was 250.

Pinning a channel

Your Team and channel list can quickly get long and overwhelming. In the mean-time, you may be paying attention to only a select few channels at any given time. To deal with that common concern, Teams provides the option to pin your favorite channels at the top of the rail in the Teams app. To pin and organize your favorite channels, follow these steps:

1. **Click Teams in the app bar.**

Your Teams appear in a list in the rail.

2. **Click the ellipsis next to a channel name to open the More Options drop-down menu; then click Pin.**

This step places the channel at the top of the rail in a section called Pinned (see Figure 2-3). You can close and expand this section at any time by clicking the caret to the left of the Pinned section. Your pinned channels still display under the Team even though they're also displayed in the pinned section.

3. **Click and drag pinned channels to reorder them.**

4. **To unpin a channel, repeat Step 2 but click Unpin.**

TIP

For deciphering similarly named channels in your pinned area (especially the General channel from multiple Teams), note that the Team icon and name are listed to the left of and below the channel name, respectively.

Muting a channel

Now comes the beauty of Teams. Don't want to hear from a not-so-relevant channel anymore? You can silence some or all of the notifications that would come from that channel except for a personal @mention that specifically references you. (@mentions are explained in "@mentioning in a conversation message," in Book 10, Chapter 3.) If someone @mentions the channel name, you won't be bothered with a notification that you don't want. To manage notifications on a channel, follow these steps:

1. **Click Teams in the app bar.**

Your Teams appear in a list in the rail.

2. **Click the ellipsis next to a channel name to open the More Options drop-down menu and then click Channel Notifications.**

A flyout menu with additional options opens.

3. Choose All Activity, Off, or Custom in the flyout menu.

If you choose Custom, you can configure which notifications will come through to you by managing these notifications in the Channel Notification Settings pane.

Expand and close pinned channels

Teams rail   Filter by Team or channel

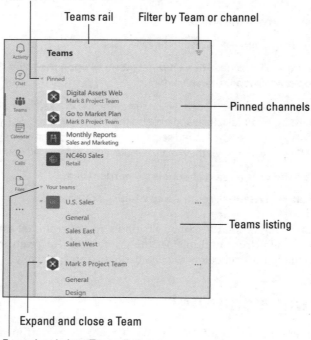

Pinned channels

Teams listing

Expand and close a Team

Expand and close Teams listing

REMEMBER

You can always change your channel notification settings if your preferences change in the future. Take advantage of this feature, because it's one of the reasons Teams can help you and your colleagues be more efficient than you can be by sticking with old-school email.

Hiding a channel

It can be a challenge to keep your channel list clean without overdoing your pinned channel list. The good news is that you can hide channels that are less relevant to you than others without losing notifications from those hidden channels. Follow these steps to hide a channel:

1. **Click Teams in the app bar.**

Your Teams appear in a list in the rail.

2. **Click the ellipsis next to a channel name to open the More Options menu; then click Hide.**

The channel gets stored in a menu called Hidden Channels at the bottom of a Team's channel list. Click the (*Number*) Hidden Channels text to open the menu of hidden channels to access it at any time. Notification badges continue to show for hidden channels, and you continue to see notifications in your activity feed.

WARNING

You can't hide the General channel, but you can hide any other channel in a Team.

3. **To un-hide a channel, click the Hidden Channels menu and then click Show to the right of the channel name.**

Chapter **3**

Communicating through Channels and Private Chat

A s noted elsewhere in this minibook, the ease of communication among colleagues is an essential feature of Teams. That communication takes two main forms: channel conversations and private chats.

In Teams, a *conversation* occurs in a channel and is a threaded list of individual messages that appear in the Posts tab of a channel. Conversations help to transform a group's old-style of communication — from email and chat apps — into centralized, organized, and strategic locations for easy access and searching as a team performs its duties over its life cycle. This approach is an efficient way to track messages from everyone.

A *private chat* takes place through the Chat app on the app bar and is useful for ad hoc, one-on-one, or group chats that don't belong within a Team. The basic feature is identical to other chat tools like Skype for Business, Slack, IRC, AOL Instant Messenger, and the chat aspects of popular social media sites like Facebook, Twitter, and Instagram. Teams chat is also similar in concept to SMS text messaging, iMessage, and Android Messenger. If your organization provides smartphones to some or all employees, chat is an excellent replacement for text messaging between colleagues to keep all content in one searchable place. It also has added features that text messaging doesn't offer.

This chapter covers how best to communicate within Teams and which features are available in channel conversations and private chats.

The Advantages of Channel Conversations over Private Chat

Although many people dive right into private chat to start conversing with colleagues in Teams, channel conversations have considerably more robust features that might entice you to perform your work-related conversations in a Team rather than in private chat. Private chat is easy and familiar, but it's often a crutch for people who may not think about organizing information in a way that considers the future.

Private chat and channel conversations both provide features like reactions, saving, praise, editing, deleting, memes, GIFs, stickers, approvals, meeting scheduling, formatting, and others. However, channel conversations come with more features than a private chat does. The following features are available in channel conversations but not private chat:

>> **Channels have more types of posts available:** Conversations in channels can consist of a standard message or an announcement. The latter stands out more and includes a large heading that you can backfill with color or an image. Click the Format icon(an *A* with a pencil) in the toolbar below a new conversation message to find and choose the option.

>> **Channel conversations can post in multiple places:** A channel conversation can be posted in multiple channels simultaneously, which creates a separate threaded conversation in each destination, including across different Teams with different audiences. Click the Format icon to see this option. If you want to post a message in multiple private chats, you'll be doing a lot of copying and pasting.

>> **You can control who can reply:** The author of a new channel conversation can restrict conversation replies to themselves and the Team owners and moderators. Click the Format icon to find this option.

>> **You can use subject lines:** Chats seemingly go on forever, offering no context as to what's being discussed unless you read the small text thoroughly

each time you stop scrolling. A new channel message can have a subject. In fact, all conversations *should* have a subject; you wouldn't send an email without a subject, right? Same with channel conversations. Click the Format icon to find this option.

» **You receive threaded replies:** Sure, you can reply in a private chat, but chat replies are disorganized conversations that could bounce around various topics in a confusing way. A channel conversation can stick to one topic. Need to ask about a semirelated question from that conversation? Start a new conversation to keep all replies on topic.

» **You can copy a link to the message:** Want to point someone directly to a message in a Team? Hover your cursor over the message and click the ellipsis to open the More Options drop-down menu for the message, copy the link, and send the link to the person. Neither private chat nor email has a way to link someone directly to a conversation or specific message at its source.

» **Uploaded files get stored in a central spot:** Although uploading a file directly to a message isn't a best practice, if you do it, at least the file will be stored in the Files tab of the channel. Doing the same in private chat dumps it in the OneDrive of the sharer, which will last only as long as the person stays in the organization. Files are better stored in a Team for long-term access. See Chapter 4 of this minibook for more information about sharing files in a Team.

Admittedly, one feature of chat that channels don't have is read receipts. If you're a fan of read receipts, only private chat supports them. You can manage your read receipts in the Privacy section of your settings. See Chapter 1 of this minibook for details on accessing settings.

Private chat has its role, but it can also be overused. In most cases, a Team is a better place to send messages or have a conversation because a channel conversation is organized, centralized, and not dependent on any individuals to remain accessible.

Private chat is best used for one-off messages that don't have a more strategic Team to take place in. Such messages could include questions, requests, or discussions that aren't closely related to work. Here are a few more aspects to keep in mind about channel conversations and chat:

» Files shared by someone in chat are removed after that person leaves the organization.

» Chats can get overwhelming, with unrelated conversations that happen simultaneously. Channel conversations keep messages better organized.

» Channel conversations have more features than chats.

- » In channel conversations, you can @mention specific subsets of the Team membership using a feature called tags. Tags make it possible to, for example, send a notification to all the project managers in a channel message without having to @mention every project manager individually.

- » Many organizations do not retain chats nearly as long as they retain conversations in a Team, which means you can't necessarily rely on a history of private chats.

- » Because chats are private, they don't foster a collaborative environment.

- » The cadence of chat implies a quicker turnaround. If you don't need an immediate response, a channel's cadence is closer to email, which can imply you'll respond within a day or two.

- » Teams can have more people in them than chats, so you can communicate to a larger audience.

WARNING

True collaboration and work-related conversation and decision-making should be occurring in a Team, through channel conversations. Don't let chat be a crutch. It has already become one in many organizations that haven't spent the time and effort training their employees and students on the best ways to use private chats as opposed to channel conversations.

Carrying on Channel Conversations

A *conversation* is a threaded list of individual messages, as shown in Figure 3-1. You can find all conversations in the Posts tab of any channel. Any message you send has a purple line along its left edge; any message addressed to you has a red line. The following sections explain how to make the most of conversations.

Starting a conversation

Starting a new conversation is easy in Teams. (Some might say it's too easy!)

Follow these steps to start a conversation in a channel:

1. **Click Teams in the app bar and then, in the rail, click the channel you want to post in.**

2. **Click the New Conversation button near the bottom of the main area.**

A text box appears, and a number of icons display in a toolbar beneath it. You can start typing your message right away, but you should really continue to the next step first.

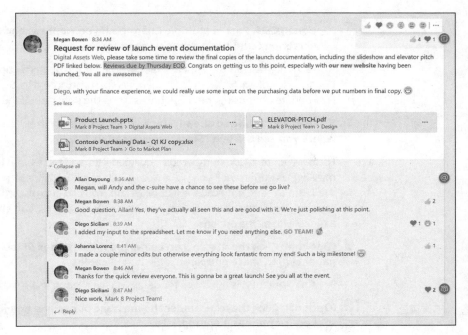

FIGURE 3-1:
Conversations
are like easier-
to-follow email
threads.

3. **Click Format, which is the leftmost icon in the toolbar (the letter *A* with a pencil next to it).**

The Add a Subject field appears along with icons for options to add formatting to the text of your message. The formatting options include Bold, Italic, and others. Hover your cursor over each option to see what it does and add the formatting as you type your message.

4. **In the Add a Subject field, enter a subject for your conversation.**

Every conversation should have a subject, just as every email does (or should). A subject keeps the conversation on topic and makes finding it later much easier when you scroll through the posts. A subject like "Quick question" is too vague. A subject is like a thesis statement: Be specific, detailed, but concise.

5. **(Optional) Click the New Conversation menu above the subject line to change your post into an announcement.**

An announcement stands out much more than a typical post because it adds a banner above the post.

6. **(Optional) Click the Everyone Can Reply menu to restrict who can reply to your message, if warranted.**

Choose You and Moderators Can Reply to limit responses to trusted members of the Team.

7. **(Optional) Click Post in Multiple Channels if you want to send this conversation to multiple channels simultaneously.**

A Select Channels button appears. Clicking the button opens a Choose Channels list of all the Teams and channels you have access to. Select the appropriate ones using the check boxes along the right side of the list.

8. **If you haven't done so already, type your message in the message box where you see the text "Start a conversation."**

Format your text, add numbered or bulleted lists, add tables, and mark your message as important if you want. You can @mention individuals, channels, or the Team to send notifications if appropriate. You can also discard a draft message by clicking the trash can icon. You may have to click an ellipsis to see a menu with all the options.

9. **(Optional) Click the Attach icon below the message box (it looks like a paper clip) to share or upload a file if applicable.**

See Chapter 4 of this minibook for details on file sharing in a conversation.

10. **(Optional) Click the icons under the message box to add emoji, GIFs, stickers, or memes if appropriate.**

You can click the applicable item in the menu that comes up; follow any prompts to finish adding the item to your message. Use these sparingly, or avoid them most of the time and dedicate a channel to fun stuff or watercooler discussion. Graphics like these take up a *lot* of space and can drown out important, work-related text amid a GIF or meme war.

11. **(Optional) Click the Send icon in the lower-right corner (it looks like a paper airplane) or press Ctrl+Enter to send your message on its way.**

If you don't open the formatting options using the A-with-a-pencil icon, you can just press Enter to send a message. When the formatting options are enabled, Enter starts a new line, hence the extra key (Ctrl) in this step.

TIP

If you copy an image from somewhere else, you can paste (Ctrl+V) the image directly in the textbox without having to upload it first. You can do this multiple times in the same message.

Figure 3-2 shows a message in a conversation including a subject, formatting, hyperlinks, an emoticon, an @message to Diego and the channel name Digital Assetts Web, and linked files.

Subject line

Formatting toolbar   Post permissions   Message content

Post type   Post to multiple channels   Discard draft

New conversation ∨   Everyone can reply ∨   Post in multiple channels   🗑

B *I* U̲ S̶ | ∀ A̲ AA | Paragraph ∨ A̲ᴮ | ⟵ ⟶ ≔ ≔ | 99 ⌗ ⟨⟩ ⤢ ⊞ | ! …

Request for review of launch event documentation

Digital Assets Web, please take some time to review the final copies of the launch documentation, including the slideshow and elevator pitch PDF linked below. Reviews due by Thursday EOD. Congrats on getting us to this point, especially with **our new website** having been launched. **You all are awesome!**

Diego, with your finance experience, we could really use some input on the purchasing data before we put numbers in final copy. 🙂

📊 **Product Launch.pptx**   ✕   📄 **ELEVATOR-PITCH.pdf**   ✕
   Mark 8 Project Team > Digital Assets Web   Mark 8 Project Team > Design

📊 **Contoso Purchasing Data - Q1 KJ copy.xlsx** ✕
   Mark 8 Project Team > Go to Market Plan

🖋 📎 ☺ GIF 🗒 ▷ 💡 ᗡ …   ▷

FIGURE 3-2:
Explore the
formatting
options available
for composing a
message.

Additional apps and features   Attachments   Post message

Attach files

Formatting button

Replying to a conversation

It's not a conversation if nobody else takes part, so you'll want to reply to conversations in a channel if you're asked for input or just have something to add. Follow these steps to reply to a conversation in a channel:

1. Click Teams in the app bar and then, in the rail, click the name of the channel where the conversation resides.

Alternatively, if you were @mentioned in the message, you receive a notification. Click Activity at the top of the app bar to display your notifications in the rail, and then click the notification, which takes you right to the conversation.

REMEMBER

2. At the bottom of the conversation, click Reply.

Be sure not to click the New Conversation button by mistake.

3. To see formatting options, click the Format icon.

The formatting toolbar above the message box opens.

4. Type your message in the message box.

Format your text, add numbered or bulleted lists, add tables, and mark you message as important, if you'd like. You can @mention individuals, channels, or the Team to send notifications if appropriate.

Communicating
through Channels and
Private Chat

5. **(Optional) Click the Attach icon to share or upload a file, if applicable.**

   See Chapter 4 of this minibook for more details on file sharing in a conversation.

6. **(Optional) Click the icons under the message box to add emoji, GIFs, stickers, or memes if appropriate.**

   You can click the applicable item in the menu that comes up; follow any prompts to finish adding the item to your message.

7. **Click Send or press Ctrl+Enter to send your reply.**

   If you don't open the formatting options, you can just press Enter to send a message. When the formatting options are enabled, pressing Enter starts a new line, hence the extra key (Ctrl) in this step.

WARNING

Never start a new conversation when you mean to reply to one. Doing so creates an orphaned conversation and splits the original arbitrarily into two competing conversations. If you start a new conversation by mistake, delete your message immediately before someone else replies. If you receive any replies, send a reply asking everyone to delete their replies and include a link to the master conversation.

@mentioning in a conversation message

One of the key features of Teams is the @mention. Taking after Twitter, Facebook, and eventually Slack, an @ in front of a person, channel, or Team name results in a notification to that person, the people who follow the channel, or are members of the Team. The notification appears in their Activity app and indicates to them that they should review the message.

Follow these steps to @mention in a channel message:

1. **Start or reply to a channel conversation.**

   See the sections "Starting a conversation" and "Replying to a conversation," earlier in this chapter, for how to do that.

2. **In the message box, type @.**

   A contact list of suggested names appears above or below the message box. If the correct suggestion displays, click it and jump to Step 4.

3. **Start typing the person's name, the channel name, or Team name and click it in the suggestions when it appears, or press Enter if it's the first suggestion in the list.**

4. **If @mentioning an individual, change how you want the name to appear in the message, if you want.**

   You can press Backspace to remove portions of the name to address a person more informally or to remove extraneous information, like the recipient's department or location. This is a good idea only if your organization's accounts display names with the first name before the last name, like *John Doe* as opposed to *Doe, John*. The latter does not play well with removing parts of a name when @mentioning.

5. **Enter the rest of your message and press Enter or click Send when you're ready to send it.**

When replying to a conversation, you may not be sure whether you should @mention an individual who's already part of the conversation. If you're in doubt, @mention them to ensure that they get the notification. They can mute the conversation notifications, but an @mention always results in a notification to them.

WARNING

Beware of overusing channel and Team @mentions. Channel @mentions notify all Team members who haven't muted the channel notifications. Team @mentions *always* notify all members of the Team. Especially in large Teams, these actions can essentially become spam. Don't be that person.

TIP

@mentions are no longer unique to Teams. You can also use them in Outlook emails as well as in files and comments in Word, Excel, and PowerPoint. In Outlook, an @mention in the body of the message automatically adds the person to the To field. In the Office apps, the @mentioned person receives an email notification that they've been mentioned with a link to the file. @mentions in these instances are useful for identifying exactly which part of a message, file, or comment is meant for whom.

Reacting to conversations

Reacting to a conversation means to add an icon as a response, just like on popular social media websites. Teams offers six reactions: Like (thumbs-up), Love (heart), Laugh, Surprised, Sad, and Angry. The most important one is Like. Like lets you acknowledge or agree with a message in an explicit but passive way; it's a minor game changer in a Team. To react to a message, hover your cursor over a message to reveal the row of available reactions and click one. If others have reacted, you can hover over each reaction to see who reacted that way, as shown in Figure 3-3.

The use of the Like reaction in Teams can meaningfully reduce the number of emails that would otherwise come to your Inbox. A large number of emails consist of low-value-but-must-be-sent acknowledgement messages, often with others CC'd. With Teams, the message author is the only recipient of the notification.

That person is likely the one who wants to know that the message was acknowl-edged. Everyone else in the Team can see the reactions if they want to.

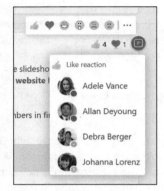

Beyond Like, the other reactions can be more open to interpretation. Incidentally, these six options — Microsoft isn't likely to provide more any time soon — are the same ones you find on Facebook (except for the times when Facebook temporar-ily adds the "caring" option). If your teammates are unsure how to use them, ask how they would use them if they were on social media as a starter.

Setting conversation options

Whenever you see an ellipsis, click it to open the associated menu. Channels and the conversations within them offer a lot of features that can help you along your way. Both the conversation (the first message) and each reply have an options menu. Hover your cursor over the message to reveal both the reactions and the options menu. For example, conversation options include some of the following key features:

>> **Save this Message:** Just like flagging an email, you can save a conversation message for later. To see your saved messages, click your profile photo or initials in the top-right corner of Teams to open the Me menu; then click Saved.

>> **Edit and Delete:** If you're the author of the message, you can edit or delete the message when you make an error or something goes out of date.

>> **Mark as Unread:** Just as you can with an email, you can toggle the message status back to unread so that you'll see it in your notifications.

>> **Copy Link:** When you want to share a message directly with someone else so that they don't have to find it or you don't need to rewrite it elsewhere, copy

the link and send it to them via private chat, email, or text message. The recipient must be a member of the Team to access the link to the message.

>> **Translate:** If you work in an organization that uses multiple languages, you can use built-in machine translation to convert the foreign text into your language. Like all automated translation, it's not perfect, but it's typically good enough.

>> **Immersive Reader:** View the message in a larger format or have it read automatically for those with visual impairment.

>> **Share to Outlook:** Send your conversation in an email to any recipient. See the "Sharing a Teams conversation to Outlook" section, later in this chapter, for details.

>> **Pin:** Pin a conversation in a channel for easy access and reference. Find the pinned conversation by clicking the information icon (a lowercase *i* in a circle) in the top-right corner of the window. You can pin only one conversation per channel, and you can pin only the first message in a conversation (replies don't have the option).

>> **Turn Off Notifications:** If a conversation goes off the rails and keeps notifying you nonstop, you can disable notifications on that conversation without impacting your notifications elsewhere in the channel. After disabling them, the only way you will get a notification from that conversation is if someone @mentions you.

Bouncing between Teams conversations and Outlook emails

Teams and email will coexist for the foreseeable future, so they should probably work together in some way, right? Well, Teams and Outlook have you covered with a few useful tricks up their sleeves. The following two sections describe how to drop an email into Teams. You have two options: forward an email to a channel or share an email to a channel or private chat. Each approach has its pros and cons. Both help you avoid having to rewrite or manually copy content into Teams. Next, you see how to send a Teams conversation via email to an outside recipient.

Forwarding an email to a channel

Follow these steps to forward an email to a channel:

1. **Click Teams in the app bar and, in the rail, find the channel you want to send an email to.**

You might have to click a Team name to see the channel names of that team.

2. **Click the ellipsis next to the channel name to open the More Options drop-down menu; then click Get Email Address.**

   The Get Email Address pane opens.

3. **Click the Copy button.**

   This copies the email address to your Clipboard.

4. **In Outlook or another email program, open the email you want to forward to Teams and, in the email's To field, paste the email address you copied in the last step.**

5. **Make any edits to the message and remove any attachments you don't want to send with it.**

   Remove any "RE" and "FW" from the subject so that it comes through cleanly. You may even want to update the subject so that the context makes sense to those who will see it in Teams.

6. **Click Send.**

TIP

Click Advanced Settings in Step 3 to manage who can send email to this address. You can limit the permissions of the email address to Team members or to certain addresses (for example, limit to @companyA.com and @companyB.com addresses), or you can allow anyone to send email.

TECHNICAL STUFF

The channel email addresses are admittedly long and ugly. There is no easy way to customize the address without using advanced IT tools. If you need to customize it, reach out to your IT team for suggestions.

Sharing an Outlook email to a channel or private chat

Follow these steps to share an email to a channel or private chat:

1. **In Outlook, double-click the email you want to share to Teams.**

   You can share an email to Teams from both the Outlook desktop version and Outlook for the Web.

2. **In the email toolbar, click Share to Teams.**

   In Outlook for the Web, you may have to click the ellipsis next to the Reply and Forward buttons to find this option in the resulting drop-down menu.

3. **In the Share to Teams pop-up that appears, enter the destination.**

   The destination can be a private chat with an individual or a group, or a channel in a Team. Search by recipient name or channel name and select it when it pops up.

4. **Above the email content, include a message.**

   You provide context to readers by describing the email and why it was sent.

5. **Select the Include Attachments check box if you want to include attachments that are already part of the email.**

6. **Click the Share button, as shown in Figure 3-4.**

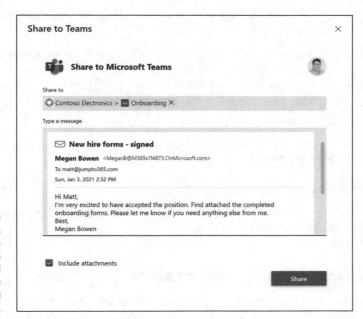

FIGURE 3-4:
Share to Teams in Outlook is a handy way to send an email to a private chat or channel conversation.

REMEMBER

Regardless of whether you choose to forward an email to a channel or use Share to Teams, after you click Share or Send, the email appears in its destination within minutes at most. The shared message begins a new conversation in a channel or posts a message in a private chat. If the email has attachments, the files are stored in the Files tab of the channel or chat. A copy of the email is also stored in the channel's Files tab if you use the channel email address. In both scenarios, the resulting message and attachments are disconnected from the original email. These are copies.

Share to Teams is useful for when you receive an email with information you need to discuss internally before responding. Have your discussion in Teams, protected and without the risk of an errant Reply All email. After the Team reaches a consensus, respond to the original email with the final response and any updated files attached.

But which option — forwarding an email to a channel or using the Share to Teams method — should you choose? Here are some suggestions.

Email a channel if

>> You want to edit the email message or subject before sending. This provides an opportunity to summarize a long email to save everyone else time.

>> You don't want to forward all attachments. You can remove any existing attachments (and even add new ones).

>> You want external people to send content directly to your channel. For example, provide the email address in a request for proposals, and all proposals are automatically submitted to your Team by anyone submitting one.

>> The email is not in your work or school Outlook account.

Use Share to Teams if

>> You need to share an email to a private chat.

>> You want to be able to edit the resulting Teams message (although you can't change the email text itself).

Sharing a Teams conversation to Outlook

In the previous sections, I cover how to send an email to Teams, but what about when you want to do the opposite: Send a Teams message or conversation through Outlook? Teams has you covered there as well with Share to Outlook, as shown in Figure 3-5. Follow these steps to share a Teams conversation or message through Outlook:

1. **Click Teams in the app bar and, in the rail, click the channel where the conversation is, or click Chat in the app bar and, in the rail, open the chat where the message is.**

2. **Hover your cursor over the message, click the ellipsis to open the More Options menu, and then click Share to Outlook.**

   This opens a new email with the Teams messages included in the body.

3. **In the To, CC, and BCC fields, enter your recipients' email addresses.**

   This feature is called Share to Outlook, but you can send these messages to any email address.

4. **(Optional) Update the subject if necessary.**

   The email will take on the subject of a conversation if there is one, but you don't have to use that.

5. **Select the Include Attachments check box if you want to include attachments.**

   Any files associated with the conversation or message will be attached to the email automatically.

6. **Click Send.**

WARNING

This feature is handy but certainly not perfect. For one thing, you may have to give Teams a moment or two to generate the email, so be patient. Second, if you choose to send any message from a channel conversation, it sends the whole conversation, not just the single message you choose. Last, the resulting email displays some — but not all — formatting that might be applied to a message, and it does not include file links.

Getting Familiar with Using Private Chats

The last section shouldn't scare you away from private chat. Chat is great for keeping connected with close colleagues, checking in with old friends, providing updates to your manager, reminding your student to hand in their work, and submitting your lunch order to the intern. Chat is also where you find the meeting chat for most meetings you attend in Teams. Figure 3-6 shows a private chat.

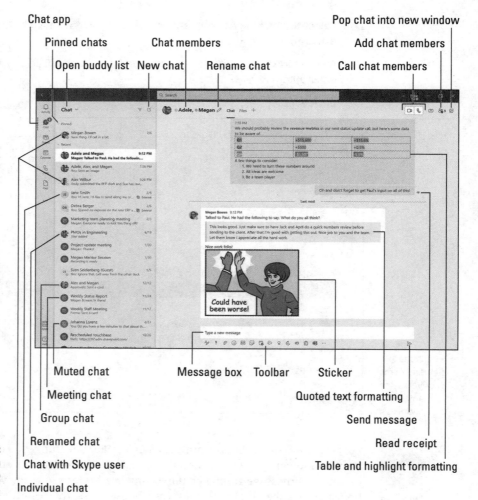

Chat app
Pinned chats
Open buddy list   New chat
Chat members
Rename chat
Pop chat into new window
Add chat members
Call chat members

Muted chat
Meeting chat
Group chat
Renamed chat
Chat with Skype user
Individual chat

Message box   Toolbar   Sticker
Quoted text formatting
Send message
Read receipt
Table and highlight formatting

FIGURE 3-6:
The Chat app with an ongoing group conversation.

Starting a chat with one person or a group

The basic chat is the one-on-one chat with another person or a group chat with multiple people in the organization. Follow these steps to start a chat:

1. **Click Chat in the app bar.**

You see any ongoing chats in the rail and the last chat you opened in the main area.

2. Click the New Chat icon (refer to Figure 3-6) at the top-right of the rail, or press Ctrl+N.

The main area changes to a blank window with the To field at the top.

TIP

3. In the To field, enter the name of the recipient.

Start typing the person's name and click it in the suggested contacts that appear under the To field, or press Enter if it's the first one in the list. If your organization supports doing so, you can send messages to external Teams and Skype users using their email address.

4. (Optional) Add more names in the To field to make this a group chat.

5. Place your cursor in the message box that says "Type a new message" at the bottom of the main area.

The chat appears in the rail under the name of the person or people in the chat, or with a custom chat name (see the "Renaming a chat" section, later in this chapter). If you've chatted with this person or group before, the message history shows up in the chat above the message box.

6. Enter your message in the message box.

REMEMBER

If you'd like to add some flair to your message, click the Format icon at the left end of the icon toolbar under the message box to display the formatting toolbar above the message box. Format your text, add lists or tables, and mark you message as important if you like. You can also @mention people if appropriate.

7. Share or upload a file if applicable.

See Chapter 4 of this minibook for details on file sharing in a chat.

TIP

8. Add emoji, GIFs, stickers, or memes if appropriate.

These visual items are more appropriate for chat than a channel conversation but can still quickly overtake a chat. Just don't allow important text to get drowned out by these (huge) graphical messages.

WARNING

9. Click Send or press Ctrl+Enter to send the message.

If you don't open the formatting options, you can just press Enter to send a message. When the formatting options are enabled, pressing Enter starts a new line, hence the extra key (Ctrl) in this step.

You can chat not only with internal people but also anyone outside your organization who is using Teams, Skype for Business, or the consumer version of Skype. These are called *external chats*. As long as you have the email of the recipient, you can send them a message. Similar to guest access in Teams, external chats must be allowed by your IT team. Reach out to them if you can't get it to work.

Reacting to chat messages

Hover over a chat message to reveal the ability to react. Chats offer the same six reactions as those covered in the "Reacting to conversations" section earlier in this chapter: Like (thumbs-up), Love (heart), Laugh, Surprised, Sad, and Angry, as shown in Figure 3-7. The most important one is Like. Like lets you acknowledge or agree with a message in an explicit but passive way, useful for replacing responses like "okay," "thanks," or "10-4," which can save you from a lot of notifications you don't need if you weren't the sender of the message people are reacting to.

FIGURE 3-7: @mentioning in a chat.

@mentioning in a chat

One of the key features of Teams is the @mention. Taking after Twitter and Facebook and eventually Slack, having an @ in front of a person's name sends the recipient a notification that they've been called out and should see the chat message. Follow these steps to @mention in a private chat:

1. **Start or reply to a private chat.**

   See "Starting a chat with one person or a group," earlier in this chapter, for details.

2. **In the message box, type @.**

   A contact list of suggested names appears above or below the message box. If the correct suggestion displays, click it and jump to Step 4.

3. **Start typing the person's name and click it in the suggestions or press Enter if it's the first suggestion in the list.**

4. **(Optional) Change how you want the name to appear in the message, if you want.**

You can press Backspace to remove portions of the name to address a person more informally or to remove extraneous information, like the recipient's department or location. This is a good idea only if your organization's accounts display names in first name-last name format, like John Doe as opposed to Doe, John. The latter does not play well with removing parts of a name when @mentioning.

5. **Enter the rest of your message and press Enter or click Send when you're ready to send it.**

WARNING

To activate the @mention, you have to select the name of the person. You'll know the @mention is activated when the @ symbol disappears and the person's name changes to purple. Using an @mention will add an @ icon on the right side of the message for the recipient. Refer to Figure 3-7 for an example.

When sending a chat message, you may not be sure whether you should @mention an individual who's already part of the chat. If you're in doubt, @mention them to ensure that they get the notification. They can mute the chat notifications, but an @mention will always notify them.

REMEMBER

You can @mention only individuals in a private chat. You cannot @mention the chat name or any groups.

Renaming a chat

Private group chats can quickly get overwhelming to manage, especially if you have a lot of group chats whose membership is only slightly different. If you have a chat with a name that's too similar to other chats, consider renaming it. Follow these steps to rename a group chat:

1. **Click Chat in the app bar and then, in the rail, click the chat you want to rename.**

The chat opens in the main area, showing a row of names of any members as well several tabs along the top (see Figure 3-8).

2. **To the left of the Chat tab, click the Name Group Chat icon (it looks like a pencil).**

The Group Name pane appears.

3. **Enter the new name in the text box and click Save.**

WARNING

Keep the name short; the rail is only so wide.

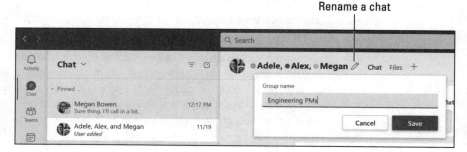

Rename a chat

FIGURE 3-8:
Rename private
group chats to
make managing
and finding
them easier.

You can rename a chat as many times as you want. Actually, anyone in the chat can rename the chat, so let others know if you change the name. However, you cannot rename a one-on-one chat (it will always display the one person's name), nor can you change the name of a meeting chat.

Adding and removing people (including yourself) from a chat

Invariably, you'll need to add people to or remove people from private chats you're in. Each chat is equally owned by all the members, so anyone in the chat can perform this action (which could be a bad thing).

Adding people to a chat

Follow these steps to add someone to a private chat:

REMEMBER

1. **Click Chat in the app bar and, in the rail, click the chat you want to invite someone to.**

   You can add people to a one-on-one chat or a group chat.

2. **In the top-right corner of the chat's main area, click the View and Add Participants icon to reveal a drop-down menu, and then click Add People.**

   The Add pane opens.

3. **Enter the name of the person or people you want to add in the Enter Name, Email, or Tag box.**

   As you add more people, they are listed in the box for now.

4. **Select how much chat history you want to share with the added members.**

   Choose Don't Include Chat History, Include History from the Past Number of Days, or Include All Chat History.

5. **Click the Add button.**

The chat appears in the new members' chat rail automatically. A status update also appears at the bottom of the chat's main area that summarizes the changes. Everyone in the chat can see the status update.

Removing people from a chat

Follow these steps to remove someone from a private chat:

1. **Click Chat in the app bar and, in the rail, click the chat you want to remove someone from.**

2. **In the top-right corner of the chat area, click the View and Add Participants icon.**

A drop-down menu opens that lists all members of the chat.

3. **Hover your cursor over the name of the individual to be removed and click X to the right of their name.**

WARNING

The person has been removed and the chat is no longer listed in their chat rail. Anyone in the chat can remove a member of the chat (which can be good or bad). You can remove someone from a meeting chat, but you may run into certain limitations depending on who the participants are, so don't depend on that possibility.

Leaving a chat

Follow these steps to remove yourself from a private chat:

1. **Click Chat in the app bar and, in the rail, click the chat you want to leave.**

You can remove yourself from any private chat except a meeting chat for which you are the organizer.

2. **Click the ellipsis next to the chat name to open the More Options drop-down menu; then click Leave.**

Anyone in the chat can add you back if you need to return.

Setting chat and message options

Whenever you see an ellipsis, click it click it to open the associated menu. Chats and the messages within them each offer a lot of features that can help you along your way. Hover your cursor over the chat or message to reveal the options menu.

Chat options include some of the following key features:

>> **Pop Out Chat:** Open an ongoing chat in a separate window so that you can keep the chat always available on your computer.

>> **Mark As Unread:** Just like with an email, you can toggle the read status of the last message back to unread so that the chat is bolded and you see any relevant notifications.

>> **Pin a Chat:** Pin your favorite chats to the top of the rail for quick access (refer to Figure 3-6). Unpin at any time.

>> **Mute a Chat:** If you're overwhelmed with all the notifications in a chat, mute it to save your sanity. You'll continue to receive notifications if someone @mentions you. A muted chat has a bell with a line through it as its icon.

>> **Hide a Chat:** When you want to clean up your chat listing, you can hide a chat. Doing so removes it from your list until someone sends a new message. Note that you can't hide a pinned chat; unpin it first.

>> **Notify When Available:** Get a Teams notification when this person's status turns green.

TIP

There is no option to delete a chat. You can leave the chat, but somebody could always add you back. If you want to be truly disassociated from a chat, your best option is to mute it and then hide it.

Message options offer their own features. Open the menu by hovering your cursor over a message in a chat. The options menu will differ whether you're working with a message someone else sent or one you sent. The options include some of the following key features:

>> **Reply:** When you reply to a message, your message will include part of the original message in a quoted format. It provides context, but it's not the same (and we'd argue not as good) as a threaded reply in a channel conversation.

>> **Save This Message:** Just like flagging an email, you can save a chat message for later. To see your saved messages, click your profile photo or initials in the top-right corner of Teams to open the Me menu; then click Saved.

>> **Edit And Delete:** If you're the author of the message, you can edit or delete the message when you make an error or something becomes out of date. Try doing that with email! And don't try to argue that email recall is a viable option; it's like the planets have to align for that to ever work.

>> **Mark as Unread:** Just like with an email, you can toggle the message status back to unread so the chat is bolded and you'll see any relevant notifications.

>> **Share to Outlook**: Send your conversation in an email to any recipient. See the "Sharing a Teams conversation to Outlook" section, earlier in this chapter, for details.

>> **Translate:** If you work in an organization that supports multiple languages, you can use built-in machine translation to convert the foreign text into your language. Like all automated translation, it's not perfect. But it's typically good enough.

>> **Immersive Reader:** View the message in a larger format or have it read automatically for those with vision impairment

>> **Read Receipts:** If you have enabled read receipts for yourself, you see read receipts for anyone else who has them enabled. You won't see read receipts from others if you don't have it enabled for yourself.

Setting Up a Buddy List

If you're familiar with using older messaging tools like Skype for Business or AOL Instant Messenger, you likely remember the concept of the buddy list. In fact, you might prefer it. The default chat listing in Teams is chronological; it shows you your most recent chats from top to bottom. A *buddy list*, on the other hand, allows you to organize individuals and groups in a manner that makes the most sense to you. You might be surprised to know that Teams includes this feature. It's just not obvious to find.

Having a buddy list can make it easier to find the people you want to chat with or call. You can even get a notification when someone is available.

Follow these steps to access and manage your buddy list:

1. Click Chat in the app bar.

2. At the top of the rail, click the downward-pointing caret next to the word Chat and then, in the drop-down menu that appears, click Contacts.

This changes your Chat rail to a list of people groups, not a chronological list of ongoing chats. You may see the "Favorites" or "Other Contacts" groups to start. Add your own people and groups following the next steps.

3. At the bottom of the rail, click Create a New Contact Group, type a name for the group in the pane that appears, and then click Create.

This group is listed in the rail, though it is empty.

4. **To the right of the Group name, click the ellipsis to open the More Options drop-down menu; then click Add a Contact to This Group.**

   The Add to Contacts pane opens.

5. **Enter the name of the person you want to add to your list.**

   Teams provides smart suggestions below the Contact box. If the correct suggestion displays, click it.

6. **Click Add.**

Repeat these steps until you've created the group listings you want to see in the list, like that shown in Figure 3-9. Group names are listed in alphabetical order (except Favorites, which appears to always stay first) as are the contacts in the group. You can change group names and membership using the More Options menu; click the ellipsis to the right of the group name to open that menu. You can close and expand groups using the caret to the left of the group name to keep your list tidy.

FIGURE 3-9:
Building a buddy list.

Chapter **4**

Organizing Your Files in Teams

Teams wouldn't be the hub for modern work if it was meant only for chat and meetings. Creating, editing, reviewing, and collaborating on files is a major aspect of workplace and educational settings. Some people feel like all they ever do is create files and pass them on. Teams is great for creating, sharing, editing, and accessing most or all of your Office 365 files, especially Word documents, Excel spreadsheets, PowerPoint presentations, and OneNote notebooks. But you can also save and access PDFs, images, video, and pretty much any other file type you can imagine in Teams (or the tool behind the scenes, SharePoint, which actually stores those files).

This chapter takes you through the files experience in Teams: creating, organizing, and sharing them. To understand collaborating on files in SharePoint and OneDrive outside the Teams app, see Book 11.

Getting to Your Files in Teams: The Files App and Files Tab

Whether you're in a Team or a private chat, you have a Files tab. In both cases, the Files tab is at the top of the main area of the channel or chat. Click the tab to see the files and folders associated with that space. From there, you can typically open, edit, download, and get a link to a file. You can also likely add certain file types — especially Office files — as a tab in the space for quick access to the file (see the section about using tabs in Chapter 1 of this minibook for more detail).

Another way to locate your files within Teams is through the Files app. Open the Files app by clicking the Files icon in the Teams app bar. When open, it lets you see various listings of files both in Teams and elsewhere in Office 365. Choose which view you want by clicking the view options listed in the rail, which you can see in Figure 4-1. After you make a selection, the list of files is in the main area. The Files app can be a great way to get to files that you use frequently or have recently worked on. Here's an overview of the different views of your files provided in the Files app:

>> **Recent:** These are the files you've most recently opened or edited in Teams, OneDrive, or SharePoint. Think of it as a digital breadcrumb trail of what you've been working on in Office 365. Figure 4-1 shows the Recent view.

>> **Microsoft Teams:** These are the files that have been most recently edited by anyone in the Teams of which you're a member or owner, regardless of who worked on those files last. This view shows you what everyone in your Team has been doing (including yourself) so that you can keep up on your projects, classes, and so on as others work.

>> **Downloads:** This view lists all the files you've downloaded from Teams. It connects to your Windows Downloads folder, so if you remove anything from that folder, it's removed from this view as well. The browser version of Teams doesn't have this view because it can't connect to your Downloads folder from a browser.

>> **OneDrive:** Wow, you can access your entire OneDrive right from Teams? Yes, indeed! You don't have to jump to File Explorer (if you're syncing your files) or open OneDrive in the browser to get to it. It's a handy integration to get you to your personal files from your central app for teamwork. To learn more about OneDrive, see Book 11, Chapter 2.

>> **Additional Cloud Storage:** Connect to external storage apps like Google Drive or Dropbox right from Teams. You'll have to add these yourself, which may depend on whether your IT team has allowed it, but having those apps can be the icing on the cake for file access in one place across multiple repositories.

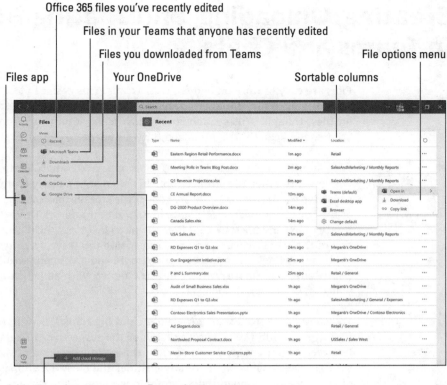

Office 365 files you've recently edited

Files in your Teams that anyone has recently edited

Files you downloaded from Teams

File options menu

Files app   Your OneDrive   Sortable columns

FIGURE 4-1:
The Recent view
of the Files app.

Add external storage apps   External storage apps

WARNING

External storage apps can be handy, but you may not be able to edit Office files directly in Teams from some of these tools. Instead, you may have to download the file, do your work, and then upload and overwrite the original one. For example, you can — somewhat ironically — edit Google Docs, Sheets, and Slides files in Google Drive in Teams, but you cannot edit Word, Excel, and PowerPoint files in Google Drive in Teams directly; you have to download a file to work on it.

TIP

You might be used to accessing files in a shared drive, network share, share file, or a multitude of other synonyms for the concept of accessing files from lettered folders in your File Explorer window. Many organizations use P ("personal") or U ("user") drives for personal files and other letter names for project, class, and work files that entire organizations can access and edit. Fear not! You can sync Teams files to your device for a similar experience, but you'll want to find out the details in Book 11, Chapter 1.

Creating, Uploading, and Sharing Files in Teams and Chats

Files are easy to work on and share in Teams. This ease can lead to a disorganized mess if you're not thinking strategically about how you should be collaborating on files, though. This section covers how to work on your files, collaborate with others, and keep things organized for your needs.

TECHNICAL STUFF

Files aren't actually stored in the Teams app. Wait, what? Teams is actually just a window into other file storage tools in Office 365, namely SharePoint Online and OneDrive for Business. These are robust file storage and sharing tools and, at least at the time of publishing, thanks to SharePoint and OneDrive, Teams can accept pretty much any file type, and files can be as large as 250GB. For files on the larger end of the size spectrum, you need to enable OneDrive sync to work on them (as explained in Book 11, Chapter 1). Learn more about the connection between Teams, SharePoint, and OneDrive later in this chapter, with added detail on when to use which in Chapter 1 of Book 11.

You can open Word, Excel, PowerPoint, and OneNote files right within Teams. The files open within the browser version of the respective Office app inside Teams; however, you if you prefer to work in the desktop version of those apps, you can set that. Open the Files tab of any channel and click the ellipsis icon to the right of an Office file to open the Show Actions menu. Click Open⇨Change Default. In the Change Default pane, choose how you want Office files to open, and then click Save. (For more on the differences between the browser and desktop versions of the Office apps, see Book 11, Chapter 1.)

In addition to Office files, many other file types either open or show previews in Team. PDFs, common image types like PNG and JPG, common video types like MP4 and WMV, and plenty of other typical file types should open or provide a preview. For more specialized file types, you want to either sync or download the files to your computer to open and edit the files; syncing is generally your best bet. Syncing is covered in detail in Book 11, Chapter 1.

Creating files in a Team

Channels in your Team are the perfect place to organize and store the files that you and your colleagues or classmates are working on or need access to. Your channels are already separating your Team into topic-, project-, or outcome-specific areas. A channel essentially is the first "folder" for organizing your files.

When you create or upload a file in a Team, everyone in the Team automatically has edit access to that file. This scenario can involve a bit of a paradigm shift for organizations used to hyper-controlling folder permissions and sending one-off email attachments, but Teams is all about transparency, access, and getting stuff done, so its permission setup is pretty open.

The first thing to know about files in Teams is how to create them from scratch. Follow these steps to create a file in your Team:

1. **Click Teams in the app bar and then click the channel where you want to create a file.**

2. **At the top of the main area, click the Files tab.**

   You see the list of files and folders in this channel. If you want to create your file within an existing folder, click the folder to open it.

3. **On the left side of the toolbar below the Files tab, click New; then select the folder or file type you want to create.**

   You see the list of files and folders in this channel, as shown in Figure 4-2.

4. **Give your file a name and then click Create.**

   The new, blank file opens in the browser version of the respective Office app. You can begin adding content to the file. All your changes are saved automatically.

You can also create folders using the same steps; choose Folder instead of a file type in Step 3 and give the folder a name.

TIP

You may also have existing files on your computer. You can drag files directly from Windows File Explorer, your desktop, or other storage spaces on your computer and drop them right in the Files tab of your channel to upload them.

Sharing files in a Team

When it's time to reference a file in a channel conversation, you'll want to attach, or share, a link to the file so that it's easily accessible to the people you're addressing in your message.

The easiest way to share an existing file in a channel is to add it as an attachment to a channel message. Follow these steps to add an attachment to a message:

1. **Click Teams in the app bar and then click the channel where you want to post.**

Upload files

See the library in SharePoint

Create folders or Office files

Pin files for quick access

Change the view and layout

FIGURE 4-2:
The Files tab in a channel has options for creating, editing, organizing, and viewing your files.

Organize files into folders

File and folder options

Tag files with custom columns

Some folders are automatically created from other actions

Sort, filter, and group by column information

2. **In the message window on the right, click the New Conversation button, or click the Reply button below an ongoing conversation.**

For more details, see the steps in Chapter 3 of this minibook for creating or replying to a channel conversation.

3. **Click the Attach icon.**

This icon looks like a paper clip and appears under the message box.

4. **From the drop-down menu that appears, choose the file source.**

There are four options to start, but it may include additional cloud storage like Google Drive or Dropbox if you've enabled them. These options are shown in Figure 4-3; this figure shows Google Drive because it was added as an option:

- **Recent:** Shows all files you have recently opened or edited. These files could stored in a Team, your OneDrive, or elsewhere in Office 365.

- **Browse Teams and Channels:** Shows the folders in your channel so that you can select files in the channel. But you can also click the upward-pointing arrow in the top-left corner of the menu to access files in other channels and Teams if you need to reference files from elsewhere.

- **OneDrive:** Lists all the files in your OneDrive so that you can upload a copy of a file to Teams.

- **Upload from My Computer:** Opens the file explorer for your computer, which lets you upload a file you might be storing on your hard drive or desktop.

5. **Choose whether to upload a copy or share a link.**

   This is an important decision. You don't want to have multiple copies of files flying around in different Teams or channels if you don't need to; people may not know which copy is the "right" copy. After you make a selection, the file is displayed as a box with an icon and filename in your message. The box looks the same whether you choose Upload a Copy or Share a Link. Here's what each does:

   - **Upload a Copy:** Uploads a copy of the file directly into the Files tab of the channel you're posting in, and the file box displayed in your message links to that file. That means, for example, if you chose a file from another channel in the same Team, you now have two copies of the same file in the same Team, accessible by the same people. Be sure that makes sense for your situation, before choosing this option.

   - **Share a Link:** Links the file box to an existing file, wherever it happens to be stored. This choice keeps one master copy of a file that everyone goes to, even if the file isn't stored in this channel.

6. **Repeat Steps 3 through 5 for any additional files you want to attach.**

   You can attach multiple files to a single message. You can't attach folders, though. To reference a folder, copy the link to it and paste that in your message instead.

7. **Click the Send icon in the lower right of the message window to post your message.**

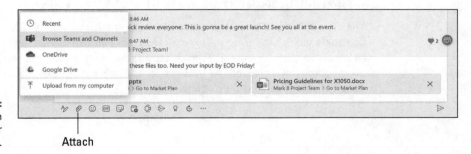

FIGURE 4-3:
Click the Attach icon to upload or link to a file.

Attach

Anytime you click Upload a Copy when attaching a file, the file gets uploaded to the Files tab of that channel, and it's not organized into subfolders in any way. From the Files tab, you can share a link through the Browse Teams and Channels option in Step 4 whenever you want to attach that file. You can attach (in this case, link to) a file using Browse Teams and Channels as many times as you want. The file doesn't get "attached" in the conversation like it would in an email, but rather just a link to it is included.

Because uploading an attachment sends your file straight into the Files tab, locating it in a list of files can be difficult. The best way to share your files is to upload them to the Files tab yourself so that you can place them in folders or subfolders in the channel. Then choose Browse Teams and Channels in Step 4 when you want to reference it in a conversation.

The file should be the only version that exists, and the links can provide easy access to it. This is a major difference from sending email attachments: typically you request feedback from multiple people and send them an attachment, perhaps a Word document. Each recipient has their own version to review and send back, and you have to go through all of them. It's a logistical nightmare. But with a Teams attachment, everyone receives a link to the one copy of that file, which everyone can edit simultaneously. It's a much more efficient way to collaborate.

Using the Files tab in a channel

The Files tab, which is located in the row of tabs in the main window of every channel, is sort of the Windows File Explorer for a channel. On this tab, you can create, upload, and access files for that channel. You can also manage the view of the files — or how they display — as shown in Figure 4-2.

In a channel's Files tab, you can create Office files and folders as well as upload files directly. In fact, you can upload many files and folders simply by selecting them on your computer and then dragging and dropping them into the Files tab. These files then become available to everyone else in the Team from any device that supports Teams (computer, tablet, smartphone).

Organizing your files within the Files tab

The files in your Files tab are the files you see if you choose Browse Teams and Channels when attaching a file to a message. You can also attach files from other channels in your Team and even other Teams when sending a message. No additional copies are created, so you retain a single version of a file no matter how many people receive the link to it.

REMEMBER

Just keep in mind that people in Team B may not have access to a file in Team A because they're not members. Permissions are always important yet sometimes difficult to traverse!

WARNING

You can use folders to organize your files, but try not to create too many levels of subfolders; those complex folder structures seemingly require an atlas to traverse, wasting the time of people who are unfamiliar with them. There is a character limit to the link length for a file, so too many layers of subfolders could cause you to break that limit. Instead, you can add columns to help organize your files with tags (refer to Figure 4-2 an example of using custom tags). Book 11, Chapter 3 tells you more about this type of organization.

Understanding where channel files are stored

The files in each channel's Files tab are not stored in Teams. When a Team is created, additional workspaces in Office 365 are created alongside it. One of those workspaces is a SharePoint team site. Each Team has a team site behind it, and all files in a Team are stored in the Documents library of that site. I cover more about SharePoint team sites in Book 11, Chapter 3.

REMEMBER

You can access your Team's SharePoint site by opening the Files tab of any channel in your Team and clicking Open in SharePoint in the toolbar. This will open your browser and show you the channel's files where they actually live: in the SharePoint site (see Figure 4-4).

The SharePoint site isn't simply another way to look at your Team's files. At least at the time of publishing, SharePoint offered more features for dealing with files than the Files tab in Teams does. You may actually need SharePoint to do your work. Some notable examples of options you have in SharePoint and not Teams are to share a file or folder to someone who's not a member of the Team; manage access of a file or folder; see a file's version history; restore a file from the Recycle bin; and receive email alerts.

TIP

You can view the rest of the Team's files by clicking Documents in the breadcrumb trail, the path of folders above the file and folder listing (refer to Figure 4-4). This will reveal a folder for each channel in your Team. You can create additional folders here, but they will not create channels in Teams. To see these extra-channel files in Teams, click the General channel in your Team, open the Files tab, and click Documents in the breadcrumb trail under the New button. This is a unique feature available only in a Team's General channel.

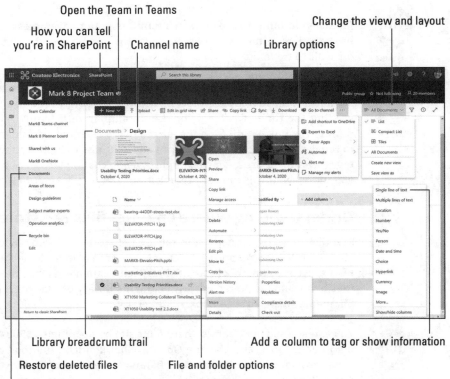

Open the Team in Teams

How you can tell
you're in SharePoint

Channel name

Library options

Change the view and layout

Add a column to tag or show information

FIGURE 4-4:
Files in your
Team actually live
in an associated
SharePoint site.

Library breadcrumb trail

Restore deleted files

File and folder options

All channel files are in the Documents library

Adding a new document library to access in Teams

The Documents library mentioned in the previous section is where all files and folders in a channel's Files tab are stored. But it's not the only library you can have in a SharePoint site, or in your Team for that matter. SharePoint is made up of pages, lists, and document libraries, as covered in more detail in Book 11, Chapter 3. Document libraries can have certain file templates, columns, permissions, and other features associated with it that other libraries in the site may not.

Sometimes you might want to have a separate library from the Documents library, and be able to access it in your Team. Follow these steps to create a new library and even add it as a tab in your channel if you want:

1. **Click Teams and then click the General channel of your Team.**

2. **Click the Files tab and then, in the toolbar below the tab, click Open in SharePoint.**

    The SharePoint team site associated with the Team opens.

3. **Click the Team icon or initials next to the site name in the top-left of the page.**

   The home page of the site opens.

4. **In the toolbar, click New and then, in the drop-down menu, click Document library.**

   In the pane that appears, provide a name and description for your library, and then click Create. Add files, folders, columns, and any other content you'd like. Book 11, Chapter 3 offers some guidance.

5. **(Optional) To add the library to your channel, return to Teams and click the channel in which you want to add the library.**

6. **To the right of the Files tab, click the + (plus sign).**

   The Add a Tab pane opens.

7. **Click SharePoint, select the Document libraries tab, choose your newly created library, and then click Save.**

   You may see another option in the initial Add a Tab pane called Document Library. That option will be retired and may already be so by the time you're reading this. Use the SharePoint option as described in this step.

WARNING

WARNING

Remember that each Team has its own SharePoint site associated with it. A Team and its SharePoint site have the same permissions, which can't be uncoupled. You can create a library in a different SharePoint site and add it as a tab in your Team, but beware that the permissions could be different. Permissions are important and sometimes difficult to work through, so always think ahead about the implications of the permissions you're working with!

REMEMBER

You can add the new library to as many or as few channels as you want. Be aware, though, that the toolbar and options in this library's new tab don't exactly match those you find in the Files tab. The Files tab is a native experience built into Teams, whereas an added library is built on top of Teams and therefore doesn't have some of the features the Files tab has. As long as you know this going in, you should be fine using your new library resources.

Sharing files in a private chat

File sharing in Teams isn't limited to channels. You may want to send a file to one or a few people you've been talking with in a private chat. Attaching a file to a private chat message is similar to attaching files to a message in a channel, but not quite the same. Follow these steps to add an attachment to a message:

1. Click Chat in the app bar and then begin the private chat or create a new one.

Follow the steps outlined in Chapter 3 of this minibook for creating a private chat or group chat.

2. Click the Attach icon.

This icon looks like a paper clip and appears under the message box.

3. Choose the file source.

You can either share an existing file from your OneDrive or upload a file from your computer. Select the file and click Open (if uploading from your computer) or Share (if sharing from OneDrive).

After you make a selection, you see the file displayed as a box with an icon and filename in your message. The box looks the same whether you choose Upload from Your Computer or OneDrive.

4. If available, choose your Share settings.

Click the permission menu under the filename. Depending on the link settings, you can manage the permissions, set an expiration date on the access, set a password, and even block the recipient(s) from downloading the file. This feature works for Word, Excel, PowerPoint, OneNote, PDF, and a limited set of other file types. See Figure 4-5; also see the warning after the steps.

5. Repeat Steps 2 through 4 for any additional files you want to attach.

You can attach multiple files to a single message, but you must attach them one at a time. You can't attach folders, though. To reference a folder, copy the link to it and paste that in your message instead.

6. Click the Send icon in the lower right of the message window to post your message.

WARNING

It's probably best to choose the People Currently in This Chat setting regardless of which option is automatically selected for you because it doesn't overshare access, nor does it require you to go through the hassle of individually selecting each person's name. Just be aware that, at least at the time of publishing, if people are added to or removed from the chat, the permissions of the file will not update. New people will not be able to access the file, and people who are removed from the chat will continue to have access to the file. The People Currently in This Chat sharing option is great for keeping the file protected, but it's not especially robust. For details on changing permissions, see Book 11, Chapter 2.

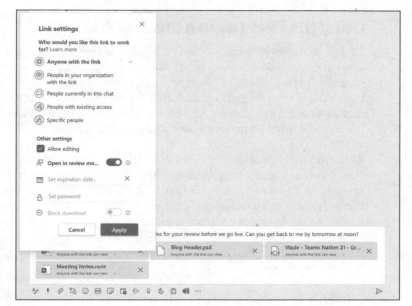

FIGURE 4-5:
Attaching a link to
a file and setting
its permissions in
a chat message.

A WORD OF CAUTION ABOUT FILE SHARING IN CHAT

REMEMBER

Sharing files is a critical aspect of any workplace or school, and a lot of times people are busy and need to *just share that file now* because they need that input or review, or they must get that document submitted. Sharing files via private chat has become a standard, just-do-it option that many people default to. Try to resist that urge. Communicating and — especially — sharing files through private chat can lead to a mess of permission and access issues that requires cleanup later.

When sharing work-related files that will ultimately require input, reviews, and other collaborative experiences, use a Team to share the files and make sure that the right people have access to this Team. Don't share those files in private chat. You can read more about when to use Teams, SharePoint, or OneDrive for file sharing in Book 11, Chapter 1.

Using the Files tab in a private chat

Like a channel in a Team, a private chat also has a Files tab at the top of the main area after you select a chat, but it doesn't work the same way as its cousin in a channel. Instead, the Files tab in a private chat is just a quick way to find files that have already been shared in that chat. As a chat goes on, scrolling up the history of messages seemingly forever to find and access a file would be difficult. The Files tab is the place to go to see all files shared in that chat.

When you click the Files tab, it shows a central listing of all the files shared in that chat, by whom, and when, as shown in Figure 4-6. You can also open a file, copy its link, or download it. In contrast to a channel's Files tab, you cannot upload files, organize them in folders, or change views. The Files tab in a private chat is strictly a way to access files, not organize them.

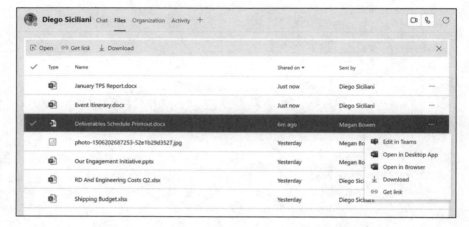

FIGURE 4-6:
The Files tab in a private chat lists all files that have been shared in that chat.

Understanding where files shared in a private chat are stored

The files shared in a private chat are not stored in Teams. Instead, any file that's shared using the Attach button in a private chat is stored in the sender's OneDrive for Business. You can either share an existing OneDrive file — which simply changes the permissions of the file and provides a link in the chat — or upload a file.

When you or anyone else in the chat uploads a file, the file gets stored in the sender's OneDrive in a folder called Microsoft Teams Chat Files, as shown in Figure 4-7. This folder is essentially a dumping zone because Teams needs to store the file *somewhere* if the sender didn't store it in a place that makes sense for others to find it when needed.

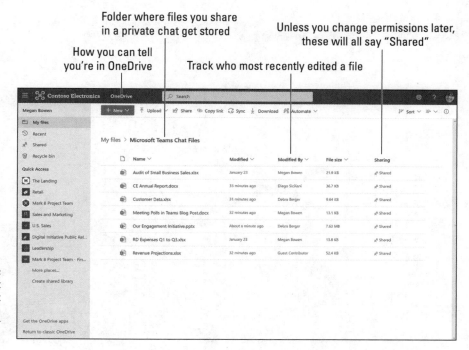

Folder where files you share
in a private chat get stored

Unless you change permissions later,
these will all say "Shared"

How you can tell
you're in OneDrive

Track who most recently edited a file

FIGURE 4-7:
The Microsoft
Teams Chat
Files folder in
OneDrive for
Business.

TIP

After you share a file in a private chat, you *can* move the file from one place in your OneDrive to another (still in your OneDrive) without breaking the link. (See Book 11, Chapter 2 for more about what you can do with OneDrive.) That said, rather than dumping files into a catch-all folder, the best experience for you is to upload a file to an appropriate folder in your OneDrive first, and then share the file from OneDrive when you click the Attach icon. You'll likely thank yourself later.

WARNING

Anyone that wants to share a file through private chat *must* have a OneDrive account. When you chat with people in a Teams meeting who aren't in the organization, or you chat with Teams or Skype users from other organizations, you often find that they can't share a file. That's most likely because those users don't have the type of Office 365 account that comes with a OneDrive account or they're not allowed to share OneDrive files with people in other organizations. Having no OneDrive account means no file sharing in a private chat or meeting chat. To get around this, *you* should share the file with everyone, or the external person can email the file to you and you can upload it in the chat.

Chapter **5**

Getting Together for Online Meetings

E ven if attending a meeting is how you were introduced to Teams in the first place, you may not be aware of all the features that come with a Teams meeting. Whether you're an attendee, a presenter, or the organizer, Teams provides many options to optimize the experience for everyone involved. All these available options can also be overwhelming, though. This chapter covers all the key features you need to know, whether you're running the meeting or simply sitting in.

Understanding Channel Meetings

Channel meetings are a unique meeting feature in Teams. Most people are used to scheduling a meeting with designated invitees — and you can still do that using either Teams or Outlook, as covered in later sections of this chapter. But a *channel meeting* is a meeting held in a channel and accessible to all members of a Team. Although you can — and should —invite key individuals to a channel meeting, the meeting in the channel is visible and accessible to anyone in the Team who wants to join it.

Once you schedule one, a channel meeting posts as a new conversation in the channel, just as if you had clicked the New Conversation button and posted a message, as covered in Chapter 3 of this minibook. This conversation, however, starts with a meeting appointment. The conversation under the initial meeting post comprises the meeting chat. When the meeting is ongoing, you see visual indicators such as a video camera icon next to the channel name in the rail and a purple bar and list of attendees at the top of the conversation in the main area (see Figure 5-1).

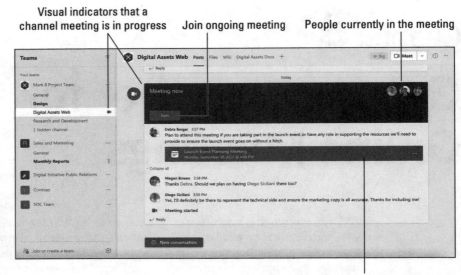

FIGURE 5-1: Channel meeting details and chat are listed in a channel, with options to join if the meeting is ongoing.

Channel meetings can be a bit confusing because for most organizations, a channel meeting does *not* automatically invite the whole Team to the meeting. Instead, it exists in the channel for anyone to join. So if you're expecting certain people to join, you need to invite them. Or if you're conducting a class, you should invite all the students in the class.

Channel meetings *used* to invite everyone until Microsoft made a change to how these meetings work. Older Teams (such as those created before the summer of 2018) may still use the older setting and invite the entire Team. Reach out to your IT team for guidance if necessary.

REMEMBER

Use channel meetings to encourage a collaborative workplace and environment. The ability to see what others are working on and join in to help and support can be surprisingly effective at increasing efficiency for your Team members.

Scheduling a Meeting

You can't have a meeting until you schedule it! You can schedule meetings ahead of time or use Teams calling features to kick off ad hoc meetings. Teams lets you create a standard meeting, a webinar (which is basically a standard meeting with a registration page and sign-up process), or a live event, which allows attendees only to watch; live events are best used for town halls, trainings, and large webinars.

Scheduling from Teams or Outlook

You can schedule a Teams meeting from both Teams and Outlook. The meeting will display mostly the same information in your Teams and Outlook calendar. The calendar entry is the same in both apps because they both use your one Office 365 calendar. Teams offers more options than Outlook to manage the meeting, though.

Follow these steps to schedule a Teams meeting in Teams or Outlook:

1. **In Teams or Outlook, click Calendar in the app bar.**

2. **In the top-right of the calendar in Teams, click New Meeting; in the Ribbon in Outlook, click New Teams Meeting.**

The new meeting window opens in the respective app.

3. **In the appropriate boxes, enter your meeting name, invitees (required or optional), date and time, description, and other meeting information.**

WARNING

You can schedule a channel meeting only from Teams, not Outlook, by selecting a channel from the Channel drop-down menu. See the "Understanding channel meetings" section, earlier in this chapter, for details.

4. **When you're done setting up your meeting, click the Send button.**

Your meeting automatically includes join information.

TIP

You can also schedule Teams meetings by clicking the Calendar icon under the message boxes in both private chat (for a private meeting) and a channel conversation (for a channel meeting).

Getting Together for
Online Meetings

Kicking off a meeting through Meet Now or a private chat

Sometimes you need to have a meeting *now,* and scheduling it from your calendar doesn't make sense. You can call a bunch of people from an ongoing chat, but the Meet Now feature is better.

A Meet Now meeting creates an ad hoc meeting without an associated calendar invitation. From the meeting, you can invite people and use all the typical meeting features outlined in the "Engaging in a meeting" section, later in this chapter. You can start a Meet Now meeting from multiple locations:

>> **From a channel:** Open the channel and click the Meet button in the top-right corner. Doing so starts a channel meeting. When meeting, all other channel members can see that a meeting is going on, which can be useful when you want people to join if they have the time or the topic is interesting.

>> **From your calendar:** Open your Teams or Outlook calendar and click Meet Now at the top of the window. Doing so starts a private meeting.

>> **From a private chat:** You don't use the actual Meet Now feature for this type of meeting, but you can call everyone in an ongoing private chat using the Audio call or Video call buttons in the top-right corner of the chat. Or you can use the Video icon that appears under the chat message box. There is no dedicated meeting chat to go along with it (just the existing chat).

REMEMBER

When you're in a Meet Now meeting, you can invite people to or share the Join link (see "Adding people to an ongoing meeting," later in this chapter). One of the benefits of a Meet Now meeting over a direct call from a private chat is that you can share the link rather than call people. That way, they can join at their convenience rather than be bothered by a direct call while in the middle of something pressing.

Managing meeting options and participant roles

When scheduling a meeting, you likely shouldn't just click Send and call it a day. Once the meeting is on your calendar, you as the organizer can manage a number of meeting options. The most important task is probably assigning roles to participants, but there are a number of other useful options as well.

To view meeting options, click the Calendar app in the Teams app bar, click the meeting in the calendar, and click the Edit button to expand the meeting from your Teams calendar. Then click Meeting Options in the toolbar at the top of the appointment to open the Meeting Options page. Any changes you make are saved automatically and applied to the meeting immediately. Here are some key options:

>> **Meeting Roles:** Each meeting has three roles: organizer, presenter, and attendee. The organizer is like a super-presenter and is the person who schedules the meeting and can manage the meeting options. Presenters have more options than attendees, but not as many as the organizer. See Table 5-1 for a list of the features available to each role.

>> **Lobby:** The lobby is a holding area for attendees before the organizer or a presenter admit them into the meeting. You can choose who can bypass the lobby automatically (including dial-in participants, if you choose that setting). The Participants pane in the meeting displays the names of anyone waiting in the lobby, and you can let them in during the meeting. Having a lobby helps avoid "Zoom bombing," which is a cheeky term for when outsiders join your meeting without your consent and cause disruption (usually because the meeting link is shared publicly, such as on a website).

>> **Hard Mute and Disabled Cameras:** These options let you limit the attendees' ability to enable their microphone or video. These limits prevent or reduce unnecessary interruptions in larger meetings like town halls, webinars, and large training sessions.

>> **Disable Chat:** Manage whether the meeting chat is always available, available only during the meeting, or exists at all.

There are other Meeting Options that you may want to explore as well.

Roles are a critical but underused feature for meetings. Attendees are essentially limited to managing only their own microphone, video, pinning, and traversing shared PowerPoint Live slides. Presenters have more control than attendees, and the organizer holds the keys to the kingdom with control of everything. Table 5-1 covers the features of a meeting and who has access to them.

Using dial-in conference lines

Teams meetings can have conference bridge lines automatically included with a meeting invitation that goes out to recipients. These dial-in lines require an additional license (and cost) for the meeting organizer, but many organizations invest in this feature for two reasons: to provide the most accessibility to join a meeting, and to allow for a more analog backup if Teams happens to be down, which definitely happens sometimes.

TABLE 5-1   **Feature Availability for Each Meeting Role**

Feature Access	Organizer	Presenter	Attendee
Share video and audio	✓	✓	✓
Use meeting chat	✓	✓	✓
Request control of a shared screen or app	✓	✓	✓
Privately traverse a PowerPoint Live presentation shared by another participant	✓	✓	✓
Pin a participant's video	✓	✓	✓
Mute other participants	✓	✓	
Share your screen or apps or start PowerPoint Live	✓	✓	
Request control of a presenter's PowerPoint Live presentation	✓	✓	
Remove participants	✓	✓	
Admit participants from the lobby	✓	✓	
Change meeting roles of participants	✓	✓	
Start or stop meeting recording	✓	✓	
Can unmute when hard mute is enabled	✓	✓	
Spotlight a participant's video	✓	✓	
End a meeting	✓		
Download meeting participant list	✓		
Change meeting options	✓		
Start and manage breakout rooms	✓		

You don't have to do anything to include a dial-in line with your meeting. If you have the license, Teams automatically provides a phone number and conference ID in the Join information included at the bottom of every meeting invitation. The conference ID is unique to the meeting, not to a person or organization. Each meeting has its own conference ID, so no one ever has to reserve conference lines.

If you have the license, all your meetings have a dial-in number, and recipients see clear instructions for joining.

Joining a Meeting

Meeting invitees can join Teams meetings from the Teams desktop app, the mobile app, or a desktop browser like Microsoft Edge or Google Chrome — no plug-ins or downloads required. This capability is helpful when you're meeting with external invitees who may not use Teams; they don't need the Teams app or a Teams account to attend a meeting. That said, the best experience is always in the Teams desktop app. Keep reading to find out the options and how to use them.

Joining from a browser

You can use the browser version of Teams to attend a meeting. This is useful for external attendees or those who use a computer that doesn't have Teams installed, or who don't want to log into the desktop app. The browser version is not as feature rich as the desktop app, but it provides all the basic tools needed for leading or attending an online meeting.

TECHNICAL STUFF

Only Microsoft Edge and Google Chrome on both Windows and macOS are fully supported for Teams meetings. Some other browsers will allow you to join, but not all browser features will work. Stick with Edge or Chrome.

REMEMBER

Each Teams meeting invitation includes a Join section at the bottom of the initial email invitation. This section includes a link to join, an associated dial-in number (if you have the feature), a Join code, and other support links. This information is automatically added to every meeting invitation. Figure 5-2 shows an example of Join meeting information in an invitation. The Join information should work for anyone as long as their device doesn't block Teams meeting web addresses. At the time of publishing, additional join options were set to launch, so yours may look a bit different.

FIGURE 5-2:
Each meeting invite includes various ways to join the meeting.

> **Join on your computer or mobile app**
> Click here to join the meeting
> **Or call in (audio only)**
> +1 212-555-1234,,123456789#   United States, New York
> Phone Conference ID: 123 456 789#

Follow these steps to join a meeting from a browser:

1. **In the browser, open the invitation or calendar appointment for the meeting.**

WARNING

If you're using Teams, you want to be logged into Teams in your browser via teams.microsoft.com. Attendees from outside the organization who do not use Office 365 need to open the meeting appointment in their email or calendar.

2. **Click the Join button (in Teams) or click the Join link at the bottom of the invitation (in any email app).**

All Teams meeting invitations include a section at the bottom with a link to join the meeting. Anyone using Teams can use this link, but it's especially useful for people who use other email tools like Gmail, Yahoo, AOL, or other email accounts.

3. **Configure your audio, video, and background.**

See the next section for more information on how to choose your meeting settings.

4. **Click the Join Now button.**

WARNING

As of the time of publishing, the browser version of Teams does not support most added apps, the modern pre-join activities covered in the next section, or various view options — including Together mode — listed in the "Changing your view and using Together mode" section, later in this chapter. Follow the prompts given to join.

Setting your video, audio, and background

After you click Join or a link to join a meeting, Teams displays one of two versions of a screen (as of the time of publishing): the modern one in the Teams desktop app, and a simpler one in the browser and mobile versions of Teams. Figure 5-3 displays both versions. The browser version will likely get an update soon to align more closely with the modern experience, so if it doesn't look exactly as shown in Figure 5-3, that's probably why.

This section covers what you see in the desktop app. Follow these steps to configure your meeting settings to participate in the meeting:

1. **Click the toggle switch next to the Video icon to enable your video (refer to Figure 5-3).**

You see a prominent preview of your video. This preview appears if you have a webcam or a camera attached to your device.

Joining in the app

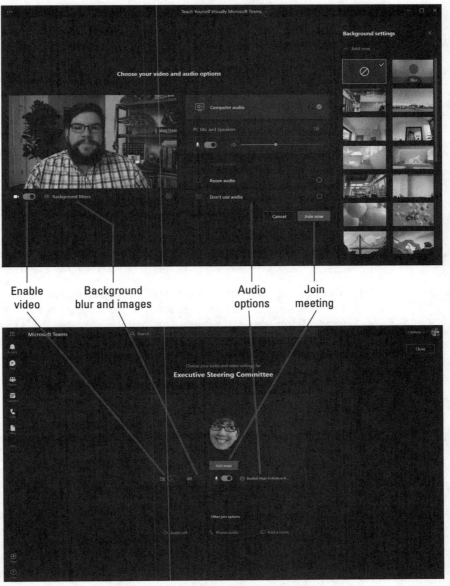

Enable
video

Background
blur and images

Audio
options

Join
meeting

FIGURE 5-3:
The view of
meeting video
and audio
options from the
desktop (top) or
the browser app
(bottom).

Joining in the browser

2. Click Background Filters and select a background if you want.

Select one of the following: Blur; a provided background image; or your own
background image that you upload from your computer. If you choose the
latter, use a JPG, PNG, or BMP image between 360 x 360 pixels and 2048 x 2048
pixels in size. The bigger, the better!

3. **Select your audio device.**

   You can use the computer or an attached audio device, or a Teams-enabled conference room that you connect to. When selecting a room, Teams may automatically detect it. If so, click Join and add this room. If the room was not detected, click Room Audio and enter or select the room name. Not all organizations support rooms.

4. **(Optional) Click the Device Settings gear icon to change your camera, microphone, or speakers.**

   This is necessary only if Teams did not automatically select the right camera, microphone, or speakers.

5. **Click Join Now to join the meeting.**

Engaging in a Meeting

After you join a meeting, there are a lot of options, best practices, and behavioral considerations to be mindful of. Many of these concepts are important for a meeting facilitator to manage, but plenty of options are available to attendees to maximize their meeting experience, too.

Changing your view and using Together mode

Now that you're in your meeting, you can set view options to see and hear all the people taking part (or at least the ones you need to see). All view options prioritize participants who turn their video on. Anyone using only audio shows up smaller, as a blank space with their profile photo or initials. Here are the available view options (see Figure 5-4):

>> **Gallery view:** Usually the default, Gallery view displays up to nine people, typically in a 3x3 format. However, when content is shared, the orientation of the videos can change.

>> **Large Gallery view:** Useful for large meetings and classes, Large Gallery view displays up to 49 people, typically in a 7x7 format. However, when content is shared, the orientation of the videos can change.

>> **Together mode:** A unique feature to Teams, Together mode takes automatic cutouts of participants' video feeds and places them on a virtual background. Click Change Scene in the bottom-left corner to update the background.

View options   Meeting toolbar

FIGURE 5-4:
Gallery view (left)
and Together
mode (right).

Gallery view   Together Mode

REMEMBER

View choices are personal to each participant. When you change your view, you're changing it only for you. You can't force a view on another participant. This is important especially for Together mode because if participants don't know others are using Together mode, they may not turn the camera on, or may not orient themselves in a way that makes the Together mode experience great. A meeting facilitator should let all participants know about Together mode if participants are likely to want to use it.

TIP

Unlike most view options, if a presenter changes the Together mode scene (its background), the scene is changed for all participants who use Together mode. Talk to your IT team about creating custom Together mode scenes.

Pinning and spotlighting participants

It can be helpful to highlight key presenters while they're speaking. Doing so not only makes it easier to follow the topic but also helps avoid promoting other participants just because they have their video on and are making noise. Because the screen may change here and there, identifying the individuals who have the floor can keep attention on the key speakers. Teams offers two options for this: pinning and spotlighting.

>> **Pin:** All participants can pin individuals they want to keep "pinned" to a visible area on the screen. When you pin a someone, you do not affect anyone else's view of the meeting. The person you pin does not know you've pinned them. You can pin as many people as the view supports (nine for Gallery view and 49 for Large Gallery view). Together mode does not support pinning.

>> **Spotlight:** Spotlighting is like a forced pin for everyone and only presenters can spotlight someone. As of the time of publishing, a presenter can spotlight up to seven participants, including that presenter. Spotlighted participants see a notification that they are spotlighted. **Note:** If any participants are joining

from a browser, as of now, the spotlighted person overtakes any shared content such as a shared screen or PowerPoint presentation. The Spotlight feature works well only if all participants are using the Teams app (desktop or mobile), not a browser, to join.

You have two ways to pin or spotlight someone:

>> **Right-click the participant's video:** This option is the easiest of the two. If the participant you want to highlight is already showing in your meeting, you can right-click that person and then click Pin or Spotlight in the menu that appears. But the person's video may not be displaying based on the circumstances of the meeting, in which case use the Participants pane (described in the next bullet). Unpin or remove Spotlight using the same steps.

>> **Participants pane:** If the video you want to pin or spotlight is not currently showing in your meeting, click the Show Participants icon on the meeting toolbar (refer to Figure 5-4), scroll through the Participants pane, click the ellipsis to the right of their name to open the More Options drop-down menu, and click Pin or Spotlight. This option involves more steps but is always available.

TIP

A good meeting facilitator makes strong use of spotlighting to ensure that speakers are promoted and always visible to the meeting's participants, as long as everyone is using the Teams app and not attending from a browser.

Muting yourself and others

Silence can be beautiful, especially in an online meeting. Background noises coming through open microphones can create mind-numbing distractions during a meeting. The worst part is that the offender is the only one who doesn't know the impact they're having on the meeting. Teams does its best to try to cancel out background sound, but it's not perfect.

Various mute buttons in Teams are highly useful. If you're not a main participant in a meeting, you should mute yourself. In fact, when you join a large meeting, Teams enables mute automatically. Following are the muting options available to participants in a meeting:

>> **Mute:** Click the Mute icon on the meeting toolbar to mute and unmute yourself. This is one of the few icons in the app that indicates its current status rather than the status after you click it. If you see a line through the icon, you're muted.

>> **Mute a Participant:** If one participant in particular is making a lot of unproductive noise, a presenter can mute that person by clicking the Show Participants icon on the meeting toolbar, scrolling through the Participants pane, clicking the ellipsis to the right of their name to open the More Options drop-down menu, and clicking Mute Participant. And no, you cannot unmute someone else; that's a major breach of privacy, which is why it's not available.

>> **Mute All:** If your meeting is large, and various unmuted individuals are making noise, muting them one by one can be difficult. Instead, click the Show Participants icon and click Mute All next to the Presenters and Attendees sections. Participants can always unmute later if they need to.

>> **Hard Mute:** Enable Hard Mute in the meeting options before the meeting or toggle it during the meeting (see the "Managing meeting options and participant roles" section, later in this chapter). Setting Hard Mute prevents attendees from unmuting; presumably, presenters would be savvy enough to know about their mute settings, but you may want to use Mute All on the presenters every so often, too.

Sharing your screen and content

Sharing content is one of the best ways to keep your meeting participants on the same page — sometimes literally! — with regard to the topic at hand. Just don't confuse this concept with sharing a file in a chat or sending a link via email; that topic is covered in Book 11. On the meeting toolbar, click the Share Content icon to see your options. You have a bunch, as shown in Figure 5-5 and explained in the following list:

>> **Share Screen:** During a meeting, you can share your entire screen or one of multiple screens if you are lucky enough to use multiple monitors. Choosing this option shares everything on that screen, so if privacy is what you're after, don't use this one.

>> **Share Window:** Share an individual window. This is useful if you want to share one app while using other apps privately, such as to take notes in Word while sharing your browser with the meeting. You can move any other windows around your screen without impacting what the meeting participants see on their end; they see only the one window you shared.

>> **PowerPoint Live:** You can share PowerPoint presentations using the previous two options, but PowerPoint Live, built right into your meeting, has special features and uses much less bandwidth, meaning crisper video and better sound quality. See the next section, "Using PowerPoint Live," for more details.

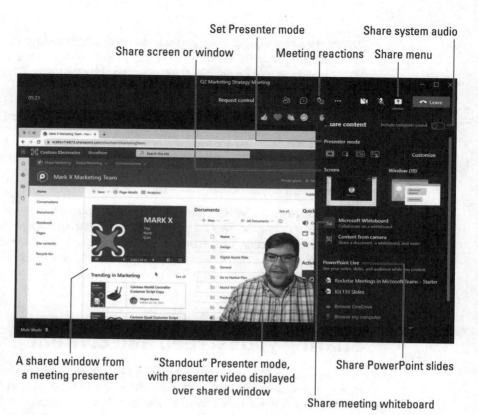

Set Presenter mode

Share screen or window

Share system audio

Meeting reactions Share menu

FIGURE 5-5:
A meeting window displaying the Share menu and another participant sharing window using Presenter mode.

A shared window from a meeting presenter

"Standout" Presenter mode, with presenter video displayed over shared window

Share PowerPoint slides

Share meeting whiteboard

>> **Whiteboard:** Choosing this option makes a whiteboard appear in the meeting. You can sketch and draw for brainstorming and notetaking. To see the whiteboard after the meeting, you open the Meeting Recap in the original appointment in your Teams calendar. Or you can open it using the Microsoft Whiteboard app in the Office 365 app launcher in your browser.

You can use a number of features with certain sharing options:

>> **Include Computer Sound:** To show a video or play music from your device, click the toggle switch next to the Include Computer Sound option. Make sure to enable this option *before* sharing.

>> **Presenter mode:** Enable this mode to display your shared content next to your video so that people know that the content is coming from you! In the Share menu, click one of the options under the Presenter mode section to turn on Presenter mode. Various ways to show your video and your shared content together are available, like placing a cutout of yourself in front of your slides, showing your screen above your shoulder like a newscaster, and more (refer to Figure 5-5 for a view of someone sharing a browser window with the

Standout Presenter mode enabled). You can enable Presenter mode before or during sharing.

>> **Presenter toolbar:** If you share your screen or window, a toolbar should display in the top-center of the screen with options. Hover your cursor in that area of the screen to reveal the toolbar and pin it to keep it there. On the toolbar, you can mute your computer audio, change your Presenter mode, and more (see Figure 5-6).

>> **Share control:** Within the Presenter toolbar, you can also click the Give Control drop-down menu to allow another participant to control your cursor and keyboard remotely. Don't give this permission willy-nilly, but it's great for tech support.

FIGURE 5-6:
The Presenter toolbar displays at the top-center of your screen when sharing a screen or window.

Presenter mode options   System audio mute   Pin toolbar

Give remote control of your device   End screenshare

Using PowerPoint Live

PowerPoint slides are probably the most common type of content shared during a Teams meeting, and PowerPoint therefore has a unique relationship with meetings in Teams. The feature is called PowerPoint Live and is available in the Share menu.

The PowerPoint Live section of the Share menu lists your recently opened `.pptx` files from OneDrive, SharePoint, and Teams. If you don't see the file you need, you can click Browse to upload it. Or, if you have the file open in the PowerPoint desktop app, you can click Send to Teams in the Home tab to launch your slides right in the meeting. Select a Presenter mode option (mentioned in the previous section) to place your video next to or on top of your slides for a better experience.

After you share your slides in the meeting, you see a "lite" version of Power-Point's presenter view, which shows the current slide, list of slides, slide notes, and other key features (see Figure 5-7). Everyone else in the meeting sees the first slide, not the details you see. Here are some key features to be familiar with:

>> **How to progress through slides:** All participants can move forward and backward through your slides. How anyone views slides is up to them and does not impact what others see. You can disable this capability by clicking

Getting Together for Online Meetings

the eye icon to the left of the Stop Presenting button near the top of the screen. You still control which slide the rest of the meeting attendees are on, even if individuals are progressing through slides on their own.

» **How to take control of slides:** Any presenter in the meeting can click the Take Control button on the meeting toolbar to manage the slides, meaning that nobody should have to say "next slide" ever again. To get control back, you have to click Take Control yourself.

» **Clickable links:** You can include a hyperlink in your slide, which will be live and clickable for everyone while the slides are shared.

» **Access to meeting chat and participant listing**: PowerPoint Live allows access to the meeting chat and the participants pane, displaying either right next to the shared slides, which are not nearly as easily accessible when you're sharing your screen or window. Learn more about these features in upcoming sections.

» **Pinning and spotlighting**: You can pin and spotlight key people so that they stay front and center while slides are shared. See the "Pinning and spotlighting participants" section, earlier in this chapter, for details.

FIGURE 5-7:
PowerPoint Live offers numerous features to control and manage your slides while presenting.

PowerPoint Live uses PowerPoint for the Web (the browser version) to render your slides. At the time of publishing, some features — especially advanced transitions and animations or complex graphics — weren't supported. You want to either design your slides for the browser experience or test running the slide show in PowerPoint for the Web to ensure that everything works as expected.

You can share PowerPoint slides through screen or window sharing for some additional presenter view features and better feature performance in PowerPoint itself, but PowerPoint Live is optimized for meetings and uses significantly less bandwidth than screensharing. The lower bandwidth use can help ensure the best audio and video quality of a meeting while you're sharing slides.

Sharing files in a meeting

Sharing a file for participants to edit during the meeting is identical to uploading a file to a private chat (for private meetings) and to a channel conversation (for channel meetings). From the meeting toolbar, click the Meeting chat icon to open the chat. Next, click the Attach icon and choose to share or upload your file.

Sharing files as described in the preceding paragraph is easy to do, but that doesn't mean it's the best option for you. When sharing files for a meeting, you should really share them ahead of the meeting — likely in a designated folder for that meeting — and share the link to the file or folder in the meeting invite. This approach keeps the files organized. When you upload a file in the meeting chat, the file ends up in an unorganized folder. Access to your file may also be limited for certain people; for example, if you shared the file before an external person joined the meeting, chances are they won't even see the file in the chat. And if your organization doesn't support external access, they wouldn't see the file at all. Learn more about sharing files in Teams (in meetings or not) in Chapter 4 of this minibook.

If you want to share a PowerPoint file for presenting — not editing live during the meeting — use PowerPoint Live, covered in the previous section.

Viewing the participants list

To see who's in a meeting, click the Show Participants icon on the meeting toolbar for a list of presenters and attendees in the meeting, as well as invitees who haven't yet joined. Each type of participant is grouped together: presenters first, and then attendees, and then invitees who haven't joined. Never again should you have to awkwardly ask someone, "Hey, are you here to give that update you promised us?" You can confidently call on someone whom you know is in the meeting. (If that attendee has started on mute, that's another story.)

The Participants pane is very helpful if you dig into the options. Click the ellipsis to the right of the pane title to open the More Actions drop-down menu and enable Hard Mute or Mute Everyone, and to download the current attendance report, among other things. Click the More Options ellipsis to the right of any participant's name to mute, pin, or spotlight them, as well as to change their role, among other options.

Viewing the meeting chat

Chat is an important aspect of your meeting. It's a place for participants to interact without interrupting ongoing discussion or presentations. Depending on your meeting type, the chat lives in different places. If you're in a private meeting, the chat is listed in the Chat app in Teams, and you can find it there after the meeting. If you're in a channel meeting, chat is part of a conversation in the host channel.

Regardless of meeting type, you access the chat the same way *during* the meeting. From the meeting toolbar (see Figure 5-4), click the Chat icon to open the chat. You will have all the features you would in a channel conversation or private chat. Additionally, messages actively pop up above the meeting at the top-center of the meeting window, so you can follow them as they come in without needing to open the chat.

TIP

Using the meeting options, the meeting organizer can disable the chat entirely or allow its use only during the meeting (see the "Managing meeting options and participant roles" section, later in this chapter).

TECHNICAL
STUFF

Access to the chat may be limited based on who someone is and when they join the meeting. The chat will state when someone has joined. If it says "*[Person's name]* has temporarily joined the chat," that person cannot see chats sent before they joined or after they leave. This scenario typically affects external attendees, but depending on your IT team's settings, it may also affect some internal meetings, too.

Recording the meeting

Meeting recordings can be useful later on for invitees who missed the meeting, for training purposes, or even as an easy way to record yourself presenting slides without needing expensive video editing software.

Follow these steps to record a meeting:

1. **On the meeting toolbar, click the ellipsis to open the More Actions drop-down menu.**

2. **Click Start Recording.**

   For privacy reasons, all participants are informed that they're being recorded. You should also verbally mention that you're going to start recording so that participants can mute themselves and disable their video if they don't want to be included in the recording.

3. **To stop the recording, follow Step 1 and then click Stop Recording.**

   If you don't click Stop Recording, the recording stops when the meeting last person leaves the meeting or the organizer ends the meeting.

   For a standard private meeting (the meetings most people schedule through Teams or Outlook), the meeting recording is saved in the OneDrive of the person who clicks Start Recording. For a channel meeting, the meeting recording is saved in the Files tab of host channel. In both cases, the file is stored in a folder called *Recordings*. Learn how to share the recording file in the "Sharing the meeting recording" section, later in this chapter.

   As of the time of publishing, the meeting recording records only standard video feeds and shared screens. It doesn't record Presenter mode or spotlighted individuals.

Using live captions and transcription

Live captions and transcription are of course useful for people with hearing impairment, but they're also handy for anyone surrounded by loud noise. Captions show what is stated. Transcription does the same but also identifies the speaker and can be downloaded after the meeting.

Follow these steps to enable captions or transcription:

1. **On the meeting toolbar, click the ellipsis to open the More Actions drop-down menu.**

2. **Click Turn on Live Captions or Start Transcription.**

   After the meeting, the transcript is available to the meeting organizer in the Meeting Recap (see the "Finding Resources after a Meeting" section, later in this chapter). If you don't need a transcript after, live captions is likely sufficient.

Adding people to an ongoing meeting

If you're in a meeting and realize you forgot to invite someone or want to pull someone in to answer an emergent question, you can add a person by calling them or sending them a link to join. Follow these steps to add someone to a meeting:

1. **On the meeting toolbar, click the Show Participants icon.**

   You have two options for adding someone: calling them to join (Step 2) or sending them a link (Step 3).

2. **Enter the person's name or email address in the Type a Name box in the Participants pane.**

   Teams provides smart suggestions below the box. If the correct suggestion displays, click it. This action calls the person; when they answer the call, they join the meeting. This is an active method for getting someone to join because answering the call brings them into the meeting.

3. **Click the Share Invite button for options to send the meeting link to the person.**

   Clicking Share Invite allows you to send the Join link using your method of choice (email, private chat, or text message). They join when they're available. This is a passive method for getting someone to join because they join the meeting at their convenience.

TIP

If the appointment for the meeting is in your Outlook Calendar, you can always forward the appointment to the person as an alternative to sharing the link.

Reacting and raising your hand

You can make your meeting more inclusive by encouraging people to react to presentations and speakers during the meeting by using meeting reactions. Anyone can Like (thumbs-up), Love (heart), Laugh, or Applaud in a meeting by clicking the Reactions icon on the meeting toolbar (refer to Figure 5-5). Although no record is kept of who reacted how or when, it's a live gauge of participants' views of the content.

TIP

Reactions (especially the thumbs-up) are also useful to get quick answers from participants, such as whether they can hear you and see your shared content without having to come off mute or muddy up the chat.

Also available in the Reactions menu is the raised hand (refer to Figure 5-5). Participants can raise their hand to indicate that they have a question or to answer an informal yes/no poll. You can view whose hands are raised by clicking the Show Participants icon on the meeting toolbar. The list of raised hands appears in the order in which people clicked the button. (The person at the top of the list has waited the longest.)

To lower a raised hand, the person who raised their hand can click the raise hand button again, or a presenter can click the Show Participants pane and then click the ellipsis to the right of someone's name. In the Show Options drop-down menu that appears, click Lower Hand.

WARNING

Beware of hand raising, however: This is a social contract that everyone in the meeting must be aware of and agree to use completely or not at all. Provide a quick briefing on hand-raising expectations by presenting a "Please raise your hand" slide at the beginning of presentations, or mention that you're not using it (whichever is applicable).

If you don't check in on raised hands every so often, people will get frustrated. Also, if participants don't use the hand but instead jump in verbally with an ad hoc question that you answer, others will see no reason to raise their hand because anyone can skip the line. Last, if participants don't know to raise their hand, they won't. You can avoid all these issues by using the tips in the previous paragraph.

Managing meeting options and participant roles during a meeting

Meeting options are available both before the meeting and during the meeting, when you can change them on the fly. A good meeting facilitator will toggle settings as necessary during the meeting to make it the best experience it can be. Meeting options can be managed only by the meeting organizer.

Follow these steps to manage meeting options during the meeting:

1. **On the meeting toolbar, click the ellipsis to open the More Actions drop-down menu.**

2. **Click Meeting Options.**

The Meeting Options pane opens.

3. **Change your meeting options as necessary.**

4. **Click the Save button.**

Getting Together for
Online Meetings

TIP

Some meeting options are more important than others when you're making changes during the meeting. Here are a few considerations:

» **Meeting Lobby:** You can disable the meeting lobby when it's time to start the meeting. Disabling the lobby is useful to avoid the *ding-ding* pop-ups of late arrivals in the lobby. You can use the lobby to block open entry while allowing key presenters into the meeting early to set up, and then disable the lobby at start time and allow everyone waiting in the lobby to join at that time from the Participants pane.

» **Hard Mute:** In large meetings, disabling attendees' ability to unmute can keep things quiet while speakers are presenting. At question time, you can disable Hard Mute so that participants can unmute to ask questions. Presenters are immune to Hard Mute, just so you know.

» **Meeting Roles**: Because attendees have fewer rights than presenters, they can't perform a lot of actions. But you may want to allow anyone to share their screen at the end of a meeting. You can manage roles meeting-wide this way. Additionally, you can manage roles individually by opening the Participants pane and clicking the ellipsis next to a participant's name to open the More Options drop-down menu and click an option to adjust their role. This is useful to promote an attendee to presenter when it's time for them to speak, but demote them back to attendee when they're done. Although it may seem draconian, it minimizes all risk of errant button clicks, screen shares, and other embarrassments.

Using breakout rooms

Breakout rooms are separated but connected mini meetings that you can split participants into during a Teams meeting. Breakout rooms are useful for breaking your meeting into smaller groups, and they're popular among teachers and people leading team-building events.

Breakout rooms can be complex, and covering them in detail is beyond the scope of this book, so you may want to learn more about them before using them live in a large event. Testing is always your friend. The meeting organizer has the most control over breakout rooms in a meeting, so make sure that whoever schedules the meeting is knowledgeable enough to use them if they are needed. Here are the general steps for using breakout rooms in a meeting:

1. **On the meeting toolbar, click the Breakout Rooms icon (it looks like two boxes together).**

The Create Breakout Rooms pane opens.

2. **Choose how many rooms you need.**

   At the time of publishing, the maximum was 50.

3. **Choose whether participants will be split into rooms automatically or manually.**

   If you choose the automatic option, you can't assign people manually at the start, though you can move people between rooms after the rooms are opened.

4. **Click Create Rooms.**

   The rooms are created.

5. **On the meeting toolbar, click the Breakout Rooms icon to display the Breakout Rooms pane.**

REMEMBER

   In this pane, you can create more rooms, delete rooms, rename rooms, manage rooms settings, send an announcement to all rooms, assign participants to rooms, and move participants to different rooms.

6. **When you're ready to open your rooms, click Start Rooms to open all rooms, or click the ellipsis to the right of the room name to open the More Options drop-down menu; then click Open Room.**

   When you open one or all rooms, anyone assigned to an open room will leave the meeting and join the room.

7. **When you're ready to close your rooms, click Close Rooms to close all rooms, or click the ellipsis to the right of the room name to open the More Options drop-down menu; then click Close Room.**

   When you close one or all rooms, the assignees of the closed rooms will leave the room and rejoin the meeting.

TECHNICAL
STUFF

There are a lot more feature and setting considerations when it comes to breakout rooms. For example, all participants in a breakout room have presenter status, even if they were an attendee in the main meeting. Each room has its own chat, whiteboard, meeting recording, and other artifacts. Investigate the setting options prior to using breakout rooms in a live meeting.

Leaving and ending the meeting

Anyone in a meeting can leave whenever they want by clicking the Leave button on the meeting toolbar. The meeting automatically ends when everyone leaves. The meeting organizer can also end the meeting, forcing everyone out when the organizer decides it's time. The organizer has a drop-down menu on the Leave button that provides the End Meeting option. If you're the organizer, you should generally end the meeting rather than wait for everyone to leave. The meeting recording, transcript, and other artifacts won't be available until everyone leaves, and sometimes people simply forget to leave.

Finding Resources after a Meeting

After your meeting is done, you gain access to the Meeting Recap, which is a window that provides information about and artifacts from a meeting (see Figure 5-8). The various tabs in the Meeting Recap quickly get you to the meeting chat, files shared in the chat, the details of the meeting, notes, the whiteboard, any poll questions that were sent, and the meeting recording, transcript, and attendance list.

Recording, transcript, and attendance report · · · · · · · · · · · Organizer options bar

Meeting artifacts tabs · · · · · Participants

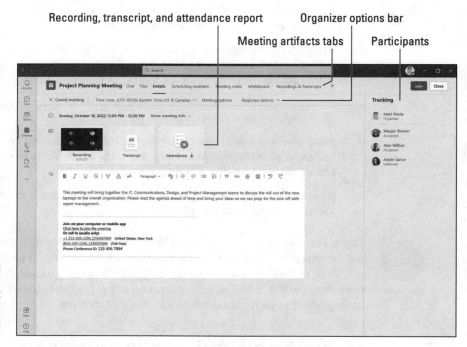

FIGURE 5-8:
Each occurrence of a recurring meeting has its own Meeting Recap.

Sharing the meeting recording

This section describes how to share a meeting recording so that everyone can access it.

Recordings of channel meetings are available by default to everyone in the Team where the channel meeting took place. Team members can find the recording in the Files tab of the host channel in a folder called Recordings. Sharing the file is as easy as clicking Open in SharePoint and then clicking the Share button for the recording.

Sharing the recording of a private meeting is a bit more involved than for a channel meeting. The recording for a private meeting is stored in a folder called Recordings in the OneDrive for Business of the person who clicks the Start Recording button in the meeting. Every internal invitee of the meeting should automatically have view access to the recording, a link to which they can find in the Meeting Recap. However, they cannot download or share the recording. Only the meeting organizer and file owner can edit or download the recording. The file owner can share a link to the file (including to external participants) by opening OneDrive and clicking the Share button.

REMEMBER

For recordings of both channel and private chat meetings, the recording can be moved or copied to a more central location by using the steps outlined in Book 11, Chapter 1. The meeting recording is just another file as far as Teams, SharePoint, and OneDrive are concerned.

Working with the meeting chat

Meeting chat is generally still available to participants after the meeting is over, which can be helpful if you want to follow up on action items or answer follow-up questions in a central location. Incidentally, all occurrences of a recurring meetings use the same, ongoing meeting chat.

REMEMBER

Accessing the meeting recordings should work well for internal participants. Guests and external participants, though, may or may not retain access to the meeting chat after the meeting has ended. You can tell whether someone will have post-meeting access to the chat based on the chat status update whenever someone joins or leaves the meeting. If the update says that someone has *temporarily* joined the chat and, eventually, that the person has *left* the chat, the chat is not available to them before or after they join or leave the meeting. Any meeting participant can also leave the chat themselves if they so choose.

TECHNICAL STUFF

Whether a guest or external participant can access the chat before or after the meeting depends on the Teams settings enabled by your IT team. Because there are unpredictable permutations when you include guests and external participants (especially if they come from multiple organizations), don't rely on the chat before or after the meeting unless your IT team can provide specific guidance to your situation.

11

File Sharing and Collaborating

Contents at a Glance

IN THIS CHAPTER

» Understanding the differences
between OneDrive and SharePoint

» Syncing your files for offline access

» Editing files in the browser versus
desktop Office apps

» Keeping track of a file's version
history

Chapter **1**

File Sharing and Collaborating

These days, many people don't just *create* documents and presentations in the Office 365 applications. Those Word documents, PowerPoint slides, and Publisher files need to live somewhere so that you and others can draft them, request outside input, send them for review, frantically update them with colleagues at 4:55 p.m. on a Friday, and ultimately finalize them for posting, submitting, or wherever your works of art need to end up.

There are a bunch of good reasons for storing and collaborating on files in the cloud: cloud storage is plentiful and cheap; you can edit certain files simultaneously with others; you can't lose them if your computer is destroyed in a fire; you get version history on files so that you can restore old ones; and you can easily share files with others on a whim, including people external to your organization.

These cloud storage tools work similarly to the file storage systems you're already familiar with in terms of navigating folder structures, viewing your files, and moving files from place to place. But the additional features for sharing and collaborating are what make these storage tools shine. In this chapter, you dive into how sharing files and collaborating on them works in the modern cloud world.

Knowing when to Use OneDrive, SharePoint, or Teams

Files in Office 365 get stored in one of Microsoft's cloud storage tools: OneDrive or SharePoint. You can still save files to C drives, flash drives, shared drives, and other local options, but most organizations that use Office 365 are moving to or already store their files in OneDrive for Business, SharePoint Online, and Microsoft Teams. If you have a personal Office 365 account, you get a consumer OneDrive account.

The most common questions for new and veteran Office 365 users alike is when to use OneDrive, SharePoint, or Teams for storing and sharing files. As Book 10, Chapter 4 notes, all files shared in Teams private chat and channels are actually stored in OneDrive and SharePoint, respectively, behind the scenes. You may think you've never used OneDrive or SharePoint, but if you're creating files in or uploading files to Microsoft Teams — surprise! — you most certainly have used them. In addition to being able to access files within Teams through the Files app or the various Files tabs, you can also share and retrieve your files from either OneDrive or SharePoint. The following sections clarify when it's best to use any of these options for retrieving, sharing, and storing files.

When to use OneDrive

OneDrive is perfect for two type of files: personal files that shouldn't be shared, and drafts of files you're not yet ready for others to see. When you're ready to share, that's when you move them to a SharePoint site or Teams channel for collaborative input or reviews.

Although you *can* share files from and collaborate on them without leaving OneDrive, it's usually not your best option. Sharing at the file or folder level, as opposed to storing all working files in one bucket with consistent access, like a Team or SharePoint site, quickly becomes a permissions nightmare. It's especially confusing when each person in a working group shares individual files from their own OneDrive account with the other members of that group as they work on them. You make things much easier for everyone if you upload and collaborate on files that are located in a central SharePoint site or in a Team in Microsoft Teams.

WARNING

Another reason to minimize sharing from your OneDrive is that when someone leaves an organization, their OneDrive is typically retired within 30 days. If your working group depends on critical files that have been shared from someone's OneDrive and that person leaves the organization, you will not be happy to find out one morning that those files are gone for good without warning.

When to use SharePoint

SharePoint consists of websites. Each site has one or a few owners and its own permissions for the whole site, which owners can change as necessary. In these sites, you can build pages, store and organize files, and do a lot more. SharePoint is best used in two ways:

>> **Team sites are best for collaborating:** Team sites have members and most — if not all — of those members have edit access to everything in the site. Team sites are for getting work done. They're also the file storage location behind Microsoft 365 Groups, including Outlook Groups, Yammer Communities, and Teams in Microsoft Teams. (Microsoft Teams is covered in Book 10.) Each member of these group types automatically has edit access to the associated team site. But you can create a SharePoint team site by itself; you don't need to use Outlook, Yammer, or Teams.

>> **Communication sites are perfect for publishing:** These sites are usually accessible to almost everyone in the organization, but most people have only view access. A few people have access to upload, edit, and delete published files. Communication sites generally make up your organization's intranet. A good example of an item published on a SharePoint communication site is a corporate policies listing. The people who write and maintain those files can update the policies when necessary, but most visitors to the site just read the policies; they shouldn't be able to edit them. Communication sites are for everyone's stuff.

If your organization doesn't already have a different process in place, consider drafting your file in OneDrive. When you're ready, move your file to your SharePoint team site where colleagues can provide input and review. You could also draft the file in the team site and leave it there for greatest visibility to your peers (if you were using OneDrive, the file would be private to start whereas in the team site, others can stumble across it and provide useful input along the way), and then call on them later to review the file.

When the file is completed and ready to be widely shared, publish the file to a communication site (if it's meant for wide distribution) or to the team site (if it's something like a template or team-specific documentation for your team to use later). Keep a working copy in your team site so that updates are easy to make and kept private from the rest of the organization while you work on any revisions.

SharePoint, OneDrive, and their integrations with Teams might seem complex. But to put it most simply, you may find yourself moving between OneDrive, SharePoint team sites, and SharePoint communication sites: me, we, us, as illustrated in Figure 1-1.

Editing & Collaborative Spaces | Publishing Spaces

FIGURE 1-1:
OneDrive for
personal drafts
(me); SharePoint
team sites for
collaboration
(we); and
SharePoint
communication
sites for
publishing (us).

My Stuff
Your private workspace

OneDrive
for Business

• Personal files
• Initial drafts

"Me"

Team's Stuff
Working groups

SharePoint

• Team sites
• Group sites

"We"

Everyone's Stuff
Wide audiences

SharePoint

• Communication sites
• Your intranet

"Us"

Syncing Office 365 Files to Your Devices

You are probably familiar with — and likely prefer — accessing files from a shared drive, C drive, or other location listed in the left side of Windows File Explorer. You might also need to be able to work on your files even when you don't have an available Internet connection. Using OneDrive, you can sync any of your files from Office 365 to any device — computer, tablet, smartphone — and locate them the same way you always have.

But isn't OneDrive just a personal storage space? No, not *just*. In an example of poor marketing that has confused millions worldwide, the name "OneDrive" is used for two distinct functions: the storage space described earlier in the chapter, and a separate tool from Microsoft that you use to sync files from *the other* One-Drive, as well as from your SharePoint sites. This other OneDrive is an app that you install on your devices, and it's a feature that you can't live without.

Installing the OneDrive app and syncing files

To sync files from Office 365, you need to have the OneDrive app installed on your device. You can get it for Windows, macOS, iOS, and Android. Follow these steps to obtain the app (if you don't have it already) and start syncing with OneDrive on a Windows computer:

1. **Check whether OneDrive is already installed.**

Most Windows devices already have it. On your computer, open your Start menu and look for OneDrive. If you have it, open it and go to Step 3.

2. **If you don't have OneDrive on your computer, follow these steps to download and install it:**

a. Browse to https://www.microsoft.com/en-us/microsoft-365/onedrive/download (or search "Download OneDrive" in your favorite search engine) and on the screen that appears, click Download.

b. **After OneDrive has downloaded, open your Downloads folder on your computer and double-click the OneDrive file. Allow it to install.**

WARNING

Work and school computers may require the IT team to install software. In fact, they may already have a way to access OneDrive, so reach out if you have questions.

3. **Sign in to OneDrive.**

After you install and open OneDrive, click the blue cloud icon in the system tray on Windows (near the clock). Provide your email address and password. OneDrive should immediately start syncing your OneDrive files.

Open Windows File Explorer to see a new section called "OneDrive" in the left-side navigation. This section lists all the folders in your OneDrive, as shown in Figure 1-2. You can also sync SharePoint and Teams files using the OneDrive app. I cover that more in the "Syncing Teams and SharePoint files to your device" section later in this chapter.

SharePoint and Teams folders

OneDrive folders   Available offline

FIGURE 1-2:
The OneDrive app provides a few features in the right-click menu.

Must download to open   File is shared   OneDrive options

Keeping files always available on your device

When you open your OneDrive folders in File Explorer, you see a little icon next to the names of files and folders. The blue cloud outline indicates that the file is available only when you have an Internet connection; to open one of these files, it has to download first. The green check mark indicates that you can access the file when you're offline. You probably want files that you use regularly to be accessible offline for times when you're disconnected from the Internet. Follow these steps to always keep a file or folder on your device:

1. **Open Windows File Explorer.**

2. **In the left-side navigation, click OneDrive.**

   You should see your OneDrive folders and files in the main area.

3. **Right-click any file or folder and click Always Keep on This Device.**

   The file or folder downloads to your device and displays a circular blue arrow icon until it's completed downloading. Depending on how much information you're downloading, it may take a while. You can view the status of your sync by clicking the OneDrive icon in the system tray.

TECHNICAL STUFF

Your OneDrive has a lot of space — 1TB for most people — but plenty of computers still don't offer that much space. So what happens if your synced files start taking up too much space on your device? Follow the preceding steps, but in Step 3, choose Free Up Space for the files and folders that take up more than their fair share of your computer.

You can sync and unsync files as you need them. If you intend to be offline for a while, you can save the files you expect to need while you're still at a location with dependable Wi-Fi. If you make edits to files while you're offline, they will sync with the source file in the cloud the next time you're on Wi-Fi.

Syncing Teams and SharePoint files to your device

You can also use the OneDrive app to sync Teams and SharePoint content to your computer or mobile devices. Teams and SharePoint files don't automatically sync to your device — that could be an insane amount of files — but you can sync the files and folders that are important to you in those Teams or sites. If you don't already have a Team or site, see Chapter 2 of Book 10 or Chapter 3 of this minibook for instructions on creating a Team or SharePoint site, respectively. Follow these steps to sync files from Microsoft Teams or a SharePoint team or communication site to your device:

1. **Open the Team or SharePoint site where the files are stored.**

   For a Team, click the channel where the files are stored and then click the Files tab at the top of the main area. For a SharePoint site, open the site in a browser. If you need access or a link, ask the site owner.

2. **Open the folder you want to sync, or follow the breadcrumb trail all the way to the top level to sync all files.**

   See Figure 4-4 in Book 10, Chapter 4 for an example of a breadcrumb trail in a SharePoint document library.

3. **In the toolbar above the files, click Sync.**

   This opens a notification from OneDrive that the sync has started. You can close it if it doesn't close automatically.

4. **Open Windows File Explorer.**

5. **In the left-side navigation, under your organization name, click the Team or Site name.**

   You should see the folders and files in the main area (refer to Figure 1-2). If needed, follow the steps in the preceding section, "Keeping files always available on your device," to choose files to always have available locally on your device, even if you're not online.

WARNING

One of the biggest risks with this feature is that you may forget that other people depend on these files. If you no longer want the files on your device, *don't* delete them! Doing so deletes the files for everyone else as well. Instead, right-click the file or folder in File Explore and click Free Up Space in the menu that appears. Alternatively, if you no longer want to see them in File Explorer at all, in your OneDrive settings on your computer, update which Teams and sites you sync: Click the OneDrive icon in the system tray and then click Help & Settings⇨Settings⇨Account.

Staying Sane When Editing Files

The previous sections cover all the great features that come with storing and accessing files in the cloud. In this section, you delve into some details on editing as well as some of the implications that come from making changes to your files.

Editing Office files in their desktop versus browser versions

If you've been using Office 365 at all, you've probably noticed that Office files — Word, Excel, PowerPoint, and OneNote — don't always open in the desktop app that you're probably used to.

Instead, these files may open in a browser version of the app. These browser versions are called Office for the Web overall, with each app having a similar name: Word for the Web, Excel for the Web, and so on. While they don't have all of the same features as their desktop counterparts, the Web apps can be pretty good for light tasks, such as to review a letter in Word or update some equations in Excel. They're faster to load than the desktop apps, they update quickly when you're editing files with someone else, and they're simpler to navigate and use.

Although the Office for the Web versions continue to progress and add features, they can be limited in what they can do, especially if you have complex needs. At some point, however, some of the app features may even be browser-only, and not available in the desktop version. For a long time, that was true of the Presenter Coach feature in PowerPoint.

REMEMBER

The takeaway here is that these apps are entirely worth using, but in the right circumstances. For example, this entire chapter was written in Word for the Web using template styles and image insertion, and it worked like a charm. Just be aware of what you need to be able to do. Unfortunately, no authoritative list exists of the feature differences between the desktop and Web apps.

Editing Office files with colleagues

One of the benefits of the cloud is the ability for Office files to be opened and edited by multiple people at the same time, which Microsoft calls *coauthoring*. This capability is a major shift from the days of shared drives, when it was not uncommon for a file to be "locked for editing" by someone, seemingly right when you most needed that file.

REMEMBER

You can coauthor in Word, Excel, PowerPoint, and OneNote in the desktop app, Web app, or directly in Teams. When someone else is currently working in a file you're editing, you see their photo or initials pop up in the Ribbon to let you know they're there. As they traverse the file, you may see a cursor or box around the content they're working on (see Figure 1-3). You also see any changes occur live, right on your screen.

List of people in the file

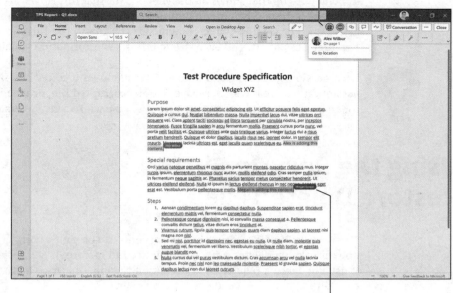

Someone actively editing

FIGURE 1-3:
Coauthoring in
a Word file in
Microsoft Teams,
which uses Word
for the Web right
in the Teams app.

WARNING

Every so often, you can run into issues with other people making edits at the same time as you. Microsoft calls this a *conflict*. When this happens, the app asks you to choose which change to keep. An easy way to prevent conflicts is to avoid working in the same part of the document as someone else — which means the same paragraph in a Word document, the same cell in an Excel spreadsheet, or the same text box or image in a PowerPoint slide show.

Keeping track of a file's version history

All OneDrive and SharePoint files provide a version history, which lets you go back in time to view or restore a previous version of your file. Version history is a great way to get a file back without needing IT intervention.

REMEMBER

To use version history, you must access OneDrive or SharePoint in the browser. If you want to access the version history of a file in a Team, starting in Microsoft Teams, click the channel where the file is stored, click the Files tab above the main area, and then click Open in SharePoint in the toolbar below the Files tab; this brings you to the Team's files in the SharePoint team site. Once you see the file in SharePoint or OneDrive, next to the filename, click the vertical ellipsis to open the Show Actions drop-down menu and then click Version History.

A menu pops up that shows all the versions for that file. Hover over a version name to expose a drop-down menu button and click that button. From that menu, you can open that version (which downloads the file to the Downloads folder in File Explorer), restore it, and even delete it if it has information you don't want saved.

TIP

Each version will also list a date and time and who edited the file, creating that version. It's a great way to recover from a corrupted file, or when someone added too many comments and you just need to go back to a clean version.

Using the Recycle Bin to Restore Deleted Files

The Recycle Bin in OneDrive and SharePoint can be your saving grace when someone mistakenly deletes a file that you need to restore. It's especially nice because it usually doesn't require IT intervention to help. OneDrive has a Recycle Bin, and each SharePoint site has its own Recycle Bin.

You can delete a file or folder in OneDrive or SharePoint by hovering your cursor to the left of a file or folder, clicking the small circular check box that appears, and then click Delete in the toolbar at the top. Sometimes clicking that button is a mistake.

To access the Recycle Bin for your OneDrive or for your SharePoint site, follow these steps:

1. **Locate the Recycle Bin in your browser:**

   - **In OneDrive,** the Recycle Bin link is near the top of the menu in the left pane of the screen.

   - **In SharePoint,** the Recycle Bin is likely at the bottom of the Quick Launch menu — the pane along the left side of the screen. If you don't see it, click the Settings gear in the top-right corner of your screen and then click Site Contents in the drop-down menu that appears. You should see the Recycle Bin in the toolbar above the list of content.

   - **In Teams,** there is no direct link to the Recycle Bin as of the time of publishing. You need to open the SharePoint team site from Teams first. In Teams, click the channel where the deleted content used to be stored, click the Files tab above the main area, and then click Open in SharePoint in the toolbar below the Files tab; this brings you to the Team's files in the SharePoint team site. Follow the steps for accessing the Recycle Bin in SharePoint in the previous bullet.

2. **Hover your cursor to the left of the file or folder that you want to restore to make a small circle appear under your cursor.**

3. **Click the circle to select the file or folder you want and then click Restore in the toolbar above the contents of the Recycle Bin.**

    When you open the Recycle Bin, you see all deleted files that can be restored from there. You should have up to 93 days to restore a file before it's permanently deleted. If you don't see a file you were hoping for and you know it was there fewer than 93 days ago, reach out to your IT team. They may have some further options.

Copying and Moving Files among SharePoint, OneDrive, and Teams

You often need to copy or move files between various locations. These actions have different outcomes, so it's important to know how and when to use each.

>> **Copy:** This feature creates an exact copy of a file in the location you select. The original version retains its version history and any unique permissions. The copy has no version history and will inherit the permissions of its new home. When you make a copy, two versions of the same file exist. That might be perfectly fine for your situation — just make sure you don't confuse people about which version they should be viewing or editing.

>> **Move:** This feature removes a file from one place and drops it in another. The file retains its version history wherever you move it, and it *may* retain its earlier permissions while also inheriting the permissions of its new home. It all depends on where you're moving it from and to; typically, OneDrive or SharePoint will ask you about the permissions before moving.

WARNING

If the file you're copying or moving is used by a number of people, always make sure to communicate the change if it could affect their ability to use that file. Communication is key!

To copy or move a file or folder, find the file or folder in OneDrive or SharePoint and click the vertical ellipsis to open the Show actions drop-down menu. Within your list of options is Copy (or Copy To) and Move (or Move To). Select the option you prefer, and the Move or Copy pane opens on the right side of the window. Choose your destination. You can choose either your OneDrive or a SharePoint site you have access to. After you select OneDrive or a site, select the document library or folder to place the content in. Finally, click the Move Here or Copy Here button.

Choosing the destination can be a bit confusing because you may not see a Team or SharePoint site you were hoping to. If you don't, open the destination site and click Not Following in the top-right corner to turn that label to Following. You should now see your Team or site listed in list of destination sites in the Copy or Move pane.

Sharing Files Outside Your Organization

For those times when you need to get a file to someone outside your organization, you have an alternative to attaching a file to an email. In many ways, sharing a file with an external person is preferred: the process is more secure, the sender has more control over the content, the information stays centralized, and you can benefit from the full features for files like coauthoring, version history, and permissions.

You still send an email, but instead of sending a copy of a file to the recipient, include a link to the file's location. You can also share a link to any file or folder and send it in another message type, such as a private chat or even a text message.

The basic share experience is available in both OneDrive and SharePoint in the browser. When you hover your cursor over a file or folder, a Share icon appears to the right of the file- or folder name (it's a box with a right-pointing arrow). Click the icon to bring up a pane that lets you send a link to specific people, people who currently have access, everyone in your organization, or anyone with the link (including external people, if external access is allowed). Sharing directly from Teams isn't available yet, so open the SharePoint site behind the Team in that situation.

Sharing a file link has a number of benefits for both the sender and recipient. All edits are made to a central copy of the file, so you don't have to merge various return copies; you can revoke permissions to the file at will; you can view and manipulate version history; you can take advantage of coauthoring; and you have access to many of the other features referenced in this chapter. An email attachment can do none of those things.

External sharing

Sharing with someone outside your organization follows the same steps as sharing with an internal recipient, except that you probably want to select a different permission option. Follow these steps to share externally from OneDrive or SharePoint:

1. **Open the OneDrive or SharePoint folder where the files are stored.**

2. **Hover your cursor over the file or folder to reveal a Share icon to the right of its name.**

   The icon looks like a box with a right-pointing arrow.

3. **Click the Share icon.**

   The Share Link pane opens, displaying the current permissions at the top.

4. **Click the existing permissions listed directly under the "Send link" title.**

   The Link Settings options appear.

5. **Select the permissions you want on the top and choose any other settings that are provided below that.**

   When sharing externally, you likely want to choose the Specific People or Anyone with the Link options. Select whether to allow editing and, if available, whether to open in review mode only (applies to Word files only), set an expiration date on the link, set a password on the link, and block download by the recipient(s).

6. **Click Apply.**

7. **If you're sharing with specific people, enter their email addresses in the To box.**

8. **To copy the link so that you can paste it in an email, chat, or other medium, click Copy Link.**

9. **To send an automatic email to the recipients informing them they have access, click Send.**

When recipients click the link you've sent, they may need to log in or provide a passcode to access the file. From there, they have the access you provided (edit or view) and should be able to download the file, unless you disabled that capability in Step 5. Talk to your IT team about the organization's rules for external sharing.

If you need to remove someone's access at some point, click the vertical ellipsis next to the file or folder to open the Show Actions menu; then click Manage Access. The pane that appears shows all the sharing links that exist for that file or folder. Hover your cursor over a link to see who has access. To remove the link, click the X next to the link to delete it. When you delete the link, the people who were listed with it no longer have access.

Note: External sharing can scare a lot of IT people, especially those in the cybersecurity realm. Although sharing files with external people might seem like a security risk, an email with an attachment amounts to the same thing, but with less control. So if external sharing is not available to you, it's likely because of an IT decision. Reach out to your IT team if necessary.

File sharing and email

Email attachments are still a thing, of course, but you can "attach" links to email so that recipients can open files that are actually stored in OneDrive and SharePoint.

To send a link when drafting an email in Outlook, click the Attach button. When Outlook displays the attachment options, look for icons that include a cloud. Any icon with a cloud indicates that the file is or will be stored in SharePoint or One-Drive. Outlook also suggests files you've recently viewed or edited; again, those with a cloud in the icon indicate the files are in SharePoint or OneDrive, and the "attachment" will actually be a link to the master file so that all recipients open the same copy. If you choose the Upload and Share option, Outlook will upload the file to the "Attachments" folder in your OneDrive and include a link to that file that all recipients can access automatically.

You can choose to send a copy of a file as an attachment if you click the Browse This Computer option, but every other option uses a link to a file, not an attachment. With so many options being about linking, Microsoft is clearly pushing you to use links rather than attachments!

TIP

When you add a file as a link attachment in an email, Outlook should handle the permission changes for you automatically, and no automated email gets sent to recipients like when you change permissions directly in SharePoint and OneDrive.

Chapter **2**

Making the Most of OneDrive

O neDrive is your personal file storage location in Office 365. Each person in your organization has their own OneDrive, and you can share files and folders with others when needed. OneDrive is also unique in its ability to bring Teams and SharePoint files together with your personal files all in one place. You can also easily access recent files and those that have been shared with you. As noted in Chapter 1 of this minibook, OneDrive files are accessible both from a browser and your Windows File Explorer. This chapter covers the browser experience because it has more features than what you find in File Explorer. This chapter covers how to create, upload, and arrange your files and folders as well as manage their settings.

Getting Started in OneDrive

To get into a personal OneDrive account or a work or school account, you first need to log in. If you're using a personal account (typical logins end in @live.com, @outlook.com, @hotmail.com, or even @xbox.com), go to `https://onedrive.live.com`. To log into a work or school account, go to `https://office.com`. In either instance, log in, and click the OneDrive icon (the blue cloud) in the app launcher in the top-left of the window. If you're using an account through the U.S. government, Germany, or China, you need to talk to your IT team for the specific link.

WARNING

If the browser asks to remember your password, feel free to let it as long as you're not using a public device (like a hotel computer). You don't want someone else to be able to log into your account and wreak havoc in the new playground they found.

TIP

When you're ready to sign out of Office 365 in a web browser, click your profile photo, name, or initials in the top-right corner of the screen and click Sign Out.

When you first log into your OneDrive account, you will likely see few or no folders. Your workplace or school may create some for you, but that depends on the organization. A personal account includes Documents and Pictures folders as well as a personal vault, which is a secure storage location in a personal OneDrive account. Figure 2-1 shows the OneDrive window with numerous folders.

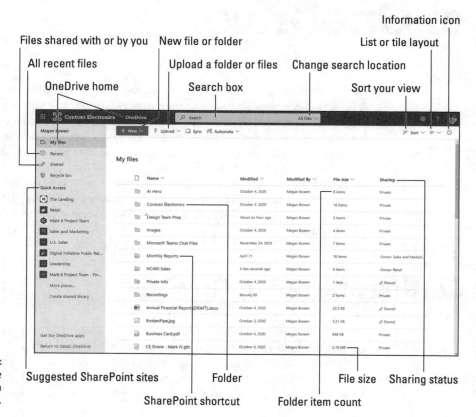

FIGURE 2-1:
The OneDrive window in List view.

OneDrive can store up to 1TB (that's 1,000GB) of files, which is the typical amount that comes with a work or school account. A personal account starts at 5GB; you can upgrade to a premium account to get the 1TB. In a personal OneDrive, a status bar in the lower-left corner of the page tells you how much space is available for storing files. Work and school accounts don't show space usage, but your IT team should be able to provide that information.

You can change the view of your files and folders by clicking the View Options button in the top-right corner of the window to open the View Options menu and choosing List, Compact List, or Tiles in the menu that appears. In Tiles view, each folder displays a number representing how many files and folders it contains. To open a folder and view its contents or to open a file, click it.

The OneDrive window contains the following options and tools for managing files (refer to Figure 2-1):

>> **Content menu:** View your files, all recent files, files shared with you, your Recycle Bin, and frequently accessed SharePoint sites under Quick Access.

>> **Create folders:** Click the New button and choose Folder to create a folder for storing files. See the "Creating a file or folder" section, later in this chapter, for details.

>> **Create files:** Click the New button and choose from various Office files. Work and school accounts also allow links, whereas personal accounts include Microsoft Forms forms. See the "Creating a file or folder" section, later in this chapter, for details.

>> **Upload files and folders:** Click the Upload button to upload files and folders from your computer to OneDrive. See the "Uploading files and folders" section, later in this chapter, for details.

>> **Arranging files and folders in the window:** Use the tools in the top-right corner of the page to arrange your files and folders. See the "Viewing and locating folders in the OneDrive window" section, later in this chapter, for details.

REMEMBER

To return to the main OneDrive page, click OneDrive in the suite bar in the top-left corner, or click Files in the Content menu along the left side of the window.

Managing Your OneDrive Content

Think of OneDrive as a cloud version of your My Documents folder. OneDrive likely gives you more space, however, and you can access your files from multiple devices, even one that's not yours, such as a computer in a hotel business center or a public library.

Viewing and locating folders in the OneDrive window

Use the OneDrive window to store and locate folders, subfolders, and files in One-Drive. The OneDrive window offers these tools for managing folders:

» **Search:** Enter a search term in the Search box to search for a folder or file. The Search box is in the top-center of the suite bar. The search engine will look through the contents of files, not just look for names of files.

» **Sort:** Click the Sort button and choose an option to rearrange folders and files in the OneDrive window. Sorting is helpful for finding a folder or file in a long list. Refer to Figure 2-1 to see this option.

» **View:** Click the View options button to switch views. Figure 2-1, shown previously, shows where to find the options, and Figure 2-2 shows the Tiles view.

  • **List and Compact List views** present detailed information about folders and files — when they were last modified, whether they are shared, and file sizes. Compact List is the same as List, but with less vertical space between each line of folders and files.

  • **Tiles view** presents folders and files in thumbnail form.

» **Details pane:** Select a folder or file and click the Information icon (the *i* in a circle at the top right) to open the Details pane (refer to Figure 2-1). You can also display the Details pane by right-clicking a folder or file and choosing Details.

After you accumulate a few folders in OneDrive, getting to the folder you want to open can be an arduous, interminable journey. To help you on your way, OneDrive offers several techniques for going to a folder:

» **The drill-down method:** Starting in the My Files view, click a top-level folder to display its subfolders. If necessary, keep drilling down this way until you reach the file you want to open.

Click to open the Details pane

File options   File preview

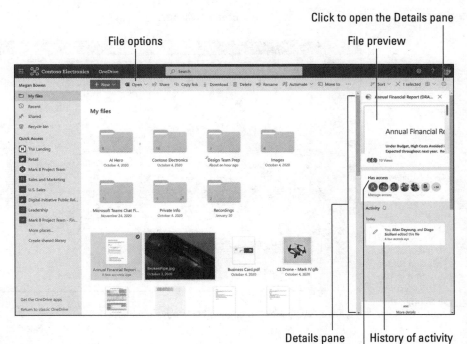

FIGURE 2-2:
The OneDrive
home page in
Tiles view with
the Details pane
showing.

Details pane   History of activity

Permissions

Making the Most of
OneDrive

>> **The breadcrumb trail method:** Most file storage pages in Office 365, including SharePoint and Microsoft Teams, have a breadcrumb trail, and OneDrive is no exception. This trail lists the path to the folder that is currently open. To backtrack, click the name of a folder on the path, as shown in Figure 2-3.

>> **The browser button method:** Click the Back and Forward button in your browser to open a folder you previously opened.

To return to the top-level OneDrive page, click My Files in the Content menu or the word *OneDrive* in the suite bar, as shown in Figure 2-1.

TIP

By bookmarking a folder in your browser, you can go straight to a folder without having to navigate to it in OneDrive. After you choose the bookmark (and enter your username and password if you haven't yet signed in), the folder opens.

Breadcrumb trail

![OneDrive screenshot showing My files > Design Team Prep > Contoso Electronics > RFPs breadcrumb trail with a list of files]

FIGURE 2-3:
Click a folder
name in the
breadcrumb
trail to open that
folder directly.

These "eyelashes" indicate a file is new in the last day

Selecting files and folders

REMEMBER

Before you can rename, delete, or move a folder or file, you have to select it. Use these techniques to select files and folders:

>> **Click the check box (it's a circle, actually) on a file or folder.** The check box appears when you move the cursor over a file or folder.

>> **In List view or Compact List view, click anywhere on a list entry apart from the file's name or folder's name.** Clicking a name opens a file or folder.

You can select more than one file or folder by clicking the check box next to multiple files or folders.

Creating a file or folder

Within OneDrive, you can create folders and various Office files. There are minor differences between a personal OneDrive account and a work or school OneDrive account, but they all let you create at least a Word document, Excel workbook, PowerPoint slide show, and OneNote notebook. Follow these steps to create a file in OneDrive:

1. **Open your OneDrive and open the folder in which you want to create the file.**

   See "Viewing and locating folders in the OneDrive window," earlier in this chapter, if you need help finding a folder in which to create a new file or folder.

2. **Click the New button in the toolbar and, in the drop-down menu that appears, choose what you want to create.**

   You can create a folder or one of multiple Office file types.

3. **Enter a name for your creation:**

   - **For a folder:** Enter a name in the Create a folder pop-up then click the Create button.

   - **For an Office file:** Click the generic filename that appears near the app name in the top-left of suite bar. In the File Name dialog box that appears, enter a descriptive title, as shown in Figure 2-4.

TIP

When you create a new Office file, the file opens in the browser version of the app. As outlined in Chapter 1, there are a number of differences between the browser and desktop versions of the Office apps. To open the file in the desktop app, find the Open in Desktop App command in the Ribbon (it may be in the Editing menu, as shown in Figure 2-4) and click it.

After a file opens in the desktop app, you should see AutoSave enabled in the top-left of the Office app. AutoSave indicates that all changes are automatically saved to OneDrive. So you don't have to remember to press Save ever again if you're working on Office files from OneDrive!

Uploading files and folders

You probably use other file types besides Office files. PDFs, photos, videos, and even AutoCad and Photoshop files need a home, too. To store other file types, you'll need to upload your files.

Although you can use the Upload button in the toolbar to move files into OneDrive, this way of moving files is a slow journey through various windows. It also lets you upload only one folder at a time. The easiest way is to simply select your files and folders (multiple folders, if you want!) in File Explorer and then drag and drop them into the browser window. The handy drag-and-drop method has worked so well for decades, why turn your back on it now?

Rename the file   Open the desktop app

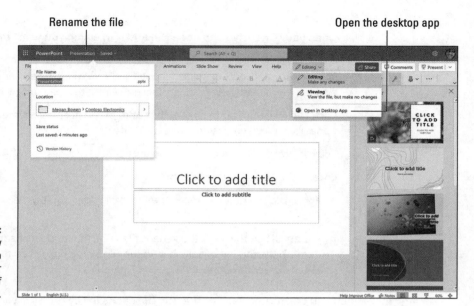

FIGURE 2-4:
In OneDrive, new Office files open in the browser version of the app.

REMEMBER

After you drop your files and folders, they immediately begin uploading. Keep an eye on the progress and don't log off your computer until the upload completes. Click the Progress menu in the top-right toolbar (see Figure 2-5) to check in on the upload process. If there's already a file with the same name as one you're uploading, that menu will ask what you want to do: overwrite the file (and create a new version in the version history), or keep both, which uploads the file but gives it a different name. This one is important because the warning is easy to miss.

WARNING

If you need to upload very large files (gigabytes in size), dozens or hundreds of files simultaneously, or many very large files, don't upload this way. Instead, drag and drop the files into OneDrive in File Explorer and let the OneDrive sync tool do the work as covered in Chapter 1 of this minibook; it will pause and resume syncing automatically if your computer is off or your Internet connection is disrupted.

Viewing file and folder options

Each folder and file offers many more options than you see when working with OneDrive files in File Explorer. Click the vertical ellipsis next to a folder or filename to see the Show Actions menu with all the available options, as shown in Figure 2-6. Some of the key actions you can take from this menu are to open a file, share it, get the link to it, manage permissions, download, delete, move, copy, rename, and view the version history. Most of these features are covered in various sections in Chapter 1 of this minibook and apply to files and folders in SharePoint as well.

Upload progress pane

Upload progress menu

Existing file with that name warning

FIGURE 2-5:
Follow the
progress of
your upload.

Making the Most of
OneDrive

	Name ∨	Modified ∨	Modified By ∨	File size ∨	Sharing
	AI Hero	October 4, 2020	Megan Bowen	8 items	Private
	Contoso Electronics	October 4, 2020	Megan Bowen	16 items	Private
	Images	Open ＞	Open in browser		Private
	Microsoft Teams Chat Files	Preview	Open in app		Private
	Monthly Reports	Share	Open in Immersive Reader		Owner: Sales and Mark...
	Private Info	Copy link	egan Bowen	1 item	Shared
	Recordings	Manage access	egan Bowen	2 items	Private
✓	Annual Financial Report (DRAF...	Download	egan Bowen	22.2 KB	Shared
	BrokenPipe.jpg	Delete	egan Bowen	5.21 KB	Shared
	Business Card.pdf	Move to	egan Bowen	846 KB	Private
	CE Drone - Mark IV.glb	Copy to	egan Bowen	2.18 MB	Private
	Contoso Patent Template.docx	Rename	egan Bowen	83.5 KB	Private
	Contoso Purchasing Data - Q1.xlsx	Automate ＞	egan Bowen	21.5 KB	Private
		Version history			
		Details			

My files

FIGURE 2-6:
Each file and folder has a lot of options in OneDrive.

Seeing Files and Folders Others Shared with You

Sharing is a major aspect of OneDrive, and you can view the files that you've shared with others and the files that they've shared with you. To view shared files, click the Shared option in the content menu on the left of the OneDrive window. You see two tabs in the toolbar if someone has shared files or folders with you: Shared with You and Shared by You. Click the one you want to open to see lists of shared content. If no one has ever shared content with you, you see only the files you've shared with others in this area. If you've never shared files, either, this area is blank.

REMEMBER

Files will show up in the Shared with You tab if the person sharing with you has selected the Specific People option when setting permissions. So if you're not seeing shared content that you believe you should see, that person's permission settings could be why. See Chapter 1 of this minibook for more details on sharing.

TIP

It's good practice to check out your Shared by You files every once in a while to make sure that people still need access to those files. Oversharing is a big problem in the modern workplace, so do your part on keeping your permissions clean by periodically removing others' permissions to files that they no longer need access to. The next section covers file and folder permissions.

Managing File and Folder Permissions

When you share a file or folder (as explained in Chapter 1 of this minibook), you may need to adjust or revoke the sharing permissions at some point. Follow these steps to change the permissions on a file or folder:

1. **Hover your cursor over the file or folder and click the vertical ellipsis next to the name to open the Show Actions menu.**

See Figure 2-6.

2. **Click Manage Access.**

In the Manage Access pane that appears on the right, you can take these actions (see Figure 2-7):

- To revoke access to the file from everybody, click Stop Sharing. Note that this option is available only for files, not folders.

- To grant access to a someone, click the plus sign button (+) next to Direct Access. In the Grant access dialog box, add the person, choose whether they can edit (click the pencil icon) or view (the crossed pencil icon), and then click Grant Access.

- To change an existing access link, click the ellipsis next to that link to view the link settings. You can change who the link works for, whether they have edit or view access, or disable the link entirely.

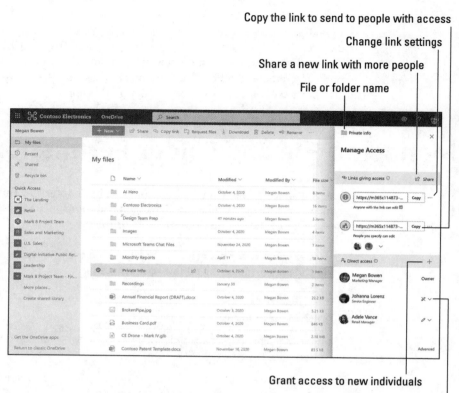

Copy the link to send to people with access

Change link settings

Share a new link with more people

File or folder name

Grant access to new individuals

Change individual permissions

FIGURE 2-7:
Change
permissions
on a shared file
or folder.

Adding SharePoint and Teams Files to OneDrive

A high-value trick to collect your files from SharePoint and Teams in OneDrive is the Add shortcut to OneDrive button. In a SharePoint library or folder, or the Files tab in a Teams channel, the toolbar always includes this option, and clicking the button makes the library or folder display in line with your top-level OneDrive folders. Follow these steps to add a SharePoint library or folder to your OneDrive:

1. **In SharePoint or Teams, open the library or Files tab you want to add as a shortcut.**

2. **Drill down to the folder you want to add as a shortcut (if applicable).**

TIP

You're more than welcome to connect the entire library (a whole Team's worth of files!), but you can also add shortcuts for individual subfolders if you don't want all the folders and files above your folder of choice mucking up your OneDrive.

3. **Click the Add Shortcut to OneDrive button in the toolbar.**

TIP

Alternatively, in SharePoint, hover your cursor over a folder name to reveal the Add Shortcut to OneDrive icon, which looks like a folder with a chainlink on top of it.

You receive a notification when the shortcut is added to your OneDrive. Go back to OneDrive, and you should see the folder or library available right in your OneDrive, as shown in Figure 2-8. You can tell it's a shortcut because it has the chainlink graphic on the folder icon.

If you sync your OneDrive to your computer so that you can access your files via File Explorer, as described in Chapter 1 of this minibook, you will see the short-cut folder there, too, and you can save those files for offline access. This is a great option for one-off folders or libraries to which you want quick access via your OneDrive without having to sync the SharePoint files separately.

Making the Most of OneDrive

FIGURE 2-8:
You can add SharePoint content as shortcuts to your OneDrive for easy access in the browser (background) and syncing in the file window (inset).

SharePoint shortcuts in OneDrive   SharePoint shortcuts in synced OneDrive

Chapter **3**

Collaborating in SharePoint

SharePoint can be a scary term for a lot of people. It may conjure bad memories of ugly web pages, messy folder structures, and bad search results. Those memories arise from the older versions of SharePoint that were installed on local servers. SharePoint Online, however, is modern, mobile friendly, and easy to use, especially compared to its predecessor versions.

SharePoint is an advanced collaboration and publishing system that stores much of the information you might work on when using Office 365. You may not directly encounter SharePoint all that often, but it does a lot of heavy lifting in the background for many Office 365 apps, especially for work and school accounts. This chapter shows you how to create a site and pages within the site. It also covers storing and collaborating on files, managing lists of information, and taking control of who can access the files and folders stored in a SharePoint site.

Getting Started with SharePoint

SharePoint Online is the Office 365 version of SharePoint; it's not a version locally installed on servers. SharePoint Online consists of *sites*, which are similar to public websites that you may use regularly, except that SharePoint in your organization is accessible only by you and your peers. Like the normal websites you're familiar with, a SharePoint site has pages and other areas to store content within the site. Organizations might create *communication sites,* which are used to publish information that needs to be widely available — like corporate policies, document templates, news, events, and resource content. An organization might also build *team sites,* which, in contrast to public websites you're familiar with, allow members to collaborate on and organize ongoing work with a project team, class, or other group. The focus of this chapter is the team site. Most of the features I discuss apply to communication sites as well, but those are likely to be in the hands of your IT or communications teams (though not always!) and are usually used for publishing finalized content to a large audience.

To get started in SharePoint, you open the SharePoint start page, which is also where you find any sites you've recently accessed or updated content in. Follow these steps to access your SharePoint start page:

1. **In your browser, type** www.office.com **to open the Office 365 home page.**

2. **Click the Sign In button to enter your work or school account and password to log in.**

3. **Click the SharePoint icon in the app bar on the far-left side of the screen, or click the app launcher (the grid of dots at the left end of the suite bar) to find and click the SharePoint icon there.**

   This page lists all sites that you're following, sites that you've been to recently or that you frequently visit, and news posts from your sites, as shown in Figure 3-1.

Every page in SharePoint displays the SharePoint app bar on the left side. The app bar gives you quick access to the following, which appear from left to right in Figure 3-2:

>> **Global navigation:** A curated list of links provided by your organization that give you quick access to all the biggest and most important sites in SharePoint. If your organization hasn't enabled this, the button links to the SharePoint start page instead. If that's the case, talk to your IT team about enabling the navigation! Click the house icon to open this pane.

>> **My Sites:** A list of the sites you follow (SharePoint's version of bookmarking) and sites you visit frequently. To follow a site, click the star icon in the top-right of any SharePoint site you're in. These are the same sites you see on the SharePoint start page (refer to Figure 3-1). Click the globe icon to open this pane.

>> **My News:** A list of news posts recommended to you based on sites you interact with the most. News posts are published by members of various sites and centralized here in the app bar. Click the newspaper icon to open this pane.

>> **My Files:** A list of recent files you've opened in OneDrive, SharePoint, or Teams. Click the files icon to open this pane.

SharePoint app bar

App launcher/Waffle

Post a news article to a site

Sites you follow

Return to SharePoint start page

Create a site

Article title

Site where article is posted

Search all SharePoint sites

Color block indicates "official" org news

News posts relevant to you

Suite bar

FIGURE 3-1:
The SharePoint start page.

Org links

Saved pages

Recent sites

Saved page

Followed site

Save a page

Follow a site

Sites you visit regularly

Collaborating in SharePoint

Introducing Team Sites

The SharePoint start page, described in the previous section, is where you can create a new site, including a team site. Team sites help people with organizing files, hosting pages to get people to their destination, and building lists to track things. You may and in fact probably will be included in multiple team sites. And, as the need arises, you can create more team sites.

REMEMBER

When I refer to a SharePoint team site, I'm not talking about a Team in Microsoft Teams. Although Microsoft (unfortunately) uses the same term for both, this chapter covers details about team sites in SharePoint. Each Microsoft Team you create comes with a SharePoint team site in the background, but the term *team site* in SharePoint doesn't derive from its connection to Microsoft Teams. You can create a SharePoint team site by itself; a Microsoft Team isn't required for a SharePoint team site to exist. In fact, the term *team site* predates Microsoft Teams; SharePoint did it first, and Teams hitched a ride. Everything in this chapter applies to the team site *behind* a Microsoft Team, if it's connected to a Team at all! Book 10 is where you find detailed coverage of Microsoft Teams.

Many organizations remove the capability to create SharePoint sites, so you have to request a site rather than create one yourself. If that's the case, follow your IT team's guidance. But if you see the Create Site button, you can follow these steps to create a new team site:

1. **From the SharePoint start page, click Create Site in the toolbar near the top-left of the page.**

See the steps for getting to the start page in "Getting Started with SharePoint," earlier in this chapter.

2. **In the Create a Site pane that appears, click the Team Site button.**

A pane opens in which you can enter information about your new site.

3. **Enter a name and description for your site.**

   As you enter a site name, fields for Group email address and Site address show up. Your site will get an email address and web address, which you can edit to simplify them if you'd like (click the pencil next to the appropriate field). Don't skimp on the site description, because it helps people understand what the site is for. Additional drop-down menus also appear, including Privacy Settings and Language.

4. **In the Privacy Settings drop-down menu, choose Private or Public, and in the Select a Language drop-down menu, choose the language of the site.**

   When selecting your privacy settings, be aware that all SharePoint users in your organizations can find public sites (for example, through the SharePoint search box); private sites can be visited only by people with explicit permissions.

5. **Click Next at the bottom of the pane.**

   The Add Group Members pane opens.

6. **(Optional) In the Add Additional Owners box, add owners by typing their name and selecting them when they pop up.**

   Owners have full control of a site. You can always add owners later if you want. A good practice is to have a total of three owners: a primary, a backup, and a secondary backup. Site ownership is a real responsibility, so choose wisely. The site creator is also an owner.

7. **(Optional) In the Add Members box, add members by typing their name and selecting them when they pop up.**

   Members have edit access to all content in the site. Your teammates would be your members. You can always add members later if you want.

8. **Click Finish at the bottom of the pane.**

   You're now the proud owner of a new team site.

Team sites are great for projects, business units, classes, affinity groups, user groups, and communities of practice (for example, project managers or customer service representatives across your organization, regardless of which departments they work in).

Safely store information relevant to who has permissions in this one central spot; add and remove people as necessary; share files with outsiders if you need to; and retain a dependable, dedicated spot for all the work that's essentially "owned" by anyone who has permission to access it at any time.

Collaborating in
SharePoint

TIP

If your organization allows people from the outside to access your SharePoint sites, you can also add email addresses in the preceding Steps 6 and 7, making them owners or members of your team sites. You should check with your IT team to review any rules that might be in place for these situations.

Understanding the connection between SharePoint team sites and Microsoft 365 Groups

To add some complexity to a seemingly easy topic, creating a team site doesn't just create a site. It creates a permission-protected collection of online workspaces called a Microsoft 365 Group. The team site and Group are forever linked, have the same name, and retain certain aspects that apply to both entities.

TECHNICAL STUFF

Groups have owner (full control) and member (edit) permissions across all the workspaces in various Office 365 apps that are connected to the Group. The SharePoint team site just happens to be one app connected to the Group, and if you create a site from SharePoint, that site was the entry point to create the Group. When you create a Microsoft Team, that, too, creates a Group and a site, though the Group works a bit differently than when you create a team site directly. But still, the underlying concept of the Group is the same.

When you create a team site in SharePoint, you get a workspace in the following Office 365 apps, as shown in Figure 3-3:

>> **Outlook Inbox:** Use the Group email address to send emails to the group as an entity (the Inbox itself) and everyone in the Group. Owners can toggle settings to push emails to all members or just to the Group as an entity. People external to the organization can email this address, too. Access the Group Inbox by clicking Conversations in the team site's Quick Launch menu on the left of any page in the site.

>> **Outlook Calendar:** Use the Group Calendar to schedule meetings or events, or to track who's out of the office. Owners can toggle settings to invite or not invite all members of the group when an event is added to this Calendar. Access the Group Calendar by clicking Conversations in the team site's Quick Launch menu on the left of any page in the site; then click the Calendar icon above the Inbox listing.

>> **SharePoint team site:** This is the website where you can create pages, edit and store files, and create tracking lists.

» **OneNote notebook:** Each team site gets a OneNote notebook for members to use. You can create more OneNote notebooks in any of your document libraries (explained in "Creating a new document library," later in this chapter). This OneNote notebook is meant to be a quick and easy one for anyone in the site to use from the start. Access it by clicking Notebook in the team site's Quick Launch menu on the left of any page in the site.

» **Planner plan:** Microsoft Planner is a simple but useful project-management tool that lets you assign tasks to people in a collaborative way (similarly to Trello). Each Group gets a blank plan. Planner uses the Kanban project management methodology and is free. You can get to the Planner home page from the app launcher at the top of the app bar in SharePoint.

» **Forms workspace:** Microsoft Forms is a survey and questionnaire tool that lets you create and get responses to forms (kind of like SurveyMonkey). Your Group gets a shared Forms workspace for collaborating on forms and viewing responses to those forms. You can get to the Forms home page from the app launcher.

FIGURE 3-3: Creating a team site also creates a Microsoft 365 Group.

REMEMBER

You may find the Microsoft 365 Group helpful as you're working in your SharePoint team site, changing permissions, or looking for other tools that might help you get work done in the team site. You get these workspaces whether you plan to use them or not, and not using them is a perfectly legitimate choice if it makes sense for you.

REMEMBER

A Microsoft 365 Group is not the same thing as a shared mailbox, a security group, or a distribution group. Microsoft 365 Groups are in some ways built on the shoulders of those earlier features, but they don't work the same way.

Finding your way around a team site

When you're in a team site, the site name displays prominently on the top of every page (see Figure 3-4). The pane on the left side of the screen contains the Quick Launch menu, which displays on all pages in the site and has the following elements:

>> **Home:** No matter where you are in the site, clicking Home takes you back to the site's home page. (Clicking the site icon next to the site name does as well.)

>> **Conversations:** This is a link to the site's Outlook Inbox, as referenced in the preceding section.

>> **Documents:** Clicking this link takes you to a document library where you can store files. It's the one document library that comes with your site, but you can add more. A document library is like a super folder and is unique to SharePoint. You can find more details about document libraries in the "Working with Document Libraries" section, later in this chapter.

>> **Notebook:** This link takes you to the OneNote notebook that comes automatically with a site. You can create more notebooks.

>> **Pages:** You can access all the pages in your site by clicking this link. Find more about pages in the "Working with SharePoint pages" section, later in this chapter.

>> **Site Contents:** This is where you can find all your document libraries, including Pages and Documents. Site Contents holds everything in your site.

>> **Recycle Bin**: When anything is deleted in your site, it goes to the Recycle Bin before being deleted forever. You should have up to 93 days to restore a deleted file, page, or other object. Chapter 1 of this minibook has more information on using the Recycle Bin in Office 365.

>> **Edit:** When you click this link, the Quick Launch changes to allow you to change the links. You can add more, reorder, or remove links as needed. Maybe you want to link to a specific page in your site, or to an outside website. If you don't see this option, you don't have the permissions to make changes.

TIP

If you're ever looking for content in a site and you don't see a link for it in the Quick Launch menu, always hop over to Site Contents. Unless someone removes Site Contents from the Quick Launch menu, the link should be there. If it's not, click the Settings gear in the suite bar (the topmost area of the screen) and then click Site Contents; you can always get there from the Settings gear.

Quick Launch · Site title · Page toolbar · Follow the site · Site privacy · Member count

Site icon · Home page · Page status · Next steps · Site settings

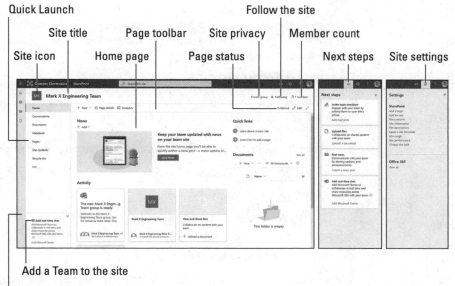

FIGURE 3-4:
A SharePoint
team site.

Add a Team to the site

SharePoint app bar

Getting familiar with site permissions

You can't talk about SharePoint without talking about permissions. Permissions represent one of the most important, although sometimes most confusing, aspects of a SharePoint site. The biggest takeaway from this section is this: Permissions can be hard to manage, and they always require thought and planning. It takes effort to keep your permissions organized and manageable. If you don't do it, you may regret it later on — in fact, you probably will.

REMEMBER

Each SharePoint site comes with a permissions setup that owners can manage. In fact, the site permissions are built atop the Microsoft 365 Group permissions (see the "Understanding the connection between SharePoint team sites and Microsoft 365 Groups" section, earlier in this chapter, for more information), but the site has additional options to use if you want. For example, the site provides permissions that are applicable only to the site; it also provides the ability for anyone in the site to share the whole site or something in the site. An owner can disable that feature, though.

Think of the basic permissions levels as buckets. The Group (and therefore the site) has two buckets: one for owners, one for members. The site offers an additional bucket for visitors; visitors have read access to content only. If you're in the owners bucket, you have full control of everything in the whole site (and the Group); members have edit access to everything in the whole site (and the Group); and visitors can read, open, and download anything in the site, but they can't

Collaborating in SharePoint

make changes. If you have a Microsoft Team connected to your site, the owners and members groups are the same across the Team and the site.

Setting permissions

To change permissions on the site or Group, you must be an owner. Follow the steps below to change permissions of your site:

1. **From the home page of your site, click the Settings gear in the suite bar.**

This opens the Settings pane.

2. **Click Site Permissions.**

The resulting Permissions pane displays a list of the three permissions groups, which you can click to expand and view who is in each one.

3. **Click the Add Members button.**

You can choose to add the people to the Microsoft 365 Group behind the site or share only the site:

a. **If you choose Add Members to Group, click Add Members, search a name in the name box, select the person when their name pops up, repeat for anyone else you want to add, and click Save.**

Anyone you add will be a full-fledged member of the site and all associated workspaces, including the Outlook Inbox associated with the Group. Note that even if you want to add an owner, you have to click the Add Members button first.

b. **If you choose Share Site Only, search a name, Microsoft 365 Group, or security group in the name box, select the item when it pops up, repeat for more names or groups you want to add, and click Add.**

Under each name or Group, choose the permission level (full control, edit, or read) and decide whether to send an email notification notifying them of this access.

You now have Group owners and members as well as site owners, members, and visitors.

There are two ways to view and manage your Group's and site's permissions, as shown in Figure 3-5. To see the Group owners and members, on the top-right of the site's home page, click the X Members icon (the X here is a placeholder for a number). Click the role under their name — owner or member — to open a drop-down menu to change their role if you need to; click Remove from Group to remove them from the Group.

To see who has full control, edit access, or read access to *just* the site, click the Settings gear icon, click Site Permissions, and in the Permissions pane, click each group name (site owners, site members, site visitors) to expand the list of people or groups in them. Names and groups listed here have access to the site only, not the Group (and therefore not any of the other workspaces listed in the "Understanding the connection between SharePoint team sites and Microsoft 365 Groups" section, earlier in this chapter). Click the role under a name — full control, edit, read — to open a drop-down menu to change their role if you need to; click Remove to remove them from the site.

Figure 3-5 shows an example team site with *Group* owners and members as well as an additional *site* owner, multiple *site* members, and in the *site* visitors, a group called Everyone Except External Users, which is a built-in security group that automatically includes everyone in your organization.

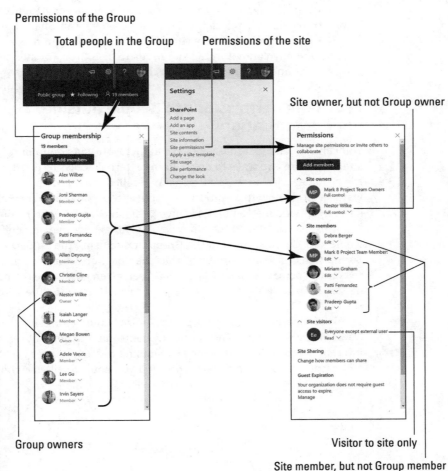

FIGURE 3-5: Permissions for a team site can get complex because the Group and the site can offer different access levels.

In the site shown in Figure 3-5, two people own the whole group, additional person owns only the site, 17 people are members in the Group, and an additional four people can edit only the site. Read access is provided to everyone else in the organization. This would be a very transparent team site because everyone in the organization can at least view it.

Setting content-sharing permissions

SharePoint offers even further flexibility — or complexity, depending on how you want to look at it — with member-sharing rights. Out of the gate, a team site lets members share parts of the site content as necessary — a file here, a folder there — for input or review from someone who isn't already a member of the Group or site. Site owners can manage this feature by clicking the Settings gear icon, and then Site Permissions, and then, in the Permissions pane that appears, clicking Change How Members Can Share. The Site Sharing Settings pane opens and you can manage these settings to meet your needs. If nothing in the site is meant to be shared, select the Only Site Owners Can Share Files, Folders, and The Site option and click Save. In that case, anyone who needs to provide input or review of any content in the site needs to be a Group or site member. More on sharing files and folders later in this chapter.

Providing permissions to people outside your organization

You can also add external people to a Microsoft 365 Group or a SharePoint team site. There are two ways to do so: grant external access or guest access. Sharing a file or folder with an external person — called *external access* — is done the same way as you share with an internal person, except you use their email address in the sharing options instead of searching for a name (see Chapter 1 of this minibook). Granting *guest access*, on the other hand, gives an external person full access to the whole site. You add them to the Group or site using the guidance in the "Setting permissions" section, earlier in this chapter, but use their email address when selecting a person. When someone has been given guest access, you can send them messages in Teams (if they use Teams) and add them to other sites.

TIP

Think of external access as a push: You're sending someone the file or folder. Guest access is a pull: You're bringing someone into your site to take part as any internal person can. Both your IT team and a Group owner can disable external and guest access, so don't be surprised if you don't see it as an option.

Working with SharePoint pages

Most people think of a team site as a place to store files, but it's also a great spot to post information to keep people updated and provide easy access to important resources. Pages in SharePoint fit the bill.

Creating a page doesn't require any knowledge of web development, coding, or HTML (though if you do have these skills, you can take SharePoint pages to the next level using the SharePoint Framework, which isn't covered in this minibook).

A good team site page can be the launching point for everyone in the site to use to get to the files and links they need, or to stay up to date with news and team status. Pages can even list popular, trending, and recent files and pages so that members can see what's going on both in your team site and in other sites in SharePoint. You can also add some useful content to the default home page. Figure 3-6 shows an example page that includes easy access to documents, important links, and a critical PowerPoint presentation as well as a list of recently edited files in the site and trending files across all sites in the Marketing department.

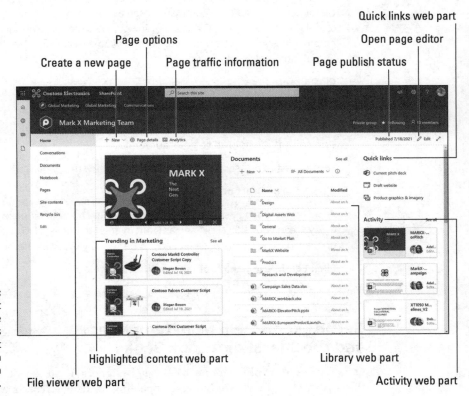

FIGURE 3-6: A SharePoint page can give members convenient information when they open the site.

Creating a page

This section presents the basic steps involved in creating a page, but subsequent sections explain more about templates as well as the various parts of a page, so you might want to continue reading before you start building pages.

Follow these steps to create a page in a SharePoint team site:

1. From the team site's home page, click + New in the page toolbar that appears under the site name.

If you don't see the page toolbar, you don't have sufficient access to create a page and need to talk to the site owner.

2. In the drop-down menu that appears, click Page or News post.

You probably want Page, unless you're posting original news articles on your site. This opens the Pages pane.

3. Choose from the available templates.

TIP

There are a few provided templates, but your organization may provide templates for you. Click a template to see a preview. You can also create a template from any page for use later in your site. See more about finding helpful templates in the upcoming "Getting some help from templates and the SharePoint Look Book" section.

4. Click Create Page.

The new page opens in Edit mode.

5. Make your edits, add sections and web parts, and organize your information so that it's helpful to your audience.

See the rest of this section for guidance on editing the page.

6. Click Save as Draft or Publish.

WARNING

If you're not ready to share a new page or update an existing page with everyone in your site, click Save as Draft instead of Publish. Don't click Publish until everything on the page is ready to be seen by everyone in the site.

7. Click Edit in the page toolbar to edit the page.

This is how you edit the existing home page, too.

Getting some help from templates and the SharePoint Look Book

Let's face it: Most of us are not webpage designers. It takes skill to make a page that is useful to the viewer but also appealing to the eye. That's where templates can come in handy. If your organization has graphic designer resources available, you may want to ask them to create a few templates for your use and even share those templates with other SharePoint owners in the organization.

But sometimes all you need is some inspiration. Microsoft provides an incredibly useful resource called the SharePoint Look Book. It offers example designs for team sites, classroom sites, organizational or department sites, and more. The Look Book examples explain how each site was built so that you can copy their lead. Visit the SharePoint Look Book at https://lookbook.microsoft.com.

Some Look Book designs are also available to install to your site as templates. From the home page of your site, click the Settings gear icon, and in the Settings pane that appears, click Apply a Site Template to see a list of available templates. Your organization may also have provided templates in the same place.

Taking a deeper look at the parts of a page

Pages are composed of sections, and each section contains *web parts*, which are building blocks that you can add to a section that display the content you want to show off. When you're in Edit mode on your page, you add sections using the toolbar on the left of the page (but to the right of the Quick Launch). Edit them by clicking the pencil icon in the section options toolbar on the left side of the section. Each section can have different layouts, so don't limit yourself to the one section the page gives you to start. Refer to Figure 3-7 as a guide as you continue reading this section.

Hover your cursor over the top of a section to reveal a plus sign icon, and click it to open the menu of available web parts. A number of web parts are available. The most obvious are text and images, but consider some of the other ones, too — such as Highlighted Content, File Preview, Quick Links, Button, Org Chart, Group Calendar, and Events. To display any document libraries or Microsoft Lists (explained in later sections in this chapter), use the Document Library or List web parts. The web parts menu also includes options that pull information from external websites like Trello, Salesforce, Google Analytics, and GitHub. Your organization may provide custom web parts, too.

REMEMBER

After you add a web part to the page, configure it by clicking it and then clicking the pencil icon in the menu that appears on its left edge. Some of the web parts offer a wide array of options, which can give you dozens of ways to apply the same web part but display information much differently. The Highlighted Content web part, for example, can display trending, recent, or most-viewed files from your site or multiple sites, and you can filter by file type: video, image, PDFs, Office files, and others. This web part can provide a lot of information to your site users for minimal effort. Also, the web part menu that appears below the pencil icon contains buttons to move a web part, make a copy of it, or delete it.

Being part of a hub provides extra content options in web parts

Web part options

Page editing toolbar

Publish your page for everyone to see

FIGURE 3-7:
Editing a
SharePoint page
provides a lot of
options.

Web part options

Section options

Add section

Each web part is indicated by dashes

Hover to add a web part

When you're ready to make your page visible to everyone in the site, click Publish. If you're working on a page that was already published, click Republish. If you're not ready to publish the page or updates, click Save as Draft instead; you can come back to it later and publish when you're ready.

Connecting an existing SharePoint team site to Microsoft Teams

As discussed earlier, each Team in Microsoft Teams comes with a SharePoint team site supporting it from the background. This chapter is about SharePoint and focuses mostly on details about the SharePoint team site, but you might also need to know how to add a Microsoft Team to an existing SharePoint team site. You might, for example, create a team site by itself or a Microsoft 365 Group to benefit from the Outlook integrations, and later decide that you need some of the benefits of Microsoft Teams associated with that team site or Group.

You can't actually *connect* an existing Microsoft Team to an existing SharePoint team site, but you can create a Microsoft Team from an existing SharePoint team site.

To add a Microsoft Team to an existing SharePoint team site, follow these steps:

1. **From the SharePoint team site's home page, click the megaphone icon in the suite bar.**

   The Next Steps pane opens (refer to Figure 3-4).

2. **Click the Add Microsoft Teams link in the Add Real-Time Chat box.**

   The Add Microsoft Teams pane opens.

3. **Click the Continue button.**

   The Pin Resources as Tabs in Teams pane opens.

4. **(Optional) Click to choose any libraries, pages, or lists that you want to see as tabs right in your new Team's General channel.**

   Book 10, Chapter 1 explains how tabs work in a Team.

5. **Click the Add Teams button.**

6. **After your Team is created, the browser asks you to choose to open the Teams desktop app or click Use the Web App instead.**

   With either choice, the General channel of the new Microsoft Team that's associated with the existing SharePoint team site opens. This is a full-fledged Microsoft Team and can be used in all the same ways as outlined in Book 10.

Working with Document Libraries

SharePoint is great for storing and sharing files in multiple ways. You can use folders and metadata tags for sorting and filtering, all within document libraries. In fact, document libraries are the lifeblood of a team site. A document library is like a super folder: it's the first level available to separate files from each other in any SharePoint site. Libraries can have their own permissions, columns for tagging files, and even template files called content types. Libraries also offer advanced settings that let you configure whether folders are allowed (you may want to use only metadata tags to organize your files), whether content will appear in search results, and whether Office files open in the browser app or desktop app when clicked.

REMEMBER

Each team site comes with a default document library called Documents. You find a link to this library in the site's Quick Launch menu on the left side of the any page. This default Documents library is where you can start storing your files from the moment your site is created. If your SharePoint team site is connected to a Microsoft Team, this library is where all your channel files are stored.

Each channel has an associated folder in the Documents library, but owners and members can add other folders as necessary.

You can create more libraries as needed, too. In those libraries, you can create, upload, edit, and share files and folders as well as sort, filter, and group content based on its columns. The following sections explain how to make the most of your libraries.

Creating a new document library

It makes sense to create a new document library when you need to keep certain files and folders in a separate location, but still within your team site. Maybe you want different permissions on this library because you're sharing it with external collaborators who shouldn't see other libraries. Or maybe you want to add specific columns to the files in this library so that you can sort and filter your files by that unique information. Follow these steps to create a new document library, also shown in Figure 3-8:

1. **From the team site's home page, click + New in the page toolbar that appears under the site name.**

   If you don't see the page toolbar, you don't have sufficient access to create a library and need to talk to the site owner.

2. **In the drop-down menu that appears, click Document Library.**

   The Create Document Library pane opens.

3. **Enter a name and description for your library in the appropriate boxes.**

   Keep the name short and descriptive. Don't skimp on the description; it sets the tone for what the library is intended for.

4. **Select the box next to Show in Site Navigation if you want the library to be displayed in the Quick Launch menu.**

5. **Click the Create button.**

REMEMBER

As site members and owners create libraries, the libraries may or may not be added to the Quick Launch, depending on the preference of the person creating the library. You can find all the document libraries created by you or anyone else in a site by clicking Site Contents in the Quick Launch menu or by clicking the Settings gear icon in the suite bar and then clicking Site Contents. Everything stored in your site is located here, including any Microsoft Lists associated with this site (we cover Lists in the "Taking a Brief Look at Microsoft Lists" section, later in this chapter).

New library

New library options

FIGURE 3-8:
FIGURE 3-8:
Create a new
document library
from your team
site's home page.

Uploading files to a document library

After you create a library, you can fill it up with good stuff. Creating and uploading files in a SharePoint library works the same as doing these things in OneDrive,
which is covered in detail in Chapter 2 of this minibook.

You have various options for adding things to your library:

>> **To create folders and Office files:** From the library toolbar, click **+ New** and
select the file type or folder you want to create.

>> **To upload multiple files or a single folder from your computer:** From the
library toolbar, click Upload.

>> **To upload multiple files and multiple folders from File Explorer:** Select the
files or folders in File Explorer and drag them into the library to upload them.
You can upload multiple folders this way, which you can't do using the Upload
button. See Chapter 2 of this minibook for more details.

>> **To sync the contents of a library to a device:** You can access your
SharePoint files right in File Explorer if you've installed and configured the
OneDrive app. Once set up, you can open and edit SharePoint files even if
you're offline. In this minibook, see Chapter 1 for more on setting up syncing
and Chapter 2 for adding SharePoint and Teams files to your OneDrive.

Collaborating in
SharePoint

Opening and editing a file in a document library

You can open Word, Excel, PowerPoint, and OneNote files from within your document library. Click a file's name to open it for viewing or editing. These Office files open in the browser version of the app. If you want to open them in the desktop app, click the vertical ellipsis to the right of a filename to open the Show Actions menu; then click Open➪Open in App. Doing so launches the desktop app and opens the file for you. All changes you make to an Office file are saved automatically.

You can also open other popular file types — such as PDFs, images, videos, and Photoshop files — from within the document library. They open in the browser for you to view, but not edit. Sync the library to your device to be able to open a file from File Explorer in its respective app, especially if you need to edit it. For example, you can open synced images in the Windows Photos app, Photoshop files in Photoshop, and PDFs in Adobe Acrobat to make changes and save them. Updates to files will automatically sync back to SharePoint so that the next person to open them will see the updated version.

Sharing files from a document library

Just as you can with OneDrive, you can share files and folders from a document library. Additionally, you can share the entire library itself if you want. Keep in mind, though, that a SharePoint team site is meant for collaborative work; ad hoc sharing of individual files and folders isn't really recommended. Instead, consider making a person a member of the site so that they can access the content they need.

Still, some situations require one-off sharing. Breaking permissions can quickly become a nightmare for the site owner, though, so it's best to discussing sharing before your group starts doing it.

Sharing is generally done internally, to people inside your organization who have accounts. However, if your site is set up to allow external sharing, you can also share the content to anyone with an email address. The next section covers how to change the permissions of your document library.

Managing permissions of a document library

Follow these steps to provide access to an entire document library to people who cannot already access the SharePoint team site (you likely have to be a site owner to perform this task):

1. **From the document library, click the Settings gear icon in the suite bar.**

   The Settings pane opens.

2. **Click Library Settings.**

   The Document Library Settings page opens.

3. **Under the Permissions and Management column in the center of the page, click Permissions for this Document Library.**

   The Library Permissions page opens, where you can change a person's or group's existing permissions or add new people individually.

4. **Click the Stop Inheriting Permissions button in the Ribbon and accept the pop-up prompt.**

   The permissions of this library are now disconnected from the SharePoint team site, so if you make changes to the site permissions, they will not apply to this library. The library is now an island when it comes to access.

REMEMBER

5. **To change permissions, select the check box next to a person's or group's name and click Edit User Permissions or Remove User Permissions in the Ribbon.**

   If you're editing permissions, stick to the Full Control, Contribute, or Read options unless you're familiar with what the other options do.

6. **To give permissions, click Grant Permissions in the Ribbon.**

   The Share pane opens, where you can invite people or groups.

7. **In the Enter Names or Email Addresses box, type names of individuals or groups and then click their name when they pop up in the suggestions. If you're inviting people from outside your organization (called "guests" in this context), enter their email addresses individually.**

   Depending on your IT policy, you may or may not have the ability to invite guests. See Chapter 1 of this minibook for more information.

8. **(Optional) Deselect the box next to Share Everything in This Folder, Even Items with Unique Permissions if you don't want the new people to see files or folders that don't inherit permissions from the library.**

   Because anyone in a site can share a file with people outside of the site or library, some content in the library may not have the same permissions as the library itself. If this box is selected, the people you're giving permissions to will be able to see those things anyway. If you deselect this box, the content with unique permissions will not show up for the people you're adding here.

9. Click Show Options.

You see more options for the new permissions you're setting up.

10. (Optional) Deselect the box next to Send an Email Invitation if you don't want to send an automated email to everyone you're giving permissions to.

If you're giving permissions to a large group of people, you may not want to send an email out to all those people automatically. Be sure that sending the email makes sense.

11. In the Select a Permission Level drop-down menu below the Send an Email Invitation box, select which level of access these people will be given.

The full control, edit, and read options are the most common selections. The other options are outside the scope of this minibook.

12. Click the Share button.

The permissions are changed and an email notification goes out to everyone if you selected the box in Step 10. If you decided not to send an automated email and the people you added need to know about the library, you should send them a message with a link to the library.

Sharing a file or folder

In many cases, you just want to share a folder or file in a library. That's a lot easier than dealing with site or library permissions and access issues, and it's something all site owners and members can do. To share a file or folder in a library, hover your cursor over the file or folder to reveal a Share icon to the right of its name (the icon looks like a box with a right-pointing arrow) and then click the Share icon, as shown in Figure 3-9. In the Send Link pane that appears, you can choose who needs access.

You have a lot of sharing options. Click the existing permissions listed directly under the "Send link" title to open the Link Settings options:

>> **Anyone with the Link:** This is the least secure way to share. Anyone who has the link can access what you're sharing and won't need to log in or provide a passcode. Sharing this way might be easier, but it's not as safe. Many organizations disable this option; if it's grayed out, it has been disabled.

>> **People in *Organization Name* with the Link:** Sharing through this option allows anyone you work with to open the file or folder if they have the link. This approach still may not be great because it means that the file is wide open to anyone in the organization who has the link.

Share   Who can access

Add individual recipients   Edit or view access

Custom message, if sending email   Send invitation via email

Copy link to send yourself   Block download (view access only)

Choose who can access

>> **People with Existing Access:** Choosing this option is useful when you want to send a link to someone who can't remember where the content is, or you just want to make it easy for them to open and edit the content. The recipient must already have access (that is, be a member of the site). This is the safest option and is useful when referencing a file or folder in an email, Teams conversation, and especially Teams meeting chats.

>> **Specific People:** This option is useful when you want to break the permissions of the site and send a link to a file or folder to a few specific people, including people outside your organization (if your organization allows it). The recipient may need to enter a one-time passcode to confirm who they are and access the content. The passcode process is automatic; you don't need to do anything to set it up or make it work.

When sharing a file or folder, you have the option to provide edit access or view access. Choose wisely. You also can either copy a link for you to share with the recipients or you can choose to send an automated email to the recipients.

TIP

It's usually best practice to click Copy Link and send the link using whichever communication method makes the most sense. The automated emails are less personal and can sometimes get caught in junk folders because they're automated. Plus, the emails just don't make it as obvious to a recipient that the message was sent by a human with a real reason.

Viewing file and folder options

Just as with OneDrive, you have a number of options you can manage for your files and folders. Click the vertical ellipsis to the right of a folder or filename to open the Show Actions menu and see all the options. This menu gives you the ability to download, delete, move, copy, rename, view the version history of a file, and more. Chapter 2 of this minibook provides more detail into what options are available and what they do.

You can also use Pin to Top to pin up to three files or folders at the top of the page for each folder level in your library. Click Alert Me to get an email when new files are created or existing ones are edited or deleted. Click Check Out to reserve a file for editing just by you (though this concept doesn't allow co-authoring, so it might not suit the practices of your organization).

Working with columns and views

The real value of document libraries in SharePoint is the ability to tag files with *metadata,* which is information *about* a file, like filename, file size, date it was created, who created it, date it was edited last, who edited it last, and so on. Metadata shows up in a library as columns. And you can add custom metadata, too, like document type, customer, or project name to tag files with appropriate categories.

With this information, you can sort, filter, and group your files into views so that you can see the correct files when you need to. For example, maybe you want to categorize all files based on which office branch manages the file so that you can group the files by office branch, then sort them by file type, and filter out files that weren't edited in a given quarter. You have a lot of power to find your files quickly and display them smartly if you put a little time into designing a robust metadata setup.

Creating or showing a column in a library

When you create or open a library, three columns automatically display under the library toolbar: Name (filename); Modified (when the file was last edited); and Modified By (who edited the file last). (Refer to Figure 3-10.) You can add more columns to serve your needs. You can reorder columns by clicking and dragging the column title left or right.

To create or show a column in your library, click +Add Column, which is on the right end of the column headers in your library. The menu that appears provides options that let you create a new column or show existing columns that Share-Point provides automatically, but hides in the background:

>> **To show an existing column,** click Show/Hide Columns. Each library comes with many more columns than the three that show from the start. In the pane that appears, select the box next to an existing column to display it. You can select multiple columns if you want. When you've finished selecting, click the Apply button at the top of the pane to see your selections displayed in the library.

>> **To create a new column,** select one of the column types in the menu and provide the required information for your column type. I can't cover all the options in this chapter, but Choice columns are great for identifying the status of a file and dividing content by organizational or regional hierarchy. People columns are useful for identifying owners of files, or who is expected to perform the next action in a task. Date columns are great for delivery dates. There are a number of other column types to explore.

REMEMBER

You can update the file's metadata by clicking the vertical ellipsis to the right of a filename to open the Show Actions menu; then click Details to open the Details pane, which shows all the column names in the Properties section of the pane (see bottom of Figure 3-11). This is your file's metadata.

Metadata can't be applied to folders, so if you're going to make strong use of metadata columns in a library, you may want to avoid using folders because they can muck up the experience. Plus, you don't *need* folders if you're using metadata. A folder is basically just another type of metadata tag, but unlike metadata, you can put a file in only one folder; you can tag a file with as much metadata as you want, meaning you can sort, filter, and group your files into whatever collection makes sense for *right now.* When someone sets up a folder structure, everyone using it is kind of stuck with a structure that made sense back when it was created, but it may not make as much sense now. Metadata is more flexible.

Creating saved views of your organized information

When you have columns set up in your library, click any of the column names to see a menu that lets you sort, filter, and possibly group by the content in those columns. You can organize the information the way you want and then save that layout as a view. You can create multiple views that display different combinations of sorts, filters, or groupings as well.

A saved view is useful to get quick access to a selection of files that's been sliced and diced to show only the ones that are relevant to that view, like having a folder for all contracts signed in a given year. With metadata, you can create a view that automatically filters a custom column called Document Type to display only contracts, and another custom column called Agreement Year to display only files for that year. Together, these two filters display only contracts from that year.

With metadata, you can tag your files by project, customer, document type, year, and any other tags that make sense. Then sort and filter any appropriate columns to show you all the files that have the tags, and save this information as a view.

Figure 3-10 shows a document library that uses some built-in and custom columns with tags. SharePoint opens the library in a default view called the All Documents view (shown in the top-right corner). Members of this site have agreed to tag every file they create or upload to this library by region (Northwest, Southeast, West Coast), lead (the person who manages the document), status (being drafted, ready for publishing, in peer review), due date, and backup lead (the person to contact when the lead is unavailable). These columns were created especially for this library, so you won't find them in a new library, but you can create similar ones yourself. The All Documents view also shows two built-in columns that list when the file was last modified and by whom. (SharePoint tracks information like this automatically, and you can display it using provided columns if you want.) The site members like this view because they can easily find what they're looking for.

FIGURE 3-10:
A library using custom and built-in columns.

Figure 3-11 shows a different view, called By Region, of the same document library. Metadata of a file is displayed in the Details pane on the right. This view groups the files by region and then sorts the grouped files by due date. It's the same content, just organized differently. The members of this team like this view because it helps them find files based on which business region they manage.

Grouped by "Region"　　　　　Sorted by Due Date　　　View name　　　File details

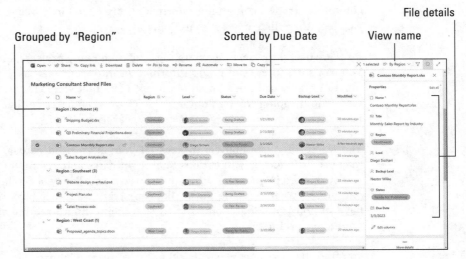

FIGURE 3-11:
The library from Figure 3-10 now grouped in the Region column and sorted by the Due Date column.

Site owners can always further change what's displayed. For example, to show the files with the viewer identified in the Lead column, you would click the Lead column and then in the drop-down menu, click Filter By. In the Filter By pane, you select @Me and click Apply at the bottom of the pane. The updated display is a version of the By Region view that shows only documents in which anyone viewing the files is listed in the Lead column. Saving this as a new view adds it to the View menu, The site owner calls it My Files By Region because it still groups the files by region, but now it filters the files based on whoever is looking at the library. Every file displayed in this view is really "my" file from the viewer's perspective.

To save a new view, click the View menu in the library's toolbar and select Save View As. In the Save As pop-up, give your view a name and decide whether to select the Make This a Public View box. If you don't select this box, your saved view is visible only to you.

You can continue to modify the layout with different sorting, filtering, and grouping preferences, and create more views based on them as the need arises. All the views for the library are listed in the View menu.

Taking a Brief Look at Microsoft Lists

We don't have the space in this chapter to cover the Microsoft Lists app in detail, but it's a useful feature to know about. Microsoft Lists is an Office 365 app that builds on a SharePoint feature (also called lists) with new branding and prettier features. A list is like a document library, but without the files. A list consists of columns and rows containing information organized in a web-friendly way. You can keep these lists in your SharePoint sites.

Lists are useful for tracking, planning, and organizing projects, events, and items. You can sort, filter, and group information into views just as you can in a document library. You can find all Microsoft Lists that were created in a SharePoint team site by going to Site Contents, which you can access either from the Quick Launch menu or by clicking the Settings gear icon.

TIP

The Microsoft Lists app centralizes all your lists from across Office 365. You may use different lists in various SharePoint sites and you might have some that you've created in your OneDrive for your own use. Easily accessing them all from one place was impossible until Microsoft Lists was introduced; now you don't have to hop from SharePoint site to SharePoint site to see the various lists you might be working on.

You find the Lists app by clicking the Office 365 app launcher in the top-left corner of the suite bar. If Lists doesn't display in the app launcher, click All Apps to find and open the app. The Microsoft Lists home page shows all your recent lists. Click the star on a list to make it a favorite and save it at the top of the page for easy access. You can create lists from here as well.

To create a list, on the Microsoft Lists home page, click the + New List button. Doing so brings up the Create a List pane, shown in Figure 3-12.

Microsoft provides a number of templates for specific uses that already include useful columns. Select one to see a preview of the list template, as shown in Figure 3-13. You can always create lists from scratch or based on an existing list, or you can import an existing Excel spreadsheet. These options are shown at the top of Figure 3-12.

WARNING

When you create a list from the Lists home, make sure you always choose the correct place for it to be created. Many people mistakenly create a list in their One-Drive when they intended to create it in a SharePoint site. If the list is not created in a site, the list isn't accessible to the people who have permissions to that site.

Import a spreadsheet

New list   Use an existing list as a template

FIGURE 3-12:
Create a list
using existing
lists or files (top)
or a template
(bottom).

Use a Microsoft template   Use an org-provided template

Template preview

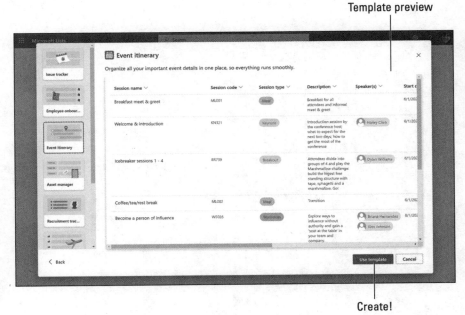

FIGURE 3-13:
If you select
a template
to start from,
Lists shows the
included columns
and dummy
information as
inspiration.

Create!

Collaborating in
SharePoint

You can avoid this problem altogether by creating a list directly in the SharePoint site where it belongs. Open your SharePoint site's home page and click + New in the page toolbar. Select List from the drop-down menu. You will see the same list creation options as shown in Figures 3-12 and 3-13. When you create a list in a site, everyone who has access to the site also has access to the list. After the list is created, it shows up in your Lists app.

TIP

You can find many resources online for guiding you on creating your list, including a number of formatting templates for showing completion status, displaying items in a bulletin board, or creating a custom profile card. There are even options for building Gantt charts. See https://github.com/pnp/List-Formatting.

Index

A

@ (at) symbol, Access, 518
* (asterisk) operator, 158
& (ampersand) symbol, Access, 518
+ (addition) operator, Excel, 269
& (concatenation) operator, Excel, 270
@@ operator, 158
/ (division) operator, Excel formulas, 269
^ (exponentiation) operator, Excel formulas, 269
= (equal to) operator
  Access, 554
  Excel, 270
> (greater than) operator
  Access, 554
  Excel, 270
  Word, 158
>= (greater than or equal to) operator
  Access, 554
  Excel, 270
< (less than) operator
  Access, 554
  Excel, 270
  overview, 158
<= (less than or equal to) operator
  Access, 554
  Excel, 270
< (left bracket) symbol, Access database tables, 518
* (multiplication) operator, Excel formulas, 269
<> (not equal to) operator
  Access, 554
  Excel, 270
% (percent) operator, Excel formulas, 269
? (question mark) operator, Word, 158
> (right bracket) symbol, Access database tables, 518
- (subtraction) operator, Excel formulas, 269
3-D diagrams, SmartArt, 649
3-D models, 682
4:3 ratio, PowerPoint slides, 372–373
16:9 ratio, PowerPoint slides, 372–373
A4 paper, printing on, 184

Access. *See also* databases, Access
  cells, 495
  creating, 499–501
  database tables
    Attachment data type, 517
    AutoNumber data type, 517, 519
    Calculated data type, 517
    choosing fields for, 506
    creating, 509–513
    Currency data type, 517
    data types for, 516–518
    Date/Time data type, 517
    defined, 495
    entering data in, 537–546
    fields, 514–528
    filtering, 548–554
    finding missing records, 544–545
    finding/replacing data, 545–546
    Hyperlink data type, 517
    indexing, 528–530
    Large Number data type, 517
    Long Text data type, 517
    Lookup Wizard data type, 517
    mapping relationships between, 507
    Number data type, 517
    OLE Object data type, 517
    opening, 513–514
    overview, 494–495
    primary key fields, 506–507
    queries, 554–566
    relationships between, 531–536
    separating information into, 504–505
    Short Text data type, 517
    sorting records in, 548
    viewing, 513–514
    Yes/No data type, 517
  databases
    defined, 494, 495
    as source files for mass mailings, 200
  deciding on information needed, 503–504
  designing, 503–507

F

lossy compression, 653
lowercase, 41, 42

M

macros, Access, 499
Mailbox Cleanup command, Outlook, 443–444
Manage Access pane, OneDrive, 861
manipulating objects
  aligning objects, 693–695
  changing size and shape, 687–688
  distributing objects, 693, 695–696
  fill color, 689–690, 692
  grouping objects, 699–700
  outlines, 692–693
  overlapping, 696–698
  rotating/flipping objects, 698–699
  with rulers and grid, 686–687
  selecting objects, 685–686
  transparent color, 690
  ungrouping objects, 699–700
manual hyphenation, 103
many-to-many relationship, Access database tables, 532
map charts, 614
margin guides, Publisher, 582
margins
  Excel worksheets, 313–314
  Word documents
    changing size of, 85
    defined, 84
    gutters, 85
    mirror margins, 85
    using ruler to change, 85–86
Mark Index Entry dialog box, Word, 215–217
mass mailings
  overview, 198
  printing, 203–204
  source files for, 198–203
    merging document with, 199–203
    overview, 198–199
    preparing, 198–199
master slides, PowerPoint
  changing layout of, 375–376
  editing, 375
  master styles and, 375
  overview, 373
  Slide Master view, 374

master styles, PowerPoint, 375
Master views, PowerPoint, 353
math expressions, drawing, 680–681
math formulas, Word tables, 140–141
Math Input Control, 680–681
matrix diagrams, SmartArt
  adding shapes to, 637–638
  defined, 632
MAX function
  Access summary query, 564
  Excel, 288, 295
Meet Now meeting, 812
meetings
  ending in Teams, 831–832
  leaving in teams, 831–832
  Outlook
    canceling, 489
    invitations to, 486–489
    rescheduling, 489
    scheduling, 486–489
  recording in Teams, 826–827
messages, Outlook email
  addressing, 461–462
  forwarding, 463
  opening, 470
  organizing, 469–471
  saving, 470–471
  sending, 459–460
metric system, displaying on ruler, 687
Microsoft 365 groups, 870–871
Microsoft account, managing, 11
Microsoft Download Center, 164
Microsoft Lists, 892–894
Microsoft Teams applications. *See* Teams application
Microsoft Viva, 729–730
MID function, Excel, 294
MIN function
  Access summary query, 564
  Excel, 288, 295
Minimize button, Word screen, 60
mini-toolbar
  applying font style to text, 38
  changing color of text, 40
  changing font size, 37
  choosing fonts for text, 35
  overview, 17

P

About the Author

Peter Weverka is the bestselling author of many *For Dummies* books, including *Windows 10 For Seniors For Dummies* and three dozen other computer books about various topics.

Dedication

For Liam

Author's Acknowledgments

Many hands went into the making of this book and I would like to thank all of them. I especially want to thank Matt Wade for writing Book 10 and Book 11, Steve Hayes for giving me the opportunity to write this and other *For Dummies* books, and Susan Christophersen for editing this book.

Publisher's Acknowledgments

Executive Editor: Steve Hayes

Project and Copy Editor: Susan Christophersen

Technical Editor: Doug Sahlin

Production Editor: Mohammed Zafar Ali

Cover Image: © PhotoTalk/iStockphoto/ Getty Images